A Companion to Renaissance Drama

Blackwell Companions to Literature and Culture

This series offers comprehensive, newly written surveys of key periods and movements and certain major authors, in English literary culture and history. Extensive volumes provide new perspectives and positions on contexts and on canonical and post-canonical texts, orientating the beginning student in new fields of study and providing the experienced undergraduate and new graduate with current and new directions, as pioneered and developed by leading scholars in the field.

Published

A COMPANION TO

RENAISSANCE DRAMA

EDITED BY **ARTHUR F. KINNEY**

Blackwell
Publishing

© 2002, 2004 by Blackwell Publishing Ltd
Editorial matter, selection, and arrangement © 2002, 2004 by Arthur F. Kinney

BLACKWELL PUBLISHING
350 Main Street, Malden, MA 02148-5020, USA
108 Cowley Road, Oxford OX4 1JF, UK
550 Swanston Street, Carlton, Victoria 3053, Australia

First published 2002
First published in paperback 2004 by Blackwell Publishing Ltd

Library of Congress Cataloging-in-Publication Data

A companion to Renaissance drama / edited by Arthur F. Kinney.
p. cm. – (Blackwell companions to literature and culture)
Includes index.
ISBN 0-631-21950-1 (alk. paper) – ISBN 1-4051-2179-3 (pbk. : alk. paper)
1. English drama – Early modern and Elizabethan, 1500–1600 – History and criticism –
Handbooks, manuals, etc.   2. English drama – 17 th century – History and criticism –
Handbooks, manuals, etc.   3. Renaissance – England – Handbooks, manuals, etc.
I. Kinney, Arthur F., 1933–   II. Renaissance drama.   III. Series.
PR651 .C66   2002
822.309 – dc21   2001043979

A catalogue record for this title is available from the British Library.

Typeset in 11 on 13 pt Garamond 3
by SNP Best-set Typesetter Ltd., Hong Kong

For further information on
Blackwell Publishing, visit our website:
http://www.blackwellpublishing.com

To the memory of Walter T. Chmielewski and for Alison, Mika, and Ben Chmielewski

Contents

Illustrations

Contributors

Ian W. Archer is Fellow and Tutor in Modern History at Keble College, Oxford. He is the author of *The Pursuit of Stability: Social Relations in Elizabethan London*, and of various articles on the history of the early modern metropolis. He is currently working on charity in early modern England, and is the General Editor of the Royal Historical Society Bibliographies on British and Irish History.

Emily C. Bartels is Associate Professor of English at Rutgers University (New Brunswick) and author of *Spectacles of Strangeness: Imperialism, Alienation, and Marlowe*, which won the Roma Gill Prize for the Best Work on Christopher Marlowe in 1993–4. She has also written articles on Shakespeare, representations of the Moor, and early English imperialism, and is currently at work on a book, *Before Slavery: English Stories of Africa*.

Lee Beier was a Lecturer in History at Lancaster University until 1990. Currently he is Professor of History at Illinois State University. He is the author of *Masterless Men: The Vagrancy Problem in England, 1560–1640*.

Herbert Berry is Emeritus Professor of English in the University of Saskatchewan. He has published many pieces about playhouses in London during Elizabethan, Jacobean, and Caroline times.

Lee Bliss is Professor of English at the University of California, Santa Barbara. She is the author of *The World's Perspective: John Webster and the Jacobean Drama* and of *Francis Beaumont*, is editor of the New Cambridge Shakespeare *Coriolanus*, and has written articles on Renaissance dramatists, the genre of tragicomedy, and Renaissance retellings of the Griselda story, and a bibliographical study of the First Folio text of *Coriolanus*.

Michael Bristol is Greenshields Professor of English Literature at McGill University. He is author of *Big Time Shakespeare, Shakespeare's America/America's Shakespeare*, and *Carnival and Theater: Plebeian Culture and the Structure of Authority in Renaissance England*.

Mark Thornton Burnett is a Reader in English at the Queen's University of Belfast. He is the author of *Masters and Servants in English Renaissance Drama and Culture: Authority and Obedience* (1997), the editor of *The Complete Plays of Christopher Marlowe* (1999) and *Christopher Marlowe: Complete Poems* (2000), and the co-editor of *New Essays on "Hamlet"* (1994), *Shakespeare and Ireland: History, Politics, Culture* (1997), and *Shakespeare, Film, Fin de Siècle* (2000). He is currently completing *Constructing "Monsters" in Shakespearean Drama and Early Modern Culture* for Palgrave.

William C. Carroll is Professor of English at Boston University. Among his books are *Fat King, Lean Beggar: Representations of Poverty in the Age of Shakespeare* (1996) and *Macbeth: Texts and Contexts* (1999), and he is editor of the forthcoming third edition of the Arden Shakespeare *The Two Gentlemen of Verona*.

S. P. Cerasano, Professor of English at Colgate University, is working on a biography of the Renaissance actor-entrepreneur Edward Alleyn. With Marion Wynne-Davies she has co-edited *Renaissance Drama by Women* (1995) and *Readings in Renaissance Women's Drama* (1998). The author of numerous articles on Renaissance theater history, she also served as a curator of the Edward Alleyn exhibition at the Dulwich Picture Gallery in London in 1994.

Mario DiGangi, Assistant Professor of English at Lehman College, CUNY, is the author of *The Homoerotics of Early Modern Drama* (1997). His essays on Renaissance drama and lesbian/gay studies have appeared in *English Literary Renaissance, ELH, Shakespeare Quarterly, Textual Practice, GLQ*, and *Shakespearean International Yearbook*, and he has contributed to many anthologies including *Marlowe, History, and Sexuality* (1998), *Shakespeare: The Critical Complex* (1999), *Approaches to Teaching Shorter Elizabethan Poetry* (2000), and *Essays to Celebrate Richard Barnfield* and *Ovid and the Renaissance Body* (both forthcoming). His current project, "Pricking out a Living," explores the erotic representation of working women on the Renaissance stage.

Richard Dutton is Professor of English at Lancaster University where he has taught since 1974. His principal research interests in early modern drama, censorship, and authorship are all reflected in his latest book, *Licensing, Censorship and Authorship in Early Modern England* (2000). He has recently completed an edition of Ben Jonson's *Epicene* for the Revels series, of which he is a general editor. He is presently editing *Volpone* for the new Cambridge Ben Jonson and, with Jean Howard, compiling four *Companions to Shakespeare* for Blackwell.

Raphael Falco is Associate Professor of English at the University of Maryland-Baltimore County. He is the author of *Conceived Presences: Literary Genealogy in Renaissance England* and *Charismatic Authority in Early Modern English Tragedy*.

Margaret Ferguson is Professor of English at the University of California at Davis. The author of *Trials of Desire: Renaissance Defenses of Poetry*, she has co-edited *Rewriting the Renaissance: The Discourses of Sexual Difference in Early Modern Europe* as well as collections of essays on Milton and on postmodernism and feminism. She has also co-edited a critical edition of Elizabeth Cary's *Tragedy of Mariam* and has recently completed a book on female literacy and ideologies of empire in early modern England and France.

Lori Anne Ferrell is Associate Professor and Co-Chair of the Program in Religion at Claremont Graduate University and Claremont School of Theology, and is on the faculty in early modern studies at the Center for the Humanities, Claremont Graduate University. She is the author of *Government by Polemic* (1998) and co-editor, with David Cressy, of *Religion and Society in Early Modern England* (1996) and, with Peter McCullough, of *The English Sermon Revised* (2000). She is currently working on a book entitled *Graspable Art: The Promise of Mastery and the Protestant Imagination in England, 1570–1620*.

Alison Findlay is a Senior Lecturer in the Department of English at Lancaster University. She is the author of *Illegitimate Power: Bastards in Renaissance Drama* (1994) and *A Feminist Perspective on Renaissance Drama* for Blackwell (1998). In addition, she is co-director of a practical research project on early modern women's drama, which has published an award-winning video *Women Dramatists: Plays in Performance 1550–1670* (1999), and she has co-authored a book on *Women and Dramatic Production 1550–1700* (2000). She is currently working on the plays of Richard Brome.

Peter H. Greenfield is Professor of English at the University of Puget Sound. He is the editor of *Research Opportunities in Renaissance Drama* and of the records of Gloucestershire, Hampshire, and Hertfordshire for the *Records of Early English Drama* (REED) project.

Eugene D. Hill, Professor of English at Mount Holyoke College, is the author of *Edward, Lord Herbert of Cherbury* (1987) and of numerous essays on Elizabethan tragedy. He co-edited *Tudor England: An Encyclopedia* (2001).

Maurice Hunt, Professor of English and Head of the English Department at Baylor University, is the author of *Shakespeare's Romance of the Word* (1990) and *Shakespeare's Labored Art* (1995) as well as the editor of *"The Winter's Tale": Critical Essays* (1995) and two volumes in the MLA Teaching World Literature series on *Romeo and Juliet* and *The Tempest* and other late dramatic romances. He is currently editing the MLA New Shakespeare Variorum edition of *Cymbeline*.

Martin Ingram is a Fellow, Tutor, and University Lecturer in Modern History at Brasenose College, Oxford. His publications include *Church Courts, Sex and Marriage in England, 1570–1640* (Cambridge, 1987) and numerous articles on crime and the law, sex and marriage, religion and popular culture. He has also published on the history of climate.

Grace Ioppolo is Lecturer in English at the University of Reading. She is the author of *Revising Shakespeare* and the forthcoming *Shakespeare and the Text* and is the editor of *Shakespeare Performed: Essays in Honor of R. A. Foakes*. She has published numerous articles on the transmission of Renaissance play-texts and is currently working on the construction of authorship in the Renaissance.

Norman Jones is Professor of History at Utah State University. With interests in the connections among religion, law, and politics, his research spans the century after Henry VIII launched the Reformation. His works include *Faith by Statute: Parliament and the Settlement of Religion, 1559, The Birth of the Elizabethan Age, God and the Money-lenders: Usury and Law in Early Modern England*, and *The English Reformation: Religion and Cultural Adaptation*, as well as numerous articles.

John Jowett is an Associate General Editor of Thomas Middleton's *Collected Works* (forthcoming). He was an editor of *The Oxford Shakespeare Complete Works* (1986) and of *Richard III* for the Oxford Shakespeare (2000). He has written numerous articles on textual theory and practical issues of editing and is presently working on cultural memory and the representation of news on stage. He is currently editing *Timon of Athens* and co-editing a *Reader in Textual Theory*.

W. David Kay is Professor of English at the University of Illinois at Urbana-Champaign. He is the author of *Ben Jonson: A Literary Life* (1995) and the editor of John Marston's *The Malcontent* for the New Mermaids (1999). With Suzanne Gossett he is editing Jonson, Chapman, and Marston's *Eastward Ho!* for the forthcoming Cambridge edition of Jonson's works.

Arthur F. Kinney is Thomas W. Copeland Professor of Literary History at the University of Massachusetts, Amherst, and Director of the Massachusetts Center for Renaissance Studies; the founding editor of the journal *English Literary Renaissance*; and Adjunct Professor of English, New York University. He has edited *The Witch of Edmonton* by Dekker, Ford, and Rowley for the New Mermaids (1998) and, most recently, *Renaissance Drama: An Anthology of Plays and Entertainments* from manuscripts and first quartos for Blackwell (1999).

Robert S. Knapp is Professor of English and Humanities at Reed College. He is the author of *Shakespeare: The Theater and the Book* (1989) and is currently writing a book entitled *Circe's Rod: Shakespeare and the Disciplines of Culture*.

Roslyn L. Knutson, Professor of English at the University of Arkansas at Little Rock, is the author of *Playing Companies and Commerce in Shakespeare's Time* (2001) and *The Repertory of Shakespeare's Company, 1594–1613* (1991) as well as numerous articles.

Lawrence Manley, Professor of English at Yale University, is the editor of *London in the Age of Shakespeare: An Anthology* (1986) and the author of *Literature and Culture in Early Modern London* (1995). His current project is *Reading Repertory*, a study of Shakespeare's plays in relation to non-Shakespearean plays in the company repertories with which Shakespeare's name is associated.

Philip C. McGuire, Professor of English at Michigan State University, is the author of *Speechless Dialect: Shakespeare's Open Silences* (1985) and *Shakespeare: The Jacobean Plays* (1994) and co-editor of *Shakespeare: The Theatrical Dimension* (1979). He chaired the seminar on "Rethinking Collaboration" at the 1999 meeting of the Shakespeare Association of America.

Lena Cowen Orlin is Research Professor of English at the University of Maryland-Baltimore County and Executive Director of the Shakespeare Association of America. She is the author of *Private Matters and Public Culture in Post-Reformation England* (1994) and *Elizabethan Households* (1995) and editor of *Material London ca. 1600* (2000).

Annabel Patterson is Karl Young Professor of English at Yale University. Her most recent book is *Early Modern Liberalism* (1997). She has just completed *Nobody's Perfect: A New Whig Interpretation of History*, which focuses on the eighteenth century.

Lawrence F. Rhu is Associate Professor of English and Comparative Literature at the University of South Carolina. He has written a book on Torquanto Tasso's narrative theory and numerous essays on Renaissance literature.

Michael Shapiro is Professor of English at the University of Illinois, Urbana-Champaign, and the director of the Sheldon and Antia Drobny Interdisciplinary Program for the Study of Jewish Culture and Society. He has also held visiting positions at Cornell, Reading, and Tamkang Universities. He is the author of *Children of the Revels: The Boy Companies of Shakespeare's Time and their Plays* (1977) and *Gender in Play on the Shakespearean Stage: Boy Heroines and Female Pages* as well as numerous essays. He is the founding artistic director of the Revels Players, an amateur acting troupe devoted to early classic theater.

Elli Abraham Shellist is a poet and doctoral candidate at the University of Illinois-Chicago. He is currently working on the relationship between mediocrity and villainy in Renaissance drama.

William H. Sherman is Associate Professor of English at the University of Maryland and author of *John Dee: The Politics of Reading and Writing in the English Renaissance* (1995). He edited *"The Tempest" and its Travels* (2000) with Peter Hulme and is currently editing *The Alchemist* with Peter Holland for the Cambridge Edition of the Works of Ben Jonson.

R. Malcolm Smuts is Professor of History at the University of Massachusetts, Boston. His publications include *Court Culture and the Origins of a Royalist Tradition in Early Stuart England* (1987, 1999) and *Culture and Power in England* (1999).

Marta Straznicky is Associate Professor of English at Queen's University, Canada. She has published articles on early modern women playwrights and is currently completing a book on women's closet drama in sixteenth- and seventeenth-century England.

John A. Twyning is Associate Professor of English at the University of Pittsburgh. He is the author of *London Dispossessed: Literature and Social Space in the Early Modern City* (1998).

Suzanne Westfall is Associate Professor of English and Theatre at Lafayette College. She is the author of *Patrons and Performance: Early Tudor Household Revels* and the editor, with Paul Whitfield White, of the forthcoming *Theatrical Patronage in Shakespeare's England*. In addition to her work in early modern theater, she directs plays and teaches acting for the Lafayette Theatre.

Deborah Willis is Associate Professor of English at the University of California, Riverside, where she teaches Shakespeare, Renaissance Drama, and Cultural Studies. She is the author of *Malevolent Nature: Witch-Hunting and Maternal Power in Early Modern England* (1995) and articles on Shakespeare, Marlowe, and Renaissance culture. She is currently working on a project about witch-families in early modern England.

Acknowledgments

One of the great pleasures of editing such a book as the *Blackwell Companion to Renaissance Drama* is to work with so many informed and cooperative scholars; this book is far richer because of their insights and their suggestions, too, along the way.

This *Companion* was first conceived by Andrew McNeillie, my editor at Blackwell, and I am grateful to him for entrusting the project to me. I want also to thank my other editor, Emma Bennett, my superb copyeditor (whose patience seems unlimited), Fiona Sewell, and my colleague for research, Walter T. Chmielewski.

Introduction:
The Dramatic World of
the Renaissance

Arthur F. Kinney

One of the most familiar lines in all Renaissance English drama is Jaques' observation in Shakespeare's *As You Like It* that "All the world's a stage." He goes on to remark further that "all the men and women [are] merely players. / They have their exits and their entrances. / And one man in his time plays many parts" (II.vii.138–41). In a time when theater was without rival as a public art form, and at a time when during the Feast of Corpus Christi, local craftsmen and townspeople donned the costumes of biblical characters to perform local theater throughout the cities, towns, and villages of England, such a comment would surprise no one. Not only playgoing was popular; so was playacting. People did play roles. They learned Latin at grammar school by acting Plautus for comedy and Seneca for tragedy. They learned to debate as different characters – often historic ones – and as proponents of differing perspectives. At the university and at the Inns of Court, they were reminded that preaching and practicing law also required a kind of drama, a staged performance. From village street and village parish to the great manor halls and Whitehall Palace in London – not to mention the public theaters like the Theatre and the Curtain, the Globe and Rose and Fortune; or the private London theaters such as Blackfriars – theater was so commonplace a cultural practice that it must have been in the blood of every person in London. And they, too, played differing roles – in their personal lives, in their married lives, in their social lives, in their political and religious lives. A man could act the role of carpenter at one moment and angry Puritan at another, could be an endearing husband and disciplinarian father by turn. In the Renaissance, all the world was a stage and all actions – from private prayers (as we see in Claudius in *Hamlet*) to staged narratives (as we see in Hamlet's advice to the players, his reaction to the speech about Priam and Hecuba, and his own revised play called "The Mousetrap") – were essentially enactments or re-enactments. This is perhaps one of the greatest challenges for understanding life in the Renaissance and the theater of the period, but it is essential to our understanding. Life was not unconscious living so much as it was, often, conscious and continuous performance.

Consequently, every space was potentially a playing space, a space for drama, so that the city streets and alleys in Thomas Middleton or the pastoral countryside in Robert Greene were inherently dramatic possibilities where life could be lived as enactment. More panoramic dramas – such as Thomas Kyd's *Spanish Tragedy*, moving from the battlefield to the court to the private arbor in the family garden, or, even more, Christopher Marlowe's *Dr. Faustus* moving from the private study at the university to the political court of the Holy Roman Emperor and the papal court itself – show how no known environment was exempt from dramatic possibility and portrayal. Hamlet's line to the players that they must hold "the mirror up to nature" because that is all they *can* do, nature being so various and so vital, may come as a metaphor to us but would have been a commonplace to those in the Renaissance. Indeed, Tudor and Stuart England made great cultural use of the mirror – in fact as well as tropically by way of metaphor. They used glass to attempt to reflect themselves; they used steel in mirrors to gain a new perspective, often thought idealistic; and in both instances, they elaborated on an earlier notion of the mirror as the soul, as God's reflection within the self. When Shakespeare's Richard II shatters the mirror at his deposition, he is shattering (at least from his point of view) his own divinity and his divine claim to rule; when Greene's Friar Bacon uses his magical mirror to call up visions, he is imitating, parodying, and perhaps even denouncing the Godly use of the mirror: it is what makes his magical glass magical rather than godly.

Actual imagined space in the theater, then, acts as a metaphor by linking the actions performed in it to actions in the lives of playgoers by analogy. In a time when theater was the only widespread public medium for commentary on religious, political, and social life (the analogy to the proclamations of kings and queens read out in market squares by heralds), theater was also especially powerful in the messages it could convey and the results it might incur – something else Shakespeare has portrayed, in the funeral orations of Brutus and Antony for Julius Caesar. What drama cannot do, in fact, is to rest on what might appear in life to be discrete, unconnected incidents and events. By isolating and then connecting scenes, working through the disjunctions of place and of varied characterizations, the playwright and actors are required to imply a kind of causality, to give to acting, and to the stage, a continuous narration that makes sense, conveys meaning, perhaps instills belief or action, as Cinna the poet learns at the cost of his life in Shakespeare's *Julius Caesar*. In this sense, all the world is *potentially* a stage rather than an actual one, for it provides all the material – and the possible agency – for drama but lacks the uncluttered sequentiality necessary to produce developing meaning and significance. Isolated, Hamlet's soliloquy "to be or not to be" emphasizes the despair and hopelessness common to all our lives, but its significance depends on what has prompted it, what has come before, and its consequences, what happens after such thoughts. It binds thought to action, as Hamlet tells the players to "Suit the action to the word, the word to the action." In this way, plays "show virtue her own feature, scorn her own image, and the very age and body of the time his form and pressure." Conversely, such plays, enacting life as re-enactment, cannot *help but* show the age to the time, reveal through words and action the real significance (at least for the playwright) of the world about them. That world is, in the hands of Dekker and Middleton, the world of Tudor and Stuart England; or, in the hands of Marlowe and Greene, clearly analogous to it. Thus all the world of Renaissance England is potentially a stage, and the stages of such plays the very world the playgoers inhabit.

What is true of space is also true of time, the other dimension in which all of us live and move and have our being. Just as playwrights could transform the bare platforms and stages of street and public theaters and work with the artificial scenery of great halls and private performances by word and action, so they could transform time with equal flexibility. Soliloquies happen in what we might call normal time, taking as long to pronounce them on the stage as in life itself, the unfolding of such speeches mutually shared by actor and audience. But time might also be expanded, as it is in Jonson's *Bartholomew Fair* when different events, happening at the same time, are nevertheless presented in sequence so that the audience is privy to only a part of the action going on at any one moment. Conversely, time on the stage could be condensed in its re-enactments: Simon Eyre's whole career and much of his life is performed for us by Thomas Dekker's art in less than two hours. Or time could be multiple: Marlowe's *Dr. Faustus* opens in real time, Faustus's discussion with his students, his meditation on the shortcoming of human knowledge, and the appearance of Mephistophilis all occurring in "real" or shared time with the audience while the following scenes follow the dizzying pace of twenty-four years before, once more, action is slowed down at the end of Faustus's life and the last few minutes, actually staged in real time, seem to us to be in expanded time, so long, dreary, and irrevocable is the outcome we have both seen anticipated and forestalled.

Thus both space and time rest initially (for the playwright) and finally (for the playgoer) on acts of imagination: the bare stages and flexible times need the trust, belief, and finally complicity of the audience in order to complete the dramatic re-enactments, to make them *work*. Plays performed on physical stages (or in the streets or before pageant wagons or in the classrooms) need performances in the mind too. The success of dramatic performance depends on concurrence, or what a later critic would call the "suspension of disbelief." But as the authors of the following chapters continually demonstrate, the enactments on the stages of theaters and in the stages of the mind found a third re-enactment, as reinforcement, in the world the theater played to, the world the audience lived in daily. Renaissance drama first spoke powerfully to its audiences because it talked to them, through metaphors, of themselves, presented (as Macbeth sees in the performance of the witches) "lies like truth." Such is the case, for example, with the anonymous play *Arden of Faversham*, performed and re-enacted for more than three decades of the English Renaissance.

"THE TRAGEDIE of Arden of Faversham & blackwill" was entered into the Stationer's Register on April 3, 1592, and, somewhat later that year, published by Edward White. The play follows closely an account of an historic event published in the *Breviat Chronicle* for 1551:

> This year on S. Valentine's day at Faversham in Kent was committed a shameful murder, for one Arden a gentleman was by the consent of his wife murdered, wherefore she was burned at Canterbury, and there was hanged in chains for that murder and at Faversham (two) hanged in chains [one of them Arden's man-servant, Michael Saunderson, who was hanged, drawn, and quartered], and a woman burned [Elizabeth Stafford, Alice Arden's day-servant], and in Smithfield was hanged one Mosby and his sister [Susan] for the murder also.

The play might have first been written about the time of the event, when the executions of those involved stretched from London across Kent to Canterbury, within possible sight of a quarter of England's population, or it might have drawn on later accounts in Raphael Holinshed's *Chronicles* printed in 1577 and 1587, fixing the sensational story indelibly in the cultural memory.

Just as intriguing and problematic as the date of composition and early performance of this play, though, is what it is primarily about. Martin White, in the introduction to his fine edition of the play for the New Mermaids (1982, 1990, xvii–xviii), first pointed this out:

> At the end of the play, Arden lies dead; eventually murdered in his own parlour, and his body dumped on his own land. From one point of view it is the mutilated corpse of a cuckolded husband, killed at the instigation of his wife. From another point of view, however, it is the body of a rapacious landowner, whose death was not only desired, but brought about, by men driven to desperate measures by his avariciousness.

There is abundant evidence within the play to establish either reading as the central one, and White resolves this matter by arguing that they represent, respectively, issues of private and public morality that work mutually within the play to reinforce each other. That is surely possible for us today; but as the writers in this collection demonstrate, it was less likely to be the case in the Renaissance. The 1551 murder occurred during the reign of Edward VI; the 1592 play was performed under Elizabeth I; and the concerns in these periods were very different. The flashpoint during the reign of Edward was the rapid accumulation of private property following the recent dissolution of the monasteries, and the fact that Arden was implicated in such historic acts might have first suggested a much earlier play – or the same play with much earlier performances.

The dissolution of church lands occurred largely between 1536 and 1540, advancing rapidly through the creation in 1536 of the royal Court of Augmentations, which gave to Henry VIII a means to isolate and control both the litigation and administration of lands which he had taken over from the church. "Having seized the lands of the monastic clergy," C. John Sommerville writes,

> Henry found a way to expropriate the lands held by the non-monastic or "secular" clergy as well, or at least to loosen their grip on it. In 1536 he began requiring bishops to yield up the London palaces which were symbolic of their former political power,

promising to compensate them with assets of equal value. By the end of his reign [in 1547] 187 ecclesiastical manors had been traded for others which were found to be noticeably inferior (1992, 25).

What followed was a landrush. David Knowles recounts "the eagerness . . . of a wealthy and land-hungry class, who had hitherto been able to buy only occasionally and locally, and who now saw an avalanche of desirable properties about to descend into the lap of the fortunate, and could only hope that by approaching Henry or Cromwell with all speed they might be among those in the running for a bid" (1976, 282–3).[1] There were three sorts of landgrabbers – local landowners wanting to extend their holdings; courtiers in high favor; officials of the Court of Augmentations itself. John Stow's account of Arden links him with the first two possibilities. As one of the clerks for Edward North, clerk of Parliament, Arden was copying out parliamentary acts for Henry VIII by 1537; by 1539 he was under-steward to Sir Thomas Cheyne, lord warden of the Cinque Ports (who appears in the play), and married to North's stepdaughter Alice. (At the time of their marriage, Arden was forty; Alice was sixteen.) Arden accumulated offices. Around 1540 he was appointed king's collector of customs for Faversham; by 1543 he was also the king's comptroller for Sandwich; he was rumored to be the *agent provocateur* at these ports for North and for the Privy Council. Arden also accumulated land. He bought the site of the virtually demolished Faversham Abbey from Cheyne and moved into the gatehouse (the site of the murder). He bought another nine acres from the former abbot; ten acres in Thornmead; the manor of Ellenden; and some lands in Hernhill in 1543. By 1545 he also owned the manor of Otterpool in Lympne and Sellindge, formerly held by Sir Thomas Wyatt; lands in the parish of Saltwood; property in the suburbs of Canterbury that had once belonged to the archbishop; Flood Mill and Surrenden Croft; and a further 300 acres by intimidating one Walter Morleyn.

Arden would then seem a prime candidate for the sort of landowner that Robert Crowley condemns in *The Way to Wealth* (1551) as "Men without conscience. Men utterly void of God's fear. Yea, men that live as though there were no God at all! Men that would have all in their own hands" (p. 132). He is the sort of man Crowley further condemns for rack-renting, engrossing, and enclosing land for profit, driving normally peaceful, God-fearing tenants to extreme and desperate measures. If so, Crowley argues in *An Informacion and Peticion* (1548), "if any of them perish through your default, know then for certain that the blood of them shall be required at your hands. If the impotent creatures perish for lack of necessaries, you are the murderers, for you have their inheritance and do not minister unto them" (White, 1982, 1990, xx). This is exactly Holinshed's portrait of Arden of Faversham when he remarks about the St. Valentine's Day Fair held at the time of Arden's death that:

> The fair was wont to be kept partly in the town and partly in the Abbey, but Arden, for his own private lucre and covetous gain, had this present year procured it to be wholly kept within the Abbey ground which he had purchased, and so reaping all the

gaines to himself and bereaving the town of that portion which was wont to come to the inhabitants, got many a bitter curse (White, 1982, 1990, 110).

Earlier Holinshed notes that "Master Arden had wrested a piece of ground on the backside of the Abbey of Faversham [from Master Greene, a character in the play], and there had blows and great threats passed betwixt them about that matter" (White, 1982, 1990, 105). Holinshed gives the history a moral lesson, making contemporary events thematic, like grammar-school lessons and church sermons of the time.

But under Elizabeth I, when *Arden of Faversham* was published and doubtless again performed, such grabbing of property was no longer an issue. Men had made peace with a land long barren of monasteries – while domestic issues of marriage were gaining rapidly in importance under the newly aggressive strictures of Puritans taking hold after the Reformation of the 1560s and 1570s. So how might we account for the publication of *Arden* (indeed, its first extant registration) in 1592 as enactment and re-enactment? We know that in that year Abel Jeffes rushed a pirated text of *Arden of Faversham* into print before Edward White could get out his publication; and that White demanded that the Stationer's Company call in all of Jeffes' copies and destroy them and confiscate the rest of the edition. Clearly *Arden of Faversham* had (once again, perhaps) become a hot property itself, its performance and its narrative staging the world of the English Renaissance. Just as the original conception can be traced back to histories from 1551 onwards, so now we can sense cultural concerns by publications of a somewhat later time. *Arden*'s performances in 1592 may have re-enacted a more recent narrative published in 1591, *Sundrye strange and inhumaine Murthers, lately committed*. As the title-page acknowledges, the work contains two stories. The first, "of a Father that hired a man to kill three of his children neere to Ashford in Kent," leads to a moral conclusion similar to that of Holinshed's and Stow's accounts of Arden and the end of the anonymous play:

> Thus may you see how murtherers are ouertaken, and their actions opened by them-selues, yea if there were no body to accuse the murtherer, the murthered coarse wold giue euidence again him. It hath bene a meane appointed by the Lord to discerne the murtherer, that when hee approched, the dead carkasse would at some issue or other bleede: many haue by this miraculous worke of the Lord bene discouered, when the proofe hath bene onely bare suspition. (sig. A4v)

The bleeding corpse of Arden is what wrings a confession from his wife Alice; but her tracks, and those of her accomplices, which showed up in the snow and remained along with a trail of blood after they dragged the body out of doors, is the provi-dential act of God that punishes the wicked. As different as the tale of Arden and the father of the pamphlet are, they work toward a common end and share a common, morally instructive purpose. Indeed, the woodcut on the title-page which shows a dog sniffing out a half-hidden corpse, also illustrates a kind of providentialism.

Nevertheless, it is the second account in this pamphlet that comes even closer to *Arden* and so may have prompted its staging (or revival). This is "of master Page of

Plymouth, murthered by the consent of his owne wife: with the strange discouerie of sundrie other murthers. Wherein is described the odiousnesse of murther, with the vengeance which God inflicteth on murtherers." Page finally meets his end on February 11, 1591, we are told, but not until many attempts have been made on *his* life, just as *Arden of Faversham* focuses on nine attempts on Arden's. One poisoning affects Page the same way Clarke's poison, which Alice places in Arden's broth, affects him:

> But God who preserueth many persons from such perrils and dangers, defended still ye said M. Padge from the secret snares & practises of present death, which his wife had laid for him, yet not without great hurt vnto his body, for still the poison wanted force to kil him, so wonderfully did almighty God woorke for him, yet was he compelled to vomit blood and much corruption, which doubtles in the end would haue killed him, and that shortlye. (sig. B2v)

Mistress Page, like Alice Arden, and George Strangwich, like Alice's accomplice Mosby, attempt to recover their losses:

> But to prosecute and that with great speed to perform this wicked and inhuman act, the said mistriss Page and Strangwidge omitted no opportunity: they wanted no means nor friends to perform it for their money, whereof they had good store, and more than they knew how to employ, except it had been to better uses. For she on the one side practiced with one of her servants named Robert Priddis, whom as she thought nothing would more sooner make him pretend the murdering of his master than silver and gold, wherewith she so corrupted him, with promise of sevenscore pounds more, that he solemnly undertook and vowed to perform the task to her contentment.

As matters turn out, Page is murdered in his bedroom rather than his parlor by Priddis and a second assassin Tom Stone; much as in *Arden of Faversham* the murderers strangle their victim, lay him in bed (as Arden is laid in the field) and break his neck, while Mrs. Page, like Alice Arden, feigns complete ignorance. But then blood is discovered on the corpse, as with Arden, and, murder at last established, the true criminals are discovered and executed.

Had the story of Thomas and Alice Arden not already been known and in wide circulation, the story of Master and Mistress Page might seem to be a source for the anonymous play. But it may have been decisive in two ways. It may have caused an earlier play to be revived or a play then being performed to be published as well. And it may have suggested the title-page of the play which would draw on both stories, one reinforcing the other for profit:

THE / LAMENTA- / *BLE AND TRVE TRA-* / GEDIE OF M. AR- / *DEN OF FEVER-* SHAM / IN KENT. / *Who was most wickedlye murdered, by* / the meanes of his disloyall and wanton / *wyfe, who for the loue she bare to one* / Mosbie, hyred two desperat ruf- / fins Blackwill and Shakbag, / *to kill him.* / Wherin is shewed the great mal- / lice and discimulation of a wicked wo- / man, the vnsatiable desire of filthie lust / and the shamefull end of all / murderers.

Like the strange and inhuman murder in Plymouth in 1591, the murder in Faversham in 1551 has now become the story of a wicked woman subject to pride and lust. The story that might first have been that of a wealthy and merciless landlord has now become, in a new age, what Catherine Belsey (1982) has called it, "Alice Arden's crime." The world as stage reflects the potentiality of the staged world, and earlier space and time transform to meet the world *Arden of Faversham* plays to.

Yet even that may not be the whole story of *Arden of Faversham*. It would seem to account for the 1592 publication and, one assumes, performances around that time, but what of the publications of Q2 in 1599 and Q3 in 1633? It may well be that the initial shift of attention historically recurred. The years 1593–6 were especially hard ones for the English economy: drought and poor harvests threatened life in the countryside and food supplies in the cities. At such a time, the complaints of Greene and Reede about their low wages and the danger of starvation could take center stage. This was apparently not the case in 1633, however. That reprinting of the play coincided with, perhaps capitalized on, the publication of a ballad claiming to be Alice Arden's confession. The pendulum had swung once more, back to Alice Arden's crime, rather than that of her husband. Touching two continuing concerns of the Renaissance – economy and marriage, excessive wealth and cuckoldry and murderous wives – *Arden of Faversham* was itself guaranteed a long and active life as a mirror held up to nature, as a re-enactment of the world of the audience, in which dramatic metaphor and trope – a "lie like truth" – helped to illuminate and even manage the playgoers' world as they watched the world of the actor.

This is not a matter necessarily of normal time, nor of expanded, condensed, or multiple time, but of contextual time. As the following chapters display, shifting contexts for Renaissance drama allow shifting meaning to those dramatic texts, while the texts themselves, mirroring the world around them outside the theater walls, provide a kind of lying that might be the greatest of truth-telling. The space of dramatic performance merges with the spaces of daily human performance. Jaques' witness to the whole world as a stage, then, in which all men and women are merely players, is a commonplace of the Renaissance, but so is his word "merely," which could, then as now, mean "simply," but which then also meant "entirely." Either way, the line separating text and context dissolves. The causes and consequences of this more lasting dissolution, the very foundation of Renaissance English theater, is the unifying subject of the book that follows.

NOTE

1   Knowles (1976) is an abridgement of Knowles (1959).

References and Further Reading

Belsey, Catherine (1982). "Alice Arden's crime," *Renaissance Drama* n.s. 13, 83–102.

Knowles, David (1959). *The Religious Orders in England, III: The Tudor Age*. Cambridge: Cambridge University Press.

Knowles, David (1976). *Bare Ruined Choirs: The Dissolution of the English Monasteries*. Cambridge: Cambridge University Press.

Sommerville, C. John (1992). *The Secularization of Early Modern England*. New York and Oxford: Oxford University Press.

White, Martin, ed. (1982, 1990). *Arden of Faversham*. London and New York: A. C. Black and W. W. Norton.

PART ONE
The Drama's World

1

The Politics of Renaissance England

Norman Jones

The English Renaissance took place against a political backdrop dominated by international conflict, dynastic questions, religious tension and economic confusion. These leitmotifs were modulated by the political styles and personal quirks of Elizabeth I and James I, and their favorites. Elizabeth refused to talk about the succession to the throne, squashed attempts to go beyond the religious settlement of 1559, and, very reluctantly, led England into a world war with Spain, putatively in defense of Protestantism. James, through adroit politics, peacefully settled the succession and took the throne of England, uniting it with Scotland through his person. He made peace with Spain, to the horror of his Protestant subjects, and tried to avoid the pitfalls of ideological warfare, despite Catholic attempts to kill him. He, too, however, was drawn into Continental conflicts in defense of Protestantism. The decisions of both monarchs stressed the economy, but probably encouraged its evolution in ways that launched British capitalism and imperialism.

By 1584 it was clear Elizabeth I would never marry. The political classes, faced with this certainty, began a new political dance around their newly designated Virgin Queen, playing the charade of eternal desirability in the face of advancing age. The queen was presiding over a court that was increasingly filled with a younger generation whose understanding of politics, and relation to the queen, differed from their parents'. Many of the leading political figures of Elizabeth's early reign died in the 1580s. Most importantly, Robert Dudley, the earl of Leicester and perhaps the one love of Elizabeth's life, died in 1588. Increasingly, William Cecil, Lord Burghley, presided over a Privy Council full of younger faces. He was grooming his son Robert to take his place as the leader of Elizabeth's government, but competition was emerging as Elizabeth was attracted to younger men like Sir Christopher Hatton and Robert Devereux, earl of Essex.

The generational dynamic in the court was magnified by religion. By the 1580s the established Church of England was under attack by Catholics, who believed it to be illegitimate, and by people, generally lumped together as Puritans, who wished to see its worship and governing structure reformed. Many of the Puritans thought the church was too like Catholicism in practice and dress, and some were prompted by their Calvinist theology to urge that England's bishops be replaced by a presbyterian system.

Catholicism represented an international threat to the queen's sovereignty. Since Elizabeth's excommunication in 1570, Catholics had been forbidden to recognize her authority over religion. Consequently, being a Roman Catholic made one a traitor *de facto*. Elizabeth never executed a Catholic for heresy, but several hundred people died for asserting that the pope was the head of the church.

The reality of this treason was brought home by the organized Catholic mission that began operating in England in the 1570s. Seminary priests were reviving English Catholicism. This was a political act, and the crown reacted accordingly. Parliament enacted new laws against those who refused to participate in the state church, and those who withdrew themselves, branded as "recusants," were fined.

The international Catholic conspiracy against Elizabeth reinforced English Protestant identity and encouraged England to do battle in defense of the faith. The more Puritanical were especially concerned to help beleaguered co-religionists in the Spanish Netherlands, where Calvinist rebels were fighting Spanish Catholic troops. As England entered the 1580s it was teetering on the brink of war with Spain. This attracted some people because it might be very profitable. On September 26, 1580, Sir Francis Drake's three-year voyage around the world ended in Plymouth harbor, his ship, the *Golden Hind*, laden with fabulous riches looted from Spanish America, triggering a national enthusiasm for voyages of trade and plunder. That same year, Richard Hakluyt advised the Muscovy Company to load their ships with English woolens and seek a northeast passage to Cathay. Meanwhile, Richard Hitchcock was urging that a fleet of 400 fishing ships should be sent to the Newfoundland Banks to harvest the "newland fish." The English nation was beginning its rapid expansion abroad, while its domestic economy acquired a new sophistication (Tawney and Power, 1963, III, 232–57).

Issues of war, peace, religion, and economics were all bound up with the problem of the succession to the throne. As Elizabeth aged, England's political classes became increasingly concerned about who would be the next sovereign. As the earl of Essex told King James of Scotland in the late 1580s, "her Majesty could not live above a year or two" (Hammer, 1999, 92).

From her accession, Elizabeth I had been reluctant to make her intentions on the succession clear for precisely the reason Essex was courting King James. To declare a successor was to give that person political power. She governed by dividing and confusing, keeping her enemies off balance. Nonetheless, it was widely believed Elizabeth's cousin, Mary, queen of Scots, a Catholic, would succeed her.

Since 1568 Mary had been a prisoner in England. She had come into the country as a refugee, escaping the revolt that put her infant son, James VI, on the throne of Scotland and established Protestantism as Scotland's faith. Once Mary arrived, she became a constant worry for Elizabeth's counselors, who were well aware that she was heir to the throne of England. From the very beginning of her stay, Mary attracted plotters. In 1572 the duke of Norfolk was executed for his second attempt to marry her, and many of England's leaders clamored for her death. Elizabeth remained unpersuaded, honoring her cousin's royal status.

In the early 1580s, as international tensions heightened, Mary became the center of more plots. Anxious for Spanish help and protection, she offered to place herself, her son, and her kingdom in the hands of Philip II if he could free her. The Spanish ambassador was drawn into a plot which called for the duke of Guise to bring a force, paid for by Spain, into England. There it would be joined by English Catholics to free Mary. Known as the Throckmorton Plot, it was uncovered in 1584, and English public opinion became hysterically anti-Spanish. After that Elizabeth began to think seriously about war with Spain.

Finally, in the summer of 1585, Elizabeth despatched 4,000 men to aid the Dutch against the Spanish, telling the Dutch ambassadors, "You see, gentlemen, that I have opened the door, that I am embarking once for all with you in a war against the King of Spain." She sent her favorite, the earl of Leicester, to lead the English army and to dominate the Dutch government. It was an important departure from Elizabeth's previous policy, leading the Tudor state into a war that lasted, in one form or another, until 1603.

In the meantime the long-running saga of Mary queen of Scots was coming to an end. In December of 1585 a Catholic exile named Gilbert Gifford was arrested at Dover. Gifford was carrying letters of introduction to Mary, for he was part of a network raising support for her. Sent to London for examination, Gifford changed sides. Thenceforth Mary's letters, smuggled out in beer barrels, were being read in London. They proved that she was urging a group of conspirators, associated with Anthony Babington, to invade England and murder Elizabeth. With this proof in hand, Elizabeth reluctantly agreed to act against Mary.

Tried before royal commissioners, Mary was found guilty of treason. Elizabeth, unwilling to execute an anointed queen put off signing the death warrant. Instead, she attempted to convince Mary's jailers to murder her. To their credit, they refused. Finally, Elizabeth signed the warrant and it was carried out in haste, before she changed her mind again. Mary was executed on February 8, 1587. There was no longer a Catholic heir to the throne of England; the legacy passed to Mary's son James VI, raised a Protestant in Scotland.

However, Philip II procured a declaration from the pope naming him the heir of Mary, rather than her son James VI, and began planning an invasion of England as a preliminary to defeating the rebels in the Low Countries. To stop Philip's Armada, Sir Francis Drake led a raid on the Spanish port of Cadiz in 1587, burning some 30 ships in the harbor.

The Armada finally put to sea on the last day of May, 1588. Half punitive expedition and half crusade, it was supposed to ferry the duke of Parma's invasion army across the English Channel. Meanwhile, Cardinal Allen, representing English Catholics from Rome, was calling on them to take up arms against Elizabeth, with God's blessing.

When the Spanish fleet was finally sighted by Admiral Howard's scouts, a running battle began. The smaller, faster, better-armed English ships harried the Spanish, preventing them from linking with Parma's army and forcing them to run for the North Sea. Somewhere near the Firth of Forth English pursuit stopped and divine wrath took over. Battered by storms, the Armada retreated toward Spain around Ireland, losing ship after weakened ship.

Meanwhile, Elizabeth was faced with a truly frightening situation. If the Spanish landed their army, it seemed doubtful that England would survive. The Spanish veterans were a much better army than those assembled hastily in England from local militias and lacking the infrastructure for keeping the field very long. They were never tested in battle, but their assembling gave Elizabeth a great opportunity for propaganda. On August 9, as the Spanish were retreating, she visited the army encamped at Tilbury. Appearing in armor and carrying a marshal's baton, she made a famous speech, declaring "I know I have the body of a weak and feeble woman, but I have the heart and stomach of a king, and of a king of England too."

It was one of England's proudest moments. God had displayed his favor by sending His winds to save His favorite nation, but the war had just begun. By fall an English fleet was sent to destroy the remnants of the Armada in the Spanish ports, to free Portugal from Spanish rule, and to attack the Azores. The fleet besieged Lisbon, but failed to take it, and in the end the expedition was a failure. However, a naval war with Spain continued through the 1590s, with English privateers attacking Spanish ships all over the world in hopes of a capture like that of the *Madre de Dios*, which returned £80,000 on Elizabeth's investment of £3,000.

England was also at war in the Low Countries, sending more and more troops to aid the Dutch Protestants against Spain. In France, where a religious civil war was being helped along by English subsidies for the Huguenots, Elizabeth was being drawn into another conflict. When Henry III was assassinated, Henry of Navarre became Henry IV of France, appealing immediately for English aid against the Catholic League. By the fall of 1588 an English expeditionary force was serving with Henry IV as he besieged Paris.

The troops came home after the siege, but Elizabeth continued to give Henry IV money for his campaigns, since a French Protestant army counterbalanced the Spanish Catholic army in the Netherlands. This strategy worked for a while, but it drew Spain into direct intervention in France. Spanish troops occupied Blavet in Brittany, giving them a base for attacks on England, so in May 1591 English troops were landed in Brittany. Poor cooperation by the French royal forces, and Elizabeth's usual reluctance to resupply and reinforce, made the operation a failure. Another English force was sent in to Normandy to aid in the siege of Rouen. That, too, failed, but Elizabeth did not withdraw all of her forces from France until 1594, a year after Henry IV had converted to Catholicism. Elizabeth had entered France because it kept pressure on Spain in the Low Countries. Spain, for its part, stirred trouble in Ireland in order to keep pressure on England. War in Ireland was nothing new. English attempts to control the island had sparked rebellion after rebellion. From 1569 until 1573, and then again from 1579 until 1583, Munster was in rebellion, led by James Fitzmaurice Fitzgerald, the earl of Desmond, aided by Spanish and Italian troops. The Desmond revolts were crushed, and in 1583, Desmond's estates began to be opened for the "plantation" of colonists. With Munster under control, the English turned their attention to mountainous Ulster, dominated by Hugh O'Neill, earl of Tyrone.

As English pressure on Ulster increased, O'Neill reacted. By 1594 he was leading a full-scale revolt known as the Nine Years' War. Seeking support from Gaels and Old English, O'Neill tried to turn the war into a Catholic crusade. This attracted the Spanish, who sent troops. The critical years of the war were 1597–9, when several Irish victories made it appear that they might win. After the disastrous defeat at the Yellow Ford in 1599, Elizabeth sent the chivalrous earl of Essex to Ireland to take command. Bragging he would quickly defeat O'Neill, he dallied. Then, when directly ordered by the queen to attack, he made a truce instead. It left the Irish in control of all that they had taken and enraged Elizabeth. Although she commanded him not to leave his post, Essex decided that he had to return to court to defend himself from his enemies there. In July 1598, abandoning the army, he arrived unexpectedly at court, bursting into Elizabeth's bedroom while she was at her toilette.

Elizabeth was enraged at his behavior, and at his failure in Ireland. She relieved him of his command and sent Charles Blount, Lord Mountjoy, to replace him. Then she stripped Essex of his patent on sweet wines, depriving him of most of his income, and appointed a commission to investigate his actions. Disgraced, Essex believed that Robert Cecil and other counselors were poisoning the queen's mind against him. If he could only get her away from them, she would understand his brilliance. He began scheming to seize the queen. To stiffen the resolve of his followers he arranged to have Shakespeare's *Richard II*, a tale of a king removed by his nobles, performed at the Globe theater. His plot was betrayed by one of his confederates, and Essex desperately led 200 men through London, calling the populace to arms in defense of Elizabeth. No one joined him. The earl and four others were executed after a treason trial that was a set piece of legal theatrics.

With Essex gone the Irish situation began to improve. In November 1601 O'Neill and a Spanish army made a joint attack on Mountjoy's forces. Mountjoy, however, surprised O'Neill as he was deploying his troops at Kinsale, ending Irish resistance and placing all of Ireland under English rule for the first time. O'Neill surrendered, on favorable terms, in March 1603, six days after Elizabeth died.

Elizabeth's government desperately needed more money than it had. In normal times the monarch paid for government out of the customs revenues, rents on crown lands, and other sources of income. By 1584 the Treasury had accumulated some £300,000 in surpluses, thanks to Elizabeth's very parsimonious management. But war ate that surplus. Consequently, Parliament was convinced, in 1589, to grant an unusual double subsidy, but the subsidy Act insisted that this was no precedent; such taxes were not to be expected as a matter of course. By 1593 Elizabeth's Council sought a third subsidy, only to be rebuffed in the House of Commons, even though the queen had spent £1,030,000 on the war and the subsidy of 1589 had yielded only £280,000. Eventually, after an arduous debate and the intervention of the House of Lords, the Commons agreed to pay, but with bad grace. The shortfalls were made up by money raised through Privy Seal loans, which Elizabeth always repaid promptly. When she died, her government was in debt by £340,000. If James I had shared her managerial philosophy, this debt would have been settled within a year, but he did not pay off the loans.

The real costs of the war were far greater than the money spent from the Treasury. Troops were levied and transported at the expense of the localities. Each recruit was armed and paid "coat and conduct" money by the town, guild, or other entity that raised him. Worse, soldiers mustered out were often discharged at the nearest port and expected to find their own way home. Many became beggars or bandits.

All this fueled resentment against the crown, and against what many localities saw as dangerously increasing central power in Westminster. The clumsiness of the system made things even worse, as did corruption and the parsimony of the crown. The entire governmental system, depending as it did on the willingness of local leaders voluntarily to govern their neighborhoods, was strained by the wars.

That the economic crisis triggered by the wars and bad harvests of the 1590s was not more profound is surprising. Although it triggered some troubles, such as the mini-rebellion in Oxfordshire in 1596, they were mitigated by changes in the economy. Agricultural production was becoming more efficient, releasing people to participate in the growing economic specialization appearing in urban areas. Iron, tin, and glass production rose, too, increasing demand for coal to such an extent that towns like Newcastle-on-Tyne boomed. On the consumer front, entrepreneurs, supported by an emerging national credit market, were displacing imported manufactured goods with native ones. These new enterprises stimulated the revival of the towns, after their long slump in the mid-sixteenth century, drawing the surplus population to them. That provided a very cheap workforce, since real wages were at an all-time low. All of this was especially evident in London, whose population exploded along with its prosperity. Taken all together, the standard of living in 1600 was remarkably higher than that of fifty years earlier.

Consumers fueled some of the boom; exports fed the rest. Companies were chartered to regulate and exploit the trade to various parts of the world. The Virginia Company, the Levant Company, the Muscovy Company, the Eastland (Baltic) Company, the East India Company, and others joined the Merchant Adventurers in dividing up foreign trade. Most of them specialized in exporting English cloth. The so-called "new draperies," light-weight woolens, were in high demand in warmer climates, and could be traded for valuable goods like spices. These brought high prices on the English market and fed the prosperity of the merchants lucky enough to own shares in these joint stock companies. Others, complaining bitterly that they were locked out of lucrative markets, were frequently attacked in Parliament.

Although there was no market for the new draperies in North America, entrepreneurs turned their eyes across the Atlantic. In 1580 perhaps 40 vessels a year fished the Grand Banks for the "newland fish." By 1604 this number had quadrupled, and by the 1620s 200 or 300 ships a year made the voyage, bringing cheap cod to the tables of England and Europe. By the early seventeenth century people were following the fishermen to North America, and by the mid-1620s tobacco was flowing into England from America, creating a return flow of manufactured goods and people. This hiccuping economic expansion was helped by the arrival of James I on the throne. He stayed out of foreign wars for a long time, allowing the domestic economy the benefits of peace.

Elizabeth went into a sudden, sharp decline in February 1603. Refusing to eat or sleep or even take to her bed, she sank into a deep depression. On March 23 she lost her voice, and early on the morning of March 24 she died. James VI of Scotland was proclaimed as James I of England that same morning.

Four issues dominated the politics of James' reign. First, religious and ideological disagreement threatened the peace and forced the king to seek new ways of resolving the tensions. Second, there was never enough money in the treasury to support a king who spent as if it was bottomless. Third, James's belief in his royal authority clashed with English political values, provoking opposition in Parliament. Lastly, there was the problem of integrating Scotland and England into a single state. James picked at these knotty problems, often making them worse.

His accession buoyed the hopes of Puritans and Catholics alike, since his policies in Scotland made him appear tolerant of Catholics and inclined toward Calvinist church discipline. As he made his triumphal way south he was presented in Northamptonshire with the Millenary Petition, signed by a thousand ministers. They asked him to reform the liturgy, clergy, and doctrine of the Elizabethan church. Coming from those who wished to see the church "purified," the petition was disliked by the bishops of the church of which James was now the supreme governor. Representatives of both sides met at Hampton Court on January 14, 1604.

James entered into the debates with relish, displaying his own theological sophistication. In the end, he ordered his bishops to reform certain things, but he also made it clear that he had little patience with attacks on the Church of England. A moderate in religion himself, he had stormy relations with the imperious Presbyterian kirk of Scotland. He preferred a church he could control, and was completely unsympathetic to any attacks on episcopacy. "No bishop, no king!" he exclaimed. Importantly, though, he did agree with them on one point – the need for a new translation of the Bible into English. Consequently, a team of academics and clerics was appointed to produce what became known as the King James Bible when it was printed in 1611.

While the Protestants argued over the form and discipline of the national church, England's Catholics had, despite the official paranoia, quietly coexisted with the regime for so long that they had evolved their own religious organization. An archpriest was, in theory, in charge of the English Catholics, although the Jesuits disagreed. Even before Elizabeth died they had been negotiating for toleration in exchange for the expulsion of missionary priests. Now they thought James, married to a Catholic and committed to religious reconciliation, might allow it.

The Catholics who tried to get tolerance in exchange for their allegiance were hated by some of their co-religionists, who wanted blood. A radical faction, led by Robert Catesby, plotted to blow up the king and Parliament. When the king came to open Parliament on November 6, 1605, they would explode 36 barrels of gunpowder beneath Westminster Hall. Wiping out the Protestant leadership would, they thought, trigger a Catholic rising that would bring the nation back to the Roman faith.

The man left to set fire to the powder in the palace cellar was Guy Fawkes. Disguised as a servant, he was waiting there when the Lord Chamberlain's men, tipped off by a Catholic who knew of the plot, captured him. The king was saved, and the nation engaged in an orgy of pious thanksgiving, cursing Catholics and praising God for His providence. Ironically, James, seeking religious peace, refused to hunt Catholics, despite the attempted assassination.

At the local level, however, religious tensions continued to stew. Scots clung to their kirk as something that made them different from their traditional enemies, the English. The English interpreted their prayer book in ways that suited each community, practicing pragmatic toleration most of the time. In those places where there was no agreed-upon local practice, tensions flared.

English local government allowed for much variation in the enforcement of religious uniformity. By the turn of the century local magistrates, increasingly convinced that their vocations demanded that they keep their communities pure, moved to outlaw swearing, drinking, and other crimes against the honor of God. For example, in 1606 Mayor Coldwell of Northampton proposed to the aldermen that the ale houses should be off-limits to the inhabitants, on pain of prison. Moreover, no swearer, drunkard, or idle person was to be eligible for public relief. The aldermen approved his proposal, so "all profaneness, dicing and carding, drinking fled clean out of the freedom of the town." This zeal for the town's good paid off, reported Richard Rawlidge, because "whereas the plague had continued in the said town above two years together, upon this reformation of the Magistrates the Lord stayed the judgment of the pestilence" (1628, sig. F1. [STC 20766]).

Similar policies were emerging elsewhere, with bans on profane actors and other irritants. Soon, Parliament began passing national legislation with the same intent. Ironically, this set the stage for a clash with the supreme governor of the church, James. In 1615, returning from Scotland via Lancashire, James discovered that zealous Puritan magistrates had banned sports on Sunday, believing they defiled the Sabbath. Horrified, James issued a national order, known as the "Declaration of Sports," protecting the right to dance, practice archery, and follow other harmless recreations on Sunday afternoons. Lumping Catholics and Puritans together as enemies was an ill political omen, upsetting precarious religious balances through central intervention.

The accession of James I to the throne of England joined the rule of Scotland and England together in the same person, but it hardly united the two countries. Neither adopted the institutions or laws of the other; nor did they invent a third way. Sharing a king, they shared little else, to the frustration of James I/VI, who dreamed of the kingdom of Great Britain.

As far as James was concerned, when he became king of England, England and Scotland became one nation. Somehow he forgot that their institutions, customs, and self-interests could not easily blend. In 1604 England's Parliament quickly made it clear to him that his actions were to be constrained by England's established legal tradition. The House of Commons produced a document known as the Apology of the Commons, designed to teach their king to respect Parliament's privileges. It was never delivered, but they refused to grant him the title of king of Great Britain. Instead, a commission on unification was created to negotiate the status of the citizens of the two nations in the unified kingdom. The English arrogantly proposed simply to annex Scotland as they had done Wales; the Scots refused, and little was done beyond erasing the laws controlling their joint borders and establishing that those Scots born after James' accession to the English throne were citizens of England in law.

One of the reasons for these actions was that the English commissioners shared the fear that James would bring a horde of Scots south to feast on England's wealth. Their fears were not unfounded. Although Elizabeth's wars, the unreformed rate book, inflation, and sheer inefficiency had drained the Treasury, James thought the English wealthier than the Scots, and made lavish gifts to his friends, spent wildly on good living, and refused to listen to the warning cries of his officials.

Robert Cecil, earl of Salisbury, had been carried over from Elizabeth's reign as the principal secretary. In 1608 he became, as his father had been, lord treasurer. But the Treasury was empty. He undertook reforms that improved the efficiency of collections and sought new ways to wring out pennies to throw into the maw of the deficit. In 1610, hoping for tax reform and new revenue, he went to Parliament. He proposed that they pay off the king's debts and increase his annual revenues by £200,000. The Commons bitterly demanded that he stop purveyance and the selling of wardships. There was intense resistance to the Great Contract, and it sank amid fears that a king with regular taxation would become an absolute monarch, able to govern without the advice and consent of Parliament.

When the attempt to get tax reform failed, Salisbury turned to drastic measures. The crown began selling titles. This "inflation of honors" allowed people to purchase titles of gentility and nobility for fixed prices. For £10,000 one could become an earl. Selling crown property, or raising the rents on it, he also began borrowing from those with crown contracts. In 1611 Salisbury ordered a "benevolence" to be collected. A forced loan, it was not expected to be repaid.

Arbitrary increases in the customs rates, forced loans and other tools were not good for trade. Neither was the habit of selling monopolies on commercial activities. The worst abuses of this system became apparent in 1614 when the Cockayne Project was launched. It was intended to enrich a small group of investors, led by Alderman

Cockayne, by giving them control of the export of colored cloth and prohibiting the export of undyed cloth. The patentees were unable to make it work, and it was an unmitigated disaster. The price of cloth collapsed in 1616.

The earl of Salisbury died in 1612, and was succeeded by the royal favorite, Robert Carr, a Scot who became earl of Somerset. Allying with the powerful Howard family through a love affair, Somerset built a position of great influence by 1613. Salisbury had been unable to pay the king's bills and Somerset was no better. Desperate for money because of his daughter's marriage and the funeral of his son, Prince Henry, James called Parliament into session in 1614. Unfortunately for the king, this Parliament was not in a mood to grant supply; it was concerned that its authority was being eroded by the crown. Ever since 1604 tension had been building between the king and Parliament over the right to tax. In 1606 in Bate's Case, the judges held the king had the right to impose custom taxes as a matter of his prerogative, without Parliament's blessing. Salisbury used this decision to augment royal revenues. In 1614 the House of Commons attacked this taxation without representation. The session was completely fruitless, passing no legislation at all. As Rev. Thomas Lorkin famously named it, it was an "addle Parliament."

Somerset failed to deliver the cash the king needed, but he, and his Catholic Howard in-laws, helped incline the king toward marrying his son Charles to the Spanish infanta, Maria. As negotiations went forward, the nation became more and more agitated about the "Spanish Match." Protestant England was horrified by the idea that Prince Charles might marry a Spanish Catholic, threatening the religion they held dear and introducing their old enemy into the kingdom.

Somerset was displaced by George Villiers, reputed to be the handsomest man in England. Son of a gentry family, his looks overcame his lack of breeding, and his backers carefully trained him to seduce the king's affections. Starting as cup-bearer at the royal table, he quickly succeeded. James knighted him in 1615 and made him a gentleman of his chamber and master of the horse. In 1616 he was made a viscount, and six months later duke of Buckingham. Buckingham applied himself with great energy to the king's affairs, gathering offices to himself and demonstrating shrewd political skill. Growing richer and richer, he married into the nobility. By 1618 he was clearly the King's favorite.

In that year the Thirty Years War began on the Continent. James I's daughter Elizabeth was married to Prince Frederick of Bohemia and, when his forces were crushed at the battle of White Mountain, it appeared that the Protestant cause was in extreme danger. James was anxious to help his son-in-law, but equally anxious not to break the peace he had striven so hard to maintain. He engaged in feverish diplomacy and, in 1621, he summoned Parliament to ask for its support in his efforts. It was happy to pass two subsidies, apparently in the belief that the nation was preparing for war in defense of Protestantism. The *quid pro quo* was to allow Parliament its head over the hated monopolies and abuses. One result of this attack on governmental corruption was that the lord chancellor, Francis Bacon, was impeached for taking bribes in court cases.

The second session of the Parliament of 1621 ended in disaster for the king. Brimming with war fever, the Commons petitioned that if the Spanish did not withdraw their troops from Bohemia, war would be declared against Spain. For good measure, they proposed that Prince Charles marry a Protestant, ending the negotiations over the Spanish Match. These demands cut too far into the royal prerogative for James to accept them and he scolded the House. It responded with cries that its traditional liberties were being violated. In frustration the king dissolved Parliament, leaving most of its work undone.

In the popular mind, the failure of the Parliament of 1621 was the result of Spanish machinations, a Jesuit plot. This stoked the anti-Catholic paranoia of the country, but James was proceeding with negotiations for the marriage of Charles and Maria, oblivious to the fear it provoked. In 1623 Charles and Buckingham went off on a boyish secret journey to Spain; Charles wished to see his bride. The nation was horrified. Philip IV of Spain found his bluff called. He was not very interested in alliance with Great Britain and now, with Charles in his court, he raised the stakes, demanding religious toleration for Catholics. After six months Charles, though an ardent lover, admitted defeat and withdrew.

Britain went mad with joy when Charles returned without a bride. He and Buckingham now followed an anti-Spanish policy, and James gave them their head. In 1624 Parliament was called in an attempt to get money for what they hoped would be a war on Spain. Once again Parliament proved truculent. Although it did grant three subsidies, it tied the money to specific conditions that usurped the royal prerogative.

Now, still desperate for money, James and Charles turned to France, negotiating a marriage with Henrietta-Maria, Louis XIII's sister. They wanted aid against Spain and a large dowry. The dowry came, but, when James I died and Charles went to war, the French failed to help. The reign of James I ended in March 1625. It left the nation in the hands of Charles I and Buckingham. They began the new reign with deep debts and political divisions. Buckingham was popularly blamed for all the trouble, and he was assassinated in 1628.

James had inherited problems from Elizabeth. The precarious finances of the crown, the religious divisions, and the succession continued to haunt him, but in different ways. He made the fiscal problems worse, irritating the parliamentary classes with his expansive lifestyle and free spending. Believing that religious peace was possible in Europe, he fed anti-Catholic paranoia at home with his attempts to marry his son to Spain. At the same time he deepened divisions among the Protestants by meddling with the locally crafted versions of the Anglican settlement. Pursuing peace was good for the economy as long as it lasted, but the final years of the reign were spoiled by his confusing attempts to deal with the Thirty Years War. At the heart of the problem was James himself. A foreigner who never seems to have understood the English constitution, he was never able to use it to best advantage.

References and Further Reading

Brenner, Robert (1993). *Merchants and Revolution: Commercial Change, Political Conflict and London's Overseas Traders 1550–1653*. Cambridge: Cambridge University Press.

Clay, C. G. A. (1984). *Economic Expansion and Social Change: England 1500–1700*. 2 vols. Cambridge: Cambridge University Press.

Cogswell, Thomas (1989). *The Blessed Revolution: English Politics and the Coming of War, 1621–1624*. Cambridge: Cambridge University Press.

Galloway, B. (1986). *The Union of England and Scotland 1603–1608*. Edinburgh: J. Donald.

Grassby, Richard (1995). *The Business Community of Seventeenth Century England*. Cambridge: Cambridge University Press.

Guy, John, ed. (1995). *The Reign of Elizabeth I. Court and Culture in the Last Decade*. Cambridge: Cambridge University Press.

Haigh, Christopher (1988). *Elizabeth I*. London: Longman.

Hammer, Paul (1999). *The Polarisation of Elizabethan Politics. The Political Career of Robert Devereux, 2nd Earl of Essex, 1585–1597*. Cambridge: Cambridge University Press.

Hindle, Steven (2000). *The State and Social Change in Early Modern England c.1550–1640*. London: Macmillan.

Hirst, Derek (1986). *Authority and Conflict. England, 1603–1658*. Cambridge, MA: Harvard University Press.

Jones, Norman (1989). *God and the Moneylenders. Usury and Law in Early Modern England*. Oxford: Blackwell.

Levin, Carole (1994). *"The Heart and Stomach of a King." Elizabeth I and the Politics of Sex and Power*. Philadelphia: University of Pennsylvania Press.

Lockyer, Roger (1989). *The Early Stuarts. A Political History of England 1603–1642*. London: Longman.

MacCaffrey, Wallace (1992). *Elizabeth I: War and Politics, 1588–1603*. Princeton: Princeton University Press.

MacCaffrey, Wallace (1993). *Elizabeth I*. London: Edward Arnold.

McGurk, John (1997). *The Elizabethan Conquest of Ireland*. Manchester: Manchester University Press.

Martin, Colin and Geoffrey Parker (1998). *The Spanish Armada*. Harmondsworth: Penguin.

Patterson, W. B. (1997). *King James VI and I and the Reunion of Christendom*. Cambridge: Cambridge University Press.

Peck, Linda Levy (1990). *Court Patronage and Corruption in Early Stuart England*. London: Unwin Hyman.

Peck, Linda Levy, ed. (1991). *The Mental World of the Jacobean Court*. Cambridge: Cambridge University Press.

Rawlidge, Richard (1628). *A Monster late Found Out*. Amsterdam.

Somerville, J. P. (1986). *Politics and Ideology in England 1603–1640*. New York: Longman.

Strong, Roy. (1977). *The Cult of Elizabeth: Elizabethan Portraiture and Pageantry*. London: Thames and Hudson.

Tawney, R. H. and Eileen Power, eds (1963). *Tudor Economic Documents*. London: Longman.

Thirsk, Joan (1978). *Economic Policy and Projects. The Development of a Consumer Society in Early Modern England*. Oxford: Clarendon Press.

Wernham, R. B. (1984). *After the Armada: Elizabethan England and the Struggle for Western Europe, 1588–1595*. Oxford: Clarendon Press.

Wernham, R. B. (1994). *The Return of the Armadas. The Last Years of the Elizabethan War against Spain, 1595–1603*. Oxford: Oxford University Press.

Wrightson, Keith (2000). *Earthly Necessities. Economic Lives in Early Modern Britain*. New Haven: Yale University Press.

Zaller, Robert (1971). *The Parliament of 1621: A Study in Constitutional Conflict*. Berkeley: University of California Press.

2

Political Thought and the Theater, 1580–1630

Annabel Patterson

Sir Epicure Mammon:	. . . when the jewels
	Of twenty states adorn thee . . .
	Queens may look pale: and we but showing our love,
	Nero's Poppaea may be lost in story!
Dol Common:	But in a monarchy, how will this be?
	The prince will soon take notice; and both seize
	You and your stone: it being a wealth unfit
	For any private subject . . .
	. . . You may come to end
	The remnant of your days, in a loathed prison.
Mammon:	We'll therefore go with all, my girl, and live
	In a free state.

Ben Jonson, *The Alchemist*, iv.141ff

Absolute wealth, absolute deprivation; prince vs. private subject; a monarchy or a republic ("free state"): these choices, parodically defined here in Ben Jonson's 1610 play *The Alchemist*, are nevertheless representative of the way in which drama and political thought are usually related in early modern England – that is to say, not very satisfactorily. Dissatisfaction consists, for readers or audiences genuinely interested in what those alternatives meant (and whether there might be any middle ground between them), in the glancing, allusive, elliptical nature of the proposition that great wealth is the prerogative of courts and denied to any private subject, unless in a republic. Conceptual dissatisfaction (which may run on opposite tracks from aesthetic satisfaction) will be generated for such readers or audiences in Jonson's and his characters' reliance on assumption rather than discussion; in the requirement that the reader know something external to the text (the history of the Roman emperor Nero, a paradigm of self-indulgence, cruelty, and lust, *and* the fact that Nero's history, especially as retailed by Suetonius, was potentially productive of complex political analysis); and above all in the realization that such venerable topics are here handed over, like stage props, to an overweight hedonist and fool, who believes he can purchase the philosopher's stone, and a thieves' whore and doxy, serving as duck's decoy.

Toward the end of the twentieth century there developed in studies of early modern drama an unusual, if not entirely unprecedented, interest in the following questions, though they may not have been posed in exactly the form that follows: what relation did a form of public entertainment, whose popularity and social importance during this period *were* unprecedented, have to public issues? Why were so many plays based on older English history in its more problematic moments, moments when the structure of government was threatened? Why did so many plays seem to allude to controversial events in current English or European affairs? That there was some relation between drama and politics seemed an unavoidable inference (although it had been avoided with considerable determination for the previous three-quarters of a century); and the new historically minded critics began to assemble the evidence, and to argue, about what that relationship was. Drama-and-politics became a lively center of activity.

Early modern drama had always been of paramount concern to the academy because of the pre-eminence of Shakespeare, whose obsessive interest in monarchy, at least at the level of plot, could not be obscured, though it could be variously explained; but a large body of contemporary criticism has subsequently emerged, much of it focused on dramatists other than Shakespeare, such as Ben Jonson, Thomas Middleton, or Philip Massinger. Perhaps because Shakespeare himself remained enigmatic on political issues, typically challenging the English system of hereditary monarchy, the law, or the constitution at the opening of a play, only to reinstate the status quo by its ending, it may have been thought that lesser dramatists and (usually) less gripping plays, produced better results – that is, if one were determined to relate the stage to the state, Elizabethan, Jacobean, or early Caroline, as the case might be. At this stage, however, the results of this inquiry still seem somewhat scattered and disputable, largely because the characteristics just displayed in Jonson's *Alchemist* are ubiquitous in the period under review. It is the very rare play in Elizabeth's or James' reign that contains an explicit debate on, still less an extended analysis of, an issue we might legitimately define as political *thought*, as distinct from political commonplace. Allusion, elision, irony, and the dilemma, as in *The Alchemist*, of unreliable spokespeople for both orthodox and unorthodox doctrine are far more common.

It would not be appropriate here to do more than name some of the landmark studies in this movement. David Bevington's *Tudor Drama and Politics* (1968) was probably the liminal work, since it actually asked whether playwrights were likely to have had political motives for writing for the stage, as distinct from merely commercial ones. Overall, though the tone of Bevington's study was cautionary, he reopened the question of how much topical allusion could be expected in the drama. More influential, since it had an axe to grind, was Margot Heinemann's *Puritanism and Theatre* (1980), a work that pioneered the thesis of an "Opposition" drama, in addition to one that worked for and in sympathy with the court. Heinemann's hero was Thomas Middleton, and her concept of Opposition was constrained by the theory that criticism of court policies would come primarily from Puritan London. Heine-mann's work reinstated the liberal assumption of the turn-of-the-century historian Samuel Rawlinson Gardiner, reinforced by her personal commitment to the Marxist historiography of Christopher Hill. It defined the school of thought that would shortly be complained of by Martin Butler in his own ground-breaking work on Caroline drama (just outside the boundaries of this anthology). In Butler's view, there had now developed "a simplified view of the seventeenth-century crisis as one continuous move-ment, a two-handed struggle between parliamentary rule and royal absolutism in politics, and patriotic puritanism and hispanophile crypto-Catholicism in religion" (1984, 9). Butler viewed this theory of Opposition drama as distorted by reading the civil war of the 1640s back into the earlier periods. Essentially Butler's point is that plays could be and were political in dozens of small ways, without relying on a polar-ized view of politics such as that implied by the division into Roundhead and Cava-lier, court and country, government and opposition (or, to return to *The Alchemist*, monarchy and free state). While this is of course true and useful, the extreme dis-persal of the idea of what was political atomizes the already elusive ingredient of polit-ical *thought* and tends to reduce it to topical griping. Any remark that contains a hint of criticism of a regime within a play becomes Oppositionist ammunition, or perhaps loyalist support by reform from within.

A decade later Rebecca Bushnell switched the emphasis from Opposition drama and the possibly retrievable views and allegiances of playwrights to political thought itself. It was, however, political thought as narrowly focused on the classical question of what differentiates a good ruler from a bad one. In *Tragedies of Tyrants* (1990), Bush-nell asked what, if any, were the connections between the many tragedies that fea-tured "tyrants" (from *Richard III* to Massinger's *Roman Actor*) and the body of prose writing (definitely not for purposes of entertainment) that had carried tyrant-theory from Plato and Herodotus to sixteenth-century writers like Sir Thomas Elyot or Thomas Starkey or George Buchanan. Yet the political thought of all these tyrant plays reduces itself to a commonplace: the difference between the tyrant and the good king is the difference between he who rules for self-interest, and he who rules for the good of his people. Not very debatable, though admittedly long-lasting, as a premise it allowed of little except unsurprising illustration on the stage. The complex and excitable thought of Machiavelli's *The Prince*, that the greatest good of a people might be political stability, best achieved through the remorseless strength of the ruler, was avoided by the playwrights, though Christopher Marlowe comes closest to it. While it could be caricatured in particular characters like the villain-heroes of Shakespeare's *Richard III* or Marlowe's *The Jew of Malta*, the proposition was untranslatable into plot in the other, Aristotelian sense.

What, then, would qualify as political thought in a fuller sense? First, I take it that political thought is abstract. Though it will be generated, rescuscitated, or cor-rected by particular examples of successful or unsuccessful polity, it must be larger than they are, and hence of transhistorical interest and duration. There will always be counter-examples to any political axiom, no matter how strong or thoughtful. Second, it must concern itself at some point with the *structures* of government, asking such questions as these: why do we have governments? For whose benefit primarily? How did government originate, and why? Is stability or evolution the more desirable goal? These primal questions had of course been raised by Aristotle in his *Politics*, and the Aristotelian approach was still the basis of most political thought in early modern England, where the claim was endlessly made that the English system of limited monarchy combined only the best features of Aristotle's three polities, monarchy, oligarchy, and democracy.[1]

After the primary questions come those that naturally evolve from them. How should the governors be chosen – by birth or some form of election? What qualified or disqualified a ruler from beginning or continuing to rule? Working within the status quo of a hereditary monarchy, political thinkers were very unlikely to raise the second alternative, of elective monarchy. Instead they ceaselessly returned to the question of the duties of monarchs and the obedience of subjects. What were the limits of each? How should transitions of rule be effected when something went askew in the system of primogeniture? When, if ever, did a monarch become so undutiful to his subjects that their responsibilities to him were cancelled? By the 1640s this had become *the* question, and it would be raised again, in spades, during the 1680s. The idea of a *contractual* arrangement between monarch and people evolved extremely slowly.

Economics, however, quickly enters the picture. Asking for whose benefit government exists leads to the issue raised by Sir Epicure Mammon and Dol Common (an aristocrat and a commoner) as to which system best permits the accumulation of private wealth – a question that dominates every modern election. This in turn leads to questions of taxation, and ultimately to the early modern assumption of no taxation without representation. But representation of whom? Should there be a slave class, as Plato and Aristotle took for granted (and so did most Renaissance monarchies, though they avoided calling their underclasses slaves)? Who should design the laws, and who should administer them? What is the relation between law and custom? In England, a country with no written constitution, and a system of common law in which precedent was paramount, the role of custom was endlessly debated in Parliament or scholarly groups like the Society of Antiquaries. It would ultimately crystallize into the theory of the Ancient Constitution, supposedly a check on monarchical overreaching. This meant, in effect, that political thought was constrained by past history (Pocock, 1957). But if England were to be ruled by custom, how could new laws, of benefit to the *res publica* as a whole, be made in response to new situations? In approaching every one of these questions, would-be political thinkers would, of course and as always, be deeply influenced by where they lived, their own social status, and their own psychological propensity toward idealism or cynicism in assessing human potential.

Now, there is no doubt that these questions were all very much "in the air" in the period under consideration here. But whereas there was a good deal of theoretical work on politics being done elsewhere in Europe, there was a dearth of it, in the formal sense, in England. The English read the work of such figures as the strong French monarchist Jean Bodin (*Les six livres de la Republique*, 1576, translated into English by Richard Knolles in 1606), or the radical Huguenot anti-monarchist Francois Hotman (*Francogallia*, 1573), or the Dutch Justus Lipsius, whose thought became increasingly influenced by the dark Roman history of Tacitus, and hence increasingly pragmatic and cynical in his pursuit of political stability. William Jones translated the *Politicorum sive civilis doctrinae libri sex* of Lipsius, first published in Amsterdam in 1589, into *Sixe Bookes of Politickes or Civil Doctrine* in 1594. In Scotland George Buchanan published a distinctively republican tract, *De jure regni apud Scotus*, in 1579, his response to the governmental crisis caused by Mary Stuart; but this had a delayed influence; it was not translated into English until 1680 and the translation was, most interestingly, republished in Philadelphia in 1766. Sir Thomas Smith's *De Republica Anglorum*, published in 1582, was essentially a *description* of the English political and legal system. Elizabeth herself strenuously opposed discussion of political issues, in or out of Parliament, and certainly in the press. When James I came to the throne in 1603, he was already known as the author of a royal tract on the virtually unlimited powers of kings: although *The Trew Law of Free Monarchies* had originally been published without his name attached in 1598, it was republished as his in London in 1603 just a few weeks after his accession. There was nothing to counter it; certainly nothing like the brief spate of "resistance" arguments that had appeared – from exile – during the reign of Mary Tudor: John Ponet's *Short Treatise of Politike Power* (1556) and Christopher Goodman's boldly entitled *How Superior Powers Ought to be Obeyd of their Subjects: And Wherein they may Lawfully by Gods Worde be Disobeyed and Resisted* (1558). Both the above were, significantly, published in Geneva, thus reminding us how powerfully political thought in the early modern period was motivated by religion and the Reformation.

It is therefore hardly surprising that Elizabethan and Jacobean drama approached political thought indirectly, enigmatically, or even frivolously. I shall not engage here with the question of what caused this reticence, comparatively speaking. Whether it was stage control and censorship, or lack of native models of political theory, or distraction by very local and topical issues, or a mixture of all three, the fact remains that, for all the critical investment in finding the politics in the plays, the results, including my own, have been inconclusive, both in particular cases and in the overall view that results from gathering together a series of inferences.

If one wants to find straightforward political thought in plays one will start earlier or continue later. One will turn to Henrician or Marian interludes, or to the heroic plays of Dryden, where increasingly the prologue or prefatory material constitutes unambiguous political doctrine. But then the theater, itself having undergone a Restoration, was notoriously politicized, with Whig plays being answered by Tory ones, and vice versa. To make a comparison between high Elizabethan and Jacobean drama and what preceded it, however, may be very instructive. One can, for example, find an extended discussion of an issue mentioned above, namely who should administer the laws, in the anonymous *Enterlude of the Vertuous and Godly Queene Hester*, first

printed in 1561, but persuasively related by Greg Walker (1991) to criticism of
Cardinal Wolsey that became near universal by the time of his fall in 1529. It is not
implied analogy to Wolsey (represented by Haman) that constitutes political thought
per se; it is the opening scene of Ahazuerus' council chamber, where the Third Gentleman argues strongly in favor of personal rule and against justice as delegated, administered by agents or proxies. Solomon, says the Gentleman, would never have acquired
such a reputation for justice had he not administered it directly from the throne:

> If by his lieutenante had been done the same,
> Hys honour shoulde never have spronge so farre . . .
> Nor yet hys subjectes to such awe and fear,
> He coulde have dryven by no meanes at all
> As he dyd by hys justice personall
>   And over thys many a noble man,
> At the prynces Wyll and commaundymente,
> To employe justice, dyd the best they can
> And yet the commons unneth coulde be content
> And why? for in their mynde they thyncke verament
> That either for riches and honour Justis will doe
> And he onely, for the Zeale that to Justis he hath to.

As translated by Walker, this argument (and that it is an argument is crucial) means
that "without such a personal involvement and commitment to good government on
the part of the one man who is above temptation, the machinery of justice will appear
to be merely an instrument of advancement employed by self-interested courtiers"
(1991, 124).[2] Proof that this speech constitutes political thought, properly speaking,
lies partly in the fact that it is delivered by a neutral, faceless, and thus virtually allegorical figure of counsel; his speech is not contradicted but borne out by the plot of
the play (and of course the biblical story that underlies it). Whether or not the writer
already knew the ending of the real history of Wolsey, its function is to confirm the
general proposition.

By the same token, one can imagine another Gentleman entering the debate in
counsel with what would constitute the exactly opposite political thought (as articulated endlessly by Algernon Sidney in his famous *Discourses Concerning Government*, the
treatise that in 1683 cost him his life) that monarchs are not always completely
upright and disinterested. Admittedly, even an anonymous playwright might hesitate to include such a riposte in an interlude designed for Henry VIII; but this does
not affect my main point — that here is a piece of political theory, one which could
theoretically invoke its own refutation, but which does not undermine itself by the
action of the play or the unreliability of the speaker, by whimsicality or irony. That
this was a *lasting* political thought, of application to many other situations than that
of the excesses of Cardinal Wolsey, is already suggested by the publication of the interlude in 1561, when it would apply (though not so neatly) to Elizabeth's determination, though a woman, to chart her own course in national, international, and religious

policy, independently of Parliament and even of her Privy Council. Monarchical autonomy vs. delegation would become pertinent again, as a wider and deeper issue, all through the eleven years of Charles I's personal rule, otherwise known (by anti-monarchists) as the Eleven Years' Tyranny. To put it in a more sophisticated way, the issues it subtends are: whether justice is best served by centralization or decentralization, and whether integrity is compatible with power, or whether it can only be maintained as it were by default, by a system of checks and balances (the theory of Algernon Sidney, and also of *The Federalist Papers* (Hamilton et al., 1999)).

One has only to compare this early interlude with Shakespeare's *Measure for Measure*, which deals with almost precisely the same question, to see that no such clarity of intention, or exegetical certainty, pertains in the relationship between the disguised Duke and his deputy Angelo. In *Measure for Measure* (which also declares, in its Solomonic title, a biblical subtext) the same advice might be deduced from the plot, but devoid of the Gentleman's confidence that the monarch himself will always have a genuine "Zeale . . . to Justis." The Duke's reason for appointing Angelo in his place is not insufficient information (such as the inadequate personnel interview conducted by Ahazuerus of Haman) but a Machiavellian strategy to deflect the blame for an overdue tightening of the laws from himself.

Another very early play, which shares with *Godly Queene Hester* the strategy of creating a dramatic scene of counsel – thus mimicking the play's intended function – is *Gorboduc*, written by Thomas Norton and Thomas Sackville, played before Queen Elizabeth early in her reign (in January 1562), and raising the theoretical issue of how, in a monarchy, the crown should descend from one generation to another. As compared to *Godly Queene Hester*, however, *Gorboduc* introduces a genuine debate. When King Gorboduc, like King Lear, proposes to resign his throne and divide his realm between his two sons, Ferrex and Porrex, he calls his counsel together to consider his proposal. The semi-allegorical structure is indicated in the names of two of them, Philander (loving one's countrymen) and Eubulus (well-advised, good counsellor). Each has more than one good point to make. Philander argues that the division of the kingdom would make each half easier to rule for the benefit of the subject, facilitating the adminstration of justice; that is to say, decentralization is positive, and may also lead to beneficial competition between the heirs. Furthermore, primogeniture (the English system) is unfair, and leads to civil strife:

> The smaller compass that the realm doth hold,
> The easier is the sway thereof to wield,
> The nearer justice to the wronged poor,
> The smaller charge, and yet enough for one.
> And when the region is divided so,
> That brethren be the lords of either part,
> Such strength doth nature knit between them both,
> In sundry bodies by conjoined love,
> That not as two, but one of doubled force,
> Each is to other as a sure defence.

The nobleness and glory of the one
Doth sharp the courage of the others mind
With virtuous envy to contend for praise.
And such an equalness hath nature made
Between the brethren of one father's seed,
As an unkindly wrong it seems to be
To throw the brother subject under feet
Of him whose peer he is by curse of kind.
And Nature, that did make this equalness,
Oft so repineth at so great a wrong,
That oft she raiseth up a grudging grief
In younger brethren at the elders state
Whereby both towns and kingdoms have been raz'd,
And famous stocks of royal blood destroyed.
                    (Tydeman, 1992, I.iii.237–59)

There is something definitely attractive in Philander's approach, with its stress on natural equality and high-minded competition; he is clearly an optimist. Eubulus, however, is not. He hews to the views that would, roughly speaking, be shared by Machiavelli, Lipsius, and Hobbes, though with very different emphases. For him, human ambition and aggressiveness are paramount, and that, he implies, is why the law of primogeniture exists, to regulate struggles over inheritance, which are everywhere illustrated in early British history. Equality itself is a cause of aggression:

Divided realms do make divided hearts,
But peace preserves the country and the prince.
Such is in man the greedy mind to reign,
So great is his desire to climb aloft,

. . .

That faith and justice and all kindly love
Do yield unto desire of sovereignty,
Where equal state both raise an equal hope.

. . .

My Lord Ferrex, your elder son, perhaps,
(Whom kind and custom gives a rightful hope
To be your heir and to succeed your reign)
Shall think that he doth suffer great wrong
Than he perchance will bear, if power serve.
                    (I.ii.329–36, 353–7)

It is actually surprising how *much* political theory is compressed into this simple-seeming dialogue, which became a classic in its own time, in a sense, going through two editions in 1565 and 1570, and being mentioned, however disparagingly, in Sir Philip Sidney's *Defence of Poesie*.

It turns out, but one cannot say of course, so open-ended has the argument been, that Philander was wrong and Eubulus was right – at least as far as these two protagonists are concerned. Philander finds himself, ironically, in Porrex's camp, hearing the news of Ferrex's animosity, and complaining that his advice was not taken. How Elizabeth I was meant to apply the play to her own situation is an intriguing matter. Was it supposed to reconcile her to the dramas of primogeniture, male primacy, and hopelessly confused legitimacy that had forced her to wait for the death of a younger stepbrother and an older stepsister before assuming the throne herself? Or was it advising her to get going – as Parliament during the 1670s constantly advised her – in creating an heir of her body to succeed herself?[3] With Mary Stuart since 1559 claiming superior title to the English crown as well as the Scottish, the issue was a real one, not least because it had been argued that to marry Mary to the duke of Norfolk would unite the two realms and strengthen England against its European neighbors. Or was the play, more probably, arguing that even in these early years, when it was still possible that the queen would marry and conceive, the temporary ellipsis in the system of inheritance should be resolved by parliamentary intervention? There are actually two versions of this proposal, again, one optimistic, the other fatalistic. At the play's conclusion, when Gorboduc and both his sons are dead, Arostus (Mr. Helpful), one of the original council, proposes a sort of self-denying ordinance whereby all the lords will suppress their own interest in the crown:

> Till first by common counsel of you all
> In parliament the regal diadem
> Be set in certain place of governance,
> In which your parliament, and in your choice,
> Prefer the right, my lords, without respect
> Of strength or friends, or whatsoever cause
> That may set forward any other's part:
> For right will last, and wrong cannot endure.
> Right mean I his or hers, upon whose name
> The people rest by mean of native line.
> Or by the virtue of some former law
> Already made their title to advance.
> Such one, my lords, let be your chosen king.
>   (V.ii.1674–86)

He thus takes on the role of Philander (who has vanished) as an optimist who believes in "common counsel"; but he leaves it uncertain whether he is proposing some kind of election, or the discovery of a *sort* of primogeniture that sounds very like Elizabeth's personal dilemma (that "his or hers" gives the game away). In contrast, Eubulus, with his tragic view of life, declares that the chances of even calling a Parliament together in this state of anarchy are now hopeless:

Alas, in parliament what hope can be,
When is of parliament no hope at all?
Which, though it be assembled by consent,
Yet is not likely by consent to end,

. . .

While now the state, left open to the man
That shall with greatest force invade the same,
Shall fill ambitious minds with gaping hope:
When will they once with yielding hearts agree?
Or in the while, how shall the realm be used?
No, no! Then parliament should have been holden,
And certain heirs appointed to the crown
To stay the title of establish'd right
And in the people plant obedience
While yet the prince did live.

(V.ii.1770–85)

In the real history of England, however, neither Arostus nor Eubulus is vindicated. Elizabeth managed to avoid having Parliament intervene in the succession, and even having to name James I as her heir until her last moments. The centralization and consolidation that the play yearned for therefore arrived by another, more arbitrary, means.

I have dwelt in such detail on a play outside this book's domain for a reason. *Gorboduc* created a precedent in how to theorize the succession in a monarchy or the transfer of power when simple primogeniture fails. It was, however, a precedent steadfastly avoided thereafter, not least by Shakespeare, who in *King Lear* might well be said to have rewritten *Gorboduc* in an anti-theoretical mode. It is, I still think, inarguable that *King Lear* was motivated by precisely the political situation that resulted from James' succession: his desire to turn an accident of history into a legal and constitutional principle, by formalizing the Union between England and Scotland (Patterson, 1984, 1990, 66–81). It seems odd to approach that topical issue by dramatizing the *division* of the kingdom. But while the play, and our sympathies, are ravaged by the evidence of what we now recognize as the Eubulus/Hobbes position, it is hard to find a single line, let alone a whole speech, in which the issues outlined in *Gorboduc* and implicitly re-enacted here are presented as political thought.

Let us now consider, in conclusion, two famous instances of plays in which political thought was detected at the time, though precisely what that thought is is harder to say than the plays' reputations would suggest. The first is Thomas Middleton's *A Game at Chess*, the heart of Heinemann's thesis of an Opposition drama, in her own words an "anti-Spanish and anti-Catholic satirical play staged by the King's Men at the Globe in 1624" (1980, 151) and a *succes de scandale* that produced a formal protest from the Spanish ambassador Gondomar; the second, though chronologically earlier, Samuel Daniel's *Philotas* (1604), an overmighty-subject play that was investigated by the Privy Council for topical allusion to the earl of Essex.

Could these messages really be called political thought in the sense we have been developing? What made *A Game at Chess* such a runaway success on the stage and so infuriated Gondomar was a topical protest – that the proposed Spanish marriage for Prince Charles was a dangerous policy, likely to bring England into Catholic hands. However, this has now to be inferred from the rather inscrutable allegory of good and bad, white and black, chess pieces. Of course, in the broader sense, chess has always been a metaphor for politics, the emphasis being on the need for strategy, the importance to a monarchy of defense (the castles and the knights) and the church (the bishops), and the complex significance (which resides in their seeming insignificance) of pawns. The problem with its application here is that you cannot determine in advance, by leaning on the different valence of black and white in a moral universe, that white will always win. In this case, white won, and all the black pieces were thrown in the "bag." As Heinemann was willing to grant, the message was frustratingly local and irrecoverable, residing in recognizable caricatures of well-known public figures. Gondomar himself was immediately seen as the Black Knight, "the turncoat De Dominis, Bishop of Spalatro," as the Fat Bishop, and the Lord Treasurer, Lionel Cranfield, as the White King's Pawn, who reveals himself to be dressed in black underneath his white.[4] The Black Queen's Pawn, however, is a secular Jesuit, really black through and through. It all gets rather crude and tiresome. As we say today, you had to be there. One could *perhaps* argue that, to a thoughtful person, the distortion by Protestant bias and jingoistic patriotism of the central notion of chess as the battle of perfectly matched equals might itself have suggested another hypothesis – that both sides were equally scheming and *politique*. But this was not a possibility likely to occur to most of those who were rolling in the (non-existent) aisles.

Daniel's *Philotas* is an entirely different matter. It is one of dozens of plays that explore the theme of the overmighty subject. That theme, especially when merged with that of the royal favorite gone bad, had become a commonplace, capable of closing down political thought rather than exciting it. We see it also in *Richard II*, in Chapman's *Charles Duke of Byron*, and in Massinger's *The Tragedy of John Van Olden Barnavelt*. All of these had real historical persons as their protagonists. It was perhaps no surprise, therefore, that Daniel was suspected of also having one in his play, despite his disguise as Philotas, the great soldier who conspires against Alexander the Great. It did not take very long for the Privy Council to suspect in this ancient story an allusion to the recent rebellion against Elizabeth of the earl of Essex, especially as, it has been demonstrated, Daniel drew on many of the details of Essex's trial and self-defense for that of Philotas (Michel, 1949, 53–65). While the Privy Council, especially Robert Cecil, would naturally object to any such deployment of recent political history (the execution of Essex was only three years in the past), one might have thought that to treat him as an overmighty subject and a traitor would have been acceptable doctrine.

But it has been proposed that the message of *Philotas*, too, is confusing; not because the governing metaphor, as in *A Game at Chess*, is awry, but because the tone changes in favor of the rebel after his cause is lost: "Whereas the first three acts seem to

establish [it] as a study in the frailty of greatness, achieved by emphasizing Philotas'
ambition, the completed Jacobean version . . . reverses this trend as the Chorus begins
to treat Philotas as the victim of the state's oppression" (Tricomi, 1989, 64). I would
put it much more strongly. Not only does the Chorus begin to suggest that Philotas
has been destroyed by the king's counselors out of private hate; not only is Philotas
tortured to make him confess his conspiracy, a strategy of which the play clearly dis-
approves; but at the beginning of act V the Chorus changes from an indiscriminate
observer to *two* commentators, one Grecian and one Persian, who discuss this case in
terms of political theory. Looking at how Alexander has handled it, the Persian
remarks:

> Well, then I see there is small difference
> Betwixt your state and ours, you civill Greeks,
> You great contrivers of free governments;
>
> . . .
>
> Those whom you call your Kings, are but the same
> As are our Sovereign tyrants of the East.
> I see they only differ but in name,
> The effects they shew, agree, or neere at least.
> Your great men here, as our great Satrapaes
> I see layd prostrate are with basest shame,
> Upon the least suspect or jelousies
> Your Kings conceive, or others envies frame;
> Only herein they differ, That your prince
> Proceeds by forme of law t'effect his end.

The Persian monarch, he continues, makes no such pretense, never tries "to give a
glosse unto / His violence." The Grecian chorus then protests that the exercise of
justice is one of the glories of kings; and the Persian, who clearly wins the whole argument, replies:

> That, by their subalterne ministers
> May be perform'd as well, and with more grace:
> For, to command it to be done, infers
> More glory than to do.
>   (Daniel, 1885, III, 166–7, ll. 1790–1808)

We are back, in other words, with the question of who shall administer the laws, and
the answer given by the Persian is the exact opposite of that asserted by *Godly Queene
Hester* and obfuscated by *Measure for Measure*. More complex still, this argument has
been nested within another, more broadly structured, whereby the supposed distinction between "free governments" in the Greek sense and such inarguably absolute
monarchies as Persia is made to vanish. For given human behavior, the difference
between them is merely formal and conventional. Thus the "tyrant" play has been, if
confusingly, rendered naive.

Daniel *was* a political philosopher. His play is difficult to read, and was never a success on the stage. He seems to have been intending to advise James I not to follow in the cruel footsteps of Elizabeth I. Daniel certainly wrote his play in stages, having completed the first three acts, which hew to his ancient sources in their judgments, by 1600, and having added acts IV and V in 1604, acts which criticize the treatment of Philotas in terms of the way Essex was actually dealt with (though torture was not used in that case). The play was performed on January 3, 1605. It therefore began as an Elizabethan play with no intended topical application; ironically acquired one in 1601, when Essex was tried; and became, by the time of its performance, a play addressed to James. Its political thought is therefore necessarily complex, negotiating as it does between ancient history and modern instance, between what was already in the sources, what came out of the courtroom, and what was in Daniel's head. The existence of a Chorus suggests some degree of pre-interpretation, of neutral statement; though the Chorus is itself dialogic, and we would not expect to be better instructed by a Persian than a Greek in ideas of freedom.

Is Daniel's play, therefore, an exception to the general argument I have been making? Yes and no. What it shows is the extreme difficulty we will necessarily have in matching political thought in the abstract to political comment in a play-text, even when that comment is, as in *Philotas*, discursive. Personally, I love political thought, but this is not where I would now go to find it. We have not yet discovered the philosopher's stone that will turn all this well-meaning effort – on behalf of history, of seriousness, of convictions we know *must* have existed – to the pure gold of the undeniably *right* (or left) interpretation.

NOTES

1   This is a vast oversimplification. To broaden the perspective, especially by taking account of the political content of Reformation polemic, readers should consult Allen (1928), Morris (1953), Sommerville (1986), and Tuck (1993).

2   The interlude was edited in 1904 by W. W. Greg, and the passage cited constitutes ll. 75–86. It can also be found in Walker (2000).

3   This is well argued by Michael Graves (1994), 94–7.

4   See also Moore (1935). Moore also observed that the title-page of the first two quartos carries pictures of the pieces which identify also James himself as the White King, Queen Anne as the White Queen, and Philip IV of Spain as the Black King.

References and Further Reading

Allen, J. W. (1928). *A History of Political Thought in the Sixteenth Century*. London: Methuen.

Bevington, David (1968). *Tudor Drama and Politics*. Cambridge, MA: Harvard University Press.

Bodin, Jean (1576). *Les six livres de la république*, tr. Richard Knolles, *The Six Books of a Commonweale* (1606, facsimile 1962). Cambridge, MA: Harvard University Press.

Buchanan, George (1579). *De jure regni apud Scotus*. Edinburgh: John Ross for Henry Charteris. Tr. Philalethes (1680, 1689). Philadelphia: n.p.

Bushnell, Rebecca (1990). *Tragedies of Tyrants*. Ithaca: Cornell University Press.

Butler, Martin (1984). *Theatre and Crisis 1632–1642*. Cambridge: Cambridge University Press.

Daniel, Samuel (1885). *Complete Works*, ed. Alexander Grosart, 5 vols, repr. 1963, New York: Russell and Russell.

Dutton, Richard (1991). *Mastering the Revels: The Regulation and Censorship of English Renaissance Drama*. Iowa City: University of Iowa Press.

Goldberg, Jonathan (1983). *James I and the Politics of Literature*. Baltimore and London: Johns Hopkins University Press.

Goodman, Christopher (1558). *How Superior Powers Ought to be Obeyed*. Geneva: n.p.

Graves, Michael (1994). *Thomas Norton: Parliament Man*. Oxford: Blackwell.

Hamilton, Alexander, James Madison, and John Jay (1999). *The Federalist Papers*, ed. Clinton Rossiter. New York: Mentor.

Hamilton, Donna (1992). *Shakespeare and the Politics of Protestant England*. Lexington: University of Kentucky Press.

Heinemann, Margot (1980). *Puritanism and Theatre*. Cambridge: Cambridge University Press.

James I (1598, 1603). *The Trew Law of Free Monarchies*. Edinburgh; London: Robert Walegrave.

Knolles, Richard (1573). *Francogallia*. London.

Levy, F. J. (2000). "Staging the news in print." In *Manuscript and Performance: The Changing Relations of the Media in Early Modern England*, eds Arthur Marotti and Michael Bristol [on *Barnevelt*]. Columbus: Ohio State University Press.

Limon, Jerzy (1986). *Dangerous Matter: English Drama and Politics 1623–24*. Cambridge: Cambridge University Press.

Lipsius, Justus (1589). *Politicorum sive civilis doctrini libri sex*. Leiden. Tr. William Jones, *Sixe Bookes of Politickes or Civil Doctrine*. London: William Ponsonby.

Machiavelli, Niccolo (1531). *Il Principe*. Rome: Antonio Blado.

Machiavelli, Niccolo (1532). *Discorsi sopra la prima deca di Tito Livio*. Florence: Bernardo di Giunto. Tr. Edward Dacres, *Machiavels Discourses upon the first decade of T. Livius* (1636). London: T. N. for Daniel Pakeman.

Michel, Laurence (1949). *The Tragedy of Philotas by Samuel Daniel*. New Haven: Yale University Press.

Moore, J. R. (1935). "The contemporary significance of Middleton's *Game at Chesse*." *PMLA* 1, 476–82.

Morris, Christopher (1953). *Political Thought in England: Tyndale to Hooker*. London and New York: Oxford University Press.

Parsons, Robert (1594). *Conferences about the Next Succession to the Crowne of Ingland*. Antwerp: R. Dolman.

Patterson, Annabel (1984, 1990). *Censorship and Interpretation*. Madison, WI: University of Wisconsin Press.

Peck, Linda Levy, ed. (1991). *The Mental World of the Jacobean Court* [Wormald and Sommerville]. Cambridge: Cambridge University Press.

Pocock, J. G. A. (1957). *The Ancient Constitution and the Feudal Law: A Study of English Historical Thought in the Seventeenth Century*. Cambridge: Cambridge University Press.

Ponet, John (1556). *Short Treatise of Politike Power*. Geneva: n.p.

Sidney, Algernon (1698). *Discourses Concerning Government*. London.

Smith, Sir Thomas (1582). *De Republica Anglorum: A Discourse on the Commonwealth of England*, ed. L. Alston (1906). Cambridge: Cambridge University Press.

Sommerville, Johan (1986). *Politics and Ideology in England 1603–1640*. Cambridge: Cambridge University Press.

Tricomi, Albert H. (1989). *Anticourt Drama in England 1603–1642*. Charlottesville: University Press of Virginia.

Tuck, Richard (1993). *Philosophy and Government 1572–1651*. Cambridge: Cambridge University Press.

Tydeman, William, ed. (1992). *Two Tudor Tragedies*. London: Penguin.

Walker, Greg (1991). *Plays of Persuasion: Drama and Politics at the Court of Henry VIII*. Cambridge: Cambridge University Press.

Walker, Greg (2000). *Medieval Drama: An Anthology*. Oxford: Blackwell.

3
Religious Persuasions, *c.1580–c.1620*
Lori Anne Ferrell

Since the 1970s, the whiggish thesis of the rapid and triumphant progress of English Protestantism in the century after Henry VIII repudiated papal authority has no longer been tenable. Its revision was provided by a new generation of social historians who argued that ordinary early modern people had the capacity to resist the inducements employed by the English monarchs, institutions, and elites who engineered the Protestant Reformation. Social history issued a blunt counter-proposal: that when viewed in the context of popular belief and practice, religious reformation represented more loss than gain – loss of sensible economies of salvation, loss of comforting rituals of death and remembrance, loss of community cohesion. Governmental policy might well have persuaded a person to *do* something, but it could never have persuaded a person to *believe* anything. This argument makes perfect sense when we recognize the remarkable individuality and diversity of early modern religious life, but it has been complicated by the findings of cultural and literary historians of the same period. Recent social histories of English religion may now present us with a contested and contestable Reformation, but they cannot revise away the fact that England's culture, its church, and its habits of thought were thoroughly Protestantized by the early seventeenth century.

Different historical methodologies produce divergent historical narratives. None of these can or should have the explanatory power to cancel another out. If most English men and women were not naturally disposed to Protestantism in the sixteenth century, and if many people in England remained Catholic right through the seventeenth century, then any analysis of Tudor-Stuart Protestantism must begin by acknowledging its characteristically paradoxical nature. By 1580, England was indeed a "Protestant nation," but, as the historian Christopher Haigh has suggested, it was no "nation of Protestants."

Faith by Statute

Under the Tudors, the population of this Protestant nation consisted primarily of ignorant, unconvinced, or dissident Christian souls. England's rapid religious acculturation may have originated in the arbitrary force of governmental legislation, but we must also recognize that Protestantism, a religion of the word preached and promulgated, possessed an enviable tactical advantage in an age of print. Enthusiastic reformers were able to capitalize on the opportunity given them by monarchs determined to be Protestant, but their evangelistic work was never easy. Protestantism did succeed in England, and remarkably swiftly, but it prevailed against a formidable competitor – a comfortable old religion with much to offer a stubbornly traditionalist society.

Successful legislation had to be followed up with successful teaching and propaganda. In those endeavors, the years 1580 to 1620 stand as the most important formative years of England's religious identity, for they mark the period of English reforming optimism: evangelical Calvinism was on the rise, and reform on its terms seemed not only possible but entirely, tantalizingly probable. In this Golden Age, the year 1580 marks a watershed: the moment historians first note the widespread public effects of a radical reconstruction of this malingering, late-medieval society, a kingdom once saturated in dramatic and pictorial religious representation, but now observably Protestant in literature and the arts. We can attribute this cultural shift in part to the entrance of a newly trained Calvinist clergy into the English church, the English court, and the English parish. This energetic clergy provided remedial teaching and influential preaching in these venues, all the while churning out a dizzying array of printed religious texts: catechisms and Latin dialogues, rude confessional propaganda, and sensitive calls to individual piety.

To understand how extraordinary the achievements of this educated clergy were and with what tools and commonplace expectations they undertook their labors, we need to cast a backward glance and to consider briefly the unsettled nature of the religious settlements of the Tudor monarchs. Religion was bred into the bones of early modern English society. It was bred, however, by habits of thought derived from a Catholic past. At the beginning of the sixteenth century, in most respects, Roman Catholicism in England was thriving. Whether or not laypeople understood the significance of the Church of England's inclusion in a western Christendom presided over by the pope, local religious activities offered them many opportunities to celebrate and honor their familial traditions, their regional singularity, and their God. For most people, religion was a matter of routine practice and the world turned on piety, tradition, and the maintenance of societal harmony.

These social and cultural assumptions were severely tested and often fractured as the century progressed. In the 1530s, Henry VIII broke legislatively with the universal western church that he now referred to contemptuously as the "Church of Rome" and took the place of the pope as supreme head of the church in his dominion of England. The Henrician reign was ultimately a trying time for nascent Protestants, especially those churchmen whose activities put them at the center of power, for Henry's enthusiasm for religious change waxed and waned with domestic politics and the patronage networks of the five wives who succeeded Katherine of Aragon.

At the time of Henry's death in 1547, the English church was already delivering a number of mixed messages, the effect of which depended on what the laity in any particular church might be primed by their priest to recognize. The mass was purged of prayers to the pope, but it was still performed in Latin. English Bibles could be found in some churches; so could plaster casts of saints. Protestants comprised a minority of the population in 1547, but under Henry's successor, Edward VI, they held governmental power for the first time. Bishops and archbishops still governed the church, but they were also its leading reformers – a reminder that the early Protestantization of the Church of England depended on changes of heart, not changes of personnel.

The brief and troubled reign of Edward VI was an age of institutional reformation first and foremost, but it also saw the publication of a Book of Common Prayer in 1549 and in 1552. With its traditional liturgical structure, stately cadences, and homely vernacular phraseology, the prayer book eventually became the premier transmitter of a uniquely English Protestant vocabulary. Its popularity by the middle of the seventeenth century may well have surpassed that of any other expressive feature of English religion. However, we should not forget that its first success could be calculated, in the fact that it was the most broadly distributed, and thus most effective, instrument of the Tudor state. Often unhappily, and nearly always with a certain amount of confusion, parishes slowly began to obey the new governmental injunctions to reform. But despite its official success, the Edwardian Reformation as outlined in its ecclesiastical canons and prayer books had no time to take hold as a cultural and social reality. Having reigned less than a half-dozen years, Edward died in 1553.

And so a Roman Catholic Reformation began under his successor, Mary I. Undoing all the acts of state that had established the new religion, the queen restored the old religion, although whether she did so with the bloody vengeance that her Protestant enemies recall is a matter of scholarly controversy. Committed Protestants faced several choices under Mary, the least desirable but most usual being grudging, acquiescent conformity. Protestants with money and Continental connections could go into exile. And a very few believers could stay home, remain obdurate, and pay the dreadful and awe-inspiring public consequences. These are the heroes of *Acts and Monuments of the Christian Faith*, one of the most influential books ever printed in English. If the blood of the martyrs is indeed the seed of the church, we might see presaged here a permanent Protestant future for England, presented in all its woodcut gore and glory, in what came to be called "Foxe's Book of Martyrs."

Time, or lack of it, also played its part. England had barely achieved full communion with the Church of Rome when Mary died in 1558, having reigned no longer than her Protestant brother. She was succeeded by her sister Elizabeth, who was well known to have Protestant sympathies. Elizabeth's Protestantism seemed peculiarly undefined and undetailed, however, and she proceeded with a deliberate caution that was often too politic to please her more evangelical subjects. Among these firebrands were many of the queen's own bishops, most of whom had returned from Marian exile with plans to effect the kind of stringent reforms they had so admired in places like John Calvin's Geneva. Elizabeth's subjects were, on the whole, Catholic, but her political and ecclesiastical ruling class was predominately Calvinist. The queen's job was to keep the social loyalty of the former without losing the political good will of the latter.

Religious Temperaments

By 1580, then, the strengths of the Protestant Church of England were well established, and they were one and the same as the elements of its weakness. It was, in the words of the historian Conrad Russell (1990), "a church designed by a committee," having tacked a thoroughly Reformed, Continentally inspired Protestant theology onto a traditional, semi-Catholic liturgical blueprint. This purpose-built architecture was thus exquisitely vulnerable to any shift, no matter how small, in the political fortunes of Protestantism. The tension created between England's self-professed identity as a member of the European Reformed tradition and its emerging sense of its national church as uniquely "English" produced the conditions of seismic instability that would increasingly characterize the condition of England's religious settlement in the early seventeenth century.

We can identify the origins of this instability in a number of key religious issues left unresolved at the time of Elizabeth's death. To begin, the pedagogical demands of the new religion created a gap in education between the clergy and many of the laity. First to be transformed were the universities, especially Cambridge, which became a hotbed of enthusiastic Reform ideas. After 1580, the fervent ministry of a rising generation of university-trained Calvinists established cohorts of increasingly Reformed believers in many parts of the country. A "Calvinist consensus" soon united most English clergy and theologically sophisticated laypeople. But theirs was a small, self-selected association, with many left outside – a few by informed choice, most in doctrinal bewilderment. The English Articles of Religion of 1563 describes the Calvinist doctrine of predestination as "comfortable." But whether most folks found comfort in, or understood, the idea that God had already decided their eternal fates before the creation of the world was a question that exercised theologians and controversialists. Their arguments were confined neither to the university table, the urban pulpit, nor to the private catechism of a godly local ministry, but went on to a life in the public domain, widely disseminated through the medium of print.

Ignorance thrived, in part because early modern print culture, impressive as it was, was hardly ubiquitous. The Protestant message, so well distributed in London and the southeast, had not yet reached all of the dark corners of England's lands. Despite the reforms enacted by three Tudor governments, and perhaps because they did not go far enough, traditional religion and community practices persisted in many localities, undisturbed by the call to Bible reading, the responsibilities of Protestant catechizing, or the arse-numbing edification of the three-hour Puritan sermon. This resistance to the new message inspired fervent debates amongst a vociferous cadre of "hot" Protestants: when was a brother's weakness, in the end, simply a cover for willful, traitorous recalcitrance? When would the monarch, the church, or the godly magistrate put an end to persistent popery?

For even after more than three decades of official Protestantism, committed Catholics were still to be found in England. Catholicism survived and even thrived in several surreptitious guises. Wealthy recusants, long-standing noble families whose attachment to the old religion could easily outlive Tudor monarchs, were able to keep priests as part of their households, and to pay the stiff fines for non-attendance at church. "Church papists" practiced their religion privately while outwardly conforming. And after the pope's excommunication of Elizabeth in 1570, Jesuit priests, most of them Continentally educated sons of English Catholic families, attempted to continue Mary I's work of Counter-Reformation, transforming it into a missionary movement.

International events, however, made possible a rapid cohesion of public Protestant opinion. The vanquishing of the Spanish Armada in 1588 was seen as a providential victory, and proved a turning point in England's religious self-fashioning. Writers, preachers, and parliamentary orators touted England's status as an "elect nation," thereby signaling the triumph of Calvinist cultural representation. England now knew what it was not — it was not Catholic. But while anti-Catholicism became a defining motif of late sixteenth- and early seventeenth-century culture, the characteristic vocabulary of this animus was eventually applied not to English Catholics (whose numbers were declining with the passing of every generation) but to those English Protestants who were less enthusiastic about Calvinism, or who resisted further liturgical reform of the church.

This polemical misapplication was made possible by the studied ambiguity of much of Elizabeth's governmental style. While professing concern over the persistence of Catholicism and ignorance, the Elizabethan government never actually promised further reforms of the English church, but simply refused to rule them out. Many extra-Scriptural worship practices hated by the Puritans for their popish provenance — signing with the cross or kneeling at prayer, for example — were ordered in the directives of the prayer book, but, as the prayer book also pointed out, they were "not to be esteemed equal with God's law." In theory, such actions were *adiaphora*, "things indifferent," important only for the maintenance of order and the authority of the royal supremacy. But no one in this period seemed indifferent to their effect in the least: the work of Reform was now fought on the battlegrounds of ceremonial, an ongoing struggle over which aspects of sacramental worship, if any, were essential to salvation. Elizabeth's conformist churchmen recommended the practices to their

Puritan brethren as a matter of decorum only. Hotter Protestants would have to content themselves with the well-Reformed state of English doctrine, recognize the queen's conservatism in matters *adiaphoric*, and wait for better times and a more thoroughly Reformed monarch.

This anti-Catholic and Reform-expectant mood sets the context for the emergence of "Puritanism" in the last decades of the sixteenth century. We should not overestimate the numerical strength of the "hotter sort of Protestants": most people in the Church of England were content with the queen's pace of reform. But Puritanism, an evangelical Calvinist movement from the early years of Elizabeth's reign through the 1620s, was a powerful if small part of the mainstream of the church, providing doctrinal quality control and persistently loyal opposition to traditional ceremonies. At the turn of the sixteenth century, Puritans were the "leaven in the loaf" of the English church. But when their demands became too many and their complaints too shrill, or when they took on issues like episcopacy that threatened the governmental structure of the church, these institutional insiders were more than capable of threatening the culture that they claimed to be a part of, and thus setting off incendiary societal conflict.

These passions remind us that "moderation" was not a spiritual ideal in early modern England: not for the hottest of Protestants, and not for the meekest of conformists. Moderation was a social ideal, connected to older traditions of good fellowship and community harmony, but it could never be applied to such a serious business as that of corporate and individual salvation. Problems arose, then, when the boundaries between social and religious categories became more blurred than usual. The intolerant disparity between this "social ecumenism" and religious conviction in the early seventeenth century led to the self-contradictory religious politics of the Jacobean era.

At the end of the sixteenth century, with the death of this cautious queen, most convinced Elizabethan Calvinists thought more liturgical reform was in the offing now that the unabashedly Calvinist James VI of Scotland was set to become James I of England. Certainly the times were auspicious. After a shaky start, with England's religion transmogrifying upon the death of every succeeding Tudor monarch, the nation had finally enjoyed nearly fifty years of confessional stability. The Catholic past was a cloudy memory: now generations were born, not converted, into Protestantism. James came to the throne in 1603 with male heirs and a stated commitment to review the concerns of England's Puritans.

An attachment to the word preached and a detestation of all things popish united Puritans to their less enthusiastic brethren in the Church of England. These were values shared by the new king, who entered his new kingdom with a genuine liking for the preaching ministry, an indifference to the more pernickety aspects of liturgical form, and a healthy regard for his own theological reasoning. James I was disinclined to persecute either Puritans or Catholics stringently, and he and the majority of his episcopate were willing to "wink" at minor issues of non-conformity in the interest of social peace. The king managed a religious settlement that was remarkable in its age for theological consensus and non-confrontational policy. Very few ministers were actually deprived for nonconformity under James; most were allowed their scruples as long as they professed allegiance to the royal supremacy.

But there were limits to James's generosity, as the Puritans found out in 1604. At a conference held at Hampton Court, the Puritan spokesmen, gathered there to ask for relief from the more onerous forms of ecclesiastical discipline, not only saw their agenda rejected but also their defense of nonconformist conscientious objection made a public mockery by some members of the Jacobean episcopate. It soon became clear that, in the stated interest of airing a broad array of opinions on liturgical conformity, James and certain of his bishops and court preachers actually intended such a display of monarchical tolerance and moderation to become a monitory example to those whose demands for further Reform could then be labeled as "immoderate." To make matters worse, the king's so-called "moderation" led him to allow some church-men, from the pulpit of the Chapel Royal and in print, to broadcast their opinion that liturgical conformity was not simply a matter of *adiaphora* but of sacramental necessity.

In the final decade of his reign, James's ecumenist tendencies in matters of international diplomacy led him to arrange a marriage between the son who would inherit England's throne and a Spanish Catholic princess. These matters of state had far-reaching religious implications. Angered by opposition to the Spanish Match issuing from Calvinist Parliamentarians, James increasingly made common cause with churchmen whose liturgical opinions were high-ceremonialist, whose doctrinal per-suasions were anti-Calvinist, and whose ever-expanding definition of "Puritanism" seemed to lump together for ecclesiastical censure opponents of the king's pacifist foreign policy, Church of England "hot" Protestants, and extremist sectarians. Their rhetoric dared to question the inclusion of the hotter sort of Protestant in the national church. The years of Calvinist ascendancy were fading; to more pessimistic observers, the sacerdotal and sacramental obsessions of the anti-Calvinists raised dark issues: of the resurgence of popery in the court and the end of English Reformation in the church.

The reign of James I has been justly recognized as a period of considerable peace at home and abroad. From 1603 to 1625, however, we can also detect the gradual dissolution of English Protestantism into increasingly bitter, irreconcilable, internal factions. In this deceptive calm before the storm of civil war, the years 1603 to 1625 became a literary laboratory for Protestant internecine warfare.

Enabled by the most prolific and innovative press in Europe, this laboratory pro-duced an unending stream of theological and polemical publications. Chief among the religious publications of this period were cheap pious chapbooks and religious broadsides: godly ballads, woodcut moralities, and simple catechisms. Their reader-ship was not confined to the less-educated classes; they appear to have been univer-sally popular. It is often hard to identify such works as specifically "Protestant," for they were an amalgam of oral and visual cultural elements and thus blended traditional and current cultural expectations. As Tessa Watt (1991) has pointed out, they operated largely outside of the church's sphere and satisfied needs other than that of religious education: they entertained, they provided inspirational models, and they taught people lessons about life. To read these tracts is to recognize the long continuities that characterized England's social world, and to understand that the religious interests of ordinary readers were not always one and the same as those that exercised their clerics and statesmen.

This is not to say, however, that complex theology was above ordinary readers' heads, or that a significant number of English men and women were unaware of, or uninterested in, the great doctrinal and sacramental issues of the day. From the last decades of the sixteenth century, we find English presses busily churning out religious pedagogical, or "how-to," books aimed at an aspiring audience captivated by Calvinist and controversial theology. Works such as William Perkins' *A Golden Chaine* (1591) featured innovative pedagogical aids: streamlined tables of contents, interactive tables that taught the difference between Protestant and Catholic doctrines, and geometric designs that made the theology of the Eucharist clear. The reach of these texts extended well beyond the relatively small ranks of the highly educated clergy, touching off a spark among a potentially influential segment of the laity. The upward expansion of the middlebrow religious print market makes a persuasive case for the power of a Calvinist minority in early modern England. To read these books is to recognize the transformative impact of a challenging and attractive theology.

Along with the Book of Common Prayer, the vernacular Bible was the most formative text of the Elizabethan and Jacobean eras, but even the Scriptures could not escape contest and competition. The Geneva Bible of 1560, with its many teaching aids and marginal theological commentary, was the favored edition of the hotter sort of Protestant, and its patterns and images can be detected in their controversial literature throughout the entire seventeenth century. The 1611 Authorized Version of the Bible represents the only concession James made to the Puritans, who had petitioned for a corrected edition of the Bible at Hampton Court, but even this grant was a backhanded one. James wanted a less theologically specific Bible for his church, and so the 1611 edition had none of the marginal theological commentary that had made the Geneva Bible so distinctively theological and so potentially revolutionary.

The most important literary religious form in this period was, without a doubt, the sermon. The sermon played a central role in all the mediations the age required: at court, in Parliament, and in the parish, preachers broadcast governmental directives, gave religious instruction, and referred subtly (or not so subtly) to current political issues. Their words often went on to a longer life in print. Theatrical, fundamentally occasional, controversial, and entertaining, sermons were perhaps best suited to capitalize on the theological and rhetorical intricacies of an uncertain age. They consistently provide the most complete glimpse into the complex nature of England's Protestantism.

Conclusion

When we review the English religious settlement from 1580 to 1620, we see a complicated picture of continuity and change, of the triumph of new doctrine and the persistence of traditional practice. We confront a Church of England marked by a dizzying array of cultural, theological, institutional, and social negotiations. The instability that was inherent in such a confusing situation is hard to detect in the confident language of legislative documentation and can be nearly impossible to identify in the historical accounts of daily life, but the undeniable fact of England's breakdown in the 1640s into civil war and regicide, and all in the name of religion, requires us to look more closely at the preceding years for the subtler evidences of conflict and strain.

Printed words may provide our clearest view of such evidence. In the religious literatures of 1580 to 1620, we see displayed to full effect the multivalent policies, the ambiguous theologies, and the contradictory character of the age itself. But ecclesiastical initiatives and statutes give us only a partial glimpse into this religious world: to understand it fully we must investigate the complex languages of doctrinal dispute, religious pedagogy, and homiletic politics. Any consideration of England's religious temperament in the age of the Renaissance must necessarily include a recognition of the public distribution and the literary influence of religious texts, and of the power these works possessed to shape all aspects of early modern culture and society.

REFERENCES AND FURTHER READING

Bossy, John (1975). *The English Catholic Community*. New York: Oxford University Press.
Collinson, Patrick (1967). *The Elizabethan Puritan Movement*. Berkeley: University of California Press.
Collinson, Patrick (1982). *The Religion of Protestants*. Oxford: Clarendon Press.
Collinson, Patrick (1988). *The Birthpangs of Protestant England: Religious and Cultural Change in the Sixteenth and Seventeenth Centuries*. New York: St. Martin's Press.
Cressy, David (1980). *Literacy and the Social Order*. Cambridge: Cambridge University Press.
Dickens, A. G. (1964). *The English Reformation*. London: Batsford.
Ferrell, Lori Anne (1998). *Government by Polemic*. Stanford: Stanford University Press.
Ferrell, Lori Anne and Peter McCullough, eds (2000). *The English Sermon Revised: Religion, Literature, and History, 1600–1750*. Manchester: Manchester University Press.
Fincham, Kenneth (1990). *Prelate as Pastor: The Episcopate of James I*. Oxford: Clarendon Press.
Fincham, Kenneth, ed. (1993). *The Early Stuart Church, 1603–1642*. Stanford: Stanford University Press.
Green, Ian (1996). *The Christian's ABC*. Oxford: Clarendon Press.
Green, Ian (2000). *Print and Protestantism in Early Modern England*. New York: Oxford University Press.
Haigh, Christopher (1993). *English Reformations: Religion, Politics, and Society under the Tudors*. Oxford: Clarendon Press.
Hamilton, D., and R. Strier, eds (1995). *Religion, Literature, and Politics in Post-Reformation England*. Cambridge: Cambridge University Press.
Lake, Peter (1982). *Moderate Puritans and the Elizabethan Church*. Cambridge: Cambridge University Press.

Lake, Peter, and Michael Questier, eds (2000). *Conformity and Orthodoxy in the English Church, c.1560–1660*. Rochester, NY: Boydell Press.

MacCulloch, Diarmaid (1990). *The Later Reformation in England, 1547–1603*. New York: St. Martin's Press.

McCullough, Peter (1998). *Sermons at Court*. Cambridge: Cambridge University Press.

Maltby, Judith (1998). *Prayer Book and People in Elizabethan and Early Stuart England*. Cambridge: Cambridge University Press.

Peck, Linda, ed. (1991). *The Mental World of the Jacobean Court*. Cambridge: Cambridge University Press.

Perkins, William (1591). *A Golden Chaine*. London.

Russell, Conrad (1990). *The Cause of the English Civil War*. Oxford: Clarendon Press.

Sommerville, J. P. (1986). *Politics and Ideology in England, 1603–1640*. London and New York: Longman.

Tyacke, N. R. N. (1987). *Anti-Calvinists: The Rise of English Arminianism*. Oxford and New York: Clarendon Press.

Wabuda, Susan, and Caroline Litzenberger, eds (1998). *Belief and Practice in Reformation England*. Aldershot: Ashgate.

Walsham, Alexandra (1994). *Church Papists*. London: Royal Historical Society.

Walsham, Alexandra (1999). *Providence in Early Modern England*. Oxford and New York: Oxford University Press.

Watt, Tessa (1991). *Cheap Print and Popular Piety, 1550–1640*. Cambridge: Cambridge University Press.

4

l Discourse and the
..anging Economy

Lee Beier

Few texts in English Renaissance studies have had the staying power of E. M. W. Till-yard's *The Elizabethan World Picture*, which was first published in 1943, went through five impressions by 1950, and was reprinted three times by Penguin in the 1960s. There were several reasons for its popularity. At just over 100 pages, it was brief and could be (and frequently was) assigned to undergraduates. Despite its brevity, it was a scholarly text, exploring sources from Aristotle and Plato through John of Salisbury and Chaucer, to Shakespeare and Spenser, and beyond to Virginia Woolf. The book was readable, wearing its immense scholarship lightly; it was spiced with quota-tions and was a model of clarity and organization. In combining the literary and the historical, moreover, it was interdisciplinary before it was fashionable. The second chapter on "Order" and the fourth on the "Great Chain of Being" – the latter acknowledging the seminal monograph by A. O. Lovejoy (1936) – were regularly assigned to students of history as well as literature. For example, in discussing the issue of order, the author told students of the drama accustomed to observing disorder in the plays of the period that, contrary to the impressions they might have formed, the Elizabethan age "was ruled by a general conception of order" (Tillyard, 1968, 18). Thus he challenged members of his discipline to look beyond their imme-diate sources.

I

Tillyard's book emphasized the static and hierarchical nature of the social world. The world picture inherited by Elizabethans was "that of an ordered universe arranged in a fixed system of hierarchies." In this scheme of things, again contrasted to the impres-sion given by Elizabethan drama, "the conception of order is so taken for granted, so much part of the collective mind of the people, that it is hardly mentioned except in explicitly didactic passages" (Tillyard, 1968, 18). Tillyard cited two memorable quotations in support of his argument. The first was from Shakespeare's *Troilus and Cressida* (1601–2), in which Ulysses observes:

> O, when degree is shaked,
> Which is the ladder to all high designs,
> The enterprise is sick. How could communities,
> Degrees in schools and brotherhoods in cities,
> Peaceful commerce from dividable shores,
> The primogenity and due of birth,
> Prerogative of age, crowns, sceptres, laurels,
> But by degree stand in authentic place?
> Take but degree away, untune that string,
> And hark what discord follows.
> (I.iii.101–10, cited Tillyard, 1968, 19,
> and Greenblatt et al., 1997, 1847)

The second was from Sir Thomas Elyot's *Boke Named the Governour* (1531): "Hath not [God] set degrees and estates in all his glorious works?"; "Behold also the order that god hath put generally in al his creatures, beginning at the most inferior or base, and ascending upward." Without order there was anarchy: "[T]ake away order from all things, what should then remain? Certes noting finally, except some man would imagine eftsones *Chaos*. Also where there is any lack of order needs must be perpetual conflict" (quoted Tillyard, 1968, 20–1; quotations here taken from Elyot, n.d. [1531], 3–4; italics original).

Recent scholarship has made significant departures from Tillyard. New Historicist literary critics consider his book to be based on dubious assumptions. Tillyard, they state, treated literature primarily as a reflection of larger historical movements such as Puritanism and Stuart absolutism. They see several difficulties with this position. It reduced literature to a handmaiden of history, and assumed that historical truths are objective and readily knowable, and that historians and critics can escape their own historicity and observe the past objectively. The truth, New Historicists maintain, is far more contingent, dependent upon the reader and interpreter (Howard, 1986, 18). In addition, they say, Tillyard's world picture was a simplistic representation of things. It was a "premature construction of a deceptively orderly social totality," which peacefully encompassed men and women, peasants and lords, Protestants and Catholics, who in reality lived in a world of "an oppressive and hierarchical totality . . . threatened by actual social disorder" (Holstun, 1989, 193). Instead of a unified social order, the critics say, the Renaissance was lacking in essentialist unity, belonging neither to the medieval nor the modern period, but rather to a boundary era that was "liminal" and conflicted in ideologies. In the Renaissance "man is not so much possessed of an essential nature as constructed by social and historical forces." Put another way, there was no "transhistorical core of being" in the Renaissance; rather, everything was contingent upon "specific discourses and social processes" which were heterogeneous rather than unified (Howard, 1986, 15 [citing the work of Jonathan Dollimore], 20, 30).

Historians, for their part, have also moved beyond Tillyard to a more nuanced picture of society. They have found that representations of social categories, unlike the rigidity of the Great Chain, were fluid, reflecting real changes in society. The law and traditional social norms emphasized the importance of land, but more and more people were not landed, as groups engaged in trade, manufacturing, and the professions were increasingly significant. In addition, contemporaries often classified people according to their political positions. Elizabethan commentators stressed the key role of the ruling elites, above all the gentry and town burgesses, and paid limited attention to those outside the magic circle of power (Cressy, 1976, 29–31). Other new issues concern social relations, namely whether loyalties cut along vertical or horizontal lines and whether social classes existed in the period. Keith Wrightson concluded that elements of paternalism and deference survived into the seventeenth century and strengthened vertical links, but that tensions between groups also existed, leading to horizontal affinities. Representations of people divided by class existed as descriptive categories, but they did not demonstrate distinct class consciousness and were not significant agents of historical changes (Wrightson, 1986a, 184, 192, 196–7; 1986b, 17ff).

These recent discussions are valuable in stimulating further thoughts on Tillyard. One observation is that the critics may overstate his simplification of Elizabethan social formations, which upon closer reading he actually portrayed in a state of flux, even under threat. He stated in the book's introduction that "though the general medieval picture of the world survived in outline into the Elizabethan age, its existence was by then precarious." Read closely, moreover, the quotation from *Troilus and Cressida* did not represent the social system as being perfectly in order. Its references to untuning strings, shaking degrees, "sick" enterprises, and "discord" suggest an order under siege (Tillyard, 1968, 16, 19). A second point is that if we shift the focus to conflict rather than harmony – for example, peasants and lords, New and Old World cultures, males and females, the Family of Love versus the Church of England – there is a tendency to lose sight of all-encompassing social models or ideologies and how they may (or may not) have changed over the long haul.[1] Certainly we should deconstruct the big picture, but once we have it in pieces we must remember how to put it back together.

A further question arising from recent discussions of representations of Renaissance society concerns chronology. Tillyard himself played rather fast and loose with the periodization of his world picture, which it turns out is really only partly Elizabethan. On the question of social hierarchies, he quoted Elyot, whose book was published almost 30 years before Elizabeth I came to the throne. Moreover, to illustrate the microcosm of the "body politic" Tillyard cited at length another Henrician humanist, Thomas Starkey, whose "Dialogue between Cardinal Pole and Thomas Lupset" was written in the early 1530s. But Tillyard completely ignored the Elizabethan social commentators William Harrison, Sir Thomas Smith, and Thomas Wilson, probably because they did not conform to the model of the Great Chain (Tillyard, 1968, 20–1, 118–20; Cressy, 1976, 29–31).

What Tillyard and other scholars have not done is to relate Elizabethan represen- tations of society to those of the early and mid-Tudor periods, which might tell us something about the development over time of social discourse in the Renaissance.[2] It is the aim of this chapter to fill that gap. My argument is that there was a discourse of social order in the period, but that contrary to Tillyard it was most evident in the reigns preceding Elizabeth I. Further, I contend that the period sees the dissolution of that discourse and its replacement by new representations of society. Ironically, as we have seen, Tillyard sensed that such developments were afoot when he referred to the "precarious" state of the old paradigm and when he quoted *Troilus and Cressida*. This chapter will not, however, present a thorough examination of the Elizabethan and later periods. This is partly for reasons of space and partly because others have undertaken the task (Cressy, 1976; Wrightson, 1986a, 1986b; Collinson, 1990). Rather it will focus on the early and mid-Tudor age, the articulation of a dominant social ideology, and the contestations of that discourse, which led to its demise. Thus some, at least, of the concerns of New Historicist critics will be met by examining countervailing as well as unitary representations of Renaissance society.

II

The *term* "society" did not exist in the Tudor period except to describe small groups such as trade guilds. Nevertheless, the *concept* of a larger society – "the body of insti- tutions and relationships within which a relatively large group of people live" – certainly did exist and can be documented.[3] A common representation of society under the early Tudors was that it consisted of elements that were specialized in function, arranged in a static hierarchy, and mutually dependent. In medieval thought three estates were usually distinguished – the clergy, the gentry, and the common people. The clergy prayed so that sinful humanity could achieve salvation, the landed elites or *milites* provided military leadership, and the populace performed manual labor so that everyone might eat. The three-estate model survived into the early Tudor period in Edmund Dudley's *The Tree of Commonwealth* (1509–10). This representation of things was no more accurate as a description of society in 1510 than in the year 1010, because the reality was a far more graduated and fluid society than that envisioned by the three-estate model. This complexity was captured in the late medieval writings of Chaucer, Langland, Lydgate, and others, who mapped out more detailed pictures of the social order, often in satirical form (Mohl, 1933, 116–49). But we are not con- sidering social realities here; rather, we are focusing on people's representations of what they thought their social world should be. We are dealing with the world of discourse or ideology, and in this world the model of specialized estates, hierarchically arranged and interdependent, was quite pervasive.

In this representation of society the estates had specialized roles that were fixed in function and place and based upon birth. None was to usurp another's role; to do so was mortal sin and rebellion. The attitude in late medieval sermons was that:

each man's first duty – be he knight or priest, workman or merchant – is to learn and labour truly in the things of his particular calling, resting content therewith and not aspiring to meddle with the tasks and mysteries of others. The social ranks and their respective duties, ordained by God for humanity, were intended to remain fixed and immutable. Like the Limbs of the Body they cannot properly exchange either their place or function. (Owst, 1933, 557)

The specialization of social roles continued to be stoutly defended under the early Tudors. Dudley admonished "every man to be content to do his duty in the office . . . or condition that he is set in, and not to malign or disdain any other." The common people in particular, he stated, "may not grudge nor murmur to live in labour and pain. . . . Let not them presume above their own degree, nor any of them present or counterfeit the state of his better" (Dudley, 1948, 40, 45–6).

Humanist opinion took a similar, although ultimately (as will shortly be seen) contradictory line on functionally specialized social hierarchies. "Has not [God] set degrees and estates in all his glorious work?" inquired Elyot. The alternative was anarchy: "Without order may be nothing stable or permanent; and it may not be called order, except it do contain in it degrees, high and base, according to the merit or estimation of the thing that is ordered" (Elyot, 1531, 4). The social body whose members took on another's role would be a monstrosity, Richard Morison observed in 1536:

A commonwealth is like a body. . . . Now, were it not by your faith a mad hearing if the foot should say, I will wear a cap with an ouch as the head doth? if the knees should say, We will carry the eyes . . . ? if the heels would now go before and the toes behind? . . . [E]very man would say the feet, the knees, the shoulders, the heels make unlawful requests and very mad petitions. (Morison, 1536, 118–19)

Morison was adamant that ranks must be maintained: "It is not meet, every man to do that he thinketh best"; "Every man doth well in his office [when] every thing standeth well in his place"; "[L]ords must be lords, commons must be commons, every man accepting his degree, every man content to have that that he lawfully may come by" (ibid.).

What held society together besides rank, function, and birth was the principle of mutual dependence, an idea as old as Aesop's *Fables*. It also appears in early Christian belief. St. Paul employed the metaphor of society as body in I Corinthians 12 to describe the spirit of Christian belief and the offices of the early church. He further implied in Romans 12 that society was a mystical body whose unity was guaranteed by the headship of Christ.[4] Medieval preachers sometimes likened society to a vineyard and a farm; other times, in architectural terms, to the parts of a church edifice; and in still others, musically, to the strings of a harp. Despite its religious radicalism, the early fifteenth-century Lollard tract *Lantern of Light* still represented society in its traditional, tripartite estates, as did the movement's founder John Wycliffe (Owst, 1933, 549, 552, 558; *New English Bible*, 1961, 295; Thomson, 1983, 367; Wrightson, 1986b, 17). Whichever image was selected, the message was that all the elements of society had to function in harmony for the order to exist. Of course, bitter arguments arose in the Middle Ages over who represented Christ on earth and exercised suzerainty – the pope or secular authorities. In the midst of the Henrician break with Rome, Clement Armstrong was in no doubt, citing II Samuel 7, that headship belonged to the king. Protestant interest in St. Paul no doubt fostered the revival of the image of a mystical body and its social correspondence (Gierke, 1987, 22; Armstrong, *c*.1536, 52).[5]

How was mutual dependence supposed to work? As described in a Caxton translation of 1481:

> *[handwritten: parts of the body must work together doing their assigned tasks]*

> The laborers ought to provide for the clerks and knights such things as were needful for them to live by in the world honestly; and the knights ought to defend the clerks and the laborers that there were no wrong done to them; and the clerks ought to instruct and teach these two manner of people and to address them in their works in such wise none do [any] thing by which he should displease God nor lose His grace. (quoted in Hale, 1971, 167)

[handwritten margin: feudal system?]

Dudley and many others also stressed the importance of mutual dependence. The clergy's prayers, Dudley wrote, were to help "every man well to prosper and speed in his lawful business"; in addition, they were to devote one-third of their income to charitable purposes. The lay elites were to be benevolent lords to their tenants and had a special responsibility to support the poor in "God's causes," especially widows and orphans. The common people were charged to "remember their rents and payments" to lords. Those better off, probably merchants, were told to be "loving and charitable" to those in their debt, while servants were commanded to be assiduous and loyal and laborers were to avoid idleness. Such mutual aid among the three estates would provide strong roots, Dudley wrote, for "this noble tree of commonwealth" (Dudley, 1948, 45–8).

The most common metaphor for social interdependence was that of the human body. "Remember that we are members of one body, and ought to minister one to another mercifully," William Tyndale wrote. Masters were to nurture their servants as their own children; to provide them with food, clothing, education; to treat them fairly, use "kind words" and moderate correction; and "when they labor sore, [to] cherish them." Landlords he enjoined not to raise rents, question customary rights, create large leasehold farms, or enclose the commons. As regards the commoner, he was to "refer his craft and occupation unto the commonwealth, and serve his brethren as he would do Christ himself." He should not cheat, nor overcharge interest on debts, and should help relieve the poor (Tyndale, 1527, 1527–8, 293–4). Armstrong took a very similar line: "And that all true members of a mystical body should work and labor in degree and order that they are called to, and none to be suffered to do anything, but only that, which might be to the wealth of the whole body and members of the same." He added medical imagery to make the point, saying it was "a grief to the general and mystical head [the monarch] to have any member sick [or] sore in the mystical body, either to suffer any member of the said mystical body to live out of order of a commonwealth of the said body." He targeted lawyers and merchants for causing disease in the body commonwealth (Armstrong, *c*.1536, 52–3).

The metaphor of the body and the principle of the interdependence of society flourished in mid-Tudor "Commonwealth" preaching and writing. Robert Crowley petitioned Parliament in Edward VI's reign to "Remember (most Christian counsellors) that you are not only naturally members of one body with the poor creatures of this realm, but also by religion you are members of the same mystical body of Christ, who is the head of us all (his members)" (Crowley, n.d., 169). Thomas Lever preached charity to the city of London in 1550, urging the citizens to "let no part or member of your Christian body be unprovided for: by reason of the which body, you be heirs of the heavenly kingdom" (Lever, 1550, 47). And Thomas Becon employed the body metaphor that same year to encourage the rich to succour the poor. To the gentry he remarked:

> For as the eyes are the principal comfort of an whole body, so likewise are the true gentlemen of the commonweal. And look, what the nose is without smelling, the tongue without speaking, the hands without feeling, the feet without going, the very same is a commonweal without them that are true gentlemen. (Becon, 1550, 599)

The idea of social interdependence even found its way into a composition by the youthful Edward VI, who in 1551, under the tutelage of the Continental Protestant Martin Bucer, wrote that: "[N]o member in a well-fashioned and whole body is too big for the proportion of the body. So must there be in a well-ordered commonwealth no person that shall have more than the proportion of the country will bear" (Edward VI, 1549–51, xxiv, 161).

III

Elizabethan social discourse diverged quite sharply from that of the early and mid-Tudor periods. Of course the old representations did not disappear overnight. Body imagery continued to be used into the seventeenth century, although with less and less frequency and with greater reference to political structures than to social ones (Norden, 1596–7, 165). Overall, the Elizabethans developed a different social vision from the old static and interdependent hierarchy of estates. The body metaphor was rarely employed after 1560 as a positive, prescriptive statement. Instead it was used as a warning and sometimes as a protest. Concerning threats to the social order, Fulke Greville told MPs in 1593 that "if the feet knew their strength as we know their oppression, they would not bear as they do." During the Midland Revolt of 1607, the feet had their chance to speak and they used some of the old vocabulary, describing themselves as "We, as members of the whole." But rather than a norma-tive observation about the way to social harmony, theirs was a protest against enclos-ing landlords or, as they put it, against "these encroaching tyrants, which would grind our flesh upon the whetstone of poverty." Judging by a report to the Privy Council by Nottinghamshire JPs, gentlemen could still occasionally use the language of the body in the 1630s, for they referred to "the endangering of the body of the com-monwealth," again by enclosers (Greville quoted in Hill, 1986, 56; Halliwell, 1966, 140–1).[6]

Elizabethan social discourse took new directions that bore little resemblance to early and mid-Tudor representations. This is even true of much of Tillyard's mater-ial. For example, he cited Davies of Hereford, who described a tripartite division of society, but on closer inspection its three members would have seemed strange to an earlier generation, consisting as they did of the ruler, the "citizens," and "rurals," and Davies made no reference to the interdependence of these groups (Tillyard, 1968, 117). Elizabethans were turning away from the prescriptive and idealized picture of the early and mid-Tudor periods to a more descriptive one. They turned, in particu-lar, to a much different social configuration, that of a society of orders or ranks, which placed greater emphasis on political power, social mobility, and conflicts between orders. Space does not permit a detailed discussion of this subject, but even a rapid look at the schemes of William Harrison (1577), Sir Thomas Smith (1583), and Thomas Wilson (1600) will show that by 1600 we are inhabiting a world with a different vision of itself.

mirrored the conflicts taking place?

IV

But the dissolution of the discourse of static hierarchy and mutual dependence actu-ally began earlier, under the early Tudors. The key pressures upon the model included, first, the growing acceptance of individualism, and specifically the principle of careers open to talent, which was espoused by humanistically trained writers and which chal-lenged the old notion of fixed hierarchies based upon birth. A second source of tension in the old discourse was the perception of rising social polarization in England in the mid-Tudor period, which cast serious doubts on the notion of mutual dependence. Third, as Wilson's comments indicate, the fortunes of one member of the three estates, the clergy, changed radically in the period, and so did the issues facing them. By the 1560s, as will be shown in the conclusion to this chapter, leading clerical spokesmen for the old discourse of interdependence, including Crowley, Lever, and Becon, found themselves facing new issues that took them away from the social question.

Birth and talent sat somewhat uneasily with one another, and the tension seemed to increase. The story line of *Fulgens and Lucres*, written in the 1490s, was the coun-terpoising of the patrician and the plebeian in a "disputation of nobleness" and whether birth should take primacy over virtue. In the end the main character concluded:

That a man of excellent virtuous conditions,
Although he be of a poor stock bore,
Yet I will honor and commend him more
Than one that is descended of right noble kin
Whose life is all dissolute and rooted in sin.
                              (Meredith, 1981, v, 68–9)[7]

In contrast with this endorsement of virtue, for medieval moralists, while they
acknowledged its value and cited instances of reconciliation between virtue and birth,
"the compromise was always one that left belief in the superiority of men of birth
intact." For example, merchants were able to gain coats of arms by being" ennobled
by virtue," but the documents making the grants "were painfully labored in their
avoidance of any reference to prosperity" being the grounds for promotion (Thrupp,
1962, 302, 307–8). Grants of arms under Henry VIII and Edward VI routinely
acknowledged that "men of virtue of noble spirit should be rewarded for their merits
and good renown," but quickly added the hereditary principle (Williams, 1967,
255–8, esp. 255–6). Dudley observed the process of plebeian promotion and with
disapproval pointed the finger at education: "the noblemen and gentlemen of England
be the worst brought up for the most part of any realm of Christendom, and therefore the children of poor men and mean folk are promoted to the promotion and
authority that the children of noble blood should have if they were meet therefore"
(Dudley, 1948, 45).

Humanists, by contrast, favored upward social mobility for the educated, even at
the expense of birth. Often they were the very same authorities who said they favored
static hierarchy in the social order, but who – possibly for rhetorical effect as well as
having things both ways – were not averse to contradicting themselves. Elyot we know
proclaimed that "[God] set degrees and estates in all his glorious works," but he
argued that careers open to talents, based upon education and intellect, should allow
people to move up the hierarchy of degrees:

> as understanding is the most excellent gift that man can receive in his creation . . . it is
> therefore congruent, and according[,] that as one excels another in that influence, as
> thereby being next to the similitude of his maker, so should the estate of his person be
> advanced in degree or place where understanding may profit. (Elyot, 1531, 5)

The justification for such elevations were governments' need to control those of
"inferior understanding":

> so in this world, they which excel other[s] in this influence of understanding, and do
> employ it to the detaining of other[s] within the bounds of reason, and show them how
> to provide for their necessary living; such ought to be set in a more high place than the
> residue where they may see and also be seen; that by the beams of their excellent wit,
> shown through the glass of authority, other[s] of inferior understanding may be directed
> to the way of virtue and commodious living. (Elyot, 1531, 5)

For Elyot the chief qualifications for social position were knowledge and reason; those who possessed these qualities should be advanced even if (the implication seems to have been) they were not born gentlemen. Of course he opposed democracy, denouncing a *Res plebeia* where "all men must be of one degree and sort," observing that potters and tinkers would make poor judges, ploughmen and carters bad ambassadors, weavers and fullers unfit captains of an army (Elyot, 1531, 4, 6).

If not birth or democracy, what was to be the basis of the commonweal? The problematic nature of this question was well articulated in Starkey's "Dialogue between Lupset and Pole," written between 1529 and 1532 by a humanist in the employ of Thomas Cromwell. Starkey saw the tension between individualism and the commonweal. His character Pole articulated the principle of individual interest, at one point saying that "if we first find out that thing which is the wealth of every particular man, we shall then consequently find out also what thing it is that in any city country we call the very true common weal." Lupset replied that Pole's statement actually contradicted what he had maintained earlier in the dialogue; namely, that individualism would "be the destruction of every common weal." In the end Pole attempted to resolve the contradiction by invoking the intervention of government: "where many, blinded with the love of themselves, regard their particular weal overmuch, it is necessary by politic persons . . . to correct and amend such blindness" (Starkey, 1529–32, x, 22–3).

The exemplary proponent of careers open to talent was Morison, who succeeded Starkey in Cromwell's favor and was an effective propagandist for the regime. Prefiguring Smith, Morison redefined virtue to the *virtù* of the Renaissance – ability, force of character, personality. In *A Remedy for Sedition*, an attack upon the Pilgrimage of Grace (1536), Morison responded to the rebels' criticism of the government for advancing new men in power at the expense of the old nobility: "they be angry that virtue should be rewarded when she cometh to men that had no lords to their fathers. They will that none rule but noblemen born." Against this he advanced the principle of competition for place based on ability and invoked the authority of the king: "who hath evermore well declared that true nobility is never but where virtue is; and . . . well testified that he will all his subjects to contend who may obtain most qualities, most wit, most virtue; and this only to be the way to promotion and here nobility to consist." In one fell swoop, Morison demolished the traditional concept of nobility. He rejected birth as the primary qualification for advancement, asking "what shall we need to endeavor ourselves unto, when whatsoever we do we must be tried by our birth and not by our qualities?" (Berkowitz, 1984, 115–16).[8]

Like Elyot, Morison was in the mainstream of Renaissance humanism in his definition of the reason for promoting those with the right qualities – good government. "But give the government of commonwealths into their hands that cannot skill thereof, how many must needs go to wrack?" he asked. He invoked the authority of the ancients: "That commonwealth cannot long stand, saith Plato, that virtue is not most honored in." Then he made his most radical statements, ranking the characteristics that suited people for power, and redefining nobility: "They must be best

rejected birth as the basis for nobility

esteemed that have most gifts of the mind, that is, they that do excel in wisdom, justice, temperancy, and such other virtues. They next that have most gifts of the body as health, strength, quickness, beauty. They thirdly that have riches and possessions" (Morison, 1536, 116). There was no place for birth in this scheme. Yet we know the same writer contradictorily stated that "lords must be lords, commons must be commons, every man accepting his degree." More humanist rhetoric, it seems. In practice Morison, like Elyot, rejected genuinely democratic access to education and power. "[E]very man cannot be kept at school," he cautioned, calling for education to focus upon the sons of the nobility and the gentry (Morison, 1536, 128).[9] Nevertheless, despite the rhetoric, contradictions, and qualifications, Morison questioned the old fixed hierarchies, establishing the foundation from which Smith could build the assumption that competition and mobility were natural to society.

[handwritten margin note: humanistic rhetoric was often contradictory]

V

Along with the acceptance of social mobility, a growing perception that the different parts of the body social were not working together also created serious problems for those supporting the old discourse. Doubts had always existed about whether the model of social interdependence could survive in relation to human realities. In medieval sermons fears were voiced about disorder leading to the dismemberment of the body of Christ and about the strings of the harp being so disarranged they would produce disharmony (Owst, 1933, 563–4). Dudley's tract, for all its organic imagery, contained numerous references to hostility between the estates. He warned the commoners not to listen to a messenger named Arrogancy, who would tell them they were of the same "mettle and mold" as the gentry, "that at your births and at your deaths your riches be indifferent," so "why should they have so much of the prosperity and treasure of this world and you so little?" Arrogancy would encourage them to take up the banner of Insurrection and "promise to set you on high, and to be lords and gentlemen, and no longer to be churls as you were before." In statements foretelling the church's clash with the monarchy, Dudley also envisioned radical reform of the first estate if it did not reform itself (Dudley, 1948, 60–6, 88–9).

Within a decade Thomas More swept aside earlier thinking about the social order in *Utopia* (1516), a radical reconsideration of social relations and government. Yet for all their novelty More's views echoed those of Dudley in blasting the first two orders for their exploitation of the commonalty and, in turn, set the table for more strident voices that would follow (Skinner, 1987, 155–6). In his "Dialogue" Starkey summed up the conflicts as follows:

[T]he parts of this body agree not together: the head agreeth not to the feet, nor feet to the hands: no one part agreeth to other: the temporalty grudgeth against the spiritual-ity, the commons against the nobles, and subjects against their rulers: one hath envy at another, one beareth malice against another, one complaineth of another. (Starkey, 1529–32, 56)

The chorus of concern about the old model of interdependence became even more vocal in the 1540s and 1550s. The background to these concerns was the "mid-Tudor crisis," a series of troubling events that raised questions about whether order would prevail. Between 1547 and 1558 the country saw the going and coming of five monarchs in just 11 years – something of a record. In addition, there were large-scale popular rebellions in the West and in East Anglia in 1549, enclosure riots that affected much of southern England between 1548 and 1551, several changes of the official religion, and a direct threat to the crown in Wyatt's rebellion of 1554. Historians have recently argued that the political system was basically viable, but their sangfroid was not, it seems, shared by many contemporary observers (Loach and Tittler, 1980; Loades, 1992). Even revisionist historians admit that the economic picture was grim. Six of the 11 years between 1547 and 1558 experienced deficient harvests, which occurred in two devastating three-year cycles, 1549–51 and 1554–6. Food prices doubled between 1540 and 1560, roughly following the increase in money supply caused by debasement of coinage. Real wages for agricultural laborers and building craftsmen dropped 25 percent between 1540 and 1560. The woolen export trade boomed in the 1540s, stimulating the conversion of tillage land to pasture and, in turn, the enclosure riots of the period. Then, as a result of currency fluctuations, the trade collapsed in the early 1550s and remained in a state of stagnation into the 1560s.[10]

Those who led discussions about England's agitated condition in the mid-Tudor period have been described as "Commonwealth-men"; they included Crowley, John Hales, Hugh Latimer, and Lever. Elton questioned whether these men formed a party and whether as a group they shared the same ideas and had specific reform policies (Elton, 1979, 23ff). Whether one answers Elton's queries in the affirmative or negative, there seems little doubt that the Commonwealth-men shared a common social discourse. They clung to the old model of interdependent estates and in those terms sought to diagnose and treat the maladies of the body social. They were greatly exercised about the conflicts they perceived between rich and poor; about the popular rebellions of Edward VI's reign, in which they perceived undisguised class hatred; about the obligations of the rich to succor the poor after the dissolutions of monasteries, almshouses, parish guilds, and hospitals; and about a multitude of offenders – middlemen, depopulators, rack-renters – who they thought violated the ideal of mutual dependence and cooperation. To look for a party with a coherent set of policies misses the point that other issues were also at stake.

The complaints of the Commonwealth-men, such as Crowley (n.d.), Lever (1550), and Latimer (1550), are too well known to require repetition here, and others besides these believed the mid-Tudor period experienced a high level of social polarization. They included tutors of the young king Edward VI, the king himself, Mary I's Privy

[handwritten margin note: disorder of estates was a reflection of disorder in the country]

Council, and a would-be advisor early in Elizabeth I's reign. The fear of social conflict was apparent in Sir John Cheke's condemnation of the rebellions of 1549. To the commoners, he wrote, "you have [de]spoiled, imprisoned, and threatened gentlemen to death, and that with such hatred of mind, as may not well be borne." The pursuit of equality would destroy the social order and the principle that all people "be parts of one commonwealth" (Cheke, 1549, 989–90, 1006). The picture drawn by William Thomas, whose writings were intended "for the king's use," went still further. He reduced the people of the kingdom to just two groups, the nobility and commonalty, whose interests he represented as diametrically opposed. The commons were "the more dangerous" because their diverse opinions made them "inconstant." They were prone to "frenzy" and "if once they attain the power, they destroy both the nobility and themselves." And they were ignorant, for "the multitude utterly knows nothing." In sum, the "faults of the nobility are nothing comparable to those of the commons" because: "[I]f the multitude prevail in power, all goes to confusion; the estate is subverted, every man's property, his possession and goods are altered, and they themselves never return to order, but by necessity" (Strype, 1822, II, ii, 372–6).[11]

King Edward himself chronicled the uprisings of 1549 and warned in a treatise on a well-ordered commonwealth that no group should be permitted to "eat another up through greediness" (Edward VI, 1549–51, 12–16, 162). A Privy Council report to King Philip in 1557 on the state of the country described the social tensions that resulted from the economic downturn. Farmers and graziers, it said, were "grown stubborn and liberal of talk," while the common people "be ready (against their duties) to make uproars and stirs amongst ourselves" (Burnet, 1824, II, ii, 456).[12] Judging by the comments of an anonymous, would-be advisor who wrote to the government, social polarization continued into the early years of Elizabeth's reign. Concerning class relations, he observed that "the wealth of the meaner sort is the very font [summit?] of rebellion, the occasion of their insolence, and of the contempt of the nobility and of the hatred they have conceived against them."[13] Here we are a long way from a belief in mutual dependence and a harmonious body or harp.

VI

The idea of mutual dependence in the social order was challenged by the internal contradiction of mobility versus a static hierarchy and by the external force of social tensions. But the demise of the old model was also the product of new contexts and issues after 1560. That the economic picture improved undoubtedly helped to ease tensions. Population and price levels combined to relieve pressure on land and employment after 1560. The population, which had increased by about 10 percent between 1541 and 1556, declined by roughly the same amount between 1556 and 1561 because of epidemics. Real wages recovered and showed a 10 percent rise in the 1560s over the 1550s as the coinage was stabilized. On the price front, wool prices showed low increases compared to grains between 1548 and 1573, thereby cutting incentives to convert tillage to pasture and to enclose. Finally, wool exports began to recover from the mid-1560s, re-energizing England's key export industry.[14] The removal of many of the conditions that polarized society in the mid-Tudor period meant the debate over the old model of mutual dependence was less relevant.

The 1560s also brought a new ideological context that engaged a number of those formerly involved as Commonwealth-men. These circumstances included the end of the Marian Catholic reaction, the coming to the throne of Elizabeth I, and the creation of a middle-of-the-road Protestant church. The Commonwealth-men who survived the Marian years found themselves facing new issues and conflicts. Articulate and often more radical in their faith than the new official church, they once again bumped up against authority. Hales became involved in the issue of the succession. Like many supporters of the new regime, he was concerned about who would succeed Elizabeth, who had fallen gravely ill in 1562. Many feared the possibility of a disputed succession and the prospect of civil war. Accordingly, with others, he became embroiled in the question of whether the house of Suffolk was first in line, and actually wrote a pamphlet in support of their claim. The upshot was a spell in the Tower and a period of house arrest (*DNB*, *sub nom.*).

But by far the most significant issue to absorb the energies of the surviving Commonwealth-men was the religious one, for Becon, Crowley, and Lever all had qualms about the Elizabethan settlement's retention of Catholic practices. Of the three Becon was the least concerned, but even he had doubts as to some "ritualisms" retained from the old church, and it is noticeable that, although he was proposed for a bishopric along with Lever, neither was chosen (*DNB*).[15] Crowley was less circumspect. When the clergy were ordered by Archbishop Parker in 1564 to wear ecclesiastical garb that Crowley felt resembled the "conjuring garments of popery," he refused. Two years later he lost his living at St. Giles Cripplegate for continued opposition to wearing the surplice, and he ultimately published a tract against the survival of Catholic vestments in the Church of England (*DNB*). Lever also objected against the surplice and was removed from his canonry at Durham Cathedral in 1567. In any case, he had probably alienated Elizabeth earlier in her reign by stating that she should not accept the supreme headship of the church (*DNB*). All told, it seems the attention of Commonwealth-men was drawn to matters other than social ideology in the remainder of their careers.

The Elizabethan period also witnessed growing attention to a great variety of groups that had not figured in the ideology of mutual dependence. As the case of the Commonwealth-men showed, the old discourse had attempted to shape social beliefs and behavior. So did the new ones, except that contrary to Tillyard they did not constitute a general social ideology. Rather, we have seen that society was now represented as consisting of ranks and orders, whose relations were ultimately lacking in coherence apart from the principles of competition and mobility. In sum, there was no dominant social ideology after the demise of the theory of mutual dependence.

Instead there developed a variety of discourses. Patriarchalism flourished in the Elizabethan and Stuart periods, encompassing family, gender, and master–servant relations, and under the Stuarts was extended to the theory of monarchy (Amussen, 1988; Wall, 1993). But patriarchy, while a pervasive ideology, did not provide a general social discourse. It left out a number of groups who nevertheless were perceived to pose challenges to the social order and who were treated as "other" in a veritable Babel of ideological positions. One question involved ethnicity, arising from encounters with non-English populations, including the native Irish, native Americans, and Africans, as England extended itself overseas. As a result of these encounters England developed a discourse of race and racism, it is argued (Hall, 1995). A second ideology focused on the poor, some of whom were deemed "worthy," while the rootless were increasingly criminalized. As fears of a vagrant underworld developed from the 1560s, stereotypes were drawn in the "literature of roguery," and large numbers of arrests were made, some in national search campaigns (Beier, 1985). A third discourse was demonology, which believed that witches threatened communities and individuals. When legislation was passed against alleged devil-worshippers, prosecutions and executions took place (Sharpe, 1996). A fourth discourse was anti-Catholicism, which focused on Catholic conspirators and the threat they posed to the crown, the church, and the Protestant community (Lake, 1989).

All four of these ideological positions had great currency in their time, but what relation they had to one another and what they add up to remains unclear. How seriously should we take campaigns against the marginal? Was the later Renaissance possibly a "persecuting society"? Did the role of government in criminalizing and policing the marginal significantly increase in the period? Besides specific discourses, what drove those in authority to act? These questions seem to be worth posing, even though answers at a general level still look remote.[16] We can, however, observe that Renaissance England moved to a vision of society in which individualism and competition were of greater significance than the discourse of status, hierarchy, and interdependence of an earlier era. Perhaps the pluralism of representations that followed the demise of the old view, however hostile in regard to those represented as marginal, may still be interpreted as a sign of the modernity of the Renaissance.

Notes

1 Greenblatt (1988) contains a number of essays that illustrate this point.
2 Ferguson (1965) is mainly early and mid-Tudor in its coverage, as is Wood (1994); Jones (2000) is chiefly concerned with political imagery. Still valuable is White (1965), although Dr. White did not treat at much length the general representations of society in the period.
3 Cf. Bossy (1982, 8–10), who supplies (p. 8) the quotation from Williams (1976).
4 The best discussion of this material remains Barkan (1975, ch. 2).
5 For St. Paul's influence, see William Tyndale in Williams (1967, 293).
6 Halliwell (1966, 140–1) is from BL, Harl. Ms. 787; see also Public Record Office, SP 16/193/79.
7 I owe this reference to my friend and former colleague Dr. Sandy Grant.
8 For the Renaissance debate on definitions of nobility, see Skinner (1987, 135–9, 154–6).
9 Cf. Zeeveld (1948, esp. ch. 8), which exaggerates the extent of "democratization" in the work of Morison and the other humanists employed by Cromwell.

10 The best recent survey is Loades (1992, chs 3–4); for harvests and other data, see Smith (1984, 433–9).

11 For Thomas as informal tutor to the King, see *Dictionary of National Biography* (hereafter *DNB*).

12 Dated 1577 but probably 1557.

13 Public Record Office, SP 12/1/66: probably the work of Armigill Waad, according to Lemon (1856, I, 119).

14 Smith (1984, 433–9) has a useful compendium of data; for wool and grain prices, see Beresford and Hurst (1971, 19).

15 The fact that Becon foolishly republished a misogynist tract in 1563 that was originally brought out against Mary I could hardly have helped his case: Haigh (1998, 11–12, 36).

16 Many of the four discourses are examined in two valuable recent collections: Kermode and Walker (1994); Fox et al. (1996).

References and Further Readings

Amussen, Susan D. (1988). *An Ordered Society: Gender and Class in Early Modern England.* Oxford: Blackwell.

Armstrong, Clement (*c*.1536). In *Drei volkswirthschaftliche Denkschriften aus der Zeit Heinrichs VIII. Von England*, ed. Reinhold Pauli. Göttingen: Dieterichsche Verlags-Buchhandlung, 1878.

Barkan, Leonard (1975). *Nature's Work of Art: The Human Body as Image of the World.* New Haven: Yale University Press.

Becon, Thomas (1550). "The Fortress of the Faithful." In *The Catechism of Thomas Becon*, ed. John Ayre. Cambridge: Parker Society, 1844.

Beier, A. L. (1985). *Masterless Men: The Vagrancy Problem in England, 1560–1640.* London: Routledge.

Beresford, Maurice W., and John G. Hurst, eds (1971). *Deserted Medieval Villages.* London: Lutterworth Press.

Berkowitz, David S., ed. (1984). *Humanist Scholarship and Public Order.* Washington, DC: Folger Shakespeare Library.

Bossy, John (1982). "Some elementary forms of Durkheim." *Past and Present* 95, 3–18.

Burnet, Gilbert (1829). *The History of the Reformation of the Church of England.* Oxford: Oxford University Press.

Calendar of State Papers, Domestic, Edward VI, Mary, Elizabeth, 1547–1580, ed. Robert Lemon. London: HMSO (1856; Kraus reprint 1967), vol. I.

Cheke, John (1549). "The hurt of sedition how grievous it is to a commonwealth." In *Holinshed's Chronicles*, ed. Henry Ellis. London: J. Johnson, 1807–8.

Collinson, Patrick (1990). *De Republica Anglorum: Or, History with the Politics Put Back.* Cambridge: Cambridge University Press.

Cressy, David (1976). "Describing the social order of Elizabethan and Stuart England." *Literature and History* 2, 29–44.

Crowley, Robert (n.d.). "An information and peticion agaynst the oppressours of the pore commons of this realme." Repr. in *The Select Works of Robert Crowley*, ed. J. M. Cowper. Early English Text Society. Extra Series, XV, 1872.

Dictionary of National Biography (1885–1900). Eds Leslie Stephen and Sidney Lee. London: Smith, Elder.

Duby, Georges (1980). *The Three Orders: Feudal Society Imagined.* Chicago: University of Chicago Press.

Dudley, Edmund (1948). *The Tree of Commonwealth*, ed. D. M. Brodie. Cambridge: Cambridge University Press.

Edward VI (1549–51). In *The Chronicle and Political Papers of King Edward VI*, ed. W. K. Jordan. Ithaca: Cornell University Press, 1966.

Elton, G. R. (1979). "Reform and the 'Commonwealth-Men.'" In *The English Commonwealth, 1547–1640*, eds Peter Clark, A. G. R. Smith, and N. Tyacke. Leicester: Leicester University Press.

Elyot, Thomas (n.d. [1531]). *The Boke Named the Governour.* London: n.p.

Ferguson, A. B. (1965). *The Articulate Citizen and the English Renaissance.* Durham: Duke University Press.

Fox, Adam, Paul Griffiths, and Steve Hindle, eds (1996). *The Experience of Authority in Early Modern England.* London: Macmillan.

Gierke, Otto (1987). *Political Theories of the Middle Age.* Cambridge: Cambridge University Press (orig. pub. 1900).

Greenblatt, Stephen, ed. (1988). *Representing the English Renaissance.* Berkeley: University of California Press.

Greenblatt, S., Walter Cohen, Jean E. Howard, and Katherine Eisaman Maus, eds (1997). *The Norton Shakespeare.* New York: W. W. Norton.

Haigh, Christopher (1998). *Elizabeth I.* 2nd edn. London: Macmillan.

Hall, Kim F. (1995). *Things of Darkness: Economies of Race and Gender in Early Modern England.* Ithaca: Cornell University Press.

Hale, John R. (1971). *Renaissance Europe, 1480–1520.* London: Fontana.

Halliwell, J. O., ed. (1966). "The Diggers of Warwickshire." In *The Marriage of Wit and Wisdom.* Shakespeare Society. Nendeln: Kraus (repr.; orig. pub. London, 1846).

Harrison, William (1577). In *The Description of England*, ed. Georges Edelen. Washington: Folger Shakespeare Library, 1968.

Hill, Christopher (1986). "Political discourse in early seventeenth-century England." In *Politics and People in Revolutionary England*, eds C. Jones, M. Hewitt, and S. Roberts. Oxford: Blackwell.

Holstun, James (1989). "Ranting at the New Historicism." *English Literary Renaissance* 19, 189–225,

Howard, Jean E. (1986). "The New Historicism in Renaissance studies." *English Literary Renaissance* 16, 13–43.

Hurst, John G. (1971). *Deserted Medieval Villages.* London.

Jones, Whitney R. D. (2000). *The Tree of Commonwealth, 1450–1793.* Madison/Teaneck: Associated University Presses.

Kermode, Jenny, and Garthine Walker, eds (1994). *Women, Crime and the Courts in Early Modern England.* Chapel Hill: University of North Carolina Press.

Lake, Peter (1989). "Anti-popery: the structure of a prejudice." In *Conflict in Early Stuart England*, eds Richard Cust and Ann Hughes. London: Longman.

Latimer, Hugh (1550). "On covetousness, being his last sermon before King Edward." In *Select Sermons and Letters of Dr. Hugh Latimer.* London: Religious Tract Society, n.d.

Lemon, Robert, ed. (1856). *Calendar of State Papers, Domestic, Edward VI, Mary, Elizabeth, 1547–1580.* London.

Lever, Thomas (1550). In Edward Arber, *Sermons.* London: English Reprints, 1870.

Loach, Jennifer, and Robert Tittler, eds (1980). *The Mid-Tudor Polity, c.1540–1560.* London: Macmillan.

Loades, David (1992). *The Mid-Tudor Crisis, 1545–1565.* London: Macmillan.

Lovejoy, Arthor O. (1936). *The Great Chain of Being: A Study in the History of an Idea.* Cambridge, MA: Harvard University Press.

Meredith, Peter, ed. (1981). *Fulgens and Lucres by Mayster Henry Medwall.* Leeds Studies in English. Leeds: Leeds University Press.

Mohl, Ruth (1933). *The Three Estates in Medieval and Renaissance Literature.* New York: Columbia University Press.

Morison, Richard (1536). "A remedy for sedition." In *Humanist Scholarship and Public Order*, ed. David Sandler Berkowitz. Washington: Folger Shakespeare Library, 1984.

The New English Bible (1961). Cambridge: Cambridge and Oxford University Presses.

Norden, John (1596–7). *A Progress Piety.* Cambridge: Parker Society, 1847.

Owst, G. R. (1933). *Literature and Pulpit in Medieval England.* Cambridge: Cambridge University Press.

Pauli, R., ed. (1878). *Drei volkswirthschaftliche Denkschriften aus der Zeit Heinrichs VIII Von England.* Göttingen.

Public Record Office, S[tate] P[apers] [Domestic] 12/1/66 (Elizabeth I); 16/193/79 (Charles I).

Shakespeare, William (1997). In *The Norton Shakespeare*, eds Stephen Greenblatt, et al. New York: Norton.

Sharpe, James (1996). *Instruments of Darkness: Witchcraft in England, 1550–1750.* London: Hamish Hamilton.

Skinner, Quentin (1987). "Sir Thomas More's *Utopia* and the language of Renaissance humanism." In *The Languages of Political Theory in Early-Modern Europe*, ed. Anthony Pagden. Cambridge: Cambridge University Press.

Smith, Alan G. R. (1984). *The Emergence of a National State: The Commonwealth of England.* London: Longman.

Smith, Thomas (1583). *De Republica Anglorum*, ed. Mary Dewar. Cambridge: Cambridge University Press, 1982.

Starkey, Thomas (1529–32). In *Thomas Starkey: A Dialogue between Lupset and Pole*, ed. T. F. Mayer. Camden 4th series, vol. 37. London: Offices of the Royal Historical Society, 1989.

Strype, J. (1822). *Ecclesiastical Memorials.* Oxford.

Thomas, William (n.d.). "A second discourse made by the same person, for king's use; whether it be better for a commonwealth, that the power be in the nobility or in the commonalty." In *Ecclesiastical Memorials . . .* , ed. J. Strype. Oxford: Clarendon Press, 1822.

Thomson, John A. F. (1983). *The Transformation of Medieval England, 1370–1529.* London: Longman.

Thrupp, Sylvia (1962). *The Merchant Class of Medieval London.* Ann Arbor: University of Michigan Press (orig. pub. 1948).

Tillyard, E. M. W. (1968). *The Elizabethan World Picture.* Harmondsworth: Penguin (orig. pub. 1943).

Tyndale, Willam (1527, 1527–8). "The parable of the wicked Mammon" (1527); "The obedience of a Christian man" (1527–8). In *Doctrinal Treatises and Introductions to Different Portions of the Holy Scriptures*, ed. Henry Walter. Parker Society, vol. 42. Cambridge: Cambridge University Press, 1848 (repr. Johnson 1968).

Wall, Wendy (1993). *The Imprint of Gender: Authorship and Publication in the English Renaissance.* Ithaca: Cornell University Press.

White, Helen C. (1965). *Social Criticism in Popular Religious Literature of the Sixteenth Century.* New York: Octagon (orig. pub. 1944).

Williams, C. H. (1967). *English Historical Documents, 1485–1558*, vol. 5. London: Eyre & Spottiswoode.

Williams, Raymond (1976). *Keywords: A Vocabulary of Culture and Society.* New York: Oxford University Press.

Wilson, Thomas (1600). "The state of England anno. dom. 1600." In *Camden Miscellany*, ed. F. J. Fisher. XVI, 3rd series, LII (London: Offices of the Society, 1936).

Wood, Neal (1994). *Foundations of Political Economy: Some Early Tudor Views on State and Society.* Berkeley: University of California Press.

Wrightson, Keith (1986a). "The social order of early modern England: three approaches." In *The World We Have Gained: Historians of Population and Social Structure: Essays Presented to Peter Laslett on his Seventieth Birthday*, eds L. Bonfield, Richard M. Smith, and K. Wrightson. Oxford: Blackwell.

Wrightson, Keith (1986b). "Estates, degrees and sorts in Tudor and Stuart England." *History Today* 37, 17–22.

Zeeveld, W. G. (1948). *Foundations of Tudor Policy.* Cambridge, MA: Harvard University Press.

5

London and Westminster

Ian W. Archer

I

From the 1590s onwards London and Westminster were an insistent presence on the London stage. A variety of plays in the emergent genre of citizen comedy took very specific metropolitan locales: thus among Jonson's plays, for example, the action of *Every Man In his Humour* takes place within a few blocks of the Royal Exchange and the Guildhall, in *Epicoene* along the Strand, and in *The Alchemist* in a house in the Blackfriars (Haynes, 1992). Citizen comedy is suffused with London images and topographical references: "men and women are borne, and come running into the world faster than Coaches do into Cheap-side upon Symon and Iudes Day, and are eaten up by Death faster than Mutton and porridge in a term time" (*Westward Ho*, II.i.171–4) (Dillon, 2000). The plays dramatized what Peter Womack (1986) has called "the centreless interchange of diverse language types" characteristic of the urban environment; in plays like Jonson's *Every Man In his Humour* the speech types of gallant, soldier, citizen, countryman, and street seller "jostle, relativize, and make fun of one another." There is a fascination with some of the distinctive features of urban living at the turn of the century: the permeability of social barriers; the difficulties of properly maintaining one's social status in a potentially anonymous urban environment; and the clash between what Susan Wells (1981) has described as "the old communal marketplace with its communal ideology and the new economy that rendered it obsolete."

The drama was reticent about some forms of social conflict within the capital. Efforts to stage the grievances of the poorer sort were uncommon, only encountered very obliquely within citizen comedy, and often displaced into the history plays where they could be neutralized by distance. Jack Cade's rebels in *2 Henry VI* or the starving Roman mob in *Coriolanus* might be said to ventriloquize the popular voice. But even in history plays there were limits to the possible: the censor insisted on the deletion of the staging of Evil May Day from the *Sir Thomas More* play in 1593 because of the power of that protest against aliens in the popular consciousness and the relevance of the anti-alien grievances to the circumstances of the troubled 1590s (Patterson, 1989, chs 2 and 6). The fault-line in metropolitan society with which the drama is most insistently concerned is not that between rich and poor but that between gentlemen and citizens. Although the distinctions cannot be absolute, citizens and gentlemen liked different types of plays. Citizens enjoyed the plays which praised noble citizens who had risen from humble origins, like Dekker's *Shoemaker's Holiday*, escapist romances incorporating tales of apprentice gallantry, like Heywood's *Four Prentices of London*, and prodigal plays like *The London Prodigal*, in which a citizen-type misled into a life of riot and disorder eventually reforms. The more select audiences of the Blackfriars seem to have developed a taste for anti-citizen burlesque. Conflict between gentry and citizens was taken as axiomatic. Standard plot lines in citizen comedy were either the maintenance of the virtue of city wives in the face of the predatory attention of courtiers or the triumph of a member of the gentry at the expense of the city's commercial classes (Gurr, 1987; Young, 1975). The fundamentally conflictual terms of the action is captured in characters like Quomodo in Middleton's *Michaelmas Term*, who talks of the enmity between citizens and gentry "which thus stands: They're busy 'bout our wives, we 'bout their lands" (I.i.106–7). Massinger's monstrous creation of the nouveau-riche Sir Giles Overreach sees the conflict as natural, justifying his efforts to abase the upper classes in terms of the "strange Antipathie / Betweene us and true gentry" (*A New Way to Pay Old Debts*, II.i.88–9).

Some of the tensions being articulated on the stage were being fought out among the audience. There is no doubting the social range of the audiences in the public theaters, and the notion that the establishment of the so-called private theaters excluded the citizenry is probably false. However far the private theaters may have sought to establish an exclusive clientele, they could not resist the pressure of the lower orders to ape the manners and lifestyles of their superiors. The Paul's boys probably had a less exclusive clientele than the Blackfriars. But even in the Blackfriars, there are references to the "six-penny mechanics" who sat in its "oblique caves and wedges" (*The Magnetic Lady*, induction). Such variegated audiences meant that both public and private theaters were themselves the sites for social conflict. In 1584 a brawl developed outside the Curtain Theatre when a gentleman's servant denounced an apprentice as scum. Dekker described the gallants seated around the stage as being a target of abuse from lower-class spectators: "our feathered ostrich, like a piece of ordnance . . . planted valiantly because impudently, beating down the mewes and hisses of the opposed rascality"; Jonson in his efforts to assert his control over the performance of his plays used his prologues to encourage audiences into criticisms of the gallants whose presence on the stage threatened to overwhelm the dramatic action (Wright, 1838, II, 227–9; Dekker, 1884–6, II, 203, 246–7; Haynes, 1992, 68–76).

II

Antagonism between citizens and gentlemen was long-standing, but it was given added edge by the dynamics of the city's growth. After a long period of stagnation, London's population began to grow around 1520, and it accelerated rapidly in the late sixteenth century. From a population of about 75,000 in 1550, it increased to 200,000 in 1600 and 400,000 in 1650. It dwarfed other English cities: in 1600 its nearest rival was Norwich with a population of 15,000, and there were only three other cities (York, Bristol, and Newcastle) with populations over 10,000. London also moved up the west European city league tables. In 1550 it was ranked sixth behind Naples, Venice, Paris, Lisbon, and Antwerp; in 1600 it was in third place behind Naples and Paris; by 1650 it was just behind Paris and poised to overtake. This increase in London's population was dependent on immigration on a vast scale. Death rates, particularly among infants and children, were very high; life expectancy in the wealthier parishes was between 29 and 36 and in the poorer parishes between 21 and 26. By 1600 London therefore needed 4,000 immigrants per annum to sustain its growth. These migrants came from every corner of the realm, and in larger numbers relative to population from the poorer pastoral districts in the north. London was thus a city of immigrants: probably only about one-fifth of its inhabitants had been born there. It was also a youthful city; and in 1600, contrary to the situation which would prevail a hundred years later, it was a masculinized city: 12 percent of the population were apprentices (Boulton, 2000; Finlay, 1981, 106–8; Rappaport, 1989, 388–93).

In the mid-sixteenth century London had been very much a satellite of Antwerp. Its fortunes rested on its near monopoly control of the export of cloth, the majority of it funnelled through the vast Antwerp entrepôt. By the 1540s London accounted for 88 percent of English cloth exports (up from 70 percent in 1510) and possibly 75 percent of all overseas trade; no fewer than 40 percent of London freemen were members of guilds involved in the production, processing, retailing, and wholesaling of cloth. Although cloth exports had surged forward in the first half of the century from 38,600 cloths per annum in the 1490s to 108,100 cloths per annum in the 1540s, the city's fortunes rested on precarious foundations, over-dependent on one commodity and on one outlet for that commodity. During the later sixteenth century increasing difficulties with the Antwerp connection encouraged some diversification of trading enterprise: English merchants returned to the Baltic and the Mediterranean, and in 1600 they began direct trading with the East Indies. The expansion of trade was increasingly import-led as the burgeoning incomes of the landed classes fueled rising demand for luxury commodities like silk, sugar, wine, and spices. Imports of wine doubled between 1560 and 1600 and doubled again by 1620; spice imports increased fourfold between 1560 and 1620, sugar threefold, and silk two-and-a-half times (Ramsay, 1975; Dietz, 1986). The availability of a greater variety of exotic goods and the dizzying fortunes to be made in trade thrilled contemporaries. "All the world choppeth and changeth, runneth and raveth after marts, markets, and merchandising, so that all things come into commerce, and pass into traffic," wrote the merchant adventurer official John Wheeler in 1601. Apologists for the city were less embarrassed by money-making, and deployed ever more concrete images of wealth and commerce. Even a writer as deferential to proper aristocratic virtue as Ben Jonson looked in wide-eyed wonderment on the new goods brought from the East: "China Chaynes, China Braceletts, China scarfes, China gfannes, China girdles, China knives, China boxes, China Cabinetts" (Wheeler, 1931; Knowles, 1999, 133).

London was not only a center of trade. It was also a center of manufacture. Increasing trade fostered a major expansion in the shipbuilding industry. At least £100,000 was invested by the East India Company in new shipping in the ten years after 1607, and the eastern suburbs came to be dominated by the maritime-related trades. Elsewhere in the suburbs manufactures proliferated, testifying to expanding consumer demand: the metal trades were prominent in St. Botolph Aldgate in the shadow of the Tower armories; silk weaving, invigorated by the skills of immigrants, expanded dramatically in the northern and eastern suburbs; and Southwark specialized in the noxious leather trades. Lee Beier has estimated that nearly three-fifths of the capital's adult male population was involved in some form of production in the seventeenth century, compared to one-fifth in exchanges, and another fifth in the transport and service sector (Beier, 1986).

The increase in trade and manufactures provide part of the explanation for the capital's renewed growth in this period, but the dominance of imports by luxury goods points to the increasing prominence of the landed elites in the life of the capital. As the author of the *Apologie of the Citie of London* explained, "the gentlemen of all shires do flie and flock to this Citty, the yonger sort of them to see and shew vanity, and the elder to save the cost and charge of Hospitality and house-keeping." This reflected several related developments: the growing centralization of patronage in the royal court over the course of the sixteenth and seventeenth centuries; the phenomenal increase in litigation in the central courts, which brought the gentry to the capital in larger numbers; the increasing attendance of the gentry at the Inns of Court; and the emergence of a London season around 1590–1630. To the despair of the crown, anxious about the failure of the gentry to discharge their traditional obligations in their local communities, the country's social elite was putting down firm roots in the capital. There was also a tendency for the location of aristocratic and gentle residence to move westward, toward Westminster and away from the city, under the irresistible pull of the court. Particularly in the early seventeenth century the aristocracy built fine palaces along the Strand. Fashionable housing developments in Covent Garden brought an ever larger number of the elite to near-permanent residence in the vicinity of the capital. By 1637 there were as many as 242 people (as many as an average English county) with claims to gentility residing in the parish of St. Martin-in-the-Fields alone. As R. Malcolm Smuts has pointed out, it would be wrong to draw the contrast between Westminster and London too starkly. There remained pockets of gentle residence in the city, like St. Botolph Aldersgate, where the Exchequer presence was strong. Although there was an elite core in Westminster, the elite needed servicing, and so a host of tradesmen lived close at hand. But what was lacking in the West End was a powerful commercial presence (Stow, 1908, II, 212; Smuts, 1991, 122; Heal, 1988).

London offered an increasing range of distractions for its gentle visitors. It was the country's premier shopping center. Shops grew more numerous, more spacious, and more specialist. With the opening of the Royal Exchange in 1568 with its gallery of shops, London acquired its first mall. The correspondence of the gentry is littered with requests for the latest in metropolitan fashion items and luxuries. In 1638–9 Sir William Calley, a Wiltshire gentleman, ordered codpiece points of musk colored silk, jordan almonds, a black tiffany hood, linen boot-hose, holland cloth, six good table knives, a pair of gold colored stockings, and a tierce of best claret, and for his wife a black satin gown and a white satin waistcoat; she independently ordered "as much of the very best and richest black flowered satin of the best worck, yet fit for an ancient woman, as will make a straight-bodied gown" (Fisher, 1990; Peck, 2000; Friedman, 2000; Matthew, 1948). Gentlewomen were seen as particularly vulnerable to the temptations of metropolitan consumerism. James I noted in 1616 that:

> one of the greatest causes of all gentlemen's desire, that have no calling or errand, to dwell in London, is apparently the pride of women. For if they bee wives, then their husbands, and if they be maydes, then their fathers, must bring them up to London because the new fashion is to be had nowhere but in London. (McIlwain, 1965, 343)

The emergence of a London season also owed a great deal to the availability of new leisure facilities. Lady Anne Clifford noted of her husband the earl of Dorset that in the capital "he went much abroad to Cocking, Bowling Alleys, to Plays and Horse Races." By the 1630s pleasure gardens with tree-lined walks and eating places had opened in Vauxhall and Lambeth, "daily resorted and fill'd with Lords and Knights, and their Ladies; Gentlemen and Gallants with their Mistresses." The concentration of so many of the social elite offered unique opportunities for socializing, and it is in the early seventeenth century that the phenomenon of the social "visit" becomes established (Clifford, 1990, 43; McClure, 1980, 138; Bryson, 1998, 129–40).

III

For all their undoubted economic and social interdependence, there were undoubtedly tensions between London and Westminster. The Westminster tradesmen looked to their aristocratic patrons to protect them against the interference of the London guilds, who in turn saw their suburban competitors as responsible for the devaluation of the benefits of the city freedom. Sir Robert Cecil played on these rivalries when he opened the New Exchange on the Strand in competition with the Royal Exchange at the heart of the old city. "When I balance London with Westminster, Middlesex, or rather with all England, then I must conclude that London might suffer some little quill of profit to pass by their main pipe." And these aristocratic patrons of fashion in celebrating the opening of their new emporium could not resist some side-swipes at the city's values. Jonson's entertainment for the opening of the New Exchange sought to differentiate it from its rival. The conventional associations of selling with fraudulence and pressure to buy worthless goods (the "mountebank tricks" used by city merchants) are neutralized by the masking of the merchant, so that at a key moment he could be unmasked as a purveyor of commodities of true worth. Likewise, the motto over the New Exchange ("All other places give for money; here all is given for love") sought to distance the shopping center from commerce and associate it with aristocratic munificence. Londoners, likewise, were aware of the contrast between the values of trade and commerce and those of the court. In the pageants welcoming James the citizens were prepared to deny their own identity for the sake of toadying to their new monarch:

> London (to doo honour to this day, wherein springs up all her happines) being ravished with unutterable ioyes, makes no accoount (for the present) of her ancient title, to be called a Citie (because that during these tryumphes, she puts off her formall habite of Trade and Commerce, treading even Thrift itself under foote) but now becomes a Reveller and a Courtier.

The contorted syntax speaks volumes for the difficulties the citizens had in negotiating their relationship with the court (Stone, 1973, 96–7; Dillon, 2000, ch. 6; Dekker, 1953–61, II, 281).

Westminster, in spite of the intervention of Parliament in 1585, lacked powerful local institutions governing the whole of the city: the court of burgesses established in that year had no power to initiate legislation and was essentially concerned with the policing of petty delinquency. The key players in Westminster government were the parish vestries, and these increasingly fell under the sway of the gentry residents. Power was perhaps more widely dispersed among the social elite after the death of Robert Cecil in 1612 (before then Westminster might be described as a Cecil fief), but it was far more subject to aristocratic interference than London ever could be. The grip of the commercial elites on the reins of London government was in fact extraordinarily firm. Meeting at least twice a week, the 26 aldermen controlled routine administration; they retained control over the initiation of city legislation; they disposed of the bulk of the city's patronage; and, assisted by their deputies, they undertook a wide range of police functions in their wards. During the later sixteenth century approximately two-thirds of London's aldermen made their fortunes in overseas trade, while the remainder were domestic wholesalers. There was no gentry presence in the court of aldermen, and the aldermen did not have to face down competing jurisdictions or a military governor in the way that the Parisians did. Venetian visitors reported in wonder on the "republic of wholesale merchants" that governed the city. Courtiers were, of course, only too eager to sink their teeth into the juicy patronage resources of the city, seeking favorable leases of the properties owned by city institutions, or the city freedom and offices in its administration, for their dependants. But the relative lack of court leverage on the capital meant that Londoners were able to keep them at arm's length (Archer, 1991, ch. 2, 2001; *Calendar of State Papers Venetian*, xv. 503).

Institutional arrangements embodied tensions that were at root economic in nature. George Whetstone warned that the readiness with which Londoners battened on the financial embarrassments of the landed elite resulted in class tensions:

> the extremitie of these mens dealings hath beene and is so cruell, as there is a natural malice generally impressed in the hearts of the gentlemen of England towards the citizens of London insomuch as if they odiously name a man, they foorthwith call him A Trimme merchaunt.

Many gentlemen found themselves caught in the toils of some "merciless griping usurer," but their difficulties owed much to the underdeveloped state of the credit market in this period. Interest rates were high; credit was only available for short periods, few moneylenders allowing longer than six months; and creditors protected their loans by the device of the penal bond, by which borrowers were forced to acknowledge a debt of double the amount borrowed should they fail to repay the principal and interest by a stipulated day. Mortgages were also fraught with peril, and only a desperate last resort. Borrowers would convey an estate in fee simple to their creditor, subject to the proviso that they could re-enter only if the debt was paid by the due date. This exposed the borrowers to the forfeiture of the estate if they were as much as a day late with their payment. Only with the establishment by Chancery of the principle of equity of redemption in the 1620s were borrowers protected against forfeiture provided that interest payments were made. The insistence of creditors on the letter of the law inevitably gave them a reputation for rapacity, but they were acutely aware of their own exposure, as regular bankruptcies reminded them of the vulnerability of commercial fortunes. Many members of London's business elite lent money only as a sideline to overseas trade or domestic wholesaling, but there were specialists like Thomas Sutton (with £45,000 on loan at his death), Baptist Hickes (the Cheapside silk dealer turned money-lender, and eventual Viscount Campden), and Paul Bayning (another beneficiary of the sale of honors, with a staggering £136,700 on loan at his death). These were the men who would have come to mind as Sir Giles Overreach stalked the stage (Whetstone, 1584; Finch, 1956, 83–92; Stone, 1965, ch. 9).

If the gentry despised the merchant classes for their avarice, the grave citizens at the Guildhall despised the prodigality and disorder of the gentleman. We are accustomed to thinking of the problem of order in the capital in terms of the difficulties posed by the apprentices. Sure enough, they were notorious for the festive misrule of Shrove Tuesday and May Day, when their targets included brothels and occasionally theaters; they threatened action against scapegoats for economic ills, like the strangers;

and in tense years like 1595 they might call into question the authority of their governors. There were also regular clashes with nobles and gentlemen and their retinues, and sometimes with the Inns of Court. The Venetian ambassador was disgusted by the spectacle of apprentices jeering at those who arrived in coaches to enjoy the spectacle of Lord Mayor's Day. These clashes, like the one outside the Curtain Theatre we discussed earlier, might have owed something to the status uncertainties of apprentices, many of them themselves younger sons from gentle backgrounds now subject to the sneers of serving-men. What we are witnessing in these clashes is competition over claims to male honor. The honor of apprentices was tainted in the eyes of the gentry and their servants by their menial occupations; the apprentices reacted by vigorously asserting their claim to honor. What is extraordinary about the incidents of violence between them and gentlemen is the apparent solidarity shown by apprentices whose social origins and trades were heterogeneous. The cry "prentices and clubs" seems to have been capable of mobilizing large numbers on the streets (Archer, 1991, 1–9).

Clashes between apprentices and gentlemen are usually reported from the biased perspective of the social elite, creating an impression of apprentice provocation. But one might well suppose that the apprentices were provoked by swaggering gentlemen and their loud-mouthed servants. Indeed, the problem of order in the capital owed a great deal more to its gentry residents and visitors than is often realized. William Harrison noted of the gentlemen of the Inns of Court that "the younger sort of them abroad in the streets are scarce able to be bridled by any good order at all." The crown's assertion of the monopoly of violence was a protracted process, and the new honor codes of virtue and civility only gradually displaced the older emphasis on lineage and violent self-assertiveness. Gentlemen and their retainers frequently came to blows in the streets of the capital, especially Fleet Street and the Strand. By the 1590s, with the adoption of the rapier, the spread of fashionable fencing schools, and the appearance of manuals on the art of self-defense, these violent impulses were increasingly channeled into the duel, which was at least confined to the principals alone. But elaborate social codes put gentlemen under pressure to mount challenges for the most trivial of verbal slips. Lodowyck Bryskett complained in 1606 that as soon as young men felt themselves ill-treated, they "fear no perill nor danger of their lives, but boldly and rashly undertake to fight"; every tavern quarrel was likely to provoke the "martiall duellists," claimed Braithwait in 1630. James I's government struggled against the "bloodie exercise of the duello," reminding the gentry in a proclamation of 1613 that "the quallities of gentlemen are borne for societie and not for batterie" (Harrison, 1994, 76; Stone, 1965, 223–34, 242–50; Kiernan, 1989, 78–88; Bryskett, 1606, 100–1; Brathwait, 1630, 39–42; Larkin and Hughes, 1973). Gentry violence was not confined to members of their own class but also expressed itself in quarrels with the citizenry, especially in confrontations between rowdy gentlemen and the watch. In 1600, for example, Sir Edward Baynham and his fellow roisterers sallied forth from the Mermaid tavern in Bread Street, and set upon the watch swearing that they "would be revenged of the said city and that they would fire the citty," and shouting that they "cared not a fart for the Lord Maior or any Magistrate in London and . . . hoped shortly to see a thowsand of the Cittizens throates cutt."[1] It is a sign of the double standards about gentry violence that when Philip Gawdy reported this episode he downplayed it, explaining that Baynham and his companions were "somewhat merry" (Jeayes, 1906, 101). Likewise, the gentry were a major obstacle to the clamp-down by the city fathers on immorality. Prostitution was another of the city's service industries oriented toward them. "Divers gentlemen with chaynes of gold" patronized Mrs. Farmer's bawdy house in St. John Street; Honman's in Southwark was the resort of "very auncyent folkes and welthye"; Mary Dornelly's was the resort of "gentlemen and wealthy men with velvet gaskins and not for the common sort."[2] The correspondence of the gentry shows them to have taken a keen interest in the "heavy newes out of Bridewell" reporting the fate of notorious prostitutes like Mall Newberry and Mall Digby; some were rescued by gangs of gentlemen as they were being carried off to Bridewell. That one of the key justifications for the playhouses was that thereby gentlemen were kept from dicing, drinking to excess, and whoring was scarcely a ringing endorsement of their morals (Jeayes, 1906, 99–100, 108–9).

What made gentry disorders so difficult to handle was the inconsistency of crown and council. The city's campaign against prostitution was compromised by the protection offered to brothels by key court interests, as several brothel-keepers were connected to aristocratic patrons. The court traffic in reprieves for convicted felons was the despair of the city's law enforcement officials: "when the court is furthest from England, then is there the best justice done in England," noted Recorder Fleetwood. The hard-line attitude of the city fathers was undermined by the council's support for theaters where drama could be tried out before performance at court. Likewise, efforts to regulate gambling were undermined by the rights granted to court concessionary interests to license dicing houses. Nor was the court establishment keen on citizens disciplining gentlewomen. Perhaps we can understand the heavy fine and imprisonment imposed on the sheriff for having a gentlewoman whipped in Bridewell for immorality. But more extraordinary was the way in which the blinkers of social snobbery could prevent the punishment of the more violent members of the elite. The Privy Council criticized the city governors for their refusal to grant bail to a gentleman who had killed the beadle carrying off one Mrs. Moody to Bridewell: impressed that Moody was "a gentlewoman of good birth and alyaunce," they astonishingly concluded that the beadle, "transported violently as it should seem by his own fury," had been at fault and deserved his fate (Archer, 1991, 230–3; Wright, 1838, II, 21, 170, 243, 245, 247; Gurr, 2000).[3]

IV

The force of social conflict was blunted, however, by a number of considerations.[4] The court was not hermetically sealed from the city. The aristocratic palaces along the

Strand stood cheek-by-jowl with tradesmen's establishments. Court culture was not always socially exclusive (at least under Elizabeth and James). Tournaments were ticketed events open to those who could afford them; the sermons at Whitehall could attract crowds of 5,000. Both Elizabeth and James were present at select city functions. James, for example, for all his supposed aversion to crowds, attended a lavish feast at Merchant Taylors' Hall in 1607 as part of the entertainment of ambassadors from the Low Countries; he was present at the launch of the great East India Company ship *Trade's Increase* in 1609; he attended the christening of Sir Arthur Ingram's son in 1614; he dined with Alderman Cockayne in June 1616; and he appeared at a Paul's Cross sermon in 1620 to launch the renewal of St. Paul's (McClure, 1939, I, 245, 292, 545, II, 8, 299). Social mobility (in particular the need for younger sons to make their way in the world) was such that many gentry families had relatives in trade. The lack of juridical definition of the gentry as a class meant that it could accommodate new sources of wealth, including the key mediators between landed and commercial society, the lawyers. The crown recruited the services of city experts like Sir Thomas Gresham, Sir Lionel Cranfield, and Sir William Russell, and it continued to depend on mercantile contacts for much of its foreign intelligence. The recipients of royal concessionary grants (for example, monopoly rights over forms of industrial production) relied on the services of business intermediaries to implement and enforce their grants. The city's constant quest for contacts in central government ensured that courtiers and government officials were invited to city functions: livery company feasts were crucial in lubricating these relationships. Humphrey Handford, sheriff in 1622–3, gained a reputation for his "magnificall" entertainment of the king's servants and the gentlemen of Lincoln's Inn. In another instance of the interchange of personnel and wealth between city and court, the lord mayor in the same year, Peter Proby, had been Walsingham's barber, enabling the lord keeper to joke at his presentation that "he was glad to see such correspondence betwixt the court and the citie that they had made choise of a courtier for their prime magistrate, and the court of a citizen for a principall officer" (McClure, 1939, II, 461, 474, 487).

More positive evaluations of merchants were emerging at the turn of the century. Commentators stressed the lawfulness and utility (in some cases even the nobility) of the merchant's calling. According to Thomas Gainsford:

> the merchant is a worthy commonwealths man, for however private commoditie may transport him beyond his owne bounds, yet the publicke good is many wayes augmented by mutual commerce, forren tyayding, exploration of countries, knowledge of language & encrease of navigation, instruction and mustering of seamen, diversity of intelligences, and prevention of forren treasons. (1616, 89)

John Wheeler argued in 1601 that merchants could trade without derogating from their nobility; Edmund Bolton in 1629 denied that apprenticeship was a mark of servitude and praised the occupations of merchants and wholesalers as "most generous mysteries." The moralists showed a greater awareness of the realities of commercial life. Thomas Cooper appended to his published sermon to the Grocers' Company in 1619 a series of cases of conscience: "whether it be not lawful to desire riches and abundance . . . whether we may use such meanes for the gathhering of riches as man's law doth tollerate . . . whether a man cannot live in the world and thrive in his calling without shipwrack of his conscience" (Wheeler, 1931, 6–7; Bolton, 1629; Cooper, 1619).

One of the indications of the softening of relations is the evidence for growing intermarriage between the landed and commercial elites in the early seventeenth century. Gainsford remarked that "citizens in times past did not marry beyond their degrees nor would a gentleman make affinitie with a burgesse: but wealth hath taught us now another lesson; and the gentleman is glad to make his younger son a trades-man and match his best daughter with a rich citizen for estate and living." Lawrence Stone has confirmed that intermarriage between the aristocracy and the merchant class was rare before 1590, but much more common from 1590 to 1630, although (con-trary to Gainsford) it was more usual for aristocratic males to marry mercantile women. Alderman Sir William Cockayne's five daughters among them married three earls, a viscount, and a baronet. Such matches were often regarded with unease by both sides. Alderman Sir John Spencer resisted his daughter's match with the feck-less Lord Compton and they were forced to elope, while Alderman Sir Christopher Harvey went to extraordinary lengths to avoid the predatory attentions of Sir Christo-pher Villiers to his daughter. Conservatives within the elite mocked those citizens who tried to "purchase so poore honor with the price of [their] daughter[s]," especially when it meant marrying a man "so worne out in state, credit, yeares and otherwise" as the decrepit Lord Effingham, married to the daughter of the lord mayor in 1620. But the existence of such matches testifies to the permeability of the social barriers (Gainsford, 1616, 27; Stone, 1965, 628–32; McClure, 1939, II, 241, 301, 347–8).

The insistence of some of the landed elite on the maintenance of the social barri-ers was a reaction to the fact that they were so loosely defined, and so regularly and successfully breached. "Whosoever . . . can live idly and without manuall labour, and will beare the port, charge and countenance of a gentleman, he shall be . . . taken for a gentleman," declared Thomas Smith. So becoming a gentleman was a matter of mas-tering the code of manners and being accepted as one. The satirists had a great deal of fun at the expense of the citizen who sought to ape the manners of his superiors. In *Every Man Out of his Humour* Fungoso, the son of the city miser sent to the Inns of Court to become a gentleman, apes the clothes and manners of the courtier Fastidius Briske, but is unable to keep up because the courtier always has a newer suit which he cannot afford. Gainsford claimed that citizens:

> are never so out of countenance as in the imitation of gentlemen: for eyther they must alter habite, manner of life, conversation and even the phrase of speche which will be but a wrested compulsion; or intermingle their manners and attire in part garish & other part comelie, which can be but a foppish mockery.

But the force of the satire is probably testimony to the citizens' success in mastering elements of the codes, which in any case were only partially adopted by the landed elite (Smith, 1982, 72; Haynes, 1992, 54; Gainsford, 1616, 27).

The realities of social interaction in the metropolitan area were therefore more complex than the antagonistic languages of court and city would suggest. When we can reconstruct the social milieux of individuals, it is the range of their contacts which surprises us. Sir Humphrey Mildmay, a regular gentleman visitor to the capital in the 1630s, socialized not only with his fellow gentry but also with his in-laws, who had connections with the aldermanic bench. Edward Alleyn, the actor and theater entrepreneur turned gentleman, was as much at ease with the vestrymen of the parish of St. Saviour Southwark as with the Surrey justices; he apparently enjoyed conversation with the earl of Arundel; he relied on the counsel of Lady Clarke, widow of a baron of the exchequer; his second marriage brought him into the kin of Dr. John Donne; and the spread of his charities across St. Botolph Bishopsgate, St. Saviour's, St. Giles Cripplegate, and Camberwell suggests that he maintained links with the parishes in which he had successively resided and built his fortune. From his "catalogue of all such persons deceased whome I knew in their life time," we learn that the social circle of the city legal official Richard Smyth included fellow legal professionals, aldermen and common councilors, and a great variety of tradesmen. The ties of neighborhood, kinship, and patronage were such that connections were maintained across the social spectrum and often straddled city and court (Butler, 1984, 113–17, 121–4; Young, 1894; Ellis, 1849).[5]

These more complex attitudes were reflected in the drama, which increasingly offers a less crudely antagonistic account of relations between gentlemen and citizens. For all that Middleton's drama often takes court–city tensions as its theme, it fails to endorse a consistent position in support of the gentry class. In *Michaelmas Term* Quomodo's pretensions are effectively punctured, but his gentry antagonists are not sympathetically presented. Jonson likewise does not confine his satire to the gentry class: his target is the greed and self-delusion present in sections of all classes of society. Citizen comedy to some extent stood in the estates satire tradition. By the 1620s and 1630s, one can detect more positive evaluations of merchant types. Thus Massinger's drama should not be seen as anti-citizen. *The City Madam* eventually upholds the values of Sir John Frugal, the merchant who restricts himself to what the law gives him, offers easy terms to those in debt to him, is a supporter of the noble Lord Lacy, and works to cure his daughters of pride above their station. In *A New Way to Pay Old Debts*, Massinger is dramatizing tensions within the aristocratic class, as Overreach does not embody the traditional city type, given his rejection of civic values like thrift. Although not entirely at ease with the city's new wealth and the mobility it released, Massinger was willing to explore means by which it could be accommodated within the traditional value system. The distinctions of social status were clearly a major source of tension in late sixteenth- and early seventeenth-century London, but the realities of permeable social barriers and the emergence of a metropolitan culture transcending status divisions meant that social realities were often more accommodating than the rhetoric of status would suggest (Chakravorty, 1996; Butler, 1982, 1995).

NOTES

1   Public Record Office, STAC5/A27/38.
2   Bridewell Court Book, III, fols. 27v, 134v, 279, 355v (microfilm at Guildhall Library).
3   *Historical Manuscripts Commission, Middleton* (1901, 158–9, 568); Corporation of London Records Office, *Remembrancia*, I, no. 318.
4   The themes of this paragraph are explored further in Archer (2000a).
5   I have developed this argument in Archer (2000b).

REFERENCES AND FURTHER READING

Archer, I. W. (1991). *The Pursuit of Stability: Social Relations in Elizabethan London*. Cambridge: Cambridge University Press.

Archer, I. W. (2000a). "Popular politics in sixteenth and early seventeenth century London." In *Londinopolis: Essays in the Social and Cultural History of Early Modern London*, eds P. Griffiths and M. Jenner. Manchester: Manchester University Press.

Archer, I. W. (2000b). "Social networks in Restoration London: the evidence from Pepys' Diary." In *Communities in Early Modern England*, eds A. J. Shepard and P. Withington. Manchester: Manchester University Press.

Archer, I. W. (2001). "Government in early modern London: the challenge of the suburbs." In *Two Capitals: London and Dublin in the Early Modern Period*, eds P. Clark and R. Gillespie. Dublin.

Beier, A. L. (1986). "Engine of manufacture: the trades of London." In *London, 1500–1700: The Making of the Metropolis*, eds A. L. Beier and R. Finlay. London: Longman.

Beier, A. L. and R. Finlay, eds (1986). *London, 1500–1700: The Making of the Metropolis*. London: Longman.

Bolton, E. (1629). *The Cities Advocate.*

Boulton, J. P. (2000). "London, 1540–1700." In *The Cambridge Urban History of Britain. Vol. II. 1540–1840*, ed. P. Clark. Cambridge: Cambridge University Press.

Brathwait, R. (1630). *The English Gentleman.*

Bryskett, L. (1606). *A Discourse of Civill Life*. London.

Bryson, A. (1998). *From Courtesy to Civility: Changing Codes of Conduct in Early Modern England*. Oxford: Clarendon Press.

Butler, M. (1982). "Massinger's *The City Madam* and the Caroline audience." *Renaissance Drama* n.s. 13, 157–97.

Butler, M. (1984). *Theatre and Crisis, 1632–1642*. Cambridge: Cambridge University Press.

Butler, M. (1995). "The outsider as insider." In *The Theatrical City: Culture, Theatre, and Politics in London, 1576–1649*, eds D. Bevington, D. Smith, and R. Strier. Cambridge: Cambridge University Press.

Chakravorty, S. (1996). *Society and Politics in the Plays of Thomas Middleton*. Oxford: Clarendon Press.

Clifford, D. H., ed. (1990). *The Diaries of Lady Anne Clifford*. Stroud: Sutton.

Cooper, T. (1619). *The Worldlings Adventure Discovering the Fearefull Estate of all Earthwormes and Men of this World in Hazarding their Pretious Soules for the Enjoying of Worldly Happiness*. London.

Dekker, T. (1884–6, rpt 1963). *Non-Dramatic Works*. New York: Russell and Russell.

Dekker, T. (1953–61). *Dramatic Works*. Cambridge: Cambridge University Press.

Dietz, B. (1986). "Overseas trade and metropolitan growth." In *London, 1500–1700: The Making of the Metropolis*, eds A. L. Beier and R. Finlay. London: Longman.

Dillon, J. (2000). *Theatre, Court and City, 1595–1610: Drama and Social Space*. Cambridge: Cambridge University Press.

Ellis, H., ed. (1849). *The Obituary of Richard Smyth, Secondary of the Poultry Compter. . . .* London: Camden Society, o.s. 44.

Finch, M. E. (1956). *The Wealth of Five Northamptonshire Families 1540–1640*. Oxford: Northamptonshire Record Society.

Finlay, R. (1981). *Population and Metropolis: The Demography of London, 1580–1650*. Cambridge: Cambridge University Press.

Fisher, F. (1990). *London and the English Economy, 1500–1700*, eds P. J. Corfield and N. B. Harte. London: Hambledon Press.

Friedman, A. T. (2000). "Inside/outside: women, domesticity, and the pleasures of the city." In *Material London*, ed. L. C. Orlin. (Philadelphia: University of Pennsylvania Press).

Gainsford, T. (1616). *The Rich Cabinet, Furnished with Varietie of Excellent Discriptions*. London.

Gibbons, B. (1969). *Jacobean City Comedy: A Study of Satiric Plays by Jonson, Marston and Middleton*. London: Hart-Davis.

Gowing, L. (1996). *Domestic Dangers: Women, Words, and Sex in Early Modern London*. Oxford: Clarendon Press.

Griffiths, P. and M. S. R. Jenner, eds (2000). *Londinopolis: Essays in the Social and Cultural History of Early Modern London*. Manchester: Manchester University Press.

Gurr, A. (1987). *Playgoing in Shakespeare's London*. Cambridge: Cambridge University Press.

Gurr, A. (2000). "The authority of the Globe and the Fortune." In *Material London*, ed. L. C. Orlin. (Philadelphia: University of Pennsylvania Press).

Harrison, W. (1994). *The Description of England*, ed. C. Edelen. Washington, DC: Folger Shakespeare Library.

Haynes, J. (1992). *The Social Relations of Jonson's Theatre*. Cambridge: Cambridge University Press.

Heal, F. (1988). "The crown, the gentry and London: the enforcement of proclamation, 1596–1640." In *Law and Government under the Tudors*, eds C. Cross, D. Loades, and J. J. Scarisbrick. Cambridge: Cambridge University Press.

Jeayes, I. H., ed. (1906). *The Letters of Philip Gawdy, 1579–1606*. London.

Kiernan, V. (1989). *The Duel in European History*. Oxford: Clarendon Press.

Knowles, J. (1999). "Jonson's entertainment at Britain's Burse: text and context." In *Re-Presenting Ben Johnson: Text, History, and Performance*, ed. M. Butler. Basingstoke and London: Macmillan.

Larkin, J. F. and P. L. Hughes, eds (1973). *Stuart Royal Proclamations. Vol. 1. Proclamations of King James I, 1603–1625*. Oxford: Clarendon Press.

McClure, D. S., ed. (1980). *A Critical Edition of Richard Brome's The Weeding of Covent Garden and the Sparagus Garden*. New York: Garland.

McClure, N. E., ed. (1939). *The Letters of John Chamberlain*. 2 vols. Philadelphia: American Philosophical Society.

McIlwain, C. H., ed. (1965). *The Political Works of James I*. New York: Russell and Russell.

Manley, L. (1995). *Literature and Culture in Early Modern London*. Cambridge: Cambridge University Press.

Matthew, D. (1948). *The Social Structure of Caroline England*. Oxford.

Orlin, L. C., ed. (2000). *Material London*. Philadelphia: University of Pennsylvania Press.

Patterson, A. (1989). *Shakespeare and the Popular Voice*. Oxford: Blackwell.

Peck, L. L. (2000). "Building, buying and collecting in London, 1600–1625." In *Material London*, ed. L. C. Orlin. Philadelphia: University of Pennsylvania Press.

Ramsay, G. D. (1975). *The City of London in International Politics at the Accession of Elizabeth Tudor*. Manchester: Manchester University Press.

Rappaport, S. (1989). *Worlds Within Worlds: The Structures of Life in Sixteenth-Century London*. Cambridge: Cambridge University Press.

Smith, D. and R. Strier, eds (1995). *The Theatrical City: Culture, Theatre, and Politics in London, 1576–1649*. Cambridge: Cambridge University Press.

Smith, T. (1982). *De Republica Anglorum*, ed. M. Dewar. Cambridge: Cambridge University Press.

Smuts, R. M. (1991). "The court and its neighbourhood: royal policy and urban growth in the early Stuart West End." *Journal of British Studies* 30.

Stone, L. (1965). *The Crisis of the Aristocracy, 1558–1642*. Oxford: Clarendon Press.

Stone, L. (1973). *Family and Fortune: Studies in Aristocratic Finance in the Sixteenth and Seventeenth Centuries*. Oxford: Clarendon Press.

Stow, J. (1908). *A Survey of London*, ed. C. L. Kingsford. 2 vols. Oxford: Clarendon Press.

Wells, S. (1981) "Jacobean city comedy and the idea of the city." *ELH* 48, 37–60.

Wheeler, J. (1931). *A Treatise of Commerce*, ed. G. B. Hotchkiss. New York: Columbia University Press.

Whetstone, G. (1584). *A Touchstone for the Time*. London.

Womack, P. (1986). *Ben Jonson*. London: Blackwell.

Wright, T. (1838). *Queen Elizabeth and her Times*. 2 vols. London: H. Colburn.

Young, A. R. (1975). *The English Prodigal Son Plays: A Theatrical Fashion of the Sixteenth and Seventeenth Centuries*. Salzburg: University of Salzburg.

Young, W. (1894). *The History of Dulwich College*. 2 vols. London.

6

Vagrancy

William C. Carroll

The poor lie in the streets upon pallets of straw . . . or else in the mire and dirt. . . . having neither house to put in their heads, covering to keep them from the cold nor yet to hide their shame withal, penny to buy them sustenance, nor anything else, but are permitted to die in the streets like dogs, or beasts, without any mercy or compassion shown to them at all.

Philip Stubbes, *Anatomy of the Abuses in England*, London, 1583 (59–60)

Philip Stubbes' horrifying description of the scene of poverty in sixteenth-century London is just one of many such contemporary accounts of the desperate condition of the poor; even in an age that must have witnessed far more everyday poverty and violence than our own, similar expressions of compassion and moral outrage were common. Yet compassion was in the eyes of the beholder. Other observers, viewing the vagrant poor, saw them not as isolated and pathetic, but as a potentially danger-ous threat to civil order; their desperation, it was argued, led directly to crimes against the person – "Men will steal, though they be hanged, except they may live without stealing," reported Richard Morison (1536, E3^v) – and to larger crimes against the state, in the form of sedition. The Privy Council, in a letter of 1571, identified the vagrant poor as the source of virtually all crime: "there is no greater disorder nor no greater root of thefts, murders, picking, stealing, debate and sedition than is in these vagabonds and that riseth of them" (Aydelotte, 1967, 157).[1] Perceptions of the poor, and hence how they were represented in cultural texts, varied enormously in early modern England.

Historical Contexts

"The poor always ye have with you," according to John 12:8, and numerous texts from the medieval period lament the numbers and condition of the poor. To observers in the sixteenth century, however, it seemed as if the numbers of the poor were increasing, and that they were not simply the old and infirm of the villages, but a more threatening, explicitly *vagrant* type. One of the standard terms for such figures – "masterless men" – conveys the social and class dislocations implicit in the problem. But were there, in fact, a greater number of poor in the sixteenth century than in the past?

The available evidence, most historians conclude, reflects a genuine crisis of poverty in the early modern period. Political, social, economic, and religious forces seem to have converged, producing painful changes, and casting more and more people into desperate conditions. One of the major factors in this change was the considerable growth in population during the century – an increase of nearly one-third the population during the 45 years of Queen Elizabeth's reign, for example. Population growth can, in the right conditions, prove a stimulus to economic growth, but while some new markets were created, the larger population could not be properly sustained and fed. Though the country as a whole suffered, London's situation was vastly more serious: the general growth in population was exacerbated by an enormous internal immigration to London. Perceived as a place where jobs or some form of relief might exist, London became a magnet for the dispossessed of the kingdom, and its unregulated growth led to the deplorable conditions lamented by Stubbes.

The steady growth in population – checked only by recurring epidemics of the plague – was accompanied by an inflation of prices so severe that some historians refer to it as a "price revolution." Rising costs of basic necessities such as food or rent devastated many people; it is symbolic of this crisis that even the official coinage was debased, with gold and silver coins adulterated with baser metals. Changing patterns of land ownership and usage also contributed significantly to the creation of a class of vagrants in the kingdom. The concept of "enclosure" – the term could stand for any of several different agricultural practices, virtually all considered destructive – was identified as early as Sir Thomas More's *Utopia* (1516) as the leading cause of displacement and vagrancy: parasitical landowners, according to the narrator Hythloday, have enclosed "every acre for pasture" of land that had previously been held in common, leaving "no land free for the plow." The effects of even a single landowner could be enormous: one "greedy, insatiable glutton . . . may enclose many thousand acres of land within a single hedge. The tenants are dismissed and . . . forced to move out." When their money ran out, "what remains for them but to steal, and so be hanged . . . or to wander and beg? And yet if they go tramping, they are jailed as sturdy beggars. They would be glad to work, but they can find no one who will hire them." What could such men do "but rob or beg? And a man of courage is more likely to rob than to beg" (More, 1975, 14–16). The enclosure movement signified an important economic shift from farming to grazing; the wool industry became, ironically, the economic engine that powered the English economy, creating in substantial ways England's economic wealth and political power. Still, for those not part of the new economy, conditions became very bleak.

Early in the sixteenth century, most of the poor were cared for by local church parishes and the monasteries throughout the kingdom. When Henry VIII disbanded the monasteries in 1536, however, he destroyed the only formal system of poor relief, leaving the poor without support; many of them necessarily took to the roads, no doubt some of them alongside the monastics forced from their retreats. (The seizure and sale of monastic lands, moreover, displaced yet more people.) The institutions of government would struggle for the next century to find acceptable ways to care for the deserving poor, but it was decades after the dissolution of the monasteries before the state's responsibility was even articulated; eventually something like an organized national taxation to support the poor was established. The City of London regained control of its hospitals in 1553, when the Royal Hospitals were chartered, among which was Bridewell. This former palace of Henry VIII was sought as a place to treat poor beggars: as one petition argued, "there could be no means to amend this miserable sort [of beggars], but by making some general provision of work, wherewith the *willing* poor may be exercised; and whereby the froward, strong, and sturdy vagabond may be compelled to live profitably to the commonwealth" (Tawney and Power, 1924, II, 307). Intended to be a "house of labour and occupations" (Tawney and Power, 1924, II, 311) – a house of "correction," as it later became known – Bridewell was, in theory, a real innovation in the early modern conception of the poor; the existence of the house presupposed that the poor were not simply sinful, but needed work. As such, Bridewell was, according to one economic historian, "the greatest innovation and the most characteristic institution of the new system" of poor relief (Leonard, 1965, 39). A statute of 1572 ordered the provision of work on a national scale, including the establishment of houses of correction in every country, "to the intent every such poor and needy person old or young able to do any work standing in necessity of relief shall not for want of work go abroad either begging or committing pilferings or other misdemeanor living in idleness" (Tawney and Power, 1924, II, 332). These noble-minded efforts, unfortunately, were either ineffectual or undermined by corruption. Bridewell itself fairly quickly became a notorious prison, where vagrants and prostitutes in particular were taken to be whipped and incarcerated, and where the torture of political prisoners occasionally took place.[2]

Representations

When early modern writers wrote of the poor, they invariably divided them into two types: the "deserving" poor – the truly sick or aged – and "sturdy beggars" – vagrants who merely pretended to be deformed or ill. The national schemes of relief were intended for the deserving poor, while the whip and the cart were reserved for the others. Official discourse was particularly harsh in its accounts of, and punishments for, idle vagrants. Idleness was reviled as a sin – the belief being that many people *chose* to be without work, when in fact there was no work to be found. The Elizabethan "Homilie Against Idlenesse" forcefully stated the official view:

> It is the appointment and will of God, that every man, during the time of this mortal and transitory life, should give himself to such honest and godly exercise and labor, and every one follow his own business, and to walk uprightly in his own calling. Man (saith Job) is born to labor. . . . [Where idleness exists,] there the devil is ready to set in his foot, and to plant all kind of wickedness and sin, to the everlasting destruction of man's soul. (Rickey and Stroup, 1968, II, 249, 251)

Idleness was not only a moral and religious failing, but a political one as well, since idleness led not to inactivity, but to the wrong kind of activity, possibly even to rebellion, as Richard Morison argued in his *A Remedy for Sedition* (1536): "The lack of honest crafts, and the abundancy of idleness, albeit they be not the whole cause of sedition, yet as they breed thieves, murderers, and beggars, so not a little they provoke men, or things like men, to rebellion" (D2ᵛ).

The problem with vagrants, as official texts argued, was not only that they were idle, but that they were loose, unattached to any geography or system of hierarchy. Since vagrants had no jobs, they were not part of an elaborate system which attempted to regulate wages, apprenticeships, clothing, food and goods, and so on. Moreover, vagrants continually crossed over geographic boundaries – they could not be fixed within any civic structure – or social ones – they were reputed to be masters of disguise who counterfeited their low condition and infirmities. A vagrant, one writer said in 1631, is "a wandering planet" (Saltonstall, 1946, 39), and just as a wandering planet contradicted and subverted what was thought to be a universally accepted conception of the universe, so the vagrant contradicted and subverted an idealized conception of the social world.

It is thus easy to see why early modern writers, across a wide political and religious spectrum, demonized the vagrant while attempting to care for the deserving poor: the vagrant was linked, even identified with, gypsies, Jews, Jesuits, and other "deviant" categories. Above all, vagrants were associated with crime and sedition. Literary and political representations of vagrants in fact frequently described an elaborate criminal underworld over which vagrants ruled; the so-called "rogue pamphlets" of John Awdeley, Thomas Harman, Thomas Dekker, Samuel Rowlands, and Robert Greene, among others, ascribed to vagrant beggars a rigidly structured organization, featuring a hierarchical list of rogue types, in which both male and female beggars were classified by skill, experience, and power. It was claimed that they held secret meetings at which they carefully planned their villainy, and elected a "king" over themselves. They were also said to have their own language, known as "beggars' cant" or "Peddler's French"; this secret language of thieves required glossing dictionaries, helpfully provided by Harman and the others, complete with sample dialogues and translations.

The social reality of vagrants, as we know it from archival sources today, is greatly at odds with the picture of organization and bureaucracy recounted above. The representations of the rogue pamphlets produce an inverted image of the very social structure which the vagrants are said to threaten: carefully delineated degrees of social distinction; a crude apprenticeship system; an "in-group" specialized language; a king or captain to rule. Thus, sovereignty, order, status distinction, regulation of employment – the vagrants resemble nothing so much as one of the craft guilds of early modern London. We might well ask why the dominant culture projected a grid of such idealized order upon these pathetic figures.

Perhaps one answer to this question is that, like any representation, this one is doing ideological work of some kind; in this vision, vagrants become the pathetic doubles of the dominant culture. Their difference from the ordinary citizenry permits (requires) their demonization, but their resemblance ironically undermines such distinctions. Hence the particular zeal with which beggars who *counterfeited* "normal" citizens were hunted down and exposed. It may be that the only way in which the dominant culture can "see" the vagrant is through its own categories, but there was a further extension of this mode of representation which is more difficult to explain in such terms – the tradition of the "merry beggar." Contemporaneous with such laments as Stubbes' and such pamphlets as Harman's is a discourse which thoroughly romanticized and idealized the beggar's life, turning every negative into a positive. This tradition dated from the early fifteenth century at least, but seemed to reach an apotheosis in the early seventeenth century. In this vision, vagrants were said to be actually superior to members of normal society: their food fell into their hands; living in a natural state, they slept better under the stars than under a blanket; they enjoyed an unfettered sexuality; they were their own masters; and so on. In John Taylor's *The Praise, Antiquity, and Commodity, of Beggery, Beggers, and Begging* (1621), even the lice on the beggar's body are said to be "Nature's gifts" (C3ᵛ). For Taylor, the beggar almost escapes the consequences of the Fall: though "A curse was laid on all the race of man" with Adam's fall, so that "of his labors he should live and eat, / And get his bread by travail and sweat," yet, Taylor wrote, "if that any from this curse be free, / A begger must he be, and none but he" (1621, D3). This pastoral freedom would surely have been news to the vagrants dying in the streets of London. Theater audiences in London, in fact, enjoyed seeing such romanticized figures on the stage, as in Richard Brome's play *A Jovial Crew* (it may have been the very last play performed before the closing of the theaters in 1642). Brome appropriated the types and language of the rogue pamphlets to produce a band of merry beggars singing their way through the countryside, happy to accept their status.

These representations of the vagrant as organized criminal or merry pastoral figure were radically contradicted by other texts of the period. It may be that the wrenching economic and social displacements of so many people, and their fall into poverty and vagrancy, required a compensatory vision of them as not actually suffering, as even being better off than others. The relation between citizen and vagrant is thus one, in part, of reflection and inversion: their thieving is a threat to, but also a symbol of, the economic practices which have produced their vagrancy in the first place, and their alleged superiority permits the dominant culture to continue content in its own status. Demonization and idealization here seem to be opposite forms of the same cultural process at work.

A related representational mode of the vagrant beggar, which was widespread in a variety of written and visual texts, paired the beggar with the image of the king – the beggar's social, economic, moral, political, and ontological opposite. The king–beggar opposition figures prominently, for example, in Richard II's bitter prison soliloquy:

> Sometimes am I king;
> Then treason makes me wish myself a beggar,
> And so I am. Then crushing penury
> Persuades me I was better when a king;
> Then am I kinged again, and by and by
> Think that I am unkinged by Bolingbroke,
> And straight am nothing. (V.v.32–8)

If to be a king is everything, then to be a beggar is, logically, "nothing," as Richard indicates. This type of oppositional dynamic has been termed "symbolic inversion" (Babcock, 1978, 14). In one sense, such inversions are an attempt to create or reinforce difference between categories; in a key speech, however, Hamlet reminds us that such oppositions also constitute equations between the terms. Here he refuses to tell Claudius where Polonius's body is hidden:

Hamlet   A certain convocation of politic worms are e'en at him. Your worm is your
           only emperor for diet. We fat all creatures else to fat us, and we fat
           ourselves for maggots. Your fat king and your lean beggar is but variable
           service – two dishes, but to one table. That's the end.
King   Alas, alas!
Hamlet   A man may fish with the worm that eat of a king, and eat of the fish that
           fed of that worm.

The meaning of his cryptic remarks, Hamlet says, is "Nothing but to show you how a king may go a progress through the guts of a beggar" (IV.iii.19–32). Again, an attempt to distinguish leads to a collapse of difference: the vagrant beggar is intimately, inextricably linked to the various forms of power in the dominant culture. Vagrancy is ultimately a culturally constructed mode of *deviance*, and as social attitudes toward such deviants vary, so do its representations: pathetic victim, criminal, potential rebel, con-man, trickster, counterfeitor, "nothing" – such was the vagrant.

Theater

Simply to *be* a vagrant constituted a crime against the state, as we have seen, but the early modern definition of a vagrant was considerably broader than our contemporary one. The 1597 statute (39 Eliz. I., c.4), for example, defined vagrants as including "all jugglers [i.e., magicians], tinkers, peddlers, and petty chapmen wandering abroad" (Tawney and Power, 1924, II, 2.355); some of these occupations were clearly "jobs," as we understand the term today, like that of travelling salesmen, but such vocations were forbidden because, in "wandering," they could not be fixed in the social field. Among those vocations officially defined as vagrant was also, somewhat surprisingly, that of the actor, though with an important exception, as the same 1597 statute explained:

> All fencers, bearwards [i.e., bear trainers for the bear-baiting pits], common players of interludes and minstrels wandering abroad (other than players of interludes belonging to any Baron of this realm, or any other honorable personage of greater degree, to be authorized to play under the hand and seal of arms of such Baron or personage). (Tawney and Power, 1924, II, 355)

Such statutes explain why companies of actors such as Shakespeare's were known as the Lord Chamberlain's Men until 1603, and thereafter as the King's Men: they had to be licensed as "belonging to" an "honorable personage" of a certain "degree." No matter how wealthy and independent they were, Shakespeare's company required the legal umbrella (or fiction) that they were the "servants" of the Lord Chamberlain – in effect, his employees – or they would be subject to the vagrancy statutes. We might not expect that the profession of actor was held in high repute, but the statutes made it potentially criminal.

Early modern opponents of the theater argued that the public theaters of London were sites of disorder and infection continually linked to vagrants: "a play," Henry Crosse wrote in 1603, "is like a sink in a town, whereunto all the filth doth run; or a bile in the body, that draweth all the ill humors unto it" (Gurr, 1987, 217). The lord mayor wrote in 1595 that the public theaters provided a place for "the refuse sort of evil-disposed and ungodly people about this city . . . to assemble together . . . [the theaters are] the ordinary places for all masterless men and vagabond persons that haunt the highways to meet together and recreate themselves" (*Collections*, 1907, 77). While the lord mayors and other city authorities continually tried to suppress the theaters, the national authorities, in the form of the Privy Council, licensed and protected (to some extent) the theaters on the grounds that the queen was "pleased at sometimes to take delight and recreation in the sight and hearing of them"; thus, the "exercise of such plays not being evil in itself may with a good order and moderation be suffered in a well-governed estate" (*Collections*, 1907, 82, 81).[3]

In attacking the theaters, writers invariably invoked metaphors of disease and infection. Some city authorities, in good conscience, opposed the public theaters on the grounds that they drew together large numbers of "the basest sort of people," as the lord mayor wrote in 1583, "many infected with sores running on them"; these people brought upon the entire city "the peril of infection" from the plague (*Collections*, 1907, 63, 62). The danger cited here was real and potentially fatal. The causes of plague were not yet known in the early modern period, but its spread had been observed to accelerate among throngs of people. As a result, the theaters were temporarily closed whenever the plague count – the number of people who died from plague per week – reached a certain level; such closings happened with some frequency.[4] One preacher in 1577 made the equation clear (if illogical): "The cause of plagues is sin, if you look to it well, and the cause of sin are plays. Therefore the cause of plagues are plays" (Evans et al., 1997, xliv).

Perhaps the most serious "infections" in the period were figurative ones, of the political body. Since playhouses were considered to be like sinkholes where masterless men and "vagabond persons" met, they represented a place where the political disease of sedition might spread as easily as the plague. The memory of previous insurrections never seemed to fade away, moreover, particularly the riots on May Day 1517: the lord mayor wrote against the Theatre (James Burbage's first theatrical venture) in 1583 because of "the danger of disorders at such assemblies, the memory of Ill [i.e., evil] May Day begun upon a less occasion of like sort" (*Collections*, 1907, 62–3), and the Recorder of London, William Fleetwood, said of one city "insurrection" of apprentices in 1586 that he had found "all things as like unto Ill May Day, as could be devised in all manner of circumstances . . . they wanted nothing but execution" (Long, 1989, 51). A few years later, a collaborative play, *Sir Thomas More*, sought to represent that same May Day riot on the stage, a prospect which led the master of the revels, Edmund Tilney, to censor it: "Leave out . . . the insurrection wholly with the cause thereof" (Gabrieli and Melchiori, 1990, 17). Shakespeare was apparently one of the several playwrights who worked on this play.

Although some city authorities exaggerated such threats, again perhaps as a way of controlling the theaters, still the period 1581–1602 in London has been described by one historian as "an epidemic of disorder" (Manning, 1988, 187), stemming from the tensions associated with social change and economic decline. The problems peaked around 1590–5, just as Shakespeare was establishing himself as a playwright. One notorious incident in Southwark (the location, on the south bank of the Thames, of several theaters) in June 1592 began, the lord mayor reported, when "great multitudes of people assembled together and the principal actors [of the riot – even the metaphors implicate the theaters] to be certain apprentices of the feltmakers gathered together . . . with a great number of loose and masterless men apt for such purposes." Problems began when authorities attempted to serve a warrant upon a feltmonger's servant who was committed to the Marshalsea prison without cause. The crowd moved to block the authorities, for "restraining of whom the said apprentices and masterless men assembled themselves by occasion and pretence of their meeting at a play which besides the breach of the sabbath day giveth opportunity of committing these and such like disorders" (*Collections*, 1907, 71). The theater – already transgressive in performing a play on Sunday, when they were forbidden – thus served as a nightmare meeting place of unstable urban youth and unruly swarms of vagrants, in an attack on civil order.

The truth of what happened that day is, of course, more ambiguous than the above account indicates,[5] but the incident was read and interpreted by civic authorities as another link in the chain of sedition, vagrancy, and theater. Essential to that interpretation is the recurring terror of the unruly mob of vagrants. In several plays of the 1590s – depicting the rebellion of Wat Tyler and Jack Straw against Richard II (the anonymous plays *Woodstock* and *The Life and Death of Jack Straw*), the Ill May Day rising of 1517 (the multiple-authored *Sir Thomas More*), and Jack Cade's rebellion against Henry VI (Shakespeare's *Henry VI, Part Two*) – the central rebellion is furthered by, though not caused by, an association with urban vagrants.[6] The London theaters, themselves the subject of attack by civic authorities, thus staged representations of the very riots most often invoked against them, but the plays did not implicate the theaters as disorderly sites.

The vagrants of London may have congregated around the theaters – which were, after all, located in the poorest, most marginal places in the urban area – but the consistent association of them with political disorder seems, in retrospect, grossly exaggerated. Still, the enduring political myth is that these masterless men represented the peril of infection – real and figurative. Represented as marginal, disorderly, and deviant, London theaters and London vagrants were closely linked throughout the period.

NOTES

1 Throughout this chapter, the terms "beggar," "rogue," "vagrant," "vagabond," and "masterless man" are used interchangeably, as they were in texts in the period. The exception is the term "poor": not all poor were considered vagrants, and not all vagrants were thought to be truly poor, as will be explained.

2 On the history of Bridewell, see Carroll, 1996; Innes, 1987; and Twyning, 1998.

3 The city authorities in London lacked legal jurisdiction over the large public playhouses, most of which were located just beyond the city limits in the so-called "liberties" of London.

4 See Barroll, 1991, on plague and the closing of the theaters. Some modern observers have speculated that city authorities at times used the plague merely as a pretext to close the theaters.

5 On this particular event, see the different interpretations by Johnson, 1969; Wilson, 1993; Manning, 1988; Patterson, 1989; and Carroll, 1996.

6 By far the most complex representation of a vagrant beggar in this period is that of Poor Tom, the disguise assumed by Edgar in Shakespeare's *King Lear* (*c*.1605). Poor Tom was supposedly from Bedlam, hence a (usually counterfeit) madman beggar.

REFERENCES AND FURTHER READING

Archer, Ian (1991). *The Pursuit of Stability: Social Relations in Elizabethan England*. Cambridge: Cambridge University Press.

Aydelotte, Frank (1967). *Elizabethan Rogues and Vagabonds*. New York: Barnes & Noble.

Babcock, Barbara, ed. (1978). *The Reversible World: Symbolic Inversion in Art and Society*. Ithaca: Cornell University Press.

Barroll, J. Leeds (1991). *Politics, Plague, and Shakespeare's Theater: The Stuart Years*. Ithaca: Cornell University Press.

Beier, A. L. (1985). *Masterless Men: The Vagrancy Problem in England 1560–1640*. London: Methuen.

Berlin, Normand (1968). *The Base String: The Underworld in Elizabethan Drama*. Rutherford, NJ: Fairleigh Dickinson University Press.

Burt, Richard, and John Michael Archer, eds (1994). *Enclosure Acts: Sexuality, Property, and Culture in Early Modern England*. Ithaca: Cornell University Press.

Carroll, William C. (1996). *Fat King, Lean Beggar: Representations of Poverty in the Age of Shakespeare*. Ithaca: Cornell University Press.

Collections Part I (1907). The Malone Society. Oxford: Oxford University Press.

Evans, G. Blakemore et al., eds (1997). *The Riverside Shakespeare*. Boston: Houghton Mifflin.

Gabrieli, Vittorio, and Giorgio Melchiori, eds (1990). *Sir Thomas More*. Manchester: Manchester University Press.

Greenblatt, Stephen (1983). "Murdering peasants: status, genre, and the representation of rebellion." *Representations* 1, 1–29.

Gurr, Andrew (1987). *Playgoing in Shakespeare's London*. Cambridge: Cambridge University Press.

Innes, Joanna (1987). "Prisons for the poor: English bridewells, 1555–1800." In *Labour, Law, and Crime: An Historical Perspective*, eds Francis Snyder and Douglas Hay. London: Tavistock.

Johnson, D. J. (1969). *Southwark and the City*. Oxford: Oxford University Press.

Judges, A. V. (1965). *The Elizabethan Underworld*. New York: Octagon.

Kinney, Arthur F., ed. (1990). *Rogues, Vagabonds, and Sturdy Beggars*. Amherst, MA: University of Massachusetts Press.

Leonard, E. M. (1965; repr. 1900). *The Early History of English Poor Relief*. New York: Barnes & Noble.

Long, William B. (1989). "The occasion of *The Book of Sir Thomas More*." In *Shakespeare and "Sir Thomas More"*, ed. T. H. Howard-Hill. Cambridge: Cambridge University Press.

McMullan, John L. (1984). *The Canting Crew: London's Criminal Underworld*. New Brunswick: Rutgers University Press.

Manning, Roger B. (1988). *Village Revolts: Social Protest and Popular Disturbances in England, 1509–1640*. Oxford: Oxford University Press.

More, Thomas (1975). *Utopia*, ed. Robert M. Adams. New York: Norton.

Morison, Richard (1536). *A Remedy for Sedition*. London.

Patterson, Annabel (1989). *Shakespeare and the Popular Voice*. Oxford: Blackwell.

Rickey, Mary Ellen, and Thomas B. Stroup, eds (1968). *Certaine Sermons or Homilies Appointed to be Read in Churches in the Time of Queen Elizabeth I (1547–1571)*. Gainesville, FL: Scholar's Facsimiles.

Salgādo, Gāmini (1977). *The Elizabethan Underworld*. London: J. M. Dent.

Saltonstall, Wye (1946). *Picturae Loquentes*. Oxford: Blackwell.

Slack, Paul (1988). *Poverty and Policy in Tudor and Stuart England*. London: Longman.

Stubbes, Philip (1877–9). *Anatomy of the Abuses in England*. ed. F. J. Furnivall. London.

Tawney, R. H., and Eileen Power, eds (1924; rpt 1965). *Tudor Economic Documents*. London: Longman.

Taylor, Barry (1991). *Vagrant Writing: Social and Semiotic Disorders in the English Renaissance*. Toronto: University of Toronto Press.

Taylor, John (1621). *The Praise, Antiquity, and Commodity, of Beggery, Beggers, and Begging*. London.

Twyning, John (1998). *London Dispossessed: Literature and Social Space in the Early Modern City*. New York: St. Martin's Press.

Wilson, Richard (1993). *Will Power: Essays on Shakespearean Authority*. Detroit: Wayne State University Press.

7

Family and Household

Martin Ingram

Allusions to household and family were ubiquitous in Renaissance plays, yet they were rarely portrayed directly save in the specialized genre of domestic tragedy. Off the stage, their social significance is attested by the burgeoning genre of books of advice on marriage, family and household government; an increasing vogue for family histories; and more graphically in the family portraits that depict parents, children, and sometimes other relatives in stiff formation. These portraits, replete with emblems, are themselves not easy to interpret. Holbein's crowded sketch of the family of Sir Thomas More, including his father and daughter-in-law, contrasts with Johnson's apparently more private vision, set against the background of a formal garden, of Lord Capel and his wife and children in 1639 (plates 1 and 2). But it should not be inferred that the period witnessed, as used to be supposed, a change from "extended" to "nuclear" families. These are simply two images of a social institution that was underlain by some enduring features but could take a multiplicity of forms and was subject to a host of accidents. In real life, household and family were both the basis of social order and personal security and the site of tension, conflict, and contest that were, in heightened form, the essence of drama.

Throughout this period the core of the family was recognized to be a husband, wife, and children. It could be fractured or eroded to something less, especially among the poor where abandoned wives and solitary widows, with or without children, were all too common. On the other hand, bereaved spouses (especially men) often wed again: perhaps a fifth of brides and grooms were marrying for the second or subsequent time. From the middling ranks upwards, the family was often extended by the presence of servants or apprentices.

To contemporaries the word "family" primarily meant a *household* of this kind, rather than simply a group of people linked by ties of blood and marriage. In the higher social strata, servants were numerous and themselves differentiated by rank and function – from lowly maidservants and serving-men to butlers, stewards, or secretaries, to the gentlemen and gentlewomen who "waited" on the great. Occasionally

FAMILIA THOMÆ. MORI ANGL. CANCELL.

Thomas Morus Æ.50. Alicia Thomæ Mori uxor Æ.57. Iohannes Morus pater Æ.76. Iohannes Morus Thomæ filius Æ.19. Anna Crisacria Iohannis Mori Sponsa Æ.15. Margareta Roperi Thomæ Mori filia Æ.22. Elisabeta Danæi Thomæ Mori filia Æ.21. Cæcilia Heronis Thomæ Mori filia. Æ.20. Margareta Gigi Clementis uxor Mori filiabus Condiscipula, et cognata Æ.22. Henricus Patensonus Thomæ Mori morio Æ.40.

Plate 1 Sir Thomas More and his family. Öffentliche Kunstsammlung Basel, Kupferstich-kabinett.

other relations by blood or marriage resided in the "family": grandfathers or grand-mothers, sisters, brothers, or cousins. Sometimes, especially among the gentry and aristocracy, a newly married couple would reside for a while beneath the parental roof. But mostly couples were expected to establish new households for themselves, and this made marriage a social transition of the utmost significance.[1]

The importance of the family household did not lie simply in procreation, child-rearing, and the transmission of property across the generations, important though these functions were in a society in which birth and dynasty were of overriding impor-tance. The family household's role extended well beyond what we think of as private concerns. Contemporary ideas were shaped in part by Aristotle and Xenephon, but were at the same time firmly rooted in practical experience of the public role of the "family." The households of princes and aristocratic families were of obvious political significance. Lower down the social scale, the families of yeomen, husbandmen, crafts-men, and traders – those who might not be taxpayers to the crown, but certainly paid their rates for the upkeep of the church and relief of the poor, and took their turn to fill local offices such as constable and churchwarden – were likewise self-evidently

Plate 2 Cornelius Johnson, *The family of Arthur, Lord Capel*. By courtesy of the National Portrait Gallery, London.

constituents of the commonwealth. It goes without saying that family households were in this period the main focus of economic activity – the country houses of the nobility and gentry were the center of their great estates; a merchant's residence was the site of commercial or financial dealings; and in the countryside, the houses of yeomen and husbandmen, with their adjacent outbuildings, were the hub of farming activities, while spinning and weaving were carried on literally as cottage industries. Contemporary churchmen saw the family as the nursery of religion (and religion itself as an element of good citizenship), laying on householders the duty of insuring that their children, servants, and apprentices absorbed the elements of Christian doctrine from the catechism. Certainly households fostered "education" in the broad sense that contemporaries used that word, embracing not only the elements of book-learning but also social skills and training in a craft, in husbandry, or in housewifery. On this view service and apprenticeship were a form of education, a means whereby young people could acquire not only some of the wherewithal to establish their own household in due course, but also essential skills to equip them for a position of some responsibility with its attendant perils. Contemporary authorities were strongly opposed to "untimely and discommendable marriages" (Tawney and Power, 1924, I, 363).

Much of what members of the household did was open, or at least susceptible, to public scrutiny. In every parish in town and country, churchwardens and their assistants or sidesmen had a duty to make presentments to the church courts: that is, to report their neighbors – a step that condemned those neighbors to a summons to court

Spying as a social function

and hence admonition, public penance, or (for the recalcitrant) excommunication – for faults such as failing to attend church, lapses of personal morality such as being pregnant at marriage, fathering a bastard, or committing adultery, or even for conniving at the sins of others by "harboring" unmarried pregnant women or allowing an unwed couple to fornicate under the householder's roof. Constables had similar duties of surveillance in the secular sphere, which in London, Westminster, and other large towns extended to certain sexual offences, especially when there was suspicion of prostitution. Adverse reports to the city authorities could result in the offenders being "carted" as "whores," "whoremongers," or "bawds" – that is, paraded around the town in an open wagon with basins ringing before them to attract the crowds. Churchwardens and constables were often aided by inquisitive and censorious neighbors, who sometimes spied on illicit goings-on through windows or through conveniently located holes in doors and walls, and who might cooperate to "stake out" a dwelling or break open the doors to secure proof positive of adultery or other scandalous activity. The obverse of these activities was that respectability – expressed as "good credit," "honesty," or "civil carriage" in the middling and lower social ranks, the analogue of upper-class notions of "honor" – was a primary source of social capital.

Even within the confines of the household, privacy was in short supply. Entries, shops, and halls were an interface with the wider world, easily accessible. Admission to the more remote spaces was restricted, and some (such as closets and counting houses) were expected to be closed off. Yet for unmarried couples to retire behind closed, and especially *locked*, doors was generally taken as a sign that they were up to no good. Moreover, for practical reasons privacy or seclusion was often impossible. Servants frequently lived cheek by jowl with their masters and mistresses, and certainly with each other, while walls, floors, and other internal partitions were often flimsy or defective. Bed curtains were becoming more common in this period, but window curtains were still rare even in the houses of the very rich. In some ways, these conditions helped to maintain household order, since they made it more difficult to indulge in secret vice. On the other hand, promiscuous living conditions could make maidservants very vulnerable to the sexual attentions of masters and fellowservants. The sexual abuse of children also occurred, although probably only rarely: the perpetrators appear to have been masters, servants in the same household, or casual visitors more often than fathers, stepfathers, or other relatives. Incest, despite its prominence in the drama, was apparently rare.

Of course houses varied greatly in size and layout, largely reflecting the wealth and occupation of the owner or tenant but depending also on their location in town or country. A common pattern, capable of infinite adaptation and elaboration, was that of hall and entry together with a number of chambers (used for other purposes besides sleeping) and parlors, buttery, kitchen, and other service quarters, outhouses for agricultural, industrial, or domestic use, and perhaps a "house of office" (latrine) in the "backside" or garden. Wealthy households might afford such additional conveniences as a gallery. These spaces were furnished with bedsteads, tables and forms, joint stools and the occasional chair; they were equipped with firedogs and irons, hooks, pots and

Plate 3 Male and female roles: hunting and spinning. From *The Roxburghe Ballads*, eds
W. Chappell and J. W. Ebsworth, 9 vols (London and Hertford, 1866–99), vol. 2, p. 411.

pans, and various other utensils of brass and iron for cooking, baking and brewing;
and were garnished with wood-, pewter-, and silverware, napery, bedding, painted
cloths or tapestries for the walls, perhaps some books, and occasionally soft furnishings such as cushions and carpets. The poor would possess only a few of the most basic
items, the "better sort" correspondingly more. The very rich could aspire to some
comfort, but even their houses would have seemed to the modern eye sparsely furnished. The luxurious visions of Sir Epicure Mammon in *The Alchemist* were pure
fantasy. More realistic is the gentry household evoked in *A Woman Killed with Kindness*. The audience infers the presence of kitchen and other offices from the servants
featured in the play, and hears directly of gate, yard, hall, parlor, study, withdrawing
chamber, and private chamber. They see the butler and other serving-men "with a
voider and a wooden knife" clear away salt and bread, tablecloth and napkins, after
supper is ended; then stools are brought in and a carpet, candles, and candlesticks laid
on a table for a game of cards (Orlin, 1994, 145–6) (plates 3 and 4).

It might be thought that, in a dynastic and authoritarian society in which marriage and household were so important, matrimony would be restricted to those of
the age of discretion and marriage laws would be carefully framed to regulate unions
and, at least for the upper ranks, insure family control over entry into the married
state. The reality was less clear-cut. Despite attempts to change the law in the sixteenth century, the age at which a valid marriage could be contracted remained 12
for a girl and 14 for a male. Moreover, it was possible for girls and boys to be betrothed

Plate 4 A family meal. From *The Roxburghe Ballads*, eds W. Chappell and J. W. Ebsworth, 9 vols (London and Hertford, 1866–99), vol.1, p. 86.

together from the age of 7. In principle they had the right, when they reached the age of 12 or 14 respectively, to repudiate the union; but obviously this might be difficult at so tender an age. "Child marriages" of this sort were still a real possibility in sixteenth-century England, at least among the aristocracy and, especially in the northwest, in the lower ranks too. But the practice was declining. Teenage marriage, especially for girls, was still common among the nobility and gentry and other wealthy groups in Elizabeth's reign, but marriage ages tended to drift upward in the seventeenth century. For the bulk of the population, the age at which people commonly married was much later than the legal minimum – on average the mid-to-late twenties, the man being commonly (but not invariably) somewhat older than the female when there was disparity. The average conceals great variation, however, and it was by no means uncommon for a woman to be married at 20. According to Alexander Niccholes, the "forward virgins of our age" claimed that 13 or 14 was the best time to marry, so the age of Juliet and other young heroines was not altogether in the realm of fantasy (1615, 11).

In church law the consent of parents, the presence of witnesses, and solemnization by a minister in church were not absolutely necessary to make a marriage: "I have heard lawyers say, a contract in a chamber / *Per verba de presenti* is absolute marriage." The Duchess of Malfi was right (I.i): it was possible throughout this period, indeed until Lord Hardwicke's Marriage Act of 1753, to contract a valid union by the mere verbal declaration of the couple in words of the present tense, characteristically taking the form of a simple ceremony called "spousals," "troth-plight," or "handfasting." This reflected the overriding importance that the church, when the law of marriage was developed in the twelfth century, had placed on the free consent of the couple. On the other hand the church had campaigned for centuries to ensure that planned unions were adequately publicized, preferably by the calls of "banns" in church, or at least sanctioned by a license issued by the ecclesiastical authorities; and that marriages were solemnized in a religious ceremony. Churchmen also assumed that in normal circumstances young people should seek the consent of their parents or other kinsfolk before they wed. These principles were in fact reinforced in the reign of Elizabeth, partly at the insistence of Protestant divines who attached greater importance to parental consent. In the canons of 1604, entry into marriage was hedged about by a dense thicket of regulations.

Yet confusions remained. Although marriage was made by consent, the precise form of words was vital. Contracts in words *de praesenti* – such as "I, John, take thee, Joan" – were immediately binding, but words *de futuro* – "I will marry thee" – were in the nature of contracts *to marry* which could in certain circumstances be broken and were superseded by any later *de praesenti* spousals or a church wedding. Moreover, while the law recognized unsolemnized or unwitnessed unions to be *valid*, they were regarded as irregular and the couple was liable to be punished, or at least harried by church authorities until they solemnized the marriage. Again, those who evaded publicity by securing what was called "clandestine marriage" – ceremonies conducted by a minister, perhaps in church or chapel, but secretly and at irregular times or seasons – were liable to be excommunicated, as were those who aided or abetted them or even attended the wedding. But such marriages were nonetheless binding.

Further uncertainties arose from the fact that spousals, often conducted in a family setting in the presence of parents and friends, masters and mistresses, and as like as not concluded with a feast or sealed with drink, could be a normal part of the marriage process: the secular conclusion of a union which would, some days, weeks, or months later, be solemnized in church. Seen in this light, spousals were the culmination of courting rituals that, at their most elaborate, included go-betweens, a carefully choreographed exchange of gifts or "tokens," and negotiations over the lands and goods that would eventually be settled on the couple. In popular parlance, spousals or handfasting made a couple "sure," "man and wife marriage in the church only excepted." Apparently there was no consensus at any social level about whether a contract licensed sexual relations before the church ceremony. Many thought it did and acted accordingly; but other individuals explicitly said no. The issue is obscured by the fact that, irrespective of the existence or otherwise of a binding contract, courting couples often had sex: parish register analysis indicates that overall about one-fifth of the brides were pregnant at marriage, although it may be assumed that the chastity of upper-class women was more closely guarded. Predictably, contemporary moralists forbade sex before marriage in church, even after a contract. However, many of them commended the practice of making a binding contract in advance of the church ceremony, as a way of ensuring adequate preparation. Although they envisaged sober ceremonies rather than the junketings that no doubt often took place in real life, they were in a sense endorsing folk custom. Ecclesiastical lawyers came to take a different view.

Marriage contracts, especially those which were unwitnessed or imperfectly attested, were liable to dispute, and cases came for adjudication before the church courts. But verdicts in favor of contested contracts were always in a minority and by the early seventeenth century were extremely difficult to obtain – virtually impossible in some courts. The judges, it would seem, viewed the evidence for unsolemnized unions with great skepticism and always tended to favor marriage in church. While in principle upholding the ancient law of spousals, therefore, in fact they gradually turned their backs on it. Popular practice gradually followed suit: in 1633 the writer of a treatise on marriage remarked that the custom of making contracts was "not now so much in use as it hath been formerly," while in 1686 the editor of the primary legal authority on the subject admitted that "spousals are now in great measure worn out of use" (Griffith, 1633, 272; Swinburne, 1686, sig. A2ᵛ). Since these legal and social uncertainties were at their height in the decades of transition around 1600, it is no surprise that all the permutations of present and future spousals, clandestine ceremonies, contested unions, and jilted lovers were depicted in innumerable plays.

For some sections of society the situation was complicated by wardship. When a landholder by knight service died leaving an heir or heiress under age, the crown stepped in to administer the estate and arrange the minor's marriage. These wardship rights, which could seriously threaten family interests and restrict the personal freedom of the individuals subject to them, were often sold to third parties. There was inevitably much scope for abuse, although by the early seventeenth century the rigors of the system were mitigated to the extent that the wardship was usually purchased by members of the family. Apart from the complications of wardship, disputed marriages, on stage and in real life, often turned on conflicts between families and individuals, and particularly between parents and children. Marriages arranged without consulting the wishes of the couple were not the norm in early modern England. Among the aristocracy and gentry and in other wealthy circles, parents or other close kin did play an extremely important, often preponderant, part in selecting marriage partners for their children. Even at this social level, however, male offspring did have some power of initiative; girls, especially if they were very young, usually had less room for maneuver. Farther down the social scale, things were even more flexible. Both prudence and obedience dictated that parents should be consulted, or at least their approval sought after the couple themselves had fixed on marriage; they might even have a powerful voice. Nonetheless there is much evidence that young people often enjoyed considerable freedom in finding a partner. In any case, late age at marriage and high rates of mortality meant that one or both parents might well be dead before a young man or woman came to choose a mate.

Individual and family interests were not necessarily at odds, of course; nor is it the case that young people were indifferent to matters of property and connection. On the contrary, material security and advancement were powerful motives for seeking marriage, while at the most basic level those who lacked the wherewithal to set up house were liable to face strong opposition to their union from parish authorities. But emotion could complicate matters. Contemporary wisdom was that love was essential *different view of "love"* (handwritten marginalia)

to a successful marriage, but consuming passion that overrode prudence or obligation to parents and friends was a disease akin to madness. One view was that, although it was essential that prospective partners had "good liking" or could undertake to "find in their heart to love" each other, it was better for love to develop after marriage had taken place. But numerous sources attest to the power, at all social levels, of something very close to modern ideas of romantic love with all its heartaches and inconstancies. The astrological physician Richard Napier recorded in his casebooks many lovesick individuals: in 1615 a certain Jane Travell "sayeth that nobody can tell the sorrow that she endureth. . . . Sometimes will sigh three hours until as sad as can [be]. . . . Should have married one, and they were at words as if she would not have him. And then bidding him to marry elsewhere she fell into this passion." On occasion love led individuals to defy parents or cast prudence to the wind. Gervase Holles recounted how his father was in hopes that his son's marriage would "bring him in a sum of money" sufficient to free him from financial embarrassment, but: "This I had not years enough either to understand or to consider; and had not only placed an unalterable love upon my first wife . . . but had secretly, without the least suspicion of my father and grandfather . . . passed a contract with her." The romantic passions that animate much contemporary drama are therefore not fantasies remote from everyday behavior but closely related to real life (MacDonald, 1981, 89; Holles, 1937, 203).

While it was perilously easy to contract a marriage, the opportunities to escape the marital bond were few and narrow. Divorce in the modern sense, the dissolution of a valid union giving the right to remarry, was not recognized. Annulment was possible on certain grounds, principally prior contract and marriage within the forbidden degrees, but cases were very few. The church courts could grant a "separation from bed and board" on the grounds of cruelty (usually the recourse of female plaintiffs) or infidelity (mostly alleged by husbands). But since these were scandalous matters and there was no right of remarriage, the remedy was not popular and cases were infrequent, especially after about 1600. The issue was a contentious one in Elizabethan England. Calvin and other Continental reformers allowed remarriage after divorce for adultery, and some English divines pressed strongly for a change in the law. During this period of debate, some individuals of whatever social rank secured remarriages in defiance of the law. In 1605 the supposed wife of Barnabe Riche, a soldier later to turn moralist, admitted that she had "heard say that he had another wife but was divorced from her . . . for [her] adultery . . . who had a child by another man in his absence at sea."[2] Some may even have thought that marriage was permissible in such circumstances. The ecclesiastical canons of 1604 were a sharp reaction to such cases and do seem to have served to clarify the situation by reinforcing the ban on remarriage. Another strand in the same controversy was the demand for the death penalty for those guilty of adultery – a sharp form of divorce that solved the problem of remarriage for the innocent party. In the event, the Adultery Act was not to reach the statute book until 1650, and even then its more draconian provisions proved largely a dead letter.

In any case, divorce was hardly an issue for many people. Harsh economic realities admittedly made the unions of the very poor extremely vulnerable. But for everyone from the middling ranks upwards, marriage was so important as an economic partnership and basis for social status that it was only in the most dire circumstances that couples would consider separation. Death was far more likely to end a union prematurely, yet even given the prevailing high rates of mortality, the median duration of marriage may have been as long as twenty years. There was thus much scope for misery if things went wrong. Establishing a satisfactory *modus vivendi* was hence of the greatest importance: the plethora of contemporary advice, the large numbers of cases bearing on marital unhappiness that in one guise or another came before the courts, and the tensions recorded in contemporary letters and diaries all bear witness to the difficulties of the task. There are a number of important reasons why it is hard to generalize about marital relations in this period. It is not merely that so much depended on personality and circumstance, and on such factors as a greater or lesser age-gap between the spouses: there were also some real, deep-seated tensions in contemporary attitudes.

The fact that marriage was supposed to be both an economic and an emotional partnership entailed many pitfalls. Men expected a portion with their brides, whether a few pounds and some household goods at lower social levels, or the hundreds or even thousands of pounds that were given with the daughters of the gentry and nobility. Women and their families, on the other hand, expected assurance of adequate support during the marriage and provision for possible widowhood. Some marriages, such as that of Francis Willoughby to Elizabeth Littleton in the reign of Elizabeth, seem to have been blighted from the outset by disappointed financial expectations. Disagreements about the disposal of the woman's property were also a factor. Married women – *femes covertes* – in theory had very few proprietary rights, but land held in their own name at marriage remained theirs (though the husband took the income), while a "separate estate" for the married woman was sometimes secured by means of a trust. Marital difficulties could result if either a husband felt his wife was withholding financial assistance or the woman feared that the man was ruining the household economy (Friedman, 1989, 54–9).

But material conditions were only one possible source of tension. The interference of relatives and the machinations of servants within the household were complicating factors in the case of the Willoughbys that must have affected many other couples too. Conventionally love was supposed to grow within marriage, but many husbands and wives can have had in advance very little real knowledge of each other and the process of mutual discovery was bound to be hazardous, not least because of the strait-jacket of contemporary expectations of husband–wife relations. It was a commonplace that husbands should exercise authority and wives owed them the duty of obedience. Yet even the most optimistic patriarchal theorist recognized that this was easier said than done, demanding not merely an unlikely degree of female compliance but also a level of skill and responsibility on the part of the husband that simply could not be guaranteed. There is much evidence that wives expected affectionate and fair dealing,

Well worth to scurge, so weake A patch, And cause the Boyes thereat make games,
Who wth So strong, A whore would match, by ryding thus, to both their shames:

Plate 5 A wife beats her husband with a bunch of keys: a "riding" occurs in the background. From *English Customs* (1628), plate 9. By permission of the Folger Shakespeare Library.

yet the law allowed a man to administer "moderate correction" to his spouse: the fact that most contemporary moralists inveighed strongly against wife-beating suggests that such behavior was by no means uncommon, and the pitiful cruelty to which it could on occasion degenerate is reflected in contemporary court records.

In relation to the drama, it is some of the more extreme expressions of marital disharmony that are most relevant. In a sense, most dramatically piquant was the situation where the wife turned the patriarchal world upside down and herself beat her husband. In real life this was the signal for a "riding" or, as the custom was called in some parts, "riding skimmington": a noisy, mocking demonstration in which a man or an effigy was carried on a pole or "cowlstaff" or ridden on a horse, sometimes face to tail, to the accompaniment of the "rough music" of pots and pans, the discharge of guns and fireworks, and derisive hoots and raucous laughter (plates 5 and 6). Some of these popular enactments were so elaborate as to qualify as a form of folk drama. The motif was occasionally displayed on stage in the professional theater, as in Thomas Heywood and Richard Brome's *Late Lancashire Witches*. Moreover the elaborate symbolism of skimmington rides, including images and inversion or reversal and discordant noise expressive of disorder, had affinities with the motifs that were, with

The world is turned, vpside downe, As by their wheeles, to gaine least riches,
When wives so on their Husbands frowne, shall forst giue leaue, to weare ÿ breeches:

Plate 6   The world turned upside down. From *English Customs* (1628), plate 12. By permission of the Folger Shakespeare Library.

infinitely more sophistication, expressed in the contemporary masque and anti-masque.

Infidelity was even more central to the drama. Neither the law nor contemporary moralists tolerated adultery in either party, but a deeply entrenched double standard was for many men a sufficient license to roam. Some wives might upbraid the errant husband, "bidding him go to his whores!" but many must have been powerless. On the other hand, suspicion of adultery on the wife's part was enough to arouse even a moderate man to passionate fury. Churchmen who denounced the double standard nonetheless conceded that in its effects the adultery of a wife was more disruptive than that of a husband, in raising doubts about paternity if not actually subverting inheritances, and in fomenting dangerous quarrels between men. Contemporaries saw cuckoldry, a man's loss of control of his wife's body, as causing possible doubts about his ability to satisfy her sexually, his capacity to govern his household, and even perhaps his fitness for any kind of public office – in brief, about his manhood. Accusations or underhand aspersions of cuckoldry – often expressed in finger signs or the actual display of horns or antlers, the ancient symbol of the cuckold – touched a man's honor to the quick. To be an unwitting cuckold was bad; to know oneself such was worse; to be exposed was a disaster, especially as failure to respond would condemn the man to the utterly ignominious status of "wittol" or complaisant cuckold. But how to react, and how to guard against the danger? To be unduly suspicious of a wife, and hence reveal the fear of being cuckolded, was itself ridiculous. To respond ineffectually was to compound disaster. A judicial response was fraught with difficulty, a violent one could lead to tragedy. The powerful emotions associated with cuckoldry, and the sheer psychological and social complexities to which the situation gave rise, ensured that the theme, with infinite variations, was ubiquitous in Renaissance drama. It was particularly piquant in the burgeoning metropolis, where – at least in dramatists' imagination – city wives, resplendent in gloves and ruffs and avid for attention, were game for town gallants. The Restoration theater, benefitting from the presence of actresses on the stage, was to develop further the dramatic possibilities of the theme.

The late age of marriage and extended lactation periods meant that most couples produced only a few children; larger families were confined to the well-off. Relations between parents and young children were less important as a theme in drama than they were in real life, but significant nonetheless. Lawrence Stone's idea that relationships were cold and harshly authoritarian, and that parents invested little emotional capital in their offspring, especially when they were very young, has been rejected. Diaries, letters, and other sources indicate that both fathers and mothers often took delight in the birth of children, doted over their infancy and childhood, anxiously strove to keep them in health, eased them as far as they could through their illnesses, and suffered much grief if they died before they grew up. (There were considerable regional variations, but on average about a quarter of all children were dead before they reached the age of ten.) Reactions to the death of an only son, especially if there was small hope of begetting another, might be colored by concerns about inheritance and the descent of estates, but this was inevitable given the economic and dynastic importance of family and household, and the sense of emotional loss was real enough. Practices such as the reusing of a dead child's name (less common than Stone thought) likewise reflect different cultural expectations, but not lack of emotion (Stone, 1977, 66–75, 105–14, 159–78, 194–5, 409; cf. Pollock, 1983; Houlbrooke, 1984, chs 6–7; Smith-Bannister, 1997, 71–4).

Conventional wisdom held that to spare the rod was to spoil the child. However, moralists were constantly chiding parents (especially mothers) for doing just that, "cockering" their children with undue leniency; and diary evidence, as far as it goes, suggests that physical punishment was a rare and usually reluctant response to childish faults. Nonetheless, this was a society in which the whipping of children was at least in principle regarded as proper. The rod was wielded with vigor by many schoolmasters, and the punishment could be administered in a family setting even to adolescent children: the newswriter John Chamberlain reported in 1612 that the bishop of Bristol's "eldest [son] of 19 or 20 year old killed himself with a knife to avoid the disgrace of breeching." His offence had been to lose money at tennis (McClure, 1939, I, 335).

Parents were, along with schoolmasters, schoolmistresses (for girls), or private tutors, vital agents in the education of their offspring – including religious and moral instruction and the rules of civility as well as book-learning. Mothers had responsibility for daughters, as well as sons until they were five or six and so old enough to be taken out of long clothes and put into breeches; thereafter, responsibility lay with the father. The duty to educate also extended to other children and youngsters living in the household, as servants or otherwise. Lady Margaret Hoby, for example, recorded in her diary for November 3, 1599, "I did read a while to my workwomen," one of many such entries (Moody, 1998, 34). By the time children reached late adolescence the focus of education shifted toward the challenges that awaited them when they were beyond the tutelage of parents. It was at this stage that so many "Letters of Advice" or "Books of Instruction" were written, often plagiarized shamelessly from the famous models provided by William Cecil, Lord Burghley, and others (Wright, 1962). Long before, the thoughts of provident parents had turned to making provision for their children's future, securing the means of professional training or binding them as apprentices if they were not to inherit sufficient land to maintain them. A good marriage was the other object in view. The anxious expectations of parents, eager to secure their children's future and the continuance of their own name before they themselves left this world, were the foil to the passions and follies of the young.

In conclusion, the sources that bear on family and household demand a comment. Peter Laslett famously warned historical sociologists that to use literary materials for this purpose was to look "the wrong way through the telescope." His preferred approach was through records such as household listings and parish registers of baptisms, marriages, and burials – sources that can be made to yield quantitative data, such as the "fact" that the average household size in England from the sixteenth to the nineteenth century was 4.75 persons. Despite suspicions that this particular figure might turn out to be a "meaningless mean," historians have undoubtedly gained much from this approach and, influenced by Laslett's general point, have shied away from using literary materials (Laslett, 1976). To supplement the demographic data, they have had recourse to autobiographies, diaries, letters, and family histories; estate papers, account books, wills, and inventories; and records from both the ecclesiastical and secular courts dealing with marriage, divorce, sexual transgressions, and property disputes within families. They have also made much use of advice literature on the themes of choosing a wife, marriage, and household government, although this material is, in fact, more varied and problematic than is often realized. The heavily prescriptive works of "godly" ministers, such as Henry Smith's *A Preparative to Mariage* (1591), William Whately's *A Bride-Bush* (1617), and William Gouge's *Of Domesticall Duties* (1622), need to be distinguished from superficially similar productions by authors of a very different stamp, such as *A Briefe and Pleasant Discourse of Duties in Marriage* (1568) by Edmund Tilney, master of the revels, or *A Discourse of Marriage and Wiving* (1615) by Alexander Niccholes. Such works, often in dialogue form, in turn relate to a variety of other forms of advice literature, and also to an extraordinary range of moral exhortations, diatribes, and satires of which only small portions have received close attention from historians. These works, designed to entertain and to provoke, address serious moral and social issues and have obvious affinities with the drama. That drama, while obviously not a simple representation of contemporary manners, did provide a commentary – sometimes glancing, sometimes direct – on issues of courtship, marriage, and family relations, and was one of the means by which people at the time were stimulated to imagine and reflect on their own experience. If love was already an important component of courtship and marriage when the period began, the experience of "seeing and reading plays and romances" (as the countess of Warwick later recalled) can hardly have made it less so (Croker, 1848, 4). Indeed, it is arguable that the drama, along with other forms of literature, not only helped to heighten an awareness of romantic love, but contributed to other changes in sensibility too. In this sense drama can itself be seen as part of the history of the family in this period, and a source that historians need to explore more fully.

↳disagrees w/ Peter Laslett

NOTES

1   For a snapshot of the variety of household forms in a single community, see Allison (1963).
2   Guildhall Library, London, MS 9064/16, fo. 64v.

REFERENCES AND FURTHER READING

Allison, K. J. (1963). "An Elizabethan village 'census.'" *Bulletin of the Institute of Historical Research* 36, 95–103.

Amussen, S. D. (1988). *An Ordered Society: Gender and Class in Early Modern England*. Oxford: Blackwell.

Ben-Amos, I. K. (1994). *Adolescence and Youth in Early Modern England*. New Haven and London: Yale University Press.

Burnett, M. T. (1997). *Masters and Servants in English Renaissance Drama Culture: Authority and Obedience*. Houndmills, Basingstoke, and London: Macmillan.

Cooper, N. (1999). *Houses of the Gentry, 1480–1680*. New Haven and London: Yale University Press.

Cressy, D. (1997). *Birth, Marriage, and Death: Ritual, Religion, and the Life-Cycle in Tudor and Stuart England*. Oxford: Oxford University Press.

Croker, T. Crofton, ed. (1848). *Autobiography of Mary, Countess of Warwick*. London: Percy Society, 22.

Erickson, A. L. (1993). *Women and Property in Early Modern England*. London and New York: Routledge.

Fletcher, A. (1995). *Gender, Sex and Subordination in England, 1500–1800*. New Haven and London: Yale University Press.

Friedman, Alice T. (1989). *House and Household in Elizabethan England: Wollaton Hall and the Willoughby Family*. Chicago and London: University of Chicago Press.

Gowing, L. (1996). *Domestic Dangers: Women, Words and Sex in Early Modern London*. Oxford: Clarendon Press.

Griffith, Matthew (1633). *Bethel: Or, a Forme for Families*. London.

Griffiths, P. (1996). *Youth and Authority: Formative Experiences in England, 1560–1640*. Oxford: Clarendon Press.

Heal, F., and C. Holmes (1994). *The Gentry in England and Wales, 1500–1700*. Houndmills, Basingstoke, and London: Macmillan.

Holles, Gervase (1937). *Memorials of the Holles Family, 1493–1656*, ed. A. C. Wood. London: Camden Society, 3rd series.

Houlbrooke, R. A. (1984). *The English Family, 1450–1700*. London and New York: Longman.

Ingram, M. (1985). "Ridings, rough music and the 'reform of popular culture' in early modern England." *Past and Present* 105, 79–113.

Ingram, M. (1987). *Church Courts, Sex and Marriage in England, 1570–1640*. Cambridge: Cambridge University Press.

Ingram, M. (2001). "Child sexual abuse in early modern England." In *Negotiating Power in Early Modern Society: Order, Hierarchy and Subordination in Britain and Ireland*, eds M. J. Braddick and J. Walter. Cambridge: Cambridge University Press.

Jones, J. (1996). *Family Life in Shakespeare's England: Stratford-upon-Avon, 1570–1630*. Stroud: Sutton.

Laslett, Peter (1976). "The wrong way through the telescope: a note on literary evidence in sociology and in historical sociology." *British Journal of Sociology* 27, 319–42.

Laslett, P. (1983). *The World We Have Lost Further Explored*. London: Methuen.

McClure, Norman Egbert, ed. (1939). *The Letters of John Chamberlain*. 2 vols. Philadelphia: American Philosophical Society.

MacDonald, Michael (1981). *Mystical Bedlam: Madness, Anxiety, and Healing in Seventeenth-Century England*. Cambridge: Cambridge University Press.

Macfarlane, A. (1970). *The Family Life of Ralph Josselin: A Seventeenth-Century Clergyman*. Cambridge: Cambridge University Press.

Moody, Joanna, ed. (1998). *The Private Life of an Elizabethan Lady: The Diary of Lady Margaret Hoby, 1599–1605*. Stroud: Sutton.

Niccholes, Alexander (1615). *A Discourse of Marriage and Wiving*. London.

O'Hara, D. (2000). *Courtship and Constraint: Rethinking the Making of Marriage in Tudor England*. Manchester and New York: Manchester University Press.

Orlin, L. C. (1994). *Private Matters and Public Culture in Post-Reformation England*. Ithaca, New York, and London: Cornell University Press.

Outhwaite, R. B. (1995). *Clandestine Marriage in England, 1500–1850*. London and Rio Grande: Hambledon Press.

Pollock, L. A. (1983). *Forgotten Children: Parent–Child Relations from 1500 to 1900*. Cambridge: Cambridge University Press.

Smith-Bannister, Scott (1997). *Names and Naming Patterns in England, 1538–1700*. Oxford: Clarendon Press.

Stone, Lawrence (1965). *The Crisis of the Aristocracy, 1558–1641*. Oxford: Clarendon Press.

Stone, Lawrence (1977). *The Family, Sex and Marriage in England, 1500–1800*. London: Weidenfeld and Nicolson.

Swinburne, Henry (1686). *A Treatise of Spousals or Matrimonial Contracts*. London.

Tawney, R. H. and E. Power, eds (1924). *Tudor Economics Documents* 3 vols. London: Longman.

Thomas, K. (1978). "The puritans and adultery: the act of 1650 reconsidered." In *Puritans and Revolutionaries: Essays in Seventeenth-Century History Presented to Christopher Hill*, eds D. Pennington and K. Thomas. Oxford: Clarendon Press.

Thomas, K. (1989). "Children in early modern England." In *Children and their Books: A Celebration of the Work of Iona and Peter Opie*, eds G. Avery and J. Briggs. Oxford: Clarendon Press.

Wright, Louis B., ed. (1962). *Advice to a Son: Precepts of Lord Burghley, Sir Walter Raleigh, and Francis Osborne*. Ithaca: Cornell University Press.

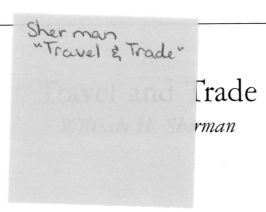

Travel and Trade

William H. Sherman

> Of voyages and ventures to enquire.
>
> Bishop Joseph Hall, *Virgidemiarum* (1599)

The extraordinary outpouring of drama between the 1570s and 1640s coincided with the dramatic expansion of England's geographical and commercial horizons. The relationship between these two developments was close and complex – never more so, perhaps, than at the turn of the seventeenth century. The Globe and Fortune theaters (the names of which are especially resonant in this context) were built in 1599–1600, just as the East India Company received its charter and the Virginia Company was granted permission for an English settlement in North America. Those years also saw the first printing of Shakespeare's *The Merchant of Venice* and the first performances of the (now lost) travel plays *Sir John Mandeville, Jerusalem*, and *Muly Molloco*, as well as the culmination of Richard Hakluyt's efforts to publish a corpus of English travel writing. The final edition of Hakluyt's *Principal Navigations, Voyages, Traffics and Discoveries of the English Nation* was completed in 1600, and its three large volumes described journeys by English explorers, traders, missionaries, and kings to every corner of the known world.

While Hakluyt made no reference to them in his anthology, Renaissance actors were themselves some of the period's most visible travelers – and not just when they were in character as Italian merchants, Turkish pirates, or native Americans. Acting was still considered an itinerant profession during the sixteenth century, and tours of provincial and even foreign cities were common until at least the second decade of the seventeenth century. Moreover, theater companies were often structured on the same "joint stock" model as the period's voyages of exploration, in which a small group of investors shared both the expenses and the profits – though very few undertakings of either kind turned out to be profitable during these formative years.

actors were travelers both on and off stage

Such striking parallels between the "wooden O" of the Renaissance theater and the "wooden world" of the Renaissance ship can only begin to prepare us for the pervasive interest in travel and trade on the Tudor and Stuart stage. Between 1500 and 1600, more than 140 plays, masques, and entertainments were printed featuring at least one traveler or trader in the cast of characters.[1] Only a few of these appeared before the 1570s, but in the course of the 1580s and 1590s more than 30 new traveling and trading roles were created. By the time Ben Jonson's *Bartholomew Fair* was performed in 1614 – only three years after Shakespeare wrote what is now considered the period's definitive travel play – he could complain about the staleness of "*Tales, Tempests*, and such like *Drolleries*." This might simply have been one of Jonson's usual jabs at a rival playwright: in 1622 John Fletcher did not hesitate to take *The Tempest* as his inspiration for two new plays (*The Prophetess* and *The Sea Voyage*), and in the 1630s and 1640s Thomas Heywood, James Shirley, and Richard Brome continued to exploit the theatrical potential of stage-voyages. But Jonson's audiences would already have recognized voyagers and venturers as stock figures.

During the last decade of Elizabeth's reign the praise of merchants became something of a literary vogue (Stevenson, 1984, 2), and they remained one of the most common types of character on the Renaissance stage – albeit sometimes in villainous rather than heroic form. The 105 merchants identified in Tudor and Stuart plays by Berger, Bradford, and Sondergard (1998) are surpassed only by soldiers (343), prisoners (168), and citizens (159). Counts of related characters offer even more surprising indications of the period's cultural preoccupations: there are nearly as many mariners (24) as kings and queens together (26), and many more travelers (40) and ambassadors (64); and there are almost as many usurers (56 – most of whom are foreigners and many Jews) as magicians (31) and witches (26) combined.

These statistics provide a crude but effective measure of the presence of travelers and traders on the Renaissance stage. For a more subtle sense of their place in the experiences, imaginations, and anxieties of early modern playgoers we need to turn to other sources. A letter from a London merchant to his agent in Turkey offers a particularly vivid glimpse not just of England's overseas ventures but of the extent to which they were bound up (from the start) with literary representations. Toward the end of August 1606, John Sanderson sent one of his ships to Robert Barton, the Levant Company's representative in Constantinople (Foster, 1931, 232–3). The cargo included five chests of tin, which was one of England's principal exports and the one which Sanderson considered "the best commodity" in an uncertain market. In the letter that accompanied the merchandise, he instructed Barton to store it until the price was right. In the meantime – perhaps to secure the credit that fully extended merchants like Sanderson needed to continue trading – he asked Barton to deliver a "jewel in a socket of ivory" and an "Indian candlestick" to a creditor he referred to as "Jacob, my Jew." If "Signor Jacob" was no longer alive, Sanderson explained, the gifts should be promptly returned in a ship whose name – the *Exchange* – recalled both the building in London where foreign goods were sold and the activity which was taking English merchants to ever more distant markets.

For his pains, Sanderson sent Barton a pair of gloves and three books, "one of which I am sure will make you laugh, being *news from Bartholomew Fair*." Richard West's pamphlet of that title, which had been published just one month earlier, was a long poem in rhyming couplets reporting the death of the fair's fictional tapster-in-chief, Maximus Omnium. Maximus is no ordinary innkeeper but an embodiment of London's expanding trade relations, lubricating the wheels of commerce by sending his ships as far as Turkey and India for "muscadel and good malmsey" – as well as the most expensive and exotic of English imports, "amber & pearl stones" (West, 1606, sigs A2^v, B1^v).

When Jonson took Londoners on another literary tour of Bartholomew Fair eight years later, he added to the alcohol and gems traded by Maximus a new set of commodities – including cloth, trinkets, tobacco, roasted pigs, and wealthy widows. Like most of Jonson's comedies, *Bartholomew Fair* depicts a world all but consumed by market forces, and driven by the mobility made possible (in part) by England's investment in commercial ventures. In the play's opening speech, the Stage-Keeper jokes that so many new products were flowing into the English capital from the countryside, the Continent, and even the New World that visiting Smithfield – the home of the fair since the Middle Ages – was now like making a voyage to Virginia.

While it is notoriously difficult to generalize about the playgoers of early modern London, it is safe to say that few of them would have had any real experience of travel beyond their immediate surroundings. Long-distance trips within the country were arduous and often dangerous, and ventures "beyond the seas" were only possible with the patronage of powerful institutions or individuals. As both advocates and critics of travel pointed out, England's physical situation meant that a trip to any country (except Scotland or Wales) required a voyage by ship. Not surprisingly, Elizabethan England struck some contemporaries as an insular nation with no interest in the wider world – or, at best, as a nation of armchair travelers. In 1599, the Swiss physician Thomas Platter visited London on the kind of Grand Tour that was not yet as popular among the English as it would later become. After attending two plays and a bear-baiting he recorded in his journal, "With these and many more amusements the English pass their time, learning at the play what is happening abroad . . . since the English for the most part do not travel much, but prefer to learn foreign matters and take their pleasures at home" (Parr, 1995, 1).

Platter's observation provides an important corrective to the popular image of Elizabethan England as the great age of maritime adventure and imperial expansion. The English were latecomers to the exploring and mapping of the wider world, and by the beginning of Queen Elizabeth's reign they had achieved virtually nothing to compare to the voyages, settlements, and narratives of Spain, Portugal, Italy, and France. By the end of her reign there were still no colonies and very few signs of an empire that would eventually surpass that of the Iberians and Ottomans; but the English had nonetheless gone some way toward catching up with their maritime rivals. In 1599 the statement that "the English do not travel much" would have seemed a little unfair: two English explorers had successfully circumnavigated the globe (Francis Drake in 1577–80, and Thomas Cavendish in 1586–8); a series of English navigators (including Martin Frobisher and John Davis) had braved the polar regions in search of a northern passage to Asia; English ambassadors had established diplomatic relations with Russian, Ottoman, and Indian rulers; English soldiers and pirates had made devastating attacks on Spanish cities and ships in the Americas; and English colonizers had made plans for several permanent settlements in the New World.

While some playwrights had direct contact with the investors behind these ventures, however, very few of "the English" had first-hand knowledge of their achievements. In a period before daily newspapers and a reliable postal service, they would indeed have turned to plays for stories from distant places. The stage was not the only source for news from abroad, of course; literate Elizabethans could also turn to the growing body of travel literature written by Englishmen (or translated by them from foreign sources), as well as the first significant products of a native map-making industry (including the first globe made by an Englishman and designed specifically to celebrate English discoveries). By the time he published the first version of his *Principal Navigations* in 1589, Richard Hakluyt had already gathered enough material from his countrymen to fill an 834-page folio, covering 93 voyages and spanning 1500 years; and in the final edition, published between 1598 and 1600, he more than doubled the number of pages and voyages (Quinn, 1974).

Hakluyt began his editorial career by translating the existing accounts of European voyagers, but he became increasingly committed to documenting the activities of English travellers. In dedicating the 1589 edition of the *Principal Navigations* to Sir Francis Walsingham, Hakluyt acknowledged that when he went to France as a young man, "I both heard in speech, and read in books other nations miraculously extolled for their discoveries and notable enterprises by sea, but the English of all others for their sluggish security, and continual neglect of the like attempts . . . either ignominiously reported or exceedingly condemned" (sigs *2–*2ᵛ). He intended his collection to set the record straight, proving that the English had not only "been men full of activity, stirrers abroad, and searchers of the remote parts of the world" but, indeed, "in compassing the vast globe of the earth more than once, have excelled all the nations and people of the earth" (sig. *2ᵛ). He concluded with a breathtaking survey of the Elizabethans' stirrings and searchings, pointing to the establishment of trading privileges with the emperor of Persia and the "Grand Signor" at Constantinople, the placement of English consuls and agents at "Tripolis in Syria, at Aleppo, at Babylon, at Balsara, and . . . Goa," and the passing of "the unpassable (in former opinion) strait of Magellan," in order to "enter into alliance, amity, and traffic with the princes of the Moluccas, & the Isle of Java . . . and last of all return home most richly laden with commodities of China" (sigs *2ᵛ–*3).

Over the next few decades the editorial labors of Samuel Purchas added still more volumes of old and new English travels (Pennington, 1997). In 1625 he published a four-volume collection, *Hakluytus Posthumus or Purchas his Pilgrims*, which at that point was the longest book ever printed in England. Hakluyt had been able to include several groundbreaking works of travel writing, including Thomas Hariot's *Brief and True Report of the New Found Land of Virginia* (published as a small pamphlet in 1588 and republished in 1590 with engravings of American people and wildlife based on the drawings of John White) and Walter Ralegh's *Discovery of the Large, Rich, and Beautiful Empire of Guiana* (perhaps the most interesting of the Elizabethan accounts, from both literary and anthropological perspectives). But it was Purchas' contemporaries who emerged as the first generation of more or less professional travel writers, the most famous of whom were Thomas Coryat, Fynes Moryson, and William Lithgow.

These texts were more often concerned with firing nationalistic sentiments, with soliciting future investments, or – as in the case of Coryat's endlessly amusing *Crudities* – with entertaining readers than with providing accurate geographical or ethnographic information (Fuller, 1995). It should also be remembered that the texts assembled by Hakluyt and Purchas would have reached a smaller proportion of the playgoing public than books describing such marvels as men with heads below their shoulders, romance quests in exotic settings, and Protestant propaganda masquerading as political reportage. As these diverse genres (and the enduring popularity of details from the imaginary voyages of Sir John Mandeville) imply, the line between fact and fiction was rarely clear in English representations of other peoples and places.

In some cases, playwrights and pamphleteers worked hand-in-hand to present breaking news of contemporary travels. In 1607, the adventures of the Sherley brothers were depicted almost simultaneously in Anthony Nixon's pamphlet, *The Three English Brothers*, and a play by John Day, William Rowley, and George Wilkins entitled *The Travels of the Three English Brothers* (Parr, 1995). Robert Daborne's play *A Christian Turned Turk* (first published in 1612) dramatized the exploits of the English pirates John Ward and Simon Dansiker, and was largely based on two sensational pamphlets published in 1609 (Vitkus, 2000, 24). The best-known example, however, is Shakespeare's *The Tempest* (1611): among the play's few identifiable sources are three pamphlets concerning the wreck of the *Sea-Adventure* off the coast of Bermuda in 1609, with the Virginia Colony's new governor on board. Two of these (Sylvester Jourdain's *Discovery of the Bermudas* and the Council of Virginia's *True Declaration of the State of the Colony in Virginia*) were published in 1610, but the third (William Strachey's *True Repertory of the Wrack*) was not published until 1625 – suggesting that Shakespeare had the interest and connections necessary to read the account in a manuscript copy.

The dramatists were also influenced by the cartographic images of England and the wider world that were newly available in the period's atlases, itineraries, chorographies, and globes; and what Platter described as a preference "to learn foreign matters and take their pleasures at home" had a particularly good pedigree among English producers and users of maps. Thomas Elyot's *Boke Named the Governour* (1531), the most influential guide to the education of English gentlemen, had commended the

study of maps from an early age, suggesting that they were essential for the reading
of histories because they brought the strange names and boring narratives to life. Maps
could bring vast spaces into small rooms, and distant or long-dead people before one's
eyes. Not surprisingly, both dramatists and cartographers found ways to exploit this
analogy, and while surprisingly few maps appear as props in Renaissance plays, they
often influenced playwrights' sense of space and the locations, and dislocations, of
their characters (Gillies and Vaughan, 1998).

The earliest English travel narratives, like many of the earliest English maps,
were concerned with pilgrimages to the Holy Land (Elsner and Rubiés, 1999,
introduction), and – as the religious frame gave way to more secular and commercial
ones – this orientation, rather than the more familiar westward drive, informed a
surprising number of Renaissance plays (Holland, 1996, 166). Even Jacobean city
comedy, which charted London's local characters and customs, revived the traditional
role of the chivalric knight and appropriated it for merchants and apprentices –
culminating in Thomas Heywood's vision, in his *Four Prentices of London* (1615), of
a mercer, a goldsmith, a haberdasher, and a grocer wandering across Europe toward
Jerusalem.

Christopher Marlowe was the earliest English playwright to attempt a systematic
exploration of the dramatic potential of travel. The conquerors, magicians, and merchants in his plays enjoy almost unrestricted movement across the globe, and – like
later tales of tempests and shipwrecks – would no doubt have offered compelling
fantasies to audiences whose own movement was extremely limited. They would also
have served as a powerful vehicle for reflection on England's place in the wider world
and, more generally, on the ethics of travel. The fates of Tamburlaine, Faustus, and
Barabas suggest that Marlowe's visits to foreign locations were motivated more by
edification than escapism. They suggest, furthermore, that travel may have played an
important role in unsettling the conventional dramatic genres by emphasizing the
tragic as much as the comic potential of the adventure narratives inherited from
romantic or pastoral models. Marlowe's plays were also among the first to confront
the dramaturgical challenges of presenting global movement in the small and fixed
space of the stage (Holland, 1996, 160–1), using choruses to take audiences through
enormous geographical leaps, and peppering his plays with cartographic details (some
designed to place his characters with remarkable specificity, and others to show them
transcending geographical boundaries altogether).

Most stage travel offered early modern audiences less challenging experiences
of imaginative travel and more comfortable images of the foreign. Crude portraits of
exotic "others" – with any potential threats dissolved in villainy, stupidity, or pure
strangeness – gave playgoers ample opportunity to consolidate their own identities.
Daubridgecourt Belchier's *Hans Beer-Pot . . . or See Me and See Me Not* (1618) featured
a typical character named "Abnidaraes Quixot," a "tawny moor" who comes on stage
just long enough to sing "a verse or two of a song" and to pronounce a sample of his
"language natural": "Hestron, pangaeon, cacobomboton, Aphnes halenon, / Mydras,
myphrasman, tyltura, pantha, teman."

This ought to suggest why Nabil Matar has recently warned against relying exclusively on drama and travel literature as historical sources for England's extensive contact with the Turks and Moors (Matar, 1999, 3). But not all plays offered such simplistic portraits as Belchier's, and even Quixot is more complicated than he seems at first. When asked about his origins, he explains that his mother was "Numedian" and his father Spanish, and that he is therefore "A Spaniard, Moor, half Turk, half Christian." Even in passing, and in such apparently superficial plays, Renaissance dramatists offered a troubling sense of the shifting borders of the early modern world, and of the ways in which identities were destabilized by travel (Vitkus, 2000, 44; Parr, 1995, 10–18). → or does traveling help create identity?

Almost from the outset, in fact, English readers and viewers of voyage literature could feel a steady undertow of skepticism about the benefits of travel, real or imaginary. If Platter had come to London late enough to see Thomas Heywood's play *The English Traveller* (1633), he would have learned that the English were themselves debating the relative merits of armchair and actual travel. In the play's opening scene the studious Dalavill ultimately defers to the traveler Young Geraldine:

> I have read Jerusalem, and studied Rome,
> Can tell in what degree each city stands,
> Describe the distance of this place from that –
> All this the scale in every map can teach –
> Nay, for a need could punctually recite
> The monuments in either, but what I have
> By relation only, knowledge by travel,
> Which still makes up a complete gentleman,
> Proves eminent in you. (I.i.7ff)

But Bishop Joseph Hall published both comic and serious attacks on the wisdom of travel, and the period's definitive anti-travel play, Brome's *Antipodes* (1638), features a character whose obsession with Mandevillean wonders can only be cured by an imaginary voyage to the other side of the world. And while Ben Jonson seems to have celebrated England's nascent colonialism and London's incipient consumer culture in some of his masques (especially in the *Entertainment at Britain's Burse*, written in 1609 for the opening of the New Exchange), he is better known for his satirical attacks on materialism and upward mobility and for his parodies of travelers who all but lose themselves in their pursuit of foreign ideas and fashions.

While Platter had observed that the English were reluctant to travel to foreign shores, he also acknowledged the fact that by 1599 Londoners were deeply involved in global trade: "most of the inhabitants are employed in commerce: they buy, sell and trade in all the corners of the globe, for which purpose the water serves them well" (Orlin, 2000, 93). Most of the period's travel was carried out, explicitly or implicitly, in the name of trade. England's early outreach, and its hopes of challenging Spanish control over trade routes and precious metals in the New World, were driven by adventuring and privateering voyages. And the remarkable rise of London as a commercial center was largely due to the expanding scope of English mercantile activity – along with a series of economic crises in the countryside, and the collapse of long-standing European entrepôts in Amsterdam and the Hanse Towns.

England's gradual transition from agrarian feudalism to venture capitalism during the sixteenth and seventeenth centuries brought with it a reconfiguration of social relations, new mechanisms of financial exchange (involving new forms of credit and risk), and an increasingly prominent role for individual entrepreneurs in overseas trade. We should not lose sight of the continuing importance of the internal (or "inland") trade: at least half of the dominant export commodity, woolen manufactures, remained within the domestic market. But at least two-thirds (and perhaps as much as three-quarters) of the gross national product derived from overseas trade between 1500 and 1700 (Chartres, 1977, 10). At the beginning of the period England occupied a peripheral position in the international network of trade, and its mercantile activity was almost entirely dominated by cloth exports to the Low Countries by the Company of Merchant Adventurers (which was not formally incorporated until the second decade of Elizabeth's reign, but was organizing English trade by the late fourteenth century). After 1550, new markets for English goods and new products for English and European consumers emerged in Russia, Persia, and the Guinea and Barbary coasts, and then in East and Southeast Asia, North America, and the Caribbean.

This expanding network was both reflected in and advanced by the official licensing of new trading companies: the late sixteenth and seventeenth centuries became the great age of companies chartered for the purpose of overseas commerce and colonization (Griffiths, 1974). The Muscovy Company was chartered in 1555 and developed trade with Russia, Persia, and Greenland before its decline at the end of the seventeenth century. In 1576–8 the Cathay Company launched an ill-fated mining venture in the Baffin Bay area. The short-lived Turkey and Venice Companies lost their grants in 1588–9 and were replaced by the Levant Company, which was chartered in January 1592 and flourished until the eighteenth century. Several African Companies pursued a lucrative trade in gold and slaves from the 1530s onward. The East India Company was chartered in 1600 and exchanged currency, silks, and spices on a truly global scale, despite persistent competition from the Portuguese and the Dutch. And the first few decades of the seventeenth century saw the advent of new companies for the explicit purpose of "plantation," including the Virginia Company (1600), the Somers Island or Bermuda Company (1615), the Plymouth Company (1620), and the Massachusetts Bay Company (1629). The impact on the London economy of the new commodities traded by these companies can be gauged by charting the changes in luxury imports between the 1560s and 1620s. The amount of sugar and tobacco more than tripled; wine, dried fruits, and spices more than quadrupled; pepper more than quintupled; and raw silk imports saw a tenfold increase (Clay, 1984, II, 124–5; Brenner, 1993, 25).

By the reign of James I English merchants were clearly playing an ever more important role in the widening world of European commerce (Brenner, 1993, 23–5, 180). In 1618, Thomas Gainsford offered English readers a comprehensive survey of foreign countries, beginning with the Tartars, Chinese, Indians, Persians, and Turks and ending with the Irish. His patriotic aims are captured in his title, *The Glory of England . . . Whereby She Triumpheth Over All the Nations of the World*, and the source of his pride is fully revealed in chapter 25 of book II, on the "greatness of English shipping." He points to the presence of English merchants in India, Japan, Persia, Africa, Europe, Greenland, and the Americas, and his concluding *tour de force* echoes and surpasses that of Hakluyt:

> Is there any place where ever Christian came, or could come, but the English merchant adventured, either for wealth, honor, or conscience . . . so that from one place or other of our country, we have not so few as 1,000 sails of ships abroad: nor so small a number as 100,000 persons dispersed under this acceptable title of merchant. (Gainsford, 1618, sigs X8–X8ᵛ)

These accounts – like Hakluyt's – were hardly objective, and they should not obscure the fact that the English mercantile economy was still extremely unstable in the early seventeenth century (Supple, 1959; Brenner, 1993). Renaissance plays engaged with the full range of old and new economic issues experienced by the stage-merchants' real-life counterparts, including the usurious money-lending that extended their credit but involved them in strange exchanges with even stranger characters; the negative balance of trade that drained the country of its hard currency; and the monopolies granted to companies and individuals that increased the gap between the rich and the poor and broke down the collective ideals advocated in the name of the "commonwealth" up through Elizabeth's reign. The new anxieties that accompanied the new mercantile activities were depicted on stage in astonishingly technical detail. It is impossible to follow the incessant economic wordplay of Dekker, Jonson, or Middleton without the help of a glossary of financial metaphors and puns (Fischer, 1985). Likewise, a full appreciation of the tensions in Marlowe's *The Jew of Malta* depends upon a fairly sophisticated sense of the mechanisms for mercantile exchange (Jardine, 1996, ch. 6).

There were certainly success stories, such as that of Sir Thomas Gresham, perhaps the period's most successful merchant and most sophisticated monetary theorist (de Roover, 1949). Gresham used his wealth to finance the building of both Gresham's College (which played a leading role in the development of geography as an academic subject) and the Royal Exchange. The construction of the latter building was celebrated in the second part of Thomas Heywood's patriotic play, *If You Know Not Me, You Know Nobody* (1606), and Heywood later produced a series of pageants as tributes to London's trading guilds and institutions: in speeches by such characters as an Indian leading an elephant and the god Mercury (patron of "trade, traffic, and commerce"), he described London as the "fountain of arts and sciences" and the "emporium" for all of Europe (Bergeron, 1986).

But the presence of foreign goods and people at Gresham's emporium, the Royal Exchange, once again produced fears that globalization would lead to the loss of English identity (Bartolovich, 2000, 14–16). Literary and social commentators were increasingly disturbed by the trade which was bringing other places to London and London to other places. Some inevitably worried that England was importing foreign vices along with foreign commodities, and that English style and language were disappearing beneath foreign clothes and accents. In light of these anxieties, it is especially useful to return to Berger, Bradford, and Sondergard (1998) for one final tally of characters. Perhaps the most surprising figure is the large number of Turks and Moors on the Renaissance stage – 45 and 55 respectively. This is just one fewer than the 101 characters identified specifically as Londoners; and when we add the 30 Venetians (and the dozens of others from Milan, Verona, and Malta), it begins to appear that in the plays attended by early modern Londoners local characters were actually outnumbered by the foreigners who were the objects of their fear and fascination.

I will conclude this brief survey by returning to the time and place where I began, in London at the turn of the seventeenth century. Thomas Dekker's *Old Fortunatus* was among the plays performed at court during the 1599 Christmas season, and it contained what may be the period's most potent emblem of the twin forces of travel and trade. The story is set in motion when the goddess Fortune gives a magical purse to a beggar named Fortunatus: like the "Indian mine" and the "Philosopher's Stone" to which Fortunatus compares it, the pouch provides its owner with an endless supply of gold. This new-found wealth allows Fortunatus not only to transform his sons and servants into gentlemen but to travel at will. As in *Dr. Faustus*, a chorus describes a magical tour that reduces the world to a small space, and invites the audience:

> To carrie *Fortunatus* on the wings
> Of active thought, many a thousand miles.
> Suppose then since you last beheld him here,
> That you have sailed with him upon the seas,
> And leapt with him upon the Asian shores. (II.Chorus.8–12)

Fortunatus' travels finally bring him to the court of the Sultan of Babylon, who has his own source of magical power – a "wishing hat" that instantly carries its wearer wherever he asks to go. Fortunatus persuades the Sultan to let him try on the hat and then wishes himself home, where he displays to his sons the unlikely sources of unlimited travel and trade:

> In these two hands do I grip all the world.
> This leather purse, and this bald woollen hat
> Make me a monarch. (II.ii.218–20)

After Fortunatus' death, the play descends into chaos as his sons and various French and English noblemen struggle for control over the pouch and hat. Fortune herself steps in to restore order by presenting them in perpetuity to the English court and transferring her own imperial power over the seas and their riches to Queen Elizabeth. This conclusion could not have been entirely satisfying to a queen who was about to die without heirs, a country which was suffering from a series of bad harvests and a dearth of cash, and a playwright who had himself been indicted for debt less than twelve months earlier. *Old Fortunatus* is generally considered to be nothing more than a quaint and shallow adaptation of an old German folktale. But Dekker's dramatic parable offers a profound meditation on the uses and abuses of gold at a moment when the English crown and its financial and foreign relations were under intense pressure.

The voyage- and venture-plays of Dekker and his contemporaries presented new fantasies of mobility – both physical and economic – and newly charged narratives of adventure. By going to the theater, citizens who never left London could travel vicariously to exotic settings for stories of fortunes gained and lost. And while dramatists used these stories to appeal to the civic and national pride of those who paid to see their plays, they also used them to question the benefits of travel, and to examine the ethics of the colonialism and capitalism that would transform their country from an isolated island at the beginning of the sixteenth century into a world power by the end of the nineteenth.

NOTE

1   This figure is derived from searches of Berger, Bradford, and Sondergard (1998) and the Literature Online (LION) database.

REFERENCES AND FURTHER READING

Bartolovich, Crystal (2000). " 'Baseless fabric': London as a 'world city'." In *"The Tempest" and its Travels*, eds Peter Hulme and William H. Sherman. London: Reaktion Books; Philadelphia: University of Pennsylvania Press.

Berger, Thomas L., William C. Bradford, and Sidney L. Sondergard (1998). *An Index of Characters in Early Modern English Drama: Printed Plays, 1500–1660*. 2nd edn. Cambridge: Cambridge University Press.

Bergeron, David M., ed. (1986). *Thomas Heywood's Pageants*. New York: Garland.

Brenner, Robert (1993). *Merchants and Revolution: Commercial Change, Political Conflict, and London's Overseas Traders, 1550–1653*. Cambridge: Cambridge University Press.

Cawley, Robert Ralston (1940). *Unpathed Waters: Studies in the Influence of the Voyagers on Elizabethan Literature*. Princeton: Princeton University Press.

Chartres, J. A. (1977). *Internal Trade in England, 1500–1700*. London: Macmillan.

Clay, C. G. A. (1984). *Economic Expansion and Social Change: England 1500–1700*. 2 vols. Cambridge: Cambridge University Press.

Elsner, Jaś, and Joan-Pau Rubiés, eds (1999). *Voyages and Visions: A Cultural History of Travel*. London: Reaktion Books.

Fischer, Sandra K. (1985). *Econolingua: A Glossary of Coins and Economic Language in Renaissance Drama*. Newark: University of Delaware Press.

Foster, Sir William, ed. (1931). *The Travels of John Sanderson in the Levant 1584–1602*. London: Hakluyt Society.

Fuller, Mary C. (1995). *Voyages in Print: English Travel to America, 1576–1624*. Cambridge: Cambridge University Press.

Gainsford, Thomas (1618). *The Glory of England*. London: Edward Griffin.

Gillies, John, and Virginia Mason Vaughan, eds (1998). *Playing the Globe: Genre and Geography in English Renaissance Drama*. Madison, NJ: Fairleigh Dickinson University Press.

Griffiths, Sir Percival (1974). *A License to Trade: The History of English Chartered Companies*. London: Ernest Benn.

Holland, Peter (1996). " 'Travelling hopefully': the dramatic form of journeys in English Renaissance drama." In *Travel and Drama in Shakespeare's Time*, eds Jean-Pierre Maquerlot and Michèle Willems. Cambridge: Cambridge University Press.

Jardine, Lisa (1996). *Reading Shakespeare Historically*. London: Routledge.

Marchitello, Howard (1999). "Recent studies in Tudor and early Stuart travel writing." *English Literary Renaissance* 29: 326–47.

Matar, Nabil (1999). *Turks, Moors, and Englishmen in the Age of Discovery*. New York: Columbia University Press.

Orlin, Lena Cowen, ed. (2000). *Material London, ca. 1600*. Philadelphia: University of Pennsylvania Press.

Parr, Anthony, ed. (1995). *Three Renaissance Travel Plays*. Manchester: Manchester University Press.

Pennington, L. E., ed. (1997). *The Purchas Handbook*. London: Hakluyt Society.

Quinn, David, B., ed. (1974). *The Hakluyt Handbook*. London: Hakluyt Society.

de Roover, Raymond (1949). *Gresham on Foreign Exchange: An Essay on Early English Mercantilism with the Text of Sir Thomas Gresham's Memorandum for the Understanding of the Exchange*. Cambridge, Mass: Harvard University Press.

Stevenson, Laura Caroline (1984). *Praise and Paradox: Merchants and Craftsmen in Elizabethan Popular Literature*. Cambridge: Cambridge University Press.

Supple, B. E. (1959). *Commercial Crisis and Change in England, 1600–1642: A Study in the Instability of a Mercantile Economy*. Cambridge: Cambridge University Press.

Vitkus, Daniel J., ed. (2000). *Three Turk Plays from Early Modern England*. New York: Columbia University Press.

West, Richard (1606). *News from Bartholomew Fair*. London: n.p.

9

Everyday Custom and Popular Culture

Michael Bristol

There was no electricity. There was no public water supply, no municipal waste disposal, no public sanitation. There was no television, no radio, no telephone, not even a daily newspaper. There were no police, no fire department, no hospitals, no such thing as a shopping mall. Early modern popular culture for the most part did not take the form of commodities or consumer goods or commercial entertainment. It was, instead, a culture of home-made artifacts, local customs, and traditional practices. And, like everything else in the early modern economy, it required skilled engagement with the tools and the materials of everyday social life.

Popular culture was the culture of ordinary people, both the "middling sort," consisting of urban merchants, well-to-do yeoman farmers, and master craftsmen, and the "lesser sort," consisting of apprentices, agricultural laborers, and tenant farmers (Burke, 1978; Leinwand, 1993). These groups represented the very large majority of the population with immediate practical knowledge of all the diverse forms of economic production. The popular element was not, however, the same thing as a working class, and it would be misleading to suggest that popular culture expressed a homogeneous set of cultural values or common ideological interests (Thompson, 1974). Cultural activity was strongly parochial in character (Rappaport, 1989). The various forms of pageantry and celebration took place within the context of the local community as a way of assuring its own survival and that of each of its members. And, not incidentally, it was a way for people who lived together for long periods of time in very close social proximity with each other to share resources, to settle disputes, and even to have fun.

For the people who lived in early modern England, cooperation, reciprocity, and mutual aid were central to their way-of-being-together-in-the-world. But the image of jolly peasants dancing together and sharing all the good things of life is a falsification of the real historical conditions in which people actually lived. It is true that the practice of hospitality was an important feature of the early modern economy (Bristol, 1986, 80–5). But it is also true that early modern society was full of dangers, not only because of unpredictable natural occurrences like disease and poor harvests, but also because of poorly understood social phenomena like price inflation and the effects of enclosure (Muchembled, 1985; Sharpe, 1997). The Protestant Reformation brought about changes in religious belief, in liturgy, and in church governance that generated chronic and often embittered animosity in many local communities (Scribner, 1987; Diehl 1997). And there were even deeper sources of conflict that arose from the complex social structure of early modern England.

The base, common, and popular element of the population had a range of obligations to the nobility and gentry who ruled over them, not always wisely, it must be said. But the social norms of deference and of noblesse oblige were no guarantee that harmonious social conditions could be sustained. And common people also lived with complex forms of social dissonance among themselves in addition to their chronic friction with hereditary elites. There were more or less permanent structural oppositions between rural and urban interests and, in addition, newer structural conflicts brought about by the introduction of new techniques and new sources of wealth. These oppositions were superimposed on traditional patterns of alliance and rivalry between particular guilds or between different towns and settlements. There were also important informal associations that figured prominently in the implementation of significant popular cultural practices, particularly the "youth groups" or confraternities composed of apprentices or of young unmarried males (Capp, 1977; Davis, 1971). Among the diverse social functions of these associations were the regulation of weddings and of sexual conduct, especially through the charivaris, organization and implementation of festive misrule, local defense, and popular justice (Thompson, 1972). The solidarity of these groups was often expressed in socially aggressive behavior, and they were often denounced for disturbing the peace. Despite the pervasive discord that characterized much of early modern popular culture, however, guilds and community associations had ways of maintaining social continuity and modulating but not eliminating social conflict.

The possibility of a meaningful popular resistance to domination by hereditary elites was linked to the accumulated power of the guilds, livery companies, and municipal corporations that regulated the various trades within the early modern economy. Guilds were voluntary associations of persons practicing a particular trade who possessed a Royal Charter or license to practice and to regulate that trade (Black, 1984). Many of the important livery companies were of very ancient standing. The guilds were also hierarchical. Members were obliged to serve a term as apprentices before they were recognized as freemen and licensed to practice a particular craft. Regulation of the company was closely held by the settled master craftsmen. Despite this, the moral culture of the guilds was based on an association of equals or corporate entity based on voluntary initiative and on fraternal solidarity (von Gierke, 1987, 36–61). Ordinary people felt entitled to take the initiative, to assemble, and to express their own characteristic sense of what constituted the good life. Much of this popular expression took the form of direct participation in a range of symbolic or ritualized social practice.

Everyday Life and the Space of Popular Culture

The customary practices of early modern popular culture were lived with the greatest immediacy within the domestic space of the household. The household was where people ate, and slept, and performed the tasks basic to their survival. And it was also the place where people sang lullabies to their children or sat before the hearth to tell stories or gathered together to dance with their neighbors. According to early modern political theorists, the household was a small model of the commonwealth, organized and governed hierarchically like the state. But the household was even more fundamentally an economic institution, and indeed the English word "economy" is derived from Greek *oikonomos*, meaning roughly "household management." In addition to its many complex domestic functions, the household also had a central role for the wider community as the privileged locus for traditional forms of conviviality, such as "keeping Christmas."

Hospitality was primarily the responsibility of women. Much of what is known about "women's work" in the context of the household comes from published manuals such as Gervase Markham's *The English Housewife*. Markham's book was itself the product of an emergent culture industry, a commodity that circulated through an anonymous market. But its economic form here is perhaps less important than its thematic content, which consists of recipes and techniques necessary for a competent housewife, including "physic, cookery, banqueting-stuff, distillation, perfumes, wool, hemp, flax, dairies, brewing, baking, and all other things belonging to a household." Women had a lot to do, but one of their more important duties was in the ordering of feasts:

> Now for a more humble feast, or an ordinary proportion which any goodman may keep in his family for the entertainment of his true and worthy friends, it must hold limitation with his provision, and the season of the year; for summer affords what winter wants, and winter is master of that which summer can but with difficulty have: it is good then for him that intends to feast, to set down the full number of his full dishes, that is, dishes of meat that are of substance, and not empty or for show; of these sixteen is a good proportion for one course unto one mess, as thus for example; first, a shield of brawn with mustard; secondly a boiled capon; thirdly a boiled piece of beef; fourthly a chine of beef roasted; fifthly a neat's tongue roasted; sixthly a pig roasted; seventhly, chewets baked; eighthly a goose roasted; ninthly a swan roasted; tenthly, a turkey roasted; the eleventh, a haunch of venison roasted; the twelfth, a pasty of venison; the thirteenth, a kid with a pudding in the belly; the fourteenth, an olive pie; the fifteenth, a couple of capons; the sixteenth, a custard or doucets. Now to these full dishes may be added in sallats, fricassees, *quelquechoses*, and devised paste, as many dishes more, which make the full service no less than two and thirty dishes, which is as much as can conveniently stand on one table, and in one mess.

Markham's description of an ordinary feast (one can only wonder what a great feast would look like) is based on a few simple principles. The feast was for entertainment of "worthy friends" rather than private domestic consumption. It reflected the rhythm of the seasons. And it reflected a bountiful life through the complex variety of dishes served. The importance of this account lies in its perhaps utopian picture of festive abundance and social generosity. It reflects the mixed resource base of that economy, setting out agricultural goods (beef, capons, "sallats") side by side with the hunter's prey (swans, venison). Even if this kind of feast was not very likely to occur in reality, it remains important as a central image of social desire, a kind of collective wishful thinking about the forms of the good life. The focal concerns of the early modern household were not linked to consumption, but rather to notions of expenditure, reciprocity, and the securing of material abundance.

Although the household was a central institution in early modern society, it was not the only location for the practice of conviviality. Related but distinct forms of sharing and celebration also took place in the inns, taverns, and public houses. The tavern had its own characteristic standards of social behavior that attached particular importance to the familiar custom of standing drinks for one's friends. Strictly private consumption was not well thought of in taverns and might even provoke active resentment. This is vividly illustrated by an incident that took place at the Red Lyon in the village of East Brent in Somerset, recorded in the quarter sessions at Ilchester in the spring of 1621. A certain Richard Dodd and his friends, incensed at the behavior of Thomas Hill, the newly appointed curate, staged a mock baptism of a dog to protest his meddling in their affairs. The offenders went to considerable trouble to carry out this act of sacrilege, even arranging for the local tailor to make a priest's coat for the dog.

Dodd's transgressive creativity illustrates the spirit of resistance to authority evident throughout early modern popular culture. It also demonstrates the importance of the grotesque forms of travesty and burlesque that were typically used by cultural agents like Dodd and his friends. Dodd had already attacked the curate, thrashing him with "leather thongs," in an earlier incident at the tavern. When asked by the court to explain his conduct, he testified "I will use all priestes so yat will come unto oure company and will not pay" (*REED Somerset*, I, 107). Hill was a spoilsport whose Malvolio-like disapproval of the Red Lyon crowd offended the community's spirit of conviviality.

The incident at the Red Lyon is a territorial dispute between the social regimes of "church" and "tavern." Richard Dodd, John Dinghurst, Emmanuel Crossman, and the other offenders were incensed at the arrogance of curate Hill, who invaded their space and breached its standards of social behavior. In effect the troublemakers at the Red Lyon were asserting the traditional privilege of the tavern as a social space exempt from priestly surveillance. The significance of the dog baptism may also reflect some kind of cultural resistance to the new administrative functions of the national church and in particular its role in the policing of social behavior. But it would be inaccurate to conclude from an affair like this that the church simply represented an alien and coercive center of authority. People did receive the sacraments along with instruction in matters of the spirit in the priest's sermons. But the parish churches were also important centers for a range of significant cultural activities that included not only baptisms, weddings, and funerals, but also festive celebrations in the form of church ales (the selling of ale and other goods), which were a customary way for the parish to raise funds for various local needs.

Church ales were typically held in the spring, most often at Whitsuntide (Laroque, 1991, 159–60). In parts of Somerset, and presumably elsewhere, the churchwardens would also go hoggling during the Christmas season. Hoggling was a means for raising funds, but it was also a form of conviviality. Hoggling resembles a number of other customs linked to the Christmas season, such as carol-singing, Christmas mummery, and hogmanay, a gathering game typically performed at Epiphany in the north of England. This was mutual entertainment: the hogglers performed and told jokes at various households and in return they were given something to eat and drink. Everybody had a good time and the church got some money to cover maintenance costs.

Neighbors looked after one another and helped each other out. But these same neighbors also gossiped, interfered, and in general kept order by continual mutual surveillance. The early modern community was in many ways nurturing and supportive of its members, but it was also coercive. At a deeper level, the customary forms of popular culture expressed a vernacular system of ethics based on maintaining social equilibrium. The various forms of conviviality, reciprocity, and mutual aid were intended to maintain a balance between husbandry and harvest, between profit and expenditure, between the skilled effort required to produce everything required for subsistence and the celebratory enjoyment of the good things of life.

The Festive Calendar

The early modern social agents who participated in the forms of popular culture understood the cycle of seasonal recurrence both in the liturgical calendar and in the traditional "labors of the months." François Laroque has suggested that the year was divided into two more or less equal halves, a "winter cycle" of sacred or religious festivals, and a "summer cycle" of secular feasts. Roughly speaking this makes sense, especially for a largely agricultural society in which most of the day-to-day work of raising crops would have to take place during spring and summer. But of course the two "halves" really overlapped and interpenetrated. The relatively abstract distinction between sacred and secular, between ritual symbolism and practical common sense, probably did not have much salience for people living anywhere in early modern Europe. And the winter cycle itself was divided between two great ritual programs: the immoveable (solar) and the moveable (lunar) feasts. The structure of the liturgical calendar is best described as an alternating rhythm between Christmas-tide and Lenten-tide.

The Christmas "season" began with the feast of All Souls, and it ended some six weeks after Christmas day with the feast of Candlemas. The onset of winter was marked by the customary practice of butchering surplus livestock roughly at the time of All Hallows and St. Martin's, at the beginning of November. This periodic killing of livestock had considerable practical importance, since the preserved and salted meat was consumed during a time when other provisions were scarce.

In many communities the start of the winter cycle at the feast of All Hallows was the time for the annual return of the lord of misrule, a custom that probably still survives in contemporary celebrations of Hallowe'en and Mischief Night. Lords of misrule were a conspicuous feature in a wide variety of social customs, ritual practices, and games, where they typically enjoyed considerable license from the customary restraints of a hierarchical society. According to Sandra Billington (1991), rule and misrule work together dialectically, with each term acting as the mirror image of the other. The annual periods of misrule corresponded to the darker period of the year, roughly from October 31 up to the time of Candlemas, a feast of lights and the beginning of the traditional cycle of outdoor work that took place every year on February 2. Of course no society can sustain three continuous months of actual misrule; in the early modern period misrule consisted mainly of traditional forms of conventional transgression. The real task of the lord of misrule who was elected each year at the time of All Hallows was to organize the seasonal performances and games like the annual Christmas mummery.

Like hoggling, Christmas mummery was a form of house-to-house canvass for the purpose of making merry, drinking, and the circulation of gifts. It could also include ritualized forms of transgression, as in the "stealing of cob loaves" reported from the village of Bathampton. This was probably a traditional variation on the customary forms of Christmas hospitality. The cob loaves were a symbolic "gift" that was "stolen" to express the mummers' sense of entitlement. Christmas mummery reminded householders that their own surplus wealth could not be withheld from those in need, but it might also involve less benign forms of mischief when the mummers had a score to settle with one of their neighbors. This helps to explain why the participants in a mummery wore disguises. Masquerade and cross-dressing are a way for people to throw off restraints and have fun, but they are also a good way to get away with slander or vandalism or petty theft. Christmas mummers may have been intent on "keeping mum" about who they were because their disguise allowed them to indulge feelings of envy or a wish for retaliation with impunity.

Christmas mummery afforded the participants a general warrant to play the fool. The irreverent disguise and transgressive behavior of the mummers were an expression of festive conviviality and the affirmation of holiday exhilaration. They were also a way to act out and to affirm the importance of gift exchange. Thus the popular transformation of Christmas solemnity into a Feast of Fools captured aspects of meaning that are simply not available either in the canonical liturgy or in other secular forms of observance. In a way the popular forms of Christmas celebration have a larger cogency as the expression of religious meaning. Gift exchange is mandated by the idea of the Nativity, Christ's incarnation, the divine "gift" that permanently binds and obligates all who receive it. This impossibly lavish expenditure paradoxically also redeems and liberates. This is the emancipatory "theological insight" captured in the popular cultural forms of Christmas folly and misrule.

The last of the annual feasts specifically connected with the Nativity was Candlemas, observed annually on February 2, marking the end of the Christmas cycle. Officially this feast commemorated the purification of the Virgin Mary, who was presented at the temple in accordance with Old Testament Law. Candlemas acknowledged Jewish law and at the same time superseded it. On a more mundane level, this was the time for taking down the Christmas decorations, for predicting the weather, for manuring the fields, for the beginning of outdoor work prompted by the noticeable lengthening of the day, and so on. This was also traditionally the last day on which candles were used at vesper services. Candlemas had its own characteristic figures of misrule, often a wild man, or a "bear" who pursued and threatened young women (Bristol, 1991). Perhaps even more important, Candlemas was the final holiday of Christmas-tide, the last important "immoveable feast" celebrated on a specific date determined by the solar calendar. The days following were traditionally set aside as the time of Carnival, a transitional period leading up to the penitential abstinence of Lent.

Carnival was an important holiday throughout early modern Europe, typically reaching its climax on Shrove Tuesday or Mardi Gras, just before the start of Lent on Ash Wednesday. One function of Carnival was to make up for the shifting relationship between the solar feasts of Christmas-tide and the lunar feasts of the Easter cycle that begin on Ash Wednesday, the first day of Lent, and conclude with Ascension Day. Easter must take place on the first Sunday after the first full moon after the vernal equinox. But this date, which determines the calendar for the entire cycle, can vary by as much as six weeks, and so there is always at least some time between the end of Christmas and the beginning of Lent. Because it is not really part of the liturgical year, Carnival is "untimely" and its onset can be signalled with customs like ringing the church bell at the wrong time. Carnival is thus a pivotal link in the festive calendar, a period of license betwixt and between the major religious cycles of Christmas and Easter. In England and elsewhere Shrove Tuesday was celebrated with misrule, inversion, and travesty. This was also a time of lavish excess – a high degree of sexual license as well as immoderate eating and drinking. Shrove-tide observances encouraged unlimited consumption of special foods, usually pancakes. Carnival was also a time for eating meat, and in fact the word itself is derived from the Latin *carnem levare*, taking away the meat, in reference to the Lenten prohibition against eating the flesh of animals. Shrove Tuesday was also a time when "things got out of hand," when apprentices rioted, damaged property, and attacked prostitutes or foreigners or other marginal groups (Bakhtin, 1968, 196ff; Laroque, 1991, 96–103).

The custom of masking, disguise, and cross-dressing made it easier for the participants to get away with violations of social order, as in Christmas mummery. But Carnival masquerade had an even more radical purpose, as it called into question all prevailing ideas of social identity and social rank. The participatory spectacles of Carnival enabled people to refuse the identity they had been assigned and to become someone else. Disguise might take the form of code-switching, in grotesque exaggeration or in the mixing of symbols from different levels of society. Religious or political insignia might be joined with or replaced by humble objects from the kitchen or the workshop. A mock-king would be crowned with a pot and hold a broom in place of a scepter. The transgressive paraphernalia of Carnival pageantry was a form of abusive mimicry of prevailing social distinctions. But it was also a way to affirm a vernacular alternative to official political ideology, a philosophy based not on hierarchy and hereditary privilege but rather on the rhythms of productive life and social labor. This was no less true of the feasts of May or midsummer than it was for the wintertime customs of Christmas-tide.

Skimmington and Social Protest

The conservative and time-binding energies of popular culture were generally directed toward maintaining and regulating social institutions such as marriage. Local communities had a stake in deciding what kind of matches were suitable and what kind of marital behavior was socially acceptable. Community standards could be enforced in the local ecclesiastical courts, but it was probably more common to maintain these conventions through gossip or public ridicule. The surveillance of marriage and sexuality was often carried out through a custom of noisy festive abuse known in England as a skimmington. This was very similar to the practice of charivari common throughout France during the same period. These funny and also intimidating performances were staged to chastise community members whose marital behavior was irregular: men who were "beaten" by their wives, "cuckolds" unable to maintain domestic order, or the seducers responsible for making women unfaithful to their husbands. A skimmington ride could be a brutal form of punishment for the offending parties, who would be forced to straddle a beam and carried through the town streets. But skimmington might also be a kind of burlesque spectacle performed by "actors" who would represent and exaggerate the shameful conduct. In the village of Cameley in 1616, the local blacksmith, John Hall, had a falling out with his wife Mary, who "stroke him uppon the back with a frying pann," causing some significant injury:

> Wherevpon afterwardes the same being knowne abroad in the parishe some men there upon a worken day usually used for makeing merry as theire Revill day there to mak some sport, had one to Ryde upon mens shoulders by the name of Skymerton without any hurt don or misdemeanors otherwise at all. (*REED Somerset*, I, 69).

The Cameley incident is a clear case of community "surveillance" that happened in a context of local gossip and scandal over the beating of John Hall by his wife. The brief court records suggest that the ride was arranged on the spur of the moment, mostly for the enjoyment of the participants.

A skimmington was usually more elaborate and theatrically colorful than the improvised horseplay at Cameley. The idea was to make a public spectacle of someone whose conduct was offensive to the neighbors. But these offenses were not exclusively limited to cases of marital or sexual misbehavior. In 1636 Oliver Chiver, a parson in Brislington, filed a complaint with archbishop Laud against Samuell and Reginald Mogg, along with several other officials of the local congregation. According to Chiver, the churchwardens of the local congregation were guilty of "wilfull contemptes" of their duties and were openly defiant of his authority. The Moggs staged an irreverent spectacle whose central figures were a domineering wife, impersonated here by Reginald Mogg, and a submissive husband, represented by a mop. The elements of female impersonation, the comical misuse of kitchen utensils, and the display of an "apron fastned to a long staffe" all expressed a general fear and resentment of insubordinate women. But the mockery was not directed exclusively against the cross-dressed "wife" and her basting ladle. An equally important target of the abusive mimicry was the mop "made like a man," significantly referred to in the text as "him" rather than "it."

The incident at Brislington was not just improvised horseplay, but a proper full-dress skimmington, complete with mops, basting ladles, a long staff with an apron for an ensign, a man (or boy) in female dress, and perhaps a horse or donkey for the boy to ride. The Moggs even went to considerable expense to hire a professional drummer. But the aim of the skimmington was not to chastise someone's wife for actually beating her husband with a ladle. The "mopp made like a man" represented a generic figure of cringing and flabby ineptitude rather than any specific henpecked husband. This thrashing was not an ordinary skimmington organized to shame a particularly feckless member of the parish, but rather a more generalized social protest over matters of church governance and financial administration. The churchwardens had refused to submit their accounts to Chiver, suggesting instead that he was but a "hireling" whose only business in the local parish church was to read prayers. Local political resistance to a novel and alien administrative regime was, however, strongly personalized. The protesters were more preoccupied with embarrassing parson Chiver than they were with any sustained project of partisan political resistance.

The rich complexity of early modern popular culture is even more vividly apparent in a series of events connected with the festivities of May and midsummer that took place in the cathedral town of Wells in 1607. In a lengthy bill of complaint submitted to the Star Chamber, John Hole, one of the local constables, brought accusations against a large number of defendants for a long list of offenses, viz:

> then and there acted not only many disordered Maygames Morice daunces long Daunces men in Weamens apparall new devised lorde and ladyes and Churchales, but further acted very prophane & unseemely showes & pastimes wherby many unruly & dangerous assemblyes were then and there gathered togeather so that outragious insolencies were then and there dailie comytted. (REED *Somerset*, I, 262)

The May games and morris dances included a number of traditional shows or pageants, including Robin Hood, Diana and Actaeon, St. George and the Dragon, the Pinner of Wakefield, and Noah's Ark. There were also a May lord and lady, a giant and a giantess, and finally a "naked feathered boy" who rode at the head of the various pro-cessions. And throughout the months of May and June various groups simply danced in the streets.

John Hole initially attempted to arrest some of the street performers, accusing them of profanation of the Sabbath as well as of disturbing the peace. But many of the townspeople, including not only the various defendants but also the mayor and several of the gentlefolk, all maintained that they were simply doing what was customary during the springtime festive season. The purpose of the May games, it was argued, was to raise funds for the church. This was largely true, but it was also a bit disin-genuous, for on June 18 a pageant of mock-tradesmen was staged by the tanners, chandlers, and butchers of Southover's wards which was decidedly untraditional. This show was in effect a skimmington ride that lampooned Hole and a number of his close associates.

The Rise of Commercial Popular Culture

Although early modern popular culture continued to express its characteristic ethos through the traditional participatory forms of festivity, dancing, and performance, it would be quite inaccurate to limit this account to a description of these ritualistic communal activities. For one thing, even at the time people were aware that these practices were in decline. Controversy over "old holiday pastimes" reveals deep an-xieties over the way social time and social labor were regulated. Furthermore, there is evidence of an increasing entrepreneurial and competitive dimension to popular culture apparent in a growing market for cultural goods and services. The existence of cultural commodities, notably in the form of printed books and broadsheets, provided an alternative to the modes of cultural experience based on direct engage-ment with others in the community. The market for printed books is an important element in the formation of a prototypical culture industry in the economy of early modern England. Perhaps equally important is the appearance of a commercial show business in the first professional theaters of sixteenth-century London (Bristol, 1996, 31–49).

By the end of the sixteenth century the reading public represented a significant fraction of England's population (Sanders, 1998). Popular ballads, which had always circulated in and through a traditional oral culture, could now be sold as mass-produced "wares" (Würzbach, 1990). Ballads were intended for the less well-educated sector in the cultural economy. They were cheap, and the content was derived from the very popular traditions that would eventually be displaced by mass culture. Ballad-mongers would stage performances at periphery fairs and carnivals in order to attract paying customers for the broadsheet copies. Street ballads were aggressively marketed to a new mass-consumption public. But the interests of that public still reflected the traditional concerns of the popular element in early modern society. Many of the printed ballads that have been preserved are concerned with themes of sexual desire, marital dissatisfaction and deception, family discord, and the regulation and surveillance of gender difference. There are ballads of shrewish wives, ballads about cuckolded husbands, ballads about how to find a husband or a wife. Ballads may derive from folklore and fairytale, but there are also many examples of topical broadsheets based on current events, scandals, and stories of adventure. Topical ballads could take the form of satirical commentary, attacking government or church officials, overbearing landlords, or shopkeepers who charged high prices. The overall picture that emerges out of this material is one of very lively and often acrimonious ideological dissension. Many of the ballads reflect an aggressive misogyny, or national chauvinism; others were basically just scurrilous personal attacks.

The concerns of popular culture were reflected in another way in the enormous popularity during the period of almanacs and manuals of prognostication. Almanacs were concerned with the scheduling of regular "red letter days," and with the system of customary practices associated with these feasts. They codified a "popular liturgy" based on the customary practices of agricultural and craft labor. The typical almanac prescribed obligations for the husbandman and the housewife and even suggested suitable menus for each feast. By consulting their almanacs, the men and women of early modern England could organize and plan for a wide range of activities. But the typical almanacs of the period were also manuals of prognostication. They were used not only to calculate the dates of the moveable feasts, but also to forecast the weather. Other entries provided guidance on the optimum timing of a long list of practices from bleeding and purgation to haircuts and clipping nails. And finally the technique of prognostication could be extended to a forecast of specific events, such as the likelihood of someone dying, or the abundance of the next harvest. Despite its outward resemblance to popular superstition, prognostication reflected a strategic orientation based on foresight and rational planning. The *aim* of these manuals was to provide reliable information about weather, market conditions, political events, and so on, all of which had obvious practical importance for their readers. The *method*, on the other hand, was obviously faulty; no one could predict the weather for the next 12 months by observing what happened during the 12 days of Christmas.

In addition to ballads and almanacs, cheap editions of play-texts were extremely popular with early modern cultural consumers. This should perhaps suggest that the theater itself was already dependent on a literate audience, and certainly one of the reasons these otherwise ephemeral performances have survived as literature is that printers could profitably sell play-quartos to people with only limited disposable incomes. By the time the first professional theaters were established in London there was already a very lively market for a diverse range of cultural products and services. The Globe, the Curtain, and the other public playhouses were part of a technological infrastructure devised for the rapid circulation of cultural goods and services. The people who went to see performances of *Mucedorus*, or *King Lear*, or *The Duchess of Malfi* were basically a heterogeneous assembly of anonymous consumers. The direct social engagement and the time-consuming effort that had been required to produce the traditional forms of popular festivity were no longer part of the experience of attending shows. In this sense show business was a very convenient alternative to the more absorbing participatory forms of traditional popular culture. This convenience does, of course, entail certain existential losses. The appearance of the commodity form and the habits of cultural consumption significantly weakened kinship affiliations and other traditional bonds of the great households, municipal guilds, and rural communes. And the growing influence of the consumer separated the domain of "culture" from the everyday practical, moral, and religious imperatives of communal life. But the theater's relationship to the anonymity of the market offered something to its public over and above the convenience of a technologically produced or reproduced cultural experience. The theater was in many ways much more congenial than the traditional participatory forms of popular culture precisely because it was able to provide an experience of social distance for its clientele. Dancing in the streets to celebrate "the rites of May" was in all likelihood a much more convivial way to expend time and energy than spending a few hours watching professional actors put on a production of *The Shoemakers' Holiday*. At the same time, however, commercial show business, though it might occasionally be offensive, carried no threat of coercion, intimidation, and public humiliation. In the public theaters of early modern London the sanctions of shame and derisory spectacle gave way to an attitude of mutual forbearance and urbane tolerance.

   The two regimes of popular culture drew from a common body of thematic and expressive content. People were equally capable of enjoying commercial entertainment and dancing in the streets. But even during the reign of Queen Elizabeth the participatory aspects of popular culture were in decline, and this fading away of conviviality was accelerating in the early decades of the seventeenth century under pressure from the absolutist state apparatus and also from an increasingly Puritanical national church.

References and Further Reading

Agnew, Jean-Christophe (1986). *Worlds Apart: The Market and the Theater in Anglo-American Thought, 1550–1750*. Cambridge: Cambridge University Press.

Archer, Ian (1991). *The Pursuit of Stability: Social Relations in Elizabethan London*. Cambridge: Cambridge University Press.

Bakhtin, Mikhail (1968). *Rabelais and his World*, tr. Helene Iswolsky. Cambridge, MA: MIT Press.

Billington, Sandra (1991). *Mock Kings in Medieval Society and Renaissance Drama*. Oxford: Clarendon Press.

Black, Antony (1984). *Guilds and Civil Society in European Political Thought from the Twelfth Century to the Present*. Ithaca: Cornell University Press.

Boulton, Jeremy (1987). *Neighborhood and Society: A London Suburb in the Seventeenth Century*. Cambridge: Cambridge University Press.

Bristol, Michael (1986). *Carnival and Theater: Plebeian Culture and the Structure of Authority in Renaissance England*. London: Methuen.

Bristol, Michael (1991). "In search of the bear: spatio-temporal form and the heterogeneity of economies in *The Winter's Tale*." *Shakespeare Quarterly* 41, 145–68.

Bristol, Michael (1996). *Big Time Shakespeare*. London: Routledge.

Bristol, Michael (1997). "Theater and popular culture." In *A New History of Early English Drama*, eds John D. Cox and David Scott Kastan. New York: Columbia University Press.

Bristol, Michael (1999). "Shamelessness in Arden." In *Print, Manuscript, and Performance: The Changing Relations of the Media in Early Modern England*, eds Michael Bristol and Arthur Marotti. Columbus: Ohio State University Press.

Burke, Peter (1978). *Popular Culture in Early Modern Europe*. London: Temple Smith.

Capp, Bernard (1977). "English youth groups and the Pinder of Wakefield." *Past and Present* 76, 127–33.

Capp, Bernard (1979). *English Almanacs 1500–1800: Astrology and the Popular Press*. Ithaca: Cornell University Press.

Davis, Natalie Zemon (1971). "The reasons of misrule: youth groups and charivaris in sixteenth century France." *Past and Present* 50, 49–75.

Diehl, Huston (1997). *Staging Reform, Reforming the Stage: Protestantism and Popular Theater in Early Modern England*. Ithaca: Cornell University Press.

Gaignebet, Claude, and Marie-Claude Florentin (1979). *Le Carnaval: essais de mythologie populaire*. Paris: Payot.

Gierke, Otto von (1987). *Political Theories of the Middle Ages*, ed. and trans. F. W. Maitland. Cambridge: Cambridge University Press.

Harrison, J. F. C. (1984). *The Common People: A History From the Norman Conquest to the Present*. London: Fontana.

Howard, Jean E. (1994). *The Stage and Social Struggle in Early Modern England*. London: Routledge.

Ingram, William (1992). *The Business of Playing: The Beginnings of the Adult Professional Theater in Elizabethan London*. Ithaca: Cornell University Press.

Ladurie, Emmanuel Le Roy (1979). *Carnival in Romans*, tr. Mary Feeney. New York: George Braziller.

Laroque, François (1991). *Shakespeare's Festive World: Elizabethan Seasonal Entertainments and the Professional Stage*, tr. Janet Lloyd. Cambridge: Cambridge University Press.

Leinwand, Theodore (1993). "Shakespeare and the middling sort." *Shakespeare Quarterly* 44, 283–303.

Manning, Brian (1988). *Village Revolts: Social Protest and Popular Disturbances in England, 1509–1640*. Oxford: Oxford University Press.

Marcus, Leah (1986). *The Politics of Mirth: Jonson, Herrick, Milton, Marvell, and the Defense of Old Holiday Pastimes*. Chicago: Chicago University Press.

Markham, Gervase. *The English Housewife*. London, 1631.

Muchembled, Robert (1985). *Popular Culture and Elite Culture in France: 1400–1750*, tr. Lydia Cochrane. Baton Rouge: LSU Press.

Patterson, Annabel (1990). *Shakespeare and the Popular Voice*. Oxford: Blackwell.

Rappaport, Steve (1989). *Worlds within Worlds: Structures of Life in Sixteenth Century London*. Cambridge: Cambridge University Press.

Reay, Barry, ed. (1985). *Popular Culture in Seventeenth Century England*. New York: St. Martin's Press.

REED (Records of Early English Drama) Chester (1979). Ed. Lawrence M. Clopper. Toronto: University of Toronto Press.

REED (Records of Early English Drama) Coventry (1981). Ed. William Ingram. Toronto: University of Toronto Press.

REED (Records of Early English Drama) Somerset (1996). Ed. James Stokes. 2 vols. Toronto: University of Toronto Press.

Sanders, Eve Rachele (1998). *Gender and Literacy on Stage in Early Modern England*. Cambridge: Cambridge University Press.

Scribner, R. W. (1987). *Popular Culture and Popular Movements in Reformation Germany*. London: Hambledon Press.

Sharpe, James (1997). "Popular culture in the early modern west." In *Companion to Historiography*, ed. Michael Bentley. London: Routledge.

Thompson, E. P. (1972). "Rough music: *le charivaru anglais*." *Annales: Economies, Sociétés, Civilisations* 27, 285–312.

Thompson, E. P. (1974). "Patrician society, plebeian culture." *Journal of Social History* 7, 382–405.

Underdown, David (1985). *Revel, Riot, and Rebellion: Popular Politics and Culture in England – 1603–1660*. Oxford: Clarendon Press.

Weimann, Robert (1981). *Shakespeare and the Popular Tradition in the Theater*. Baltimore: Johns Hopkins University Press.

Würzbach, Natascha (1990). *The Rise of the English Street Ballad, 1550–1650*, tr. Gayna Walls. Cambridge: Cambridge University Press.

10

Magic and Witchcraft

Deborah Willis

In 1563, early in the reign of Elizabeth I and a year before the births of William Shakespeare and Christopher Marlowe, Parliament passed the Act Against Conjurations, Enchantments and Witchcrafts, making it a crime punishable by death to conjure evil spirits for any purpose or to use any "witchcraft, enchantment, charm, or sorcery" to kill another person. Although not the first secular anti-witchcraft legislation to be enacted in England, it was the first to stay on the books for more than five years and to be enforced actively through the courts.[1] A few years later, in 1567, John Brayne (the future partner of James Burbage) oversaw the construction of what now appears to be the first public playhouse in London, the Red Lion. In the decades that followed, as more playhouses were built and play companies formed, as the theater developed into a potent and influential cultural institution, prosecutions of witches and other magical practitioners also gathered force.

It is not surprising, then, that the theater would find in witchcraft and magic a prime source of material. By the 1580s and 1590s, witchcraft was a hot-button issue, the topic of an increasing number of religious tracts, philosophical treatises, and popular pamphlets as well as plays. In both the courtroom and the theater, magical practitioners were figures of fascination and danger, put on display to be probed and tested, at the center of conflicting beliefs, perceptions, and debates. Both the laws and the theater's treatment of these figures spoke to a new anxiety about a wide variety of magical practices that had been tolerated or ignored in preceding decades and centuries. While always subject to some sort of regulation, such practices seemed increasingly widespread and newly dangerous to many observers, exerting a powerful hold on the people, requiring a more vigorous response.[2]

But what, more precisely, was meant by the term "witchcraft" and others mentioned in the Act? The meanings we give to these terms and the associations we bring to them today are not necessarily those of Elizabethan or Jacobean England. The language of the Act itself contains a certain profusion of terms that overlap though are not quite identical. "Witchcraft" could be an umbrella term, used to refer to all manner of magical practices, including the use of conjuration, spirits, image magic, or charms and spells, and a "witch" could be either male or female, good or bad, book-learned or illiterate, depending on context. "Magic" was an even broader term, inclusive of witchcraft, sorcery, or necromancy but also such occult practices as alchemy and astrology. Nevertheless, the terms were frequently used in narrower senses, and the witch and the magician tended to be differentiated by gender, class, and method. Witches were typically women, usually old, poor, and uneducated, who used familiars or "imps" – spirits who appeared to them in the form of small animals – to cause sickness, death, or other misfortunes to their neighbors. They practiced *maleficium* – harmful magic. The magician, on the other hand, was more likely to be male, an educated "middling sort" who gained his skills from books. He too might use magic to harm or to kill, but more often he used it to gain wealth, power, or knowledge. Typically, he raised spirits – angels, demons, spirits of the dead – by means of a magic circle and complicated incantations and rituals. He might also make astrological predictions or use other forms of divination. The magician's less-educated counterparts at the village level were the cunning folk (known also as wizards, white witches, or merely witches) who used magical techniques to cure sickness, tell fortunes, find lost treasure, achieve success in love, or protect from bad luck and witchcraft.

Not all the magician's practices were equally forbidden. The Act prohibited only the raising of "evil" spirits, leaving an opening for those who wanted to contact spirits they considered more benign. Charms and amulets, it was assumed, drew upon occult forces but did not necessarily require spirits. The fundamental beliefs of astrology were widely accepted, although some aspects of it were controversial. The Act gave more weight to the ends of magic than to its methods. Only when witchcraft or other magical practices resulted in death were they punishable by execution. Causing sickness or injury merely led to a year's imprisonment and quarterly appearances in the pillory (at least for a first offense). Similarly, imprisonment was the punishment for using magic to kill livestock, find stolen treasure, or procure unlawful love.

One of the first persons examined after the Act went into effect was John Walsh of Dorsetshire, servant to a Catholic priest.[3] Although no records have survived to tell us whether Walsh was tried or convicted after his examination, he confessed that he used a "book of circles" and a familiar spirit to find stolen goods – a deed punishable by a year's imprisonment, according to the Act. Until the book of circles was taken from Walsh by a constable, the familiar had stayed with him for five years, appearing to him variously as a pigeon, a dog, and a man with cloven feet. In exchange for its help, Walsh had to give it "living things," and, upon first receiving the spirit from his master, he had been required to give it a drop of his own blood. Yet Walsh also emphatically denied using the spirit – or any other form of magic – "to harm man, woman, or child," a statement he was willing to affirm by solemn oath.

John Walsh's case was unusual in that he was male, and it is tempting, though speculative, to conclude that the absence of records means leniency was shown to him and that his case was not pursued further. Although Walsh's relationship with his familiar resembles descriptions in many confessions by accused women, his examiners appeared willing to accept that he had not used his spirit to cause sickness or death. By and large, it was the female witch and not the male magician who was prosecuted under the Act. It was the homicidal use of witchcraft, rather than the conjuration of evil spirits or the less overtly harmful types of magic, that moved villagers to inform against witches and authorities to prosecute them. Nearly all known trials in England focused on acts of *maleficium* believed to end in human death, and most of those executed for such acts were women.

The deadly legacy of the witch-trials has led many historians studying witchcraft and magic in the early modern period to focus on the prosecution process and to attempt to identify the causes of the trials. Skeptical about supernatural agency or occult power, they have typically seen prosecution as persecution, and "witch-hunt" has become a term for the scapegoating of innocent victims. Historians in the early to mid-twentieth century, who usually focused broadly on European witch-hunting, saw the prosecutions as primarily a top-down affair, the work of the elite class, who imposed their beliefs on the common people. By the 1970s, however, Alan MacFarlane and Keith Thomas showed conclusively that authorities in England were responsive to popular fears of the witch's *maleficium*, and villagers often actively accused witches, pressuring authorities to take action. In their analysis, the impetus for witch-hunting came primarily "from below" and was to be explained by social and psychological factors, catalyzed by economic tensions. Other historians have built on their work, integrating both approaches, while feminist historians have focused on the role of gender in the hunts, asking why so many accused witches were women, and finding at least partial answers in patriarchal codes, misogynist attitudes, and/or anxieties about mothers (Sharpe, 1996; Hester, 1992; Purkiss, 1996; Willis, 1995). More recently, historians have moved away from speculating about causes, turning instead to investigate patterns of belief, mentalities, or representational systems, in order to render magical beliefs more intelligible to the modern reader (Clark, 1997; Gaskill, 2000; Gibson, 1999).

Whatever their approach, most historians would agree that the typical witchcraft case in England followed a fairly predictable trajectory. Many cases began with a quarrel between neighbors, after which the winner of the quarrel fell victim to certain types of misfortune: the milk went sour, the butter would not come, hogs died "strangely," a child fell sick, a wife or husband died. The loser of the quarrel was suspected of using magic to retaliate for a perceived injury or slight, especially after several such incidents. Before the Act of 1563, neighbors fearful of a witch might turn to one of the local cunning folk for protection, procuring some sort of counter-magic to undo the witch's *maleficium*. But afterwards, they could also appeal to the local justice of the peace to open an inquiry. Depending on his findings, a trial would be held. The accused woman was on her way to imprisonment, execution, or sometimes acquittal.

In England, conviction was by no means automatic. Juries were well aware that such things as sickness or death might have natural causes, and that the relation between a quarrel and subsequent misfortune might be purely coincidental. The evidence against the accused was necessarily circumstantial, and as Frances Dolan (1995) has pointed out, the legal system had to adjudicate between competing narratives: a woman's fate was determined by who told the most compelling story. Along with the details of quarrels and subsequent misfortunes, other types of evidence could be used as corroboration. Sightings of small animals, first in the presence of the accused woman, then on the bewitched person's land, helped to support the idea that witchcraft was the cause of a particular illness or death: familiar spirits, or "imps" as they were often called, which carried out the witch's requests, were widely believed to appear in animal form. Once an investigation was underway, the accused woman's body might be examined for the devil's mark, or "teat" – a place on her body where the familiar would suck blood. Any unusual fleshly protuberance, especially one in a private place, provided further confirmation of the charge of witchcraft.

But the most crucial piece of evidence was generally the witch's confession – the story told by the accused woman herself. In a great many investigations, women confessed to keeping familiar spirits, often after receiving them from other witches, just as John Walsh had received his from his master. The spirit might live with a woman for many years, being fed milk or beer along with the witch's blood, and being kept warm inside a wooden box or wool-lined pots. In exchange for this quasi-maternal care, the spirit would carry out the witch's requests to bring sickness or death to the homes of her enemies.

Historians have tended to distinguish English popular beliefs from those on the Continent, where witches were believed to make pacts with the devil, belong to covens, fly to sabbaths, and have sexual relations with demons. Such beliefs were elaborated in the works of demonologists, such as Kramer and Sprenger's *Malleus Maleficarum* (1486) or Guazzo's *Compendium Maleficarum* (1608), and were featured in many European trials. The English witch, on the other hand, seldom confessed to making a pact, and sabbaths or lurid sexual activities were almost never mentioned by accused women or their village-level accusers. Instead, familiars settled into long-term domestic relationships with their witch, and though accused women frequently reported receiving familiars from other witches, they held no regular meetings and did not claim the power to fly. In many confessions the familiar was not clearly linked to the devil or even regarded as a demon, more closely resembling a mischief-making fairy. The so-called devil's mark was not necessarily the sign of a pact with the devil, but a teat by which the witch fed her imp.

The historian Robin Briggs, however, has recently argued that a sharp division between "English" and "Continental" is mistaken. Basing his argument on a close study of documents from French witch-trials, Briggs shows that popular beliefs about witches are a key part of many cases. Continental witch-hunting was not exclusively a top-down affair, any more than English witch-hunting was. At the same time, Briggs goes on to argue that claims about the absence of the pact from English documents are false, and that "the animal familiars or imps which appear in almost every well-documented case quite clearly performed the role of the devil. The witch made an effective compact with him" (1996, 29). It is true that John Walsh, for example, told his examiners his master had required a drop of blood when he first received his familiar – a one-time occurrence suggestive of a pact. Joan Cunny, examined in 1589, reported that she had learned the witch's craft from Mother Humphreys, who had required her to make a circle on the ground and invoke Satan, "the chief of devils," in order to receive her familiar spirit. When they appeared, she promised them her soul in exchange for their services (Rosen, 1991, 183). But in many other confessions, accused women made no reference to a pact or even to the devil, describing more informal arrangements, in which spirits performed services merely to get the witch's quasi-maternal care. Another example, which at first glance seems to support Briggs's claim, in fact more strongly suggests the coexistence of two related, yet distinct threads in popular belief: when the devil appeared to Joan Prentice in the likeness of a ferret and demanded her soul, she refused to give it to him (Rosen, 1991, 187). Instead, she allowed him occasionally to suck blood from her cheek. In exchange, the ferret spoiled the drink of a neighbor's wife, and later killed a neighbor's child (even though Joan had asked him only "to nip it but a little"). Familiars, this confession suggests, might carry out the witches' *maleficium* without requiring an oath of allegiance or their soul.

All the same, even when the pact is absent, confessions are narratives of temptation and fall. Elizabeth Bennett, one of the women accused in the St. Osyth trials, confessed to becoming a witch after she called upon the name of God and "prayed devoutly" to get two spirits to stop pestering her (Rosen, 1991, 122). They had been causing her mischief for several months. For a while her prayers succeeded and they left her alone. But after a series of increasingly serious quarrels with her neighbor, William Byatt, who called her names and abused her cattle, she gave in to the temptation to take revenge, asking the spirits "to plague Byatt's beasts to death." They did so, but went even further and killed Byatt's wife. Bennett denied responsibility for this death, saying the spirits did it only "to win credit" with her, after telling her they knew that "Byatt and his wife [had] wronged thee greatly." Suffering further harassment, Bennett finally asked one of the spirits to go after Byatt himself. After his death, she gave the spirit "a reward of milk."

Although Bennett's confession does not make it explicit, the underlying story of temptation and fall is evident. The spirits initiated contact with Bennett and pressured, coaxed, and seduced her into committing an intentional act of murder. Once she actively called them to do her bidding, she had crossed the line separating victim from perpetrator. Many Protestant clergymen were anxious to go one step further by making the familiar's link to the devil utterly clear. In sermons, treatises, and prefaces to witchcraft pamphlets, clerics such as George Gifford and William Perkins argued that however inoffensive these animal spirits might seem, with their wool-pots, endearing names, and shows of pity for human suffering, they were all merely deceptive disguises of none other than Satan himself. If he takes on the form of "paltrie vermin," suggests Gifford, "it is even of subtiltie to cover and hide his mightie tyrannie and power" and entrap old women and ignorant people (1593, C2). Moreover, the cunning folk who used magical practices and seemed to do good were even more dangerous than the witch guilty of *maleficium*. The common people knew enough to avoid the harmful witch. Yet the action of the devil could also be detected in the white witch's charms and magical cures, and those who thought they were conjuring angels or "good" spirits were deceived. Similarly, the elite magician was a danger. James VI and I in his *Daemonologie* condemned all astrology (except the kind used to predict weather) and all forms of conjuration, concluding that magicians and necromancers deserved punishments at least as severe as those for witches. In fact, echoing Gifford, he believed they were worse than witches, for "their error proceeds of the greater knowledge, and so draws nerer to the sin against the holy Ghost." Moreover, he that "consults, enquires, entertaines, and oversees" the magician was as guilty as the magician himself (1597, 26).

Yet many in early modern England remained unconvinced, and accepted such practices as astrology, divination, and the conjuration of angelic spirits. Well-respected men such as the mathematician, navigator, and philosopher John Dee or the physician and Anglican clergyman Richard Napier employed magical practices at times and believed doing so to be consistent with the highest Christian principles (French, 1987; Macdonald, 1981). Others felt that no wrong was done by raising demons with a "binding spell." The notion of the pact, alive in English intellectual circles if not always so among villagers, in fact helped some magical practitioners defend their conjuring; as long as demons were under their control and no bargain was made, they were not doing the devil's work. And even after the anti-witchcraft laws were toughened in 1604 (by, among other things, making it a crime punishable by death not only to conjure an evil spirit but also to "consult, covenant with, entertain, employ, feed, or reward any evil and wicked spirit to or for any intent or purpose"), prosecutions remained almost entirely focused on the witch who practiced *maleficium*.

Still others viewed many magical beliefs with skepticism. Reginald Scot thought witches' confessions should be understood as the delusions of old women. Demonic possession might be madness or fraud. George Gifford was highly critical of evidence used in witch-trials and thought most accusations the "devil's testimony." William Perkins, more generally supportive of the trials, nevertheless thought some identifying techniques were suspect and urged caution in assessing evidence (Perkins, 1608). Educated gentlemen viewed many of the beliefs of villagers as ignorant superstitions. Fortune-tellers and conjurers were frequently suspected of being con-artists.

Where, then, does the theater fit in this complex, shifting landscape of debates about magical practices? As Barbara Traister has shown, from 1570 to 1620 magicians appear as major characters or as significant minor ones in over two dozen plays (1984, 33). Witches appear in at least a dozen others. References to magical practices or metaphorical allusions occur widely in plays throughout the period even when the human figures of magician or witch are absent. Playwrights were well aware that theatrical practices resembled that of the magician, and drew analogies between the stage and the magic circle, spirits and actors, conjuration and the play-company's craft.[4] At the same time, however, playwrights sought to draw distinctions. The aims of the theater were to entertain and edify, by presenting fictions, not lies. As Sir Philip Sidney put it in his *Apology for Poetry*, "the poet never maketh any circles about your imagination, to conjure you to believe for true, what he writeth . . . What child is there that, coming to a play, and seeing Thebes written in great letters upon an old door, doth believe that it is Thebes?" (1595; 1973, 124). The magician's methods were far more suspect, his aims less lofty and disinterested.

There was, of course, great diversity in playwrights' treatment of magical themes and characters. They were by no means in agreement on questions of magic's moral or spiritual status. Yet some generalizations seem reasonably safe to make. Most stage-plays did not participate in sweeping Calvinist denunciations of the cunning folk or white magicians. Magicians could appear as benevolent and virtuous figures, their practices consistent with the highest spiritual and ethical principles. In many plays, astrology, charms, or even conjuration are used for constructive or at least neutral ends. Few, if any, seem designed to promote witch-trials or to foster fear of the witch.

At the same time, however, the most probing and sophisticated early modern playwrights do not by any means adopt an uncritical or romanticizing stance when they treat the subject of magic in depth. In most of these plays, the magician appears as a complex, humanly sympathetic, yet morally problematic figure. Prospero in Shakespeare's *Tempest*, having lost his dukedom by becoming "rapt in secret studies," is a man walking a moral tightrope, and the price of his redemption is the adjuration of his magic art. Jonson's Doctor Subtle in *The Alchemist* is a wily con-artist whose manipulation of the spurious promises of alchemy works to expose greed, gullibility, and self-delusion in the social world around him. Dr. Faustus's expansive humanist aspirations, but also his egotism, leave him open to the devil's entrapment.

Moreover, major characters who "consult with witches" or seek out other magical practitioners typically do so out of criminal desire. Macbeth goes to the weird sisters in search of "security" after becoming a usurper and serial killer. Alice and Mosby in *Arden of Faversham* plot to murder Alice's husband by engaging the services of a cunning man. In *The White Devil*, Brachiano consults a conjurer in his quest to murder his wife and marry Vittoria Corombona. Corrupt suitors seek out witches for love potions or to render rivals impotent in Middleton's *The Witch* and Marston's *Sophonisba*.

In contrast, then, to the law courts, which primarily targeted the female witch, the early modern theater tended to focus on male characters when it took up the practices prohibited by the anti-witchcraft statute, targeting male desire instead of women's unruly nature. While the witch featured in pamphlet literature was most likely to be motivated by anger and revenge, in stage-plays magical practitioners and those who consulted them typically sought shortcuts to power, status, wealth, and/or sexual conquest. To the extent that these plays were understood as cautionary tales, they could be said to supplement the anti-witchcraft laws, performing a regulatory function. If the courts lacked the resources to enforce the laws against conjuring or consulting evil spirits, the theater could at least warn of the tragic outcomes for those who did so. But plays such as *Dr. Faustus* and *Macbeth* produced more complex and

ambiguous effects, offering a rich meditation on the psychology of temptation, exploring paradoxes of the will and testing the limits of agency. Faustus and Macbeth are
doomed by a complex intersection of internal and external forces, in which their own
desires and propensity for wishful thinking combine with cultural influences and
human relationships to make them acutely vulnerable to "supernatural soliciting" and
the manipulations of the devil or his agents. Ultimately, they are plays that raise more
questions than they answer, punishing the apparent reprobate yet also arousing sympathy for him, along with uneasiness about the mysteries of the divine plan.

Unlike magicians, witches on the early modern stage seldom were given such subtle
or extensive treatment. Nor do stage witches resemble their off-stage counterparts
very closely. While magicians such as Prospero or Dr. Faustus employ practices that
can be found in the books of real-life magicians, the stage witch is often a broad stereotype with monstrous traits and fantastical powers, a hybrid of medieval romance, classical tradition, and Continental demonological treatises as well as of pamphlets or
other documents about village-level witches. Middleton's Hecate in *The Witch* has
animal familiars with names that come straight from village trials, yet her own name
comes from classical tradition and she uses Latin incantations and necromancy. Her
aggressive sexual appetites and lurid relations with incubi who take the shape of young
men has roots in Continental demonology. The chief source for Marston's witch
Erichtho in *Sophonisba* is book VI of Lucan's *Pharsalia*, and the witches of Jonson's
Masque of Queenes are also shaped primarily by classical tradition.

Rowley, Dekker, and Ford's *Witch of Edmonton* comes the closest to giving a village-
level witch-figure some depth and complexity. Its chief source is a pamphlet by a
Protestant clergyman, Henry Goodcole, who examined Elizabeth Sawyer in prison
after she had been convicted of witchcraft. In some ways, however, Mother Sawyer's
story as constructed by the play seems more closely modeled on the confession of Elizabeth Bennett, available in an earlier pamphlet which the authors may also have consulted. Like Bennett, Sawyer is called names such as "old witch" and "old trot" before
she actually becomes a witch. She is poor and subject to abuse from her neighbors.
The devil, appearing to her as Dog, initiates contact with her and actively pressures
her into becoming a witch, through a mix of sly manipulations and offers of com-
panionship and sympathy. As Bennett's familiars do, Dog eventually succeeds in
coaxing Sawyer into intentional acts of witchcraft by appealing to her desire for
revenge upon her abusive neighbors. From thereon the play rewrites her story as
revenge tragedy. Coming after so many plays constructed around narratives of temptation and fall, *The Witch of Edmonton* has little truly original to offer. Yet its representation of Elizabeth Sawyer is well nuanced and often moving, and though she is
punished with death at the play's end, she is also an effective voice of social critique,
calling attention to corruption in the world around her.

By the 1630s and 1640s, the theater was losing interest in magical practices;
witches and magicians appear, if at all, in very marginalized roles. Nor do they resur-
face on stage after the Restoration. Belief in the reality of spirits or occult powers was
on the wane in elite circles, and after the 1640s the anti-witchcraft laws in England

were seldom enforced, although they remained on the books until 1736 (Bostridge, 1997). Yet it would be a mistake to relegate the theater's concern with magical themes to an exotically distant past, given the global context of today's classrooms and stage and screen productions. Evidence of the modernity of witchcraft and magical beliefs is all around us. The New Age repackaging of astrology and other early modern beliefs is apparent in many aisles of surburban Barnes & Noble bookstores, and internet websites devoted to alchemy and magic make available the works of men such as John Dee and Cornelius Agrippa, finding them of more than historical interest. Echoes of old debates about white witchcraft can be heard in the controversies surrounding wiccan and neo-pagan groups on US campuses. Some postcolonial states such as Burkina Faso and Cameroon have passed anti-witchcraft laws in the name of indigenous beliefs; elsewhere, as in post-apartheid South Africa and post-glasnost Russia, the state gives no official sanction to such beliefs but reports incidents of witch-killings. It is an odd testament to the insularity of the academic world, then, that even some very recently published books on early modern witchcraft and magic treat these beliefs as relics of a long-dead, pre-scientific world. Really, it should be no surprise that, in their subtle interrogations of magical themes and identities, Shakespeare and his fellow dramatists have again become our contemporaries.

NOTES

1   The Act is reprinted in Rosen (1991, 54–6).
2   Thus, for example, John Jewel proclaimed in a sermon before Queen Elizabeth shortly before the passage of the Act that witches and sorcerers were "marvellously increased within your grace's realm. These eyes have seen most evident and manifest marks of their wickedness" (quoted in Kittredge, 1972, 252). A similar remark is included in the Act Against Conjurations.
3   The main source for Walsh's case is *The Examination of John Walsh* (1566), reprinted in Rosen (1991, 64–71).
4   Cf. the Prologue to Shakespeare's *Henry V* or Prospero's revels speech in *The Tempest*.

REFERENCES AND FURTHER READING

Bostridge, Ian (1997). *Witchcraft and its Transformations c.1650–c.1750*. Oxford: Clarendon Press.
Briggs, Robin (1996). *Witches and Neighbors: The Social and Cultural Context of European Witchcraft*. New York: Viking Penguin.
Clark, Stuart (1997). *Thinking with Demons: The Idea of Witchcraft in Early Modern Europe*. Oxford: Oxford University Press.
Corbin, Peter, and Douglas Sedge, eds (1986). *Three Jacobean Witchcraft Plays: The Tragedy of Sophonisba, The Witch, The Witch of Edmonton*. Manchester: Manchester University Press.
Dolan, Frances E. (1994). *Dangerous Familiars: Representations of Domestic Crime in England, 1550–1700*. Ithaca: Cornell University Press.
Dolan, Frances E. (1995). "'Ridiculous fictions': making distinctions in the discourses of witchcraft." *Differences: A Journal of Feminist Cultural Studies* 7.2, 82–110.
French, Peter (1987). *John Dee: The World of an Elizabethan Magus*. London: Ark.

Gaskill, Malcolm (2000). *Crime and Mentalities in Early Modern England*. Cambridge: Cambridge University Press.

Gibson, Marion (1999). *Reading Witchcraft: Stories of Early English Witches*. London: Routledge.

Gifford, George (1593, rpt 1931). *A Dialogue Concerning Witches and Witchcraftes*. London: Oxford University Press.

Goodcole, Henry (1621). *The Wonderful Discoverie of Elizabeth Sawyer, a Witch, Late of Edmonton*. London.

Greenblatt, Stephen (1993). "Shakespeare bewitched." In *New Historical Literary Study: Essays on Reproducing Texts, Representing History*, eds Jeffrey N. Cox and Larry J. Reynolds. Princeton: Princeton University Press.

Harris, Anthony (1980). *Night's Black Agents: Witchcraft and Magic in Seventeenth-Century English Drama*. Manchester: Manchester University Press.

Hester, Marianne (1992). *Lewd Women and Wicked Witches: A Study of the Dynamics of Male Domination*. London: Routledge.

James VI and I (1597; rpt 1966). *Daemonologie*. New York: Barnes & Noble.

Kieckhefer, Richard (1990). *Magic in the Middle Ages*. Cambridge: Cambridge University Press.

Kinney, Arthur F., ed. (1998). *The Witch of Edmonton*. London: A. & C. Black; New York: W. W. Norton.

Kittredge, George Lyman (1972). *Witchcraft in Old and New England*. New York: Atheneum.

Larner, Christina (1981). *Enemies of God: The Witch-Hunt in Scotland*. London: Chatto and Windus.

Macdonald, Michael (1981). *Mystical Bedlam: Madness, Anxiety, and Healing in Seventeenth-Century England*. Cambridge: Cambridge University Press.

Macdonald, Michael (1990). *Witchcraft and Hysteria in Elizabethan London: Edward Jorden and the Mary Glover Case*. London: Routledge.

Macfarlane, Alan (1970). *Witchcraft in Tudor and Stuart England: A Regional and Comparative Study*. New York: Harper and Row.

Mebane, John (1992). *Renaissance Magic and the Return of the Golden Age: The Occult Tradition and Marlowe, Jonson, and Shakespeare*. Lincoln: University of Nebraska Press.

Perkins, William (1608; rpt 1970). "A discourse of the damned art of witchcraft." In *The Works of William Perkins*, ed. Ian Breward. Abingdon: Sutton Courtenay Press.

Purkiss, Diane (1996). *The Witch in History: Early Modern and Twentieth-Century Representations*. London: Routledge.

Rosen, Barbara, ed. (1991). *Witchcraft in England, 1558–1618*. Amherst, MA: University of Massachusetts Press.

Scot, Reginald (1584). *The Discovery of Witchcraft*. London.

Sharpe, James (1996). *Instruments of Darkness: Witchcraft in Early Modern England*. Philadelphia: University of Pennsylvania Press.

Sidney, Sir Philip (1595; 1973). *An Apology for Poetry*. Ed. Geoffrey Shepherd. Manchester: Manchester University Press.

Thomas, Keith (1971). *Religion and the Decline of Magic*. New York: Scribner's.

Traister, Barbara (1984). *Heavenly Necromancers: The Magician in English Renaissance Drama*. Columbia: University of Missouri Press.

Willis, Deborah (1995). *Malevolent Nurture: Witch-Hunting and Maternal Power in Early Modern England*. Ithaca: Cornell University Press.

Woodbridge, Linda (1994). *The Scythe of Saturn: Shakespeare and Magical Thinking*. Urbana: University of Illinois Press.

PART TWO
The World of Drama

11
Playhouses
Herbert Berry

I Introduction

English Renaissance playhouses, often now described as Shakespearean, were the first commercial theaters in the British Isles and those for which Shakespeare and his rivals wrote plays. They were in gestation when he was born in 1564, and they had nearly reached their final form when he died in 1616. Organized companies of professional actors had been performing plays and other entertainments in England from at least the latter half of the fifteenth century. But they performed relatively briefly in any one place, employing buildings or open spaces mainly used for other things.

Building or adapting structures for the regular performance of plays required large amounts of money, which required large numbers of spectators and financiers looking for quick profits. Since London was much the most populous place in the country and both its literary and financial center, it was there that Renaissance playhouses mainly appeared, the first in 1567, when Shakespeare was three years old. The last of them there, the twenty-third, opened in 1630, 14 years after his death. Even though acting and attending plays was illegal from 1642 to 1660, several of them continued in irregular use, and three reopened legally in 1660.

From medieval times, drama in England had been of two kinds (see chapter 17 below). One consisted of plays for public consumption, performed by professionals who toured the country or by amateurs in local festivals. The other consisted of plays meant for the elite, performed by children who belonged to either a choir or grammar school. Performances usually took place indoors, often with candlelight and music. So the playhouses eventually built or adapted for the commercial performance of plays were also of two kinds, public and private. In the public ones, anybody with the price of admission could attend a play. In the private, for many years performers were supposed to play only for the monarch but could take money from people who wanted to attend so-called rehearsals.

The defining characteristic of public playhouses was that their stages stood in open unroofed yards surrounded by galleries; people stood in the yards on at least three sides of the stages and stood or sat in their galleries. Except for children, who played either children or women, their actors were professional men. Private playhouses were in large rooms. Each also had a stage, an equivalent of the yard called the pit, and galleries, but how these things related to one another architecturally is obscure. Their actors at first were boy choristers from St. Paul's Cathedral or royal chapels, who acted by candlelight to small, elite audiences, usually with music. Seventeen public and six private playhouses were built, in new or existing buildings.

II 1567

The first commercial playhouse was built in 1567. It was a public playhouse, now called the Red Lion because it was in the yard of a farmhouse of that name. It was in Whitechapel, an eastern suburb of London, and nearly a mile east of the city wall at Aldgate, not far from open fields at Mile End where Londoners amused themselves and the trained bands (militia) of the city held often festive musters. John Brayne, a grocer, had the playhouse built, spending, it seems, about £15 on it. One carpenter built scaffolds for spectators, on which Brayne spent £8 10s., and another built a stage for which Brayne demanded a performance bond of £13 6s. 8d. (such bonds were customarily for twice the investment). Brayne then quarreled with both carpenters, and the papers of these quarrels provide virtually everything known about the place – nothing about the scaffolds, apart from their cost, but a good deal about the stage. It was 5 feet high, 40 feet in length, and 30 feet in breadth, had an unboarded space, perhaps for a trap door, and a turret rising over it 30 feet from the ground, with a floor 7 feet under the top and with four compass braces on the top, perhaps to make an onion dome. These structures were to be finished by July 8, 1567, so that a play called *The Story of Samson* could take place there. Brayne apparently meant his playhouse for more than the performance of one play, but he may have abandoned it by the autumn of 1568.

III 1575–8

Brayne's playhouse was before its time. Apparently no other was in use in London until about 1575, but from then to 1578 nine commercial playhouses appeared there, two of them very large and expensive. It was an astonishing event. Nothing of the kind had happened anywhere or would happen again in London for centuries. Shakespeare was between 11 and 14 years old. Four of these playhouses were inns that became public playhouses as well between 1575 (or a little earlier) and 1578; two were rooms in existing buildings that became private playhouses in 1575 and 1576; one was a public playhouse that had been built out of a "messuage" between 1575 and 1577; one was a large and expensive public playhouse purpose-built in 1576; and one was another large public playhouse probably purpose-built in 1576 or 1577. The four inns and two private playhouses were all within the city of London, five actually within the walls, where the civic authorities were usually hostile to playhouses. The three other places were in suburbs governed by the usually less zealous magistrates of the counties of Middlesex and Surrey.

The first inn to become also a playhouse was the Bel Savage, which was on the north side of Ludgate Hill, about 100 yards west of Ludgate. It was in business as a public playhouse in 1575. The second was the Bull on the west side of Bishopsgate Street. It was a playhouse in 1577 and eventually was the inn from which Milton's carrier, Thomas Hobson, left weekly for Cambridge. It was also the Renaissance playhouse whose vestiges above ground were the last to disappear, when the inn was demolished in 1866. The third and fourth were the Bell and the Cross Keys, which adjoined one another on the west side of Gracechurch Street, north of Lombard Street. The Bell was a playhouse early in 1577 and the Cross Keys by the summer of 1578. Presumably plays took place in the inn-yards of all four, but nothing is known about how these inns were adapted for plays or who financed the work. All housed reputable companies of actors from time to time and apparently continued as playhouses until the city authorities closed not the inns but the playhouses in them in about 1596.

The first private playhouse was the work of the master of the choristers of St. Paul's Cathedral, Sebastian Westcott, a musician. He had led the ten boys in his charge frequently in theatrical performances at court from the 1550s onward, and by December 1575 he provided a place in the city for their performances. It was apparently on an upper floor in the almonry, which adjoined the south wall of the cathedral nave, just west of the wall around the chapter house. Contemporaries described the stage as small; the room could have been about 29 feet wide and much longer. The playhouse continued until 1589 or 1590, then resumed in the autumn of 1599 and continued until the summer of 1606.

The second private playhouse was the work of another musician, Richard Farrant, master of the boy choristers of Windsor Castle and deputy master of those of the Chapel Royal. In August 1576, he leased rooms in two adjoining buildings in the former Blackfriars monastery to have, as he told the landlord, a place in which he could rehearse his charges. He did not add that they would be rehearsing plays before paying spectators. This playhouse, which opened in the winter of 1576–7, was at the south end of the upper floor of the old buttery, in two rooms that Farrant made into one, measuring 26 feet east to west, and 46 feet 6 inches north to south. The playhouse continued until the spring of 1584, when the landlord reclaimed the lease because Farrant had lied about his intentions and he and successors had not observed the terms of the lease. The building burned in the great fire of 1666.

Jerome Savage, an actor who led the Earl of Warwick's Men, built a playhouse in Newington, a village in Surrey a mile south of London Bridge, probably in the spring of 1576, but possibly in 1575 or early 1577. It was in an enclosed field, containing a "messuage," garden, and orchard, that measured 99 feet along the east side of New-ington Butts, the high street of Newington, 144 feet on the north and south, and 126 feet on the east. Savage bought a sublease on the field in 1575 and had it put into his name in March 1576, and his company (first noticed in London in February 1575) were in the playhouse by May 1577. The playhouse had to do with the mes-suage and was apparently along Newington Butts, a few yards south of the famous inn, the Elephant and Castle. The playhouse seems always to have gone by the name of the village or the street in which it stood. For brief periods the most celebrated actors played there: Lord Strange's Men for three days in 1593 and the two compa-nies into which that company had divided, the Lord Chamberlain's and Lord Admiral's Men, for ten days in June 1594. The latter companies played there unprofitably because, as they complained, the way from the city was tedious and the playhouse had long not been used on working days. It closed in the fall of 1594.

In April 1576, James Burbage, a joiner and an actor among the Earl of Leicester's Men, set out to build what proved to be the definitive public playhouse and the origin of a great theatrical business. The playhouse was in Shoreditch, a suburb outside the northeast boundary of the city, and Burbage appropriately called it the Theatre, English for the Latin word *Theatrum*. He leased part of the dissolved Priory of Holy-well containing some old buildings and, for the Theatre, an open space. He meant to spend about £200, much more, probably, than anyone had yet spent on a play-house. Because such a sum was well beyond his means, he took as a partner his brother-in-law, John Brayne, the grocer who had built the Red Lion. Burbage would add Brayne's name to the lease, and Brayne would supply most of the money; plays would yield profits that would go mostly to Brayne until his and Burbage's expenditures were the same, after which the two men would share the place equally. This scheme, however, was hopelessly inadequate because they could never agree on how much each had spent or received, and together they spent not £200 but about £700. Brayne died bankrupt in 1586, and Burbage, who grew rich, squeezed Brayne's widow out of own-ership in 1589. The quarrel between Burbage and the Braynes bedeviled the play-house virtually throughout its history, sometimes spectacularly, as did another between the Burbages and the landlord, Giles Allen, from 1585 until four years after it was no more.

The Theatre probably opened late in 1576. It was a polygonal timber-frame build-ing that seemed round. It had three galleries, one above the other (the top one with a tile roof), around the yard, and a stage and tiring house. In the Christmas season of 1598–9, the Burbage family had it demolished and its timbers (girders) and other useful parts taken to the Bankside in Southwark for use in a new playhouse, the Globe. Since the Theatre's girders became the Globe's, and the Globe was eventually rebuilt on the same ground and then continued until Parliament closed all playhouses in 1642, the plan of the Theatre probably survived from almost the beginning of Renais-sance playhouses to the end. In 1635, James Burbage's son, Cuthbert, described his father as the first builder of playhouses. He was obviously wrong in a literal sense, but if cost and influence are important, he was probably right.

Soon after the Theatre opened, another public playhouse was being built only some 200 yards to the south or southeast, also in Shoreditch on land in the dissolved Priory of Holywell. It was called the Curtain because it was in a large field of that name (meaning that the field was surrounded by a wall) on the south side of Holywell Lane and beyond the houses along the west side of Shoreditch High Street. It opened in the autumn of 1577 and from the beginning was paired with the Theatre as representative of all public playhouses. It, too, was seen as round and had three galleries one above the other around an open yard. It must have been roughly the same size as the Theatre, because in 1585 the owner of the Curtain, Henry Lanman, a yeoman of the queen's guard, agreed with Burbage and Brayne to pool and share equally the profits of the two playhouses for seven years, and the agreement was in force without apparent objection in 1592. The Curtain is probably the playhouse shown on the left side of *The View of the Cittye of London from the North towards the South* (*c*.1600 or later; Wickham et al., 2001, 404). That playhouse is octagonal, has three stories served by two external staircases, and a big rectangular hut on top from which a large flag flies. Who built the Curtain, at what cost, and even exactly where are unknown, as are what actors played in it for most of its history. Yet its survival was remarkable: it was in regular theatrical use until 1625 (longer than any other playhouse) and, converted into housing, was apparently still standing in 1698.

IV 1587, 1594

This great setting forth of playhouses sated London playgoers. Centuries would pass before more than nine playhouses would be simultaneously available there for plays.

In 1585, a year after the demise of the Blackfriars playhouse, Philip Henslowe leased ground called the Little Rose, about 94 feet square, on which he would build a public playhouse called the Rose. He was officially a dyer, actually a financier, who was founding the only theatrical business to rival James Burbage's. He and eventually his stepdaughter's husband, Edward Alleyn, the actor who led the Lord Admiral's Men, would be concerned with five playhouses and the Beargarden. Henslowe was also creating a new theater district, for the Rose was the first of five public playhouses on Bankside, the south bank of the Thames west of the south end of London Bridge.

Henslowe hired John Griggs, a carpenter, to build the Rose, and on January 10, 1587, as work began, he drew up a contract by which he protected himself against great losses. He agreed that a grocer, John Cholmley, could sell food and drink to spectators from a building on the southwest corner of the property for eight years if he paid Henslowe a huge rent (£102 a year) and joined Henslowe as an equal partner in the costs and profits of the playhouse. But although the two men had "great zeal and good will" for one another, by 1592 Cholmley had nothing to do with the playhouse.

The Rose opened in the fall of 1587, and for much of its history Alleyn's players used it. From 1592 its day-to-day finances are better known than those of other playhouses, even modern ones, because Henslowe recorded his costs and takings there in a "diary" that survives. Henslowe did not reopen the Rose after the horrendous plague of 1603–4, nor did he renew his lease on the property in 1605. Successors did not use it for plays and may have pulled it down in 1606 or in the 1620s.

The Rose was a timber-frame building of thirteen or fourteen sides that contemporaries saw as round. It was probably smaller than the Theatre, but it too consisted of three tiers of galleries, one over the other, around an open yard. It may have been some 73 feet across, its yard 45 feet across, and its lower galleries on either side 14 feet. Its stage, which was on the north side of the yard, was about 37 feet wide at the back, tapered to about 27 feet at the front, and was about 16 feet 6 inches deep. In 1592 Henslowe spent more than £100 enlarging the Rose. He rebuilt the northern half of the galleries and the stage so that the playhouse grew 10 feet northwards and became rather egg-shaped. The stage was much the same size as before but more rectangular. In 1595 he built or rebuilt a roof over the stage and put a throne in it that could descend to and rise from the stage.

Toward the end of 1594, Francis Langley set about building the second playhouse on Bankside, the Swan. The playhouse in Newington Butts had just closed, and plays had not been performed in the one at St. Paul's for several years. Langley was officially a draper, actually a financier, who repeatedly sought to enrich himself by reckless ventures of dubious legality. He finished the Swan in 1595, and the next year a Dutch tourist, Johannes de Witt, called it "the largest and most distinguished" of the London playhouses. He drew a picture showing the place on the inside and sent it to a friend at home, who copied it into a commonplace book that survives (Wickham et al., 2001, 437). This copy of de Witt's drawing has made the Swan the main source of ideas about what other public playhouses looked like, including the Theatre.

The Swan was, however, one of the least successful of the public playhouses, perhaps because it was some 500 yards farther than the other Bankside playhouses from the centers of population in the city and at the south end of London Bridge. Langley had trouble keeping players in the Swan, and it was a regular playhouse for only nine years. Players, some of whom were perhaps the Lord Chamberlain's Men (among them Shakespeare), were in the playhouse in 1595 and 1596, and Pembroke's Men in February 1597. Playing, however, ceased there in 1598, and Langley died bankrupt in 1602. Playing resumed in 1610 but went on sporadically for only six years more, ending finally in 1621.

The Swan was a timber-frame building whose interstices were filled with flints and cement rather than the usual wattle and daub. The drawing shows it as round and consisting of three tiers of galleries one above the other around an open yard. Built into the galleries and rising above them is a tiring house of three stories, one at stage level with two doors leading onto the stage, another just above with a window right across at which apparently sit spectators, and the third at the top with a door at the right side out of which steps a man probably blowing a trumpet. A rectangular stage extends from the tiring house perhaps halfway across the yard so that spectators can stand on three sides of it. Thatched roofs cover the galleries, tiring house, and stage; the stage roof is held up by two pillars on the stage. According to de Witt, the Swan accommodated 3,000 spectators.

V 1596, 1598–1600

By 1596, only the Theatre and Curtain remained of the nine playhouses built from 1575 to 1578, and they competed with only the Rose and Swan. Moreover, James Burbage's lease on the Theatre property was running out, and the landlord was refusing to renew it on suitable terms. So Burbage decided to make a huge investment on a theatrical project elsewhere. If he and his brother-in-law, John Brayne, had effectually invented the public playhouse, he would now reinvent the private one. On February 4, 1596, he bought for £600 the medieval hall and other parts of a building formerly belonging to the Blackfriars monastery and adjoining that in which the first Blackfriars playhouse had been. He meant to put a second Blackfriars playhouse in the hall, one of the grandest rooms in the country where several Parliaments had met. It was at least as high as two rooms on top of one another, and it may have had a hammer-beam roof. It was in the upper story at the northern end of the building. The first Blackfriars playhouse had been in the upper story at the southern end of the other building, and the "great" stone staircase that led to the first led also to the second.

Burbage meant to enhance not only the private playhouse but performances in it, for his players would not be boy choristers but the Lord Chamberlain's Men, led by Burbage's son, Richard. Burbage was, however, more than a decade before his time. While the work of making the playhouse was still proceeding in November 1596, his wealthy and influential neighbors in Blackfriars successfully objected to a playhouse in their midst. Burbage died in 1597, leaving a useless private playhouse to his son Richard.

In 1598 the Theatre finally closed and the Swan went into hibernation, and perhaps for a moment early in the summer only the ancient Curtain and 11-year-old Rose were available in London for plays. So the Burbages, Henslowe, Alleyn, people who had been associated with St. Paul's and the first Blackfriars, and others all set about theatrical projects. The result was a second remarkable coming of playhouses from the summer of 1598 to 1600, consisting of three new public playhouses, one new private playhouse, and one reopened private playhouse.

The people first off the mark were new to the business. Oliver Woodliffe, haberdasher and financier, had in 1594 bought a lease on most of an inn, the Boar's Head, to make a public playhouse in the inn-yard, which was about 55 feet square. This inn, unlike the earlier playhouse inns, did not remain an inn and was in Middlesex, a few yards outside the eastern boundary of the city. In April 1598, Woodliffe made a yeoman, Richard Samwell, a partner and made himself invisible: he sublet most of his part of the inn to Samwell, appointed him to build and manage the playhouse, and went abroad. Woodliffe paid for a tiring house, with a gallery for spectators over it, on the west side of the yard, also for the stage. Samwell paid for galleries on the north and south sides and for adapting the existing gallery along a building on the east side, all of which were on posts so that people could stand under them. Woodliffe would have half the takings in his western gallery and Samwell half those in the other galleries; the players would have the other halves and the takings in the yard. Samwell spent only about £40 for his part of the place. His northern and southern galleries were only about 3 feet deep, and the stage was in the middle of the yard like a boxing ring.

This unpretentious place opened in the summer of 1598 and apparently was a success, for when Woodliffe returned early the following summer he proposed and Samwell agreed to enlarge it. Samwell now spent £260 making his northern and southern galleries bigger and building a new gallery over the existing eastern one. Woodliffe made his western gallery bigger, too, and moved the stage so that it adjoined the tiring house. The work was done in July and early August 1599. The single galleries on the north and south were now about 6 feet deep and ran on posts from the eastern gallery, into which they led, to the western gallery, which they abutted but did not lead into. The eastern galleries were about 8 feet deep and the western one about 7 feet. The stage was 39 feet 7 inches wide and about 25 feet deep; and beside it were strips of the yard about 8 feet wide in which people could stand.

The place was now a recognizable if rather intimate public playhouse. Woodliffe and Samwell, however, had spent more on it than they wanted and sought ways to leave it. Samwell had borrowed money for it from Robert Browne, an actor who led Derby's Men, and in mid-October 1599 conveyed his part to him for £360 in all. Woodliffe sold his part for £400, more than it was worth, on November 7, 1599, to Francis Langley, who had built the Swan. Langley promptly made the playhouse a legal and literal battleground that persisted until the fall of 1603, when, thanks to the great plague of 1603–4, the playhouse fell into the hands of Browne's and Woodliffe's widows. It then continued apparently peaceably until the leases expired in 1616, after which it became a collection of small holdings. It was on the north side of Whitechapel High Street and the east side of a street leading north, then Hog Lane, later Petticoat Lane.

While the Boar's Head was in its first season, James Burbage's heirs solved their problems at the Theatre. They leased property on Bankside, and a few days after Christmas 1598 had the Theatre pulled down and its useful parts, including its girders, taken there, more or less across Maiden Lane from the Rose. There they built the famous Globe, the third public playhouse on Bankside. It was much the same size and shape as the Theatre, but with thatched, instead of tiled, roofs. It was complete or nearly so by May 16, 1599.

The Burbages essayed a new kind of ownership at the Globe, perhaps because a lot of Burbage money was tied up in the unused playhouse in Blackfriars. Rather than lease the property and build and manage the playhouse themselves, they organized a group of sharers to do so: five players among the Lord Chamberlain's Men, one of them Shakespeare, acquired one share each, and James Burbage's sons, Cuthbert and Richard, acquired two and a half shares each, so that they owned half the venture. These sharers, according to their successors, spent £700 building the playhouse, and hence contributed £70 per share.

Thus owned, the Globe was a stable and unlitigious enterprise in which the Lord Chamberlain's, later called the King's Men played until the afternoon of June 29, 1613, when during a performance of Shakespeare's *Henry VIII* it burned spectacularly to the ground. A burning wad from a small cannon fired as a salute had set the thatch alight. Although the Globe was a classic public playhouse like the Theatre, Curtain, Rose, and Swan, not much else is known about it (see the second Globe below). One can only speculate, therefore, about the authenticity of "Shakespeare's Globe," built recently by Sam Wanamaker and associates some 225 yards west of the site of the original one.

In the autumn of 1599, the boy choristers of St. Paul's Cathedral began acting again at their old playhouse. It was a notable event, because no private playhouse had operated in London since they had ceased acting in 1589 or 1590.

The Burbages concluded, therefore, that if adult actors could not use their private playhouse in Blackfriars, child actors might. On September 2, 1600, they leased it to Henry Evans, one of Richard Farrant's successors at the first Blackfriars. By December 1600, he was presenting plays in the second Blackfriars acted by the boy choristers of the Chapel Royal.

The boys at the second Blackfriars and St. Paul's were apparently the "little eyases" who, Rosencrantz tells Hamlet, "are most tyrannically clapped" and "are now the fashion." The boys' success, however, did not last. Those at the second Blackfriars played there less than eight years, about as long as their predecessors had played at the first. The scheme was dogged with problems from the start that led to lawsuits involving almost everybody in it, including Richard Burbage. It came to an end in March 1608 because the boys had been acting plays that offended people in high places and had finally acted two that outraged the king. The Burbages then decided that the time had come to carry out James Burbage's plan for the playhouse. On August 9, 1608, they reacquired Evans' lease and the next day organized ownership to echo that at the Globe. Richard Burbage granted seven identical leases on the property, the rent for which yielded him £40 a year. The lessees were himself, Cuthbert Burbage, four actors among the King's Men, including Shakespeare, and, apparently, Evans.

Because of plague, the King's Men could not begin at the playhouse until late 1609. Neighbors objected again but now did not prevail. The company came to play at Blackfriars in the winter months and at the Globe in the summer ones. Although the shares passed from hand to hand, the playhouse was not troubled by lawsuits or financial problems. It became the most important playhouse of its time and one of the most important in the history of English drama. The hall comprising the playhouse measured 66 feet north to south and 46 feet east to west, so that at floor level the second Blackfriars playhouse was more than two and a half times the size of the first one. The main entrance was at the northern end and the stage at the southern end. The playhouse had a pit in which people sat on benches, and galleries that perhaps ran around three sides of the room above the pit. Boxes were adjacent to and on a level with the stage, perhaps at the back. The stage was famous for spectators who stood, sat, and even reclined on it, and somewhere there was a tiring house.

The second Blackfriars closed with the other playhouses in 1642 by order of Parliament and, unlike most of them, was not used for plays again. Richard Burbage's son, William, sold it in 1651 for £700; the great fire of 1666 destroyed the building.

Soon after the Globe opened, Philip Henslowe and Edward Alleyn, neighbors at the Rose, set about building a public playhouse called the Fortune for Alleyn's players. Alleyn, who was to invest about £100 more than Henslowe, acquired a lease on property in Middlesex, some 100 yards beyond the northwest boundary of the City, on December 22, 1599. The two of them then drew up a contract (which survives) on January 8, 1600, with a builder, Peter Street, who had pulled down the Theatre for the Burbages and probably built the Globe. Henslowe saw to the construction, which was to cost £440, and Alleyn negotiated with objecting neighbors. Alleyn eventually said that the Fortune had cost £520, some of the extra £80 probably being for painting, which the contract excluded. Street could not finish by July 25 as agreed, partly because of complaints by neighbors, and Alleyn's players opened the Fortune in, apparently, November 1600. These players, successively called the Lord Admiral's, Prince Henry's, and Palsgrave's Men, remained in the playhouse throughout its history.

The contract provides more reliable information about the structure of this playhouse than is available about any other. It, too, was a timber-frame building consisting of three tiers of galleries around an open yard, but unlike other large public playhouses it was square, 80 feet on each side. The bottom gallery was 12 feet 6 inches deep, and, because of jutties over the yard, the middle one was 13 feet 4 inches and the top 14 feet 2 inches. The bottom gallery was on a foundation rising a foot or more above the ground and was 12 feet high; the middle and top galleries were 11 feet and 9 feet high. The yard was 55 feet square. The stage, which adjoined one side of the yard, was 27 feet 6 inches deep and 43 feet wide, so that 6 feet of the yard lay on each of its left and right sides. Behind the stage was the tiring house, which had glazed windows. The galleries and stage had tile roofs, as did the staircases, which were outside the frame. The contract, however, omits many details because they were explained in a missing "plot" and others because Street was to use the Globe as a model for them.

Like the Globe, the Fortune burned to the ground – late on the night of December 9, 1621. Alleyn by then owned it outright, having inherited Henslowe's interest in 1617 and bought the freehold. It was between Golden Lane and Whitecross Street, its entrance by way of Golden Lane.

VI 1607, 1614

Replacements appeared in 1607 for the Rose, which had not reopened after the plague of 1603–4, and for St. Paul's, which had closed in 1606. They were the Red Bull, a public playhouse, and Whitefriars, a private one.

Thinking perhaps of the Boar's Head, Aaron Holland, a servant of the earl of Devonshire, leased the Red Bull, an inn in Clerkenwell in Middlesex, at Christmas 1604, and began erecting a playhouse in it. He had the help of Martin Slatier, a player who would lead a new company of players sponsored by the duke of Holstein, Queen Anne's brother. When the playhouse was "all framed and almost set up," however, the Privy Council ordered the work to stop. Slatier protested, saying that he and Holland had spent £500 on construction and pacifying objectors, but the duke left England on May 31, 1605, and Slatier's hopes apparently collapsed. Holland completed the playhouse by the autumn of 1607, when it was first demonstrably in use. He apparently financed it by selling leases on eighteenths of the profits. If all alike, these sales yielded him £450 at the start and £45 a year. Around 1610, the playhouse took £8 or £9 a day, of which about £3 went to leaseholders.

Slatier said that the playhouse was in the square yard of the inn where Holland had turned "some stables and other rooms" into galleries. Holland said that he had "set up . . . divers buildings and galleries for a playhouse." The playhouse shown in a famous drawing of a performance of drolls at night in the 1650s is probably the Red Bull (Wickham et al., 2001, 565). The stage is rectangular and surrounded on three sides by spectators; it is against a wall with a curtained doorway at stage level and a gallery above occupied by spectators. The Red Bull was some 575 yards north of the city boundary at Smithfield and lay behind buildings on the west side of St. John Street. Its main entrance was a "great gate" through those buildings.

Holland had sold his lease and other interests in the Red Bull by 1623, but his successors are unknown. It was "re-edified" in the 1620s and closed when playing became illegal in 1642. It was often used surreptitiously until playing became legal again in 1660. It then reopened but ceased to be a playhouse in 1663.

The originator of the Whitefriars playhouse was Thomas Woodford, a financier who had once had an interest in St. Paul's and would have one in the Red Bull. During the Christmas season of 1606–7, he subleased the hall of the former Whitefriars monastery for eight years from Sir Anthony Ashley, brother-in-law of Francis Langley, who had built the Swan and harassed the Boar's Head. Woodford divided the sublease into six parts and sold three of them to Michael Drayton, the poet, and three to Lording Barry, a prospective playwright. Drayton would lead a company of children who were not choristers. He and Barry sold shares and half-shares to businessmen and another prospective playwright, John Mason. To keep the venture afloat, most of these people borrowed money from Woodford.

The playhouse was open during the summer of 1607, but plague closed it during the autumn and the sharers had trouble finding money to feed the boys. So early in

1608 they reorganized themselves. They sold a share to a rich silk weaver, George Andrewes, and gave one to Martin Slatier, the actor who, having failed to lead a company at the Red Bull, would now lead the boys at Whitefriars. These people signed documents on March 10, 1608, putting the place on a businesslike footing. The scheme, however, collapsed within a month because Woodford had not paid the rent to Ashley, and Ashley ejected them all. Sometime in 1609, the boys who had aroused the king's ire at Blackfriars moved into Whitefriars, and, despite local objections, remained there until 1614, when Ashley's lease and the playhouse probably ended. The boys had combined in 1613 with an adult company associated with Philip Henslowe, Lady Elizabeth's Men, so that Whitefriars, like Blackfriars, had become a private playhouse where men acted.

The playhouse was in the city of London but closer to the West End than any other playhouse so far, some 330 feet south of Fleet Street. The hall was, with a kitchen and cellar, in the lower story (measuring inside about 90 feet by 17 feet) of a stone building; upstairs were ten rooms where Slatier's family and no doubt the boy actors lived.

As the Whitefriars playhouse was closing, and two months after the Globe had burned, Henslowe began a venture on Bankside that would provide a place for the actors from Whitefriars. He, Edward Alleyn, and Jacob Meade, a waterman, had dealt in animal-baiting at the Beargarden since the 1590s. Now Henslowe and Meade would pull down the Beargarden and on the site (just west of whatever remained of the Rose and more or less across Maiden Lane from the charred ruins of the Globe) build the Hope, which could at will be either a public playhouse or a Beargarden. They agreed on August 29, 1613, with Gilbert Katherens, a carpenter, that he would do the work, which included pulling down and rebuilding a structure for bulls and horses, for £360 and materials from the Beargarden and elsewhere. At least partly because Katherens did not finish in the three months allowed him, the Hope did not open until the spring of 1614.

The contract with Katherens survives, as does a drawing of the Hope by Wenceslaus Hollar (Wickham et al., 2001, 608), but the contract often instructs Katherens merely to do what had been done at the Swan, and the drawing is from the outside. Like other public playhouses, the Hope seemed round and consisted of three tiers of galleries around an open yard. The stage, however, was removable, and its roof was held up without stage pillars (the drawing shows a cowl-like continuation of the tiled gallery roof where the stage roof should have been). The bottom gallery, which rested on a brick foundation 13 inches high, was, like the one at the Fortune, 12 feet high. The upper galleries were probably also like those at the Fortune in height, and the staircases leading to them were likewise external.

Henslowe was wrong to think that plays and baiting could coexist. Actors quarreled with him and, after he died in 1616, with Meade, because they lost money when they gave way to baiting. Both companies Henslowe put into it left in anger. After 1617 no company played there regularly, and it became increasingly associated with baiting only. Parliament ordered the Hope to stop baiting on December 12, 1642, and again on November 30, 1643. It was pulled down before 1660 and another Beargarden built over it in 1663.

After the Globe burned in 1613, the lease required the sharers to replace it with a building as good or better within a year. They reckoned that such an expenditure required a 15-year extension of the lease, until Christmas 1644. Because the landlord, Matthew Brend, was a minor, they went to his trustee, who gave them six years on October 26, 1613. They then went to Brend himself (now 14 years old) on February 15, 1614, and extracted from him a document promising that if they spent £1,000 rebuilding the Globe and gave him £10 when he was 21, he would confirm the trustee's six years and give them nine more. With this dubious assurance, the sharers, including Shakespeare, taxed themselves £120 a share and spent £1,400 on the playhouse, twice as much as they were bound to spend, and £200 more on an adjacent building for refreshing spectators. The King's Men, who had been burned out of the first Globe, opened the second, "the fairest playhouse that ever was in England," by the end of June 1614 and remained until Parliament closed the playhouses in 1642.

They used it only during the summer from at least 1616, generally from mid-May until early September, and the second Blackfriars the rest of the year, but the second Globe remained valuable. When Brend (now Sir Matthew) threatened to replace it after Christmas 1635 with "fit dwelling houses," the sharers took great pains maneuvering him into extending their lease for nine years at nearly triple the former rent. Moreover, when none of the sharers was an actor in 1635, the principal actors complained and the lord chamberlain arranged that five actors could buy shares.

The second Globe was the fifth playhouse on Bankside. It occupied the lines on the ground of the first and was also a polygonal timber-frame building that appeared round and consisted of three tiers of galleries around an open yard. Unlike the first, it was covered with tiles, not thatch. People said it could accommodate 3,000 spectators, but little is known of its interior, except what appears in Wenceslaus Hollar's persuasive drawing of its exterior (Wickham et al., 2001, 608): it has two massive gables over where its stage and tiring house should be, extending over at least half the yard; between the gables over the tiring house is a small polygonal tower covered by an onion dome; and it has two external staircases. The people who have rebuilt the first Globe have studied this drawing minutely, assuming that the second was in many ways identical to the first, as it may or may not have been, and that Hollar always drew with mathematical precision, as he clearly did not. The second Globe was probably pulled down after Christmas 1644, and other buildings were on the site by 1655.

VII 1617, 1623, 1630

The Renaissance playhouse entered its final moment with the opening in 1617 of the Phoenix (often called the Cockpit), a private playhouse in the city of Westminster meant for the sophisticated people who increasingly lived there. It was also the first professional theater in the West End, the present theater district, and was used by adult actors from the start.

From 1616, one public playhouse after another ceased to house plays: the Boar's Head (1616), the Hope (*c*.1617), the reborn Swan (1621), and the everlasting Curtain (1625). The London stage that had consisted largely (and during the 1590s entirely) of public playhouses came to consist of three public playhouses (the Fortune, Red Bull, and Globe) and three private. Public playhouses, even the Globe, were associated with crude spectators, fustian, and stage battles. In private playhouses, the best writers and players offered refinements of language and plot to elite spectators who paid more money to see plays indoors by candlelight.

An actor among the Queen's Men, Christopher Beeston, built the Phoenix. On August 9, 1616, soon after the closing of the Boar's Head, he took a sublease on property where a cockpit, house, and garden were. He converted the cockpit into the Phoenix, and the Queen's Men had just opened it on March 4, 1617, when rioting apprentices wrecked it. Three months later, with the place repaired, the company returned. They were the first of five companies successively there, for Beeston began a new way of operating a playhouse that eventually would apply everywhere. He was master not only of the playhouse but of the enterprise in it, hiring and dismissing players, acquiring plays, and contenting officials like those of the parish and revels office. Artistically his methods were a success, for the Phoenix achieved a standard second only to that at the second Blackfriars.

Beeston died in 1638, leaving the Phoenix to his widow. She made their son, William, manager, but he produced an unlicensed play that criticized royal projects in May 1640, and the king replaced him with William Davenant. When Davenant's involvement in the Army Plot — a plot in 1641 among disbanded officers of the English army and some courtiers to encourage the discontented against Parliament — caused him to flee London a year later, William Beeston returned to the Phoenix and stayed until the playhouses closed in 1642. It was then sometimes used illegally and in 1658–9 semi-legally. In 1660 it was the first playhouse to open legally. It could not, however, compete with the Drury Lane Theatre, built about 100 yards away in 1663, and may have become housing.

The Phoenix apparently had brick walls and probably appears on Wenceslaus Hollar's "Great Map" (*c*.1658) as roughly 40 feet square and of two main stories covered by three pitched roofs side by side (Wickham et al., 2001, 624). It was midway between Drury Lane and Wild Street.

Edward Alleyn was organizing the building of a second Fortune four months after the first burned in December 1621, and the company in the first from start to finish (called since 1613 the Palsgrave's Men) opened the second by March 1623. Alleyn financed it by selling 12 shares, each a lease, expiring in 1673, on a twelfth of the property and playhouse. Every share cost £83 6s. 8d. paid to the builders and £10 13s. 10d. a year paid to Alleyn, so that the builders received £1,000 to erect the building and Alleyn £128 a year. The holder of a share then paid a twelfth of the expenses of the playhouse and received a twelfth of the profits. Alleyn originally kept a share for himself but later only half of one. Little is known about the playhouse itself. It occupied much the same site as the first, and spectators also got to it through Golden Lane, but it was a round brick building, not a square timber-frame one. After 1625, when the Palsgrave's Men dissolved, it suffered the decline of public playhouses in general. It closed with the other playhouses in 1642. Some illegal performances took place in it until 1649, but it was ruinous in 1656 for lack of repairs.

Alleyn died in 1626, leaving his interest in the playhouse to his College of God's Gift in Dulwich, which, as sharers ceased to pay their rent after 1642, became outright owner. The college eventually had the site redeveloped, and by 1662, 20 new "messuages" stood where the playhouse had been and on "other ground thereunto belonging."

Only five playhouses resumed after the plague of 1625, with a sixth opening in November 1630. It was a private playhouse, Salisbury Court, the last Renaissance playhouse built and the only one partly a venture of the royal establishment. William Blagrave, deputy to the master of the revels, and Richard Gunnell, a veteran actor, created it. Behind Blagrave was the master himself, Sir Henry Herbert, and behind both was the earl of Dorset, the queen's chamberlain. The playhouse was in the grounds of the earl's London House, Dorset House, which was in Salisbury Court.

The earl agreed that Blagrave and Gunnell should build a playhouse on a plot that lay 42 feet along the east side of Water Lane and extended 140 feet eastward to the garden wall of Dorset House. He granted them a lease until 1670, and they spent some £1,000 making a barn into a playhouse and building a residence nearby. They raised a company, the King's Revels, ostensibly boys but mainly men, who used it in 1630–1 and 1634–6. Two new companies promoted by the earl, Prince Charles's Men and Queen Henrietta Maria's Men, used it otherwise, the former in 1631–4 and the latter from 1637 until Parliament closed the playhouses in 1642. Gunnell died in 1634, Blagrave in 1636. They were succeeded by Richard Heton, who, if they had not, instituted the dictatorial management that Christopher Beeston had imposed at the Phoenix. Gunnell and then Heton hired Richard Brome to write plays for the playhouse, with litigious results, but one play, *Sparagus Garden*, made, Brome said, £1,000 in profit. Because the lessee of the property in 1649 tried to make the playhouse into a brewery, the earl urged William Beeston to buy the lease, as he finally did in 1652. He reopened the playhouse, restored and enlarged, in 1660, but it was destroyed in the great fire of 1666.

The playhouse was small and less successful than its two rivals, the second Blackfriars and the Phoenix. Eventually a room 40 feet square was built over it, prompting ideas about its size and shape. It was in the city of London near where the Whitefriars playhouse had been.

REFERENCES AND FURTHER READING

A great many articles and books have appeared about Renaissance playhouses. Below are the most useful compilations of them.

Bentley, G. E. (1941–68). *The Jacobean and Caroline Stage*. Oxford: Oxford University Press.

Chambers, E. K. (1923). *The Elizabethan Stage*. Oxford: Oxford University Press.

Hotson, Leslie (1928). *The Commonwealth and Restoration Stage*. Cambridge, MA: Harvard University Press.

Wickham, Glynne, William Ingram, and Herbert Berry (2001). *English Professional Theatre, 1530–1660*. Cambridge: Cambridge University Press.

The Transmission of an English Renaissance Play-Text

Grace Ioppola

As the cultural historian Robert Darnton argues, while a book moves from author to publisher to printer to distributor to reader, its path is actually a circuit because it will inevitably return in some way to the author, if only as reader (1990, 111). Renaissance play-texts, by their very nature, returned culturally and textually to their authors throughout their circuit of transmission, including and excluding print, because their transmission was not usually linear, that is from author to acting company to theater audience to printer to literary audience, but circular. Unlike poems, novels, short stories, and prose tracts, written for print for individual readers, plays are written for performance before communal audiences. By the time a play reached print in the English Renaissance, it usually had exhausted its theatrical run and was reincarnated into a literary text, its secondary and, for some dramatists, its lesser form.

Many theorists and historians of the book who examine the impact of Elizabethan and Jacobean play-texts on culture often concentrate only on this later reincarnation in print, oblivious of the numerous stages in the progress of the text before it became a literary or "material" text. Those actually responsible for this privileging of the printed text were the most prominent and influential figures in the "new bibliography," including R. B. McKerrow, A. W. Pollard, W. W. Greg, and Fredson Bowers, who derived their theories about dramatic textual transmission from their work on Shakespeare's *printed* texts. Although three pages that may be in his hand appear in the extant collaborative manuscript of the unacted play *Sir Thomas More*, no extant contemporary manuscripts of any of Shakespeare's plays exist. These textual scholars worked backward by examining his early printed texts (published as Quartos and in the 1623 First Folio) and then *imagining* from them what his manuscripts looked like.

Autograph or scribal manuscripts of plays by Middleton, Jonson, Chettle, Munday, Dekker, Massinger, Heywood, Fletcher, and other colleagues and sometime collaborators of Shakespeare do survive, so we do not have to imagine what dramatic manuscripts from this period looked like. The ample evidence about the transmission of the play-text that these documents provide has often been ignored, misinterpreted, or dismissed by many of the new bibliographers, either because they chose to focus on Shakespeare or because they lacked the skills to examine this archival material themselves.[1] But we need to focus on *all* stages, giving equal weight to authorial, scribal, licensing, theatrical, and print stages in the transmission of a play-text. An examination of all these usually unrecognized stages, and the historical and cultural forces at work within them, demonstrates that the final printed text is often the least interesting, and the least informative, stage of a play's circuit from author to audience and back to author.

[margin handwriting: focus on transmission of play, Not just the play as a text]

The Author and his Text

The *Diary* and financial papers of Philip Henslowe, as sharer in the Rose and other theaters and in the Lord Admiral's Men, note that his payment to a dramatist for a new play in the late 1590s ranged from £5 to £7, with the price rising to £20 in the 1610s. Acting companies performed plays in repertory, with any given play performed approximately eight to twelve times over a four- to six-month period;[2] thus, acting companies had to have on hand a large supply of new and old plays. Henslowe hired both company dramatists (those attached for a long period to a particular acting company) and freelance authors to write new plays for him, as well as to "mend," "alter," or make "addicians" to plays he had already acquired. Writers could approach Henslowe to offer him plays that they had already written or planned to write, or he could approach writers and commission them to work for him.

Henslowe usually provided the writer with an advance on his total fee when contracting the play, paying the rest upon receipt of the finished manuscript. Many plays contracted by Henslowe either were not completed or do not survive in print, although he provides information about the performance history of some of the now-lost plays.[3] He employed most of the major dramatists of the age, including Jonson, Marston, Rowley, Bird, Daborne, Chapman, Drayton, Heywood, Webster, Munday, Dekker, and Chettle. As most of these writers also worked at various times for other major acting companies, such as the Lord Chamberlain's/King's Men, and other major theater owners–sharers, such as the Burbages, his direct competitors, Henslowe's practices were probably standard in the profession. Most noticeably, Henslowe's records suggest that the act of playwriting was a *financial* rather than a *creative* enterprise for employer and employee. His writers often seemed to have approached him simply when they needed a loan, offering an unwritten play, which they may never have intended to finish, as collateral. Henslowe occasionally records that the writer(s) (he records numerous sets of collaborators as well as single authors) read aloud an outline, and sometimes later the finished play or "book" (the correct term for a "prompt-book" in this age), of the contracted play to the acting company. Such practices may have been common rather than occasional, especially since some, such as Jonson and Shakespeare, wrote with particular company actors in mind and would want their reactions to the new plays.[4] Once purchased by an acting company, a play became its property, and the author had no further fees from or claims to it.[5]

If two or more writers were working in collaboration, they most likely used the play's outline to divide up acts or scenes, rather than sitting down and writing each scene together (although this may have happened on occasion). Some dramatists specialized in comic and others in tragic scenes; some may only have checked or revised the finished work of their collaborators. In short, collaborators probably wrote in a number of ways, but studies of extant manuscripts and of contextual stylistics in printed texts suggest that collaborators indeed usually wrote "shares" of the text, dividing up acts or scenes (Hoy, 1956–62; see chapter 36 below). Even those known for working regularly in collaboration, such as Fletcher, who wrote a number of plays with Beaumont and with others after Beaumont's death, also wrote plays alone. Heywood claimed to have had a "maine finger" in 220 plays, but if his estimate seems high (he may have included plays by others that he revised slightly for revival), some professional dramatists wrote between 30 and 70 plays each, alone or in collaboration, during their careers (Bentley, 1971, 27–8). The composition of a play took approximately six weeks, although Jonson used the Prologue to boast of completing *Volpone* in a mere five weeks "*in his owne hand without a* Co-adiutor / Nouice, Iorneyman *or* Tutor."

We know from at least two uses in this period of the term "foul" papers and numerous uses of the term "fair" copy or sheet that authors distinguished between different stages of the manuscripts that they (and/or their copyists) produced.[6] By "foul" papers authors meant the first complete draft of a new play, full of the types of cuts, additions, revisions, confusions, false starts, and inconsistencies commonly made in composition and afterwards. These foul papers could contain *currente calamo* changes (that is, changes made as the author composed) or later changes made after the scene or entire play was finished. Extant foul-paper or fair-copy manuscripts such as *The Captives* (in Heywood's hand), *John a Kent and John a Cumber* (in Munday's hand), and *Believe as You List* (in Massinger's hand) show revisions made interlinearly, in the margin, and on interleaved or pinned- or glued-in sheets of paper. Cuts sometimes were signalled by crossing out lines of text, but more often were marked by a simple vertical line in the margin next to the text. Authors wrote most of the text (especially the dialogue) in the standard script of the period, secretary hand, a much more stylized and elaborate form of cursive handwriting than we are used to today. By convention, writers were supposed to use "italic" hand (the precursor of our modern handwriting style) for formal features such as act–scene notations, stage directions, speech-prefixes, and character names within dialogue, but in practice, judging by the surviving manuscripts, most composing authors wrote in secretary hand throughout. Authors or scribes recopying foul papers do use italic hand when required.

Although some scholars have claimed that no extant example of foul papers exists, Heywood's manuscript of *The Captives* (British Library Egerton MS 1994) is clearly a foul-paper text (see plate 7). Heywood is in the act of composing, unsure as he writes

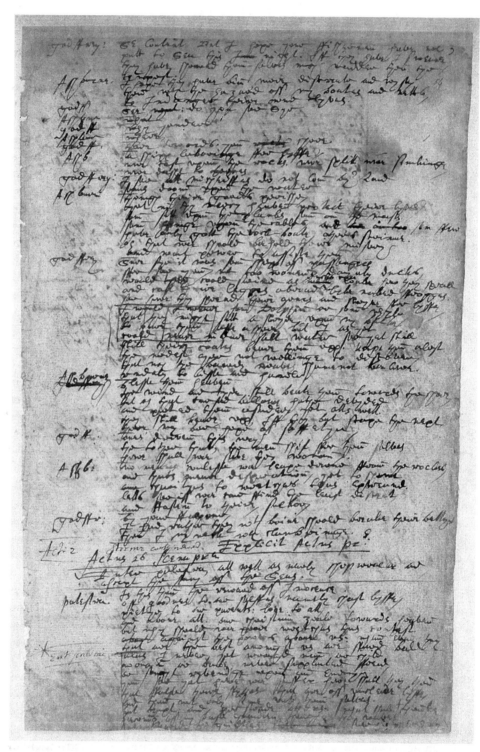

Plate 7 A page from Heywood's foul papers of *The Captives* (BL Egerton MS 1994), showing authorial *currente calamo* revisions and a few later additions of stage directions by the book-keeper. Reproduced by permission of the British Library.

which characters will appear in which scene, at what point they will enter, what they will say, and even what relationship they bear to the others.[7] That the manuscript has some light notation (in act–scene breaks and in stage directions) by another hand, probably a playhouse scribe responsible for keeping the "book" (the acting company's master copy), does not disqualify it from the category of foul papers. Other foul-paper manuscripts also survive, although they have not been recognized as such.[8] Heywood's characteristics in composing can also be seen in his portions, and revisions to Munday's original portions, of the "book" of *Sir Thomas More* (British Library Harley Manuscript 7368). This "book" is one of the many extant examples of mixed foul- and fair-copy manuscripts; all of the portions (excluding Heywood's) written by the original author, Munday, and by Dekker, Chettle, and probably Shakespeare, appear to be fair rather than foul copies. That is, these portions of the text show very little revision or alteration in the act of writing and instead show much more of the coherence, consistency, and uninterrupted fluency typical of a recopied text. However, an authorial fair copy can show both correction (rectification of errors) and revision (changes of text) at times, since a dramatist, like any writer, could and did make occasional changes as he recopied his text. Two other extant partly foul-paper manuscripts, which are also, curiously, partly fair-copy, show a mix of the composition of new material and the revision of existing material. In *Believe as You List* (British Library Egerton MS 2828), Massinger satisfied the censor's objections by revising his modern Spanish characters and setting to those of the ancient world, but simply recopied other sections. In *The Escapes of Jupiter* (British Library Egerton MS 1994), Heywood recycled material from two of his previous plays already in print, *The Silver Age* and *The Golden Age*. Even though Heywood could have pasted in and annotated the printed portions of the texts he was reusing, he chose to make a fair copy of them, revising them as he went. Not surprisingly, the sections of these manuscripts in which the author is composing, rather than incorporating his older material, show *currente calamo* alterations and confusions.

The reasons that a dramatist would make a fair copy of his text, as Heywood's foul-paper manuscript of *The Captives* suggests, might be many. His handwriting while composing might be illegible to others (Heywood elsewhere acknowledged his "difficult" hand), or the text might have had so many changes (including marginal additions written any which way, and not on the line where they belonged) that it would seem confusing, or there might be a combination of these or other reasons. It was probably a rare dramatist who wrote his first draft so legibly and fluently that it could be passed along to his theater company without being recopied. In fact, the playhouse scribe who tried to use Heywood's foul papers of *The Captives* to make a company "book" (largely by adding stage directions) without recopying it evidently did not succeed, as this manuscript lacks the censor's license, suggesting instead that a fair copy of it was made for him to read. Not surprisingly, more fair copies of manuscripts in the authors' hands exist than of foul-paper texts, as foul papers were relatively unimportant and likely discarded once they had been neatly copied. These fair copies include the Trinity College Cambridge manuscript (wholly in the author's hand) and the Huntington Library manuscript (partly in the author's hand) of Middleton's *A Game at Chess.*

However, professional scribes were also paid to copy manuscripts, and if a theater company did employ a playhouse scribe, like Edward Knight (who worked for the King's Men in the 1620s), it could find one at the local "scriptorium" (or copy-house).[9] Scribes were trained to copy a text more or less as they saw it, not to alter a text's fundamental literary or theatrical features. They may have regularized the placement of stylistic or formatting features (such as speech-prefixes, stage directions, act–scene notations, and character names), but they did not alter plot, setting, dialogue, or other authorial features. We can even find scribes who fail to correct obvious errors or who retranscribe inconsistencies. If a scribe did so, he was, in fact, doing his job properly. The idea that a scribe "collaborated," "intervened," or "interfered" in the composition of a play is not supported by evidence in any extant dramatic manuscripts of this period.

The Acting Company and their Text

An acting company was obliged to submit a copy of any new play, or a newly revised licensed play, to the theatrical censor, the master of the revels, before it could be performed publicly (and probably privately, although some government decrees concentrated on "publick" shows). This copy could be either foul papers or a fair transcription of them. Experienced dramatists and the acting companies for which they wrote apparently knew just how far they could press the master of the revels, and thus probably practiced some self-censorship before the text reached the censor. Of course, it is always possible that, now and then, they tested the censor with particular material, otherwise manuscripts would not show the number of censor's cuts which they do.

The extant manuscripts of the plays *Sir Thomas More, Sir John Van Olden Barnavelt, The Second Maiden's Tragedy, The Lady Mother,* and *The Launching of the Mary (or The Seaman's Honest Wife)*, among others, tell us what the censor did or did not contribute to the transmission of a play-text. In each of these, he has marked objectionable passages with an "X" or a vertical bar in the margin, and sometimes written ominous warnings such as "Mend this" or "I like not this" next to offensive lines. Herbert, for example, granted his license to the "book" of *The Launching of the Mary* on the condition that all the "Oaths left out In ye action as they are crost In ye booke & all other Reformations strictly obserud may be acted not otherwyse." Herbert then signed his name, thereby granting the official license, yet remained so irritated that he then instructed the company book-keeper (responsible for preparing and regularizing the "book") to "leaue out all oathes, prophanite & publick Ribaldry as he will answer it at his perill."[10] A few other manuscripts, including those of Fletcher's *The Honest Man's Fortune* and Massinger's *The Parliament of Love,* carry the censor's comments, although his signature was later removed by collectors or someone else. The censor would

[handwritten marginal note: notion of self-censorship in Renaissance plays]

usually sign on the last page of the text, immediately below the last line of dialogue (or the notation "Finis," if it appeared), but he may have sometimes signed elsewhere, such as on a separate sheet or title-page. Thus, some extant manuscripts that no longer carry a license may once have done so.

Some manuscripts that have been through the censor's hands show very little actual censorship, other than an occasional "X" or vertical line, so the task of reading through a play may not have been as onerous for the censor as it seems to us now. Censors did not serve as literary editors or collaborators, and did not advise the author on how to improve dramatic or thematic elements of the plays, or criticize or correct errors or inconsistencies. Instead they confined themselves almost entirely to *cutting* offensive material. With the exception of *Sir Thomas More* (which never apparently satisfied the censor no matter how many hands tried to improve it), we have no extant manuscripts with censor's licenses that demanded that the play be submitted again. While a dramatist and censor may have trusted each other to operate under a set of mutual guidelines, each or both may have been lax (or even complicit) on occasion. Jonson, Middleton, Chapman, and Daniel, among others, tempted the various censors over the years with plays that they knew would provoke controversy. However, of the 900 or so plays written for the London professional stage in this period (Bentley, 1971, 25), we have few examples of those provoking serious censorship before or after performance. On the whole, dramatists and their acting companies seemed to have stood little risk of serious punishment for crossing whatever strict or lax line existed between their desires and the censor's obligations. They may have had a lot to gain in increased notoriety, publicity, and admissions.[11]

[margin handwritten note: Censors did not rewrite plays c but they cut offensive material]

[margin handwritten note: Very interesting]

Once the censor had returned his licensed copy of the play, the acting company had to prepare it to use in rehearsal and performance. At this point the text returned to the author if he was attached to the company. The dramatist could have also assisted the scribe who had made a fair copy before it went to the censor (any scribe copying Heywood's foul papers, for example, would have needed to have consulted him frequently). If the company had submitted to the censor a fair copy, from which he required few cuts or changes, the book-keeper (or another scribe, or even the author) could adjust that manuscript to suit the censor, and still use it for a company "book." Otherwise the book-keeper or another scribe, or the author himself, could recopy the text, making any required changes. What is apparent from the different hands often found in a single manuscript carrying a license is that the author has more often than not made the corrections required by the censor, as in *The Launching of the Mary*, *Believe as You List*, *The Soddered Citizen*, and *The Honest Man's Fortune*, among others, all of which apparently contain post-licensing revisions made by or with the guidance of the original authors.[12] Thus a manuscript did not go simply to the book-keeper (as Herbert assumed in his license to *The Launching of the Mary*) after it left the censor's hands but returned via the book-keeper to the author(s) if they were still in the acting company's employ.

Once the post-licensing authorial corrections had been made to the text, the book-keeper could adjust the text to suit performance. For example, he could add act–scene divisions or marginal notes about the properties (such as a table) or actors (by writing in their names) to be made ready for some or all scenes. He could also correct, enlarge, or cut stage directions and regularize character names. In short, he would perform any task required to make the company "book" both comprehensive and consistent for use in rehearsal and performance, when he was required to read through it in case an actor needed prompting to remind him of his lines. From this legible, complete, consistent, and coherent manuscript, whether foul or fair copied, he or other scribes could also transcribe actors' "parts" (their characters' lines and preceding cue lines). We have no significant evidence in any extant dramatic manuscript of this period that the company book-keeper or another scribe rewrote or revised an author's text (although he may have recopied it), unless it was to suit the censor's demands.

An acting company with an attached dramatist (who sometimes also acted in his own plays, as Jonson and Shakespeare did) almost certainly relied on him to deal with changes to his own text. This point is repeatedly made clear by Henslowe, who used original authors, when possible, to "mend" plays at a later date. Actors could and did suggest or make changes, not always to the satisfaction of the authors, some of whom later complained.[13] Jonson (in *Every Man Out of his Humour*) and Richard Brome (in *The Antipodes*), among others, took exception to actors cutting their texts in performance, but neither notes that actors added or revised any material (although company clowns were notorious for enlarging their parts). Changes made in rehearsal or performance were probably accepted, however reluctantly, by an author who participated in the staging of his own plays.

Even after a play had been in performance for some years, it did not cease to attract the attention of its original author or authors. As noted above, Heywood, among others, used material from earlier plays to write new ones, and the majority of company dramatists seemed to have had no compunction about retouching or rehandling their earlier work, either to update it for revival or to recast it in some way. This is not to say that a text could be rehandled by anyone; company dramatists seem to have kept some control over their own texts, but they may also have revised the plays of authors who had worked on a freelance basis or had died. In addition to foulpaper and fair-copy versions (possibly used for the licensed "book"), the acting company could have simultaneously possessed numerous other texts of a play, some slightly or highly variant. Although some scholars posit that all revisions would have been made to the company "book," it is possible that new transcripts were made instead. Although the censor was supposed to relicense any revised play, we have no evidence that he did so regularly, so the company may have kept its licensed copy locked up for safekeeping, making one or more transcripts of it through the years. Their chances of being caught out if they had revised a play without relicensing it were apparently minuscule, unless they provoked controversy. Nor could the censor be expected to keep track of whether any given line in 900 or so plays had been altered.

An acting company, or the author of its play, would also have had reason, on occasion, to make special reading or "presentation" copies of plays to give to the monarch or other aristocratic patrons; these would usually include an ingratiating dedication page. Copies could also be specifically commissioned (for a price) by friends and others. Extant presentation or commissioned copies often show a text nearly flawlessly written and beautifully bound in vellum, with elaborate title-pages and, sometimes, gilt-edged leaves.[14] As dedicatees or commissioners would be given copies of plays they had admired in performance, their copies apparently offered the text as used in performance, that is, the "book." A presentation or commissioned copy is a fair copy in its neatness and consistency, but it is supposed to look like a book, rather than a manuscript. Its material form, including its binding and gilt-edged pages, makes it a literary and not a theatrical object. Only the form, and not the text itself, has been usually adapted for a reader. Manuscripts especially made to serve as printer's copy are also literary copies, designed to present a reading text that can compete with the best poetry and prose, and presented in a form (no binding or decoration required) that would ease the printer's job. In major or minor ways, copies made strictly for print may have been altered to suit literary convention, rather than preserved to reflect performance, particularly if made by the original author.[15]

The Printer and his Text

In deciding to print a play still in repertory, a company had to weigh what they would lose (exclusive access to the text) against what they would gain (a small amount of money but more prestige or publicity).[16] Although acting companies were not supposed to steal each other's plays, they did so anyway (as comically noted in the induction to Marston's *The Malcontent*), and, once in print, the text could be used by any set of actors. A notorious play, like *A Game at Chess*, which attracted 3,000 people each day for nine consecutive days to the second Globe theater, would be profitable in print, even though banned from being printed. Companies (and sometimes authors) could approach a "stationer" to print their plays, or they could be approached. In this period, printing was an industry highly regulated by the government, and most London-based members of the profession belonged to the Stationers' Company, whose rules they had to follow (but which did not extend to those outside the Company). The person who acquired the play (paying about 40 shillings for title to it)[17] and undertook all other expenses for producing and distributing the book would be what we now term the "publisher" (and he would be male – women were not members of this or the playwriting profession until after the Restoration). A publisher could also be a printer and/or a bookseller (the Stationers' Company had all three types of entrepreneur among its members), or he could hire others to print and to distribute and sell the books for him.

In order to print, the publisher would first need to seek the permission or "authority" of the print censor, either the archbishop of Canterbury or the bishop of London (or their deputies), paying 6–10 shillings (in the case of a single play) for the privilege. The publisher would then need a "license" from one or both of the wardens of the Stationers' Company.[18] During some periods, the master of the revels, the theatrical censor, also served as print censor for plays only (Dutton, 1991, 233, 235). In theory, the publisher was required to seek a print license "authority" in addition to the theatrical license already given to a play-text. But, in practice (as suggested by Stationers' Company records), the wardens may have approved for publication some or many play-texts that carried only the theatrical license. Once having registered his claim with the Stationers' wardens and received their approval or "license," the publisher could assume the exclusive right, among his brethren in the Company, to print it. This did not mean he had to or did print it, but that he was registering his intent to print it, and in an age before copyright, the Company's license offered him some protection against others laying claim to the play. The publisher would pay another 6 pence for the wardens' license (for a single play) and as further insurance, could pay 4 pence to "enter" it into the Stationers' Register.[19] A typical example from this period of the entering of a play in the Register is this one:

7 Decembris [1593]

John Danter/
This copie is put
ouer by the
consent of **John**
Danter to
Cuthbert Burbye.
vt patet. 28 maij.
1594

Entred for his copie vnder th[e h]andes fo the wardens, a plaie booke, intituled, *the historye of ORLANDO ffurioso. / one of the xij / peeres of Ffraunce* **vj**[d]

(Arber, 1875, II, 303)

Here we see John Danter's original entry on December 7, 1593, of *Orlando Furioso* (sold by its author to both the Queen's Men and the Lord Admiral's Men, according to a satirist).[20] Danter did not print the play, perhaps because he lacked title to it (he often violated Stationers' Company's rules), or because the two acting companies were still fighting over who had exclusive title to it and therefore could sell it to a publisher. On the following May 28, Danter surrendered his claim (perhaps for a fee) to Cuthbert Burby, on the condition that "the saide **John Danter** to haue th impryntinge thereof." Danter published the first quarto of the play in 1594.

In some entries in the Register, the wardens (or their clerks) use the formula of "a book called . . ." or "a book entitled . . ." for plays, poems, and prose works; in other entries they use a more specific formula for plays, such as "a book of the book called . . ." or (as above) "a playbook entitled . . ." This suggests that on this occasion and others, perhaps when the wardens were not satisfied that a publisher had the permission of the owners to print a play (as in James Roberts' entry of *The Merchant of Venice* on July 22, 1598), the acting company's "book" had to be produced. This "book" was usually far too valuable to be used for the printing process (unless the play was no longer active in the repertory). So even if it had been given the "authority" of the print censor, and the "license" of the Stationers' wardens, another copy would be used to print from. But at least the appearance of the acting "book" in the hands of a publisher wishing to register his claim to a play would probably have been more persuasive to a doubtful warden than another type of manuscript copy. Any other Stationers' Company member who felt that his right to a licensed play (or any other type of text) had been infringed could complain and seek redress. However, as Peter Blayney (1990) has demonstrated, members of the Company often worked out private deals among themselves that were never overseen or recorded by the Company's wardens. If the publisher who had been granted the censor's "authority" and the Stationers' Company's "license" for a play was not a printer, he would need to hire a master printer (who may have had one or more apprentice printers in his shop) to do the job for him. The publisher would usually supply the paper, at least, and his cost for producing the book had to be weighed against this and other expenses and what he would make from selling it.

The largest format (producing the largest book) used by printers was the folio, which would be printed from formes set with two pages per side, producing four pages in all (on both sides of a single sheet). A folio format would be appropriate for a large, expensive, and prestigious history book, such as Holinshed's *Chronicles* (1577), or a large set of literary works, such as the collected works of Jonson (1616), Shakespeare (1623), and Beaumont and Fletcher (1647). But plays printed individually were not as commercially profitable or marketable as other types of literary works, so they were usually printed using the cheaper format, the quarto, set from formes with four pages per side, with eight pages per sheet. Other common formats, in descending order of size from the folio and quarto, were octavo (with eight pages per side, 16 pages per sheet), and duodecimo (12 pages per side, 24 pages in total). The costs in paper and labor of printing a folio would be considerably more than those for a quarto. But, conversely, the smaller the format became, the more intricate and time-consuming the layout of the forme, for pages were not set in numerical order but in the order required to make them numerical once the sheet of paper was folded.[21] The format would also determine where the watermarks (resulting from the shape of wires in the frame or mould in which paper was made from a mixture of wet rags) and chain lines (the vertical lines from the frame) would appear. In a folio page, the watermark could appear in the middle of one or more pages, and the chain lines would run vertically. However, in a quarto, the watermark could end up sideways in the middle (and thus partially or wholly obscured by the binding) of two pages, with the chain lines running horizontally.

Numerous types of texts served as printer's copy in this period. If an acting company still had access to a dramatist's foul papers, perhaps made obsolete by a later fair copy, they could submit those to a printer, to avoid risking the loss of a more important copy. Or they could submit a transcript of any stage of a play's transmission: an early or later fair copy (authorial or scribal) of the foul papers or of the "book" or another transcript, or the manuscript especially copied for the printer (by a conscientious dramatist like Jonson or a scribe), or even an annotated copy of an early printed edition of the play. As noted above, the copy they could not afford to submit to the printing house would be the actual "book" or whatever other copy contained the license of the master of the revels, for once they surrendered this copy, they would have no protection against prosecution should a performance of the play provoke controversy in the future. Some acting companies may have loaned copies of their plays to printers, but the actual process of using a text to set type would incur some damage to it. This may be the reason no printer's copy (except for a few non-dramatic texts of this period) survives.

Before beginning to set type, the compositor would need to "cast off" his copy. That is, he would have to count off and mark (usually with a small symbol in the margin) the number of lines in the copy that he could fit onto each page. For example, a quarto usually contained between 38 and 39 lines of type per page. Casting off verse lines in a manuscript would be easy, but casting off prose lines (and long stage-directions as in dumb shows) would be more difficult. The more experienced a compositor was, the easier he would find it to cast off prose lines, or to squeeze in or stretch out type whenever he had not cast off correctly. Type was hand set, line by line, by the compositor, who picked up the correct letter, numeral, punctuation mark, or blank space type from his "case" and put it into his composing stick, which would accommodate a few lines. The compositor's case had its contents laid out in specific ways, with upper-case letters usually at the top and lower-case at the bottom. Letters were not always laid out alphabetically, but a compositor would become as familiar with the case's layout as a professional typist is with a computer keyboard. Thus he could set type into his composing stick by reaching for a piece of type without looking at the case. (This explains why words are occasionally misprinted with a wrong piece of type in place of the correct one to which it is adjacent in the compositor's case.) Once his compositor's stick was full, he would transfer the type to a page-sized tray (or a longer "galley" tray) until it was full, and then tie it up with string. When he had finished all the other pages to be printed in the forme, he would enclose the pages within a "chase" or frame, and then the forme would be ready to use.

When it came time to print, the forme would be locked into the printing press, with all the type daubed with ink. The pressmen would crank the press so that it would force a sheet of paper against the type. They would usually print off sample copies of each forme, proofread them, mark errors, and then stop the press to adjust the type and make corrections. But those sheets that were being run off before the press was stopped for correction would not be wasted, even though uncorrected, and would still be used. Nevertheless, careful proofreading seems to have been more common in the printing of the more luxurious folio-sized book, for some play quartos in this period show little stop-press correction. We know that at least one author, Jonson, stood in the printing house and read his own proofs. We also know of another dramatist, Chettle, who was himself a printer and member of the Stationers' Company. While we may not have as much direct or implied evidence about other dramatists, we cannot always conclude with certainty whether they did or did not concern themselves with the process of putting their plays into print.

For example, extant copies of printed quartos of Philip Massinger's plays *The Duke of Milan* (1623), *The Bondman* (1624), *The Roman Actor* (1629), *The Renegado* (1630),

The Picture (1630), and *The Emperour of the East* (1632) all show numerous corrections (and a few revisions) in his own hand (Greg, 1966a, 1966b). Whether Massinger took as much time correcting other errors during printing as he did afterwards is difficult to prove because we lack the corresponding evidence. It is only because these authorially annotated quartos still survive that we can see his continuing concern with the quality of his text, long after the foul papers left his hands. That such quartos may have once existed for the numerous other dramatists of this period, including Shakespeare, should at least be considered. Most Elizabethan and Jacobean dramatists probably continued to see their plays as their own artistic and intellectual property, perhaps without a finished or final form but as a continual work in progress.

With or without stop-press correction, the forme would be used to print as many copies of the pages as were required for the number of books to be sold. The sheets from this impression on the outer forme would then be hung to dry, and, once dry, the sheets could be turned over and pressed on to the inner forme for the next set of pages, and then dried again. Then the sheets would be bundled into like piles so that a worker could construct a book by picking up one sheet from each pile in the correct order. The sheets could then be left unfolded, if going to a binder, or folded, if being sent out for sale. For an expensive book, the publisher would usually be willing to pay a binder to sew the pages carefully together and then cover the book with leather or some other type of decorative material. Other copies could be left unbound so that buyers could later choose their own binding. However, most quartos were usually stitched lightly together through the spine, with a front cover consisting only of its title-page, or blank pages left over on a forme from printing the title-page, or some other scrap paper.

Pages were not usually numbered individually but carried "signatures" (used by printers to keep track of the order of pages printed), consisting of a numbered letter (such as "B3") printed on each recto page. Thus, in a quarto (in which, for example, the A signature has been reserved for prefatory material), for the first eight pages, there can be found signatures B1, B2, and B3 on the first three recto pages, with the fourth left blank, although it assumed the signature of B4. (We now identify the verso pages by the previous signature; hence the verso of B1 would be considered B1ᵛ.) This process would be repeated with each letter of the alphabet (except "J," which was usually seen as identical to "I," and "V," which would seem identical to "U"), until the correct number of pages was printed off. One or more sheets sewn together constitute a "gathering." If the sheets have been laid inside each other, rather than just situated on either side of each other, the gathering is "quired." If quired, the pages have not been printed by single sets of an inner and outer forme (to print four pages, for a folio, or eight, for a quarto, at a time), but by multiple sets of formes (for example, three sets of an inner and outer forme to create 12 folio pages at a time), in a grouping sufficient to place the pages in the proper order when bound.

Unless the book had been printed illegally, the publisher would usually include on its title-page a notice of the bookseller who would act as the book's distributor, selling it wholesale (for about 4 pence per quarto) to other Stationers' Company members or retail (for about 6 pence per quarto) (Blayney, 1997, 411). For example, the title-page of the anonymous play *The Taming of a Shrew* (either a source play or analogue of Shakespeare's *The Taming of the Shrew*) notes that copies have been "Printed at London by Peter Short and *are to be sold by Cuthbert Burbie, at his* shop at the Royall Exchange." While this imprint tells us that Peter Short was the printer and Cuthbert Burby the bookseller, we cannot distinguish which of them (or what other person) served as publisher. Some title-pages offer more information, using the formula "Printed for . . . by . . . and are to be sold by . . . ," for example, but imprints cannot always be trusted to give us the exact (or even the correct) information about who was involved in a play's publication.

Folios would, of course, fetch a much higher price than the 6 pence for quarto texts. Blayney notes that the 1616 Jonson folio sold for between 9 and 10 shillings unbound, and 13 to 14 shillings with a calf-skin binding, while the 1623 Shakespeare folio probably sold for 15 shillings unbound, 16–18 shillings with a plain binding, and £1 with a leather binding. Blayney estimates that a publisher would need to spend approximately £9 to acquire the authority and license, purchase the paper and pay all printing expenses (to compositors, proofreaders, pressmen, etc.) for a run of 800 books printed in quarto format. Even if he sold all his copies, he would have made relatively little profit (Blayney, 1991, 2, 32; 1997, 406–9, 410–11, 422, n. 61). Neither did folio publishers become rich from their endeavours, even when they pointed out how cost-efficient their texts were for buyers. For example, the very experienced printer Humphrey Moseley noted in the 1647 Beaumont and Fletcher folio: "Heretofore when Gentlemen desired the copy of any of these Playes, the meanest piece here . . . cost them more than foure times the price you pay for the whole Volume" (Beaumont and Fletcher, 1647, sig. A3ᵛ). The type of person who had the spare cash to purchase quartos and folios could vary from a nearly impoverished university or law student to a middle-class businessman (or his wife) to a prosperous aristocrat. Moseley also claims that had he included too many plays, "it would have rendred the Booke so Volumnious, that *Ladies* and *Gentlewomen* would have found it scarce manageable, who in Workes of this nature must first be remembred" (sig A3). Whether Moseley was worried about the intellectual or the physical weight of the books for female readers is not clear, but his admonition that gentlewomen must be remembered "first" in the publication of plays suggests that they were avid consumers of this theatrical-turned-literary product.

Jonson participated in the printing of his plays in folio, but the Shakespeare and the Beaumont and Fletcher folio editions were put together after their deaths by their fellow actors. These three dramatists did not contribute to the enshrining of their rep-utation in expensive, luxurious, and prestigious volumes for literary audiences. Ben Jonson claims in his elegy to his fellow dramatist and actor in the Shakespeare folio, "Thou art a Moniment, without a tombe, / And art aliue still, while thy Booke doth liue, / And we haue wits to read." Two pages earlier, Heminge and Condell had acknowledged to their readers that one of their main aims in collecting Shakespeare's works was financial: "It is now publique, & you wil stand for your priuiledges wee know: to read, and censure. Do so, but buy it first. That doth commend a Booke, the Stationer saies" (Hinman, 1968, 9, 7). A dramatist who engaged in a financial agreement with an acting company manager or sharer (such as Henslowe or Burbage) in composing a play eventually engaged, with or without his consent, in a financial agreement with his publishers. Another elegist in the Shakespeare folio claimed, "This Booke, / When Brasse and Marble fade, shall make thee looke / Fresh to all Ages" (Hinman, 1968, 15). All of those English Renaissance dramatists whose plays survived in print past their own generation have stayed fresh to the succeeding generations of readers, and their play-texts have been preserved not solely for reading audiences, but as theater scripts, for they remain, primarily, performing texts for generations of theater audiences. Here we have the final reminder that play-texts, which returned to their authors at various stages throughout their original transmission, move continually, and circularly, back to the theater, from whence they came.

NOTES

1   Two works I place in this category are Bowers (1966) and Werstine (1997). Bowers sets out numerous authoritative theories about their composition and transmission in his book, drawing from other scholars' work. Werstine, likewise, relies almost entirely on the work of others in discussing the characteristics and provenance of manuscripts.

2   Roslyn L. Knutson argues that this is typical "for a new play or a revival" (1997, 468).

3   In 1602, for example, Henslowe's entry for a 5-shilling advance to "antony monday & thomas deckers" in "earnest of a booke called Jeffae" is followed by another entry for a 20-shilling payment to "harey chettel for the mendynge of the fyrste parte of carnowlle wollsey" (purchased new from Chettle, Munday, and Michael Drayton in 1601). Thus he has contracted a new play called *Jeffa* (probably *Jephthah*) and has paid for revisions of an old one, *The First Part of {the life of} Cardinal Wolsey*, which he already owned. Neither play survives in print or manuscript, although Henslowe records payments he made to license, provide costumes for, and/or pay for wine at the first reading of the plays (Foakes and Rickert, 1961, 202, 183, 181, 201).

4   Robert Daborne promises in his correspondence with Henslowe, "One Tuesday night if y^u will appoynt J will meet y^u & m^r Allin [Edward Alleyn] & read some [portions of a new play] for J am vnwilling to read to ye general company till all be finisht" (Greg, 1907, 70).

5   A satirist chastised Greene in 1602 for "cony-catching" (or double-dealing one play to two buyers), demanding indignantly, "Ask the Queens Players, if you sold them not *Orlando Furioso* for twenty Nobles [worth about 10 shillings each] and when they were in the country, sold the same play to the Lord Admirals men for as much more" (Anon., 1592, C3—C3'). Henslowe records only one 1592 performance of the play by the Admiral's Men, collecting 16 shillings and 6 pence. If this was the total return on his investment, Henslowe paid dearly for Greene's "cony-catching" (Foakes and Rickert, 1961, 16).

6   Edward Knight, an experienced playhouse scribe and official book-keeper of the King's Men acting company, consulted the "fowle papers of the author" in recopying Fletcher's play *Bonduca* (British Library Additional MS 36758), and Daborne used the term "foule" sheet in correspondence with Henslowe. Daborne also refers repeatedly to the more polished "fayre" sheets he will supply Henslowe of his foul papers (Greg, 1907, 78, 69, 72). The theatrical censor Sir Henry Herbert demands a "fayre" copy of the next play he is expected to license while chastising the writer of the manuscript of *The Launching of the Mary* (British Library Egerton MS 1994).

7   See the original manuscript (British Library Egerton MS 1994) or Brown's Malone Society printed facsimile (1953).

8   Other foul papers I would include are Walter Mountfort's *The Launching of the Mary* and the first two and a quarter pages (which I believe to be in the author's hand) of the manuscript of Jonson's 1609 *Entertainment at Britain's Burse* (Public Record Office Manuscript, State Papers 14/44/62*).

9   Both Beal (1998) and Woudhuysen (1996) discuss the role of scribes in English Renaissance literary culture.

10 British Library MS Egerton 1994, f. 349ᵛ. On Herbert's fairly typical treatment of one manuscript see Walter's preface to his Malone Society Reprints edition of *The Launching of the Mary* (1933, x).

11 Jonson, with *Eastward Ho*, and Middleton, with *A Game at Chess*, profited from the notoriety of their scandalous plays. See "Life of Jonson" and *Conversations with Drummond* in Herford et al. (1925, I, 38–9, 140), and Bald's edition of *A Game at Chess* (1929, 162). For other cases, see Dutton, (1991, 182ff).

12 See the Malone Society Reprints' edition of each of the first three, Vols 65 (1933), 55 (1927), 71 (1936), and Gerritsen's facsimile edition of *The Honest Man's Fortune* (1952).

13 Humphrey Moseley, who printed the collected plays of Beaumont and Fletcher in 1647, notes in his address to readers, "When these *Comedies* and *Tragedies* were presented on the Stage, the *Actours* omitted some *Scenes* and Passages (with the *Authour's* consent) as occasion led them" (Beaumont and Fletcher, 1647, sig. A3).

14 These include manuscripts made by professional scribe Ralph Crane of Middleton's *A Game at Chess* and *The Witch* and of Fletcher's (?) *Demetrius and Enanthe*.

15 Ben Jonson noted in prefaces to *Sejanus* and *Epicoene, or The Silent Woman* exactly what he had done to make them suitable for *reading* audiences (Herford et al., 1925, IV, 351, V, 161). If we can trust Jonson, dramatists who prepared printer's copy could provide a text of the play as first composed, or they could slightly or extensively correct or amend the text used in the theater. In any case, they would be reclaiming their texts to suit their own artistic requirements.

16 Greg notes that the King's Men asked the lord chamberlain to prevent publication of their plays in 1619, 1637, 1641, and possibly 1600 in order to keep them out of the hands of other acting companies (1956, 77).

17 This is the amount offered by the character John Danter (named for the notorious printer) in *The Second Part of the Return from Parnassus*, I.iii. Blayney (1997, 395–6) offers other contemporary allusions to this amount.

18 Blayney disputes Greg's interpretation of the contemporary terms of "authority," "license," and "entrance"; I cautiously use Blayney's definition and interpretation of these terms (Blayney, 1997, 400–4).

19 Blayney (1997, 404) disagrees with Greg (1956) that entry in the Stationers' Register was required. I am not entirely convinced by Blayney's argument here, but I use his figure of 4 pence for entries, even though the entries of individual plays give the fee as 6 pence. Unless this fee records the "license" and not the "entry" fee, Blayney is in error.

20 See n. 5.

21 I draw most of my discussion of printing-house practices from McKerrow (1927) and Gaskell (1978).

References and Further Reading

Anon. (1592). *The Defence of Conny Catching*. London: Printed by A. I. for Thomas Gubbins.

Arber, Edward, ed. (1875). *A Transcript of the Registers of the Company of Stationers of London, 1554–1640*. London: privately printed.

Bald, R. C., ed. (1929). *A Game at Chess*. Cambridge: Cambridge University Press.

Beal, Peter (1998). *In Praise of Scribes: Manuscripts and their Makers in Seventeenth-Century England*. Oxford: Clarendon Press.

Beaumont, Francis and John Fletcher (1647). *Comedies and Tragedies Written by Francis Beaumont and John Fletcher*. London: Humphrey Moseley.

Bentley, G. E. (1971). *The Profession of Dramatist in Shakespeare's Time, 1590–1642*. Princeton: Princeton University Press.

Blayney, Peter (1990). *The Booksellers in Paul's Cross Churchyard*. London: Bibliographical Society.

Blayney, Peter (1991). *The First Folio of Shakespeare*. Washington, DC: Folger Library Publications.

Blayney, Peter (1997). "The printing of playbooks." In *A New History of Early English Drama*, eds John D. Cox and David Scott Kastan. New York: Columbia University Press.

Bowers, Fredson (1966). *On Editing Shakespeare*. Charlottesville: University Press of Virginia.

Brown, Arthur, ed. (1953). *The Captives by Thomas Heywood*. Oxford: Oxford University Press.

Darnton, Robert (1990). *The Kiss of Lamourette: Reflections in Cultural History*. London: Faber and Faber.

Dutton, Richard (1991). *Mastering the Revels: The Regulation and Censorship of English Renaissance Drama*. Iowa City: University of Iowa Press.

Foakes, R. A., and R. T. Rickert, eds (1961). *Henslowe's Diary*. Cambridge: Cambridge University Press.

Gaskell, Philip (1978). *A New Introduction to Bibliography*. Oxford: Oxford University Press.

Gerritsen, Johan, ed. (1952). *The Honest Man's Fortune*. Groningen: J. B. Wolters.

Greg, W. W. (1907). *The Henslowe Papers: Being Documents Supplementary to the Henslowe's Diary*. London: A. H. Bullen.

Greg, W. W. (1956). *Some Aspects and Problems of London Publishing between 1550 and 1650*. Oxford: Clarendon Press.

Greg, W. W. (1966a). "Massinger's autograph corrections in *The Duke of Milan*, 1623." In *The Collected Papers of Sir Walter Greg*. Oxford: Clarendon Press.

Greg, W. W. (1966b). "More Massinger corrections." In *The Collected Papers of Sir Walter Greg*. Oxford: Clarendon Press.

Herford, C. H., Percy Simpson, and Evelyn Simpson, eds (1925). *Ben Jonson*. Oxford: Clarendon Press.

Hinman, Charlton, ed. (1968). *The Norton Facsimile: The First Folio of Shakespeare*. London: Paul Hamlyn.

Hoy, Cyrus (1956–62). "The shares of Fletcher and his collaborators in the Beaumont and Fletcher canon." *Studies in Bibliography* 8–15.

Knutson, Roslyn L. (1997). "The repertory." In *A New History of Early English Drama*, eds John D. Cox and David Scott Kastan. New York: Columbia University Press.

McKerrow, Ronald B. (1927). *An Introduction to Bibliography for Literary Students*. Oxford: Clarendon Press.

Walter, John Henry, ed. (1933). *The Launching of the Mary*. Oxford: Oxford University Press.

Werstine, Paul (1997). "Plays in manuscript." In *A New History of Early English Drama*, eds John D. Cox and David Scott Kastan. New York: Columbia University Press.

Woudhuysen, H. R. (1996). *Sir Philip Sidney and the Circulation of Manuscripts 1558–1640*. Oxford: Clarendon Press.

13

Playing Companies and Repertory

Roslyn L. Knutson

A playing company in early modern England was known by the name of its patron, as in the "Earl of Oxford's Men," or by its playing venue, as in "the Children of Paul's." Occasionally a company was known by its players: the title-page of *A Knack to Know a Knave* advertised the play by way of its lead, Edward Alleyn, and its clown, William Kempe.[1] Also, according to Scott McMillin and Sally-Beth MacLean, a company established its identity by means of its "acting style, its staging methods, its kinds of versification, [and] its sense of what constructed a worthwhile repertory of plays."[2] Unfortunately, most of the play titles and even more of the texts owned by companies have not survived; it is therefore difficult to identify early modern English playing companies by their dramaturgy. Nevertheless, a few repertory lists do exist: for example, the titles in the accounts of the Revels Office for productions by various companies at court, 1572–85; titles in the performance lists and payments to dramatists in the book of accounts kept by Philip Henslowe at the Rose and Fortune playhouses, 1592–1603; and titles licensed by Sir Henry Herbert, master of the revels, and entered in his office-book, 1622–42. It is from these, supplemented by the attribution of company ownership on the title-pages of plays in print, that a discussion of playing companies and their repertory may begin.

The adult companies with a significant presence at court in the 1570s and early 1580s included the Earl of Leicester's Men, the Earl of Sussex's Men, and the Earl of Warwick's Men; also at court were boy companies including those from the Merchant Taylors School, the Queen's Chapel, and Paul's School. The kinds of plays performed by the boys appear similar, if the titles of their offerings are a fair measure. Each relied on classical materials, romances, and the moral play: *Ariodante and Genevora* and *Perseus and Andromeda* (Merchant Taylors); *Narcissus* and *Loyalty and Beauty* (Chapel); *Scipio Africanus* and *The History of Error* (Paul's). In the mid-1580s John Lyly began to write for the company at Paul's and the Children of the Chapel (now at Blackfriars). A number of Lyly's plays survive, including *Campaspe* (Q1584), *Endimion* (Q1591), and *Midas* (Q1592). These texts suggest that the repertories of the boy companies, which continued to be identified with stories from classical history and mythology, acquired a witty edge that perhaps masked commentary on political issues.

Repertory evidence for the early men's companies also comes primarily from the titles of plays in the revels accounts at court. But a somewhat fuller picture of their business is possible because, in their desire for a license and a place to play in the London area, they left more of a paper trail. In 1572 Leicester's Men, a touring company since their formation in 1559, asked their patron, Robert Dudley, to certify them with a license. Six players signed the letter: James Burbage, John Perkin, John Lanham, William Johnson, Robert Wilson, and Thomas Clarke. By this time Leicester's Men probably had already occupied the Red Lion playhouse (see chapter 11 above). The repertory of Leicester's Men included offerings at court such as *Philemon and Philecia*, *The Collier*, and *A Greek Maid*; *The Three Ladies of London* (if its dramatist, R. W., was their Robert Wilson), and *Samson* (if they played at the Red Lion). These titles suggest a repertory like those of the boy companies in its romances and moral plays, broadened by the inclusion of biblical subjects and folk or estate characters.

The Earl of Sussex's Men, under the patronage of Thomas Radcliffe, were a touring company at their inception in 1569; when Radcliffe became the lord chamberlain in 1572, the company also began to play at court, making 13 appearances through 1582–3. Judging from the titles recorded in the revels accounts, 1578–80, Sussex's Men (also known as the Chamberlain's Men) performed classical and romance materials mixed with commoner subjects: *The Rape of the Second Helen*, *Sarpedon*, *Portio and Demorantes*, *The Cruelty of a Stepmother*, and *Murderous Michael*. The famous clown Richard Tarlton played with the company in the 1570s; his talents might account for the large crowd at a performance of another of their offerings, *The Red Knight*, at Bristol in 1575. Sussex's Men appeared at court in 1591–2 (now under the patronage of Thomas' brother, Henry) and at the Rose playhouse from December 27, 1593, through February 6, 1594 (now under the patronage of Robert, son of Henry). In a joint venture with the Queen's Men, with whom they had played occasionally while touring in 1590–1, Sussex's Men played again at the Rose for the first eight days of April 1594.

Philip Henslowe recorded the titles of twelve plays performed at the Rose by Sussex's Men, 1593–4, and all are different from the plays entered for the company in the revels accounts, 1572–83. In comparison, Sussex's Rose repertory appears much more diverse in materials popular with general audiences. Two of the plays show the influence of the latest fashion in tragedy, the revenge play: *The Jew of Malta* and *Titus Andronicus*. Five suggest the recent fashion of English chronicles: for example, *Buckingham* and *King Lud*. One of these plays survives, *George a Greene, or the Pinner of Wakefield*; its text features a stout-hearted patriot in the title character, George, plus the folk hero, Robin Hood.[3] Other of Sussex's offerings appear compatible with the 1570s court repertory in that they suggest the Corpus Christi and moral plays, medieval romance, love stories about fetching female commoners, and true crime; yet the titles of the plays at the Rose suggest that the material was given a more contemporary spin: for example, *Abraham and Lot*, *God Speed the Plough*, *Huon of Bordeaux*, *Fair Maid of Italy*, and *Friar Francis*.

The earl of Warwick, Ambrose Dudley, patronized a company contemporaneous with that of his brother, the earl of Leicester. In the 1570s Warwick's Men, like Leicester's, acquired experienced players in Jerome Savage and the Dutton brothers (John and Lawrence). Also like Leicester's, the company acquired a playhouse, which was built in 1576 in Newington, about a mile south of London Bridge.[4] Although that playhouse was arguably the more significant to the development of commercial theater, the performances of Warwick's Men at court in 1576–80 provide the only record of their repertory offerings. By title, these plays sound like items that would succeed with both public and royal audiences: for example, familiar romance material (*The Irish Knight*, *The Knight in the Burning Rock*, and *The Four Sons of Fabius*) and a love story or two (*The Painter's Daughter*, *The Three Sisters of Mantua*). In 1580 the Dutton brothers transferred their affiliation to Oxford's Men; however, other members of Warwick's Men (or perhaps new ones) played in the provinces for a few more years.

A significant event in the history of English playing companies occurred in March 1583 when Sir Francis Walsingham authorized Edmund Tilney, master of revels, to form a company under the patronage of Queen Elizabeth. More is known about their players and repertory than about any company until the formation of the Admiral's Men and Chamberlain's Men in 1594.[5] Tilney chose players from Leicester's Men (William Johnson, John Lanham, Robert Wilson), Sussex's Men (John Adams, Richard Tarlton), and the former Warwick's Men (John Dutton, later also Lawrence). In addition, John Bentley, Lionel Cooke, John Garland, Tobias Mills, John Singer, and John Towne joined the Queen's Men in 1583. For the next five years, if not the next ten, the Queen's Men dominated theatrical activity at court, in the provinces, and possibly also in London. At a provincial performance in Norwich in June 1583, several players challenged a customer who did not want to pay, and a by-stander was killed in the resulting affray. In London, the Queen's Men did not establish themselves at a particular playhouse, but to civic officials they seemed to be everywhere. The Privy Council heard complaints in November 1584 that the previous year "all of the places of playeing were filled with men calling themselues the Quenes players" (Chambers, 1923, IV, 302).

Despite their hegemony, the Queen's Men faded as a court and London presence after 1588. One possible reason is that several leading players died, including Richard Tarlton. But another, according to McMillin and MacLean, is the challenge to their dramaturgy presented by new theatrical talents such as Christopher Marlowe. Walsingham's motive in the formation of the Queen's Men had been to use the theater "in the service of a Protestant ideology . . . [and] the 'truth' of Tudor history" (McMillin and MacLean, 1998, 33). Nine plays with title-page advertisements of the Queen's Men and printed between 1590 and 1599 suggest how that agenda was carried out. Four were specifically British history plays: *The Famous Victories of Henry V*, *King Leir*, *The Troublesome Reign of King John*, and *The True Tragedy of Richard III*. In a fifth, *Three*

Lords and Three Ladies of London, England defeats the Spanish Armada. A sixth, *Friar Bacon and Friar Bungay*, features an English wizard and a sub-plot of royal romance; a seventh, *The Old Wives Tale*, is a series of English folktales. In these plays there is evidence of the acting style, staging, and versification that made the Queen's Men the premier troupe of their time; yet by 1590 that very dramaturgy led to their commercial decline. These plays are highly visual, depending on the skills of the players with "standard gestures, intonations, costumes, wigs, false noses, dialects, postures, gags, songs, and pratfalls" (McMillin, 1972, 14). The stories are overplotted, and a common verse form is the fourteener (McMillin and MacLean, 1998, 124–54). This dramaturgy could not compete for long with the high astounding terms and moral ambiguity of Marlowe's *Tamburlaine* or Shakespeare's *Richard III*. Remnants of the old company – invigorated with recruits such as Francis Henslowe, George Attewell, Robert Nichols, and Richard Alleyn – continued as a provincial company. They might have played briefly at the Swan playhouse, built in 1595 by Francis Langley. But after 1603, when some of the Queen's players acquired a new patron in the duke of Lennox, the company slipped further into commercial insignificance.

The Queen's Men, having dominated performances at court since their formation in March 1583, had company in the winter of 1588–9: the Children of Paul's gave one performance, and the Admiral's Men gave two. Over the next few years, the balance of court appearances continued to shift away from the Queen's Men. In 1590–1, Strange's Men performed at court twice; in 1591–2 Strange's Men gave six performances, Sussex's Men one, and Hertford's Men one. In 1592–3 Pembroke's Men appeared at court for the first time, adding two performances to the three by Strange's Men (who would become Derby's Men in September 1593). Although the Queen's Men gave the only performance at court in 1593–4 (on Twelfth Night), the transition to other men's companies was accomplished: in 1594–5 the Admiral's Men and the Chamberlain's Men divided the five court performances.

In a sense, then, the story of playing companies and repertory for 1588–94 is the story of companies that were not the Queen's Men. The names of these "other" companies are known: the Admiral's Men, Sussex's Men, Pembroke's Men, Strange's/Derby's Men. The players are also known: Edward Alleyn, Richard Burbage, Richard Cowley, George Bryan, William Kempe, Thomas Pope, Augustine Phillips, John Sincler, and William Sly (to name a few). What is unclear is the match of companies and players. Alleyn, for example, belonged to the Admiral's Men in 1589 (his career probably began with Worcester's Men *c.*1583), but he was touring with Strange's Men in 1593. Will Sly and John Sincler played with Strange's Men in 1592–3 (if the plot of *2 Seven Deadly Sins* belonged to this company at this time), but they were apparently Pembroke's Men in 1593–4 (if Pembroke's Men at this time owned texts in which these players' names occur). The advertisement of company ownership on the title-page of the 1594 quarto of *Titus Andronicus* illustrates the instability of lines dividing companies: the title-page assigns the play to "the Earle of *Darbie*, Earle of *Pembrooke*, and Earle of *Sussex* their Seruants." This advertisement may reveal serial company ownership, or it may reveal an amalgamation in one company of players who retained their discrete patronage (for example, in 1593 Edward Alleyn called himself an Admiral's man although he was touring with Lord Strange's Men). Either way, it suggests the expediencies characteristic of the business of playing in the early 1590s. The instability was temporary: out of this reservoir of players and patrons came two companies – the Admiral's Men and the Chamberlain's Men – that survived into the reign of Charles I with a relatively stable membership, a solid financial structure, their own playhouses, and a huge repertory of commercially tested plays. But in 1588–94 this longevity could not have been confidently foretold.

Plagues in 1588, 1592, and 1593 contributed to the uncertainty of theatrical conditions by taking star performers such as Richard Tarlton and forcing playhouse closures, thus reducing the opportunities for companies to sustain runs in London. Political, financial, and perhaps even personal disputes contributed to a volatility in the playhouse world. The Martin Marprelate controversy of 1588–90 played a role by engaging companies in political arguments against anti-theatrical critics. It may be that John Lyly, by his participation in the controversy, inadvertently caused the closure of the playhouse at Paul's at this time (the Children of the Chapel had ceased playing *c.*1584; Dutton, 1991, 76–7). In 1589 James Burbage was involved in a tangle of lawsuits over matters including revenue at the Theatre, the playhouse in Shoreditch built in 1576 largely with money from his brother-in-law, John Brayne. In 1592 John Alleyn, older brother of Edward and player with the company currently at the Theatre, was drawn into the suit as a witness, and his testimony did not help the Burbages. In 1590–1 Alleyn had had his own dispute with Burbage over revenue owed to Alleyn's company for playing. Perhaps as a result of these events, or perhaps by coincidence, a company under the patronage of Ferdinando Strange began to play at the Rose, a relatively new playhouse in Southwark constructed in 1587 by Philip Henslowe. Just prior to the arrival of Strange's Men, Henslowe had remodeled the playhouse, enlarging the area of the yard and the capacity of the galleries. Due to forced playhouse closings, Strange's Men received a license for touring in May 1593; the company, becoming Derby's Men in September when Ferdinando's father died, played in the provinces into the winter. In 1592 a company under the patronage of Henry Herbert, earl of Pembroke, began to appear in the provinces, at court, and perhaps in London. On September 28, 1593, Henslowe wrote to Edward Alleyn that Pembroke's Men had aborted their summer tour for financial reasons: "they cane not saue their carges . . . & weare fayne to pane the⟨r⟩ parell for ther carge" (Foakes and Rickert, 1961, 280). A Pembroke's company toured in the provinces in 1595–6, and perhaps that same version of the company played at the Swan playhouse in 1597. In late summer, however, the players broke with Francis Langley, owner of the playhouse, and many joined the Admiral's Men, effectively bringing Pembroke's Men to an end. The quarrel with Langley and related events are known as the "Isle of Dogs Affair," from the name of a coincidentally controversial play by Thomas Nashe, Ben Jonson, and one or more other players.

Had there not been disruptions of playing due to plague and other factors, it is possible that the emergence of stable companies settled in London for lengthy runs might have occurred much sooner than 1594. Certainly the repertories of the companies in the years from 1588 to 1594 suggest the availability of generically diverse, theatrically innovative, and poetically exciting material. The repertory of Strange's Men at the Rose in 1592–3 is exemplary. The company performed 27 plays, three of which appear to have been tragedies, nine to have been history plays, and the remainder some form of comedy. Two of the tragedies were revenge plays: *The Spanish Tragedy* and *The Jew of Malta*; the third, *Machiavel*, might have been. The history plays represented material as diverse as the English chronicles (*Harry of Cornwall*, *Henry VI*), the Mediterranean world (*Titus and Vespasian*, *Muly Mollocco*), empire in the Far East (*Tamar Cham*, parts one and two), and European religio-political turmoil (*Massacre at Paris*). The comedies were equally diverse, including a magician play (*Friar Bacon*), a romance (*Orlando Furioso*), a moral history (*A Knack to Know a Knave*), a biblical moral (*A Looking Glass for London and England*), a pastoral (*Cloris and Ergasto*), a craft play (*The Tanner of Denmark*), and a "wonders" narrative (*Sir John Mandeville*).[6] In addition to illustrating a range of popular formulas, the repertory of Strange's Men contained multi-part plays. *Four Plays in One* was possibly a set of related playlets like *2 Seven Deadly Sins*. *The Comedy of Don Horatio* was a prequel to *The Spanish Tragedy*. *Tamar Cham* was a two-part serial. *Friar Bacon*, if it was *John of Bordeaux*, was a sequel of sorts to *Friar Bacon and Friar Bungay* in the repertory of another company, the Queen's Men. *Machiavel* was perhaps a spin-off of *The Jew of Malta*, which Strange's Men were themselves playing.

Pembroke's Men had *Edward II*, *The Taming of a Shrew*, and *The True Tragedy of Richard Duke of York* (that is, *3 Henry VI*) in repertory in 1592–3; advertisements of the company appear on the title-pages of these plays in print.[7] Probably Pembroke's Men also had the companion to the latter play, *The First Part of the Contention of . . . York and Lancaster* (that is, *2 Henry VI*), although its quarto title-page does not so declare. These few plays are slender evidence of the company's identity in dramaturgy,[8] but they are nonetheless suggestive. *Edward II* draws on the material of the English chronicles. But, unlike the plain truth of Protestant Tudor ideology in repertory by the Queen's Men, this historical tragedy features male lovers, Ovid's erotic language, and a horrific on-stage death. The serial histories of *2* and *3 Henry VI*, which are likewise chronicle plays but epic in scope, dramatize the War of the Roses by staging the rebellion of Jack Cade, the adultery of a queen, the incantations of a sorceress–duchess, the rise of the ruthless Yorks, and one pyrrhic battle after another. The one comedy, *The Taming of a Shrew*, offered a flamboyant battle of the sexes, a testing of the bride in the wedding wager, and the carnival frame of a drunkard who is lord for a day.[9]

But even more than by the specific items in their repertory, the companies of Strange's Men and Pembroke's Men signaled by their commerce with dramatists that something unprecedented was happening: the number of talented young poets who expected to make a living from their pen was growing, and their scripts were being acquired by companies who were not the Queen's Men. Strange's Men in 1592–3 had plays by Robert Greene, Thomas Lodge in collaboration with Greene, Thomas Kyd,

Christopher Marlowe, and William Shakespeare. Pembroke's Men had one play by Marlowe and two by Shakespeare. Furthermore, both companies had the services of stage-savvy writers who now are known only as "anonymous" but who could turn out a script by themselves or with collaborators in a few weeks' time. The availability of these dramatists to companies with openended leases at London playhouses enabled the expansion of the market that distinguishes the decade of 1594–1603.

On May 14, 1594, the Admiral's Men performed *The Jew of Malta* at the Rose playhouse. Except for a brief run at the playhouse in Newington in June, the company thus began a six-year run at the Rose, which extended to a run of more than 20 years at the Fortune playhouse (built by Edward Alleyn and Philip Henslowe in 1600 for the company's exclusive use). The Admiral's Men were not an entirely new company in 1594. Charles Howard, their patron, had sponsored a company in 1576 while he was deputy to the earl of Sussex, then lord chamberlain. Howard became lord admiral in 1585, and his company appears in records of provincial and London performances into 1591, when its lead player, Edward Alleyn (and no doubt others) performed with members of Strange's Men until the reconstitution of the company in May 1594. Sometime after 1585, the Admiral's Men acquired *Tamburlaine* by Christopher Marlowe, and soon afterwards *Tamburlaine, Part II*;[10] they also acquired *The Battle of Alcazar* by George Peele and *The Wounds of Civil War* by Thomas Lodge. In October 1592 Alleyn married Joan Woodward, stepdaughter of Philip Henslowe, thus cementing the professional and family ties that would guarantee the Admiral's Men a playhouse, quality players, and smart financial management.

The repertory acquired by the Admiral's Men is *the* measure of successful theatrical commerce, 1594–1603. Henslowe's book of accounts contains a calendar of performances for the company from May 14, 1594, to November 5, 1597; it contains entries of payments for playbooks, apparel, and properties from August 25, 1597, to May 9, 1603. These records indicate much of the activity at the Rose and Fortune playhouses. The playlists of 1594–7 show that the company performed an average of 33 plays a year, divided fairly evenly between offerings being continued from the previous season and new plays, plus a couple of revivals. Most of the plays were comedies or histories, but the few tragedies tended to receive the longest runs. The titles suggest trends in popular subject matter and genre to which all the companies responded. For example, in November 1595 the Admiral's Men acquired a chronicle play called *Henry V*, which they performed 13 times through July 15, 1596. Perhaps in this same year, the Queen's Men were performing *The Famous Victories of Henry V* at the Swan, and the Chamberlain's Men were performing *1 Henry IV* at the Theatre. In May 1597 the Admiral's Men acquired *The Comedy of Humours* by George Chapman (a.k.a. *A Humorous Day's Mirth*), and soon the Chamberlain's Men acquired Jonson's *Every Man In his Humour*. The domestic prodigal play, *Patient Grissel*, which the Admiral's Men performed in 1599–1600, was soon copied by Worcester's Men with the offerings of *How a Man May Choose a Good Wife from a Bad* and *A Woman Killed with Kindness*. Furthermore, the repertory of the Admiral's Men illustrates the popularity of the multi-part play, not only in the genre of history (for instance, the four-part *Civil Wars of France*, 1598–9) but also in comedic material (for instance, *The Blind Beggar of Bednal Green* and its parts).

The company of Henry Carey, lord chamberlain, first appears in theater records in Henslowe's book of accounts in a set of performances in June at the Newington playhouse with the Admiral's Men. They appeared at court over Christmas, 1594–5, and three members served as payees: Richard Burbage, William Kempe, and William Shakespeare. Other documents indicate that George Bryan, Henry Condell, John Heminges, Augustine Phillips, Thomas Pope, John Sincler, and Will Sly also joined the company at its start. The company played at Burbage's Theatre until 1597, then moved to the adjacent Curtain until the Globe was built in 1599. At the Newington playhouse, the Chamberlain's Men performed *Titus Andronicus*, *Hester and Ahasuerus*, *Hamlet*, and *The Taming of a Shrew*.[11] No doubt their players brought additional play-books from their former companies, and presumably Shakespeare's works to date were among these, but otherwise there is no sure way to identify the company's acquisitions. The Chamberlain's Men's repertory in subsequent years included the anonymous plays *Mucedorus*, *A Larum for London*, and *A Warning for Fair Women*; Ben Jonson's *Every Man In his Humour* and *Every Man Out of his Humour*; and Thomas Dekker's *Satiromastix*. Indirectly, Heminges and Condell provided an approximation of a repertory list for the Chamberlain's Men by publishing the First Folio in 1623, for Shakespeare's collected works probably mimic the company's general holdings. In 1594–1603 specifically, the majority of his plays were comedies or histories. The comedies covered the popular forms of Roman street drama, pastoral, and humours. One comedy, unique for the genre in 1595, appears to have had a sequel, now lost (*Love's Labor's Won*). Another, a satire, exploited the matter of Troy. Eight of the nine histories were serial chronicle plays. The tragic characters, except for the star-crossed lovers in *Romeo and Juliet* and the political assassins of *Julius Caesar*, were revengers.

Two men's companies in London took advantage of a new theater, the Boar's Head, built in 1598 (see chapter 11 above). One, Derby's Men, may be traced only in the provinces after their patron died in April 1594 and after many of their players joined the Admiral's Men or Chamberlain's Men in May–June 1594. The other, Worcester's Men (under the patronage of William and Edward Somerset, earls of Worcester, 1548–89 and 1589–1628), offered the Queen's Men some provincial competition in 1583–5 with players such as Edward Alleyn, Richard Jones, and James Tunstall. Alleyn and Tunstall were Admiral's Men in 1589 and 1594, a fact that suggests some permutation of Worcester's Men into the Admiral's company; but through the 1590s until 1601, Worcester's Men performed primarily (if not exclusively) in the provinces. The construction of the Boar's Head provided an opportunity for Robert Browne of Derby's Men to become a theatrical entrepreneur. In 1599 Browne leased the playhouse (now remodeled) and established his company not only with plays such as the two-part *Edward IV* but also with comedies penned by their patron (William Stanley, earl of Derby, 1594–1642). The company appeared at court, 1599–1601. In the autumn of 1601, Browne sublet the Boar's Head to Worcester's Men (now merged with Oxford's Men), and the company performed plays such as *The Weakest Goeth to*

the Wall and *How a Man May Choose a Good Wife from a Bad*, with scripts by Thomas
Heywood. Worcester's Men appeared at court, 1601–2; in the late summer of 1602,
they moved to the Rose, where they played until the death of Queen Elizabeth in
March 1603 and the onset of plague in May shut down the playhouses. By October
of 1603 Robert Browne had died of that plague. Browne's wife, Susan, later married
Thomas Greene, who became a leader in Queen Anne's Men in 1605 (formerly
Worcester's Men), thus belatedly joining the companies that had played at the Boar's
Head since 1599.

When Worcester's Men moved to the Rose, Philip Henslowe began to keep payments for their scripts, properties, and apparel in his book of accounts, August
1602–May 1603. Some of these plays undoubtedly remained in performance when
the company returned to the Boar's Head. While at the Rose, Worcester's Men
acquired at least one tragedy from Thomas Heywood in 1603, *A Woman Killed with
Kindness*. No other play-texts survive from Worcester's listings, as far as is known, but
the presence of titles such as *Shore's Wife*, the two-part *Lady Jane*, and the two-part
Black Dog of Newgate suggest the continuing popularity of both stories from the
English chronicles and multi-part plays. The proverbial titles of *Christmas Comes but
Once a Year* and *The Blind Eats Many a Fly*, as well as *Medicine for a Curst Wife* (if it
was a "shrew" play), suggest familiar comedic folk materials. Further, it is possible to
assume that Worcester's Men were as competitive in the theatrical marketplace as the
Admiral's Men because they shared dramatists: for example, Henry Chettle, John Day,
Thomas Dekker, Richard Hathaway, Thomas Middleton, Wentworth Smith, and John
Webster. Also, Worcester's Men had veteran players: Christopher Beeston, John Duke,
William Kempe, and Robert Pallant. Heywood was both a player and a playwright.
By 1605, the company had acquired the patronage of Queen Anne and authoriza-
tion to play at the Boar's Head, Curtain, and new Red Bull playhouses. Christopher
Beeston became the manager, took the company to the new Cockpit playhouse in
1617, and held it together until the death of Queen Anne in 1619.

Two of the boys' companies that had been prominent at court in the 1580s reap-
peared as commercial companies in 1599–1600. The Children of Paul's, having
acquired the services of John Marston, opened at Paul's playhouse in 1599 with *Antonio
and Mellida*, followed soon by its second part, *Antonio's Revenge*. In addition to *Jack
Drum's Entertainment*, the company performed *The Maid's Metamorphosis*, *The Wisdom of
Doctor Dodypoll*, *Satiromastix* (also played by the Chamberlain's Men), and *Blurt, Master
Constable*. The Children of the Chapel, having acquired the services of Ben Jonson,
opened at Blackfriars in 1600, and they soon produced *Cynthia's Revels* and *Poetaster*.
Other repertory offerings included John Lyly's *Love's Metamorphosis*, and comedies by
George Chapman (such as *All Fools* and *May Day*). Business by the Children of Paul's
moved along without significant controversy until its close in the summer of 1606.
However, business by the Children of the Chapel – known as the Children of the
Queen's Revels in 1604 – soon attracted unwanted attention from powerful nobles,
who were offended by the increasingly harsh political satire in the company's plays.
The company persisted, following performances of Samuel Daniel's *Philotas* with the

collaborative *Eastward Ho*, and John Day's *Isle of Gulls* with Chapman's two-part *Byron*. Consequently, the queen withdrew her patronage. Henry Evans, who had leased Blackfriars for the company in 1603, relinquished the playhouse in 1608, and the company folded. Some of the players probably moved to the company of the King's Revels, newly formed at Whitefriars.

Soon after King James I came to the throne in March 1603, the royal family became the patrons of the men's companies: the Chamberlain's Men became the King's Men; the Admiral's Men became Prince Henry's Men (the Elector Palatine's Men in 1613, also Palsgrave's Men); and Worcester's Men became Queen Anne's Men. The Chamberlain's/King's Men, who had built the Globe playhouse in 1599, acquired the lease of Blackfriars in 1608.[12] Plague delayed all theatrical business until the fall of 1609, but presumably the King's Men then began to perceive their repertory in terms of both a small indoor playhouse and a large outdoor one. At about this time, the company started buying plays from the new collaborative team of Francis Beaumont and John Fletcher. Their innovation, the tragicomedy, contained masque elements and narrative motifs from the Greek romances. The First Folio (plus *Pericles* and *Two Noble Kinsmen*) shows that many of Shakespeare's scripts in this period reflect the innovations of Beaumont and Fletcher. The chamber accounts of performances at court, 1612–13, record that nine of the 20 performances by the King's Men were given to plays in this general category: *Philaster* (twice), *The Maid's Tragedy*, *The Tempest*, *A King and No King*, *The Twins Tragedy*, *The Winter's Tale*, *The Nobleman*, and *Cardenio*. Yet many of the old repertory items remained popular. Performances of *The Knot of Fools*, *Much Ado about Nothing* (twice), *The Merry Devil of Edmonton*, *Sir John Falstaff* (*Merry Wives of Windsor*?), *Othello*, *Caesars Tragedye* (*Julius Caesar*?), *A Bad Beginning Makes a Good Ending*, *The Captain*, *The Alchemist*, and *The Hotspurr* (*1 Henry IV*?) suggest the durability of the revenge play, classical history, chronicle history, magician play, and all varieties of comedy. A fire at the Globe on June 29, 1613, during a performance of Shakespeare's *Henry VIII* destroyed the play-books and apparel of the Chamberlain's/King's Men, but the company continued undiminished at Blackfriars and a rebuilt Globe, except by the loss of its long-time poet, William Shakespeare, who retired in the year of the fire and died in 1616.

Sir Henry Herbert, master of the revels, entered the titles of licensed plays in his office-book, 1622–42, and this list identifies the London playing companies and some of their repertory in the Stuart period. For the King's Men, Herbert issued licenses for 56 old and new plays for the company. For the Admiral's/Prince's/Palsgrave's Men, Herbert licensed 15 plays, only one of which is extant (*The Duchess of Suffolk*, Q1631). A fire at the Fortune playhouse on Sunday, December 9, 1621, destroyed the company's play-books and apparel; and, though the playhouse was rebuilt and the company continued, the players from Elizabethan and Jacobean configurations of the company had retired or died. In one way or another, Christopher Beeston is the common denominator in the history of several companies for which Herbert licensed plays. Beeston, after managing Queen Anne's Men at the Red Bull until 1617 or so, continued a theatrical enterprise at the Cockpit with players under the patronage of

Prince Charles. Herbert licensed four plays for the company in 1623, which ceased to exist after its patron became king in 1625. At the Cockpit, Beeston replaced Prince Charles's Men with a company formerly of boys, Lady Elizabeth's Men. Before 1622, Lady Elizabeth's Men had played at the Swan, where they performed Middleton's *A Chaste Maid in Cheapside*. Herbert licensed 13 plays for Lady Elizabeth's Men from May 1622 to February 1635. Queen Henrietta's Men and Beeston's Boys were also ventures by Beeston, who died in 1638. Herbert licensed four plays for Queen Henrietta's Men, 1625–8, and ten in 1633–4; after 1637, another configuration of the company played at the Salisbury Court playhouse until 1642. Beeston's Boys, also known as the King and Queen's Young Company, appear in Herbert's office-book in 1636–7. After Beeston died, his son William managed Beeston's Boys, who played at the Cockpit.

If the identity of companies in the Stuart years was determined by repertory, staging, and versification, as Scott McMillin and Sally-Beth MacLean suggest was true in the heyday of the Queen's Men in 1583–92, there is little in the entries of licenses by Herbert to differentiate one company from another by the time the playhouses were officially closed in 1642. Evidence of a sameness is the employment of dramatists across company lines. Plays by Beaumont and Fletcher appear in the repertory of the King's Men, Lady Elizabeth's Men, Queen Henrietta's Men, and Beeston's Boys. Plays by Ford, or Dekker and Ford, appear in these repertories plus that of Palsgrave's Men. Plays by Heywood, Middleton, Massinger, Rowley, and Shirley are likewise ubiquitous. A few companies still were performing Marlowe and Shakespeare but the plays new in 1588 or 1590 or 1600 were now into their fourth decade of reruns. Therefore, after nearly 75 years of business, the early modern English playing companies and their repertories were blended into slight variations of one another.

NOTES

I am indebted throughout this chapter to E. K. Chambers's masterful *Elizabethan Stage* (1923) and Andrew Gurr's wide-ranging and updated treatment of the subject, *The Shakespearian Playing Companies* (1996); I refer readers to both for information on companies not discussed here and for further detail on those that are.

1 The title-page phrase is "ED. ALLEN . . . [and] *Kemps applauded Merymentes*"; title-page advertisements are quoted from Greg (1939).
2 McMillin and MacLean are speaking specifically of the Queen's Men in the 1580s (1998, xii).
3 Sussex's *William the Conqueror* may survive under the title *Fair Em*, which includes a plot with King William (however, the title-page of the quarto advertises Lord Strange's Men).
4 For a fuller description of the Newington playhouse enterprise, see Ingram (1992, 150–81), and chapter 11 above.
5 For a comprehensive study of the company, see McMillin and MacLean (1998). Unless otherwise noted, I rely on this source.
6 Greg suggests the title, "Cloris and Ergasto" (1904, II 152).

7   I omit *Titus Andronicus* from discussion in the belief that the attribution to Pembroke's company on the title-page of the quarto derives from the presence of some of Pembroke's players in the company of Sussex's Men in January 1594 when the play was performed at the Rose.

8   Karl Wentersdorf (1977) attributes *Dr. Faustus*, *The Massacre at Paris*, *Soliman and Perseda*, *Arden of Faversham*, and *Richard III* to Pembroke's Men in 1592–3.

9   I take the title-page of the 1594 quarto of *The Taming of a Shrew* at its word and assume that the accompanying printed text, not Shakespeare's *Taming of the Shrew*, was the play owned and performed by Pembroke's Men.

10 During a London performance in 1587, a feigned on-stage shooting went terribly wrong; a man in the audience was wounded, and a child and a pregnant woman were killed. Andrew Gurr hints at a connection with the performance of *2 Tamburlaine* (1996, 232).

11 I trust Henslowe less than title-pages, and I assume that the Chamberlain's Men had Shakespeare's play, not Pembroke's.

12 James Burbage had bought Blackfriars on February 4, 1596, shortly before his death; Richard Burbage inherited it, but leased it to Evans until Evans relinquished the lease in 1608.

REFERENCES AND FURTHER READING

Beckerman, Bernard (1962). *Shakespeare at the Globe, 1599–1609*. New York: Macmillan.

Bentley, G. E. (1941–68). *The Jacobean and Caroline Stage: Plays and Playwrights*. 7 vols. Oxford: Clarendon Press.

Berry, Herbert (1986). *The Boar's Head Playhouse*, illus. C. Walter Hodges. Washington, DC: Folger Shakespeare Library.

Carson, Neil (1988). *A Companion to Henslowe's Diary*. Cambridge: Cambridge University Press.

Cerasano, S. P. (1994). "Edward Alleyn: 1566–1626." In *Edward Alleyn: Elizabethan Actor, Jacobean Gentleman*, eds Aileen Reid and Robert Maniura. Dulwich: Dulwich Picture Gallery.

Chambers, E. K. (1923). *The Elizabethan Stage*. 4 vols. Oxford: Clarendon Press.

Dutton, Richard (1991). *Mastering the Revels: The Regulation and Censorship of English Renaissance Drama*. Iowa City: University of Iowa Press.

Dutton, Richard (2002). "The licensing of the boy companies 1600–1612: a reconsideration." *English Literary Renaissance* 32.

Foakes, R. A., and R. T. Rickert, eds (1961). *Henslowe's Diary*. Cambridge: Cambridge University Press.

Gair, W. Reavley (1982). *The Children of Paul's: The Story of a Theatre Company, 1553–1608*. Cambridge: Cambridge University Press.

Greg, W. W. ed. (1904). *Henslowe's Diary*. 2 vols. London: A. H. Bullen.

Greg, W. W. (1939). *A Bibliography of the English Printed Drama*. 4 vols. London: Bibliographic Society.

Gurr, Andrew (1996). *The Shakespearian Playing Companies*. Oxford: Clarendon Press.

Harbage, Alfred (1952). *Shakespeare and the Rival Traditions*. New York: Macmillan.

Hillebrand, H. N. (1926). *The Child Actors: A Chapter in Elizabethan Stage History*. Urbana: University of Illinois Press.

Ingram, William (1992). *The Business of Playing*. Ithaca: Cornell University Press.

Ingram, William (1997). "What kind of future for the theatrical past: or, what will count as theater history in the next millennium?" *Shakespeare Quarterly* 48, 215–25.

Knutson, Roslyn (1991). *The Repertory of Shakespeare's Company, 1594–1613*. Fayetteville, AR: University of Arkansas Press.

Knutson, Roslyn L. (1997). "The repertory." In *A New History of Early English Drama*, eds John D. Cox and David Scott Kastan. New York: Columbia University Press.

Knutson, Roslyn (1999). "Shakespeare's repertory." In *A Companion to Shakespeare*, ed. David Scott Kastan. Oxford: Blackwell.

McMillin, Scott (1972). "Casting for Pembroke's Men: the *Henry VI* quartos and *The Taming of a Shrew*." *Shakespeare Quarterly* 23, 141–59.

McMillin, Scott (1988). "The Queen's Men and the London theatre of 1583." In *The Elizabethan Theatre, X*, ed. C. E. McGee. Port Credit, ON: P. D. Meany.

McMillin, Scott and Sally-Beth MacLean (1998). *The Queen's Men and their Plays.* Cambridge: Cambridge University Press.

Pinciss, G. M. (1970). "Thomas Creede and the repertory of the Queen's Men, 1583–1592." *Modern Philology* 67, 321–30.

Shapiro, Michael (1977). *Children of the Revels: The Boy Companies of Shakespeare's Time and their Plays.* New York: Columbia University Press.

Wentersdorf, Karl P. (1977). "The repertory and size of Pembroke's company." *Theatre Annual* 33, 71–85.

14

Must the Devil Appear?: Audiences, Actors, Stage Business

S. P. Cerasano

In *The Rare Triumphs of Love and Fortune* (1589) the god Mercury conjures up a series of magical shows. At this point in the play, Vulcan, sneering at what had become such a familiar spectacle, comments: "Lord have mercy upon us! Must the devil appear?" (I.i.215). The on-stage audiences of Renaissance plays have been well studied, especially in texts such as Shakespeare's *Taming of the Shrew* or *Hamlet*. But what were the actual audiences like? What characterized them and how did they respond to the plays they attended? And what elements shaped the interface between the actors who brought the plays to life and their viewers? Although the nature of the Renaissance audience has prompted fascinating speculation, some aspects of these questions are finally unknowable. Nonetheless, the conjectures and hypotheses about audiences and performance constitute the most enticing part of the inquiry surrounding them.

[margin note: questions to ask about Renaissance play audiences]

Imagining an Audience

Over the years historians have constructed many hypothetical audiences, especially for the public playhouses, which – being open throughout the year, costing less, and drawing many more spectators – attracted a more diverse audience than their private counterparts. The conversation began in 1941 when Alfred Harbage envisioned an audience made up of London's most prevalent group, the "craftsmen," as he characterized them. Yet simultaneously, Harbage, ever cognizant of the noblemen who lent their names to the actors' patents, was eager to suggest that this elite echelon would have been represented as well, thus creating an audience at once plebeian and courtly. In later times this equation has become inadequate for describing Renaissance audiences. Furthermore, it clouds the question with modern assumptions on the educational and cultural backgrounds of those who heard plays at the public theaters. Moreover, Harbage's scheme is concerned with demonstrating Shakespeare's talent, in part, by arguing for his universality, for his ability to reach all spectators. Not only has such thinking been superseded by more complex discussions, but the method-ological difficulties raised by Harbage's assessment fail to address the problems in-herent in any attempt to identify English class structure of the period 1550–1650 using modern constructions of hierarchy. What defined a "citizen"? Did all "citizens" respond to a theatrical performance similarly? What assumptions can we reasonably adopt concerning "noblemen" and their responses to the drama? These difficulties have plagued conversations about Shakespeare's audience from the beginning.

For many years Harbage's view went unchallenged, until Ann Cook published *The Privileged Playgoers of Shakespeare's London* (1981). Here, she argued for an audience populated largely by the upper strata of the population; that is, those with education, a moderate income, and a more elevated social status than that of tradesmen or crafts-men. (She does not, however, rule out the presence of tradesmen amongst the specta-tors.) More recently, Andrew Gurr and others have argued for the presence of the social elite at the private playhouses, the dominance of an "average citizen" (my terminol-ogy) at two public playhouses (the Fortune and the Red Bull), and an amicable mixture of both social groups at the Globe. The difficulty with these arguments, as with Harbage's, lies in the attempt to construct – from sparse evidence – a group of spectators on the basis of their social background. Moreover, in exploring the Renais-sance audience it has been difficult for theater historians to stick to their agenda – who were these spectators? which theaters did they attend? how did they respond? – without straying into a defensive position that seeks, openly or covertly, to defend Shakespeare as anomalous (somehow more highbrow, more talented, more deserving of permanence) when compared with other dramatists. Yet perhaps the best way to revisit the issue is simply to review the evidence and to articulate some new ques-tions. For instance, we might ask how large the potential audience of playgoers was. This, in turn, raises questions of the geographical distribution of residents and playgoers, and the potential effect upon the composition of a particular playhouse audience. We might also wonder not only about the audience's behavior inside of the playhouse, but about their expectations of what would transpire on stage.

A review of the evidence on London's inhabitants and their residences is instruc-tive in building the larger picture. In 1590 the city of London contained approxi-mately 200,000 residents. Thirty years on this number had almost doubled. It included tradesmen and local merchants, as well as a sizeable transient population of foreign merchants, dignitaries, and travelers. As for the social status of this reference group, part of the difficulty in describing London's residents emanates from the glaring differences between the Renaissance classification of social groups and our contemporary hierarchy. Moreover, it is hard to characterize an audience by its geographical proximity to any particular playhouse, or even to Southwark. In general, London's residents were not segregated by class. Whereas some precincts – such as the Blackfriars – boasted an elite citizenry, many areas were not exclusive in terms of properties or the types of persons who inhabited them. For instance, the neigh-borhood surrounding the Fortune playhouse, north of London wall just outside of

Cripplegate postern, contained a jail, tenements rented by workaday citizens (as well as some of the players who performed at the playhouse), and an impressive house owned by Lord Willoughby; but the area also contained more than the usual quota of London poor.

Additionally, London's citizens did not remain within the boundaries of their parishes. Instead, people traveled around the city, from Westminster in the west to Smithfield market in the east; and from north of London Wall (where they attended the Theatre and the Curtain) to Bankside. Additionally, although the suburbs were home to large numbers of vagrants, they were not the only social group there. Finally, while it has been claimed that apprentices figured prominently in the playhouse audiences, there seem to have been fewer than 10,000 apprentices among the 15 livery companies between 1570 and 1646. This is not a weighty portion of the population, and does not convey a clear sense of what percentage of any audience might have been composed of apprentices.

The diversity of the potential playgoers who happened to be in London at any one time suggests that the playhouses attracted a broad cross-section of the population. Available evidence reminds us that the earl of Essex and his followers attended a performance of Shakespeare's *Richard II* on the eve of their rebellion in 1601. A Dutchman made, in his own crude way, the only representation of the inside of the Swan. The Spanish ambassador and his troupe saw a play at the Fortune in 1621, and Simon Forman, the notorious astrologer, saw plays at several theaters, wooed and won his wife in their gardens, and even dispensed medical advice to Philip Henslowe, the owner of the Rose. Shrove Tuesday riots – promoted largely by apprentices – became legendary during the period. Yet, concurrently, John Chamberlain, London's famous gadfly reporter, noted his avoidance of the playhouses because he became bored and hated to sit still for such a long time. Opponents of the playhouses continually referred to the pickpockets and prostitutes there (who, by their very presence, were thought to lower the quality of the audience) and to those persons diverted from church services by the attractions of the theaters. So a variety of spectators who never lent their names to posterity seem to have attended plays. Consequently, any attempt to characterize the audience in absolute terms will ultimately fall short. Only its many types of persons can be suggested.

The size of an average audience can only be estimated within limits. The capacity of most public playhouses seems to have varied from 1,000 to 3,000. (Some historians argue that the Globe was at the high end of these estimates while the other playhouses were smaller.) Again, however, much of the evidence for this is anecdotal, although a recent excavation of the foundations of the Rose suggests that the number of spectators there fell somewhere in the middle range of these estimates. Regardless of the fact that historians know the dimensions of two playhouses – the Rose and the Fortune, both more or less the same size (see chapter 11 above) – mathematical calculations are ultimately misleading. First, Elizabethan spectators were physically smaller than modern ones; and attendance levels in Elizabethan playhouses varied from day to day. Receipts collected by Philip Henslowe on performances of the 1590s

very difficult to estimate the size of audiences [margin annotation]

indicate that the Rose was rarely full, except during the Christmas holiday season, and perhaps during the performances of certain wildly popular plays such as *Tamburlaine the Great* and *Dr. Faustus*. (Even then, Friday and Saturday performances regularly drew larger audiences than those earlier in the week.) Owing to all these factors, even the best estimates of the size of playhouse audiences are probably in error.

A handful of early spectators will be remembered for comments that have shaped the history of the playhouses. The best known of these is doubtless John Chamberlain, mentioned above, whose reports of the Globe and Fortune fires have been much scrutinized. Others include John Manningham, whose diary of the Middle Temple preserves an allusion to a performance of *Twelfth Night*; Thomas Platter, a Swiss traveler whose diary records a performance of *Julius Caesar* (as well as the jig following the play); and Simon Forman, who recorded plot summaries of several plays performed at the Globe and elsewhere. Also extant are the comments of various foreign ambassadors who observed plays performed at court. Nevertheless, while such documents offer scant insight into specific dramatic moments, historians lack the type of extended commentary that would allow them to determine how an audience responded to the whole of one specific play or performance.

Other evidence of spectatorship appears in visual form. The engraving used by Henry Marsh as a frontispiece to *The Wits* (plate 8, 1662) depicts a performance in a theater used much earlier than the Restoration. Preserved in this illustration is the sense of artifice that historians imagine as being part of any early performance, along with the intimacy we imagine the spectators to have enjoyed. In fact, the engraving suggests a structure very like the private, indoor playhouse, the Cockpit-in-Court, used in the 1630s. There is one curtained entrance onto the stage, and spectators sit above the platform in sections divided by pilasters. Above the central stage is another curtained area, partially open, perhaps to reveal a music room. A painted frieze of battle scenes frames the area just below the spectators' gallery. The stage is lit by two candelabra and a row of double candles at the front of the stage. (This is the earliest stage illustration to include stage lights.) Seven figures on the stage are identified by their names, or by the play to which they belong. The figure emerging through the curtains is from John Cooke's *Greene's Tu Quoque* (1614); the character to his left at the rear of the stage is presumably Antonio from Middleton and Rowley's *The Changeling* (1622); at the front left of the stage is "S[i]r J. Falstafe" with the hostess of the tavern, both probably from a droll based on Shakespeare's *Henry IV, Part I*. Clause, the king of beggars, is drawn from John Fletcher's *The Beggar's Bush*, acted before 1622, and published in 1647. The remaining figures (Simpleton and French Dancing Master) are taken from later entertainments printed in the 1640s and 1650s. In addition to illustrating a seventeenth-century playing space, the engraving represents a group of spectators, both in the gallery above the stage and surrounding it. Their attire seems to reflect an audience of the late 1640s.

Although no handbook of stage principles existed, the expectations of the audience are probably mirrored, at least partially, in the play-texts that survive from the period. Yet these texts can provide only glimpses of a much fuller dramatic

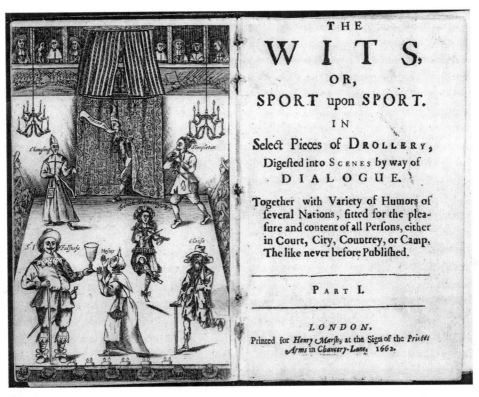

Plate 8 Title-page illustrations from Henry Marsh, *The Wits* (1662). Reproduced by permission of the Huntington Library.

experience. Clearly some dramatic elements were expected. Among other things, theatrical expression was distinguished by spectacle. Dumb shows and bed-tricks – to name but two elements – were conventional. Concurrently, the actors demanded that spectators play an active role. Their imaginative participation was essential to the success of any performance. It is difficult to reconstruct the influence of actors on their Renaissance audiences, in large measure owing to the scantiness of extant evidence. Unhappily, the biographical research concerning specific actors does not ultimately help to "cast" the plays. This notwithstanding, some hypotheses have become popular. One theory is that some (if not all) plays were designed to be performed at specific playhouses, which in turn drew specific audiences. Regardless of the attractiveness of such a theory (which often commends the Globe and Blackfriars and denigrates other playhouses), the primary characteristic of plays written for the public stage seems to have been flexibility.

Even if this theory is not water-tight, it does help to answer the question of how the spectators knew which play would be performed on a specific date. Playbills were posted around and near the playhouses, but other means of predicting which play would be performed were also possible. Evidence from Henslowe's *Diary* suggests that there was a pattern in the rotation of plays so that spectators knew in advance that end-of-the-week or weekend performances, when audiences were their largest, tended to feature popular plays, whereas a new play might premier on a day when fewer spectators would be in attendance. Of course, as a play gained popularity it was probably performed more frequently during the holiday and weekday periods, after which word-of-mouth became a powerful influence. But here there is also room for assuming diversity among the audience. Whereas some spectators probably went to the playhouses in anticipation of viewing a specific play, others doubtless went during their free hours and were happy to see whatever was being performed.

Aside from the play itself, there were many attractions at the public playhouses. Most of the theaters were surrounded by decorative gardens, pleasant for walking during clement weather, and adjoining the playhouse was a tap house where spectators could eat and drink. Doubtless various types of assignations took place among the spectators, and the playhouses provided a place where one could both see others and "be seen." Anecdotal evidence indicates that there was a fair amount of movement into and out of the audience throughout a performance; and also, that the audience was altogether more openly responsive than modern audiences. The famous "nut-cracking Elizabethans" shouted at players, responded to jokes with wisecracks of their own, and (metaphorically) nipped at the heels of the actors standing close to the edge of the stage. Yet regardless of the popular image of Renaissance spectators as "the rabble," there was some sense of etiquette involved in playhouse attendance. Again, anecdotal evidence points to the sense that a "proper" woman did not attend plays unaccompanied by a man, and that women frequently sat together during the actual performance. As for children and attendant servants, few accounts suggest that either group was included in the audience.

The spectators watched the actors, but the actors also observed their audiences. Perhaps some of the well-known on-stage audiences represent the players' impressions of their spectators; and perhaps when these representations are unlikable, this was the players' (and the dramatists') way of getting back at the audience. It is no coincidence that the players occasionally implicate their spectators along with some characters in the plays. At the end of *The Merchant of Venice*, when Portia states that "I am sure you are not satisfied / Of these events at full" (V.i.296–7), she is clearly speaking to the spectators, as well as to other on-stage characters. Her rhetorical strategy indicates an acute awareness of the theatrical process, the spectators, and their responses.

Actors and Orality

The terminology of play-going is filled with words and phrases related to the visual elements of dramatic production, what contemporaries would have termed "gazing." Yet if the playhouse experience was constructed from mortar and boards, from props

and costumes, it was also an aural world created by poetry and human voices. In addition to gazing "upon the secrets of the deep," the audience of *Richard III* would also
have said that they "heard" a play. Linguists identify the language of the stage during
the Renaissance as "early modern English," but the acoustical dimension of the theater
was more complicated than this label implies. In part, this is because Shakespeare's
spectators lived in a different acoustical world than our own; and, in part, they construed what they heard differently than we do now. Social historians remark that
Renaissance Londoners were probably more attuned to the sounds they heard around
them; however, they were also accustomed to a different set of sounds than modern
urbanites. The soundscape of London was characterized by church bells, the clatter of
rolling carts, the piercing street-cries of hawkers. As it was a port city overflowing
with mercantile activity, accompanied by the cross-currents of multiple speech
communities (together with the many languages of foreigners living in or visiting
London), many of London's soundscapes competed for the aural attention of its inhabitants. Nonetheless, while writers reveled in this rich linguistic environment, seizing
upon the fluidity of sound and sense that was a natural part of the English language,
others (notably Puritanical commentators) were disturbed by such aural richness and
display. Of course – despite the anxiety of Puritanical critics – these same traits made
rhetorical cleverness a natural element of stage performance, analogous to the metamorphosis and transformability of actors who played many roles.

While the actual voices of Renaissance actors have been lost to us, a few players
were distinguished especially for their rhetorical talents. The most notable of these
was Edward Alleyn, the actor who played the larger-than-life roles in Christopher
Marlowe's plays. His "strutting and bellowing" were well known to his audiences,
and one commentator remarked that he equaled the Roman actor Roscius "for a
tongue." Richard Burbage, who immortalized many of the leading roles in Shakespeare's plays, possessed speech that "became him." Just over 50 years after Burbage's
death, Richard Flecknoe remembered him as "an excellent orator" whose voice was
"music to the ear." Andrew Cane, who belonged to the next generation of performers, possessed "the tongue of Mercury." But even in an era in which poetry was so
central to theatrical experience, few voices or styles of delivery were preserved in any
way that allows us to imagine exactly how actors sounded.

Regardless of this void, it is clear that the public playhouses were constructed so
as to maximize the aural experience of the spectators. First, most of the public playhouses were apparently constructed on the scale of the Rose and Fortune, that is, with
an 80–85-foot diameter, which accommodates the natural range of the human voice
better than larger areas. Second, most theaters were built in a shape (a polygonal arena-
style space) that was conducive to the distribution of sound, even though the actors
probably shifted their position on stage frequently in order to project sound around
the playhouse. Third, the building materials (the large wooden beams, together with
the plaster-over-lath surfaces) returned a large proportion of the sound waves that
struck them. Lastly, the stage acted as a sounding board, and the sound waves also

reflected off the underside of the canopy. For this reason the musicians' gallery was located near the stage in order to distribute sound to the audience; and trumpet blasts were probably played from the front of the arena.

Of course, the volume level in early modern performances was a function not only of narrative line but of subject matter, acoustical space, the time of year in which the performance took place (subject to weather and general atmospheric conditions), and the ages of the actors. Boy players (if they were on the young side) necessarily had a different vocal profile than adult players. Moreover, many historians suggest that comedies offer a wider range of vocal pitches than do the histories or tragedies. It appears too that bold sound was a feature for which the northern playhouses (the Theatre, Curtain, Fortune, and Red Bull) were particularly known. The Fortune's actors were noted for their deep bass sound. When the Theatre opened in the 1570s the popularity of performances was attributable, in part, to this new type of sound. Overall, the outdoor playhouses accommodated local sounds much better than did the smaller, private playhouses of the same period.

Acting Styles, Training, Rehearsal

The space in which Renaissance actors performed offered different theatrical possibilities than the more modern, proscenium arch theater. Because the public playhouses were so much smaller than most of our contemporary theaters, and also because the actors stood close to the spectators, the actors shared an intimate relationship with the members of their audience.

For many years historians have differed in their assessment of how actors would actually have looked and sounded on stage. Some of the earliest historians, in deference to the magnetic quality of Shakespeare's verse, have imagined that any gesture would have been secondary to the oral dimension of a performance. Others have defined acting styles in terms of the two major stage personalities who performed with the two big playing companies of the 1590s – Edward Alleyn and Richard Burbage. Because the roles associated with Alleyn were bombastic, some historians have taken the comment that he "strutted and bellowed" literally. Implicit in this is the sense that his stage presence was mono-dimensional, employing stiff, stereotyped gestures, and driven by a booming delivery that lacked subtle variation. Also implicit in this is the sense that Alleyn "out-Heroded Herod" (in Hamlet's words), creating a stage tradition that quickly became outmoded in the 1590s and thereafter became the butt of ridicule. By contrast – and no doubt strongly influenced by the Shakespeare-centric bent of many early commentators – historians have concurrently imagined that Richard Burbage's stage presence was more naturalistic than Alleyn's, and that the roles Burbage played showed greater subtlety. However, these polarities are now being put aside by contemporary historians who acknowledge that both actors probably performed a variety of roles, and that even within roles such as Doctor Faustus or Henry V much variation exists. The comparison between Renaissance actors and Proteus (the classical god of changing shapes) made by Shakespeare's contemporaries implies that the best actors were gifted with versatility.

Yet several, general elements of Renaissance acting are verifiable. First, the principal actors in a company seem to have played single parts, with greater numbers of lines and more exposure to the audience. A leading adult actor played one of the largest roles and that role only. (However, not all principal actors necessarily performed in every play.) Supporting players divided up the remaining roles, not only doubling and tripling, but performing many mute roles. For example, there is evidence that, in *Sir John van Olden Barnavelt* (1619), seven men probably played 16 minor speaking roles and 12 mutes. These conventions seem to have remained customary from the early 1590s through the 1630s.

A second theory that can be advanced with some certainty is that actors performed many plays within a repertory. Therefore they were doubtless quick to learn their lines, able to remember them over a period (regardless of a limited preparation time), and capable of improvising convincingly when necessary. In addition, the actors also probably relied on some stereotypical gestures, movements, and even blocking in order to get them through a performance. (It has been suggested that John Bulwer's *Chirologia, or the Naturall Language of the Hand* (1644) – written to help the deaf communicate – demonstrates some of the standard gestures that actors might have employed.) Certainly what some theater historians refer to as "gestural phrases" (such as "what is that noise?") are common in dramatic texts. Such cues strongly suggest general types of stage movement, although the finer points of acting remain mysterious.

Third, conventional terminology describes actors as "personating," "imitating," and "counterfeiting," rather than "performing" in the modern sense. Therefore it is debatable whether spectators shared the expectations of today's audiences, who are accustomed to the extreme intimacy and intrusiveness of film as a medium. In holding the mirror up to nature, the sense of "personating" is closer to "representing to the life" than "becoming in actuality." Consequently, while the best Renaissance actors possessed enormous charisma, together with the ability to move their audiences, roles were not so tied to specific actors that they were not performable by other actors. *Dr. Faustus* was performed for many years after Edward Alleyn played the lead; yet he clearly immortalized the role during the time that he performed it.

Finally, implicit in all discussions regarding the players' style is one hidden, though persistent question: what was the quality of performances? For many reasons it would appear that the players were both skilled and blessed with abundant natural talent. To begin with, it was difficult to acquire a position in one of the London playing companies. Actors were asked to bring with them theatrical talent *and* a substantial sum of money in order to purchase a share, usually £50. (Companies were normally comprised of ten to twelve sharers.) Not only this, but the public playhouses were legendary in their time, attracting foreign visitors (such as Thomas Platter) who made it a point to visit them when they were in London. Last but not least, the major companies performed regularly at court to entertain aristocratic audiences and distinguished foreign ambassadors, and there are also records of foreign ambassadors visiting the public playhouses while they were resident in London. All this appeal, to diverse but selective (and seasoned) audiences, suggests that actors were genuine professionals.

Other obscure areas of inquiry include the players' origins and training. In some cases boys were apprenticed to master players within the established companies, and a few of the adult players were committed to training boys. However, few boys went on to make a career on the stage as adults, and the vast majority of adult actors apparently joined the London companies with no traceable formal training. Of course, the cathedral schools that sponsored theatrical companies – such as St. Paul's – offered young men some of the training that they carried with them into adult careers. Nonetheless, the first school established to train players was not founded until the Restoration, in Middlesex, on the site of the former Fortune Playhouse.

It is unclear how much time was given over to a formal rehearsal with all members of the cast. Most historians conjecture that productions were put together at breakneck speed, because many plays were in a repertory concurrently. While preparing for rehearsals, actors worked off of rolled parchments called "sides," which consisted only of the lines of a single character. Doubtless the actors would have spent private time memorizing their speeches; and presumably, the masters rehearsed their apprentices. When the company met as a group to rehearse a play it was probably during the morning hours because – at the public playhouses, and sometimes at the private ones as well – the afternoons were given over to performing. There is some evidence that other company business was carried out in the evenings. Then informal readings of plays or meetings with dramatists to review work in progress occurred.

As only one copy of the completed play manuscript was prepared (a matter of much expense), historians believe that a "book-keeper" or "book-holder" literally "held" the book and followed the text during rehearsal. In extant play manuscripts it is not uncommon to see the book-keeper's hand in the occasional insertion of a particular actor's name – usually connected with a minor role – or in a stage direction beyond the usual "enter" or "exit," which was presumably supplied by the author of the play. (However, early manuscripts were not as complete as a modern prompt-book, and do not represent a performance fully.) In addition, it was common for dramatists to submit their text to the company in sections as it was completed. Playwrights were frequently paid in portions – by the act, scene, or "sheet." Consequently, it is probable that members of the company who commissioned dramatists to write plays familiarized themselves with the plot and also the play-text as it was being written. However, the actors did not study the play until it was completed and the individual "sides" were copied out. Beyond these details, it is difficult to know where to turn for evidence of the rehearsal process. The traditional loci in dramatic texts do not necessarily reflect actual practice. Hamlet's advice to the visiting players is vague at best, and he is, by his own admission, an inept actor. The "rude mechanicals" in *A Midsummer Night's Dream* are such a comic representation of players in production that it would be surprising if they bore any resemblance to real actors at work.

Celebrated Actors

Austin Dobson, the popular nineteenth-century poet, deduced both the talents and the celebrity status of Shakespeare's lead actor from the play-texts that have been handed down:

> When Burbage played, the stage was bare
>   Of fount and temple, tower and stair;
> Two backswords eked a battle out;
> Two supers made a rabble rout;
> The throne of Denmark was a chair!
> And yet, no less, the audience there
> Thrilled through all changes of Despair,
>   Hope, Anger, Fear, Delight, and Doubt
>   When Burbage played!
>   (Dobson, 1895, 232)

The Renaissance was the first era in which celebrity actors are identifiable in England and, not surprisingly, the first in which acting became a full-time profession; however, the actors' experiences were not uniform. There were at least three "generations" who performed in the period between 1590 and the 1640s, when the playhouses were closed by Puritanical opposition. The first generation was distinguished by the talent of Richard Burbage and Edward Alleyn, the lead actors of the Lord Admiral's Men and the Lord Chamberlain's Men. During this period players inherited the experience of their predecessors, who led a more peripatetic existence, performing in inn-yards and throughout the countryside in town halls; but by the late 1580s the construction of permanent, purpose-built public playhouses meant that actors were thoroughly familiar with the venue in which their plays would be performed much of the time. This also assisted the players in cultivating a returning audience who knew where to find them, which players performed with a specific company, and which roles an actor performed in the course of his career. In turn, the players could exact a fee from every person who entered the playhouse. Ultimately this guaranteed the companies a more substantial income, which could be spent on acquiring plays and costumes, and which increased the players' personal fortunes.

It is from this combination of increased wealth and regular performance that the repertory system was born. Consequently, the construction of the public playhouses put the acting profession on a more secure footing altogether. An increasing tendency toward stability in company membership was partially an outgrowth of this impulse. Master players tended to remain with a company, as did dramatists, and specific parts were doubtless written with specific actors in mind. A change in the players' legal status furthered this increasing sense of stability. Formal patents, issued by prominent noblemen, allowed the actors to perform in their London playhouses regularly, and to go on tour during periods when plague forced the closure of the theaters. This first generation of players were pioneers who turned playing into a formidable and a potentially lucrative profession, despite the fact that they did not enjoy the same secure professional footing as the London guilds or as other, more traditional professions, such as the law.

The second generation was constituted, in part, from the first; however, they saw one substantial change. The companies were patronized by the royal family under King James, several of whom genuinely appreciated theater. Queen Anne was interested in theatrical performance more than any previous member of a royal family. Furthermore, it was her for whom the many, extravagant court masques were staged. Even the king's oldest son, Prince Henry, sponsored a significant company (the former Lord Admiral's Men). Not least, this second generation, represented by Shakespeare at the end of his career, witnessed the construction of a new generation of public playhouses – the first Fortune and the first Globe. Judging from contemporary commentary by such Londoners as John Chamberlain, these new theaters met with considerable excitement; they also presumably reflected the practical experience of the players who had performed in the earlier structures. Hence, the second generation of players enjoyed playing as an established profession, both aesthetically and economically. The system by which the players owned shares in the company, and collected income from the return on these, had become accepted practice.

The third generation of players became prominent around 1615, by which time previous generations had largely retired or died, and a new generation of dramatists (such as John Webster and John Ford) was well established, and were well acclimatized to the smaller, private playhouses that had become fashionable. Although the period between 1615 and 1640 was greater than that of previous "generations" of actors, in many ways the profession seems to have come full circle. This third generation was faced with problems of change and instability that haunted their colleagues in the 1570s and 1580s. Eventually, those who lived long enough would have seen Puritanical sentiments prevail, and the playhouses closed.

Cracks began to show in the profession late in the second decade of the seventeenth century. First, the deaths of Queen Anne and Prince Henry dealt a substantial blow to the political infrastructure of two major companies, sending them scrambling for patronage. The patrons they acquired finally were not as illustrious as their predecessors, and King James' tepid attitude toward dramatic performance probably did not do much to assist their artistic cause. Second, the first 25 years of the new century saw both loss and transition, in terms of theatrical personnel, on many levels. Two major playhouse owners and a substantial number of significant sharers in the two major companies died during this period. The influential mastership of the revels saw three office-holders, the last of whom, Henry Herbert, seemed interested primarily in discovering how lucrative the position could become. Third, the solid economic bases of the theaters (and thus, of the companies) began to erode. Shares in playing companies began to be inherited by non-players, instead of being passed from player to player, as formerly. Thus, in some instances the control of the companies began to flow away from the actors, in the direction of the company's owners, some of whom had little interest in, or experience of, playing as a business.

Despite the triumph and turmoil experienced by Renaissance actors as a group, individual actors were very much appreciated by their audiences. Their celebrity was expressed frequently in poems and epithets and occasionally in portraiture. Other "tributes" resided in the work of the many fine dramatists of the era who wrote for the public playhouses, which was dedicated to showcasing the lead players.

Celebrity status – while it lasted – brought with it certain privileges. In economic terms, the lead players were rewarded with sizeable fortunes in fluid assets and property. At the time of his death in 1619 Richard Burbage was worth £300, in addition to his shares in the company and in the Globe and Blackfriars. Christopher Beeston (d. 1638) also ended his career as an actor and a playhouse owner, with a substantial estate. John Shank outlined gifts in his will totaling just over £240. At a time when a schoolmaster might only earn £20 per annum, these sums suggest that celebrated actors were often well compensated; that a career of shareholding, court performances and occasional touring offered an income in excess of many a London tradesman's, at least during periods devoid of plague or political intervention.

In personal ways celebrity brought a combination of pleasure and security, punctuated by the anxiety of having to perform well consistently. In addition to the public exposure and the privilege of performing at court was the simple pleasure of fraternity. Many of the well-known actors, such as John Heminges, remembered their compeers in their wills. He bequeathed ten shillings to "every of my fellows and sharers" to make "rings for remembrance." Nicholas Tooley (d. 1624) cleared his debts to his fellow players and passed on to the daughter of his former master, Richard Burbage, a moderate sum that was owed him by another player. Shakespeare, in one of the period's most famous wills, left 26s. 8d. to his "fellows" – John Heminges, Richard Burbage, and Henry Condell – "to buy them rings."

Nevertheless, not all theatrical relationships, whether between actors or between players and their public, were so positive. Scholars who have reconstructed the actors' psychological dimensions have found evidence that for some, acting was – then as now – an escape, an attempt to master decay and death, to remodel the most negative aspects of the human condition. Metaphorically and to their detractors, players were cast as exhibitionists, jugglers, hustlers, tempters, and even whores. Their opponents described them simultaneously as proud beggars and sly procurers of their audiences' attention.

Clowns and Clowning

While some actors were typed as tragic heroes, no playing company could function without at least one actor who was an adept clown. In *The Defence of Poesy* (published first in 1595) Philip Sidney objected to clowns who conversed with kings on the same stage; however, dramatists and their audiences seem not to have shared this concern. In fact, the clown was a significant character in many plays, both singly and in combination with aristocratic characters. Feste and Touchstone, Lear and his fool, or Hamlet and the gravedigger give only a few examples of clowns whose importance loomed much larger than their limited exposure on stage would suggest.

Describing a tragedian's performance is complicated by conflicting evidence and a paucity of available material; characterizing the clown's craft is even more difficult, largely because their roles are partly (and scantily) preserved in extant texts. Much of the clowns' attractiveness was due to their talents in improvisation; and their routines probably changed with each performance. Unhappily, much of what actually occurred on stage has been lost to us; and, as in the case of other types of actors, few specifics of actual performances are noted. Observers' epithets, while occasionally interesting in terms of theatrical biography, rarely answer our most probing questions.

Clowns developed their own traditions of stage performance over time, and some well-known clowns passed their artistic mantles on to others. Audiences of the 1570s and 1580s enjoyed Richard Tarlton and Robert Wilson, who were remembered for their improvisational talents long after they left the companies with which they achieved fame. Their successors included Will Kempe, who performed with Strange's (then the Chamberlain's) Men in the 1590s. Robert Armin, who seems to have been encouraged early on in his career by Tarlton, joined the Chamberlain's Men around 1599 when Kempe was on his way out. But apart from this artistic lineage, these clowns differed in background and in the specific type of clowning they provided for the companies with which they performed, and the dramatists who wrote their parts were acutely aware of these differences.

A drawing of Richard Tarlton (plate 9, ?1588) depicts a small, open-faced man in rustic costume tooting on a pipe while simultaneously banging on a tabor. (He was described by one contemporary as being squint-eyed and having a flat nose.) A poem in the right-hand margin notes that "Of all the Jesters in the lande / he bare the praise awaie." Doubtless some of this extravagant praise was a reference to Tarlton's many diverse abilities – as an improviser, tumbler, composer of ballads, dramatist, and master of fencing. In 1585 his play *The Seven Deadly Sins* (now lost) was so popular that a second part was written, which survives only in a "plot," or outline. Numerous jest-books of the time include anecdotes, real or rumored, that are attributed to Tarlton. If nothing else they testify to his legendary wit. The playing company with which he has been customarily associated was the Queen's Men.

Robert Wilson, a contemporary of Tarlton's, belonged to both the Earl of Leicester's Men and Queen Elizabeth's Men. His performances seem to have been marked by a style that some found more "academic" than Tarlton's. Wilson's lost play *Short and Sweet* was described by Thomas Lodge as " a piece surely worthy praise, the practice of a good scholar." On stage he was described by Francis Meres as "our witty Wilson, who for learning and extemporal wit in this faculty is without compare or compeer," a sentiment echoed later by Edmund Howes, who described Wilson's stage presence as marked by "a quick delicate refined extemporal wit."

Plate 9   Richard Tarlton, from a drawing by John Scottowe (?1588), in BL Harleian MS 3885, fo 19. Reproduced by permission of the British Library.

Because of their association with Shakespeare's plays and the companies that performed them, the next generation of clowns (Will Kempe and Robert Armin) were better remembered. Kempe, "Jestmonger and Vice-gerent generall to the Ghost of Dick Tarlton," was already distinguished by 1594 when the printed version of the play *A Knack to Know a Knave* was advertised as containing "Kemps applauded Merrimentes of the men of Goteham." This was performed by Lord Strange's Men, who took up the lord chamberlain's patronage around the same time; and when the company was paid in March 1595 for performances at court, Kempe was joint payee along with Richard Burbage. While in the Chamberlain's Men, Kempe appeared in plays by Jonson and Shakespeare. The accidental substitution of his name for those of two characters in early printed dramatic texts leads theater historians to conclude that he performed the role of Peter in *Romeo and Juliet* and of Dogberry in *Much Ado About Nothing*. Not only this, but he was renowned as a writer and a performer of jigs. These short pieces contained substantial amounts of dancing, one of Kempe's particular strengths, and one that he continued to display until his death. He apparently left the Chamberlain's Men around 1599, gaining notoriety when he danced from London to Norwich. (His personal account of this was published in 1600.) A Continental tour followed, and then Kempe joined Worcester's Men, which was apparently the last company-based activity before his death.

Kempe's successor was Robert Armin, who began his career as an apprentice to a goldsmith and came to the public's attention early on as a writer. In theatrical circles he was first associated with Lord Chandos's Men. It appears that he had probably joined the Chamberlain's Men by 1599, and he was still among them in 1603, when he was named in the license for the King's Men. Armin was listed among the players for Jonson's *Alchemist* (1610) and in the "Principall Actors" of the First Folio of Shakespeare's plays (1623). Although few of his roles are known, Armin played melancholic clowns. Historians conjecture that he succeeded Kempe in the part of Dogberry, that he probably played Feste in *Twelfth Night* and the clown in George Wilkins' *Miseries of Enforced Marriage* (c.1605), and possibly the fool in *King Lear* (whose lines the fool mimics in *Miseries*), performed around the same time. Armin died in 1615, just a year before Shakespeare's death signaled the end of the theatrical era that began in the late 1580s.

John Singer joined the Queen's Men when it was established in 1583, and he remained with that company for at least five years. By 1594, however, he had joined the Lord Admiral's Men, where he served as one of the company's payees for court performances during the Christmas season, 1594–5. Like Tarlton and Wilson, Singer also wrote at least one play (*Singer's Voluntary*), for which the Admiral's Men paid him £5 in January 1603. Later, Singer was associated with Tarlton and Kempe in the *Gull's Horn-Book* by Thomas Dekker: "Tarlton, Kempe, nor Singer, nor all the litter of fools that now come drawling behind them, never played the clowns more naturally than the errantest sot of you all shall."

By the 1630s improvisational clowning was out of fashion; but throughout the time that it was popular it was revered as a distinct specialty that complemented other types of stage performance.

Impersonating Women

Few theatrical conventions intrigue and confuse modern readers as much as the concept of the boy actor who performed female roles. Moreover, with few eyewitness accounts to shed light on this historical phenomenon, and few modern analogues outside of Japanese kabuki theater, there is little chance that the ongoing controversies concerning boy players will ever be settled.

The common use of boy players in English Renaissance companies touches both theoretical and practical matters. Theoretical questions include "Why did English culture resist the use of women on the stage during the Renaissance?" and "What sociosexual elements were invoked in the performance of women's roles by boys?" More practical are questions relating to how boy players functioned in specific roles, and how the spectators responded to them.

Gender critics remind us that cross-dressing, in itself, was considered a misdemeanor, or certainly a tell-tale sign of such. In the extant evidence, it is abundantly clear that women who cross-dressed as men were often accused of covering up some immorality through their adoption of male dress. Almost no evidence of transvestite men has been preserved, and the occasional reference to a masquerade or seasonal festival in which men are described as cross-dressed female characters always seems to appear in the context of events authorized by the civic authorities. On the university and public stages a few references to boy players by their female roles indicate, according to some historians, that the boys were essentially invisible, absorbed into the performance. Aside from an acceptance of cross-dressing within certain conventional situations – the well-worn tradition of all-male companies in ancient Greece and Rome, and male productions of mystery plays and university drama in England – the shrill rhetoric of Puritanical critics crescendoed around the topic of boy players who displayed themselves on stage as women. More than other aspects of theatrical commentary, modern historians attribute these outbursts to anxiety in relation to female sexuality. The boy actor destabilized cultural binarisms and boundaries, they note. However, other theoreticians argue that theatrical transvestism works finally to insulate the audience from genuine lustful feelings, rather than arousing them. From a political standpoint, Puritanical critics had other ends in mind when they disparaged boy players: the closure of the theaters, which finally took place by 1642. In this context cross-dressing was one obvious element that critics could fix upon easily, as a symbol of the more general sense of the theater as a locus of sociopolitical subversion. For the most damning commentators, whether a person was on stage or in the audience was ultimately indistinguishable; involvement in theater imperiled the virtue of actors and spectators, men and women, alike. For the Puritans, theater was an assured gateway to inciting desire, whether heterosexual or homosexual. It is therefore difficult to read between the lines of political polemics in an attempt to reconstruct, from these treatises alone, any historical sense of how boy players functioned on stage. A sense of the theoretical complexities raised by what some term the "transvestite theater" finally presents the most useful picture.

On a practical level, theater historians remind us that, from 1558 on, companies of boy players performed regularly at court and in London, although they fell in and out of fashion. In this context, boys performed all of the characters in the plays, including female parts. Like adult players, boys utilized a range of performance styles suitable to the roles they performed, and were capable of dealing with sophisticated rhetorical locutions. "Boys" could well have been between ten and 20 years of age, beyond what we define as boyhood. Still, some historians speculate that perhaps owing to slower maturation "boys" might have retained their childlike voices for longer than is the case today. In some ways the establishment of the boys' companies – which performed in small, indoor playhouses – must have presented a different aural palette than that of the adult actors. The boys who came out of the cathedral schools, or from the Chapel Royal, were trained as singers and musicians, and they exploited these talents in their theatrical performances. When the King's Men took over Blackfriars in 1609, after the Children of the Blackfriars had been playing there, the adults preserved this tradition. The musical consort performed before plays, between acts, and possibly after the performances as well.

Boy players must have brought their own limitations to the stage, but female roles are limited in different ways. Actual displays of passion (kissing, particularly) were minimal, as evidenced in extant dramatic texts. Romeo and Juliet are separated by a balcony, while Cleopatra draws attention to "some squeaking" boy actor who will perform her role in a play when she is dead. Of course, historians speculate that some adult female roles, especially those strong female leads that seem to demand sustained vocal and physical strength (Cleopatra and Lady Macbeth among them), or those female characters of advanced age who are so frequently the objects of fun (such as Juliet's Nurse), might well have been played by older boys or by adult actors. If it is true that, in some cases, this male sexuality was meant to "cut through" the feminine attributes of the characters then, at times, older women were played for comedy that stemmed from gender confusion, while at other moments, strong female rulers gained power, in part, through the use of a decidedly male resonance.

Yet despite the controversy concerning the boy players – both in earlier times and in our own – and despite our limited sense of their stage presence, what is certainly true is that spectators were intrigued by them; and some spectators were affected deeply by their performances. When *Othello* was performed in Oxford in 1610, one of the spectators, a scholar named Henry Jackson, noted that Desdemona's death "moved us still more greatly; for when she fell back upon the bed she implored the pity of those watching with her countenance alone."

Conclusion

Theater historians might find themselves asking Vulcan's original question: "Must the devil appear?" It would seem that, for some Renaissance spectators, such display was expected and even enjoyed; and in a play such as *Dr. Faustus*, the appearance of the devil was crucial to the performance. But beyond this, the relationship between audience and actor was ultimately much more complex than Vulcan's high-handed joke would suggest. A performance was not only influenced by the moment, with its intricately nuanced display; it was also framed by the actor's professional history, his current and past performances. And even more than this, the relationship between actor and audience was complicated by the spectators' own individual histories of playgoing, and by their shifting expectations and demands. Therefore Vulcan's remark cuts in two directions, at once allowing him to pretend that he is the discriminating spectator, while ironically undercutting him as the ham-fisted playgoer who is out of step with contemporary fashion.

That being said, even acknowledging these many facets does not do justice to all the shadings of complexity in the relationship between actor and audience. The many intriguing portraits of Renaissance spectators are complicated by our own contemporary assumptions; and these are continually challenged by the knowledge that the historian's legacy is an uneven collection of evidence. Yet amid all of this uncertainty there is one thing of which historians can be reasonably confident: the devil *must* and *did* appear.

REFERENCES AND FURTHER READING

Bentley, G. E. (1941–68). *The Jacobean and Caroline Stage*. Oxford: Clarendon Press. (See esp. vol. II.)

Bradbrook, M. C. (1979). *The Rise of the Common Player*. Cambridge: Cambridge University Press.

Cerasano, S. P. (1994). "Edward Alleyn." In *Edward Alleyn: Elizabethan Actor, Jacobean Gentleman*, eds Aileen Reid and Robert Maniura. Dulwich: Dulwich Picture Gallery.

Chambers, Edmund K. (1923). *The Elizabethan Stage*. 4 vols. Oxford: Clarendon Press. (See esp. vols II and III.)

Cook, Ann Jennalie (1981). *The Privileged Playgoers of Shakespeare's London, 1576–1642*. Princeton: Princeton University Press.

Dessen, Alan (1984). *Elizabethan Stage Conventions and Modern Interpreters*. Cambridge: Cambridge University Press.

Dobson, Austin (1895). *Collected Poems*. New York: Dodd, Mead.

Foakes, R. A., and R. T. Rickert, eds (1962). *Henslowe's Diary*. Cambridge: Cambridge University Press.

Gurr, Andrew (1987). *Playgoing in Shakespeare's London*. Cambridge: Cambridge University Press.

Gurr, Andrew (1996). *The Shakespearian Playing Companies*. Oxford: Oxford University Press.

Harbage, Alfred (1941). *Shakespeare's Audience*. New York: Columbia University Press.

King, T. J. (1992). *Casting Shakespeare's Plays: London Actors and their Roles, 1590–1642*. Cambridge: Cambridge University Press.

Nungezer, Edwin (1929). *A Dictionary of Actors and Other Persons Associated with the Public Representation of Plays in England before 1642*. New Haven: Greenwood Press.

Orgel, Stephen (1996). *Impersonations: The Performance of Gender in Shakespeare's England*. Cambridge: Cambridge University Press.

The Rare Triumphs of Love and Fortune (1589, rpt 1930). Malone Society Reprints. London: Oxford University Press.

Shapiro, Michael (1994). *Gender in Play on the Shakespearean Stage: Boy Heroines and Female Pages*. Ann Arbor: University of Michigan Press.

Skura, Meredith (1993). *Shakespeare the Actor and the Purposes of Playing*. Chicago: University of Chicago Press.

Smith, Bruce R. (1999). *The "O" Factor: The Acoustical World of Early Modern England*. Chicago: University of Chicago Press.

Wiles, David (1987). *Shakespeare's Clown: Actor and Text in the Elizabethan Playhouse*. Cambridge: Cambridge University Press.

15

"The Actors are Come Hither": Traveling Companies

Peter H. Greenfield

In 1572 the Earl of Leicester's Men asked their patron for a license that would identify them as "your household Servaunts when we shall have occasion to travayle amongst our frendes as we do usuallye once a yere" (Chambers, 1923, II, 86). The spelling of "travayle" suggests a pun playwrights of the period would have liked: to travel might well be travail, as the actors were at the mercy of the weather and their audiences' generosity, not to mention local authorities who might clap them in jail as vagabonds. The less successful companies might well feel like Sir Oliver Owlett's men in Marston's *Histriomastix*, who complain that they "travell, with pumps full of gravell . . . And never can hold together" (Wood, 1939, III, 264). Yet the very fact that an annual tour was the usual practice of Leicester's Men suggests that there must have been rewards for traveling that balanced the hardships. In fact, Leicester's Men continued to tour each year after the Theatre was constructed in 1576 as their London base.

In doing so, they were following a tradition of itinerant performing that predated the purpose-built theaters of London by centuries. Visiting minstrels appear in the earliest records that survive from many provincial towns and households: from as early as 1277 at Canterbury, 1307 at Leicester, and 1337 at Worcester. Minstrel troupes visited the dowager Queen Isabella at Hertford Castle in 1357, and others entertained Elizabeth Berkeley's household at Berkeley castle at Christmas in 1420 (Gibson, 2001; Hamilton, n.d.; Klausner, 1990, 396; Greenfield, n.d.; Douglas and Greenfield, 1986, 347). "Stage players" began to appear in the records in the late fifteenth century, and their travels about the country followed routes already established by the minstrels. Touring was thus the normal mode of operation for acting companies until the last quarter of the sixteenth century, and it remained important even after some companies established themselves in London playhouses.

The Purposes of Playing

Aesthetically the players' purpose may have been "to hold the mirror up to nature," as Hamlet suggests, but the practical purposes of traveling were to make a living and to serve their patron. The former purpose is apparent from the way that Owlett's Men "cry their play" – that is, announce their performance:

All they that can sing and say,
Come to the Towne-house and see a Play,
At three a clocke it shall beginne,
The finest play that e're was seene.
Yet there is one thing more in my minde,
Take heed you leave not your purses behinde.
(Marston, *Histrio-Mastix*, in Wood, III, 268)

If the audience did leave their purses behind, the players might suffer a fate similar to Pembroke's Men, whose 1593 tour failed to meet expenses, forcing the company to return to London and disband, selling off their costumes to pay their debts (Foakes and Rickert, 1961, 280). Most companies, however, must have managed to break even or make a modest profit on the road. Unfortunately, the surviving evidence provides only a partial picture of any particular company's finances, even for brief periods. The Queen's players received 12s. from Lord Berkeley when they visited his seat at Caludon Castle on July 1, 1594, and the city of Coventry gave them 40s. on July 4 (Greenfield, 1983, 16; Ingram, 1981, 341). The 52s. total for these four days could have meant a considerable loss if they had no other source of income. Actors on the road around 1600 would have had to spend a minimum of a shilling a day per man for room and board. If they rode or had a horse to pull their wagon of costumes and props, food and stabling would cost another shilling per horse (Ingram, 1993, 58–9). Since the Queen's Men probably numbered 14 at that time, their expenses would have come to at least 56s., and probably much more, as we would expect the monarch's players to have horses and be otherwise well equipped. No touring company could long sustain such losses, and the Queen's players must have done considerably better, by both making more and spending less.

Most likely they did spend less than the above estimates, since players visiting aristocratic households could expect to be fed and lodged. Hamlet asks Polonius to "see the players well bestowed" – that is, lodged – and accounts from the Duke of Buckingham's household at Thornbury for 1507–8 and Francis Clifford's at Londesborough for 1598 show that players were often present at meals for several days, though only a single reward is recorded (Douglas and Greenfield, 1986, 356–8; Wasson, n.d.). In fact, an itinerant singer claimed that he could maintain himself simply by going "from gentilmans house to gentilmans house vpon their benevolence" (Somerset, 1994a, 280). Success, even survival, depended as much on a company's reception in gentlemen's houses as in the towns, or more so.

Players also had income beyond the rewards recorded in civic and household accounts. Willis' description of a performance at Gloucester tells us that the first performance by a visiting troupe was "called the Mayors play, where every one that will comes in without money, the Mayor giving the players a reward as he thinks fit to shew respect unto them" (Willis, 1639, quoted in Douglas and Greenfield, 1986, 363). At Leicester, though, the official reward is usually recorded as being "more than was gathered," and enterprising players may have used the tactic employed by the actors of *Mankind*, who stop in the middle of performance to take a collection or "gathering" (Hamilton, n.d.). Sir Oliver Owlett's Men may have had a gathering in mind when they urged their potential audience to bring their purses, or they may have intended to charge admission to the performance space. The Queen's Men charged admission to their performance at the Red Lion inn in Norwich, where "one wynsdon would have intred in at the gate but woold not haue payed," starting a fight with the gatekeeper that eventually involved sword-bearing actors and ended in the death of an audience member.

Players could increase their income by giving several performances during a single visit to a town. Norwich gave companies permission to play for periods ranging from a single day to a week or more, though the civic accounts mention only a single official reward. The Queen's Men may thus have boosted their receipts for the first week of July 1594 by giving several performances at Caludon Castle and Coventry, at the same time cutting their expenses by lodging with Lord Berkeley. This combination of multiple performances in towns with free food and lodging in gentlemen's houses made financial survival possible.

That survival also depended on the players' having a patron. His (or, rarely, her) name on a letter or warrant kept the players out of jail and got them into guildhalls and aristocratic residences across the land. Without a license from someone holding at least the rank of baron, travelling players faced imprisonment as wandering rogues and vagabonds, under the 1572 "Acte for the Punishemente of Vacabondes" (Chambers, 1923, IV, 270). With such a license, the first thing they did on coming to a town was to visit the mayor "to enforme him what noble-mans servants they are, and so to get license for their publike playing," as Willis tells us. Then, "if the Mayor like the Actors, or would shew respect to their Lord and Master, he appoints them to play their first play before himself and the Aldermen and common Counsell of the City" (Douglas and Greenfield, 1986, 362–3). The identity of the players' "Lord and Master" thus often determined whether and how much they would be allowed to perform. In 1582 Leicester prohibited performers other than "the Quenes maiestes: or the Lordes of the Privye Counsall" (Hamilton, n.d.). A 1580 Gloucester ordinance permitted the Queen's players to perform three times over three days, but players whose patron held the rank of baron and above could perform only twice over two days, and other players could play but once (Douglas and Greenfield, 1986, 306–7).

It was also the patron's name, rank, and influence – and not the size or skill of the company – that determined the size of the reward the players received. Civic and household accounts rarely mention the title of the play or the identity of individual players; the one piece of information they nearly always record to identify an expenditure on players is the name of the patron. The largest rewards were given to the players of the monarch: at Gloucester in 1582–3, the Queen's Men received 30s., while the earl of Oxford's players got 16s. 8d. and Lord Stafford's 10s. Local influence might count as much as rank, for Gloucester gave 20s. to the players of Lord Chandos, who lived nearby at Sudeley Castle and represented the county in Parliament. Lord Berkeley also had extensive local holdings but was less in favor at court than Chandos, so his players received only 13s. (Douglas and Greenfield, 1986, 308).

If the patron's influence could help the players make a living on the road, their traveling could serve the patron by spreading that influence. At a time when power and influence were maintained largely through theatrical means, actors who could move about the country provided an inexpensive equivalent to the royal progress. Just as the size and richness of the monarch's entourage when on progress reminded people where power and authority lay in the nation, so – in a lesser way – did the livery the players wore and the license they carried. In addition to advertising the patron's prestige, the players might make useful local connections, and even act as informants. Traveling players were, after all, "the abstract and brief chronicles of the time," who could report to their powerful patron just how much respect particular individuals and towns had shown to them and to him. The ambitious earl of Leicester fully realized this capability of traveling players, and his company was the best known and most widely traveled during the years when he was striving to become royal consort (McMillin and MacLean, 1998, 20–3).

The players' traveling performances could likewise serve their civic and aristocratic hosts in ways beyond entertaining them. The players, in presenting the mayor with their license, asked the town to recognize their patron's influence by allowing them to perform and paying them a reward. Yet the players' request simultaneously recognized the authority of the mayor and council over what happened within the town. Each arrival of a traveling troupe thus involved a negotiation of the power relations between patrons and towns. It is not surprising, then, that when the relationships between the crown and urban elites became strained in the seventeenth century, touring became a much riskier business.

In the second half of the sixteenth century, however, towns were still largely receptive to traveling players, at least partly because urban elites found that the symbolic effect of a tour performance as advertisement of the patron's power could also provide much-needed support of their own authority. Most provincial towns suffered economic decline in the sixteenth century, as London came to dominate the economy. At the same time, immigration from the countryside swelled their populations, resulting in widespread poverty and increasing social tension (Clark, 1969, 10). The Reformation had brought an end to most of the public ceremonies that ritually reaffirmed the hierarchical social structure of the community – ceremonies that, much like those used by the crown, had a definite theatrical quality. The Corpus Christi procession, in which the civic officials and guild members marched in order in ceremonial garb, had advertised their position in the hierarchy. So urban elites had to find new ways to ensure recognition of their authority, including giving the mayor a chair of office, enlarging the ceremonial mace, and building or renovating the town hall (Tittler, 1991, 98–128). When traveling players were licensed to perform in that town hall, in a space that itself represented civic authority, they too became a representation of that authority, especially when the performance was a "mayor's play" like that described by Willis, which the audience attended for free – effectively as guests of the mayor. This effect was all the stronger because the players in some ways represented the very forces which theatened the dominant order. They traveled freely, they made their living by playing, and that playing involved temporarily taking on a range of social positions, while outside their roles they did not fit anywhere in the social order (Montrose, 1996, 55–6). Yet because they did their playing as servants of a noble patron, and under the auspices of the local authority, they offered the urban audience a representation of potentially subversive forces that in fact served and reaffirmed the existing social order.

Playing Places on Tour

Traveling players had to adapt to a variety of playing places. Bristol had two purpose-built theaters in the early seventeenth century – the Wine Street playhouse and Redcliffe Hall – but they were exceptional (Pilkinton, 1997, xxxvii–xl). The "mayor's play" Willis saw at Gloucester took place in the "Bothall," and similar performances were staged in town halls or guildhalls like the surviving ones at Leicester, Norwich, and Southampton. The players must also have performed in halls in the private house-holds they visited – spaces such as the Great Hall of Berkeley Castle or the High Great Chamber of Hardwick Hall (McMillin and MacLean, 1998, 67–83; Somerset, 1994b, 54–60).

Since the audiences that typically kept accounting records – mayors and aristo-crats – saw the players in such halls, they are the best attested places for traveling players to play, but not the only ones. Performances also occurred in churches, private houses, and especially inns, but these usually went unrecorded unless they caused a disturbance or property damage. In smaller towns or parishes, the players might use the church itself, as at Doncaster, or the church house, as at Sherborne, Dorset (Hays, 1992, 12–23; Wasson, 1997, 36). At Norwich players performed at the Common Hall, but also at the Red Lion inn, as we know from the court testi-mony regarding the "affray" in 1583. Southampton prohibited performing in the town hall in 1620, blaming players for broken benches, "fleas and other beastlie things." The council ordered "That hereafter yf anie suche staige or poppett plaiers must be admitted in this towne That they provide their places for their representa-cions in their Innes," the use of "their Innes" suggesting that inns were a familiar place to play.[1]

Repertory and Company Size

What the players performed in these halls and inns is rarely known. The names of plays almost never appear in accounts or even in highly detailed records of court cases. The only touring performance that is both named and described in considerable detail is the one Willis saw at Gloucester in the 1570s:

> The play was called (the Cradle of security,) wherin was personated a King or some great Prince with his Courtiers of severall kinds, amongst which three Ladies were in speciall grace with him; and they keeping him in delights and pleasures, drew him from his graver Counsellors, hearing of Sermons, and listning to good counsell, and admonitions, that in the end they got him to lye downe in a cradle upon the stage, where these three Ladies joyning in a sweet song rocked him asleepe, that he snorted againe, and in the meane time closely conveyed under the cloaths were withall he was covered, a vizard like swines snout upon his face, with three wire chaines fastned thereunto, the other end whereof being holden severally by those three Ladies, who fall to singing againe, and then discovered his face, that the spectators might see how they had transformed him, going on with their singing, whilst all this was acting, there came forth of another doore at the farthest end of the stage, two old men, the one in blew with a Serjeant at Armes, his mace on his shoulder, the other in red with a drawn sword in his hand, and leaning with the other hand upon the others shoulder, and so they two went along in a soft pace round about by the skirt of the Stage, till at last they came to the Cradle, whereat all the Courtiers with the three Ladies and the vizard all vanished; and the desolate Prince starting up bare faced, and finding himself thus sent for to judgement, made a lamentable complaint of his miserable case, and so was carried away by wicked spirits. This Prince did personate in the morall, the wicked of the world; the three Ladies, Pride, Covetousnesse, and Luxury, the two old men, the end of the world, and the last judgement. (Douglas and Greenfield, 1986, 363)

Two titles mentioned in the Bristol records from the 1570s sound like similar moral interludes: "what mischief worketh in the mynd of man" and "the Court of Comfort" (Pilkinton, 1997, 116). Such plays may well have remained the staple of smaller companies that played only in the provinces, but the major companies toured with the repertory developed for their London theaters. When Edward Alleyn and Lord Strange's Men performed "hary of cornwall" at Bristol in 1593, they had already performed it several times at the Rose (Pilkinton, 1997, 144; Foakes and Rickert, 1961, 16–18). Presumably Alleyn would have played Tamburlaine and his other famous Marlowe roles on tour, and Shakespeare must have performed in his own plays on the extensive tours of the Lord Chamberlain's/King's Men.

The records show these companies went on tour with enough actors to perform plays from their London repertory without cutting the text extensively. Early in the period touring companies were probably small in number – the "four men and a boy" who act the play within a play in *Sir Thomas More*. The play Willis saw at

Gloucester in the 1570s, *The Cradle of Security*, requires a cast of six, and *The Murder of Gonzago* – clearly meant to represent an older kind of play than *Hamlet* – calls for a company of from five to seven. Some companies may have remained small right through the period. As early as 1577, however, Leicester's Men appeared at Southampton with 12 actors, Bath's 11, and Worcester's, Stafford's and Delawarre's 10 each. The Queen's Men were formed in 1583 with 12 sharers, and the Earl of Derby's Men numbered 12 when they visited Francis Clifford at Londesborough in 1598. Seventeenth-century troupes might be even larger: 20 players of Lady Elizabeth visited Plymouth in 1617–18, and Norwich saw 28 in the King's Revels Company in 1635 (McMillin and MacLean, 1998; Wasson, n.d.; Gurr, 1996, 43).[2] Touring companies probably did cut the number of plays they performed, however. Unlike in London, where the audience demanded a constant diet of new plays, on tour they could rely on a few tried-and-true favorites.

Itineraries

London-based companies took to the road most often in the summer, particularly as that was the season when the authorities sometimes closed the playhouses down due to the increased threat of plague. Other companies toured throughout the year, as the Southampton mayor's accounts for 1593–4 suggest: the mayor rewarded the earl of Worcester's players on October 18, 1593, the Queen's players on November 26, and Lord Chandos' on November 28. Lord Montegle's players visited Southampton in March 1594, those of Lord Morley and the earl of Derby in May. The Queen's players returned in August, and Worcester's in September.[3] Two years earlier the Queen's Men had also visited in August, and Lord Morley's in May, showing that the itineraries particular companies habitually followed frequently brought them to the same places at the same time of year.[4]

The routes the players followed were determined by topography and roads, and by the prospects for profit. Many of the companies that played in Southampton bypassed Winchester, no doubt because the main road from London to Southampton's port ran several miles to the east. To visit the cathedral city meant a detour on a rough road over some considerable hills. The ruggedness of the North Downs was probably responsible for the dearth of companies visiting Guildford and Farnham, and the steepness of the Cotswold Edge prevented easy travel between Oxford and Gloucester. Water courses, on the other hand, meant relatively easy travel, so that players visiting Gloucester were usually following the Severn from Bristol to Worcester and Shrewsbury.

Of course the roads and rivers were only worth following if the players knew that at least the chance of substantial rewards lay along their path. Undoubtedly they took aim at the most populous towns – Norwich, Bristol, and the like – and great houses where they could expect a warm – and lucrative – reception. Smaller towns and households would sustain them along the way to the big paydays. Places as small as

Bridgwater (Somerset) and Ashburton (Devon) saw players often because they lay on the roads from Bristol to Exeter and from Exeter to Plymouth.

Itineraries might also reflect the geographical spread of a patron's influence, since that was where they could expect the largest rewards. The monarch's players ranged most widely, matched only by those of ambitious lords like the Earl of Leicester. The players of lesser patrons might concentrate near their master's residences and holdings: the majority of the recorded appearances of Lord Berkeley's players occurred in Gloucestershire, Somerset, and Warwickshire.

Companies that had London playhouses and appeared at court developed itineraries that looped out from London and back again. One of the most popular loops led to Norwich – England's second-largest city – with stops at Ipswich, Cambridge, and elsewhere in East Anglia, including towns and aristocratic residences. Another led southeast through Canterbury to the Cinque Ports. To the southwest, the usual route went to Southampton and west to Exeter and perhaps Plymouth, then looping northeast to Bristol, the third-largest town. From there the tour might return to London, or proceed north along the Severn to Gloucester, Worcester, and Shrewsbury, then turn south via Coventry and Leicester, or continue north as far as York or beyond. When Lord Strange's Men went on tour in 1593, they knew their itinerary well enough that Edward Alleyn could write his wife from Bristol and confidently ask her to send to him at Shrewsbury or York (Foakes and Rickert, 1961, 276).

The End of Traveling

The seventeenth century brought changes that disrupted the players' traditional routes and practices, so that touring steadily declined, and had all but disappeared by the time Parliament banned public performing in 1642. Coventry rewarded traveling players more often than any other provincial town – an average of six a year in the 1590s and eight a year in the first decade of the seventeenth century. But that average shrank to four between 1610 and 1619, then to two in the 1620s and 1630s. Other towns saw similar drops in the number of tour visits, as the number of companies on tour decreased, and many that remained reduced the amount of traveling they did.

The causes of this decline are various and complex. They include James I's attempt to limit patronage of players to the royal family. Shortly after his accession in 1603, he issued royal patents that transformed the Lord Chamberlain's Men into the King's Men, the Lord Admiral's Men into Prince Henry's Men, and the Earl of Worcester's players into Queen Anne's Men. A revision of the Elizabethan statute against vagabonds eliminated the legal right of the nobility to license players. In theory, James had reduced the number of licensed companies to three, and given provincial towns legal justification to prevent performances by anyone else. In practice, touring patterns changed little for the first five years of James' reign. By 1610, however, both Norwich and Leicester had begun to pay companies without royal patrons to leave town without playing; other towns denied such troupes any reward at all. Before long even royal companies found some towns using this tactic of paying the actors not to act.

The towns' antagonism toward players resulted largely from the growth of Puritanism among urban elites, though that Puritanism expressed itself as much in economic concerns and in resistance to the king as it did in moral or theological anti-theatricalism. The 1580 Gloucester ordinance that restricted the number of performances a company could give reveals what worried civic authorities. Gloucester's council felt it should put restraints on players because they "allure seruauntes, apprentices and iorneyman & other of the worst desposed persons to leudenes and lightnes of life." But the ordinance also complains that players encourage "the maintenance of idelenes" among these same persons, and "Drawe awey great Sommes of money from diuerse persons" – directly away from the servants, apprentices, and journeymen; but also indirectly from their employers, whose work sat neglected. In the sixteenth century these moral and economic objections to players were balanced by the civic authorities' desire to maintain good relations with the players' patrons and exploit some of the symbolic effect of the players' visits to reaffirm the local social order. Increasing tension between the crown and urban elites meant that by early in the seventeenth century mayors might no longer wish to "shew respect to [the players'] Lord and Master" or to associate their own authority symbolically with that of the king and his family.

Many other towns passed ordinances designed to regulate or even eliminate public performance. In 1595 Canterbury prohibited playing on the sabbath and after nine o'clock at night, and restricted visiting companies to performing only two days out of any 30. These restrictions effectively eliminated Canterbury from the players' itineraries. Between 1603 and 1642, only 20 companies received rewards at Canterbury, and 15 of those were to leave town without performing (Gibson, 1995, 7–8). As long as such restrictions were relatively rare, players could still survive on the road, performing where they could, and making brief forays into less receptive towns to pick up their payments not to play. As more and more towns paid them not to play, traveling became less and less viable, since the official rewards alone had never met expenses. The southeastern route long popular with itinerant entertainers could still make money without Canterbury. When Maidstone, Hythe, and other towns also restricted playing, setting off for the southeast coast became a risky business, even if the players still had hope of a decent payday at Dover, Lydd, or Rye (Gibson, 1995, 2–3, 11).

Only companies with royal patrons continued to tour consistently into the 1620s and 1630s, and the towns that welcomed them tended to be those that remained sympathetic to the crown. In general, traveling players were more welcome the farther they went from London – into areas where the old religion and old traditions lived on. Even non-royal companies could still find receptive households in remote places like Workington, Cumberland, where Sir Patricius Curwen rewarded Lord Wharton's players in 1629, or Dunkenhalgh Manor, Lancashire, where Thomas Walmesley hosted

Lord Strange's players in 1634 and 1636 (Douglas and Greenfield, 1986, 129; George, 1991, 207, 210). Finally, though, even the most receptive town of all, Coventry, gave its last reward to visiting players early in 1642, and that entry in the civic chamberlains' accounts is followed by an ominous one: "given to the trumpeters of the troopes which came with the Lord Brooke & the lord Gray x s. the xxviij[th] of August 1642" (Ingram, 1981, 447). With the troops came the end of the long tradition of traveling players.

NOTES

1 Southampton Court Leet Book, SRO: SC6/1/37, f. 16v.
2 Southampton Record Office: SC5/3/1, f. 167r.
3 Southampton Record Office: SC5/3/1, ff. 247v–250v.
4 Southampton Record Office: SC5/3/1, f. 237r.

REFERENCES AND FURTHER READING

Chambers, E. K. (1923). *The Elizabethan Stage*. 4 vols. Oxford: Clarendon Press.

Clark, Peter, ed. (1981). *Country Towns in Pre-Industrial England*. Leicester: Leicester University Press.

Douglas, Audrey and Peter H. Greenfield, eds (1986). *REED (Records of Early English Drama) Cumberland, Westmorland, Gloucestershire*. Toronto: University of Toronto Press.

Foakes, R. A. and R. T. Rickert, eds (1961). *Henslowe's Diary*. Cambridge: Cambridge University Press.

George, David, ed. (1991). *REED (Records of Early English Drama) Lancashire*. Toronto: University of Toronto Press.

Gibson, James M. (1995). "Stuart players in Kent: fact or fiction?" *Records of Early English Drama Newsletter* 20. 2, 1–12.

Gibson, James, ed. (2001). *REED (Records of Early English Drama) Kent*. Toronto: University of Toronto Press.

Greenfield, Peter, H., ed. (n.d.). "REED (Records of Early English Drama) Hertfordshire." Unpublished transcriptions.

Greenfield, Peter H. (1983). "Entertainments of Henry, Lord Berkeley, 1593–4 and 1600–05." *Records of Early English Drama Newsletter* 8, 16.

Greenfield, Peter H. (1988). "Professional players at Gloucester: conditions of provincial performing." In *Elizabethan Theatre X*, ed. C. E. McGee. Port Credit, ON: P. D. Meany.

Gurr, Andrew (1996). *The Shakespearian Playing Companies*. Oxford: Clarendon Press.

Hamilton, Alice, ed. (n.d.). "REED (Records of Early English Drama) Leicester." Unpublished transcriptions.

Hays, Rosalind C. (1992). "Dorset church houses and the drama." *Research Opportunities in Renaissance Drama* 31, 12–23.

Ingram, R. W., ed. (1981). *REED (Records of Early English Drama) Coventry*. Toronto: University of Toronto Press.

Ingram, William (1993). "The cost of touring." *Medieval and Renaissance Drama in England* 6, 57–62.

Klausner, David N., ed. (1990). *REED (Records of Early English Drama) Herefordshire, Worcestershire*. Toronto: University of Toronto Press.

MacLean, Sally-Beth (1988). "Players on tour: new evidence from Records of Early English Drama." In *Elizabethan Theatre X*, ed. C. E. McGee. Port Credit, ON: P. D. Meany.

MacLean, Sally-Beth (1993). "Tour routes: 'provincial wanderings' or traditional circuits?" *Medieval and Renaissance Drama in England* 6, 1–14.

McMillin, Scott and Sally-Beth MacLean (1998). *The Queen's Men and their Plays*. Cambridge: Cambridge University Press.

Montrose, Louis (1996). *The Purpose of Playing: Shakespeare and the Cultural Politics of the Elizabethan Theatre*. Chicago: University of Chicago Press.

Murray, John Tucker (1910). *The English Dramatic Companies, 1558–1642*. 2 vols. London: Constable.

Pilkinton, Mark C. (1997). *REED (Records of Early English Drama) Bristol*. Toronto: University of Toronto Press.

Somerset, J. A. B. (1994a). *REED (Records of Early English Drama) Shropshire*. Toronto: University of Toronto Press.

Somerset, J. A. B. (1994b). "'How chances it they travel?': provincial touring, playing places, and the King's Men." *Shakespeare Survey* 47, 45–60.

Tittler, Robert (1991). *Architecture and Power: The Town Hall and the English Urban Community c.1500–1640*. Oxford: Clarendon Press.

Wasson, John (n.d.). "Records of Early English Drama: Clifford family." Unpublished transcriptions.

Wasson, John M. (1997). "The English church as theatrical space." In *A New History of Early English Drama*, eds, John D. Cox and David Scott Kastan. New York: Columbia University Press.

Willis, R. (1639). *Mount Tabor, or Private Exercises of a Penitent Sinner*. London: printed by R. B. for P. Stephens and C. Meredith, at the gilded Lion in S. Paul's Church-yard. STC 25752.

Wood, H. Harvey, ed. (1939). *The Plays of John Marston*. Edinburgh: Oliver and Boyd.

16

Jurisdiction of Theater and Censorship

Richard Dutton

One of the delights of the movie *Shakespeare in Love* (dir. John Madden, 1998) is that it resurrected Edmund Tilney, master of the revels to Queen Elizabeth and James I. It is no fiction that this court official exercised a careful authority over the theater of his day. But it is a slander to suggest he did so boorishly or with a posse of men-at-arms to enforce his will. Nor was it ever part of his remit to keep budding Gwyneth Paltrows off the stage: the convention which prevented women from acting was a cultural practice of obscure origin, not a matter of regulation. But the issues to which Tilney and his successors *did* attend, and how they handled them, were crucial to the development of the drama – to its very survival – in the last 20 years of Elizabeth's reign and down to the Civil War.

In attending to the nature of their office we can better appreciate the kinds of control, and the limits of toleration, which were actually applied to the professional theater of the era: the kinds of pressure which in fact fostered the work of Marlowe, Shakespeare, Jonson, Heywood, Webster, Fletcher, Middleton, Massinger, Ford, and their fellows. Some important features of this emerge from the scrabble eventually to succeed Tilney. In 1597 it became clear to former playwright John Lyly that he was never going to do this. He bemoaned how "Offices in reversion [i.e. promised to someone when the current holder died] are forestalled, in possession engrossed, and that of the Revels countenanced on Buc" (Hunter, 1962, 78). Lyly knew that the reversion was going to Sir George Buc, the man who actually succeeded Tilney; in a petition to the queen he lamented that he had been passed over, recalling how she herself had urged "that I should aim all my courses at the Revels, (I dare not tell with a promise, but a hopeful item of the reversion), for which these ten years I have attended with an unwearied patience" (Hunter, 1962, 85–6).

This sorry episode underlines first that the authority involved derived from the court, the nub of power and patronage in the country: the nature of what was permitted, and on what terms, was largely determined by the court's own interest in drama as a recreation and as a means of conspicuous display. Second, the award of this post was affected by precisely the same considerations as any other middle-ranking position at court: many applicants would be vying for it, and the decision would hinge on the influence of patrons and a history of loyal service to the crown. As a former impresario with Oxford's Boys and Paul's Boys, a man of letters, and a courtier with substantial connections (including the earl of Oxford), Lyly was ideally qualified. But he lost out to Buc, a man without theatrical experience; critically, Buc was a diplomat who had served the powerful Robert Cecil for some time, while also being (like Tilney) a client of Lord Admiral Howard. Third, as often at the time, the authority of the crown was a pretext for making money: in regulating the theaters Tilney and his successors generated a significant income for themselves. Hence the competition for the post. But hence also a relationship between the acting companies and their regulator marked as much by mutual interdependence as by antagonism.

The master of the revels was originally and primarily an official in the lord chamberlain's office, charged with providing suitable entertainment at court, like Philostrate, Theseus' "usual manager of mirth" in *A Midsummer Night's Dream* (V.i.35).[1] Prior to Tilney's appointment in 1579 the Revels Office was in disarray: it was expensive to run, some of the shows it sponsored were unsatisfactory, and some of the aristocrats who patronized acting companies brought pressure to bear to have their own "servants" selected for court performances. In 1581 the queen gave Tilney a special commission, which authorized him:

> to warne commaunde and appointe in all places within this our Realme of England, aswell within francheses and liberties as without, all and every plaier or plaiers with their playmakers, either belonging to any noble man or otherwise, bearinge the name or names or using the facultie of playmakers or plaiers of Comedies, Tragedies, Enterludes or whatever other showes soever, from tyme to tyme and at all tymes to appeare before him with all such plaies, Tragedies, Comedies or showes as they shall in readines or meane to sett forth, and them to recite before our said Servant or his sufficient deputie, whom we ordeyne appointe and aucthorise by these presentes of all suche showes, plaies, plaiers and playmakers, together with their playing places, to order and reforme, auctorise and put downe, as shalbe thought meete or unmeete unto himself or his said deputie in that behalf. (Chambers, 1923, IV, 285–7)

This was the basis of Tilney's role as licenser and censor of the professional theater in the London region. Some have seen it as a step toward absolute state control of players and playing, in the wake of efforts in the provinces to eradicate the mystery cycles and other religious drama closely associated with Roman Catholicism (Wickham, 1959–81, II, 1, 94). But the pressures which required an end to the church- and guild-sponsored playing in the provinces were actually very different from those which governed the control of professional theater in London: these activities belonged to different spheres of life, attracting the attention of different authorities. As W. R. Streitberger (1978) has shown, Tilney was given his powers specifically to reinforce his primary role as the provider of theatrical entertainment at court: and to do it both economically and with consistent quality.

At the heart of his policy for achieving this was a greater reliance than hitherto on the professional actors, whose newly purpose-built theaters marked the growth of the industry in London. The commission gave Tilney the power to compel these troupes to rehearse their repertory before him, against possible performance at court during the festive season. Until 1607 he had capacious quarters in the old palace of St. John's, where, as Thomas Heywood recalled in *An Apology for Actors,* "our Court playes have been in late daies yearely rehersed, perfected, and corrected before they come to the publike view of the Prince and the Nobility." So the office of the master of the revels developed symbiotically with the growth of the theatrical profession. The structure of licensing and censorship that grew up around him was precisely one that enabled successful professional actors to become adjuncts of the court, while also providing them with a relatively stable environment within which they could cater for a wider audience in the public theaters.

The competition at court between the actors' influential patrons was largely resolved in 1583 by a decision to create a new troupe under direct royal patronage, the Queen's Men (McMillin and MacLean, 1998; Gurr, 1996, 196ff). Powerful figures in the Privy Council (Sir Francis Walsingham and the earl of Leicester) instructed Tilney to create this elite company, who received the lion's share of performances at court over the next several years. The Queen's Men were specifically subject to Tilney's authority (and protection) both in London and in the extensive touring operations which were, from the outset, part of their remit: they carried the queen's livery, and her government's view of the world, throughout the kingdom.

Tilney, however, remained only one figure in a complex array of authorities in the London region. One key competing authority in respect of the theaters was the court itself, represented by the Privy Council: the serving lord chamberlain always had a brief for acting matters, while Lord Charles Howard (patron of both Tilney and Buc) continued to take an interest in them when he moved on from that post to become lord admiral. On the other side was the city of London, variously represented by its lord mayor, Common hall, Court of Common Council, and Court of Aldermen. The received picture of this contest has it that the court staunchly supported the actors, while the Puritan-inclined city tried to put them out of business. But this is misleading. The court only supported actors patronized by its own senior members, regarding their commercial activities as in effect rehearsals for performance before the queen; it readily followed the city in stigmatizing unlicensed actors as rogues and vagabonds. In the city there were legitimate concerns about the maintenance of order and the threat of disease (which the Privy Council sometimes shared), as well as the promotion of crime and lewd behavior. But there was also a shrewd sense that these enterprises might be licensed and so taxed to support the hospitals for the poor and diseased (Ingram, 1992, 119–49). At times negotiations between the parties also boiled down to a contestation over their respective prerogatives, in which the theaters were almost an incidental issue.

Because of such tensions, all the early purpose-built theaters were constructed outside the jurisdiction of the city authorities, in the liberties to the north and south (see chapter 11 above). Even here they were not outside the framework of authority: they came under the magistrates for Middlesex and Surrey.[2] But until at least 1596 there was also regular playing at inns within the city's jurisdiction, notably the Bell, the Bull, the Cross Keys, and the Bel Savage (Ingram, 1978, 140–1). The role of the master of the revels evolved in the midst of these conflicting authorities and agendas, and not without competition. As early as 1574 the Common Council of London argued that playing places in the city should be licensed, and that plays performed there should be "first perused and allowed" by persons appointed by the lord mayor and the Court of Aldermen. This was to rebut the lord chamberlain's proposal (before Tilney was in post) that "one Mr Holmes" should take on such a role. They wanted to preserve the city's own authority and to control profits from the licensing, rather than promote "the benefit of any private person" (Ingram, 1992, 127, 142). There is no evidence, however, that such persons ever were appointed.

In 1589, the Privy Council instructed Tilney to act in consort with nominees of both the lord mayor and the archbishop of Canterbury in a commission for the censoring of all plays to be performed "in and about the City of London"; but the articles setting it up are all we ever hear of this. By 1592 Tilney's importance was such that the city authorities saw him as an impediment to the kinds of restraint they wanted to exert themselves, and they sought (without success) to buy him out. By then, he was certainly receiving regular fees from the theatrical financier Philip Henslowe, indicating his relationship with the most established companies. It seems Tilney was receiving separate fees for licensing the theaters, the acting companies, and each play – which he would "peruse" (that is, read rather than see in rehearsal) and then "allow" when he was satisfied with it, appending his signature to what became the only "allowed copy" for performance purposes. Tilney kept records of licenses, but his office-book and that of Buc have been lost. Only from the time of Sir John Astley (1622), who quickly sold his office to Sir Henry Herbert (1623), do we have information from their shared office-book. But even that is unreliable, as the original long since disappeared (Bawcutt, 1996, 13–26). We often have to infer from it what may have been earlier practice. The precise fees changed a good deal over the period as a whole, but a significant economic symbiosis between the master of the revels and those whose livelihood he licensed remained throughout (Dutton, 1991, 52, 116; Bawcutt, 1996, 38–40).

Precisely which companies Tilney licensed in the 1580s and early 1590s we do not know, apart from the Queen's Men: probably only those who actually performed at court, notably Leicester's, Strange's, the Admiral's and the boy companies (Chapel Royal/Oxford's and Paul's), though their licenses differed from those of the adult players. As early as 1574 Leicester's Men received a patent allowing them to perform anywhere in the country, providing that their plays had been "sene and allowed" by the master of the revels (Chambers, 1923, II, 87–8; Gurr, 1996, 187–8). The company sought this as defense against civic authorities (including London's) that tried to prevent them from playing; the master's license certified that their plays were fit for court, and ought not to be challenged elsewhere. It reinforced their status as servants of a patron like Leicester, whose livery they wore. Patronage by an influential aristocrat was an important adjunct to commercial viability for any company, and a form of control in that no patron would stand for behavior which reflected badly on him. Earlier, members of the gentry had patronized actors, but from 1572 this privilege was restricted to the aristocracy (barons and those of higher degree), though companies could locally get permission to perform from two justices of the peace. Those without patronage or permission were subject to punitive laws against rogues, vagabonds, and sturdy beggars (Chambers, 1923, IV, 270; Beier, 1986).[3]

In this context we can see why the city authorities might see the master of the revels as protector of the most successful actors, as much as their regulator. And we may suppose that the actors appreciated this themselves; his license gave them protection against hostile authorities, an opportunity of lucrative performances at court, and the sole right to perform plays "allowed" to them – a version of performing copyright. As a censor it seems that each of the masters was scrupulous, could on occasion be strict, but on the whole applied relatively broad criteria of what was permissible. At the start of her reign Elizabeth issued a proclamation (May 16, 1559) which instructed royal officers everywhere on what was not acceptable:

> And for instruction to every one of the sayde officers, her majestie doth likewise charge every one of them, as they will aunswere: that they permyt none to be played wherein either matters of religion or of the governaunce of the estate of the common weale shalbe handled or treated, beyng no meete matters to be wrytten or treated upon, but by menne of aucthoritie, learning and wisedome, nor to be handled before any audience, but of grave and discreete persons. (Chambers, 1923, IV, 263–4)

Note the implication that such matters *might* be put on stage in privileged contexts, an implicit *court* standard of what was acceptable. This explains how a play like *Gorboduc*, which clearly if mythologically treats of matters "of the governaunce of the estate of the common weale" (the need for the queen to marry, or otherwise provide for the succession), could be performed in the Inns of Court. Yet the play passed into the professional repertory after it was published, circumventing notional restrictions.

So masters of the revels, who were supposed to be reviewing plays for performance before the monarch, implicitly applied a court standard in their licenses. A clear demonstration of this comes in Herbert's office-book (January 1631): "I did refuse to allow of a play of Messinger's, because itt did contain dangerous matter, as the deposing of Sebastian king of Portugal by Philip the ⟨Second,⟩ and ther being a peace sworen twixte the kings of England and Spayne" (Bawcutt, 1996, 171–2). So he refused to license a play he deemed overtly hostile to the king's current foreign policy. Yet five months later he licensed a play called *Believe as You List*, which is transparently a reworking of the play he had turned down, merely transposed to classical antiquity. It is unlikely this was an oversight. All the masters were literate and sophisticated men – Tilney a diplomatic genealogist, Buc a respected historian, and Herbert the brother of the poets Edward and George. Herbert probably judged that the play, as reworked, was no longer an open affront to the royal prerogative or to a friendly foreign power. In that context, it was acceptable. He was not concerned to second-guess either Massinger's *intentions* or what audiences might *infer* from material that was not openly provocative.

There is something patrician about all this – Herbert, a representative of the privileged classes, not deigning to notice what did not strictly require to be noticed. Such assumptions were openly expressed by the caste-conscious Spanish ambassador who complained about Middleton's *A Game at Chess* (1624), writing that the play was "offensive to my royal master (if, indeed, the grandeur and inestimable value of his royal person could receive offense from anybody, and especially from men of such low condition as ordinarily are the authors and actors of such follies)" (Howard-Hill, 1993, 193). The English might not put such attitudes into words, but we should not doubt they lived by them. In such a context, as Annabel Patterson puts it: "there were conventions that both sides accepted as to how far a writer could go in explicit address to the contentious issues of his day, how he could encode his opinions so that nobody would be *required* to make an example of him" (1984, 11).

There is, then, always something disingenuous about censored dramatists' protestations of innocence, of having been misunderstood. When Jonson laments how "nothing can be so innocently writ or carried but may be made obnoxious to construction" (Epistle to *Volpone*, ll. 57–8), he is at least partly inviting the very reading between the lines that he decries. There are similarly provocative disavowals in many plays, most famously in Massinger's *The Roman Actor* (1626), where Casesar's spy, Aretinus, accuses the actors: "You are they / That search into the secrets of the time, / And under feigned names on the stage present / Actions not to be touched at" (I.iii.36–9). Paris the Tragedian denies this, arguing that it is wrong to hold the actors to blame for meanings which are unintentional and not aimed at individuals. Yet in *A Game at Chess* the actors indisputably did satirize known individuals.

It was normally the masters' function to ensure, not exactly the innocence of a play, but that its fictional veiling was adequate, that serious offense might not be offered to members of the court or to friendly foreign dignitaries. The masters also needed to be alert to contentious issues with public order implications; but in other respects they could be quite relaxed. The only extant manuscript censored by Tilney is *Sir Thomas More*, about a man seen by many as a Catholic martyr to Henry VIII; the play depicts More going to his death for refusing to accept the Act of Supremacy, but tactfully does not go into detail about this delicate subject. We might have supposed that Tilney would ban the play outright, but his markings suggest he was careful about its main theme, though not overly disturbed. But the opening scenes, depicting anti-alien riots, brought this strict warning: "Leave out the insurrection wholy & the Cause ther off & begin with Sr Tho: Moore att the mayors sessions with a reportt afterwardes off his good service don being Shrive [Sheriff] of London uppon a mutiny Agaynst the Lumbardes only by A Shortt reporte & nott otherwise at your perilles. E. Tyllney" (Dutton, 1991, plate 7). His concern is almost certainly similar riots in London when the play was first drafted (Long, 1989). Feelings against French immigrants were particularly strong, so references to the Lombards might be less inflammatory; but the main thrust is to replace graphic scenes of rioting with a brief *report* of More's actions. Tilney seems more concerned by the public order resonances of the play than by its broader ideological implications.

We may see something analogous in the censorship of the 1597 quarto of *Richard II*. We do not know if the abdication scene was cut by Tilney or by the press censor (Dutton, 1991, 124–7). But we have the apparent anomaly of allowing the murder of a king to be shown openly, while cutting the non-inflammatory abdication. The most compelling explanation is that the scene shows Richard's abdication being sanctioned by Parliament, its authority apparently outweighing that of the crown (Clegg, 1997b). At the time, with no agreed successor to Elizabeth, this was highly contentious; but it was a non-issue in 1608, when the play was printed with the scene restored. Again, the censor's attention seems to be on immediately provocative matters rather than on *potentially* subversive subtexts in the play as a whole.

The fraught situation as Elizabeth's reign neared its end affected a sequence of Privy Council initiatives concerning the theaters, which finally installed the master of the revels center-stage. In July 1597 they issued an extraordinary order that all the theaters should be "plucked down" (Wickham, 1969; Ingram, 1978, 167–86). The timing suggests this was linked with the lost play *The Isle of Dogs*, denounced by the Council as "sclanderous," "lewd" and "seditious." But perhaps more than one agenda was in play. The notorious torturer and chief of the secret police, Richard Topcliffe, was involved, the only known instance of such brutal realities bearing on theatrical affairs. It seems likely that broad anti-court satire lampooned known individuals (Nicholl, 1984, 242–56). But Sir Robert Cecil also had a separate dispute with the owner of the Swan where it was staged, while the Lord Admiral's Men objected that Pembroke's Men, the actors, were luring away sharers from their company (Ingram, 1978), both factors which may have affected the Privy Council's actions.

Their order was never enforced. Instead, they restricted the number of companies authorized to play regularly in London to two (February 1598), both licensed by Tilney – as Pembroke's Men had not been – and patronized by two of their own number, the lord chamberlain and lord admiral, both cousins of the queen.[4] And Parliament removed the right of justices of the peace to authorize playing: patronage was restricted exclusively to the peerage, while penalties against masterless men became even more draconian. In June 1600 the two companies were restricted to playing at their "usual houses" – for the Chamberlain's the Globe, for the Admiral's the new Fortune. And the number of performances was limited. The intention was clear: to restrict London playing to two select companies, both patronized by senior privy councillors, in fixed locations and at known times, conditions which Tilney could easily police (Dutton, 2000, 16–40).

The reality was rather different: the Children of the Chapel and Paul's Boys, both defunct for a decade, were revived under their different licensing arrangements. Then Derby's Men played at the Boar's Head, and even performed at court. Soon Worcester's Men replaced them. Worcester, also a privy councillor, secured his men a place among the "allowed" companies – making three adult and two boys' companies, all answerable to Tilney (Dutton, 2002). This was as many as the master of the revels was ever responsible for, usually four and sometimes five, as companies and patronage fluctuated. Tilney and his successors expanded their authority (and revenue) by licensing first non-theatrical shows and latterly actors traveling in the provinces (Dutton, 1991, 116, 235–6). But their central concern was always the London-based companies, the most successful of their time, who bequeathed the great majority of plays which have survived.

When James I succeeded Elizabeth he took four of the London companies into royal patronage: the Chamberlain's became the King's Men, the Admiral's Prince Henry's, and Worcester's Queen Anne's. The Children of the Chapel became the Children of the Queen's Revels.[5] This has been seen as an act of royal absolutism, pulling the theaters away from their popular roots and redirecting their repertories toward courtly tastes. In fact it was only an extension of the policy of the Elizabethan Privy Council, taking into account the multiplied royal households, and probably reinforced the economic instincts of the companies affected. The adult companies remained answerable to Tilney, but the Queen's Revels Boys had their own licenser, Samuel Daniel. This company provoked some of the most notable theatrical scandals of the era. They consistently fostered a repertory of politically charged satirical drama, which may have found encouragement under Queen Anne's patronage (Lewalski, 1993, 24). Daniel's own *Philotas* (1604) was seen as commenting on the Essex rebellion and he was questioned by the Privy Council. *Eastward Ho* (1605) landed Jonson and Chapman in prison, under threat of mutilation; their satire of mercenary Scots courtiers was compounded by failure to have the play licensed at all: much could be overlooked within the circle of licensed authority, but not the flouting of authority itself. Only representations to powerful people at court effected their release. We presume Daniel lost his post as licenser, but the company continued to cause scandal, with Day's *Isle of Gulls* (1606), Chapman's *Byron* plays (1607/8), and other works. Other parts of the profession resented their threat to the collective livelihood. Heywood's *Apology for Actors* urges them "to curbe and limit this presumed liberty," while the "little eyases" additions to *Hamlet* have been convincingly linked to this period (Knutson, 1995). In 1608 the company was stripped of its license (Dutton, 2002).

In 1606 Sir George Buc began licensing plays *for the press*; this was formerly done by clerics of the Court of High Commission, who licensed all other printed works (Clegg, 2001). It has been supposed that Buc also acted as the aging Tilney's deputy, but there is no evidence of this, and Tilney continued to function at court until his death (Eccles, 1938; Streitberger, 1986). Only then, in 1610, can we be confident that one man, Buc, was licensing all the London companies, as well as play-texts for the press. He inherited from Tilney a system of licensing and control that did not change in essence until the closing of the theaters. From 1606 this included attending to Parliament's "Acte to restrain the Abuses of Players," prohibiting blasphemous language on the stage. Most texts licensed or relicensed after this are more careful (see, for example, the differences between the quarto and folio *Volpone* and *Othello*). The manuscript of *The Second Maiden's Tragedy* (1611), with Buc's license, shows him alert to the issue, marking places where changes were necessary, perhaps expecting the actors to change others (Dutton, 1991, 194–209).

Sir John Van Olden Barnavelt (1618) is another manuscript where Buc's hand is visible; we see a careful method of penciled markings, some later reinforced in ink, with crosses in margins where he perhaps intended to consult the actors (Howard-Hill, 1988). Where he finds objectionable material he tries to find alternatives, and only crosses it out as a last resort. He is most alert to depictions of the Prince of Orange, losing patience in an initialed note: "I like not this: neithr do I think that the prince was thus disgracefully used. besides he is too much presented" (Dutton, 1991, 208–17, plate 9). We learn during the *Game at Chess* controversy that "there was a commaundment and restraint given against the representinge of anie moderne Christian kings in those Stage-playes" (Howard-Hill, 1993, 200). But Buc only draws a line when faced with outright provocation, as in a strongly anti-monarchist passage with the loaded suggestion (ostensibly for those on stage, but available to an audience) "you can apply this" (Dutton, 1991, 214–15). He tinkered, redrafted, but finally crossed out the whole passage. The play (like Chapman's *Byron* plays) was doubly problematic since it depicts recent Dutch history, and might be diplomatically sensitive; but it probably also shadowed the death of Walter Ralegh, like Barnavelt a "patriot" who had fallen from royal favor and been executed.

Buc finally went mad, probably from the pressures of trying to run an office in a bankrupt court. This perhaps explains how some actors managed to circumvent the Revels Office, and obtained licenses by other routes – a situation which lord chamberlain Pembroke tried to rectify with a 1622 warrant, confirming the exclusive theatrical authority of the Revels Office throughout the country (Dutton, 1991, 225–6). Perhaps because of such problems, Buc's successor, Sir John Astley, quickly sold the post to Herbert (Dutton, 1990; Bawcutt, 1992). He was the client and kinsman of his lord chamberlain, the powerful third earl of Pembroke; even when Pembroke was succeeded in 1626 by his brother, the earl of Montgomery, essential ties of patronage and kinship remained. This perhaps helped to maintain a continuity of practice in the Revels Office at times when the supremacy of Buckingham and later the personal government of Charles I created very different political atmospheres from that in which the largely consensual role of the master of the revels had evolved.

Middleton's *A Game at Chess* was the most resonant theatrical scandal of the era; it performed to packed houses until Spanish protests had it stopped.[6] The play is a lively satire on Jesuit wiles, and contrived to review Anglo-Spanish relations in unusually close detail. The previous Spanish ambassador, Gondomar, and the archbishop of Spalato were impersonated in some detail, while other characters (under the allegory of chess pieces) represented the leading figures of the Spanish and English courts. We know that Herbert gave the play a license in the usual way, but commentators then and scholars since have supposed it may have been specially sponsored at the highest level. This is unprovable, and not a necessary conjecture. England and Spain were on the brink of war, a context in which Herbert had no need to protect Spanish sensitivities; he may have felt that the depiction of the English court was acceptably patriotic. Perhaps the lengths to which the actors went to impersonate Gondomar (acquiring a cast suit of clothes and a "chair of ease" for his anal fistula) breached the fictional veiling on which he normally insisted, and created a popular scandal which could not be ignored. In 1632 he recorded: "In the play of *The Ball*, written by Sherley, and acted by the Queens players, ther were divers personated so naturally, both of lords and others of the court, that I took it ill" (Bawcutt, 1996, 177).[7]

Middleton may have spent some time in prison over *A Game at Chess*, but the King's Men suffered no more than a brief suspension of playing.[8] They were clearly not over-awed, since in December 1624 they staged the lost *Spanish Viceroy* without Herbert's license. He was so incensed – and so sensitive to the implications for his own stand-ing – that he required all patented members of the company to subscribe to a letter (transcribed in his office-book) acknowledging their fault and submitting to his authority (Bawcutt, 1996, 183). Yet again, however, no one actually suffered the harsh penalties potentially available either for libeling someone important on stage or for flouting the licensing regulations. Although dramatists and actors spent brief periods in prison, no one in the theater suffered the grim mutilations of John Stubbes or William Prynne, or the prolonged imprisonment of John Hayward, who all trans-gressed in print (Finkelpearl, 1986). Which is a testament of sorts to the Revels Office as an instrument of regulation, and to the general good will of the court towards the actors it patronized.

In October 1633 something about a revival of Fletcher's *The Woman's Prize* (*c.*1611) severely strained Herbert's relations with the actors (Bawcutt, 1996, 182–3; Dutton, 2000, 41–61). Normally where the actors followed their "allowed copy," a play need not be relicensed. Yet he stopped this revival at short notice, which "raysed some dis-course in the players, though no disobedience." His recorded objections were to "oaths, prophaness and ribaldrye." But something more serious was probably at issue: almost certainly the play's strong anti-Catholicism and its husband-taming heroine (it is a continuation of *The Taming of the Shrew*), called Maria. In 1633, the play probably glanced at Queen Henrietta-Maria, her overt Catholicism, and her influence over Charles I. The fact that the King's Men and Herbert were already in dispute over Jonson's *The Magnetic Lady*, which had been referred to archbishop Laud himself in the Court of High Commission, is probably also relevant and evidence of tension for the whole profession during Charles's personal rule (Butler, 1992). Herbert now insisted that old plays should be relicensed, "since they may be full of offensive things against church and state, ye rather that in former time the poetts tooke greater liberty than is allowed them by me." The actors concerned later apologized for their "ill manners"; they knew how things stood.

One effect of the growing identification of the leading companies with the court was the emergence of gentlemen or courtier playwrights, in a position to challenge the authority of the master of the revels.[9] Astley had problems with *Osmond the Great Turk* by Lodowick Carlell, a courtier with connections, and referred it to lord chamberlain Pembroke (Bawcutt, 1996, 137). Herbert's changes to Davenant's

The Wits caused problems, and it was reviewed by King Charles himself: "The king is pleasd to take *faith*, *death*, *slight*, for asseverations, and no oaths, to which I doe humbly submit as my masters judgment; but under favour conceive them to be oaths, and enter them here, to declare my opinion and submission" (Bawcutt, 1996, 186).

Herbert also recorded his own referral of *The King and the Subject* (1638), by the professional dramatist Massinger, to the king: "who, readinge over the play at New-market, set his marke upon the place with his owne hande, and in thes words: 'This is too insolent, and to bee changed'. Note, that the poett makes it the speech of a king, Don Pedro kinge of Spayne, and spoken to his subjects" (Bawcutt, 1996, 204). The passage in question concerns royal taxation without parliamentary sanction, a very sensitive issue at the time. The wonder is that Herbert did not simply rule the passage, or even the entire play, out of court. In fact, like his predecessors, he did his best to make it playable – allowing it on the condition that "the reformations [be] most strictly observed, and not otherwise," including that the provocative title be changed. Yet he took the precaution of referring it to the king. Charles's "too inso-lent" implies that he was used to insolence, but that this crossed the limits of toler-ation. (And Herbert notes for future reference that the context – a king speaking to his subjects – contributes to the insolence.) But majesty rarely acknowledges such flea-bites. Even, as here, when it did so there were no recriminations: Massinger was not to be punished for what he very likely thought. There is no evidence of *any* drama-tist of the period being punished for his ideas, opinions, or intentions. If this seems suspiciously liberal, we may have to settle for an unpalatable truth: that in early modern England, players and playwrights were normally too insignificant for those in power to take all that seriously, except when they were far "too insolent" and con-trived to offend someone with influence (Yachnin, 1991). And the masters of the revels were adept at preventing that from happening too often. It is that which made them, perhaps paradoxically, such an important element in the formula which produced early modern drama. Without their protective presence, giving the theatrical profession a degree of creative and expressive space, it is unlikely that the plays they licensed could have been as culturally vigorous as so many of them actually were.

Tensions surrounding *The King and the Subject* clearly foreshadow the Civil War and the closing of the theaters. But it is a mistake to see what happened in 1642 simply as the revenge of parliamentary Puritans, now in the ascendant. On January 26 (before the final breach with the king), an order was moved in the Commons "that in these times of calamity in Ireland and the distractions in this kingdom, that all interludes and plays be suppressed for a season." But it was "laid aside by Mr Pym his second-ing of Mr Waller in alleging it was their trade" (Coates et al., 1982, 182). The leading parliamentarian John Pym resisted a ban on playing as an infringement of the players' trade, and the House backed him. The whole business underlines the complex mix of political, economic, and social pressures within which the theaters had operated to this point. Parliament finally passed the critical ordinance for the cessation of playing on September 2, 1642. But this only required that "while these sad Causes and set times of Humiliation doe continue, publike Stage-Plays shall cease" – referring to the rebellion in Ireland, the most important matter before the Commons that day. There was no move against the playhouses themselves, and it seems "the prohibition was intended to be a temporary one, to last as long as the crisis which occasioned it" (Roberts, 1997). In all probability it was the behavior of the acting companies themselves which turned a temporary prohibition into a state of affairs lasting 18 years: even before the ordinance they started to disintegrate (Gurr, 1996, 385–6). Those who had controlled them also parted company. In 1643 Henry Herbert joined the royalist Parliament at Oxford (but never, as was once supposed, fought for the king); by late 1645 he decided that the royalist cause was lost, and by 1648 he had made his peace with Parliament in London. His kinsman and superior, lord chamberlain Pembroke, sided (however reluctantly) with Parliament from the start.[10] Only as positions hardened did a vindictive anti-theatricality overtake Parliament: in 1647 they chose to regard the old legislation against *masterless* players as applying to all of them; the next year they ordered the demolition of all the playhouses.

NOTES

1   References to Shakespeare are to *The Riverside Shakespeare* (Evans, 1974). Philostrate's role is much more prominent in the 1599 quarto text; most of his role is redistributed among other characters in the 1623 folio.

2   Mullaney (1988) argues that "[w]hen popular drama moved out into the Liberties, it . . . converted the moral license and ambivalence of the Liberties to its own ends, translating its own cultural situation into a liberty that was at once moral, ideological and topological" (p. ix). But the argument that the theaters enjoyed a special "liberty" because of where they were situated is questionable: for most purposes they were not subject to interference from the city authorities, but this did not remove them from the wider structures of control in early modern England.

3   These restrictions only applied to professional players performing in public. The gentry might still retain household servants who would sometimes perform as entertainers.

4   The Queen's Men lost their special status at court after the deaths of Leicester and Walsingham, though they continued as a touring company.

5   Paul's Boys were in decline and disappeared around 1606.

6   It ran August 5–14, barring only August 8, since performances were not allowed on Sundays. Performances were normally also suspended for much of Lent, though in later years dispensations could be bought from the master of the revels (Bawcutt, 1996, 213). Playing was also stopped when the weekly plague bills exceeded a given number – the years of 1593–4, 1603, and 1608–9 were particularly bad (Barroll, 1991). There is evidence the Privy Council and others sometimes exploited this excuse for other reasons (Freedman, 1996).

7   Only people of substance could expect to be protected from malicious "personation." We know Chapman's lost *The Old Joiner of Aldgate* (1603) shadowed real events and that participants saw "themselves" on stage. Anne Elsden fruitlessly complained about the portrayal of herself in *The Late Murder in the White Chapel, or Keepe the Widow Waking* (1624), by Dekker, Rowley, Ford, and Webster (Dutton, 1991, 129–32).

8   Dramatists (rather than actors) often carried the blame for "personations," perhaps because some of them coached the actors in their performances. Over *The Ball*, Herbert records the assurance of Christopher Beeston, manager of the Queen's Men, "that he would not suffer it to be done by

the poett any more, who deserves to be punisht" (Bawcutt, 1996, 177). The actors surely knew what they were doing.

9   In arguing that the leading companies were increasingly identified with the court I do not suggest either that the court was itself a monolithic entity, or that the actors and their dramatists endorsed Stuart absolutist government, but rather that the economic and social dependence of the companies on the court affected their theatrical styles and strategies. Within this – as *The King and the Subject* amply demonstrates – there remained room for a considerable range of political views (Butler, 1984).

10 The earl of Montgomery succeeded his brother to the senior title of Pembroke in 1630.

REFERENCES AND FURTHER READING

Barroll, Leeds (1991). *Politics, Plague, and Shakespeare's Theater: The Stuart Years.* Ithaca: Cornell University Press.

Bawcutt, N. W. (1992). "Evidence and conjecture in literary scholarship: the case of Sir John Astley reconsidered." *English Literary Renaissance* 22, 333–46.

Bawcutt, N. W. (1996). *The Control and Censorship of Caroline Drama: The Records of Sir Henry Herbert, Master of the Revels 1623–73.* Oxford: Clarendon Press.

Beier, A. L. (1986). *Masterless Men: The Vagrancy Problem in England, 1560–1641.* London: Methuen.

Burt, Richard (1993). *Licensed by Authority: Ben Jonson and the Discourses of Censorship.* Ithaca: Cornell University Press.

Butler, Martin (1984). *Theatre and Crisis, 1632–1642.* Cambridge: Cambridge University Press.

Butler, Martin (1992). "Ecclesiastical censorship of early Stuart drama: the case of Jonson's *The Magnetic Lady*." *Modern Philology* 89, 469–81.

Chambers, E. K. (1923). *The Elizabethan Stage.* 4 vols. Oxford: Oxford University Press.

Clare, Janet (1997). "Historicism and the question of censorship in the Renaissance." *English Literary Renaissance* 27.2, 155–76.

Clare, Janet (1999). *"Art Made Tongue-Tied By Authority": Elizabethan and Jacobean Dramatic Censorship.* 2nd edn. Manchester: Manchester University Press.

Clegg, Cyndia Susan (1997a). *Press Censorship in Elizabethan England.* Cambridge: Cambridge University Press.

Clegg, Cyndia Susan (1997b). "'By the choise and inuitation of al the realme': *Richard II* and Elizabethan press censorship." *Shakespeare Quarterly* 48, 432–48.

Clegg, Cyndia Susan (2001). "Burning books as propaganda in Jacobean England." In *Literature and Censorship in Renaissance England*, ed. Andrew Hadfield. Basingstoke and New York: Palgrave.

Coates, Willson H., Vernon F. Snow, and Anne Steele Young, eds (1982). *The Private Journals of the Long Parliament Vol. 1.* New Haven: Yale University Press.

Dutton, Richard (1990). "Patronage, politics, and the master of the revels, 1622–40: the case of Sir John Astley." *English Literary Renaissance* 20, 287–331.

Dutton, Richard (1991). *Mastering the Revels: The Regulation and Censorship of English Renaissance Drama.* London and Basingstoke: Macmillan.

Dutton, Richard (2000). *Licensing, Censorship and Authorship in Early Modern England: Buggeswords.* London and Basingstoke: Palgrave.

Dutton, Richard (2002). "The Revels Office and the boy companies, 1600–1613: new perspectives." *English Literary Renaissance* 32.

Eccles, Mark (1938). "Sir George Buc, master of the revels." In *Sir Thomas Lodge and Other Elizabethans*, ed. C. J. Sisson. Cambridge, MA: Harvard University Press.

Evans, G. Blakemore et al., eds (1974). *The Riverside Shakespeare.* Boston: Houghton Mifflin.

Finkelpearl, Philip J. (1986). "'The comedians' liberty': censorship of the Jacobean stage reconsidered." *English Literary Renaissance* 16, 123–38.

Freedman, Barbara (1996). "Elizabethan protest, plague, and plays: rereading the 'Documents of Control.'" *English Literary Renaissance* 26, 17–45.

Gildersleeve, Virginia Crocheron (1908). *Government Regulation of the Elizabethan Drama*. New York: Columbia University Press.

Gurr, Andrew (1996). *The Shakespearian Playing Companies*. Oxford: Clarendon Press.

Howard-Hill, T. H. (1988). "Buc and the censorship of *Sir John Van Olden Barnavelt* in 1619." *Review of English Studies* n.s. 39, 39–63.

Howard-Hill, T. H., ed. (1993). *A Game at Chess*, by Thomas Middleton. Manchester: Manchester University Press.

Hunter, G. K. (1962). *John Lyly: The Humanist as Courtier*. London: Routledge and Kegan Paul.

Ingram, William (1978). *A London Life in the Brazen Age: Francis Langley, 1548–1602*. Cambridge, MA: Harvard University Press.

Ingram, William (1992). *The Business of Playing: The Beginnings of the Adult Professional Theater in Elizabethan London*. Ithaca: Cornell University Press.

Knutson, Roslyn L. (1995). "Falconer to the little eyases: a new date and commercial agenda for the 'little eyases.'" *Shakespeare Quarterly* 46, 1–31.

Lewalski, Barbara K. (1993). *Writing Women in Jacobean England*. Cambridge. MA: Harvard University Press.

Long, William B. (1989). "The occasion of *Sir Thomas More*." In *Shakespeare and "Sir Thomas More": Essays on the Play and its Shakespearian Interest*, ed. T. H. Howard-Hill. Cambridge: Cambridge University Press.

McMillin, Scott and MacLean, Sally-Beth (1998). *The Queen's Men and their Plays*. Cambridge: Cambridge University Press.

Mullaney, Steve (1988). *The Place of the Stage: License, Play, and Power in Renaissance England*. Chicago: University of Chicago Press.

Nicholl, Charles (1984). *A Cup of News: The Life of Thomas Nashe*. London: Routledge and Kegan Paul.

Patterson, Annabel (1984). *Censorship and Interpretation: The Conditions of Reading and Writing in Early Modern England*. Madison: University of Wisconsin Press.

Roberts, Peter (1997). "William Prynne, the legal status of the players, and the closure of the playhouses by the Long Parliament." Unpublished paper given at the Shakespeare Association of America conference, Washington DC, April.

Streitberger, W. R. (1978). "On Edmond Tyllney's biography." *Review of English Studies* n.s. 29, 11–35.

Streitberger, W. R. (1986). *Edmond Tyllney, Master of the Revels and Censor of Plays: A Descriptive Index to his Diplomatic Manual on Europe*. New York: AMS Press.

Wickham, Glynne (1959–81). *Early English Stages 1300–1600*. 3 vols. London: Routledge and Kegan Paul.

Wickham, Glynne (1969). "The Privy Council order of 1597 for the destruction of all London's theatres." In *The Elizabethan Theatre*, ed. David Galloway. London: Macmillan.

Yachnin, Paul (1991). "The powerless theater." *English Literary Renaissance* 21, 49–74.

PART THREE
Kinds of Drama

17
Medieval and Reformation Roots
Raphael Falco

Theater historian Glynne Wickham some time ago complained that "where common sense tells us that Shakespeare and his contemporaries reaped the harvest of the seed, tilth and growth of preceding centuries, most modern criticism, with its heavy literary bias, has in fact severed Elizabethan drama from its roots" (Wickham, 1980, I, xxi–xxii; cf. Weimann, 1978, xxii). Wickham's point is well taken in regard to the theatrical significance of the early drama, as is his forceful statement that "the public theatres of Elizabethan London were the crowning glory of the medieval experiment" (1980, I, xxvii). He is referring to the open stage which was superseded by the stage of the proscenium arch and perspective scenes, "translated," as Wickham says, from "an old theater of poetry and visual suggestion . . . into a new one of pictorial realism and prose" (1980, I, xxvii). But this very translation, this newfangledness, makes the term "roots" misleading in the context of medieval and Reformation drama in England. Roots suggest a definite course of development, an organic link between earlier and later growth. The metaphor implies a subterranean quality and a promise of ongoing nourishment, while it is impossible to dissociate the idea of roots from the notion of belonging to and flourishing in a native soil. But, as division among critics continues to reveal, all of these associations are problematic when we analyze the relationship between the drama before and after 1580 (more or less). Wickham is surely right to object to heavy literary bias in criticism of the medieval drama, but literary bias is difficult to avoid when reading backward from Marlowe, Shakespeare, Jonson, and others whose work became the standard by which literary-dramatic criteria were set.

Medieval theater was neither childlike nor primitive, but in fact highly sophisticated (cf. Twycross, 1994, 37). Yet that sophistication is manifest in modes of artistry – from open staging to pageantry to characterological abstraction – less appreciated in the post-Marlovian theater. The prejudice against drama thought to be more primitive is not, however, a recent development. We find evidence of it throughout the Elizabethan period. Philip Sidney's objections in the *Defence* are probably the most familiar examples of a burgeoning literary bias among English intellectuals. "Our comedies and tragedies (not without cause cried out against)," he says, "observ[e] rules neither of honest civility nor skilful poetry" (1973). He singles out one play only, *Gorboduc*, which he considers above the common run. But his praise is very faint indeed: "notwithstanding as it is full of stately speeches and well-sounding phrases, . . . in truth . . . [it] is very defectuous in the circumstances" – that is, in the Aristotelian unities of place and action. If *Gorboduc* is "defectuous," much more so are all the rest according to Sidney. He goes on to castigate the decorum of contemporary plays, always from a literary, neo-Aristotelian perspective: thus he complains "how all their plays be neither right tragedies, nor right comedies, mingling kings and clowns . . . with neither decency nor discretion, so as neither admiration and commiseration, nor the right sportfulness, is by their mongrel tragi-comedy obtained." There is no doubt that "mongrel tragi-comedy" remained in vogue, as the gravedigger in *Hamlet* or Lear's fool attests – and we are grateful that it did. But, paradoxically, Sidney's prejudice has also remained in vogue, both as a basis for literary bias and as a justification for regarding pre-Shakespearean drama as primitive.

Nor was Sidney alone in his prejudice. There is a curious passage in George Puttenham's *Arte of English Poesie* (1589) that reveals a similar attitude, but more subtly, in the form of an evolutionary historical argument. In a chapter on the ancient theater called "Of the places where their enterludes or poems drammaticke were represented to the people," Puttenham claims that "The old comedies were plaid in the broad streets upon wagons or carts uncovered, which carts were floored with bords and made for removable stages to passe from one street of their townes to another, where all the people might stand at their ease to gaze upon the sights." This is a description not so much of Greece or Rome as of Tudor England and of the mystery cycles in particular. It seems likely that Puttenham is ascribing the pageant-wagons of the Corpus Christi Day festivities, which he might have witnessed as a child, to an earlier theatrical tradition. The parallel between antiquity and older English theater, if we can call it that, suggests an evolutionary hypothesis: by association, both ancient drama and traditional English drama representing earlier steps in a progressive literary history.

The implication of progress, of primitive roots that develop over time, has stigmatized medieval drama from Puttenham's era to our own. For the last 30 or 40 years, as Wickham's remarks indicate, this problematic view of medieval drama as the early form of Renaissance drama has been a popular topic of discussion among medievalists and theater historians. Literary critics, at least since the publication of David Bevington's *From Mankind to Marlowe* (1962), O. B. Hardison Jr.'s *Christian Rite and Christian Drama in the Middle Ages* (1966), and V. A. Kolve's *The Play Called Corpus Christi* (1965), have rejected the naive approach, fostered chiefly by E. K. Chambers' *The Medieval Stage* (1903), that saw medieval drama as the embryo or primitive ancestor of Renaissance drama (cf. Emmerson, 1988, 23). Chambers propounded an evolutionary thesis of dramatic development from the very early liturgical *Quem quaeritis* to the Corpus Christi cycles of the fifteenth and sixteenth centuries. Hardison objected to what he called the "evolutionary analogy" of Chambers' book – the introductory chapter of *Christian Rite* is titled "Darwin, mutations, and medieval drama" – and he proceeded to historicize Chambers himself, linking him to historians and cultural theorists of the last quarter of the nineteenth century, such as E. B. Taylor, Herbert Spencer, T. H. Huxley, and James Frazer. According to Hardison, the teleological character of Chambers' hypothesis has little support in the period, once a wider experience of documents is gained.

Recent scholars have continued to challenge the evolutionary hypothesis and to warn that regarding literary chronology in terms of cause and effect, or as a progression from simple to more complex forms (cf. Hardison, 1965, 182), it is necessary to ignore much contemporary manuscript evidence. Such practice can result, as Richard Emmerson has noted, in an elision of the medieval, or in a failure to recognize the continuation of so-called "medieval" drama in the sixteenth century (1998, 33). For instance, John Wasson has rejected Chambers' notion of a chronological progression of dramatic sites from church to marketplace to banqueting-hall, which supposedly occurred in tandem with a developmental progession of performers from clergy to folk to professional actors (cf. Wasson, 1997, 35). Although, as Wasson notes, Chambers argued that "all vernacular plays were moved outside for the laity, to be performed in marketplaces, theaters-in-the-round, on pageant wagons, or elsewhere," scholarship has established that "more than half of all vernacular plays of the English Middle Ages and Renaissance were in fact performed in churches" (Wasson, 1997, 26). This last fact reminds us that churches did not begin to incorporate pews or stalls until the late sixteenth century, before which the nave was a large open space conducive to dramatic activity (cf. Wasson, 1997, 28). But it should also alert us to the coexistence of Renaissance drama and that entity which we insist on referring to as medieval drama chiefly because it is associated with ecclesiastical doctrine or folk traditions rather than with neoclassical humanism or narrowly defined courtly conventions of playing. In actuality, as we will see below, both "medieval" and "Renaissance" are porous boundaries where the drama is concerned, all the more so when we approach the subject from a theatrical rather than a restrictively literary perspective.

In regard to the theatrical perspective, one of the most significant scholarly developments in recent decades has been the massive effort to collect and publish the documents relating to the mystery cycles, each of which is associated with a particular town in England. Known as REED (Records of Early English Drama), this project "aims 'to find, transcribe, and publish external evidence of dramatic, ceremonial, and minstrel activity in Great Britain before 1642'" (Emmerson, 1998, 28). The editors of the *York* volume note that "no attempt has been made to interpret the documents," although they admit to a necessarily strict selectivity (Johnston, 1979, ix). Moreover, they note the "familiar paradox of all collections of records. Although they are voluminous, they are also fragmentary" (1979, xv). The REED volumes, despite the high quality of the archival scholarship, have raised several questions about the nature of the historical record. Theresa Coletti, for example, has questioned the editorial aims of the REED project from the perspective of New Historicist and cultural studies theories. She is uneasy with notions of historical objectivity, comprehensiveness of dramatic records, and the supposed "neutral quality of evidence" assumed by the REED editors (Coletti, 1991; see also 1990). Coletti's objections have been vigorously met, however, by Greg Walker and Peter H. Greenfield, both of whom acknowledge the selective nature of the documentary evidence and its sometimes doubtful relevance to the drama. But both also note the promising value of the material so far collected; and, as Greenfield puts it, even if we can no longer believe in "'objective' historical evidence untouched by interpretation, . . . the experience of the past decade suggests that REED's policy of offering accurate transcriptions, selected and presented with a minimum of interpretation, has produced a series versatile enough to provide material for our stories despite changes in critical fashion" (1991, 21). The "stories" Greenfield refers to are the literary histories by which scholars explain medieval drama to themselves. How successfully the transcribed documentary evidence will lend itself to accurate interpretations is yet to be seen. A measure of REED's success, however, is the extent to which the volumes can prevent the imposition of sweeping theories like Chambers' while at the same time shoring up the fragmentary record against neglect.

I

The most commonly used generic designations for medieval drama are liturgical drama, mystery cycle, morality play, saint's play, and court or household interlude. Much of this drama, both Latin and vernacular, survives only in fragments of texts, if at all. Some of it, notably the cycle dramas, was not written down to be read by anyone except the performers and therefore was deliberately not preserved. These were ephemeral texts, literally, meant for a production to be staged one day only (although repeated throughout the day and perhaps saved from year to year). The liturgical drama, on the other hand, was preserved in monasteries and used annually and in large measure for the instruction of the monks and clergy, although perhaps with popular edification as a complementary objective.

The earliest evidence of what we would term dramatic activity is the ritual used at the dedication of a church. Chambers claims that it was found in various forms in England from the ninth century onward:

> The bishop and his procession approach the closed doors of the church from without, but one of the clergy, *quasi latens*, is placed inside. Three blows with a staff are given on the doors, and the anthem is raised *Tollite portas, principes, vestras et elevamini, portae aeternales, et introibit Rex gloriae*. From within comes the question *Quis est iste rex gloriae?* and the reply is given *Dominus virtutum ipse est Rex gloriae*. Then the doors are opened, and as the procession sweeps through, he who was concealed within slips out, *quasi fugiens*, to join the train. It is a dramatic expulsion of the spirit of evil. (Chambers, 1903, II, 4)

Chambers speaks of the evolution of this dedication ritual into the tropings – also called tropes or tropers – of the medieval liturgy, which were sung interpolations in the Mass. He posits the subsequent development of these early interpolations into the antiphonal *Quem quaeritis*, which he deemed an Easter trope. The *Quem quaeritis* ("Whom do you seek?") is an exchange between the three Marys and two angels at the tomb of Jesus, the text of which is derived from the gospels of Matthew (28:1–7) and Mark (16:1–7):

> Quem queritis in sepulchro, o Christicole?
> Ihesum Nazarenum crucifixum, o celicola.
> non est hic, surrexit sicut ipse dixit; ite, nuntiate quia
>   surrexit.

> [Whom seek you in the tomb, O followers of Christ?
> Jesus of Nazareth who was crucified, O Heaven-Dwellers.
> He is not here, he has arisen as he said; go announce that he
>   has arisen.] (Hardison, 1965, 178–9)

This early version of the *Quem quaeritis* comes from a manuscript at St. Gall dating from *c*.950. Chambers believed that this simple version of the exchange evolved into the more complex versions of the eleventh and following centuries. But here as elsewhere the concept of evolution is problematic, since there may well have been simultaneous development of tropings and other kinds of ceremonial and ritualistic dramatic activity. Hardison in fact insists that "there is not the slightest evidence that the tenth-century liturgists favored the association of the *Quem quaeritis* with the Easter Mass. If anything," he concludes, "the manuscripts suggest that the *Quem quaeritis* was regarded as an independent composition to be included wherever convenient" (Hardison, 1965, 189). He proves that the version quoted by Chambers and placed in St. Gall is both later and simpler than a Limoges version of 923. Thus the notion of a chronological evolution from simpler to more complex falls apart, leading Hardison to several plausible conclusions in opposition to Chambers and his followers, not least that the *Quem quaeritis* was not a trope at all, but a ceremony sometimes but not necessarily attached to the Mass (1965, 198–9). That it eventually emerged as the full dramatic text of the *Visitatio Sepulchri*, used at matins, apparently underscores Hardison's notion of dramatic independence from the Mass (cf. Hardison, 1965, 184).

But perhaps it would be useful at this point to remind ourselves what exactly we mean by drama in the context of the medieval church. Hardison emphasized that the boundary between religious ritual and drama posited by Chambers and Karl Young (author of the influential *The Drama of the Medieval Church* [1933]) did not exist: "religious drama," according to Hardison, "*was* the drama of the early Middle Ages and had been ever since the decline of the classical theater" (1965, viii). More recently, yet in the same vein, Simon Trussler has argued that troping was not intended to create dramatic illusion but to create a "microcosmic version of an enduring macrocosmic reality" (Trussler, 1994, 20). He recommends that troping not be seen as an "embryonic" form of drama that developed in the later medieval period, but rather as evidence that the church was responding to the "infiltration of more secular demands at every level of life" and that it sanctioned new kinds of dramatic activity when it recognized that "Christ's humanity could communicate itself to the laity more readily than his divinity" (1994, 20). It remains to wonder, however, whether in creating a microcosmic version of macrocosmic reality, the church's intentions notwithstanding, the anonymous authors of the liturgical tropings could have avoided the simultaneous creation of dramatic illusion. After all, the staging of the scene at the tomb is undeniably a dramatic illusion, regardless of how present and enduring the putative religious truth of the resurrection might have been to the congregational audience. "To the contemporary mind," as William Tydeman argues, "all worship could be deemed dramatic in character, not least the rite of the Mass, which was written in terms of a divine drama by Amalarius of Metz prior to 850" (Tydeman, 1994, 6). Yet Tydeman wonders whether "a combination of sung text and a series of ritual actions [can] be truly regarded as forming a play, when it is nowhere alluded to as constituting one and we possess no evidence to suggest that at its inception it was perceived as something separable from the remainder of the liturgy" (1994, 6). His answer is equivocal, though he emphasizes that scholars are inclined to agree that clerics created the earliest medieval drama.

Not all early drama was written by clerics, however, even if until the late fifteenth century the drama confined itself to religious subjects. As both Wickham and Trussler have noted, there were two separate kinds of medieval religious drama, that of the "Real Presence" within the liturgy and that of Christ's humanity in the outside world, the latter, which was written in the vernacular, being the more "imitative" (Trussler, 1994, 20). The mystery cycles are the most striking example of this vernacular drama, not least because these elaborate town-centered festivals continued to thrive for 200 years until outlawed in 1576. Four cycles are fully extant in English: the York cycle, with 48 episodes, dating from the last quarter of the fourteenth century; the Towneley cycle (named for the family who owned the text and associated with Wakefield in East Anglia), with 32 episodes, including a half-dozen episodes by the so-called "Wakefield master"; the Chester cycle, with 25 episodes; and the N-town cycle ("N" from *nomen*, meaning "fill in the blank with your town name"), with 42 episodes (cf. Trussler, 1994, 39; Happé, 1999, 35–41). Known to scholars as processional drama, these plays were performed on Corpus Christi Day, the Thursday after Trinity Sunday (between May 21 and June 24). Meg Twycross refers to the cycles as a moveable feast (1994, 38), because the individual plays were repeated serially at different sites throughout a town in the course of a very long day. They were played on large pageant-wagons, or floats, that could be pulled to as many as 40 sites. These wagons could be two or three stories high and varied in shape, made to look like ships or Jesse trees or a stable (as in one of the rare pictures we have of the 1615 Triumphs of Isabella in Brussels) (Happé, 1999, 49). The subjects of the plays were drawn from

Judeo-Christian history; thus we find plays on the Creation, the Last Judgment, Noah and the flood, the Nativity of Christ, the Resurrection, the Harrowing of hell, and so forth. Plays were sponsored by various guilds, such as the Plasterers, Tilers, Bricklayers, Bakers, Coopers, Innkeepers, Cordwainers, or Glovers, who also supplied most of the performers. Professional actors and minstrels also participated, as the REED volumes have shown.

Like all religious drama, the processional plays were meant to instruct the audience and also to celebrate glorious moments in putatively sacred history. The audience included members of the clergy and the aristocracy, as well as burgesses and peasants, all gathered in the streets for the holiday festival (cf. Kolve, 1966, 6–7). Wealthy citizens might pay to have a staging site placed in front of their house, so that they could watch with their friends, perhaps from an upper window (cf. Twycross, 1994, 48). Because the plays were repeated at different sites throughout the town, the number of spectators was kept to a reasonable size, probably no more than 100 people at each staging. Nevertheless it would have been difficult for everyone to see everything happening on the lower stages of the pageant-wagons or of the open-air "place and scaffold" stages; the upper stories would have afforded better views, as would the scaffolds on the open-air *platea* stage (cf. Twycross, 1994, 60). No doubt many of the townspeople would have known players from the guilds, increasing the audiences' interest in the production. In the absence of amplification, or of an enclosed theatrical space, actors depended on their voices. In contrast to audiences for morality plays or courtly entertainments, which would have been both more homogeneous and more stable, the audiences for processional drama were free to come and go, and probably viewed the plays out of sequence (cf. Carpenter, 1997, 3).

The writing varies widely in the extant mystery cycle texts, as might be expected with multiple authorship, and the dramatization or expansion of biblical episodes ranges from the banal to the inspired. The most acclaimed work is that of the anonymous author of the Wakefield Group, whose six plays in the N-Town cycle display, in A. C. Cawley's words, "a lively use of gesture and action, an outspoken criticism of contemporary abuses, a bold rehandling of secular material for comic purposes, and an unusual skill in characterization" (1958, xx). In the *Mactacio Abel* (Cawley, 1958), for instance, Cain is selfish and profane, an impious ingrate whose murder of his brother comes after the audience has had ample proof of Cain's deviant attitude. The expansion of the meager passage from Genesis contains historical anomalies meant undoubtedly to suggest contemporary life, such as the presence of Garcio, Cain's servant, and the entrance of Cain behind a plow-team: the first is problematic since Garcio would also have had to be a brother (or some close kin), while the second, the technologically advanced existence of a plow and team, is of course absurd. But these anomalies link the story to the present day, adducing identifiable realities to the cryptic outcome of the brothers' sacrifices to Yahweh; the burnt offerings are in fact referred to in the play as "tithe-sheaves," yet another familiarizing detail. Abel warns his brother to tithe correctly (the word for *tithe* is *teyn* or *tend*):

Abell	Caym, thou tendys wrang, and of the warst.
Cayn	We! com nar, and hide myne een!
	In the wenyand, wist ye now at last!
	Or els will thou that I wynk?
	Then shall I doy no wrong, me thynk.

> [*Finishes counting with his eyes closed*

	Let me se now how it is – [*Opens his eyes*
	Lo, yit I hold me paide;
	I teyndyd wonder well bi ges,
	And so euen I laide.
Abell	Came [Cayn], of God me thynke thou has no drede.
Cayn	Now and he get more, the dwill me spede! –
	As mych as oone reepe –
	For that cam hym full light chepe;
	Not as mekill, grete ne small,
	As he myght wipe his ars withall.
	For that, and this that lyys here,
	Haue cost me full dere;
	Or it was shorne, and broght in stak,
	Had I many a wery bak.
	Therfor aske me no more of this,
	For I haue giffen that my will is.

(ll. 224–44)

Despite the oppressively normative interpretation of the biblical scene, the Wakefield author manages to create a very human Cain who looks out for himself while coarsely suggesting what the deity can use his sacrifice for. His language is that of the churl, familiar and probably amusing to the local audience, while at the same time recognizably inappropriate.

The earthiness of the language in the *Mactacio Abel* is not unusual. Many of the vernacular plays of the period contain obscenity and profane speech, although, judging from extant material, it was more prevalent in the morality plays than in the mystery cycles. This earthy language may serve as a technique of negative characterization, but it also connects the artificial stage language with the spoken language of the day. The drama of Shakespeare and his contemporaries probably owes a genuine debt to this license with dramatic speech. Roman and Greek drama supplied the models for both the exalted language of tragic figuration and also, through Plautus in particular, for the vulgar tongue of comedy. But, whereas the language of tragedy had no homegrown equivalent, comic speech had English sources as well: Chaucer, the fabliau tradition, and the vernacular drama. The clowns of the Renaissance stage, even when they are meant to duplicate Roman antecedents, are obvious imports from the medieval stage. They simultaneously represent the *vulgus* and the theatrical past. If we can speak of roots at all, then the linguistic license of medieval and Reformation drama merits the term: the raw obscenity of such plays as *Mankind* is detectable behind not only such early Elizabethan plays as *Gammer Gurton's Needle* but also the more restrained vulgarisms of many later works written for the public theater, from *The Merry Wives of Windsor* to *The Knight of the Burning Pestle*.

The morality plays tended to be written for court or by schoolmasters for their students to perform (Wasson, 1997, 28). These plays might have been staged in open-air performances in fixed locations using "place and scaffold" construction, which afforded a large space for action; or they might have been performed indoors in the halls of great houses or in college halls; it was even possible that some morality plays might have been performed by itinerant actors in what Peter Happé calls "unlocalized impromptu" staging (Happé, 1999, 48). The Macro collection (named for the Reverend Cox Macro, a late seventeenth-century antiquarian) contains three of the five surviving fifteenth-century texts: *The Castle of Perseverence*, *Mankind*, and *Wisdom*. The other two plays are *The Pride of Life*, which is fragmentary, and *Everyman*, which is now thought to be a translation from the Dutch play *Elckerlijc*, "one of hundreds of surviving Rederijkers" (rhetoricians') plays, which were encouraged and supported in the low countries by local Chambers of Rhetoric from the second quarter of the fifteenth century until the beginning of the seventeenth" (Coldewey, 1993, 43). Characterization in the moralities is broad and allegorical, with figures like Fellowship, Mind, Lucifer, Will, Mercy, Mischief, and Mankind. The action — mostly conversational — is obviously didactic and characters' speeches tend to be explanatory. Thus in *Mankind* (Coldeway, 1993) the eponymous protagonist enters (carrying a spade) and announces:

> My name ys Mankynde. I have my composycyon
>   Of a body and of a soull, of condycyon contrarye.
> Betwyx them tweyn ys a grett dyvisyon;
>   He that shulde be subjecte, now he hath the victory.
>
> Thys ys to me a lamentable story
>   To se my flesch of my soull to have governance.
> Wher the goodewyff ys master, the goodeman may be sory.
>   I may both syth and sobbe, this ys a pytuose remembrance.
>   (ll. 194–201)

The play's agon is here revealed, and the action develops around the resolution of Mankind's "condycyon contrarye." The metaphor of the wife as master over the husband represents the imbalance between the carnal and the spiritual in Mankind himself. That the metaphor is sexist goes without saying, but it is nonetheless indicative of the author's attempt to link the human "composycyon" to the composition of society. This underscores the palpably social character of the morality drama, its pointed didacticism, and its presumed value as an application in daily life. The allegorical quality of the characterization alienates the play from post-Marlovian drama; rather, it seems a precursor of *Pilgrim's Progress*.

We should be careful, however, not to separate the morality tradition from later drama. As David Bevington noted in *From Mankind to Marlowe*, "almost all pre-

Marlovian plays of the sixteenth century which bear convincing evidence of popular commercial production are in fact moralities or hybrids" (Bevington, 1962, 10). William Wager's *The Longer Thou Livest* (1569; 1967), for example, calls itself "A Very Merry and Pithy Comedy" and cites Aristophanes in the first line of the Prologue. But the characters are straight from the morality tradition: for example, Moros, Discipline, Piety, Exercitation, Wrath, Fortune, Ignorance, and so on. The main character is Moros (whose name means *fate* or *destiny* in Greek), over whose behavior there is a struggle between the good and the bad characters. The play contains an interesting insight into characterization, as well as a series of lugubriously instructive speeches. The complex character Fortune, enraged, berates Incontinence, who claims to have "nuzzled [Moros] in carnality" (l. 1071). Incontinence begins to leave the stage when Fortune enters; Fortune asks "Are you blind? / Am I so little a mote that you cannot see?" (ll. 1086–7). Incontinence, alarmed, asks for mercy, to which Fortune replies:

> Well, at this time I hold you excused,
> Glad to see you do your duty so well.
> If all other had themselves so used,
> It had been better for them, to you I may tell.
> I trow your name is Incontinency,
> One of the properties of Moros.
>
> (ll. 1094–9)

The notion that the other characters, both good and bad, are properties of Moros is a remarkable insight. It reflects a fundamentally different concept of dramatic representation from that which we encounter in the more naturalistic conceptualizations of late Elizabethan and Jacobean drama. We would never think of asking whether Ophelia is a property of Hamlet, or Bosola of Ferdinand in *The Duchess of Malfi*, and undoubtedly literary bias persuades us to see even partial naturalism as more advanced than allegory, or than the "property-ism" of Wager's play. Yet, at the level of abstraction *The Longer Thou Livest* is both playful and sophisticated. Like the bulk of the morality tradition, the messages are all very clear. The dramatization serves less to advance the plot than to increase awareness of the reality of abstract principles in daily life. Thus Wager's figure called Discipline can lecture Moros simultaneously on piety and on Piety, the character or "property" of Moros himself:

> Piety will teach you your duty to kings,
> To rulers and magistrates in their degree,
> Unto whom you must be obedient in all things
> Concerning the statutes and laws of the country.
> It is piety your parents to obey,
> Yea, your prince and country to defend,
> The poor to comfort ever as you may,
> For the truth's sake your blood to spend.
>
> (ll. 441–8)

According to the stage directions, Moros should "between every sentence say 'Gay gear,' 'good stuff,' 'very well,' 'fin-ado,' with such mockish terms." The mockery dramatizes Moros' dubious moral condition, while the speech plainly outlines the social value of piety to the right functioning of the rigid hierarchy of degree. The dialogue admits no question about Discipline's veracity; his sententiousness is not ridiculous and Moros' mockery seems drastically wrong.

In contrast, we might think of Polonius' sententiousness, more or less naturalized by Shakespeare and thereby made ridiculous. The morality tradition (including the hybrid moralities) thrives in abstraction rather than naturalistic characterization. Even within the tradition, however, there is a difference between symbolic names and full personification. John N. King concludes that there is a distinction between the medieval use of personification, such as that found in *Everyman* or *The Castle of Perseverance*, and the Reformation practice of assigning what he calls "generic type-names" (King, 1982, 284). The characters in *The Longer Thou Livest* seem to fall into the second category. As properties of Moros, they are not full personifications, nor are they quite the same as such figures as Ben Jonson's Lady Would-Be or Everill and his characters based on the humors. But we should be wary here. To see the generic type-names as constituting a transitional status of characterization courts the danger of seeing sixteenth-century dramatic development as strictly evolutionary. As we noted in discussing Chambers, this sort of naive evolutionism can distort our analysis. It would be better to recognize the Reformation practice as a viably alternative form of characterization; and it would be better not to transmute chronology into evolutionary development, but rather to recognize parity among medieval, Reformation, and Renaissance styles of characterization. The use of personification or type-names changes the dramatic effect, yet the range of responses evoked is just as wide, if not always as subtle, as that of more naturalistic characterization. For example, whereas the morality tradition is by no means humorless, its humor too is abstracted and laden with meaning (usually negative). It is tempting to call such abstraction (or such humor) primitive, or transitional, but we should resist doing so. If, as literary-minded critics, we were to neglect the theatrical power of symbolic abstraction, we would be committing the same error as those who deem Cycladic sculpture or African art primitive.

II

Although humanist practices, specifically in regard to revival of the Greek and Roman classics, made little impact on the morality tradition (despite a seasoning of Latin) until the sixteenth century, interludes performed at great houses and at courts began turning to classical models in England by the end of the fifteenth century. The term "interlude" is very slippery: as F. P. Wilson observes, it might mean either "a play (*ludus*) conducted between (*inter*) two or more actors or a play performed between the courses of a banquet" (1969, 10). Henry Medwall's *Fulgens and Lucres*, a secular English comedy acted in 1491 and printed by John Rastell between 1512 and 1516, is called an interlude, as is his *Nature*. It is the former play, however, which is of interest as unique in fifteenth-century England. Whereas *Nature* traces the course of human life, recording the struggle between virtue and vice in the morality tradition, *Fulgens and Lucres* is the earliest secular drama to have survived (cf. Wilson, 1969, 6–7). The play takes the form of a Ciceronian debate. The topic of the debate is nobility, whether birth or merit makes a noble human being. A popular topic (even Chaucer takes it up), the nobility question will be taken up with gusto by later writers from Castiglione to Ben Jonson. Although, as Wilson suggests, we should resist calling Medwall a humanist, his play reflects the thematic secularity and the classical turn of much later writing which we routinely term humanist (cf. Wilson, 1969, 8).

The main plot of Medwall's play is drawn from Buonaccorso da Montemagno's Latin treatise *De vera nobilitate* (1428), which had been translated into English by John Tiptoft and printed by Caxton in 1481. The play is clearly a household drama which would have been presented during the course of a banquet in a great hall (Nelson, 1980, 2; Happé, 1999, 110). There is a possibility that Thomas More, as a teenage page in the house of Thomas Morton, archbishop of Canterbury, might have acted in *Fulgens and Lucres* in a subordinate role. Set in ancient Rome, the play dramatizes Lucres' choice between two suitors, the wealthy patrician Publius Cornelius and the commoner Gaius Flaminius. That she should be permitted to choose is itself extraordinary and her choice of the commoner Gaius Flaminius stands conventional expectation on its ear. As one character puts it:

> What? Will they afferme that a chorles son
> Sholde be more noble than a gentilman born?
> Nay, beware, for men wyll have therof grete scorn.
>
> (ll. 130–2)

Fulgens, Lucres' father, justifies his permissiveness regarding his daughter's right to choose with biblical authority. Somewhat surprisingly, not least because the play is set in Rome, he paraphrases 1 Corinthians 12, St. Paul's discussion of the nine charisms of the congregation of Christ. Fulgens' speech is a translation of the Vulgate:

> To some he lendith the sprete of prophecy,
> To some the plenty of tongues eloquence,
> To some grete wisdome and worldly policy,
> To some litterature and speculatyf science,
> To some he geveth the grace of preemynence
> In honour and degree, and to some abundance
> Of tresoure, riches, and grete inheritance.
> Every man oweth to take gode hede
> Of this distribution, for who so doth take
> The larger benefite, he hath the more nede
> The larger recompense and thank therfor to make.
>
> (ll. 210–20)

In addition to editing the original charisms – "litterature and speculatyf science" are particularly newfangled – Fulgens folds honor and degree into a socialized utopian ethos. The distribution of various privileges and powers makes for a somewhat complacent view of social stratification. Yet Fulgens, an aristocrat, is more accepting of Lucres' choice than the play's common characters. *Fulgens and Lucres* includes a subplot, not derived from Buonaccorso, in which characters designated A and B pursue Ancilla, Lucres' maid. The subplot is typically comic, full of mishaps and beatings and rambunctious language. It seems at once Chaucerian and proto-Elizabethan in its spirited jests and confusions. It should be noted too that *Fulgens and Lucres* includes a play within a play, or what might be termed a mumming within a mumming.

Other secular plays soon followed *Fulgens and Lucres*. John Rastell's *Four Elements* (1517), *Calsito and Melebea* (1523), and *Gentleness and Nobility* (1523), and John Skelton's *Magnyfycence* (1519), all appeared within a decade of the printing of Medwall's play. *Magnyfycence* takes up the subject of kingship in a political allegory, concentrating on the cardinal virtue of *fortitudo* in rulers. The play might be seen in the *speculum principi* or perhaps *de casibus* tradition, concerned as it is with demonstrating the dangers of bad advisers to a king. In addition, Skelton draws on the French *sotie* (fool's play) tradition and introduces fools to the English stage (cf. Happé, 1999, 113). John Heywood's plays also began appearing at this time: *Witty and Witless, The Pardoner and the Friar, The Four PP, Johan Johan, The Play of the Weather*, and *A Play of Love*. Thomas Warton said of Heywood, who was Rastell's son-in-law, that he was "among the first of our dramatists who drove the Bible from the stage, and introduced representations of familiar life and popular manners" (Wilson, 1969, 27–8). This is a bit overstated insofar as the Bible provided many subjects for Reformation dramatists; and, while it is true that morality plays avoided "familiar life and popular manners," some of the mystery plays, as we noted above, deliberately exploited familiar practices to drive home their instructional message. Yet Heywood is noteworthy for his lively wit and for his probable debt to French farce, the latter of which reflects the incipient dependence of English literary culture on Continental models. His plays are mostly structured as disputations or debates, more sophisticated in language than *Fulgens and Lucres* and complicated by more characters taking part.

The Bible was certainly not driven from the English stage, unless we take "the stage" in the narrow sense and apply it only to the public theaters. Not only were there translations of religious plays, such as Arthur Golding's of Theodore Beza's *Abraham sacrifiant*, but there were also many native works on biblical themes. Once the Reformation gathered strength, religious drama flourished – that is, Protestant drama – and biblical themes appear throughout the period in Latin and vernacular plays. Perhaps the days of the old mystery plays were numbered because of their papish content; and perhaps liturgical drama, which continued well beyond the banning of the mystery cycles, lost its dramatic primacy. But the Reformation dramatists of the mid-sixteenth century, as King has noted, "passed on . . . the themes and conventions of the early moral interlude in a form suitable for adaptation by the Elizabethan dramatists" (1982, 272). King considers *Dr. Faustus* "the last avowedly religious

drama in Renaissance England" and, citing Bevington, he concludes that "the achievement of Marlowe and his contemporaries springs from their synthesis of new secular
subjects with traditional doubling patterns and the psychomachia form of the
medieval morality play and Tudor moral interlude" (1982, 272–3).

Religious dramatists included George Buchanan, tutor to James VI (later James
I of England) and sometimes called the best Anglo-Latin poet of the century, who
wrote the Latin tragedy *Baptistes sive Calumnia* (1541). The clerics John Bale, John
Foxe, William Baldwin, Nicholas Udall, and Nicholas Grimald all wrote plays. Udall
in fact wrote the secular *Ralph Roister Doister* while also editing and translating religious texts (King, 1982, 275). John Bale wrote many plays in both Latin and English
on Protestant themes. Most of the plays are heavily didactic, overburdened by the religious controversies of the day. In *King Johan*, for example (Bale, 1985–), the title character (who is a man) speaks with the female allegorical figure, Englande:

K. Johan	say forth thy mynd now
	And show me how thow art thus becum a wedowe.
Englande	Thes vyle popych swyne hath clene exyled my hosband.
K. Johan	Who ys thy husbond? Tell me, good gentyll Yngland.
Englande	For soth, God hym selfe, the spowse of every sort
	That seke hym in fayth to ther sowlys helth and confort.
Sedicdyon	He ys scant honest that so may wyfes wyll have.
K. Johan	I saye hold yowre peace and stond asyde lyke a knave!
	Is God exylyd owt of this regyon? Tell me.
Englande	Yea, that he is, ser: yt is much more pete.
K. Johan	How commyth it to passe that he is thus abusyd?
Englande	Ye know he abydyth not where his word ys refusyd.

                                                          (ll. 105–16)

The intertwining of the political and the religious, as well as hostility toward Catholicism, are typical of Bale's plays, The old religious metaphor of marriage – Christ wed
to the church, the bishop to his diocese, the wife to the husband – gains a chauvin-
istic dimension in *King Johan*. While it may be difficult to see an allegory such as this
one as a precursor to Shakespearean, or even Marlovian, characterization, we should
not underestimate the influence of the allegorical psychomachia, the inner struggle
projected onto stage figures. The later dramatists naturalized these projected struggles, creating what we now think of as characterological identity.

Attacks on the theater, the well-documented anti-theatrical prejudice, did not
begin until the opening of the public theaters in 1576 (see chapter 11 above).
Until that time – until the physical space became a threat to morals – even such
austere Protestant figures as John Foxe approved of drama. Moreover, contrary to
expectations, the pre-public, Protestant drama includes not only religious plays, but
also the first comedies in English (cf. King, 1982, 277–9). Biblical themes might
supply the foundation of such plays as *Nice Wanton* or *Lusty Juventus* or George
Gascoigne's *Glass of Government*, one of many prodigal son dramas. But, in contrast to

Bale's writing, the matter of these plays tends to be more secular than religious. Indeed, it could even be coarse or scatalogical, as in the university drama *Gammer Gurton's Needle*.

III

Prejudice against the theater coincides not only with the opening of the public spaces but also roughly with the increase in Continental influences on English drama. This is a valuable, if somewhat neglected, coincidence. Although it is by no means assured that the Puritan attacks would have been lessened if the drama had retained a more exclusively native tradition, the influx of foreign, ostensibly papist influence probably stoked the anti-theatrical fires. In any case, the evidence of Continental influence is clear and abundant. As is well known, the second half of the sixteenth century witnessed an extraordinary efflorescence of generic imitations of classical genres, with literary models drawn from Greece, Rome, Italy, and France. The drama, while never losing touch entirely with native traditions, nonetheless began to complicate its literary genealogy by adopting both ancient and Continental ancestors. The works of the Greek tragedians, Aristophanes, Terence, and Seneca all became available in sixteenth-century editions, in the original languages as well as in English. Italian and French plays were translated, and Continental poetic treatises helped to codify and even to modernize the rules of decorum about which Philip Sidney was so exercised. *Gorboduc*, Sidney's solitary grudging exception to the generally dismal state of English drama, provides a good example of the new Elizabethan trends. While retaining dumb shows not unlike those in the morality and mystery plays, *Gorboduc* is a five-act tragedy in blank verse, an imitation of Italian *intermezzi*, with a chorus and deliberately elevated rhetoric. Norman Rabkin calls it "a sophisticated and self-conscious attempt at native classical drama" (Fraser and Rabkin, 1976, 81).

The phrase "native classical drama" says it all. It is both self-contradictory and curiously accurate. The influence of Continental sources such as *commedia dell'arte* or the French morality tradition, in tandem with the increasingly prevalent acceptance of humanist ideals of classical revival, refashioned the family tree of Elizabethan drama. The idea of English roots, and particularly of national rootedness, became much more complicated. Consequently, any organic connection between, for example, the mystery cycles or the morality plays and Kyd, Marlowe, Shakespeare and their contemporaries is difficult to establish with certainty, as is the exclusively English rootedness of the later Elizabethan theater. Once English writers had begun to feel the influence of humanist pedagogy, they, like their Italian and French contemporaries, grafted themes, techniques, and forms from ancient Greek and Latin authors onto native (even local) literary tradition. If a play like *Fulgens and Lucres* already reflects a classical influence, then later works make it nearly impossible to disentangle English from Continental-cum-classical influences. As a result, we are obliged to complicate the notion of rootedness itself, rejecting, as in any other literary history, indefensible ideas of purity and native progress in favor of a more flexible concept of cultural interdependence.

Finally, it must be emphasized that the roots of drama need not be confined to dramatic representation. It can be unduly restrictive to limit ourselves to dramatic roots, particularly in a period so complexly indebted to classical revival and to what might be termed the importation across genres of *materia poetica*. In innumerable works of the fifteenth and sixteenth centuries from *Magnyfycence* to Marlowe's *Dido, Queene of Carthage*, from Henry Medwall's use of Ciceronian debate to Shakespeare's *Antony and Cleopatra*, authors drew on other-than-dramatic sources. Vergil, Plutarch, Ovid among the ancients, the Italian and French *novelle* tradition, *The Mirror for Magistrates* — all supplied material for Renaissance drama. Similarly, the Bible continued to be an important source of dramatic themes throughout the late Elizabethan and Jacobean periods. But it would be fruitless to try to establish whether, for example, Elizabeth Cary's *Mariam, Queene of Jewry* drew more from its biblical source than from Senecan tragedy or from the contemporary closet drama. At the same time we must recognize the growth of interest in authorship and in literary (as opposed to theatrical) practice. In 1616 Ben Jonson published his plays along with his poems in his *Works*, with the conscious objective of making his works analogous to the collected editions of ancient poets; in 1623 the First Folio of Shakespeare's plays was published. These are patently literary events, canonizing the Author with a capital A, and as such are in striking contrast to the anonymity and practical–theatrical concerns of the medieval drama. Moreover, the self-consciously literary approach to playwriting, as to poetry in general, bespeaks a Continental humanist influence contrary to the communal folk traditions.

Still, even as we temper our definition of native rootedness, it would be rash to deny the influence of the earlier English dramatic forms on the Elizabethan and Jacobean dramatists — or, if "influence" is too strong a term for it, perhaps we can speak of discernible threads of continuity between these apparently disparate forms and theatrical practices. The continuity is often highly mediated, or compromised, by changing fashions and contemporary polemics. But the threads of continuity are visible nonetheless, indeed may be rendered more visible by the accompanying contrasts. For instance, John Wasson has suggested that "the clearest medieval influence on Renaissance drama is that of the saints' lives on history plays" (1982, 322). He even goes on to propose that the now lost Thomas à Becket plays, which were abundant in medieval England, supply a model for Renaissance tragedy. But, if valid, the continuity Wasson suggests between the medieval plays and Renaissance tragedies is invisible, thus truly subterranean and deserving the name "roots." This is a difficult concept to accept from the standpoint of criticism, for we might say the same for the invisible influence of the ongoing gospelling tradition in the sixteenth century or even for the liturgical drama. It is pointless to argue for continuity if the threads have become too exiguous to identify. In any case, the practice of *Quellenforschung* has limited value when the sources are almost completely lost.

The continuity between medieval and Renaissance drama is both more subtle and more distorting than one expects in a search for sources or roots. Perhaps Puttenham's pageant-wagons, supposedly built in antiquity but in likelihood modeled on local English floats, are more emblematic of the kind of continuity we find between medieval dramatic practice and the Renaissance stage. The older medieval forms do not simply drop away; they undergo a complicated process of integration into the plays of the public theater. In the course of that integration they also undergo significant distortion, so that threads of continuity coexist side by side with deliberate rejections of native tradition. Analogous versions of Puttenham's pageant-wagons can be found in every aspect of the Renaissance drama – in themes, diction, character projections, humor, and much more. Just as distorted as those antique wagons, these traces of continuity are all the more important as historical markers because of the distortions they embody.

References and Further Reading

Bale, John (1985–). *The Complete Plays of John Bale*, ed. Peter Happé. Cambridge: D. S. Brewer.

Bevington, David (1962). *From Mankind to Marlowe: Growth of Structure in the Popular Drama of Tudor England*. Cambridge, MA: Harvard University Press.

Carpenter, Sarah (1997). "The sixteenth-century court audience: performers and spectators." *Medieval English Theatre* 19, 3–14.

Cawley, A. C., ed. (1958). *The Wakefield Pageants in the Towneley Cycle*. Manchester: Manchester University Press.

Chambers, E. K. (1903). *The Medieval Stage*. 2 vols. Oxford: Clarendon Press.

Coldewey, John C., ed. (1993). *Early English Drama: An Anthology*. New York and London: Garland.

Coletti, Theresa (1990). "Reading REED: history and the Records of Early English Drama." In *Literary Practice and Social Change in Britain, 1380–1530*, ed. Lee Patterson. Berkeley and Los Angeles: University of California Press.

Coletti, Theresa (1991). "'Fragmentation and redemption': dramatic records, history, and the dream of wholeness." *Envoi* 3, 1–13.

Emmerson, Richard K. (1988). "Dramatic developments: some recent scholarship on medieval drama." *Envoi* 1, 23–40.

Emmerson, Richard K. (1998). "Eliding the medieval: Renaissance 'New Historicism' and sixteenth-century drama." In *The Performance of Middle English Culture: Essays on Chaucer and the Drama in Honor of Martin Stevens*, eds James J. Paxson, Lawrence M. Clopper, and Sylvia Tomasch. Cambridge: D. S. Brewer.

Fraser, Russell and Norman Rabkins, eds (1976). *Drama of the English Renaissance, vol. 1*. New York: Macmillan.

Greenfield, Peter H. (1991). "'But Herefordshire for a Morris-daunce': dramatic records and the New Historicism." *Envoi* 3, 14–23.

Happé, Peter (1999). *English Drama before Shakespeare*. London and New York: Longman.

Hardison, O. B., Jr. (1965). *Christian Rite and Christian Drama in the Middle Ages: Essays in the Origin and Early History of Modern Drama*. Baltimore: Johns Hopkins University Press.

Johnston, Alexandra F., ed. (1979). *REED (Records of Early English Drama) York*. 2 vols. Toronto: University of Toronto Press.

King, John N. (1982). *English Reformation Literature: The Tudor Origins of the Protestant Tradition*. Princeton: Princeton University Press.

Kolve, V. A. (1966). *The Play Called Corpus Christi*. Stanford, CA: Standford University Press.

Nelson, Alan H., ed. (1980). *The Plays of Henry Medwall*. Cambridge: D. S. Brewer.

Puttenham, George (1589). *The Arte of English Poesie.*

Sidney, Philip (1973). "A defence of poetry." In *Miscellaneous Prose of Sir Philip Sidney*, eds Katherine Duncan-Jones and Jan van Dorsten. Oxford: Oxford University Press.

Trussler, Simon (1994). *The Cambridge Illustrated History of British Theatre.* Cambridge: Cambridge University Press.

Twycross, Meg (1994). "The theatricality of medieval English plays." In *The Cambridge Companion to Medieval English Theatre*, ed. Richard Beadle. Cambridge: Cambridge University Press.

Tydeman, William (1994). "An introduction to medieval English theatre." In *The Cambridge Companion to Medieval English Theatre*, ed. Richard Beadle. Cambridge: Cambridge University Press.

Wager, William (1967). *The Longer Thou Livest, and Enough is as Good as a Feast*, ed. R. Mark Benbow. Lincoln: University of Nebraska Press.

Walker, Greg (1995). "A broken reed?: Early drama records, politics, and the old historicism." *Medieval English Theatre* 17, 42–51.

Wasson, John (1982). "The morality play: ancestor of Elizabethan drama?" In *The Drama of the Middle Ages: Comparative and Critical Essays*, eds Clifford Davidson, C. J. Giankaris, and John H. Stroupe. New York: AMS Press.

Wasson, John (1997). "The English church as theatrical space." In *A New History of Early English Drama*, eds John D. Cox and David Scott Kastan. New York: Columbia University Press.

Weimann, Robert (1978). *Shakespeare and the Popular Tradition in the Theater*, ed. Robert Schwartz. Baltimore and London: Johns Hopkins University Press.

Wickham, Glynne (1980; first pub. 1959–72). *Early English Stages 1300–1600.* 3 vols. London: Routledge and Kegan Paul.

Wilson, F. P. (1969). *The English Drama 1485–1585*, ed. G. K. Hunter. Oxford: Clarendon Press.

Young, Karl (1933). *The Drama of the Medieval Church.* Oxford: Clarendon Press.

18

The Academic Drama

Robert S. Knapp

Francis Meres' famous list of the best English authors has little critical value beyond establishing what minimally well-educated gentlemen could have known about their literary heritage in 1598, yet a telling peculiarity in its order of names helps us situate the academic drama. Modern scholarship has tended to make Tudor academic drama into a niche topic, segregated by its dominant language (Latin) and its ordinary venue (the college hall) from what is normally taught and studied as constituting the English dramatic tradition. Meres, however, takes a more promiscuous view. Although Shakespeare has pride of place as "the most excellent in both kinds for the stage," Meres' list of "our best for Tragedie" otherwise begins with "the Lorde *Buckhurst*, Doctor *Leg* of Cambridge, Doctor *Edes* of Oxforde, maister *Edward Ferris*" before proceeding to "*Marlow, Peele, Watson, Kid, Shakespeare*, . . . and *Beniamin Iohnson*." His enumeration of "best for comedy" has a similar extension: from "*Edward* Earl of Oxforde, Doctor *Gager* of Oxforde, Maister *Rowley* once a rare Scholler of learned Pembrooke Hall in Cambridge, Maister Edwardes one of her Maiesties Chapell, eloquent and wittie Iohn Lilly" on to "Greene, Shakespeare, Thomas Nash . . . and Henry Chettle" (Allen, 1933, 76, 78–9).

Ordering his comparisons partly by social status and partly by chronology, Meres sets Thomas Sackville, the co-author of the English *Gorboduc*[1] (performed in 1562 before the queen by the lawyers and students of the Inner Temple), next to the authors of two Latin tragedies – Legge's *Richardus Tertius* (at Cambridge, 1578/9) and Edes' *Caesar Interfectus* (at Oxford, 1582).[2] Then he sandwiches Thomas Watson, author of the Latin *Absolom* (the earliest extant play written at Cambridge [*c.*1539–40]), among a number of contemporary playwrights for the commercial stage. In the sequence of comedians, Richard Edwardes, author of the English *Damon and Pithias* (1565) and of the lost *Palamon and Arcite* (1566 or before),[3] keeps company with John Lyly.[4] Then come Shakespeare and his principal critics among "university wits," and William Gager, whose Latin plays, strategically staged during Shrove-tide 1592, helped provoke the older Rainolds into the first of several polemical letters collected and published as *The Overthrow of Stage Plays* (Middelburg, 1599). Like Rainolds' former student, Stephen Gosson – and like Gosson's opponents in the domestically printed, London version of the Oxford controversy over the propriety of plays and playacting – Meres seems to see the drama as one institution and one series of texts, amateur and commercial, Latin and English, all intertwined and all to be judged by the same standards.

Yet the social hierarchy reflected in Meres' naming lords, doctors, and masters before other playwrights reminds us that academic drama occupied a privileged position within late Tudor cultural practice. Every text associable with those named first and given prefixed titles in Meres' lists can count as an academic play, whether written in Latin or in English. Academic drama had by the late sixteenth century become forcefully distinguished from what the unemployed scholars of the *Return from Parnassus* call that "basest trade" practiced by the likes of Will Kempe and Richard Burbage (Leishman, 1949, 343). Not only had university authorities generally succeeded by at least the 1580s in preventing commercial players from invading a five-mile radius with anything that might "hinder the quiet of the Vniuersitie, and drawe our Studentes from their bookes" (Nelson, 1989, 342), but by contrast with the works of the commercial theater that developed after 1576, academic plays were each acted on special and often unique occasions,[5] by amateurs, in contexts where the educational, the ceremonial, and the festive all intermingled.

In the late fifteenth and early sixteenth centuries, no similarly clear line could have been drawn (cf. Boas, 1914, 25). Not only did no properly commercial theater exist, but most of the surviving early drama was tied to particular locales or audiences, had explicit persuasive and didactic purposes, was written by a member of the educated elite, and was probably staged either during one of the festal periods traditionally devoted to plays and games or for a specific occasion.[6] To be sure, college and school regulations from the mid-fifteenth century forbid fellows and scholars from attending taverns, shows, and other shameful places (Lancashire, 1984, 131). Within the larger context, however, and building on a long but sparsely documented late medieval tradition of dramatic entertainment at schools and universities (including remunerated visits of various "pleyars," "lusores," and "interlusores"), the production of plays on models and for purposes recommended by humanist educational reformers cannot have seemed an altogether new and separate kind of activity.

The Elizabethan statutes refounding St. Peter's College, Westminster (1561), clearly indicate the mixture of aims that academic drama was supposed to satisfy. "In order that the youth may spend the time of Christmas with better profit and may become better accustomed to proper action and pronunciation," the masters of the grammar school were to produce a Latin play and the master of the associated choir school a play in English. Either play could be a tragedy or a comedy and both should be acted in the hall, either privately or in public, during the twelve days of Christmas or later, at the masters' discretion (Motter, 1929, 86–7). One such performance occurred (January 17, 1565/6) in celebration of the seventh anniversary of Elizabeth's coronation. Before an audience of the queen, her Council, and the visiting Swedish princess Cecilia, the grammar school boys performed an expanded and slightly adapted version of the German schoolmaster Sixt Birck's Latin tragicomedy, *Sapientia Solomonis*. The choristers provided the music, probably sang the *Hymnus* that concludes act III, and may have performed as members of the crowd (Payne, 1938, 1–48). A *Sapientia Solomonis*, presumably the same play, had been performed at Trinity College, Cambridge (with which Westminster had close ties and whose own statutes requiring the performance of plays were drawn up two years earlier), during the Christmas season of 1559/60, with Euripides' *Hecuba* (possibly in Greek but probably in Erasmus' translation), Seneca's *Oedipus*, Plautus' *Mostellaria*, and a set of English plays (Nelson, 1989, 208–9).

Thus by mid-century, at both grammar schools and universities, the acting of plays in Latin, English, and occasionally Greek had not only become commonplace but was a statutory obligation (Nelson, 1989, 712, 205).[7] It is possible to chart a fairly steady growth in this dramatic activity during the first two-thirds of the sixteenth century. The performance of Roman comedy in college halls can be dated as early as 1510/11 at King's Hall, Cambridge, and perhaps at Eton before 1519 (Nelson, 1989, 84; Lancashire, 1984, 131). Aristophanes' *Plutus* was performed in Greek at St. John's, Cambridge, in 1536 and his *Pax* was staged at Trinity in 1546 by John Dee, subsequently famous as scholar, alchemist, and natural philosopher (Lancashire, 1984, 95, 97). Evidence for the composition and performance of original plays in Latin – sometimes a requirement of employment for schoolmasters – appears by 1512/13 (Lancashire, 1984, 17). In support of their efforts to gain appointment as fellows and teachers, both Nicholas Grimald and John Foxe transmitted manuscripts of their original Latin plays to influential academics. Some works in turn came to be assessed by neoclassic standards: Roger Ascham, himself the author of a lost *Philoctetes*, praised Watson's *Absolom* together with Buchanan's *Jepthes* (*c.*1543) as uniquely able to "abyde the true touch of *Aristotles* precepts, and *Euripides* examples" (Wright, 1904, 284).

Participation in theatrical performance was not left to mere statutory admonition. In the same year (1546) as Queen's College, Cambridge, staged a Latin version (*Laelia Modenas*) of the racy Italian play *Gl'Ingnannti*,[8] college authorities undertook to fine or expel any undergraduate who refused a role or who failed to attend performances (Lancashire, 1984, 98; Nelson, 1989, 147). Partly to discourage participation in any "awful and unbelievable pleasure" (Nelson, 1989, 1113) that might distract from a literary education, the colleges had established "Christmas lords" (successors to the boy bishops, abolished in 1541) to produce these festival plays and speeches, creating what appears to have been a climate of communal enthusiasm for theater. Thus Nicholas Grimald, fresh out of Cambridge and living at Brasenose College, Oxford, claimed in 1540 to have been approached by younger students "eager to enter the field of drama, that they might stimulate their minds, and that they might give some representation of life to the citizens" (Merrill, 1925, 99). Much later (1607), when the tradition of college plays had become controversial, the St. John's, Oxford, students who reinstated the Christmas lord after a thirty-year hiatus still felt the obligation to plan a program that involved everyone. Intermingled with the serious Latin (and English) plays was a "Mock" play allowing even those "whose voyces or personages would not suffer them to act any thing in publicke" nonetheless to "doe something" (Boas, 1923, 135).

As the "astonishingly early" (Wilson, 1969, 114) Cambridge production of *Laelia Modenas* suggests, the development of academic drama in the sixteenth century, in all its modes, was an international affair. The *Christus Redivivus* that Grimald released for performance at Brasenose, Oxford, was soon printed in Germany (1543), where its ambiguous influence continues as the earliest extant source for the Oberammergau play. Thomas Kirchmayer's ferociously anti-papal *Pammachius* created a scandal when staged at Cambridge in 1545. Foxe's *Christus Triumphans*, probably influenced by Kirchmayer, was published in Basel just after the martyrdom of Ridley and Latimer; upon the accession of Elizabeth, the president of Magadalen College, Oxford, asked permission to perform it, but the only known staging of the play was at Trinity College, Cambridge, in 1562/63 (Smith, 1973, 33–4). Works by the German and Dutch schoolmaster playwrights of the "Christian Terence" movement appear in England at least as early as Palsgrave's textbook translation of Gnapheus' *Acolastus* (1540), a dramatization of the prodigal son story recast with the scheming parasites and grieving fathers of Roman comedy. With *Ralph Roister Doister* (1547?), *Gammer Gurton's Needle* (at Christ's College, Cambridge, 1550) – probably by William Stevenson – vies for the distinction of being the first comedy in English written on a Roman model. But like the later Cambridge play *Misogonus* (also in English, after 1564), *Gammer Gurton* may owe some inspiration for its condescending treatment of peasant life to the Continental playwrights, especially to the rustic comedies of Macropedius (Wilson, 1969, 102).[9] And George Gascoigne's English translation of Ariosto's *I Suppositi*,[10] which played both at Gray's Inn (1566) and at Trinity College, Oxford (1582), reminds us again of the dramatic traffic between academic institutions as well as continents and languages.

Perhaps the most ambitious of the mid-century academic playwrights was Ralph Radcliffe, who founded the short-lived school at Hitchin, Hertfordshire, in 1546. Although his program of theatrical activity (to which the public was invited) could not have been as extensive as that of Ascham's correspondent Johann Sturm at the famous Strasbourg Gymnasium,[11] Radcliffe too taught Latinity through the annual performance of plays. John Bale's list of Radcliffe's works ranges from an early *Bellum Gramaticale*, or war between nouns and verbs, to adaptations of Chaucer and Boccaccio, dramatized versions of the biblical stories of Dives and Lazarus, Job, and Susanna, and a play on the condemnation of John Huss (Motter, 1929, 225–6). Thomas Ashton, master at the Shrewsbury School,[12] staged weekly plays at the school, and with his schoolboys took over the annual Corpus Christi plays in the "Quarry," which Queen Elizabeth twice tried to visit in order to see his *Passion of Christ* (Motter, 1929, 210, 215). Yet for all this activity at Tudor grammar schools, the only surviving play certainly known to be from the pen of a Tudor schoolmaster is Nicholas Udall's Plautine *Ralph Roister Doister*. Udall's most influential student, Richard Mulcaster, also incorporated drama in his pedagogy, as we know from Sir James Whitelocke's testimony: "Yeerly he presented sum playes to the court, in which his scholers wear only actors, and I on among them, and by that meanes taught them good behaviour and audacitye" (Motter, 1929, 110).

Whitelocke's account lets us deepen and refine our description of the purposes of academic playing. Begun partly in continuation of a festival tradition and partly as one component in what we would now call a program of total immersion in the study of ancient languages, the academic drama also became a favored medium for instruction in proper behavior. This instruction had at least two not always fully compatible dimensions. On the one hand, as Bruce Smith analyzes the effect of acting classical plays in the context established by Erasmian methods of teaching, where every character is taken as illustrating a particular virtue or vice, "the moral program came to rhetorical life, casting the audience in the role of jurors" (Smith, 1988, 26). On the other hand, as contemporaries repeatedly urged, acting in plays exercised ingenuity, developed skills in oratory and gesture, and promoted bold and confident behavior in public, inestimably valuable at college and at court, in the pulpit, and in every domain of early modern social and political life. In this respect, as in the structure of their plots, it seems right to say that such plays "taught future statesmen about the structure of Elizabethan society" (Smith, 1988, 106).

Roger Ascham is hardly alone, however, in noticing the tension between these ways of using drama. The "base stuffe" of the action in classical comedy – "the thoughtes and conditions of hard fathers, foolish mothers, vnthrifty yong men, craftie seruants, sotle bawdes, and wilie harlots" – is hardly suitable for utterance by the "scholer, that should becum hereafter, either a good minister in Religion, or a Ciuill Ientleman in seruice of his Prince and contrie," yet in Plautus and especially in Terence there appear ideal examples of "the pure fine talke of Rome, which was vsed by the floure of the worthiest nobilitie that euer Rome bred" (Wright, 1904, 287–8). Not surprisingly, therefore, most of the early modern academic scripts sharpen the moral program. Birk's *Sapientia Solomonis* emphasizes the precocious judgment and constant humility of the young Solomon: the serenity of his face makes him irresistible to other minds, a model to the schoolboys and an exemplar that the still youthful Elizabeth follows in her own noteworthy mercy and wisdom (Payne, 1938, 57, 129). Watson's Absolom, Gnapheus' Acolastus, Gager's Meleager, each a young man in perilous circumstances, all pay for rage or arrogance or even an almost justifiable failure of self-control. In an atmosphere of increasing theatrical experimentation, questions of behavioral decorum also received a greater range of treatment. The comic rustics of *Gammer Gurton's Needle* – like the ignorant and hypocritical townsmen of *Club Law* (*c*.1600) – offered a merry opportunity for undergraduates simultaneously to act out and to stigmatize the stereotypic speech and gesture of social inferiors, distancing themselves both from their own atavistic tendencies and from townsmen and country folk outside the academy (cf. Cartwright, 1999, 75–91).

Like *Club Law*, some plays from the later Tudor period become more explicitly satirical, not only differentiating the academic community from its other in morals and manners, but (as one might expect from the higher proportion of economically privileged students within that body) distinguishing true insiders from supposedly ridiculous parvenus, like the rope-maker's son, Gabriel Harvey. Using the devices of Roman comedy to pillory a prominent scholar and would-be courtier, Forsett's *Pedantius* (1581) mocks the pretensions, turns of phrase, and attitudes of its unfortunate hero. As schoolmaster, Pedantius/Harvey wishes to sleep and be buried with his favorite lexicon; as lover, he offers Lydia philosophical reasons why she should be moved to copulate with him; as deluded courtier, he is reduced to selling his books in order to pay his tailor. Frustrated in every way, he leaves for Ulyssean shores, bidding farewell to an academy that was blessed on his arrival, miserable on his departure (George Smith, 1905). From Thomas Nashe's report (and from college accounts) this kind of satiric drama could also inspire undergraduate riot and mayhem (Nelson, 1989, 713, 848–50).

Although it appears that academic drama after the 1560s went into partial decline, at least at some of the university colleges, this is also the period in which some of the most ambitious and well-attended performances occur. These are less frequently associated with the older Christmas-tide observances than with extraordinary dramatic festivals connected either with such more strictly academic ceremonies as the Bachelor's Commencement (at Cambridge, a month before Ash Wednesday and on Ash Wednesday itself), or with Shrove-tide, or with the ceremonial entertainment of visiting dignitaries. All these occasions provided a special opportunity for displaying the prowess of students, fellows, and masters before an audience that William Gager characterizes as a "learned, grave, worshipful, and sometimes honorable presence." And in each of these contexts, plays were either staged in association with disputations, public oratory, and literary declamation, or were themselves disputatious and performative assertions of the importance of literary drama for the life of the university college (Sutton, 1994, IV, 273, II, vi–xiv).

Of all these products of unusual activity, Legge's *Richardus Tertius*, the commencement play written by the master of Gonville and Caius College, has been characterized as "perhaps the most ambitious dramatic performance ever attempted in England (before or since)" (Nelson, 1994, 61). His tragedy was a month in rehearsal, its 70 named parts and unnamed choristers and extras involving over 100 men and boys in a performance that extended over three nights and was received with "great applause." Legge not only invented the chronicle play, he devised a drama of considerable influence and genuine power. Extant in 11 different manuscripts, one of which was probably meant as copy-text for Cambridge University Press, the play is cited by John Harington in his *Apologie of Poetrie* (1591) as able to move "Phalaris the tyrant, and terrifie all tyrannous minded men from following their foolish ambitious humours." Marlowe, Greene, and Nashe must have known the play, and the scene in which Richard woos Elizabeth is the only identifiable source for the comparable scenes (II.ii and IV.iv) of *Richard III* (Boas, 1914, 129–31; Sutton, 1993, vii–xlvii). One recent critic, discussing Legge's anticipation of strategies used in *Tamburlaine*, remarks upon its skillful manipulation of viewpoint, its way of converting victims into witnesses, and its success in making Richard into a fearsome and dominating spectacle that outruns the audience's expectations (Cartwright, 1999, 202).

Three other Latin dramatists from the final quarter of the Tudor era, none as influential as Legge, have received particular praise in modern times. William Alabaster's *Roxanna* (Trinity College, Cambridge, *c.*1592), singled out by Dr. Johnson as the one Latin work "worthy of notice" before Milton's elegies, manages its Senecan bombast with evident skill. Matthew Gwinne's *Nero* (printed 1603), rejected for performance at St. John's College, Oxford, is a Senecan dramatization of Tacitus and Suetonius (Binns, 1990, 131–6). Of all the academic playwrights in this period, William Gager, active at Oxford 1582–92, had the greatest generic and poetic range. Tucker Brooke even claims that the "graciousness and melody" of his Latin verse rivals Marlowe's English (Brooke, 1946, 236). One wonders what Sir Philip Sidney (and the earl of Leicester, far less a Latinist) made of the early *Meleager* (1582; revived for their visit in 1585), with its repeated unmaskings of the terror that lies just beneath aristocratic honor, familial loyalty, and noble expressions of love. There is the poignant and politically sophisticated *Dido* (1583), staged to entertain the Polish palatine Pfalzgraf, with theatrical materials supplied by George Peele. Tantalizing notices of the *Rivales* as involving "cuntry wooinge," "drunken mariners," and a "bragging soldier" (Sutton, 1994, I, 232) indicate that academic audiences could have seen comedies taking contemporary English life as their subject, perhaps in the manner of *The Merry Wives of Windsor* or with a version of Stephano and Trinculo.

During the highly unusual three-day dramatic festival produced at Christ Church during Shrove-tide 1592, Gager proved himself adept at tragicomedy, comedy, and Senecan tragedy, in the process constructing a dramatic trilogy, thematically and intertextually linked (Sutton, 1994, II, xiv–xvi). His *Ulysses Redux*, published with suggestive speed by the university press, seems part of a rejoinder to critics of the academic stage. Appropriately enough, the play begins with a theatrically self-conscious speech in which Ulysses reflects upon the mystery of his having been deposited in this strange place where no one seems to hear or answer him. Demonstrating a "thorough knowledge and considered rejection of . . . academic theories of tragedy," Gager mixes genres and affective responses within *Ulysses Redux* in a way that anticipates and parallels the strategies of vernacular dramatists (Binns, 1990, 130–1). As with his additions to Seneca's *Hippolytus* or with the raucous epilogue that brings the trilogy to an end, Gager also used these shifts of tone and mimetic strategy in order to call attention to the subtlety, artifice, and necessarily interactive character of all representational (and ethical) activity. Thus by the end of the innovative period of academic drama in England, playwrights for the university stage had achieved a literary sophistication and theatrical self-awareness that fit well with what we attribute to the great writers for the commercial stage. As that stage became more prominent, academic dramatists – partly in an effort to preserve an important aspect of college life, and partly as an exaggerated statement of the gentleman amateur's self-understanding – came sharply to distinguish their efforts from those that soiled the dyer's hand. But over the course of the sixteenth century, academic drama – both in

Latin and in English – was a vital and influential part of that larger intellectual culture which we now appreciate mainly through its "popular" and vernacular synecdoche.

NOTES

1 In 1598 Sackville was also the current Oxford chancellor.
2 *Caesar Interfectus* is alleged by some critics to have influenced *Richard III* and *Julius Caesar*.
3 It was in *Palamon and Arcite* that the young John Rainolds received a favorable notice from the queen for his acting of Hippolyta during her 1566 visit to Oxford.
4 Lyly was the playwriting grandson of the grammarian who was first high master of St. Paul's grammar school, of which the schoolboys acted in 1527 what appears to be the first original Latin tragedy by an Englishman, John Ritwise.
5 Gager's *Meleager* and his now lost but twice revived *Rivales* are exceptions, not the rule.
6 The festal periods included the twelve days of Christmas, when *Mankind* and *Fulgens and Lucres* were performed: see chapter 17 above. One such specific occasion was the visit of the French ambassadors, for which Ritwise's elaborate grammar school production at Greenwich was designed.
7 The earliest statute requiring Latin plays at Cambridge appears to be in 1544/5 and for Greek in 1558/9 at Queen's.
8 *Gl'Ingnannti* was acted in 1531 in Siena, published in 1537, and translated again for the same college in 1595. It is probably one source for *Twelfth Night*.
9 *Gammer Gurton* was famous enough to appear in Sir Oliver Owlet's Men's repertory in Marston's *Histrio-Mastix*.
10 *I Suppositi* is one source for *The Taming of the Shrew*.
11 After 1538 Sturm annually staged all the plays of Plautus and Terence, as well as many Greek texts.
12 Shrewsbury School was attended by Abraham Fraunce, Philip Sidney, and Fulke Greville.

REFERENCES AND FURTHER READING

Allen, Don Cameron, ed. (1933). *Francis Meres's Treatise "Poetrie": A Critical Edition*. Urbana: University of Illinois Press.

Binns, J. W. (1990). *Intellectual Culture in Elizabethan and Jacobean England: The Latin Writings of the Age*. Leeds: Francis Cairns.

Boas, Frederick S. (1914). *University Drama in the Tudor Age*. Oxford: Clarendon Press.

Boas, Frederick S., ed. (1923). *The Christmas Prince: Account of St. John's College Revels at Oxford in 1607–1608*. London: Malone Society Reprints.

Brooke, Tucker (1946). "Latin drama in Renaissance England." *ELH* 13, 233–40.

Cartwright, Kent (1999). *Theatre and Humanism: English Drama in the Sixteenth Century*. Cambridge: Cambridge University Press.

Elliot, John R. Jr. (1997). "Drama." In *Seventeenth-century Oxford*, ed. Nicholas Tyacke. Oxford: Clarendon Press.

Harington, Sir John (1591). "An Apologie of Poetrie." In L. Ariosto, *Orlando Furioso*, trans. Sir John Harington. London: R. Field.

Lancashire, Ian (1984). *Dramatic Texts and Records of Britain: A Chronological Topography to 1558*. Toronto: University of Toronto Press.

Leishman, J. B., ed. (1949). *The Three Parnassus Plays (1598–1601)*. London: Ivor Nicholson & Watson.

Merrill, L. B., ed. and trans. (1925). *The Life and Works of Nicholas Grimald*. New Haven: Yale University Press.

Motter, T. H. Vail (1929). *The School Drama in England*. London: Longmans, Green.

Nelson, Alan H., ed. (1989). *REED (Records of Early English Drama) Cambridge*. 2 vols. Toronto: University of Toronto Press.

Nelson, Alan H. (1994). *Early Cambridge Theatres: College, University, and Town Stages 1464–1720*. Cambridge: Cambridge University Press.

Payne, Elizabeth Rogers, ed. and trans. (1938). *Sapientia Solomonis: Acted before the Queen by the Boys of Westminster School January 17, 1565/6*. New Haven: Yale University Press.

Sharratt, P., and P. G. Walsh, eds and trans. (1983). *George Buchanan Tragedies*. Edinburgh: Scottish Academic Press.

Smith, Bruce R. (1988). *Ancient Scripts and Modern Experience on the English Stage 1500–1700*. Princeton: Princeton University Press.

Smith, George Charles Moore, ed. (1905). *Pedantius: A Latin Comedy Formerly Acted in Trinity College, Cambridge*. In *Materialien zur Kunde des älteren Englischen Dramas*, vol. 8, gen. ed. W. Bang. Louvain: A. Uystpruyst.

Smith, George Charles Moore (1923). *College Plays Performed in the University of Cambridge*. Cambridge: Cambridge University Press.

Smith, John Hazel, ed. and trans. (1973). *Two Latin Comedies by John Foxe the Martyrologist: Titus et Gesippus, Christus Triumphans*. Ithaca: Cornell University Press.

Sutton, Dana F., ed. and trans. (1993). *Thomas Legge: The Complete Plays*. 2 vols. New York: Peter Lang.

Sutton, Dana F., ed. and trans. (1994). *William Gager: The Complete Works*. 4 vols. New York: Garland.

Walker, Greg (1991). *Plays of Persuasion: Drama and Politics at the Court of Henry VIII*. Cambridge: Cambridge University Press.

Wickham, Glynne (1959–81). *Early English Stages 1300–1600*. 3 vols. London: Routledge and Kegan Paul.

Wilson, F. P. (1969). *The English Drama 1485–1585*. Oxford: Oxford University Press.

Wright, William Aldis, ed. (1904). *Roger Ascham, English Works: Toxophilus, Report of the Affairs and State of Germany, The Scholemaster*. Cambridge: Cambridge University Press.

19
"What Revels are in Hand?": Performances in the Great Households
Suzanne Westfall

Until recently, theater historians barely mentioned early modern household theater, but the fact that this chapter exists indicates that we are finally recognizing the importance of these venues in our new historical studies of the period, and making our previously implicit assumptions more explicit. At royal courts, at rural innyards, at New Year's concerts in the earl of Northumberland's castle, at Cardinal Wolsey's great hall, at a royal banqueting house for Queen Anne, retainers and administrators presented performances to the members of their households and to the public at large. Since we have been indirectly discussing this topic for some time, a slight shift of the focus will foreground auspices and patronage, will restore the households to their rightful places as primary producers of early modern theater. *Records of Early English Drama* (*REED*) publications have certainly opened up our study of household and patron theater, and have demonstrated clearly that performances sponsored by the aristocracy continued to thrive and indeed to increase throughout the years when public theaters were flourishing in the city, a fact that disputes the popular notion that the public stage replaced the private.

Here, I will begin by exploring the nature of the great household as a political and economic unit, then provide several examples of the entertainments we might expect the great households to produce. Ultimately, of course, the issue of patronage informs my entire study – household theater is, after all, patron theater. Looking at early modern theater from the perspective of patronage and households allows us to re-evaluate the meaning and purpose of theater, to better understand the power structures and hierarchies of Elizabethan England, and to reassess noblemen's and especially noblewomen's roles in creating Renaissance theater.

Entertainments in great households were almost always occasional, multimedial, frequently non-textual, and ephemeral, as Jonson himself acknowledges at the end of the *Masque of Blackness*, which "had that success in the nobility of performance as nothing needs to the illustration but the memory by whom it was presented" (Jonson, 1999, 367). Since we have very few visual representations, musical scores, or first-hand descriptions for entertainment outside the royal courts, we recover these performances only with great difficulty and with creative research in financial and historical accounts. In addition, many performances at the great households have not been considered theater at all, though they are, of course, theatrical. Tournaments, disguisings, ceremonialia – all these seem trivial in comparison to extant play-scripts, and are difficult to assess by scholars who hold highly rhetorical concepts of drama, since these entertainments rarely survive in published form. Discussion of household theater, therefore, requires interdisciplinary approaches, since it engenders a profusion of other issues, from the influence of patronage (ideology, religion, touring), to the aesthetics of non-verbal performance (jousts, disguisings, masques, cookery, heraldry, ceremony), to architectonics (great halls, chapels, outdoors, domestic vs. public space).

Household books of ordinances do give us some idea of the structures of occasional theater and the household staff who were expected to provide it. Edward IV's *Black Book* is an early and particularly valuable record of household management for resident and non-resident performers. *The Second Northumberland Household Book*, ordinances for Henry Algernon Percy, fifth earl of Northumberland (1478–1527), also gives detailed instructions about every aspect of family ceremonial occasions. Some household accounts from the Stafford dukes of Buckingham survive, as does an earlier household book (1311–12) for Queen Isabella. So, although we may not have play-scripts, we do have a few stage managers' "bibles" and business manager's account books to guide us, to confirm that household theater was not improvisational, but rather meticulously planned and precisely stage-managed.

A great household, whether ecclesiastical or aristocratic, was not a place *per se*, not a specific architectural structure. Rather, these "sites" of culture were collections of people assembled to serve an aristocrat in the maintenance of person and property. So the Tudor noblemen and noblewomen (for many women kept their own courts within the household auspices of husbands, brothers, and fathers) formed an epicenter for a semi-itinerant company of family, bureaucrats, officers, and servants. Static and active, private and public, domestic and commercial, the superstructure of servitors and household "stuff" moved from property to property, from manor to castle to London townhouse. As such, the household constituted an economic unit, to manage the noble's estate; a political unit, to serve as an expression of power and to provide the links between and among the patronage networks; and a social unit, to supply the trappings of culture that would indicate the aesthetic and intellectual sophistication of the patron. As Machiavelli observed, an aristocrat ought to "neglect no circumstance of sumptuous display," but rather "should show himself a patron of merit" who will "entertain the people with festivals and shows . . . offering an example of courtesy and munificence" (1992, 41, 61).

The numbers in a household could range from the small group of servitors for a country knight to 250 or more for Edward Stafford, third duke of Buckingham, 86 of whom formed the household of his duchess, Eleanor Percy; royal households could be, of course, much larger, and encompass several sub-households. For example, 9-year-old (and doubtless beardless) Edward VI retained his own barber, and as a toddler danced to the music of his own minstrels, provided by his father Henry VIII, whose chamberlain also administered households for the queen (whoever she might be at the time) and the princesses Mary and Elizabeth. These servants expected to be given food, livery, lodging, entertainment, and sometimes protection at the expense of the patron.[1] Small wonder that provincial families panicked when the royal household was headed their way, expecting the country hosts to foot the bill for the support of two entire households – their own and the traveling monarch's. In fact, when Edward VI was on the verge of bankruptcy, he headed for the shires in an extended progress, a stratagem probably practiced frequently by the frugal Queen Elizabeth, who seems to have mastered the art of getting other people to pay for her entertainment.

Although the geographical space of the household was changeable, the duties and privileges of the personnel are rigidly prescribed by household regulations. While resident in the household, a retained performer could expect a salary, gratuities from the patron and his friends, lodging (and perhaps employment and lodging for family members while the performer was touring), meals, candles, fuel, and a suit of livery once a year. One actor even expected burial costs from the countess of Pembroke (McMillin and MacLean, 1999, 29). Successful households were economically practical, so often resident entertainers served in more than one occupational capacity. For example, in 1311 Richard Pilke and his wife Elena were retained by the royal court as both minstrels and pastry chefs; much later the duke of Rutland provided Anthony Hall with board for four weeks because he was "lernyng a play to pley in Christemes" and "scowrying away the yerthe and stones in the tennys playe." Many have noted Richard Gibson's metamorphosis from player to yeoman of the wardrobe, or John English's as Henry VII's interluder and tailor (Westfall, 1990, 126–7).

Edward IV's *The Black Book* furnishes us with a detailed job description for heraldic trumpeters, directing them to provide:

> blowinges and pipinges, to such offices as must be warned to prepare for the king and his houshold at metes and soupers, to be the more redy in all seruyces, and all thies sitting in the hall togyder, whereof sume vse trumpettes, sume shalmuse and small pipes. (Edward VI, 1857, 131)

The king also warned his minstrels not to "be too presumptuouse nor to famiier to aske any rewardes of the lordes of his lond"; further orders are given that some minstrels come to court only at the "v festes of the yere," to take "iiijd ob. a day," and to "auoyude the next day after the festes be don" (1857, 132), showing that the household was not inclined to support all its entertainers on a full-time basis. So here we have an institutional reason for many of those touring minstrel troupes we find in civic and household financial accounts.

Performances were customarily required on specific occasions. Northumberland's chapel, for example, was directed to perform the Nativity play on Christmas morning, the resurrection play on Easter morning, and an unspecified play in the great hall on Shrove Tuesday. Records of precisely what these entertainers performed do not survive, but it seems plausible to assume that the Christmas and Easter plays resembled the appropriate episodes of the cycle plays, while the Shrove-tide play could offer more secular treats. Northumberland's almoner was a "maker of interludes," and his chaplain apparently assisted in the writing of the Beverley plays, so it is not difficult to imagine aesthetic exchanges between civic and household producers (Lancashire, 1980, 7–45, 13n.). As I have argued elsewhere (Westfall, 1990), *The Second Shepherd's Play*, with its complex musical requirements, seasonal allusions, and explicit references to chapel functions, seems a particularly good candidate for such household production. Indeed, virtually every known playwright (and probably most of those "anons") occupied some position in one or more patronage networks, so that to some extent we might say that the great household patrons were fundamental to Renaissance public theater.

Even though the great household was not always situated in a specific geographical place, various manors and castles provided platea and loci for performance. In actuality any space, from Queen Katherine's bedchamber, to King Henry VIII's tents at the Field of Cloth of Gold in France, to the Thames River for Edward VI's water tournaments, could and did become stages. In 1591, the earl of Hertford even reconstructed a few acres of his landscape at Elvetham in Hampshire to provide a four-day entertainment for Queen Elizabeth, including a crescent-shaped lake with three islands, a ship, sea creatures, and verses that Shakespeare may have recalled when he wrote *A Midsummer Night's Dream*.[2] Clearly, early modern patrons were not as limited in their conception of "appropriate" theater space as today's audiences are; rather, early modern aristocrats conducted their lives with a complex understanding of "public privacy."

Household revels too often blur the distinction between communal and personal space, actor and audience, public and private experience, liturgical and secular activities. Henry Medwall's interlude *Fulgens and Lucres* actually depends upon such ambiguities for its initial jest, and makes an astute political comment on fashion at the same time:

> *A.*   I trowe your owyn selfe be oon
>   Of them that shall play.
> *B.*   Nay, I am none.
>   I trowe thou spekyst in derision
>   To lyke me thereto.
> *A.*   Nay, I mok not, wot ye well,
>   for I thought verely by your apparell
>   That ye had bene a player.
> *B.*   Nay, never a dell.
> *A.*   Than I cry you mercy;
>   I was to blame. Lo, therefore, I say
>   Ther is so myche nyce aray
>   Amonges these galandis now aday
>   That a man shall not lightly
>   Know a player from a nother man. (ll.43–56)

In one of the most popular household entertainments, the disguising or masque, performers and spectators mingled more unambiguously. Henry VIII, who was extremely fond of fancy dress, once burst into Queen Katherine's bedchamber dressed as Robin Hood to perform for the Spanish ambassadors (Hall, 1809, 723–4). On many other occasions, Hall records that the king broke both social and theatrical "fourth wall" conventions to choose dancing partners from among the spectators, an innovation that first caused alarm, then quickly became quite popular, as the later extravagant masques of Ben Jonson and Inigo Jones demonstrate.

Various household spaces were also natural settings for theater. Chapel choirs and lofts as well as the great halls where banquets took place (thus prompting some scholars to interpret the Latin term *interlude* as entertainments *between* courses), were frequent sites for theatrical activities. John Astington (1999) shows that platform stages constructed for specific events were intricate, often trompe l'oeil and equipped with innovative mechanical devices that did not invariably use the screens or the full expanse of the hall, as Richard Southern (1973) had assumed. The reusable stages at Cambridge, as Alan Nelson (1994) has demonstrated, were complex and sophisticated; Sally-Beth MacLean and Scott McMillin (McMillin and MacLean, 1999) have beautifully photographed a variety of spaces that indicate the diversity and adaptability of household space.

At family occasions or royal progresses, entire properties became theater space: ceremonial processions wound through the house; divine service or liturgical plays occupied the chapel; banquets, concerts, and entertainments filled the great hall. Tournaments, often highly allegorical, were staged with elaborate sets by the royal household, which could afford the economic and political expense of mock battle, but some notable exceptions to the royal venue for jousts occur among the upper, most trusted nobility.[3] Hunting, al fresco banqueting, and dancing erupted into the parks and meadows outdoors. Great household performances, like the great cycles and psychomachia, were "environmental" theater.

The most ubiquitous troupes in the great households were the musicians without which no respectable household could function, or so it appears from period household accounts. Heraldic minstrels were indispensable for martial and ceremonial occasions, and the nobility almost always traveled with trumpets and drums. In addition, most families employed soloists, frequently players on harp, psaltery, lute, organ, or virginals; richer families also retained "mixed consorts," usually comprising rebec, lute, tabor, viols, and fiddles. These musicians had a variety of responsibilities, including preserving family history, carrying messages (or perhaps spying?), providing music for dancing and singing, repairing instruments, and teaching music to family members, who frequently purchased song-books.

Music was also provided by resident chapel clergy and children of the chapel, literate musicians in both English and Latin, who were responsible primarily for religious service, but also performed as a theatrical company. In great household disguisings, such as those for the wedding of Prince Arthur and Princess Katherine, and later in the elaborate masques of Jonson and Jones, chapel children and gentlemen (most likely along with household actors) must have taken the singing and speaking roles. Noblemen and noblewomen could be expected to dress in elaborate costumes and to dance, but would probably not have memorized lengthy speeches or sung tenor, treble, or harmony. Households who did not retain resident chapels could import boy companies, as when Edward Seymour, lord protector, hired Paul's boys for New Year's Day; Sir William Petre did the same for his daughter's wedding in 1560 (Emmison, 1964; Jackson, 1875, 140–207, 174). Chaplains, almoners, and chapel gentlemen, such as John Redford, John Heywood, Nicholas Udall, and William Hunnis, were also known as playwrights.

We know from financial accounts (not to mention Hamlet's famous complaint) that these choristers were popular actors on the public and private stages and frequent performers in plays and disguisings at royal and aristocratic courts. Chapel involvement seems required, in fact, for many interludes from the mid-fifteenth to the mid-sixteenth centuries, including *Wisdom*, *Youth*, *Fulgens and Lucres*, *Godly Queen Hester*, *Wit and Science*, *Roister Doister*, *Respublica*, and *Jacob and Esau*. Most of these plays are polemical, arguing specific political or religious agendas (another luxury of great household performance), require large casts that cannot be doubled, and specify music and dance, ingredients specific to chapel productions.

What sorts of entertainments would we expect to find in the great households? The program is as varied as the personalities that produced it. Northumberland's *Household Book* requires the services of actors, singers, dancing henchmen, and musicians in the ordinances for spectacular occasions such as family weddings and for Twelfth Night, when the household enjoyed hierarchical processions, a banquet, a masque, a morris dance, and a concert by the gentlemen of the chapel. Many household accounts note the popularity of novelty entertainers such as court fools (like Queen Mary's Jane, who had her head shaved) and animal trainers.[4] The court fool Bernard and 54 others danced naked before King Edward I, and odd references to such antics as "minstrelsy with snakes" and to the multi-talented Roland le Fartere (who was rewarded for "making a leap, a whistle, and a fart") (Bullock-Davis, 1978, 66–7; 1986, 108–9), show that human appetite for the coarse or exotic never changes. Dancing women, puppet shows, storytellers, water combats, and maypoles appear as frequently as "highbrow" banquets, disguisings, classical pageants, and Latin interludes. A payment to William Cornish for "paving gutters of lead for urinals" for a 1516 Greenwich joust (Streitberger, 1994, 244–5, 249, 252, 263, 272 *passim*) both brings us down to earth and demonstrates the foresight of those charged with producing household performances.

Households also heard plays, of course. Certainly from 1580 onward we find at the royal court many of the same plays that we find on the London public stages, for, after all, the premier household in England is the queen's, and her revels demand that the best troupes in the city perform before her. Naturally, I do not suggest that all plays were written specifically for households or patrons, but there was clearly a financial advantage in offering texts simultaneously to both private patrons and the general public. But before the 1570s, many of the interludes or moral plays do seem to have been commissioned by aristocratic patrons, performed within their households, and, if the production values of the text warranted, toured by their players.

Since the 1950s, many scholars have been working to attribute anonymous early Tudor play-texts to patrons and great household auspices. Alexandra Johnston (1986) makes a persuasive case that *Wisdom* was commissioned by local nobility, perhaps by the duke of Norfolk or the duke of Suffolk, both of whom lived nearby.[5] David Bevington's argument in *Tudor Drama and Politics* (1968) that drama was naturally polemical and that patrons either chose or commissioned works that would communicate their own ideologies has become an assumption for scholars studying patronage and player repertories. T. W. Craik (1953) and Ian Lancashire (1976) have made strong cases for household auspices for *Temperance and Humility*, *Wealth and Health*, *The World and the Child*, *Youth*, and *Hick Scorner*. More recently, Scott McMillin and Sally-Beth MacLean (1999), in their detailed discussion of the repertory of one particular company, the Queen's Men, connect players to specific texts, showing that the Queen's Men (with the support of radical Protestants like Walsingham and Leicester) were engaged in promulgating ideological state apparatuses, in discouraging simultaneously both recusancy and more extreme Puritanism, positions which also happened to be the ideological concerns of their patrons. Paul Whitfield White explores the relationship between John Bale and the household of Thomas Cromwell during the 1530s. Sir Richard Cholemeley's players were called before the Star Chamber for producing *King Lear*, *Pericles*, a seditious interlude, and a saint's play at the household of the recusant Sir John Yorke *c.*1609–10 (Takenaka, 1999).[6]

Sidney Anglo's *Spectacle, Pageantry, and Early Tudor Policy* (1969) describes in detail the court entertainments of Henry VII, indicating the complexity, both in structure and in content, of royal household entertainments. While we do not have (or have not as yet unearthed) similarly detailed accounts of entertainments at provincial noble households, we can assume from the household account and ordinance books that the wealthier great households lavishly celebrated major religious and secular festivals; Henry VII actually fined Northumberland for excessive displays (Brennan, I, 141, 168–9). Performances, because they tended to be occasional, could be made specific to social, liturgical, and political events and aimed at specific audiences, to "self-fashion" (to use Stephen Greenblatt's [1980] term) the aristocratic patron. Sets and costumes were supplied by wealthy households; retained entertainers encouraged collaboration in design and performance among various types of artists. Most important, household theater was non-profit theater, at least in hard cash, which left the designers considerably freer to experiment and overproduce, since the patron absorbed the cost. These factors make private household drama different from civic and public stages.

Masques (or their earlier form called disguising) demonstrated production values and techniques that made them extremely popular at the great households. Masques were generally commissioned to celebrate a specific occasion by referring to particular events and people and by employing allegory complementary to the interests of the household. A play performed by a small troupe of interluders could never hope to be as extravagant a theatrical display as could a masque that involved a greater number and variety of performers. Chapel gentlemen and chapel children, singing and perhaps speaking, joined with minstrels and dancing gentlemen and gentle-women on elaborate sets and scenic devices to create a visual and aural extravaganza that interluders could not match, as Sydney Anglo (1969), W. R. Streitberger (1994), Stephen Orgel (1967), and John Astington (1999) have all amply demonstrated in their work on the masque and disguising. Expensive masques, which were never intended for general admission audiences, could not be recreated for touring, could not return a profit or even meet expenses, so the household absorbed the entire expenditure. In addition, the masque involved household guests in a fashion that a play could not. Some, such as Queen Anne and Prince Henry, participated themselves as disguisers in works commissioned from notable creators like Ben Jonson and Inigo Jones. The masque not only entertained but flattered the elite as well, complimenting their intellect with its often classical themes, and reflecting their own courtly lifestyle. The sole profit to the patron, the grandeur of the impression, made it a splendidly wasteful display.

Patron troupes also served aristocratic interests. By 1583, as McMillin and MacLean (1999) have shown, the earls of Leicester, Sussex, Oxford, and Derby had retained all the most prominent actors in England, and contributed their best players to an amalgamated troupe under the queen's titular patronage. This "monopoly" (later to be replaced by the "duopoly" of the Lord Chamberlain's Men and the Lord Admiral's Men) increased Privy Council control over public playing, thereby ensuring that the political and religious ideologies of the patrons were advanced, and, ironically, reducing both recusant themes and radical Protestant attacks. The actively touring Queen's Men once again functioned to affirm the importance of household theater even while the public theaters of London were at full strength; touring players were far more effective as spies, emissaries, and messengers, stopping at towns and other noble households all over the kingdom, rather than staying home in London.

Touring players have been a matter of record and a focus for early modern theater studies for the past century (see chapter 15 above), so I will not belabor the issues here, except to reiterate that civic and aristocratic account books continually indicate the presence of actors not by their geographic origins or their names or their texts, but by the names of their patrons. For years theater historians ignored this fact, or perhaps assumed that patrons acted in name only, in spite of the fact that the law specified that patronage was essential to traveling players. As early as 1285, the Statute of Winchester addressed the problem of masterless vagabonds, and the statute was reactivated by royal proclamation in 1527 with a reminder in 1531. Years later Elizabeth I once again renewed the Act against Retainers and the Act for the Punishment of Vagabonds. The crown also began issuing patents to control the patronized troupes and regulations to control seditious content in plays (Great Britain Records Commission, 1963, I, 97, III, 328; Hughes and Larkin, 1964, I, 172).

In fact, recent studies make it clear that the patron–retainer relationship was quite complex. Andrew Gurr (1996) reconstructs the histories of almost 20 patron companies, noting their composition, repertories, and touring details, which allows us to form a much sharper picture of the interactions we have long simply surmised. Richard Dutton's *Mastering the Revels* (1991) shows that the central government assumed that the nobility had some control over their entertainers, for potentially seditious materials were sometimes permitted to be performed within household auspices. Aristocratic patronage might also inspire higher wages and rewards on tours. In 1540–1 the city of Dover rewarded the troupe of their local patron, the duke of Suffolk's players, with six shillings and eight pence, whereas more far-flung communities gave them only the typical 12 pence. The earl of Northumberland's household book institutionalizes this practice, specifying that performers retained by a "speciall Lorde Frende or Kynsman" receive higher rewards than others (Blackstone, 1988, 112–32; Dawson, 1965, 39, 69, Grose, 1809, 253).

Focusing on households as producers of textual and non-textual entertainments also allows us to revise our view of women as creators and producers of theatrical art and accord them new prominence. While we know that women were forbidden to perform on the public stage, we also know that women were very active in private theater on the extremes of the social hierarchy, from traveling entertainers and fools to noble dancers in masques and disguisings. Many women also served as patrons, such as the queen-mother, Margaret Beaufort, patron of the poet–playwright John Skelton during the reign of Henry VII, and Queen Anne, patron of Jones and Jonson to produce Stuart court masques. Can we perhaps contemplate Queen Anne's, not just Ben Jonson's, *Masque of Blackness* (1999), when the queen, desiring some exotic (and erotic?) fantasy, requested Jonson to compose a masque in which she and her ladies could appear "all paynted like Blackamores face and neck bare," inspired perhaps by an assumed spectacle of Africans dancing "naked in the snow in front of the royal carriage" at her own wedding (Hall, 1991, 4)?

Many women, including seven queens, created household entertainments through their retained artists and playwrights. Many noblewomen performed. Even after the government closed the theaters in 1642, women continued to produce domestic theatricals in their salons. David Bergeron has identified, through dedications of dramatic texts, at least 14 women who served as patrons (1981, 274–90). And in more indirect fashion, women in the audiences, both public and private, served as patrons, a situation satirized in quite controversial style in *The Knight of the Burning Pestle*. Through control of the purse strings, women did indeed have a say in the theatrical art of their era. Denied acting roles in the civic and public theater, women sang, played musical instruments, spoke text, and danced in disguisings and masques. Matilda Makejoy, one of the very few female minstrels on record, entertained the royal court with dances and acrobatics in the early fourteenth century. Aemilia Lanyer, feminist poet and, according to A. L. Rowse (1978) at least, Shakespeare's "dark lady," was a member of the recorder-playing Bassano family who served Henry VIII, receiving lucrative properties and monopolies in return (Lewalski, 1991, 59–78). Countless prologues and epilogues demonstrate that women, particularly queens, often provided the raison d'etre for entertainments. John Lyly's compliments to the chastity of Queen

Elizabeth and the devotion of her courtiers in *Endymion*, and George Peele's *The Araygnement of Paris* (in which the prize golden apple rolls to the queen's feet), demonstrate appeals to feminine influence.

Extant plays, more familiar to the general reader than chronicles or financial account books, provide us with impressions, albeit in fictional form, of the ways in which great households administered performance. The most often-quoted example is Duke Theseus in *A Midsummer Night's Dream*, who asks Philostrate, his master of the revels, "What masque? What music?" Theseus then selects a play, providing his rationale:

> "The battle with the Centaurs, to be sung
> By an Athenian eunuch to the harp."
> We'll none of that. That have I told my love
> In glory of my kinsman Hercules.
> "The riot of the tipsy Bacchanals,
> Tearing the Thracian singer in their rage."
> That is an old device, and it was played
> When I from Thebes came last a conqueror.
> "The thrice three Muses, mourning for the death
> Of Learning, late deceased in beggary."
> That is some satire keen and critical,
> Not sorting with a nuptial ceremony.
> "A tedious brief scene of young Pyramus
> And his love Thisby; very tragical mirth."
>   (V.i.44–56)

This literary analogue clarifies some of the principles of selection: patrons required fresh materials, preferably in praise of family members or histories, suitable to the occasion and uncritical of household policies.

Other Shakespearean plays also represent scenes of patron–player interaction. Hamlet is clearly delighted to welcome players to Elsinore, and greets them as old friends, suggesting that players, with their regular circuits, had friends and acquaintances all over the country. Besides debating aesthetics with Polonius, the prince also compliments the player troupe's adaptability, assuming that they can and will insert a patron's emendations into their script. Prospero prepares the ubiquitous wedding masque for his daughter, as so many noble patrons actually did. Just as in the real world of courtly marriage, the masque on the fictional island employs classical goddesses, learned allusions, and appropriate themes: Venus and Cupid, representatives of sexual love, are excluded in favor of Iris, Ceres, and Juno, representatives of home, hearth, and fertility. Middleton and Rowley's *The Changeling* also contains the requisite wedding masque for Don Vermandero's three-day wedding celebration, this one commenting ironically on the marriage; unlike the virtuous Miranda, who gets an harmonic masque of marriage blessing, Beatrice-Joanna ends up with a cacophonous masque of fools and madfolk from the local asylum.

The framing scenes from *The Taming of the Shrew*, almost always omitted from performance, show the interactions of a lord and his household in the elaborate joke on the drunken beggar:

Lord	Sirrah, go see what trumpet 'tis that sounds.
	Belike some noble gentleman that means,
	Traveling some journey, to repose him here.
	Enter Servingman
	How now, who is it?
Servingman	An't please your honor, players
	That offer services to your lordship.
	Enter Players
Lord	Bid them come near. – Now, fellows, you are welcome.
Players	We thank your honor.
Lord	Do you intend to stay with me to-night?
A Player	So please your lordship to accept our duty.
Lord	With all my heart. This fellow I remember
	Since once he played a farmer's eldest son.
	'Twas where you wooed the gentlewoman so well.
	I have forgot your name, but sure that part
	Was aptly fitted and naturally performed. . . .
	Well, you are come to me in happy time,
	The rather for I have some sport in hand
	Wherein your cunning can assist me much.

(Ind.i.72–91).

Again, we see the same sort of welcome and the same expectations that Shakespeare writes into other plays drawn, no doubt, from his own days on the road. And perhaps the scene is so often omitted because it serves no plot function, but merely contextualizes the means of theatrical production – of little interest to current audiences, perhaps, but of paramount interest to historians interested in patronage theater.

These analogues indicate that patrons may have actively chosen their ludi for specific reasons (taste? novelty? politics?) and did not scruple to interfere actively with performance details. To a certain extent, reality once again supports fiction, as a closer look at the household revels during the brief reign of the boy-king Edward VI indicates. Although Edward was well educated (multilingual, well read in history, philosophy, and divinity, skilled in sports, music, and dancing), his favorite entertainments nevertheless remained "boyish." John Allen, yeoman of the prince's beasts, staged fights and bearbaitings once a month; revels accounts record frequent parades and masques of wild Irishmen. The king, like most boys, was fond of martial displays. At Shrove-tide 1548, John Stow records a castle storming "to shew the King the manner of Warres wherein hee had great pleasure," and in June of 1550 Edward, lord Clinton and the new admiral of England, staged a water tournament, which Edward enjoyed enough to describe in detail in his journal (Edward VI, 1857, II, 279,

383; Stow, 1631, 595; Anglo, 1969, 300–1). Within the circumscribed structure of the lengthy coronation pageant, it seems Edward was already making a patron's space for himself by stopping the procession to watch a tumbler walk a tightrope (Hume, 1889; Edward VI, 1857, I, ccxc). At the coronation banquet, revels accounts note expenses for the sort of entertainment we should expect from the newly empowered Protestant household – an anti-clerical and anti-papal masque, in which Edward himself played a priest (Feuillerat, 1963, 3–8). Extant plays from Edward's reign also reflect his personality. *Jacob and Esau*, *Lusty Juventus*, and *Nice Wanton* all address matters specific to the reign of a boy-king reformer. Again we see that the patron's tastes and ideologies affected the themes and aesthetics of the entertainments. The plays and entertainments certainly flattered the boy, self-centered no doubt by nature and nurture, using theater to reflect and refract policy, as did all the Tudor entertainments.

A study of household theater leads constantly to speculation about its function within the political system, and ultimately its value to the people who paid the pipers. Clifford Geertz, writing from the anthropological wing, puts it best:

> At the political center of any complexly organized society . . . there is both a governing elite and a set of symbolic forms expressing the fact that it is in truth governing. No matter how democratically the members of the elite are chosen (usually not very) or how deeply divided among themselves they may be (usually much more than outsiders imagine), they justify their existence and order their actions in terms of a collection of stories, ceremonies, insignia, formalities and appurtenances that they have either inherited or, in more revolutionary situations, invented. It is these – crowns and coronations, limousines and conferences – that mark the center and give what goes on there its aura of being not merely important but in some odd fashion connected with the way the world is built. (1983, 124)

Clearly, great household performances are exactly the "set of symbolic forms" that express the political power of the patrons. Rather than one unified ideological state apparatus, we find many – sometimes competing and conflicting. In spite of repeated attempts by the city and crown, we find that theater eluded control. In fact, we find that tight control was undesirable, as Richard Dutton (1991) has demonstrated in his investigation of the Tudor Revels Office. Instead of the Revels Office as censor, we find a commission dedicated to balancing patronage and patrons to produce the most profit for all concerned.

Approaching theater from the perspective of households also refocuses our perspective on the public stage in London as the center and epitome of performance in the sixteenth and seventeenth centuries. London public theater was not the only high-quality performance in the land. Just as the public theater is not the only game in town, neither is elite private theater. By the end of the sixteenth century, companies like the Queen's Men, the Lord Chamberlain's Men, and the Lord Admiral's Men clearly had two patrons – the monarch *and* the paying public, in most cases quite comfortable as bedfellows, implying that aristocratic patronage offered perquisites that the public could not, and that the public offered economic rewards that the patrons were reluctant to distribute.

A new view of household revels as auspices for theater provides us with greater understanding of politics and art in the early modern era. In multimedial, occasion-specific events, patrons employed their retained artists – performers, painters, writers, cooks, and carpenters – as collaborators in theater that could not return a financial profit but might well score sociopolitical points. Perhaps the increasing competition among patrons and the replacement of the feudal system with incipient capitalism, based heavily on patronage politics, finally encouraged some actors to market their commodities in more lucrative and rewarding ways, leading to the heyday of the public theater. But for the recusants in the provinces, the noblewomen stuck in country households or glittering courts, the aristocrats with political and religious ideologies they felt compelled to express, and the player troupes touring the land with passports from their patrons, households offered opportunities not only to "connect with the way the world is built" but also to contribute to the construction of early modern culture.

NOTES

1 For more detailed information on the structure and workings of households, see Westfall (1990).
2 For a convenient new edition of the Elvetham revels, see Kinney (1999, 139–54).
3 Henry Herbert, second earl of Pembroke, and Sir Philip Sidney produced tilts at Wilton; Pembroke's son William celebrated his wedding to Mary Talbot, daughter of the privy councillor earl of Shrewsbury, with emblematic tournaments (Brennan, 1902, I, 108).
4 For various payments, see Feuillerat (1963).
5 For a thorough discussion of staging, see Riggio (1986).
6 See also *Star Chamber Accounts* (London: Public Record Office), Stac 18 19/10, fos 51–6.

REFERENCES AND FURTHER READING

Anglo, Sydney (1969). *Spectacle, Pageantry, and Early Tudor Policy*. Oxford: Clarendon Press.
Astington, John (1999). *English Court Theatre 1558–1642*. Cambridge: Cambridge University Press.
Bergeron, David (1981). "Women as patrons of English Renaissance drama." In *Patronage in the Renaissance*, eds Guy Fitch Lytle and Stephen Orgel. Princeton: Princeton University Press.
Bevington, David M. (1968). *Tudor Drama and Politics: A Critical Approach to Topical Meaning*. Cambridge, MA: Harvard University Press.
Bevington, David M. (1997). *The Complete Works of Shakespeare*. 4th edn. New York: Addison Wesley Longman.
Blackley, F. D., and Gustav Hermansen, eds (1971). *The Household Book of Queen Isabella of England for the Fifth Regnal Year of Edward II, 8 July 1311 to 7 July 1312*. Edmonton: University of Alberta Press.
Blackstone, Mary (1988). "Patrons and Elizabethan dramatic companies." In *Elizabethan Theatre X*, ed. C. E. McGee. Port Credit, ON: P. D. Meany.
Brennan, Gerald (1902). *A History of the House of Percy from the Earliest Times down to the Present Century*. 2 vols. London: Freemantle.

Bristol, Michael (1985). *Carnival and Theater: Plebeian Culture and the Structure of Authority in Renaissance England.* New York and London: Methuen.

Bullock-Davis, Constance, ed. (1978). *Menestrellorum Multitudo: Minstrels at a Royal Feast.* Cardiff: University of Wales Press.

Bullock-Davis, Constance (1986). *Register of Royal and Baronial Domestic Minstrels 1272–1327.* Woodbridge: Boydell Press.

Collier, John Payne (1844). *The Household Book of John, Duke of Norfolk, and Thomas, Earl of Surrey.* London: Roxburghe Club.

Craik, T. W. (1953). "The political interpretation of two Tudor interludes: *Temperance and Humility* and *Wealth and Health.*" *Review of English Studies* NS 4, 98–108.

Craik, T. W. (1958). *The Tudor Interlude.* Leicester: Leicester University Press.

Dawson, Giles, ed. (1965). *Records of Plays and Players in Kent.* Malone Society Collections 7. London: Clarendon Press.

Dutton, Richard (1991). *Mastering the Revels: The Regulation and Censorship of English Renaissance Drama.* London: Macmillan.

Edward VI (1857). *Literary Remains of King Edward the Sixth,* ed. John Gough. 2 vols. London: Roxburghe Club/J. B. Nichols.

Emmison, Frederick G. (1964). *Tudor Food and Pastimes.* London: Ernest Benn.

Feuillerat, Albert (1963). *Documents Relating to the Revels at Court in the Times of King Edward VI and Queen Mary.* Vaduz: Kraus Reprint.

Gage, John (1834). "Extracts from the household book of Edward Stafford, duke of Buckingham." *Archaeologia* 25, 311–41.

Geertz, Clifford (1983). *Local Knowledge.* New York: HarperCollins.

Great Britain Records Commission (1963). *The Statutes of the Realm.* 11 vols. London: Dawson of Pall Mall.

Greenblatt, Stephen (1980). *Renaissance Self-Fashioning: From More to Shakespeare.* Chicago: University of Chicago Press.

Grose, Francis, comp. (1809). "The earl of Northumberland's household book." In *The Antiquarian Repertory,* IV. London: E. Jeffery.

Gurr, Andrew (1996). *The Shakespearian Playing Companies.* Oxford: Clarendon Press.

Hall, Edward (1809). *The Vnion of the Two Noble and Illustre Famelies of Lancastre and Yorke.* London: G. Woodfall.

Hall, Kim F. (1991). "Sexual politics and cultural identity in *The Masque of Blackness.*" In *The Performance of Power: Theatrical Discourse and Power,* eds Sue-Ellen Case and Janelle Reinelt. Iowa City: University of Iowa Press.

Hughes, Paul, and James Larkin, eds (1964). *Tudor Royal Proclamations.* 3 vols. New Haven: Yale University Press.

Hume, M. A. S., ed. (1889). *Chronicle of King Henry VIII of England, Being a Contemporary Record of Some of the Principal Events of the Reigns of Henry VIII and Edward VI.* London: G. Bell and Sons.

Jackson, J. E. (1875). "Wulfhall and the Seymours." *Wiltshire Archaeological and Natural History Magazine* 15, 140–207.

Johnston, Alexandra (1986). "Wisdom and the records: is there a moral?" In *The Wisdom Symposium,* ed. Milla Cozart Riggio. New York: AMS Press.

Jonson, Ben (1999). *The Masque of Blackness.* In *Renaissance Drama: An Anthology of Plays and Entertainments,* ed. Arthur F. Kinney. Oxford: Blackwell.

Kinney, Arthur F., ed. (1999). *Renaissance Drama: An Anthology of Plays and Entertainments.* Oxford: Blackwell.

Lancashire, Ian (1976). "The auspices of *The World and the Child.*" *Renaissance and Reformation* 12, 96–105.

Lancashire, Ian (1980). "Orders for Twelfth Day and Night *circa* 1515 in the second Northumberland household book." *English Literary Renaissance* 10, 7–45.

Lewalski, Barbara (1991). "Re-writing patriarchy and patronage: Margaret Clifford, Anne Clifford, and Aemilia Lanyer." In *Patronage, Politics and Literary Traditions in England: 1558–1658*, ed. Cedric. C. Brown. Detroit: Wayne State University Press.

McMillin, Scott, and Sally-Beth MacLean (1999). *The Queen's Men and their Plays*. Cambridge: Cambridge University Press.

Machiavelli, Niccolo (1992). *The Prince*, trans. N. H. Thomson. New York: Dover.

Medwall, Henry (1980). *The Plays of Henry Medwall*, ed. Alan H. Nelson. Cambridge: D. S. Brewer.

Myers, Alec Reginald (1959). *The Household Book of Edward IV: The Black Book and the Ordinance of 1478*. Manchester: Manchester University Press.

Nelson, Alan (1994). *Early Cambridge Theatres*. Cambridge: Cambridge University Press.

Orgel, Stephen (1967). *The Jonsonian Masque*. Cambridge, MA: Harvard University Press.

Orgel, Stephen, and Roy Strong (1973). *The Theatre of the Stuart Court*. 2 vols. Berkeley: University of California Press.

Riggio, Milla Cozart, ed. (1986). *The "Wisdom" Symposium*. New York: AMS Press.

Rowse, A. L., ed. (1978). *The Poems of Shakespeare's Dark Lady: Salve Deus rex Judaeorum by Aemilia Lanier*. London: Cape.

The Second Northumberland Household Book, Bodleian MS Eng. Hist.b. 208.

Southern, Richard (1973). *The Staging of Plays Before Shakespeare*. London: Faber and Faber.

Stow, John (1631). *Annals*. London.

Streitberger, W. R. (1994). *Court Revels, 1485–1559: Studies in Early English Drama 3*. Toronto: University of Toronto Press.

Takenaka, Mashahiro (1999). "The Cholemeley players and the performance of *King Lear* in Yorkshire in 1609–10." Paper given at the Lancastrian Shakespeare Conference, Lancaster University, July 21–3, 1998.

Westfall, Suzanne (1990). *Patrons and Performance: Early Tudor Household Revels*. Oxford: Clarendon Press.

White, Paul Whitfield (1993). *Theatre and Reformation: Protestantism, Patronage, and Playing in Tudor England*. Cambridge: Cambridge University Press.

20

Progresses and Court Entertainments

R. Malcolm Smuts

General Characteristics of Court Theater

Renaissance courts employed a wide variety of theatrical forms, including some shared with the public stage and others that were quite distinctive, which by the seventeenth century included the English masque, the French *ballet de cour*, and the north Italian opera. These complex genres incorporated spectacular acoustical and visual effects well beyond the range of ordinary plays. They were set to music and included lengthy dances, from which modern ballet evolved, along with stage machinery, painted scenery, and extraordinarily opulent costumes (Meagher, 1966, ch. 4; Ravelhofer, 1998). This scenic paraphernalia evoked a fantasy world peopled by gods and heroes and also expressed philosophical ideas through emblematic formulas derived from manuals like Caesar Ripa's *Iconologia*: court theater shared the visual language of historical and allegorical painting. Lighting effects further contributed to its painterly quality: indeed, Inigo Jones once described masques as "nothing else but pictures with light and motion" (Chambers, 1912, 119). Many productions culminated in a "scene of light," in which the main performers were suddenly revealed within an enclosure lit by dozens of hidden candles, as if suffused by supernatural radiance, like religious figures in certain baroque canvases (Meagher, 1966, 199, ch. 5 *passim*; Astington, 1999, 96–7).

The visual impact of a court production was integrated through the use of a proscenium arch, an invention of Italian court theaters, introduced into England by Inigo Jones. The proscenium defined a boundary between the imaginary world on stage and the real world of the audience, in much the manner of a picture frame. But this boundary remained much more permeable in court entertainments than in the later public theaters that adopted the proscenium stage. At least some illumination always suffused the entire hall, instead of being concentrated solely on the stage, so that the audience remained in view, competing with the actors for attention. The admiring of richly dressed playgoers that now takes place during intermissions went on throughout performances at early modern courts, forming one of the main attractions. This was especially true of the main royal spectator, who watched the performance from a raised dais at the opposite end of the hall from the playing space. A court entertainment effectively had two stages, one for the actors and one for the king (Orgel, 1981).

The entertainment itself also invariably gestured toward the ruler, representing him and his companions under mythical guises and addressing him from the stage as a divine source of virtuous order. The appearance of prominent courtiers and members of the royal family in leading roles further emphasized this connection. Although Elizabeth and James I never danced in a masque, Queen Anne and Prince Henry, Charles I and Queen Henrietta Maria, did so frequently. An invitation to perform in a masque provided both a special mark of favor and an opportunity for special access to royalty during intervals in lengthy rehearsals (Barroll, 1998). At the end of a performance the boundary between actors and spectators collapsed, as masquers descended from the stage to select partners from the audience for a final dance. This action led into the revels, when other spectators joined in the dancing, which preceded a final banquet.

Even though their plots were less realistic than those of most ordinary plays, court entertainments were therefore more closely connected to their audiences' lives. Rather than fictive stories enacted on a stage, they were spectacles that reflected the court to itself, denying any clear separation between theater and reality. As we move back toward the early Tudor period, the boundary separating court theatricals from ordinary court life becomes even more indistinct. The court of Henry VII was already familiar with entertainments known as disguisings, which included recited speeches and dances by costumed performers in spaces equipped with moveable stage machinery. Disguisings anticipated all the key features of later Stuart masques, except for the proscenium stage and painted scenery (Kipling, 1974, Anglo, 1968). But the form actually known as a "mask," which Henry VIII introduced a few years later, had a much less developed structure. As E. K. Chambers remarked, the early mask "is not primarily a drama; it is an episode in an indoor revel of dancing," in which costumed figures enter a court gathering and demand to dance with the ladies present (Chambers, 1923, 1965).[1] Although some masks included speeches, many did not: the mysterious dancers simply added a twist of fantasy to a festive occasion. In cases like this it becomes difficult to decide whether we are dealing with a dramatic form at all.

Many older discussions of court theater resolved the problem by treating Tudor entertainments as embryonic forms from which more mature dramatic genres later developed. This approach risks imposing modern concepts of theater upon the historical evidence, however. An alternative is to begin by examining how court society worked, with an eye to identifying the topographical and social contexts in which dramatic entertainments developed.

Settings and Occasions

The court is best pictured not as a single environment but as a series of concentric zones, of which the outermost lay in the city streets and other spaces surrounding the main palace of Whitehall (Thurley, 1999). For court life frequently spilled beyond the confines of the palace, into public places where ordinary subjects might see it. The Thames and London streets provided staging grounds for great state rituals, like coronations and openings of Parliament, as well as sites for public celebrations of events like royal weddings and great military victories. They also connected White-hall to other royal palaces and to satellite households belonging to the monarch's consort and great ministers of state. A royal palace was a place from which people were constantly coming and going, often in theatrical processions of considerable splendor. Royal excursions tended to be elaborate and provided a form of public enter-tainment. On April 23, 1559, for example, Elizabeth took supper at the earl of Pem-broke's London house and then took a boat trip on the Thames, attracting "hundreds of boats and barges rowing about her and thousands of people thronging at the water-side . . . rejoicing to see her and partaking of the music and sights" (Nichols, 1823, I, 67). A few months later another large crowd joined the queen at Greenwich as she watched military exercises by the London militia, tilts by the court guard, fireworks displays, and a masque performed within a newly erected timber banqueting house. (Nichols, 1823, I, 73).

Events within the palace were, inevitably, witnessed by fewer people, who were generally of higher rank than most of those who watched outdoor events. But palace interiors were themselves sudivided into regions with different functions and rules of access, so that some rooms were far more exclusive than others. Anyone dressed as a gentleman might normally enter the court's outer precincts, which included service rooms, areas inhabited by lesser household servants, and the hall, a great structure more than 100 feet in length. Halls had once formed the social and ceremonial center of palaces, where kings presided over great public feasts. They had gradually lost this function in the Middle Ages, however, as the real center of court life moved up a flight of stairs into the king's chamber. At Whitehall and other large palaces, the chamber actually consisted of both an ornately decorated great chamber, at the top of the stairs, and an adjacent throne room known as the presence chamber (Thurley, 1999, 8–10, 29–30, 76). From here a guarded door led into the ruler's private apartments, which had been given their own staff and organized into a separate household department, known as the privy chamber, under Henry VII. In 1603 James I introduced a further division by creating a separate bedchamber, which thereafter became the innermost sanctum of the Stuart court (Thurley, 1993, chs 7 and 8; Starkey et al., 1987; Adamson, 1999b; Bucholz, 2000).

The character of any event in the court's life, including a theatrical performance, was largely determined by its location within this structure. The further the distance from the bedchamber, the larger and more heterogeneous the attending crowd became and the more elaborate the apparatus of formality and magnificence. Most indoor entertainments took place in halls or in three successive Whitehall banqueting houses, which were also relatively public rooms. The earliest of these was a timber structure erected in the 1570s to house feasts and entertainments associated with the courtship of Elizabeth by the Duke of Alençon. James I rebuilt it in stone at the start of his reign, and replaced it again with Inigo Jones' famous structure after a fire in 1618 (Thurley, 1999, 68, 81–2, 82–90). The hall accommodated about 800 spectators, while Jones' banqueting house may have seated 1,200. Plays and masques performed in these spaces were therefore witnessed by fairly large audiences, including gentry and wealthy Londoners who were not regular courtiers. But some entertainments took place in the great chamber, which limited the audience to about 300, while Henrietta Maria performed pastoral dramas within the privy chamber at St. James, before a tiny group of invited guests.[2] This privacy limited, without entirely eliminating, the scandal caused by the queen's appearance on a stage. Great courtiers also produced theatrical performances in their own houses, inviting the monarch to attend (Wright, 1998; Raylor, 1999). These provided opportunities for the host to appeal for continuing favor and advance his own political viewpoint.

Theatrical entertainments were also shaped by the occasions on which they took place. Many dramatic productions accompanied events like coronations, visits to England by foreign monarchs, and royal weddings, and their themes naturally reflected these settings. Princess Elizabeth's marriage in 1613 to the elector palatine gave rise to three masques, several tournaments, a mock naval combat on the Thames, and fireworks fashioned to present moving images of warriors, ships, fire-spouting whales, and monstrous serpents.[3] All celebrated the nuptials as a union of "the Thames and the Rhine," uniting Britain to Protestant Germany. Ben Jonson's *Hymenaei* and Thomas Campion's *The Lord Hay's Masque*, by contrast, were written for weddings arranged by James I between Scottish courtiers and brides from English noble families. They employed an imagery of love and marriage to commemorate the union of England and Scotland, as well as the particular marriages they graced (Lindley, 1979; Gordon, 1975).

Most court masques and plays took place during the Christmas season, traditionally a time of lavish hospitality in great households. Christmas festivities also frequently involved rituals of social inversion, like the antics of lords of misrule: as the second earl of Essex once remarked, Christmas was a season when "disorder is not only allowed but, in a manner, warranted" (Spedding et al., 1862). The first Tudor mask on Twelfth Night in 1512, when Henry VIII and several attendants invaded a court ball wearing frightening disguises, must have seemed to those present an ingenious variant on this tradition (Chambers, 1923, 1965). Even in the Stuart period Jonson's anti-masques retained a strong connection with the concept of the Christmas revel, a protracted episode of disorderly merrymaking welcoming in the new year.[4] By overcoming the anti-masque through his miraculous power to transform vices into virtues, the king therefore also contained the anarchic spirit of Christmas itself. At least in theory: contemporary reports suggest that the effort at containment did not always succeed. A Venetian spectator who saw *The Masque of Blackness* reported that the night's entertainment ended "with a banquet in the Great Chamber, which was so furiously assaulted that down went the table and tresses before one bit was touched," to the sound of crystal platters shattering on the floor (Nichols, 1828, I, 473).

Whether performed at Christmas or on some other occasion, masques were always associated with royal hospitality, liberality, and magnificence. A different set of theatrical forms developed around military exercises that displayed the monarch as a leader of warriors and patron of courage and prowess. These included mock battles framed by a theatrical plot, staged by militia companies in London and some provincial cities. The main vehicle for warlike entertainments was, however, the court tournament (Young, 1987, 23 and *passim*). In the late Middle Ages a practice had developed of beginning tournaments with disguisings, in which knights wearing fanciful costumes enacted stories patterned after chivalric romances, leading up to challenges to combat. Early disguisings sometimes took place on large mobile stages, like one constructed for a tournament in 1511, which measured 26 by 16 feet and contained artificial trees, birds and beasts, a forester, and a castle inhabited by a maiden (Young, 1987, 53–5). In England wheeled stages fell into disuse after the early 1520s, but disguisings employing fixed scenery and mechanical props remained popular into the seventeenth century: *Prince Henry's Barriers* is a late example, with speeches by Jonson and scenery by Jones.

Young princes, like Henry VIII before about 1525, Edward VI and Prince Henry, especially favored tournaments as a way of displaying their skills and future military aspirations. But the form was also associated with chivalric ideals of courtly love, which made it suitable for royal weddings and courtships. This romance element became important during the latter part of Elizabeth's reign, when a tradition developed of honoring the anniversary of her accession on November 17 with an annual joust, in which knights from all over England assembled to pay homage to the royal mistress of English chivalry (Yates, 1975b; Strong, 1977b). Participants approached the queen in fanciful costumes, delivered speeches and presented her with impressas, wooden shields bearing symbolic pictures and mottoes that obliquely expressed the jouster's devotion and hopes for her favor. By the end of the reign the task of devising impressas and tournament speeches had become sufficiently demanding for many jousters to hire expert assistance. The earl of Essex employed Francis Bacon and other scholars to create a skit for a tournament in 1595; Robert Cecil asked Sir John Davies to write him a speech for a tournament in 1601; and in 1614 the earl of Rutland paid Shakespeare 44s. to devise an impressa for a Jacobean court tournament (Hammer, 1998; Young, 1987, 123–43).

Accession Day tournaments provide an example of entertainments devised by the queen's subjects rather than the royal household. Civic pageants performed during royal entries and progress entertainments also fall into this category. The greatest royal entries normally occurred on the day before a coronation and involved a procession through London by the royal court, the nobility, bishops, and other dignitaries. Members of the city's livery companies assembled in ceremonial robes along one side of the route, while the other was left open for ordinary spectators (Smuts, 1989; Manley, 1995, 217–58). Although an entry procession included numerous heraldic insignia, it was in origin essentially a liturgical rite. The king rode beneath a canopy similar to that which would be placed over the consecrated host during a Corpus Christi Day procession, along a route connecting the site of the ancient Roman cathedral of London to its successor church of St. Paul's (Manley, 1995, 221–41). As he passed, the crowd shouted "God bless your grace." Late medieval entries were modeled specifically on the Epiphany and included mechanical angels that descended from elevated platforms to bless the king as he passed by (Kipling, 1997).

From an early date, London guilds and resident communities of foreign merchants produced allegorical pageants along the processional route, emphasizing moral and religious virtues associated with good rule. The Reformation rendered much of this imagery problematical and led to the removal of overtly popish symbols, like the mechanical angels. But for Elizabeth's coronation entry, the London guilds fashioned an alternative Protestant imagery. As she processed through the city Elizabeth encountered the Old Testament heroine Deborah and a child who presented her with an English Bible, which she took in her hands and kissed. At Temple Bar, while listening to a speech imploring God to maintain Truth and eradicate Error, she "held up her hands to heavenward and willed the people to say amen" (Mulcaster, 1559). During a visit to Coventry in 1566, the queen was similarly entertained by pageants representing biblical stories of "the sacred council of Sion" and St. John's vision of the seven churches of Asia (Colthorpe, 1985). The pageants at James I's coronation entry, postponed because of plague until March 15, 1604, were superficially secularized. But even they emphasized philosophical ideals of kingship with strong theological overtones.

A royal progress reversed the situation prevailing during the winter at Whitehall, since the monarch now became a guest of provincial landowners and civic corporations (Cole, 1999). Most hosts simply feasted their royal visitor and presented her with an expensive gift, but a few took the additional step of devising poems and theatrical skits. The early history of progress entertainments remains obscure, since few texts survive before 1575. It is clear, however, that traveling monarchs enjoyed dramatic performances long before that year. In August 1559, the earl of Arundel entertained Elizabeth with a "banquet and masque, with drums and flutes and all the music that could be" (Nichols, 1848). In 1573, Warwick provided a pageant and fireworks that almost ended in disaster when a missile misfired and ignited several tenements in the town (Nichols, 1823, I, 319–20). The same year Sandwich decorated its streets with garlands of flowers and poems honoring the queen, stuck up "on every post and corner from her first entry to her lodging" (Nichols, 1823, I, 338). From this point on our documentation becomes fuller. Thomas Churchyard published the text of an entertainment he devised for a royal visit to Bristol in 1574, involving a series of mock combats between forces of peace and war, impersonated by the city's militia (Churchyard, 1575, pt 12). The entertainments at Kenilworth and Woodstock performed during the 1575 progress also gave rise to printed texts, as did the five days of pageantry Elizabeth witnessed while visiting Norwich in the summer of 1578, and several later progress entertainments.

Interpretations

Despite the enormous variety of court entertainments, certain general characteristics do emerge from this survey. Truly private performances, witnessed only by members of the court, were rare. Although some dramatic events were more public than others, nearly all took place before mixed audiences and were somehow associated with the ruler's public roles, as a dispenser of hospitality and largesse, a leader of warriors, a divinely appointed upholder of justice, or an accessible lord or lady perambulating the realm to make contact with its people.

Should we therefore regard court theater as propaganda? In certain respects this conclusion seems inescapable. Entertainments addressed monarchs through a language of compliment, while celebrating virtues associated with chivalric and Christian ideals of kingship: in that sense they undeniably sought to project a favorable image of the ruler. But we need to beware of oversimplifying. The entertainments with the largest audiences, performed during tournaments, progresses, and entries, were those over which the crown had the least direct control. Rather than court propaganda directed toward the public, these spectacles often provided opportunities for courtiers, country landowners, or civic corporations to address the monarch. Even court masques reflected the viewpoints of patrons including Queen Anne, Prince Henry, and Henrietta Maria, who did not agree on all matters with James I and Charles I (see, e.g., Holbrook, 1998; Parry, 1993; Sharpe, 1987; Butler, 1993; Veevers, 1975). For obvious reasons court entertainments did not present blatant attacks on royal policies or flagrantly subversive ideological statements; but in more oblique ways, they often did present advice and criticism.

Scholars have gradually moved away from interpretations stressing the role of court theater as a vehicle for royal cults, toward interpretations stressing ways in which productions voiced multiple viewpoints and attempted to intervene in factional rivalries. The first approach characterized several pioneering studies written between 1945 and 1980, by scholars including D. J. Gordon, Frances Yates, Sydney Anglo, Roy Strong, and Stephen Orgel. Their work reflected the strong interest in ideological propaganda of the Cold War period, as well as the then dominant interpretation of the early modern centuries as an age of growing absolutism, when courts and their cultural resources drew provincial elites more firmly within the orbit of royal power (Gordon, 1975; Yates, 1947, 1975a; Strong, 1973, 1977a; Orgel, 1965, 1975; Orgel and Strong, 1973). Research since the 1960s has undermined this view, by revealing the degree to which even the strongest monarchs needed the cooperation of local elites to rule effectively. Rather than centers of autocratic power, courts have increasingly emerged in recent studies as arenas of negotiation, where kings worked out arrangements for sharing power with royal ministers, great nobles, leading ecclesiastics, and other powerful subjects (e.g., Adamson, 1999a). Literary scholars have meanwhile become more aware of undercurrents of criticism and dissent in the work of writers like Philip Sidney and Ben Jonson, who used to be regarded as much more unequivocally supportive of royal authority.

These revisionist trends have combined to produce more complex perspectives on court entertainments. Particularly for the Elizabethan period, certain conclusions seem to be emerging. To a striking degree, most Elizabethan theatricals for which significant documentation survives focused on closely linked issues involving the queen's marriage, the problem of the succession, and England's role in European affairs (Axton, 1977; Doran, 1995). During the 1560s, several masques and plays performed before Elizabeth during Christmas revels at the Inns of Court hinted that she should marry and produce an heir (Axton, 1977, ch. 4). These included Thomas Sackville and Thomas Norton's *Gorboduc*, the first blank verse tragedy in English, produced during the 1561–2 season, which portrayed a mythical ancient king of Britain who failed to heed the advice of his council to name a single heir to his throne. The result was a disastrous civil war between his sons. One spectator reported that a dumb show between acts hinted more directly that "it was better for the Queen to marry with L.R. [lord Robert, earl of Leicester] than with the King of Sweden," her leading foreign suitor at the time (James and Walker, 1995). Leicester presided over the revels as Pallaphilos, the lover of Pallas, goddess of wisdom, and evidently tried to use them to promote his courtship of the queen.[5]

In 1575 he tried again to woo Elizabeth through entertainments presented while she visited his seat at Kenilworth. She spurned his plea by departing before the planned theatrical events were completed. Later in the same progress an entertainment at Sir Henry Lee's house at Woodstock urged her to avoid all marital entanglements, a message she obviously found more congenial, since she asked that a text be prepared for the press. Three years later the court was seriously divided over whether Elizabeth should marry the duke of Anjou, brother to Henry III of France. Several privy councillors who wanted an ally in any future war with Spain supported the match, but the queen's favorites, Leicester and Christopher Hatton, opposed it, as did staunch Protestants like Francis Walsingham. A pageant during the queen's visit to Norwich that summer depicted the triumph of Dame Chastity and her attendants over Venus and Cupid, and ended with Cupid's arrows being presented to Elizabeth, to show her absolute power over the hearts of her subjects. Other Norwich pageants advanced belligerent Protestant themes and warned against false friends. The political message was clear: Elizabeth should reject foreign suitors and rely on her own subjects. Two years later she signaled her final rejection of Anjou's suit through a court tournament, at which knights calling themselves "the four foster children of desire" failed to storm the "fortress of true beauty." It cannot be entirely coincidental that the progress pageants of 1575 and 1578 were among the first commemorated in printed texts, while *The Four Foster Children of Desire* was the first tournament disguising of the reign recorded in print. The publication of pageant texts dealing with Elizabeth's marriage was itself a political act (Smuts, 2000).

The pageants of 1575 and 1578 and *The Four Foster Children of Desire* all relied on imagery deriving from medieval romance traditions. In doing so they helped redefine Elizabeth as a perpetually virgin mistress of English chivalry. The Accession Day jousts, which developed in the same period, further expanded this trope. At one level such imagery made excellent wartime propaganda, but as Richard McCoy and Paul Hammer have shown, it also provided a formula that bellicose courtiers, like Sir Philip Sidney and the earl of Essex, might use to complain of Elizabeth's failure to support her champions. Hammer has demonstrated that in 1595 Essex employed an Accession Day celebration to appeal over the queen's head to the watching crowd, in hopes that by gaining popular support he might pressure Elizabeth into accepting his advice (Hammer, 1998). This was a high-risk strategy that eventually backfired disastrously, but it illustrates how court theater might be turned against the interests of the monarch.

The substantially increased use of the press to provide published texts of court entertainments from the 1570s onward reflects not only political motivations but two other important developments: a growing interest in poetry and drama produced by the humanist culture that had grown up around the court, and the court's increasing reliance on professional writers. Churchyard and George Gascoigne, the main author of the Kenilworth entertainment, were early pioneers in this field, but others soon eclipsed them. In the 1580s John Lyly wrote several comedies performed at court by child actors, which quickly reached print. By 1603 several established playwrights, including Thomas Dekker, George Chapman, Thomas Campion, and Ben Jonson, were competing for the Jacobean court's patronage and using the press to advance their claims. In addition, a self-styled architect named Stephen Harrison, who devised the triumphal arches for the street pageants during James' coronation entry, lovingly prepared a folio of engravings to commemorate his work (Harrison, 1604). Although Harrison subsequently disappeared, another self-trained architect of London artisanal background, Inigo Jones, soon took his place.

The partnership of Jonson and Jones that began with Queen Anne's *Masque of Blackness* in 1604 brought English practices more closely into line with an established European tradition, through which humanist poets and artists devised court theatricals, turning them into didactic spectacles of classical learning. Their masques displayed a much greater consistency and philosophical coherence than earlier Tudor entertainments, deriving from a platonized symbology in which the king consistently appears as a source of order and harmony in both the physical and political domains, who banishes dissonance by his mere presence, in ways reminiscent of God's rule of the cosmos. In this way the masque became an expression of ideas of divine right (Orgel, 1965; Strong, 1973, 218–20).

It also appears to have gradually eclipsed other forms of court theater, such as the progress entertainment and tournament disguising. This impression may, however, be partly an illusion created by the assiduity of Jonson and a few other poets in publishing masque texts. Accession Day jousts continued through James I's reign, while progresses occurred into the 1630s. In August of 1634, for example, the Florentine

ambassador reported that the king and queen were on progress enjoying "great banquets [*festini*] that the nobility have prepared in the provinces through which they
pass."[6] But only a few texts of entertainments associated with Stuart progresses and
jousts are now known.[7] Is this because such entertainments had actually become rare,
or simply because they were not often preserved through print? The answer is not
altogether clear. The texts for the majority of the masques produced by noble households in this period also seem to have disappeared, although one manuscript has
recently come to light and additional discoveries probably await future researchers
(Raylor, 1999).

Important gaps will probably always exist in our sources for Stuart court entertainments, making generalizations difficult. The textual and other evidence that survives, however, shows clearly enough that masques often continued to reflect
disagreements within the court itself. The pacific tone of Jonson's masques for James
I, for example, does not always coincide with the tenor of other entertainments written
by authors like George Chapman, for Prince Henry, Prince Charles, Princess Elizabeth, and major courtiers (Butler, 1998; Holbrook, 1998; Parry, 1993; Norbrook,
1986). Yet a coherent reinterpretation of Stuart court theatricals as vehicles for court
factional struggles has yet to emerge, partly because historians have still not fully
investigated the court's internal politics, particularly during the early Jacobean period,
when many of the most interesting masques were performed. Even the most sophisticated recent work on this subject has sometimes oversimplified political alignments
at court, especially over foreign policies. Like all powerful politicians, James I and
Charles I frequently needed to keep open divergent and even contradictory policy
options, to cope with a constantly shifting European situation. They had to choose
between competing objectives and must often have entertained real doubts about how
best to respond to specific contingencies. Ambiguities and tensions in court entertainments may often have reflected genuine conflicts within the king's own mind, as
much as clear rivalries between factions at his court.

Even more than other types of Renaissance drama, court theatricals require thoroughly interdisciplinary forms of investigation, combining close textual analysis,
investigation of surrounding historical circumstances, and attention to the role of
stage scenery, music, and dance in shaping a performance's meaning. Perhaps for this
reason, work on this subject has often been in the vanguard of innovative historicist
scholarship. Frances Yates' pioneering studies of Renaissance court festivals, Roy
Strong's essays on Elizabethan Accession Day jousts, and Stephen Orgel's seminal work
on the Jonsonian and Caroline masque have become major landmarks of interdisciplinary cultural history. Yet the very quantity and quality of the research stimulated
by these pioneering studies has also demonstrated how much additional work still
remains to be done. Undiscovered source materials, still buried in archival repositories, will almost certainly enlarge our understanding of the subject in the future. Far
more attention needs to be paid to the role of music and dance in court theater, and
to the role of various European influences in shaping English practices.[8] Above all,
interpretations of court theatricals need to be integrated within even more precise

historical contexts, through the integration of deeper historical research and careful critical analysis. This has been a very productive field of scholarship for over 40 years, but it is one that is still far from exhausted.

NOTES

1 The terms "mask" (or "maske") and "masque" were interchangeable; I have followed the convention of using "masque" to refer to the Stuart form and "mask" to its Tudor ancestor.
2 *Calendar of State Papers Venetian, Charles I* XIX, 345–6.
3 British Library Royal Manuscripts 17.C.XXXV.
4 OED *sub* revel, definitions 1 and 2. Revel was occasionally used as a synonym for riot (definition 3). For an especially elaborate early Elizabethan example, held at the Middle Temple in 1561–2, see Nichols (1823, I, 131–41).
5 In addition to works previously cited see Bevington (1968, 141–6); Jones and White (1996); and Vanhoutte (2000).
6 British Library Add. Mss. 27, 962, f. 124.
7 The chief exception is Jonson and Jones's *Prince Henry's Barriers*.
8 The best recent studies along these lines are Peacock (1995) and Veevers (1989).

REFERENCES AND FURTHER READING

Adamson, John, ed. (1999a). *The Princely Courts of Europe, 1500–1700*. London: Weidenfeld and Nicolson.

Adamson, John (1999b). "The Tudor and Stuart courts, 1509–1714." In *The Princely Courts of Europe, 1500–1700*, ed. John Adamson. London: Weidenfeld and Nicolson.

Anglo, Sidney (1968). "The evolution of the early Tudor disguising, pageant and mask." *Renaissance Drama* n.s. 1, 3–44.

Astington, John (1999). *English Court Theatre 1558–1642*. Cambridge: Cambridge University Press.

Axton, Marie (1977). *The Queen's Two Bodies: Drama and the Elizabethan Succession*. London: Royal Historical Society.

Barroll, Leeds (1998). "Inventing the Stuart masque." In *The Politics of the Stuart Court Masque*, eds David Bevington and Peter Holbrook. Cambridge: Cambridge University Press.

Bevington, David (1968). *Tudor Drama and Politics: A Critical Approach to Topical Meaning*. Cambridge, MA: Harvard University Press.

Bucholz, R. O. (2000). "Going to court in 1700: a visitor's guide." *Court Historian* 5, 181–216.

Butler, Martin (1993). "Reform or reverence? The politics of the Caroline masque." In *Theatre and Government under the Early Stuarts*, eds J. R. Mulryne and Margaret Shewring. Cambridge: Cambridge University Press.

Butler, Martin (1998). "Courtly negotiations." In *The Politics of the Stuart Court Masque*, eds David Bevington and Peter Holbrook. Cambridge: Cambridge University Press.

Chambers, E. K., ed. (1912). *Aurelian Townshend's Poems and Masks*. Oxford: Oxford University Press.

Chambers, E. K. (1923; 1965). *The Elizabethan Stage*. Oxford: Clarendon Press.

Churchyard, Thomas (1575). *The Firste Part of Churchyarde's Chippes*. London.

Cole, Mary Hill (1999). *The Portable Queen: Elizabeth and the Politics of Ceremony*. Amherst, MA: University of Massachusetts Press.

Colthorpe, Marion (1985). "Pageants before Queen Elizabeth I at Coventry in 1566." *Notes and Queries* 32, 458–60.

Doran, S. (1995). "Juno vs. Diana: the treatment of Elizabeth I's marriage in plays and entertainments, 1561–1581." *Historical Journal* 38, 257–74.

Gordon, D. J. (1975). "*Hymenaei*: Ben Jonson's masque of union." In *The Renaissance Imagination*, ed. Stephen Orgel. Berkeley: University of California Press.

Hammer, Paul (1998). "Upstaging the queen: the earl of Essex, Francis Bacon and the Accession Day celebrations of 1595." In *The Politics of the Stuart Court Masque*, eds David Bevington and Peter Holbrook. Cambridge: Cambridge University Press.

Harrison, Stephen (1604). *The Arches of Triumph*. London.

Holbrook, Peter (1998). "Jacobean masques and the Jacobean peace." In *The Politics of the Stuart Court Masque*, eds David Bevington and Peter Holbrook. Cambridge: Cambridge University Press.

James, Henry and Greg Walker (1995). "The politics of *Gorboduc*." *English Historical Review* 110, 109–21.

Jones, Norman and Paul Whitfield White (1996). "*Gorboduc* and royal marriage politics: an Elizabethan playgoer's report of the premier performance." *English Literary Renaissance* 26, 3–16.

Kipling, Gordon (1974). "The early Tudor disguising: new research opportunities." *Research Opportunities in Renaissance Drama* 17, 3–8.

Kipling, Gordon (1997). "Wonderful spectacles: theater and civic culture." In *A New History of Early English Drama*, eds John D. Cox and David Scott Kastan. New York: Columbia University Press.

Lindley, David (1979). "The Lord Hay's Masque and Anglo-Scottish union." *Huntington Library Quarterly* 43, 157–86.

Manley, Lawrence (1995). *Literature and Culture in Early Modern London*. Cambridge: Cambridge University Press.

Meagher, John C. (1966). *Method and Meaning in Jonson's Masques*. Notre Dame: Notre Dame University Press.

Mulcaster, Richard (1559). *The Quene's Majestie's Passage through the Citie of London to Westminster the Daye before her Coronation*. Rpt in *Elizabethan Backgrounds: Historical Documents of the Age of Elizabeth I*, ed. Arthur F. Kinney. Hamden: Archon.

Nichols, John (1823). *Progresses of Queen Elizabeth*. 3 vols. London: J. B. Nichols.

Nichols, John (1828). *Progresses of James I*. 4 vols. London: J. B. Nichols.

Nichols, John Gough, ed. (1848). *The Diary of Henry Machyn, Citizen of London*. Camden Society Publications o.s. 42.

Norbrook, David (1986). "*The Masque of Truth*: court entertainments and international Protestant politics in the early Stuart period." *Seventeenth Century* 1, 81–110.

Orgel, Stephen (1965). *The Jonsonian Masque*. Cambridge, MA: Harvard University Press.

Orgel, Stephen (1975). *The Illusion of Power*. Berkeley: University of California Press.

Orgel, Stephen (1981). "The royal theatre and the role of king." In *Patronage in the Renaissance*, eds Guy Fitch Lytle and Stephen Orgel. Princeton: Princeton University Press.

Orgel, Stephen and Roy Strong (1973). *Inigo Jones: The Theatre of the Stuart Court*. London: Sotheby Parke Bernet.

Parry, Graham (1993). "Politics of the Jacobean masque." In *Theatre and Government under the Early Stuarts*, eds J. R. Mulryne and Margaret Shewring. Cambridge: Cambridge University Press.

Peacock, John (1995). *The Stage Designs of Inigo Jones: The European Context*. Cambridge: Cambridge University Press.

Ravelhofer, Barbara (1998). "'Virgin wax' and 'hairy men-monsters': unstable movement codes in the Stuart masque." In *The Politics of the Stuart Court Masque*, eds David Bevington and Peter Holbrook. Cambridge: Cambridge University Press.

Raylor, Timothy (1999). *The Essex House Masque*. Pittsburgh: Duquesne University Press.

Sharpe, Kevin (1987). *Criticism and Compliment*. Cambridge: Cambridge University Press.

Smuts, R. Malcolm (1989). "Public ceremony and royal charisma: the English royal entry in London, 1485–1642." In *The First Modern Society: Essays in English History in Honour of Lawrence Stone*, eds A. L. Beier, David Cannadine, and James M. Rosenheim. Cambridge: Cambridge University Press.

Smuts, R. Malcolm (2000). "Occasional events, literary texts and historical interpretations." In *Neo-Historicism: Studies in Renaissance Literature, History and Politics*, eds Robin Headlam Wells, Glenn Burgess, and Rowland Wymer. Cambridge: Brewer.

Spedding, J., R. L. Ellis, and D. D. Heath, eds (1862). *Works of Francis Bacon*, vol. IX. London.

Starkey, David, D. A. L. Morgan, John Murphy, Pam Wright, Neil Cuddy, and Kevin Sharpe (1987). *The English Court: From the Wars of the Roses to the Civil War*. London: Longman.

Strong, Roy (1973). *Splendor at Court*. Boston: Houghton Mifflin.

Strong, Roy (1977a). *The Cult of Elizabeth: Elizabethan Portraiture and Pageantry*. London: Thames and Hudson.

Strong, Roy (1977b). "Fair England's knights: the Accession Day tournaments." In *The Cult of Elizabeth: Elizabethan Portraiture and Pageantry*. London: Thames and Hudson.

Thurley, Simon (1993). *Royal Palaces of Tudor England*. New Haven and London: Yale University Press.

Thurley, Simon (1999). *Whitehall Palace: An Architectural History of the Royal Apartments, 1240–1698*. New Haven and London: Yale University Press.

Vanhoutte, Jacqueline (2000). "Community, authority, and the motherland in Sackville and Norton's *Gorboduc*." *Studies in English Literature* 40, 227–39.

Veevers, Erica (1989). *Images of Love and Religion: Queen Henrietta Maria and Court Entertainments*. Cambridge: Cambridge University Press.

Wright, Nancy (1998). "'Rival traditions': civic and courtly ceremonies in Jacobean London." In *The Politics of the Stuart Court Masque*, eds David Bevington and Peter Holbrook. Cambridge: Cambridge University Press.

Yates, Frances (1947). *French Academies of the Sixteenth Century*. London: Weidenfeld.

Yates, Frances (1975a). *Astraea: The Imperial Theme in the Sixteenth Century*. London: Routledge.

Yates, Frances (1975b). "Elizabethan chivalry: the romance of the Accession Day tilts." In *Astraea: The Imperial Theme in the Sixteenth Century*. London: Routledge.

Young, Alan (1987). *Tudor and Jacobean Tournaments*. London: Sheridan House.

21

Civic Drama

Lawrence Manley

Civic drama in the English Renaissance comprised an enormous variety of performative activities, from simple public proclamations and processions to civic "history plays" performed by professional actors in the new commercial theaters. These activities converged and interacted, however, in the most distinctive kind of Renaissance civic drama, which involved elaborate public shows and spectacles making use of decorated arches, tableaus and scaffolds, triumphal cars and barges, and symbolic programs and speeches crafted by leading scholars and theater professionals. In a manner that imitated the splendor of the Tudor–Stuart court but also called attention to the urban wealth and security on which such courtly splendor depended, these shows and spectacles rendered public life theatrical: they displayed the political and economic power of the urban community and its leadership, commemorated and redefined its values, enacted governmental decisions and procedures, and addressed matters of domestic concern.

The concentration of wealth, power, and population in London made it "the spectacle of the realm whereof all other places and cities take example."[1] Officially styled *caput regni* and *camera regis*, the capital was, in terms of ceremonial splendor, most "fit and able to entertaine strangers honourablie, and to receiue the Prince of the Realme worthily" (*An Apologie of the Cittie of London*, in Stow, 1908). The splendid pageants of early modern London were rooted, however, in local civic traditions and in a fiercely guarded municipal status that London shared with other English towns possessing the liberties of freeman citizenship and local self-government. In London as elsewhere in England, a *longue durée* of customary civic events, together with an ancient calendar of religious feasts and observances, had shaped traditions of civic performance long before the coming of the Renaissance and Reformation. The practices associated with these traditions had acquired a quality of liturgical invariance. They were endowed with an aura of timelessness, a canonical authority that enabled participants to transmit but not themselves encode the permanent meaning of the rituals they performed.[2] In the highly theatrical and politicized rituals of Renaissance civic drama, however, it was never simply the case that performance straightforwardly re-enacted tradition or that tradition alone dictated the choices acted out in performance. An element of improvisation contributed to the continual reinvention of tradition. But this reinvention proceeded against a background of customary events and practices, which had endowed urban time and space with ritual significance. I propose, then, to examine the development and interaction of different forms of civic performance in terms of the ritual significance of urban time and space, focusing on the common ritual site in London where the development of civic drama and the divergence of its main varieties were played out.

City, Crown, and Royal Entry

The two grandest types of pageantry in sixteenth-century London were both inaugural celebrations. One, the royal coronation entry, was a rarely held event that had nevertheless been in practice for centuries.[3] The other, the so-called Lord Mayor's Inaugural Show, was a relatively recent way of gracing an almost equally ancient and far more regularly celebrated event, the annual installation of the city's newly elected lord mayor.[4] Both forms ritually acknowledged a symbiosis between the crown and a local government that enjoyed its defining liberties, immunities, and privileges in exchange for political and financial support of royal policy. In their very forms, the two ceremonies embodied this quasi-constitutional arrangement (Kipling, 1977). The entry of monarchs into London preceded by a day the actual ceremony of anointing and consecration at Westminster Abbey, thereby reflecting both the general importance of popular acclamation in the making of a monarch and the crown's particular dependence on the support of London, whose lord mayor, "nexte vnto the kynge in alle maner thynge," became the chief legal authority in the kingdom upon the death of a monarch (*Gregory's Chronicle*, in Gardiner, 1876; see also Bradbrook, 1981, 63). The Lord Mayor's Inaugural Show, reflecting a different but equally important legal arrangement, took place in London only *after* the new mayor's return from Westminster, where he had taken an oath of fealty before the monarch or the barons of the Exchequer.[5] As the recorder of the city of London explained in presenting the new mayor to the queen for such a ceremony in 1593, "we enjoy our jurisdictions and privileges derived from your imperial crown" ("The recorder of London's speech to Queen Elizabeth, after the election of Sir Cuthbert Buckle to be lord mayor, 1593," in Nichols, 1823, II, 228). By underlining mutual needs and obligations, both forms celebrated a politico-economic rapprochement that was for each party more desirable than the unpredictable alternative of summoning Parliaments into session.

At the same time, however, the different purposes and practices of the two ceremonies could articulate, and sometimes sharpen, the differences between these two jurisdictions and forms of government. Viewed against their longer-term ritual background, the changing relationships between the relatively novel form of the "loud voyc'd inauguration" (*Londini Status Pacatus*, in Heywood, 1874, V, 363) and its older counterpart, the royal entry, reflect a number of important early modern developments: the transformation of civic ritual and pageantry in the wake of the Reformation, the increased prestige of secular authority, and, in the case of London, with its far-flung economy, emerging freedoms, and innovative modes of life, the establishment of a leading role in shaping the nation's destiny.

By the sixteenth century, ritual practice had determined a canonical processional route, which included both customary pageant stations and a well-established ceremonial "syntax" that connected them. The most important portion of the ceremonial route began at the top of Gracechurch Street at the corner of Leadenhall, and followed, from the Conduit or Tunne in Cornhill along Cheapside to the Little Conduit at the gate into Paul's Churchyard, the main east–west route through the city. A basic syntax of pageant stations was clearly laid out around the same invariant landmarks that punctuated the route – the Conduit in Cornhill, the Great Conduit at the head of Cheapside, the Standard and the Cross in Cheapside, the Little Conduit at Paul's Gate.[6] Progress westward along this series of landmarks involved a gradual heightening of symbolic significance. Although they actually began outside the city and processed through its entire length, royal entries reached their symbolically climactic moments along the portion of the route between the Cross and Standard in Cheapside and the Little Conduit at the gateway into Paul's Churchyard, where the pageants of the entries unfolded themselves before the eyes of the City's chief officials.

As Gordon Kipling has demonstrated, these climactic pageants symbolically enacted, through a blend of classical and biblical symbolism, a quasi-magical event that Ernst Kantorowicz has called "the King's Advent" (Kipling, 1985, 88; Kantorowicz, 1944, 210). The imagery of advent ceremonies derived from Christ's biblical entry into Jerusalem and from the *adventus*, or prayer for the dying in the Roman office, wherein the anointed soul, departed from the body, is received into the New Jerusalem by companies of angels and saints. In the coronation entry of Richard II in 1377, an angel descended from a tower to offer the king a golden crown, while in Richard's reconciliation entry of 1392, "an Aungell come a downe from the stage on hye bi a vyse and sette a croune upon ye Kinges hede."[7] The monarch's advent was thus understood as a salvific event that brought about a *renovatio* or *initium seculi felicissimi*. Henry VII's entry, for example, transformed London into a metaphoric temple, God's "chyeff tabernacle and most chosyn place" (Thornley, 1937, 308–9). As royal entries grew more elaborate, pageants of graces, virtues, and heroes were mounted at stations preceding these climactic advent symbols; but the virtues represented in these pageants were understood less as desiderata in the Mirror of Princes tradition than as manifestations of the rejuvenating powers and virtues emanating from the *roi thaumaturge*, whose presence in the city caused the local conduits to run not with water but with wine (Bloch, 1973, 114).

Despite the miraculous events that transpired there, however, the climactic portion of the ceremonial route also became the locus for a different sort of ceremonial activity, in which London officials not only offered the city's loyalty and support but asserted the city's power and represented its wishes to the monarch. Gift-giving, deriving ultimately from the gifts of the magi, was a traditional way of symbolizing the acclamation, bonding, and epiphany enacted during entry ceremonies (Kipling, 1998, 117, 161). But the presentation of the gift also provided opportunities for speeches in which officials could represent the city's interests and establish the terms of rapprochement with the monarch. Between the two apocalyptic Cheapside pageants in the "reconciliation" entry of Richard II in 1392, the king received a gift but also a harangue from the city officials who lined this stretch of the route, an oration in which there was never "the least hint that London was wrong in the initial quarrel" between king and city that the ceremony was designed to lay to rest (Wickham, 1959–81, I, 70). Such speeches had become a common feature by the sixteenth century, so that at the heart of their enactment, the arcane mysteries of the advent were balanced by a conspicuous display of the underlying political realities; monarchs found themselves engaging in the process of dialogue, exchange, and contractual obligation.

Such contractual exchange played a crucial role in the coronation entry of Elizabeth I in 1559, as the traditional salvific tropes of the sacred advent were transformed into tokens of political covenant. A pattern of discursive give-and-take, of moral reasoning and political argument, ran throughout the entry, and, in keeping with the covenantal theme, the felicities promised in the pageants were presented in a morally and politically conditional light. A pageant on the "uniting of the houses of Lancaster and Yorke," for example, insisted less on Elizabeth's genealogy than on her role as an "heire to agreement." The point was sealed by such Latin tags as *omnium gentium consensus firmat fidem* and by the queen's (allegedly improvised) "promise, that she would doe her whole endeavor for the preservation of concord." A pageant on the virtues of governors made a similarly conditional claim that the queen "should sit faste in the . . . seate of government . . . *so long as* she embraced vertue and helde vice vnder foote" (*The Quenes Majestie's Passage through the Cittie of London*, in Kinney, 1975, 20–1).

The covenantal argument of the entry came to a head in the climactic Little Conduit pageant, which represented Truth and his daughter Veritas, who bore in her hands a Bible with the motto *Verbum veritatis*. While suggestive of miraculous revelation, this pageant was in fact a polemical revival of a controversial pageant first planned and then censored from the entry for Queen Mary's husband Philip II, in which the Protestant author of the pageant, Richard Grafton, had given offense by representing Henry VIII as having in his "hande a booke, whereon was wrytten *Verbum Dei*" (*Chronicle of Queen Jane and Mary*, 78, quoted in Anglo, 1969, 329–30). By resurrecting this pageant for the entry of Elizabeth, the city of London was reaffirming its commitment to the Henrician reformation. With her shrewdly theatrical response that "Tyme hath brought me hither," Elizabeth gracefully transformed the political lesson lurking in this pageant into her own epiphanic arrival as the vessel of revealed truth, a providentially ordained daughter who was the temporal fulfillment and incarnation of the Revelation.

Yet another set of analogies lay beneath those of Elizabeth the Daughter of Henry and Truth the Daughter of Time: if the scriptural *Verbum veritatis* descended from Henry–Time to Elizabeth–Truth, it also descended to her from the patriarchs of the city of London itself. As Elizabeth approached the Little Conduit pageant station, and "understoode that the Byble in Englishe shoulde be delivered unto her: *she thanked the Citie for that gift*, and sayd that she would oftentimes reade over that booke" (Kinney, 1975, 26; italics mine). The covenantal basis of the exchange was then immediately underlined, for the queen – restrained from sending an attendant to take the Bible – did not receive the book until she first received the city's financial gift, accompanied by a speech from the city recorder to the effect that the:

> Lord maior, hys brethren, and comminaltie of the citie, to declare their gladnes and good will towardes the Quene's majestie, did present her Grace with that gold, desyering her grace to continue their good and gracious Quene. (Kinney, 1975, 26)

In presenting their financial gift as a preliminary to the pageant in which the queen received the Bible from a youthful female Veritas (the daughter of a masculine Time), the city fathers were drawing an important analogy and reinforcing the policies commended in the pageants, from the call to Protestant reform to an insistence on the Merchant Adventurers' privileges over those of the foreign Hanseatic league, which Queen Mary had favored.[8]

Significantly, Elizabeth responded to the "positional skirmishing" (Kipling, 1998, 127) represented by this gift in discursive kind, highlighting the genuine political exchanges and contractual logic that counterbalanced the advent pattern:

> I thanke my lord maior, his brethren, and you all. And whereas your request is that I should continue your good ladie and quene, be ye ensured, that I wil be as good unto you, as ever quene was to her people. (Kinney, 1975, 27)

Throughout his account, the reporter of the entry emphasized the quasi-contractual undertakings, the promises and assurances which, depending on the perspective taken, either manifested the charismatic magnificence of the monarch whose pleasure it was to grant them or demonstrated the power of the city to demand them. The whole entry was conceived by its reporter as forming a connected discourse of moral and political reasoning: interspersed summaries related each pageant to the ones preceding, stressing that "the matter . . . dependeth of them that went before" (Kinney, 1975, 29). The entry was concluded at Temple Bar by the city's twin giants – identified as "Gotmagot" and "Corineus" – who bore up "a bryffe rehearsall of all the said pagauntis," a discursive summary of "theffect of all the Pageantes which the Citie before had erected" (*Two London Chronicles*, 1910, XII, 38).

Time, Space, and Civic Ritual

The discursive "argument" of Elizabeth I's entry and the interaction between the queen and London's chief officials were reinforced by a nexus of traditional meanings that had accumulated around the ritual site itself. When the city's chief lawyer, the recorder William Fleetwood, observed that "it hath euer been the vse in . . . gouerning mens doynges and policies alway to follow the ancient presidentes and steps of the forefathers," he had in mind primarily the importance of legal precedent or custom (Fleetwood, 1571, sig. A2). But in a traditional community like London, these customary "steps of the forefathers" could literally be followed along the routes and pathways where generations of calendrical reiteration had traced a pattern of civic precedents onto the urban space.

In London, as Charles Pythian-Adams has shown was also the case in Coventry, government was organized ritually in the form of a "ceremonial year," a complex cycle of events, divided into secular and religious semesters (Pythian-Adams, 1971). The secular semester began with the shrieval election and the confirmation of the chamberlain, clerk, and chief sergeant. These events coincided with the feasts of John the Baptist (June 24) and Sts Peter and Paul (June 29), which had also become by the later fifteenth century the occasion of London's grandest civic procession, the Midsummer Marching Watch, in which the lord mayor and two sheriffs, each accompanied by dancers, musicians, and several pageants sponsored by the London guilds, led midnight processions of horsemen, archers, and halberdiers through the streets while hundreds of constables and citizens maintained a standing watch with cresset lights along the way and at the city's defensive chains and gates. Thus began the connected series of civic events that created a new city government – the swearing-in of the sheriffs on Michaelmas Eve, the Michaelmas mayoralty election, and the installation of the new lord mayor on the feast of Sts Simon and Jude (October 29) and its morrow.

This round of secular events, lasting from June through the end of October, left the new city government in place just in time for it to preside over the semester of religious feasts that began with All Saints on November 1. This religious semester included the series of fixed religious feasts between All Saints and Candlemas (February 2), and extended through the moveable events of Easter week and the religious processions of Rogationtide, Whitsuntide, and Corpus Christi, the last of which could be dated as late as June 24. In many English towns, cycles of guild-sponsored Corpus Christi plays had developed around the religious procession of the sacred host; guild sponsorship of the plays served to assert secular and civic power in the face of ecclesiastical authority and to establish an order of precedence among the individual guilds within the town hierarchy. Towns with the most elaborate cycles (York, Coventry, Chester) were those in which the guilds were in fiercest competition with the power of the church (Clopper, 1989). The apparent absence or early disappearance of a major Corpus Christi drama cycle in London, the greater importance of the processions and pageants of the Midsummer Watch on June 24 and 29, and a relatively early shift in emphasis from the religious to the civic semester of the year have all been taken to indicate an early dominance over church authority by the London government, guilds, and merchant elite (James, 1982, 34–41).

Calendrical observance of ritualized time in government transformed the city into a sacred space, a physical embodiment of the community's history and civic spirit.

This space was both defined and maintained by the liturgically invariant routes of public processions and ceremonies, through which the leaders of London traced a highly ordered ritual space and established such "places accustomed" for pageants and speeches as the conduits, standards, and crosses used in royal entries and mayoral shows.

The main civic event in London until the mid-sixteenth century, the Midsummer Marching Watch, took in the longest east–west route in the city, processing, as the Tudor antiquarian John Stow observed, "from the litle Conduit by Paules gate, through the west Cheape, by ye Stocks, through Cornhill, by Leaden hall to Aldgate" (1592, I, 102). On its return to St. Paul's from the Priory of the Holy Trinity, Aldgate, the Midsummer Watch passed, in the same sequence, by all the principal pageant stations that were used in coronation entries, from the Tunne or Conduit near St. Peter's and the Leadenhall in Cornhill to the Little Conduit at Paul's Gate.

A second civic processional route, followed on Whitsuntide, corresponded exactly with this main axis of the coronation route. On Whitsun Monday the rectors, lord mayor, and aldermen of London had traditionally processed from St. Peter's to St. Paul's, where, according to the *Liber Albus*, "the hymn *Veni Creator* was chanted by the Vicars to the music of the organ in alternate verses; an angel meanwhile censing from above" (Riley, 1862, 26). Following the Reformation, the Whitsuntide processions atrophied into a series of sermons attended by London officials, but antiquarians remained keenly aware of the ecclesiastical history that had made St. Peter's and St. Paul's (whose twin feasts on June 29 came near the June 24 Midsummer Watch, and whose twin effigies, Stow noted, were "of olde . . . rudely engrauen" on the city's seal, 1592, I, 221) the two anchors of the Whitsun processional route. As Stow also noted, St. Peter's and St. Paul's commemorated, respectively, the first and second Christianizations of Britain (1592, II, 125–7); in John Speed's *Theatre of the Empire of Great Britaine* (1611), these twin hilltop churches, the one "vpon the East," the other "in the west part" of the city, formed a diptych representing London's British and Saxon roots, and they were so featured in the illustration of London in Michael Drayton's *Polyolbion* (1622). Between the two churches lay what Stow called "the high and most principall streete of the cittie" (1592, I, 117). In the architectural conceit that would transform London into a "Court Royall" in Thomas Dekker's account of the coronation entry of James I, the series of pageant stations along this route defined a ceremonial crescendo, as the king passed from the "great Hall" of Cornhill, to the "Presence Chamber" of Cheapside, to the "closet or rather the priuy chamber" framed by the passage from the Little Conduit into St. Paul's Churchyard.

While the writer who recorded the coronation passage of Elizabeth I reported that "a man . . . could not better term the City of London that time than a stage," his dramatic metaphor was attributing as much to the theatrical setting, a public stage defined by civic custom, as to the charismatic performance of the queen. The climactic portion of the coronation entry route was frequently traversed by city officials, not just at Whitsuntide and midsummer, but much more often on what Stow called the "dayes of attendance that the fellowships doe giue to the Maior at his going to Paules"

(1592, II, 190). These "dayes of attendance" originated in a ritual recorded in the city's fourteenth-century *Liber Ordinationum* – the series of civic processions on fixed religious feasts between All Saints and Candlemas along Cheapside to St. Paul's from St. Thomas de Acon in Cheap, the hospital and church raised to the memory of Thomas à Becket, the famous London saint whose effigy remained on the city's official seal until 1539, and who was still believed in Tudor times to have been born on the spot of the high altar on the feast of St. Thomas the Apostle. In its account of these ritual processions, the *Liber Ordinationum* explained that the mayor led a procession to St. Paul's, where he "offered prayers for Bishop William, led the Aldermen in a ritual chant at the Becket grave, and [then proceeded] in a torchlight procession through Cheap to the house of St Thomas" (*Liber Ordinationum*, fo. 174, cited in Williams, 1963, 30–1).

The civic importance of the shrines of the sainted Becket and Bishop William (whose "great sute and labour," Stow explained, had won "the Charter and liberties" enjoyed by Londoners) explains not only the regular processions on religious feast days, but the route of the traditional ritual that marked the annual installation of London's lord mayor. On his inauguration day in late October, the lord mayor processed between St. Paul's and St. Thomas de Acon, the purpose being to combine religious veneration with public display of the symbolic regalia that were the real focus of civic life: the common crier's mace, the city's sword, and the lord mayor's collar.[9] Following the suppression of Becket's cult at the Reformation (when the saint's name was blotted from the city's fourteenth-century *Liber Albus* and the church of St. Thomas de Acon was transferred to the Mercers' Company), the traditional processions to St. Paul's took on a more purely civic character by departing from the Guildhall, north of Cheapside in Ironmonger Lane, rather than the old church itself. The practice of processional tributes to Bishop William ended on "the feast of All Saints" in 1552, when "the lord maior, aldermen, and crafts in their best liveries" heard Bishop Ridley preach on the promulgation of the new prayer book at Paul's Cross, "which sermon continued till almost fiue of the clocke at night, so that the maior, aldermen, and companies entered not Paules church as had been accustomed, but departed home by torchlight" (Stow, 1592, 1028). But even in the wake of these reforms, much of the old processional pattern remained, including virtually all of the original route, from the foot of Ironmonger Lane at the Mercers' Chapel to Paul's. Even after the Reformation, moreover, the city's officials continued to process regularly to the cathedral on fixed religious feasts between All Saints and Candlemas, still doffing their gowns before entering, and circling the cathedral before donning them again.

Thus hallowed by civic routine, the portion of West Cheap between the Great Conduit and Paul's Gate formed the central core of the city's ceremonial space. Its very sacredness also made it an important scene for the staging of rebellion and disorder. The market cross or "Standard in Cheap," from which proclamations were commonly read, was a site where entering rebels – Wat Tyler in 1381, Jack Cade in 1450 – had executed their victims. The Cheapside Cross, the focus of iconoclastic incidents in the 1580s and 1640s, was the site where in 1591 the fanatic William Hacket proclaimed himself messiah and king of the world; it became, a few days later, the site where he was hanged, drawn, and quartered (Breight, 1989). Violent events like these were probably important to the way the civil order was both enforced and symbolized during coronation entries, when this most sacred portion of the ceremonial route in western Cheapside was double-railed and lined with the city companies, "beginning with the mean and base trades, and ascending to the worshipful companies. Highest stood the mayor and aldermen" (Hall, 1548, sig. Aaaiiv). It was here, by forming a buffer between the tumultuous London crowds behind them and the nobility and royalty passing before them, that the orderly ranks of London officials, in full regalia, served as a symbolic reminder of the city's essential role in maintaining civil order. It was here, with the performance of the climactic pageants dramatizing the *renovatio* of the monarch's advent, that London officials delivered the gifts and harangues embodying the element of popular *acclamatio* essential to the making of English kings. But it was here, too, that the status of London's mayoralty was affirmed, when the lord mayor received from entering monarchs the sword or mace with which he then preceded the remainder of the procession (Smuts, 1989, 72–3). And so it was here, finally, that the Lord Mayor's Inaugural Show, a novel development in Stow's lifetime, reached its culminating phase, as "the whole fabric of the Triumph" (*The Triumphs of Health and Prosperity*, in Middleton, 1964, VII, 409) was finally assembled in processional order.

From Civic Ritual to Civic Drama

The first Inaugural Show known to have made use of speeches as well as pageants dates from 1541, the very period in which the older and traditionally more important pageants and processions of the Midsummer Watch were suppressed by royal edict. The 1539 order that suppressed the London Midsummer Watch in favor of a royally controlled military muster cited the excessive expense of the Watch and the greater need for genuine military preparedness in the face of the threat of Catholic invasion. But these were probably reinforced by religious factors, including the 1538 injunctions against the abuse of images. The June dates of the Watch were after all saints' feasts, and the pageants traditionally associated with the Watch included religious subject matter, both biblical figures (such as Jesse, Solomon, and Christ's Disputation) and saints (such as Our Lady and St. Elizabeth, the Assumption, or the local saint Thomas à Becket, whose cult was explicitly targeted in the 1538 injunctions) (Robertson and Gordon, 1954, xx–xxii).[10] Even prior to the Reformation, the primary significance of the Watch was civic rather than religious. The cadres of marching and standing watchmen as well as the fearsome giants who accompanied the mayor and sheriffs, turning "from side to side and looking in every direction," were designed to symbolize the vigilance of civic authority (Lindenbaum, 1994). And there is evidence that even prior to the suppression of the Watch, occasional use of pageantry may already have been associated with the mayoral inauguration in October (Lancashire, 1997). Nevertheless, it appears that for a period of more than 30 years, coinciding with the period of the greatest religious instability in England, there was considerable uncertainty regarding the ceremonial priority of the Midsummer Watch and the mayoral inauguration. From 1539 to 1568, one ceremony or the other, but seldom both in a single year, received the primary emphasis with fully fledged pageants and processions. It is not surprising, in view of this uncertainty, that one of the most lavish of the older Midsummer Watch pageants, the restored Watch of 1541, was the first to have made use of speeches, or that, just as crucially, the first Inaugural Show to have made use of speeches was staged in that same year. The suppression of the earlier ceremony, marking the beginning of the civic semester in June, may have influenced the amplification of the newer ceremony at the end of the civic year in October. What is new in both forms from about this time, and points forward to the eventual dominance of the mayoral feast, is the appearance of scripted texts – commissioned from local humanists like Nicholas Grimald and Richard Mulcaster, and later from professional playwrights – to accompany the pageants. The new articulateness of the pageants bespeaks a new quest for ideological influence and magisterial prestige.

These were achieved as the Inaugural Show finally superseded the Midsummer Watch in the early Elizabethan reign. The Watch was once more allowed in London in 1548, the year when religious fraternities and the remaining Corpus Christi processions were suppressed, but was then again discontinued (Hutton, 1994, 83, 88). At nearly the same time, from 1553 onward, the London records "definitely indicate substantial pageant structures" accompanied the newly prestigious inaugural processions (Lancashire, 1997, 91). The pattern in London was mirrored in other English towns. In Norwich, for example, the traditional Watch was replaced in 1556 with standing pageants and speeches for the inauguration of the mayor at the parishes of St. Peter and St. John (Galloway, 1984, 38–43; Lancashire, 1984, 239).

Final attempts to revive the London Watch in the 1560s reflect a decisive and irreversible transition in the city's ceremonial order resulting from the Reformation. In 1564, for the first time since 1548, according to Stow:

> there was on the Vigile of Saincte Peter a certayne kynde of watche in the Citie of London, which did onely stand in the hyghest stretes of Cheape, Cornhyll, and so forth towardes Algate, whyche was to the commons of the same citie (for the most parte) as chargeable as when in tymes past it was most commendablie done, where as this beyng to so very smal purpose, was of as smalle a number of people wel liked.[11]

The following year, Stow notes with similar dissatisfaction, "was the lyke standinge watche in London as was the same night .xii. moneths or very lyttle better" (247v). After an apparent hiatus in 1566, a final attempt in 1567 to restore the ceremony to something like its former glory through the use of pageants appears to have met with disaster:

On Saint Johns euen at night being the like standing watche in the Citie of London as
on Saint Peters euen in the year last before passed, certayne Constables of euery warde,
beynge very well appointed with the handsomest of their watchemen cleane armed in
Corslets, and also diuers prety showes done at the charges of youngmen in certaine
parishes aweighted on the Lord Maior, he ryding from the Guildhalle through Cheape
to Algate and backe agayne, which being lyke to haue made a very handsome sight, was
for lack of good order in keping their array muche defaced.[12]

Mayor Thomas Rowe laid the Watch aside in the following year, allegedly because of
rogues and pickpockets and a fear of spreading the plague (Strype, 1720, I, 257); but
from what the Catholic Stow says, the "lacke of good order in keeping their array"
may been caused by some conflict over the "diuers prety showes" by "youngmen in
certaine parishes." In any event, the Watch of the following year was reduced to a
lonely vigil, when alderman John White, a Catholic and former lord mayor under
Queen Mary, "rode the circuit, whiche the Maiors of London in time past had vsed
to do" (or as Stow's *Chronicles* of 1580 more forcefully put it, "as the Lord Maior *should
haue done*").

Sir John White's lonely ride may have been connected to the fact that the lord
mayor who suppressed the Watch that year, Sir Thomas Rowe, had celebrated his own
inauguration the preceding October in the manner that had come to rival the old
Watch as the primary civic event – with a fully fledged inaugural pageant, including
accompanying speeches commissioned from Edmund Spenser's teacher Richard Mulcaster. These speeches, articulating a new civic ideology to accompany the new ceremonial form, are only the second set that survive. In them, St. John the Baptist, on
whose feast the former Midsummer Watch occurred, leads the way before the mayor,
and the pageant text proclaims the coming of a new and godly order wherein the
preaching of the word is bestowed upon the city by the queen:

> God save oᵉ quene oᵉ maiden Prince
> > whom he hathe sett in place,
> That Iohn maye preache, yᵗ Roe maye heare
> > The gyftes of heavenly grace
>
> The Courte forbad Iohn ones to speake,
> > A mayden made the meene,
> The Courte nowe biddes Iohn Baptist preache,
> > Vnder our mayden Quene.
> > > (Robertson and Gordon, 1954, 49)

As the Catholic court and the maiden Salome who had once silenced the Evangelist
gave way to a new court and virgin queen, the ceremonial life of London came to focus
not on corporate rites of the past but on a new dispensation of Protestant preaching
and public deference to the secular authority of London's chief magistrate.

In view of the disordered Watch of summer 1568, the godly Protestant ideology
of the mayoral pageant that autumn, and the lonely ride of Alderman John White at

Midsummer the following year, it cannot be an accident that 1568 marks another important date in the ceremonial history of London – the appearance of the first printed calendar, regularly issued thereafter by city printers, of London's civic holidays. Known as *The ordre of my Lorde Mayor, the Aldermen & the Sheriffes, for their meetings throughout the yeare*, the calendar marks the beginning of the civic year not at the customary Midsummer events, but with a shrieval election set at August 1; it omits Midsummer altogether, elaborates at length on the mayoral inauguration, and sets the pattern for processions on high religious feasts, when the magistracy processes from the Guildhall to St. Paul's, "goeth vp to the Queere, & there heareth ye Sermon" (sig. B2). The publication of these ceremonial orders may have been part of a concerted effort by London's leaders at about this time to revive and transform London's civic memory (Cain, 1987).

This moment of civic consolidation coincided with a general reformation in the nature of civic drama throughout England, when traditional religious theater was being transformed into secular performance sponsored or controlled by municipal authorities. Reformed in 1561, the traditional Corpus Christi plays at York and Coventry ended in 1569 and 1579, those in Newcastle and Lincoln in 1568–9 (Gardiner, 1946, 65–93; Ingram, 1981, xix). Many of these older performance traditions were altered to suit the needs of the godly Protestant civic regime. At Chester, for example, the processional route and subject matter of the traditional Whitsun plays were several times altered "to reflect the greater glory of the Mayor and his brethren" before they were discontinued in 1575; a civic-oriented Midsummer Show replaced them and continued into the early seventeenth century (Tittler, 1998, 316–17; Mills, 1991). In Essex, during the Vestments Controversy of the 1560s, church vestments (which Bishop John Jewel had called "theatrical habits") were transformed into players' garments for use in reformed sacred dramas that continued to be performed until the Protestant "prophesyings" of 1574–6 led to their suppression (Coldeway, 1975). The Coventry "Hock Tuesday" play depicting the conquest of the Danes, disallowed in 1561, was declared to be "without ill exampl of mannerz, papistry, or ony superstition" and presented before Queen Elizabeth at Kenilworth in 1575; it was thereafter intermittently revived by town authorities. The town council of Coventry also allowed, from 1584, the performance of a *Destruction of Jerusalem* at midsummer, and from 1591 a *King Edward IV* (Griffin, 1999). In such performances of national and biblical history, as in widespread sponsorship of traveling players by many towns in the mid-Elizabethan years, a new relationship between towns and professional playing emerged.[13]

Permanent public theaters began to appear in London from the 1570s; their repertory included urban morality plays like Robert Wilson's *Three Ladies of London* (1584), the *Three Lords and Three Ladies of London* (1590), and Thomas Lodge and Robert Greene's long-running *Looking-Glass for London and England* (1594), not to mention countless works that reinterpreted history, politics, religion, economics, and society for the burgeoning metropolis. Though players and playing became, with the emergence of the first Puritans in the 1580s, a source of worry and aggravation to civic authorities,[14] they were also, as Thomas Heywood noted in 1612, "an ornament to the citty" (*An Apology for Actors*, in Hardison, 1963, 226).

The Lord Mayor's Show

One of the new professional theater's novel contributions to civic life was the Lord Mayor's Inaugural Show of the late Elizabethan and Jacobean periods. The very route of the Inaugural Show, based on civic rituals that had themselves been transformed in the course of the sixteenth century, provided an underlying syntax for the argumentative and triumphal logic of the new form. The show began when the lord mayor returned by barge from taking his oath in Westminster and arrived at the first pageant station, the waterside at Baynard's Castle or Paul's Wharf. He then proceeded northward on land to Paul's Chain, from there through the Churchyard (where one or two pageants were performed), and then to Cheapside and St. Lawrence Lane, the sites where the climactic pageants of the shows were staged. Most crucially, however, after attending a feast at the Guildhall, the mayor returned to St. Paul's for evening prayers, following a route which led down St. Lawrence Lane and then along Cheapside to the Little Conduit. This route retraced, as the older civic processions from St. Thomas de Acon to St. Paul's had done, the portion of the processional route where royal entries reached their climax.

In contrast to the royal entry ceremony, modeled on the pattern of the Christian and Roman imperial advent, the lord mayor's shows were modeled formally on the Roman republican *processus consularis* and the military "triumph." The mayor's "triumph" was understood not as a once-and-for-all salvific miracle, but as an annual renewal in an ongoing history of orderly transitions and exceptional achievements. In the mayor's triumphal show, the pageants were not, as in the coronation entry, fixed tableaus and arches stationed along the route, but mobile pageant-wagons, symbolic elements that could be inserted seriatim into the moving procession itself. The title of George Peele's *Device of the Pageant Borne Before Wolston Dixi* indicates that after each pageant along the route was performed, it was "borne before" the mayor as in triumph, providing for the construction of longer discursive strings, as four or five pageants were inserted to form a continuous sequence by the end of the day's events. In most of the fully fledged Jacobean shows the pageants were performed and inserted into the procession on the way to the Guildhall feast. It was only after the return from the Guildhall feast to evening prayers at St. Paul's, on a westbound route mirroring the climactic phase of the entry route, that "the whole fabric of the Triumph" was finally and fully assembled. In "Cheapside; at which place the whole Triumph meets," the inaugural procession of the mayor became most strikingly a formal alternative to the royal advent, as the city's chief official went "accompanied with the Triumph before him, towards St Paul's, to perform the noble and reverend ceremonies which divine authority religiously ordained" (*The Triumphs of Health and Prosperity, The Triumphs of Honour and Industry*, and *The Triumphs of Love and Antiquity*, in Middleton, 1964, VII,

409, 305, 329). In contrast to the royal entry, whose individual stationary pageants could have been experienced immediately only by the royal entourage and only after the fact by readers of the printed accounts, Londoners all along Cheapside could have witnessed first-hand "the whole body of the Solemnity." In the passing echelons of city officials and company members who accompanied the pageants, they could observe the physical embodiment of a citizen's lifetime, the *cursus honorum* by which an apprentice might become lord mayor (Darnton, 1985, 122–3).

According to the logic of the triumphal trope, as each new element took its place in the procession, it was understood as following from but also superseding the one before it. As the lord mayor processed "from court to court before you be confirm'd / In this high place" (*The Triumphs of Honour and Virtue*, in Middleton, 1964, VII, 364), his progress thus formed a narrative sequence of symbolic events. In contrast to the monarch's passage through a series of static arches and tableaus, moreover, the mayor's progress stressed sequence and causality, as each mobile pageant joined the procession, displacing the ones before it in pride of place, just before the *triumphator* himself, the lord mayor. In contrast to the royal entry, the final phase of the Inaugural Show always led, after prayers at St. Paul's, to a unique destination: the private home of the individual that year chosen to lead the city. Rotated among the companies whose candidates were chosen, and sponsored by the company's bachelors, who were themselves raised in mayoral years from the yeomanry to the livery in recognition of the company's achievement, the Show thus combined practices of reciprocity and commensality with glorification of the chief official exalted from their ranks.

Supporting this glorification was a new kind of civic myth-making that, both in pageantry and on the popular stage, extolled the feats of London citizens and mayors past. William Nelson's 1590 pageant for the fishmongers, celebrating Mayor William Walworth's killing of Jack Straw and defeat of the rebel Wat Tyler in 1381, shared its subject matter with an anonymous play on *The Life and Death of Jack Straw* published in 1593 (Withington, 1915; Bergeron, 1968). A host of popular theater plays, from *The Book of Sir Thomas More* and Dekker's *The Shoemaker's Holiday* (1600) to Heywood's *1–2 Edward IV* (1599) and *1–2 If You Know Not Me You Know Nobody* (1605) and Dekker and Webster's *Sir Thomas Wyatt* (1607), depicted the heroic and politically decisive participation of Londoners in historical events of national moment: Sheriff Thomas More putting down the May Day riots of 1517, Simon Eyre feasting the king on the traditional Shrove Tuesday pancake feast; Sir John Crosby (a hospital orphan become lord mayor) leading mercers, drapers, grocers, and hosts of apprentices against the Falconbridge rebellion; Sir Thomas Gresham lending his support to the Elizabethan regime; the Fluellen-like Captain Brett leading Londoners in resistance to the Wyatt rebellion (see Knights, 1968, ch. 8; Leggatt, 1973; Stevenson, 1984, 108–29; Dillon, 2000, ch. 2).

In their Inaugural Show commissions for the London companies, the authors of these plays devised pageants paying similar tribute to a pantheon of civic heroes whose worthy acts and benefactions were visible in the fabric of churches, schools, halls, and hospitals that formed the pageant's backdrop. Thomas Munday, an author of *The Booke*

of Sir Thomas More, revived the memory of the former guildsman and mayor Nicholas
Farringdon in his *Cruso-Thriambos* for the goldsmiths in 1611; Simon Eyre, already
popularized in Thomas Deloney's novel and Dekker's play, found his place among the
mythical heroes of the drapers in pageants prepared for that company by Middleton
in 1623 and by Heywood in 1639; Webster's *Monuments of Honour* (1624) for the
merchant taylors (formerly the "Merchant Taylors of Saint John the Baptist") revolved
around a series of company heroes extending from its founder Henry de Royall to the
Elizabethan mayor Sir Thomas White, founder of "the Colledge of Saint John Baptist
at Oxford." As the mayoralty rotated annually from company to company, each Inaugural Show contributed to a common fund of civic myth its own version of a story
leading from past to present. Each new lord mayor, exhorted to "spend the Houres to
inrich future story / Both for your own grace and the Cities glory" (*Londini Status
Pacatus*, in Heywood, 1874, V, 365), was at once symbol of both the city's timeless
capacity for annual self-renewal and the historical providence that culminated in the
crowning achievements of an individual citizen.

By annually retelling the story of a shared civic achievement, the Inaugural Shows
exemplified the tendency of all renewal rites to "re-enter the time of origin" and to
repeat the paradigmatic act of the creation, the "passage from chaos to cosmos" (Eliade,
1959, 77, 88). In the pageants fashioned by dramatists like Munday, Middleton,
and Dekker, this passage was enacted in the form of a primordial agon between the
forces of creation and destruction. The pageant that typically began the day's events,
the rough and boisterous celebration of the mayor's return by river from Westminster, where he had taken his oath to the crown, was a transitional event that marked
a successful negotiation between political jurisdictions, and more broadly, between
the dangers of the external world and the community's inner stability. This rite of
arrival provided the occasion for constructing narratives of arrival – myths, stories,
and symbolic tableaus staging the historical passage from rude nature to urban
culture, from the violence of pagan origins to the serenity of Christian community,
from a barbarous past to a civilized present. Giants, sea-beasts, pagan deities, and
exotic infidels usually presented themselves in the early stages of the triumph, to be
superseded by later representations of London's Christian virtues and civic harmony.
But in the Inaugural Shows, which were rougher affairs than royal entries, the threat
of reverting to primordial chaos was repeatedly emphasized in the elements of license
and saturnalia surrounding the day's events. The route of the procession was not railed,
as in royal entries; instead a cadre of whifflers, green-men, devils, and beadles cleared
the way ahead with staves and fireworks, while sweetmeats were thrown to the crowd.
The symbolic vices and evils depicted at the pageant-stations, moreover, were not left
behind (as were the static royal entry tableaus) but incorporated into the procession,
according to a Roman custom dictating that only the *triumphator*, or entering victor,
was empowered to bring inside the city the *spolia opima*, the magically hostile and
dangerous enemy captives and arms (Versnels, 1970, 309–11). Like the earlier Midsummer Watch, which carried the dangerous element of fire through the heart of the
city, the Inaugural Shows brought with them the symbolic tokens of the dangers that

actually invaded the civic space on such historically momentous occasions as rebellions and royal entries.

The incorporation of such symbolic evils into the mayor's triumph revealed an ultimate faith in the city's virtues and destiny. Yet the incomplete realization of this destiny was figured in the setbacks, delays, symbolic retrogressions, and saturnalian eruptions that continued to occur even as the pageants unfolded. The persistence of evil and disorder became, in fact, the most striking feature of the most allegorically elaborate, magnificent, and expensive of the shows ever staged, Dekker's *Troia-Nova Triumphans* for the merchant taylors (1612) and Middleton's *The Triumphs of Truth* for the grocers (1613).[15] In the former, the lord mayor's progress along Cheapside, from the Throne of Virtue at the Little Conduit to the Temple of Fame at Cheapside Cross, was blocked by a Forlorne Castle or Fort of Furies at the Little Conduit, where Envy breathed out a poisonous speech until a volley of rockets enabled the procession to pass. On the return from the Guildhall feast to St. Paul's, with the Show marching in the "same order as before," the procession was once again threatened at the Little Conduit by a revived "Enuy and her crue" until a climactic volley of pistols shot by the armed representatives of the twelve great livery companies brought the pageant to its narrative conclusion. Similarly, in Middleton's extravaganza of the following year, which began with pageants on the East India Company's outposts in Asia and the arrival of a Moorish king, the mayor was led along by Zeal in a progress toward London's Triumphant Mount, where he was presented to Religion; but as the assembled procession moved along Cheapside to the Guildhall feast and then back toward the Little Conduit and evening prayers at St. Paul's, the Triumphant Mount continued to be shrouded with mists cast over it by Error and his monstrous companions. Only at the lord mayor's doorstep did Zeal, "his head circled with strange fires," set Error's chariot afire and offer up the glowing embers as "a figure or type of his lordship's justice on all wicked offenders in his time of government" (Middleton, 1964, VII, 262).

In the agonistic means by which they staged the passage from primitive chaos to a civilized present, these pageants inaugurated a profane, material time that, in contrast to the once-and-for-all salvific time of the royal advent, required an annual renewal of commitment to the virtuous labor of citizenship. As annual responsibility for the pageant rotated among the leading companies, and the election of new officeholders enabled "the maine Authoritie of Government" to survive "in other Pellicanes of the same brood" (*Chrysanaleia: The Golden Fishing: or, Triumph of Fishmongers*, in Munday, 1985, 107), the pageants continued in a new form the celebration of commensal values that had been part of the city's older ceremonial traditions. But at the same time, as the inaugural pageant ended at the mayor's private doorstep, the ceremonial renewal of civic life took a narrative shape in which history was represented as having propelled a single representative of London's mercantile elite to the apex of the *cursus honorarium*. The triumphal procession was thus a trope for the historical providence by which commensality was completed and fulfilled in personal achievement, as "In great Processions many lead the way / To him who is the triumph of the day" ("To Doctor Alabaster," ll. 3–4, in Herrick, 1963, 338). The developing symbolic logic of civic drama in London thus reflects the increasing prominence of London's wealthiest elite on the national scene. In celebrating the values of a city on whose wealth and stability the splendor of the Tudor–Stuart court had been built, civic drama had come not only to rival its courtly counterparts, the royal entry and the masque, but to imitate them.

NOTES

1   Corporation of London Records Office, *Journals of the Common Council*, fo. 65 (1572–3), quoted in Berlin (1986, 23).
2   On the ritual qualities of invariance and canonicity, see Rappaport (1979, 176, 179, 193, 194, 200–4).
3   The standard studies of English royal entries are Withington (1926), Anglo (1969), and Kipling (1998).
4   The seminal studies are Williams (1959) and Bergeron (1971).
5   On the importance of oath-takings as a basis for civic ceremony, see Knowles (1993, 163–4).
6   On the use of these structures as stages, see Wickham (1959–81, I, 58).
7   Bodleian MS Ashm. 793, fos 128b–129, quoted in Withington (1926, I, 130).
8   On the economic messages of the entry and the view that "it is the London elites – the liveried companies, the aldermen, the Merchant Adventurers – that triumph in this text," see Frye (1993, 27, 40, 48–53).
9   On the ceremonial and historical importance of such regalia, see Tittler (1998, 272–5).
10 The pageant of St. Thomas associated with the Midsummer Watch at Canterbury since 1503 was replaced by marching giants in 1537, briefly revived in 1554, and then finally suppressed in the early part of Elizabeth's reign (Sheppard, 1878).
11 *Summary of English Chronicles* (1565), f. 245ᵛ.
12 *Summary of English Chronicles* (1570), f. 411.
13 On town sponsorship of professional playing in the Elizabethan period, see Tittler (1998, 325–7) and McMillin and MacLean (1998, 41–2).
14 On the paradoxes arising from the City's patronage of playwrights, see Leinwand (1982); on changing Protestant attitudes toward cultural institutions like theater, see Collinson (1988).
15 On the moral and satiric implications of these pageants, see Tumbleson (1993, 56–9) and Lobanov-Rostovsky (1993).

REFERENCES AND FURTHER READING

Anglo, Sydney (1969). *Spectacle, Pageantry, and Early Tudor Policy.* Oxford: Clarendon Press.
Bergeron, David M. (1968). "Jack Straw in drama and pageant." *Guildhall Miscellany* 2, 459–63.
Bergeron, David M. (1971). *English Civic Pageantry, 1558–1642.* London: Edward Arnold.
Berlin, Michael (1986). "Civic ceremony in early modern London." *Urban History Yearbook* 15–27.
Bloch, Marc (1973). *The Royal Touch: Sacred Monarchy and Scrofula in England and France*, trans. J. E. Anderson. London: Routledge and Kegan Paul.
Bradbrook, Muriel (1981). "The politics of pageantry: social implications in Jacobean London." In *Poetry and Drama 1570–1700: Essays in Honour of Harold F. Brooks*, eds Anthony Coleman and Anthony Hamond. London: Methuen.

Breight, Curtis (1989). "Duelling ceremonies: the strange case of William Hacket, Elizabethan Messiah." *Journal of Medieval and Early Modern Studies* 19, 35–67.

Cain, Piers (1987). "Robert Smith and the reform of the archives of the City of London." *London Journal* 13.1, 3–16.

Clopper, Lawrence M. (1989). "Lay and clerical impact on civic religious drama and ceremony." In *Contexts for Early English Drama*, eds Marianne G. Briscoe and John C. Coldeway. Bloomington: Indiana University Press.

Coldeway, John C. (1975). "The last rise and final demise of Essex town drama." *Modern Language Quarterly* 36, 239–60.

Collinson, Patrick (1988). *The Birthpangs of Protestant England*. New York: Macmillan.

Darnton, Robert (1985). *The Great Cat Massacre and Other Episodes in French Cultural History*. New York: Vintage Books.

Dillon, Janette (2000). *Theatre, Court and City 1595–1610: Drama and Social Space in London*. Cambridge: Cambridge University Press.

Eliade, Mircea (1959). *The Sacred and the Profane: The Nature of Religion*, trans. Willard R. Trask. New York: Harcourt.

Fleetwood, William (1571). *The Effect of the Declaration made in the Guildhall by M. Recorder of London*. London.

Frye, Susan (1993). *Elizabeth I: The Competition for Representation*. Oxford: Oxford University Press.

Galloway, David (1984). *REED (Records of Early English Drama): Norwich, 1540–1642*. Toronto: University of Toronto Press.

Gardiner, Harold C. (1946). *Mysteries' End: An Investigation of the Last Days of the Medieval Religious Stage*. New Haven: Yale University Press.

Gardiner, James, ed. (1876). *The Historical Collections of a Citizen of London in the Fifteenth Century*. London: Camden Society.

Griffin, Benjamin (1999). "The breaking of the giants: historical drama in London and Coventry." *English Literary Renaissance* 29, 3–21.

Hall, Edward (1548). *The Union of the Two Noble and Illustre Famelies of Lancaster and Yorke*. London.

Hardison, O. B., Jr, ed. (1963). *English Literary Criticism: The Renascence*. Englewood Cliffs: Prentice-Hall.

Herrick, Robert (1963, rpt 1968). *The Complete Poetry of Robert Herrick*, ed. J. Max Patrick. New York: W. W. Norton.

Heywood, Thomas (1874, rpt 1964). *Dramatic Works*, ed. R. H. Shephard. 6 vols. New York: Russell and Russell.

Hutton, Ronald (1994). *The Rise and Fall of Merry England: The Ritual Year 1400–1700*. Oxford: Oxford University Press.

Ingram, R. W. (1981). *REED (Records of Early English Drama): Coventry*. Toronto: University of Toronto Press.

James, Mervyn (1982). *Society, Politics, and Culture: Studies in Early Modern England*. Cambridge: Cambridge University Press.

Kantorowicz, Ernst (1944). "The 'king's advent' and the enigmatic doors of Santa Sabina." *Art Bulletin* 26, 207–31.

Kinney, Arthur F., ed. (1975). *Elizabethan Backgrounds: Historical Documents of the Age of Elizabeth I*. Hamden: Archon.

Kipling, Gordon (1977). "Triumphal drama: form in English civic pageantry." *Renaissance Drama* 8, 37–56.

Kipling, Gordon (1985). "Richard II's 'sumptuous pageants' and the idea of the civic triumph." In *Pageantry in the Shakespearian Theater*, ed. David M. Bergeron. Athens: University of Georgia Press.

Kipling, Gordon (1998). *Enter the King: Theatre, Liturgy, and Ritual in the Medieval Civic Triumph*. Oxford: Clarendon Press.

Knights, L. C. (1937; rpt 1968). *Drama and Society in the Age of Jonson*. New York: Norton.

Knowles, James (1993). "The spectacle of the realm: civic consciousness, rhetoric, and ritual in early modern London." In *Theatre and Government under the Early Stuarts*, eds J. R. Mulryne and Margaret Shewring. Cambridge: Cambridge University Press.

Lancashire, Anne (1997). "Continuing civic ceremonies of 1530s London." In *Ludus: Medieval and Early Renaissance Theatre and Drama*, eds Alexandra F. Johnston and Wim Hüsken. Amsterdam: Rodopi.

Lancashire, Ian (1984). *Dramatic Texts and Records of Britain: A Chronological Topography to 1558*. Toronto: University of Toronto Press.

Leggatt, Alexander (1973). *Citizen Comedy in the Age of Shakespeare*. Toronto: University of Toronto Press.

Leinwand, Theodore B. (1982). "London triumphing: the Jacobean Lord Mayor's Show." *Clio* 11, 137–53.

Lindenbaum, Shelia (1994). "Ceremony and oligarchy: the London midsummer watch." In *City and Spectacle in Medieval Europe*, eds Barbara A. Hanawalt and Kathryn L. Ryerson. Minneapolis: University of Minnesota Press.

Lobanov-Rostovsky, Sergei (1993). "The triumphs of gold: authority in the Jacobean Lord Mayor's Show." *ELH* 60, 879–98.

McMillin, Scott and MacLean, Sally-Beth (1998). *The Queen's Men and their Plays*. Cambridge: Cambridge University Press.

Middleton, Thomas (1964). *The Works*, ed. A. H. Bullen. New York: AMS Press.

Mills, David (1991). "Chester ceremonial: re-creation and recreation in the English 'medieval' town." *Urban History Yearbook* 18, 1–19.

Munday, Anthony (1985). *Pageants and Entertainments of Anthony Munday*, ed. David M. Bergeron. New York: Garland.

Nichols, John, ed. (1823). *The Progresses and Pageants of Queen Elizabeth*. London: J. B. Nichols.

Pythian-Adams, Charles (1971). "Ceremony and the citizen: the communal year at Coventry, 1450–1550." In *Crisis and Order in English Towns 1500–1750*, eds Paul Slack and Peter Clark. London: Routledge and Kegan Paul.

Rappaport, Roy (1979). "The obvious aspects of ritual." In *Ecology, Meaning, and Religion*. Richmond, CA: North Atlantic Books.

Riley, H. T., ed. (1862). *Liber Albus*. London: Longman, Brown, Green, Longmans, and Roberts.

Robertson, Jean, and D. J. Gordon, eds (1954). *A Calendar of Dramatic Records in the Books of the Livery Companies of London*. Oxford: Malone Society.

Sheppard, J. Brigstocke (1878). "The Canterbury Marching Watch with its pageant of St. Thomas." *Archaeologia Cantiana* 12, 27–46.

Smuts, Malcolm (1989). "Public ceremony and royal charisma: the English royal entry in London, 1485–1642." In *The First Modern Society: Essays in Honour of Lawrence Stone*, eds A. L. Beier, David Cannadine, and James P. Rosenheim. Cambridge: Cambridge University Press.

Speed, John (1611). *Theatre of the Empire of Great Britaine*. London.

Stevenson, Laura Caroline (1984). *Paradox and Praise: Merchants and Craftsmen in Popular Elizabethan Literature*. Cambridge: Cambridge University Press.

Stow, John (1592). *Annals*. London.

Stow, John (1908, rpt 1971). *A Survey of London*, ed. C. L. Kingsford. 2 vols. Oxford: Oxford University Press.

Strype, John (1720). *A Survey of the Cities of London and Westminster*. 2 vols. London.

Thornley, I. D., ed. (1937). *The Great Chronicle of London*. London: George W. Jones.

Tittler, Robert (1998). *The Reformation and the Towns in England: Politics and Political Culture, c.1540–1640*. Oxford: Clarendon Press.

Tumbleson, Raymond D. (1993). "The triumph of London: Lord Mayor's day pageants and the rise of the city." In *The Witness of Times: Manifestations of Ideology in Seventeenth-Century England*, eds Katherine Z. Keller and Gerald J. Schiffhorst. Pittsburgh: Duquesne University Press.

Two London Chronicles (1910). In *Camden Miscellany*. London: Offices of the Society.

Versnels, H. S. (1970). *Triumphus: An Inquiry into the Origin, Development and Meaning of the Roman Triumph*. Leiden: Brill.

Wickham, Glynne (1959–81). *Early English Stages, 1300–1600.* 3 vols. New York: Columbia University Press.

Williams, Gwyn A. (1963). *Medieval London: From Commune to Capital.* London: Athlone.

Williams, Sheila (1959). "The Lord Mayor's Show in Tudor and Stuart times." *Guildhall Miscellany* 10, 3–18.

Withington, Robert (1915). "The Lord Mayor's Show for 1590." *PMLA* 30, 110–15.

Withington, Robert (1926, rpt 1963). *English Pageantry: An Historical Outline.* 2 vols. New York: Benjamin Blom.

22

Boy Companies and Private Theaters

Michael Shapiro

Under the first Tudor monarchs, troupes of boy actors from London grammar schools and choirs began performing plays in the banqueting halls of royal residences as part of the court's annual season of winter revelry, a season which usually ran from late November to early February. Adult troupes performed as well, but only the children offered that special mixture of pertness and naivety, audacity and innocence, which Roger Ascham felt was overly prized in upper-class English families. Elizabeth herself is said to have savored this combination of cheekiness and charm, a quality which probably accounted for the widespread appeal of boy companies in early modern London.

Whether by boy companies or adult troupes, all court performances were arranged and supervised by the master of the revels and often received logistical support from the Revels Office. Court accounts record payments to the schoolmasters and choirmasters who directed these companies, but it is unclear whether these payments were recompense for expenses, donations to the institutions, supplementary income for the troupes' masters, or some combination of the above. Shortly after the accession of Elizabeth, several grammar school and chorister companies also presented plays before paying audiences in venues other than royal banqueting halls. They maintained, as did professional adult companies and their supporters, that such performances were essential if the queen was to have her usual fare of theatrical entertainment each winter and on other special occasions. It is still not clear precisely when and how, at least for the boy companies, these rehearsals evolved into fully fledged commercial enterprises, for motives of patronage and profit are inextricably intertwined throughout the lives of these troupes. Indeed, even after two of the London companies resumed playing around 1599 after an eight- or nine-year hiatus, clearly under commercial auspices, their success still depended at least in part on the notion that they were purveyors of theatrical entertainment to the court. In the decade after this resumption of playing, "an aery of children, little eyases," as Rosenkrantz calls the boy company which has forced Hamlet's favorite company of adult players to leave the city and tour the provinces, had become an integral part of the commercial world of the London theater. While they never actually supplanted adult troupes, they were the avant-garde theater of their day. They performed plays by most of the leading playwrights of the period (Shakespeare excepted), of which about 70 are extant. Their repertories are dominated by satiric comedies, for the combination of high-ranking spectators and saucy diminutive players evoked a spirit of mockery which could be directed at figures of authority in their plays and in the real world, at their audiences, at rival companies or playwrights, and even at themselves. Such mockery, which tended to become ever more acute, attracted spectators but often brought punitive measures from official quarters and eventually led to the cessation of playing by boy companies on a commercial basis. Nevertheless, in their brief but glittering heyday, they established the indoor playhouse as the norm for commercial theater in London, and sounded the death-knell of the larger open-roofed amphitheaters used by their adult rivals.

Grammar Schools

Many humanist educators of the period believed that their pupils might develop poise and improve their skill in speaking Latin by acting in dialogues or even in entire plays, either those by Plautus or Terence, or neo-Latin imitations of Roman comedy (see chapter 18 above). Eventually some schoolmasters translated or adapted Roman comedies into English and some even wrote vernacular plays for their pupils. In London, Henry VIII and his guests were entertained in 1527–8 by the students of the newly established grammar school at St. Paul's; they also performed before Cardinal Wolsey and his guests. Nicholas Udall brought his grammar school students from Eton to play before Cromwell in 1538, and his pupils from Westminster grammar school to play before Mary in 1554. One such occasion witnessed the performance of Udall's original Terentian comedy, *Ralph Roister Doister*.

The statutes of the Westminster grammar school dating from about 1560 require that the students perform a Latin play each year. On January 17, 1566, they presented a *Sapientia Solomonis* before Queen Elizabeth, her guest Queen Cecilia of Sweden, and other members of the court circle. The previous year, the queen had seen a Roman comedy at the school, but *Sapientia Solomonis* was a neo-Latin work by Sixt Birck, a German schoolmaster. The play dramatized the relationship between King Solomon and the Queen of Sheba in a way appropriate for schoolboys, with additional material developing an allegorical parallel to the queen of England and her royal Swedish guest.

The Westminster performance of *Sapientia Solomonis* seems more like a gift offering than a commercial enterprise. Elizabeth was clearly the school's patron, having restored her father's foundation shortly after her accession. On this occasion, the troupe presented her with a richly decorated manuscript copy of the text written in red and black ink and bearing her arms on its vellum binding. The abbey itself, along with the Revels Office, bore some of the expenses involved in supplying and transporting sets, props, and costumes. Thomas Brown, then headmaster of the school, was reimbursed for expenses by the abbey, but no court record of payment to him for staging the play has been found.

Richard Mulcaster, headmaster from 1561 to 1586 of the grammar school established by the guild of merchant taylors, encouraged acting on pedagogical grounds and often brought his pupils to perform before Elizabeth at court in the 1570s and early 1580s. For such performances, he evidently used the guildhall as a rehearsal space and charged admission of a penny. He admitted the general public until forbidden to do so by the masters of the guild in March 1574, on the grounds that outsiders were taking seats which should have been reserved for officers and members of the guild. None of the plays performed by the merchant taylors' troupe in their own hall or at court survive, but the few extant titles, such as *Timoclea at the Siege of Troy*, indicate a preference for plays focusing on the pathos of captive women. His troupe's use of the merchant taylors' guildhall represented the first commercial "private theater" in London. That is, aside from inns and banqueting halls at court, it was the first small indoor playhouse in the city, and as such differed from the larger open-roofed "public" theaters established in London after 1576 and used exclusively by adult troupes (see chapter 11 above). Mulcaster's merchants taylors' pupils were the last grammar school troupe to entertain the court. In 1596, he became headmaster of the grammar school at St. Paul's, but its students never performed at court or in their own hall, nor is there any evidence that he was instrumental in the revival of the chorister troupe at the cathedral.

Chorister Troupes (1)

William Cornish, master of the Chapel Royal under the early Tudors, used adult and boy choristers in the entertainments he fashioned for his royal patrons. Like her father and grandfather, Elizabeth was entertained by her own Children of the Chapel Royal, but more frequently by the boy choristers from St. Paul's Cathedral, from the Chapel Royal at Windsor, and from Westminster Abbey. As boy choristers from all these institutions were highly trained in singing and playing instruments, their plays were much richer in song and music than the plays by adult troupes, as Austern (1992) has demonstrated.

The most frequent payee for court performances in the first half of Elizabeth's reign was Sebastian Westcote, almoner and choirmaster at Paul's from 1547 to 1582. He seems to have continued the theatrical tradition established by the previous almoner and choirmaster, John Redford, whose extant play, *Wit and Science*, was probably performed by the Children of Paul's. But it was Westcote who attracted Elizabeth's patronage. On February 12, 1552, he led the Paul's choristers in an appearance before the then Princess Elizabeth at Hatfield House, her official residence, for which he received the rather large payment of £4 19s. After Elizabeth's accession in 1558, Westcote and the Paul's boys were frequent entertainers at court, appearing on about two dozen occasions over the next two decades. For these productions, Westcote was listed in the court records as payee, and probably functioned as producer-director and perhaps as playwright as well, although the only extant play ascribed to him is *The Marriage of Wit and Science*.

Westcote was granted the power to impress, or draft into his service, talented boy choristers from any choir in the land, and on one occasion the Privy Council interceded when someone else tried to impress one of his choristers. Like Mulcaster, he had his children rehearse before paying spectators, probably in a hall somewhere on the cathedral grounds. Such an arrangement is suggested by Westcote's will, which records bequests to the men who kept the cathedral gate and watched the hall door during plays. Whether solely for profit or out of a desire to please the royal patron, or for the usual mixture of both motives, Westcote followed the example of Mulcaster in establishing a fee-charging indoor playhouse for his choristers to use when they rehearsed for court performances.

Richard Farrant also established a private theater for the Children of the Chapel Royal to use in rehearsing for their visits to court. He did so by renting space in 1576 in the precinct known as Blackfriars, a former Dominican priory. There is no evidence that any of Farrant's predecessors as choirmasters of the Chapel Royal had anything like their own private rehearsal space or playhouse. Not even Richard Edwards, who held the position from 1561 to 1567 and who was noted as an author of comedies, of which only *Damon and Pythias* is extant, is known to have had such a space. When Edwards' successor, William Hunnis, took some sort of temporary leave from 1576 to 1580, the post was filled by Farrant, who had been master of the Children of the Chapel of St. George at Windsor since 1564. Under his leadership, the Windsor boy choristers appeared at court at Shrove-tide 1567, as they did nearly every year until 1575. On January 6, 1577, the court records document a joint performance of a lost play entitled *Mutius Scevola* by the Children of the Windsor Chapel and the Children of the Chapel Royal, and for several years thereafter Farrant was associated with the latter troupe in their frequent court appearances. His one extant play, *The Wars of Cyrus*, dramatizes the plight of Penthea, a royal captive, whose musical lamentations are also preserved.

When Farrant died in 1580, Hunnis resumed his post as master of the Chapel Royal, and acquired the lease to the first Blackfriars theater in order to continue Farrant's practice of training his choirboys to entertain the queen. For the next four years, the playhouse was used by a combination of Chapel and Paul's choristers playing not directly under his supervision but rather under the sponsorship of the earl of Oxford and his retainer, John Lyly. At one point in the early 1580s, Henry Evans, a scrivener and close friend of the late Westcote, became involved in the management of the troupe. Working on his own, or perhaps in partnership with Oxford and Lyly, Evans acquired the lease for the first Blackfriars theater from Hunnis and sold it to

Oxford around June 1583. In 1584, however, the original owner of the property regained control of the Blackfriars playhouse and evicted the children's troupe, probably a combination of Paul's and Chapel boys playing under Oxford's name. Perhaps it was Evans' past association with Westcote at Paul's that permitted the troupe, or its Paul's contingent, to shift its operations back to the playhouse on the cathedral grounds, now under the control of Westcote's successor, Thomas Giles.

Throughout the 1580s, Lyly's plays were performed by the amalgamated or separate children's companies both at court and in the private theaters at Blackfriars and Paul's. Early printed texts often include different prologues and epilogues for the different venues, but whether written for court or private theaters, these extra-dramatic speeches sound the trope of *sprezzatura*, the self-deprecating ploy advocated by Castiglione for use when a courtier is entertaining his patron. To judge from the courtly tone of these extra-dramatic addresses, the ambience of the first Blackfriars theater and of the playhouse in Paul's approximated that at court, and that approximation may indeed have been the basis of whatever commercial success the Children of Paul's achieved in their own playhouses. Several of Lyly's plays, *Campaspe*, *Sappho and Phao*, and *Endimion*, reflect a courtier's point of view, for they dramatize the power gap between remote and celibate sovereigns or deities and their mortal subjects or admirers. Another of Lyly's plays, *Gallathea*, anticipates Shakespeare's interest in cross-dressed heroines by having two women disguised as boys fall in love with each other. Nearly every one of Lyly's plays follows the practice of Richard Edwards and earlier dramatists for boy companies by counterpointing the main action with short, low-comic scenes for pages, apprentices, and maidservants, roles evidently played by the youngest and smallest boys in the troupe, probably about 9 or 10 in age.

As an amalgamated company or as separate troupes, the Lyly–Oxford–Evans enterprise went downhill after their loss of the Blackfriars lease. One reason for the decline may have been the establishment in 1583 of an adult troupe, the Queen's Men, more directly under royal patronage than either of the two leading children's troupes. This company was created by Edmund Tilney, the master of the revels, out of the best adult talent available. The Queen's Men gave three performances at court in 1583–4, when the Chapel Children and Oxford's boys gave one each, and the following year the adult troupe gave four. The Chapel Children did not perform at court under their own name after February 2, 1584, and Oxford's boys, perhaps an amalgamation of Paul's and Chapel choristers, appeared at court for the last time during the following Christmas season, 1584–5. The Children of Paul's came to court regularly each Christmas season from 1586–7 to 1589–90, but in 1591 the publisher of the quarto of Lyly's *Endimion* declared that "the Plaies in Paules were dissolved."

Most scholars believe that the troupe was silenced because some of its plays were part of the Martin Marprelate controversy, a spirited if scurrilous exchange over questions of hierarchy within the Anglican Church. Like Lyly, the Children of Paul's are thought to have taken a conservative position in support of the bishops, but may have done so with too much satiric zeal. Despite sporadic records of provincial appearances, both children's companies were dormant in the 1590s.

Chorister Troupes (2)

When the two leading children's troupes resumed playing in and shortly after 1600, they did so as somewhat more commercialized enterprises than they had been a decade earlier. The directorates of both revived troupes involved entrepreneurs who surely expected a return on money invested in the companies. The legal fiction that their performances were primarily rehearsals for court performances was therefore harder to maintain. Still, both troupes maintained a nominal if not stronger affiliation with a prestigious religious choir, and their choirmasters retained the right to impress new personnel. Functioning more or less as small commercial playhouses, they charged much more for admission than did the public theaters and thus catered to a more exclusive clientele. Their locations within the precincts of St. Paul's Cathedral and Blackfriars made them immune from municipal control yet closer than the public theaters in Shoreditch or Bankside to fashionable districts nearer the center of London. With high admission fees and fashionable locations, the private playhouses used by the two revived boy companies probably attracted an up-scale audience. It must have comprised members of the aristocracy and gentry along with their entourages, whether they were London-based or there temporarily for sessions of the law courts or for pleasure, as well as members of the legal profession, students at inns of court, and (then as now) foreign tourists. The same cohort of spectators no doubt also saw plays in the public theaters, but in these large amphitheaters they were greatly outnumbered by lower- or middle-class spectators. At Paul's and Blackfriars, the audience was, and wanted to think of itself as, decidedly elite.

This self-image is most clearly seen in a Blackfriars play, Beaumont's *Knight of the Burning Pestle*, which ridicules a grocer, his wife, and his apprentice who wander into that very private playhouse. Beaumont pokes fun at them for being out of their element, and for their fondness for escapist and episodic dramas of love and adventure with middle-class apprentices as chivalric heroes. His relentless mockery of these middle-class interlopers suggests that his own up-scale audience harbored considerable anxiety about its social position and that such ridicule was meant to (re)affirm his audience's precarious sense of its own status.

The resumption of playing at Paul's is usually dated sometime after May 1599, when Edward Pearce succeeded Thomas Giles as choirmaster. It is not clear whether the resuscitated troupe performed in the same hall used by Westcote or in some other space, neither of which has been convincingly identified. Court appearances followed within a year of revival, during the winter revels of 1600–1, and the company played at court several more times until its demise, probably in 1607 or 1608. Its last court performance, July 30, 1606, was of a lost play entitled *The Abuses*, on the occasion of a visit by James' brother-in-law, Christian of Denmark.

Pearce's precise role in the theatrical activities at Paul's is problematic, but his choristers were probably the same boys who performed plays, or the nucleus of the company known as the Children of Paul's. A strong connection with the choir is

suggested by the lavish use of song and instrumental music in the company's repertory. One of the members of the troupe was a chorister named Thomas Ravenscroft,
who went on to become a well-known composer and among whose published compositions are songs from plays performed by the troupe. Although the choir at Paul's
usually numbered around 10 or 12, the acting company evidently needed more actors.
Antonio's Revenge, for example, requires 17, assuming that boy companies did not normally double roles.

Pearce claimed, perhaps disingenuously, that he was only marginally involved in
the theatrical activities at Paul's. Testifying during a libel suit, arising from a lost
play by George Chapman, *The Old Joiner of Aldgate*, performed at Paul's in 1603, Pearce
minimized his role in the troupe's management, perhaps to evade responsibility for
any damages awarded the plaintiff. He claimed that the burden of the company's management had fallen on the shoulders of Thomas Woodford, a businessman who entered
the picture in 1603 or 1604 and who subsequently fell out with Pearce. Edward
Kirkham, a yeoman of the revels, was also involved in the affairs of the company, as
he was later at Blackfriars, but in what capacity is unknown. Pearce's ability to revive
the company even after its demise, and hence his centrality to the operation, is suggested by the annual payment of £20 he was offered in "dead rent" in 1608–9 from
rival children's troupes to keep the Paul's playhouse dark.

About two dozen plays survive from the second phase of theatrical activity at Paul's.
When the troupe resumed playing, the first plays were revivals of anonymous older
plays, such as the morality *The Contention Between Liberality and Prodigality*, and the
Lylyesque pastoral romance *The Maid's Metamorphosis*. But the company soon thereafter found a new voice in the work of John Marston, a young resident of Middle
Temple, who wrote Juvenalian verse satire and an Ovidian epyllion, or little epic,
which proffers erotic material even while it chastises the reader's desire to read it.
Whether Marston was part of the directorate of the resuscitated troupe, as Gair (1982)
has argued, remains conjectural, but his earliest plays surely demonstrate a familiarity with the Paul's boys and the architecture of their playhouse.

One of Marston's first plays for the reopened playhouse at Paul's, *Jack Drum's Entertainment*, in fact pokes fun at the archaic quality of other plays performed at the same
playhouse as "the mustie fopperies of antiquity." Such old-fashioned fare, it is charged,
is unworthy of "the audience that frequenteth there." The reopened playhouse is not
like one of the public theaters, where "a man shall not be choked / With barmy stench
of garlic, nor be pasted / To the barmy jacket of a beer-brewer." In another of his early
plays for the revived Paul's boys, *Antonio and Mellida*, Marston initiated a mode of
drama analogous to the absurdist drama of our own day, and did so with flamboyant
linguistic inventiveness. These plays used children to burlesque the futile and inappropriate posturing of the adult world, and to parody the portrayals of such posturing in plays acted by adult companies. In *Antonio's Revenge*, Marston applied burlesque
and parody to the concept of revenge and its dramatic representation in such popular
adult plays as Kyd's *The Spanish Tragedy*, and perhaps *Hamlet* (Caputi, 1961; Foakes,
1962).

At about this time, Marston seems to have begun feuding with Ben Jonson in an exchange of satirical caricatures known as "the War of the Theaters." In such Paul's plays as *What You Will* and *Satiromastix*, Marston directed the ridicule of his audience not so much toward other plays or adult acting companies as toward a gallery of satiric victims. Of these, the most noteworthy are characters who, like satirists such as Jonson, seemed to collect fools in order to mock them. His last play for Pauls was probably *The Fawn*, another Italianate anti-court satire, which was also performed by the children's troupe at Blackfriars. This play, like Thomas Middleton's *The Phoenix*, featured a disguised nobleman who denounces the vice and folly of his world. Middleton, who succeeded Marston as the principal dramatist for the Paul's boys, continued to offer the spectators objects of ridicule in a new type of satiric comedy which later critics call "city comedy." In a series of such plays, *Michaelmas Term*, *A Trick to Catch the Old One*, *A Mad World, My Masters*, and perhaps *The Puritan*, Middleton pitted impoverished but attractive young prodigal gallants against a host of predatory authority figures — merchants, lawyers, usurers, uncles, and grandfathers. These plays invite audiences to share in the oedipal triumphs of the young over the old, triumphs usually marked by the restoration of wealth and status, and the conquest of attractive young women.

The importance of city comedies in the repertories of both major boy companies can be witnessed by the "Ho" plays. When Thomas Dekker and John Webster wrote *Westward Ho*, the first for the Paul's boys, it elicited a response from the Blackfriars troupe in the form of *Eastward Ho* by Jonson, Marston, and Chapman, to which Paul's, again relying on Dekker and Webster, responded with *Northward Ho*. All three plays dramatize the familiar rivalry between merchants and gallants over women and money, while *Eastward Ho* includes a satiric and parodic treatment of the prodigal son parable, a motif treated more didactically in city comedies performed by adult troupes at the same time.

The most anomalous play in the entire repertory of the Children of Paul's is Chapman's *Bussy D'Ambois*, a tragedy based on recent French history. The title character, a kind of natural hero, is taken up by the king and his courtiers for his candor, simplicity, valor, and military prowess, but is later destroyed by them when he has a passionate affair with a courtier's wife. The sequel, *The Revenge of Bussy D'Ambois*, was performed by the Blackfriars children's troupe. Both plays seems like odd choices for boy companies, and in fact the first of these works was later acquired and performed by one of the adult troupes, the King's Men, in whose repertory it flourished for many years. Despite the heroic aspects of the hero's trajectory, however, *Bussy D'Ambois* includes a good deal of anti-court satire, and as such embodies the spirit of ridicule which informs and animates nearly all of the plays performed by the Children of Paul's in the second phase of its existence.

The second phase of the boy company at Blackfriars parallels that of the troupe at Paul's, but with some significant differences. In the latter part of 1600, about a year after the resumption of playing at Paul's, the Children of the Chapel Royal also began performing in their own playhouse in Blackfriars. This second Blackfriars theater was

located in a different part of the priory from that used by Ferrant's Chapel Children
and by the combined Chapel–Paul's–Oxford children's company between 1576 and
1584. It was twice the size of the earlier theater and, like Paul's, evidently charged
much more for admission than either the first Blackfriars theater or the "public" theaters used by adult troupes. Like Paul's, it was a blatantly commercial enterprise but
still preserved vestiges of the older, patronage-based mode of theater associated with
the name of Children of the Chapel Royal. Like the Children of Paul's, the Chapel
Children, under its various names, performed at court during the winter revels in
1600–1 and nearly every year thereafter until 1608–9.

Relying on impressions recorded by a German visitor, Wallace (1908) argued that
the second Blackfriars theater was established and maintained by royal sponsorship.
Later scholars, Harbage (1952) most strongly, believed that the playhouse was a purely
commercial enterprise designed to exploit the opportunity to play at court and to
market access to "rehearsals" for those performances. As a further commercial advantage, the company would use child actors whose maintenance could be charged to the
Chapel Royal and who, unlike the shareholders of an adult company like the Lord
Chamberlain's Men, would not expect to share in the profits. Whatever the motiva-
tion, probably mixed, the moving force behind the revival of the Chapel Children was
Henry Evans, formerly associated with Westcote at Paul's and subsequently with
Oxford, Lyly, and the children who performed at the first Blackfriars (see chapter 11
above). Evans' partners in this enterprise included his son-in-law, Alexander Hawkins,
Edward Kirkham of the Revels Office, and Nathaniel Giles, choirmaster of the Chapel
Royal following the death of William Hunnis in 1597.

Like all previous choirmasters, Giles held the right to impress boys into his service.
Just as Pearce did at Paul's, Giles used his impressment privileges to augment the 12
boy choristers of the Chapel Royal, for several plays call for 18 to 20 actors to be
onstage at once and one of the legal documents refers to a troupe of 18 or 20. In one
ill-fated instance, the power of impressment was exercised against a boy named
Clifton, whose father used his considerable political influence to have his son released.
From extant records of the case we know the names of other boys impressed into the
company. One was Salomon Pavy, who joined the company at the age of 9 or 10, specialized in playing the roles of old men, and died at the age of 12 or 13, to become
the subject of a touching epigram by Ben Jonson. Another boy impressed into the
Blackfriars troupe was Nathan Field, who went on to become one of the leading adult
actors of the period and something of a dramatist. As an aftermath of the Clifton affair,
Evans was compelled to withdraw from the active management of the Blackfriars
theater and at least ostensibly passed his interest and authority on to his son-in-law,
Hawkins.

One of the earliest plays performed by the resuscitated Chapel Children at the
second Blackfriars playhouse was Jonson's *Cynthia's Revels*. Like *Jack Drum's Entertainment*, this play flatters its spectators by invidiously comparing them to public
theater audiences in its prologues. Its induction mocks the company's own repertory
as "the umbrae, or ghosts of some three or four plays, departed a dozen years since,

[which] have been seen walking on your stage here." Other early plays at the second Blackfriars theater include Jonson's *Poetaster*, which satirizes inept or corrupt poets like Marston, forced to vomit forth examples of his own idiosyncratic diction, as well as a series of satiric "humors" comedies by George Chapman: *May Day*, *Sir Giles Goosecap*, *All Fools*, *Monsieur D'Olive*, *The Widow's Tears*, and *The Gentleman Usher*. A few years after the reopening of both private theaters, Marston switched his allegiance from Paul's to the Chapel Children, from whom the Lord Chamberlain's Men stole his comic revenge play *The Malcontent*, performing it with additions by Webster. Marston also provided the Chapel Children with *The Fawn* (mentioned above); *The Dutch Courtesan*, a city comedy; and *Sophonisba*, the tragic drama of a Roman wife which called for elaborate musical effects.

Around 1604, two new investors joined the syndicate, William Rastell, a merchant, and Thomas Kendall, a haberdasher. Later, Robert Payne and Robert Keysar, a goldsmith, entered the picture, as did John Marston. Like Evans, most of these men invested in the boy company at Blackfriars in hope of a profitable return, and most of the legal action concerns the recovery of their investments from one another or from the troupe's assets. In 1604, the Blackfriars children's company also received a patent which permitted it to call itself the Children of the Queen's Revels. Queen Anne evidently wished to set up a household establishment parallel to the king's, which would have her own acting company, her own lord chamberlain, and, under his jurisdiction, several other officers, including the equivalent of a Revels Office. A patent of 1604 made Samuel Daniel something like Anne's master of the revels, with responsibilities to provide her with theatrical entertainment, providing that the texts first obtained his approval.

Daniel was an unfortunate choice, for he soon found himself in trouble over his own Blackfriars play, *Philotas* (1605), which seemed to allude to the rebellious end of Essex, a still dangerous topic. The company also offended the king, first over alleged anti-Scots allusions in *Eastward Ho* (1605) by Jonson, Marston, and Chapman, then over highly personal anti-court satire in Day's *The Isle of Gulls*, and finally over mockery in a lost play of James' drunkenness, silver mines, and love of hunting. In 1606, James was angry enough over these attacks to forbid Thomas Giles to allow any of the Chapel Children to perform at Blackfriars, and the acting troupe, no longer having a claim to royal patronage, renamed itself the Children of the Revels or the Children of Blackfriars. Two years later, when the company staged unfavorable representations of the French court in Chapman's *Conspiracy and Tragedy of Charles, Duke of Byron* (1608), all playing in London was temporarily suspended.

As Dutton (1991) has argued, the impudence involved in satiric thrusts at King James and his Scots friends may have seemed like a kind of licensed abuse when launched by a company patronized by Queen Anne, and possibly performed before at court. Personal satire, also called "application" and "railing," was quite prevalent too in plays performed at the second Blackfriars and at Paul's. Such abuse suggests that the private theater audiences welcomed satire sharp enough to risk offending, if not actually to offend, figures of authority who were or imagined themselves to be targets of ridicule. In his *Apology for Actors*, Thomas Heywood chastised the children's troupes from satirizing individuals from behind the protection of their juniority, and a number of their plays contain prologues which deny personal satire, a sure sign that it was inferred even if unintended.

In 1608, after a lengthy closing of the playhouse on account of plague, Evans returned the Blackfriars lease to the Burbages. Keysar moved the company to the theater in Whitefriars, which in 1607–8 had been the home of another troupe of boy actors, the shadowy Children of the King's Revels, a thoroughly commercial enterprise having not even the slightest connection with any sponsoring academic or religious institution. (The same can be said for Beeston's Boys, a company of boys or youths run entirely along commercial lines as an adult company between 1637 and 1642.) Like the other boy companies, the Children of the King's Revels specialized in satiric city comedies, but the derivative quality of such works as Day's *Law Tricks* and Barry's *Ram Alley* suggest that this vein had long since played itself out. Court performances by a troupe styling itself the Children of the King's Revels are recorded during the winter revels of 1609–10 and 1611–12.

In 1610 a patent was granted to Keysar's new syndicate, which now included Philip Rosseter, a royal lutenist, and several marginal theatrical figures, for a company to be called the Queen's Revels Children. By this time, the actors who had once been part of a boy company were growing long in the tooth. Nathan Field, who had acted in *Cynthia's Revels* in 1601 at Blackfriars at the age of 13, was now 22. Some of the actors joined adult troupes, such as the King's Men, and some merged with a group of adult actors in a new troupe, the Lady Elizabeth's Men, formed around 1613. Rosseter and his associates held on to their patent for the Queen's Revels Children, and a troupe playing under that name performed four or five plays at court during the winter of 1612–13, and may also have toured the provinces. But in 1617–18 three different troupes claiming the same title arrived in Leicester, suggesting that in the provinces, if not at court or in London, juvenile troupes claiming some prestige as former purveyors of entertainment to royalty and nobility apparently still retained a trace of commercial value.

References and Further Reading

Armstrong, W. A. (1959). "The audience of the private theatres." *Review of English Studies* NS 10, 234–49.

Austern, L. P. (1992). *Music in English Children's Drama of the Later Renaissance.* Philadelphia: Gordon and Breach.

Bevington, D. (1962). *From "Mankynd" to Marlowe.* Cambridge, MA: Harvard University Press.

Bloom, G. (1998). "'Thy voice squeaks': listening for masculinity on the early modern stage." *Renaissance Drama* 29, 39–72.

Caputi, A. (1961). *John Marston, Satirist.* Ithaca: Cornell University Press.

Clare, J. (1990). *"Art Made Tongue-Tied by Authority".* Manchester: Manchester University Press.

De Molen, R. L. (1972). "Richard Mulcaster and the Elizabethan theatre." *Theatre Survey* 13, 28–41.

Dutton, R. (1991). *Mastering the Revels.* Iowa City: University of Iowa Press.

Finkelpearl, P. (1969). *John Marston of the Middle Temple*. Cambridge, MA: Harvard University Press.

Foakes, R. A. (1962). "John Marston's fantastical plays: *Antonio and Mellida* and *Antonio's Revenge*." *Philological Quarterly* 41, 229–39.

Gair, N. R. (1982). *The Children of Paul's*. Cambridge: Cambridge University Press.

Gurr, A. (1996). *The Shakespearian Playing Companies*. Oxford: Clarendon Press.

Harbage, A. (1952). *Shakespeare and the Rival Traditions*. New York: Macmillan.

Hillebrand, H. N. (1926). *The Child Actors*. Urbana: University of Illinois Press.

Hunter, G. K. (1962). *John Lyly*. London: Routledge and Kegan Paul.

Hunter, G. K., ed. (1964). *The History of Antonio and Mellida*. London: Edward Arnold.

Ingram, W. (1985). "The playhouse as an investment, 1607–14." *Medieval and Renaissance Drama in England* 2, 209–30.

Knutson, R. (1995). "Falconer to the little eyases." *Shakespeare Quarterly* 46, 1–31.

Lennam, T. (1975). *Sebastian Westcott, the Children of Paul's, and "The Marriage of Wit and Science"*. Toronto: University of Toronto Press.

Marston, John (1601). *Jack Drum's Entertainment*.

Payne, E. R., ed. (1938). *Sapientia Solomonis*. New Haven: Yale University Press.

Shapiro, M. (1977). *Children of the Revels*. New York: Columbia University Press.

Sisson, C. (1936). *Lost Plays of Shakespeare's Age*. Cambridge: Cambridge University Press.

Tucker, K. (1985). *John Marston: A Reference Guide*. Boston: Hall.

Wallace, C. W. (1908) *The Children of the Chapel at Blackfriars, 1597–1603*. Lincoln: University of Nebraska Press.

Wharton, T. F. (1994). *The Critical Fall and Rise of John Marston*. Columbia, SC: Camden House.

23
Revenge Tragedy
Eugene D. Hill

The English revenge tragedy, which emerged in the last decade and a half of Queen Elizabeth's life and continued to flourish through the reign of her successor James I (1603–25), lent itself all too readily to satiric mockery. In the anonymous play *A Warning for Fair Women* (published 1599), a character standing for Comedy offers the following quite merciless sketch of her counterpart. Tragedy, she tells us, represents:

> How some damned tyrant to obtain a crown
> Stabs, hangs, imprisons, smothers, cutteth throats;
> And then a chorus too comes howling in,
> And tells us of the worrying of a cat;
> Then too a filthy whining ghost,
> Lapt in some foul sheet or a leather pilch,
> Comes screaming like a pig half sticked
> And cries "Vindicta! Revenge! Revenge!"
> With that a little rosin flasheth forth,
> Like smoke out of a tobacco pipe or a boy's squib
> Then comes in two or three like to drovers,
> With tailor's bodkins stabbing one another.

Though hardly a fair portrayal of the best works in the revenge genre, this sketch does indicate the conventional elements that have led many to dismiss the genre as fundamentally an exercise in hair-raising, in blood-and-guts-mongering. The foundational work in the genre (to judge from surviving texts), *The Spanish Tragedy* (published 1592, attributed to Thomas Kyd), used to be described in just such a way. *The Revenger's Tragedy* (published 1607–8, attributed to the minor poet Cyril Tourneur or the major dramatist Thomas Middleton) used to be seen as a decadent exercise in murderous one-upmanship illuminated by some splendid verse passages. Only *Hamlet* (second quarto published 1604–5) has been exempted from this charge, but at the risk of missing fundamental features that it shares with its fellow revenge plays.

Revenge tragedy is extraordinarily simple in some respects, built upon a handful of motifs (ghosts, madness, delay, horrible killing) that it derives from its ancient progenitor, the Roman tragic poet Seneca. At the same time, it bears a complexity of implication that will keep playgoers and readers intellectually stimulated and puzzled as well as thrilled by the exhibited gore. Revenge tragedy looks in two directions, much as Hamlet does in the play-within-a-play. The old tragedy that Prince Hamlet has mounted in the Danish court allows him to search, here and now, the conscience of the king. Hamlet's position exemplifies that of the observer of all of these plays, from Seneca to the Roman's Elizabethan and Jacobean descendants. It is an old story being represented, in which we take horrid delight; if we are of a moralizing bent, we can say that we are viewing a monitory example of what happens when reason gives way to passion. That is our alibi. But the keen observer knows that Seneca, tutor and victim of the dreadful emperor Nero, represented nothing in his plays of legendary heroes that did not take place in their own lives, in the horror-show of Nero's Rome. Such doubleness – old story, present-day application – affords revenge tragedy some of its keenest pleasures.

The bedeviling complexities of the English revenge drama derive from its very nature. Take the issue of madness. In one of the standard books on the genre, entitled precisely *The Revenger's Madness*, Charles and Elaine Hallett (1980) argue that the would-be revenger, in his imagining of killing his victimizer, becomes so overwrought that he truly falls into insanity. The mind separates itself from the real world, and from the traditional moral codes that condemn private revenge. Moral-minded critics will find this account to their liking, and they can cite to their purpose Seneca's memorable remarks near the opening of his treatise *De ira* ("On anger"). Other emotions, the philosopher argues, have in them some "element of peace and calm"; not so anger, which proves "eager for revenge though it may drag down the avenger along with it." Then comes the bravura passage:

> [Y]ou have only to behold the aspect of those possessed by anger to know that they are insane. For as the marks of a madman are unmistakable – a bold and threatening mien, a gloomy brow, a fierce expression, a hurried step, restless hands, an altered colour, a quick and more violent breathing – so likewise are the marks of an angry man; his eyes blaze and sparkle, his whole face is crimson with the blood that surges from the lowest depths of the heart, his lips quiver, his teeth are clenched, his hair bristles and stands on end, his breathing is forced and harsh, his joints crack from writhing, he groans and bellows. (Seneca, 1928, 106–9)

The description, too lengthy to cite in full, wonderfully evokes a passion "unfit to discern the right and true – the very counterpart of a ruin that is shattered in pieces where it overwhelms." (Seneca's words here will remind some readers of Ophelia on Hamlet's overthrown mind.)

But of course that is exactly what the avenger (Hieronimo, Hamlet, and any number of their analogues) wishes his intended victim to believe. As Claudius says in *Hamlet*, madness in great ones must not go unwatched – especially since the feigned madness of the Roman Brutus represents the archetypal menace to a tyrant. Here the moralist's line (vengeance equals madness) protects the aspiring tyrannicide; madness disguises, and thus enables, vengeance.

This characteristic doubleness of revenge drama may be observed even in small details. Near the end of the opening act of *Hamlet*, the prince obliges Marcellus and Horatio to swear not to reveal what they have observed that night. Their mere promise will not suffice – they must swear, and on his sword. At that moment, as the stage direction prompts, *Ghost cries under the stage*, "Swear." Hamlet's impromptu comment goes:

> Ha, ha boy, say'st thou so? Art thou there, truepenny?
> Come on. You hear this fellow in the cellarage.
> Consent to swear.

The passage haunts the memory. It is utterly literal: there is one of the fellows or shareholders of the acting company, perhaps (according to an old tradition) William Shakespeare himself, precisely in the woodwork under the stage. The phrase also works symbolically: the foundations of Denmark are themselves haunted. Not often noted is that the phrase, so striking in its pertinence and particularity at this moment in this play, in fact echoes an idea that was already conventional in the first century BC. Cicero mocks a political enemy who wished not to be seen entering the gladiatorial exhibitions: "He used to emerge all of a sudden after he had crept along under the planks [*sub tabulas*], so that he looked as if he were going to say, 'Mother, I call you,'" that last phrase a quotation from a lost Roman tragedy in which a ghost visits his mother (Hickman, 1938, 81). From this remark of Cicero's it is evident that Hamlet's ghost in the cellarage could not be more ancient – it is the sort of echo that a politically minded student of classics like Hamlet of Wittenberg would produce. The context of political enmity in the Ciceronian text (*Pro Sestio* 59) heightens the wit here. Not every viewer will catch the allusion in Shakespeare's day, but some might, including the character Horatio.

Traditional criticism often missed this vital Janus-like quality. A generation or two ago, commentators typically dated *The Spanish Tragedy* before 1588 – since, they argued, a later production would surely have taken account of the English defeat of the Spanish Armada in that year. Revisionist scholarship has turned the argument on its head, suggesting that the downfall of the royal house of Spain that occurs in the play echoes the Armada events. But since the entire play is enacted on the Iberian peninsula, the characters cannot recognize the larger revenge at work. The wheel of history is turning, and tiny England will replace Spain as the ascendant power. It is left for us, the English audience, to understand what the Spaniards and Portingales on stage cannot recognize: their Senecan downfall functions as the counterpart to the Vergilian rise of the English nation. That is one of the reasons why the allegorical figure Revenge, who observes the action along with the ghost of Don Andrea, falls asleep. Morally, the saying went that God's vengeance may delay, but will surely be taken. Politically, though, the sleep suggests a certain boredom on the part of Revenge; these plotters and quarrelers really do not have a clue about the macro-revenge that is taking place. No wonder a recent scholar considers a date for *The Spanish Tragedy* as late as 1591 (Norland, 1998, 68). The entire play, of course, involves *our dream*, as English audience *c*.1590. The real tragic emotion, here as so often in revenge drama, is not purging terror but *Schadenfreude*, our pleasure at the Spaniards' collapse. Indeed, in his *Rhetoric* (often a better guide to our plays than the *Poetics*, which deals explicitly with drama), Aristotle noted that "anger is always accompanied by a certain pleasure, due to the hope of revenge to come . . . and also because men dwell upon the thought of revenge, and the vision that rises before us produces the same pleasure as one seen in dreams" (*Rhetoric* 1378b).

Of course moralists of the age condemned revenge. William Baldwin is typical; in *A Treatise of Moral Philosophy* (1547; often reprinted) he writes a chapter "Of wrath" offering such pithy comments as these: "Wrath and revengement taketh from man the mercy of God, and destroyeth and quencheth the grace that God hath given him," and (borrowing from Seneca) "Forgetfulness is a valiant kind of revengement." But from the ancient world to our own, the sweetness of revenge has stood as a commonplace; and the major revenge plays exhibit a veritable museum of devices carried and displayed with a view to forestalling forgetfulness. These include the bloody handkerchief in *The Spanish Tragedy*, Hamlet's pocket notebook, and the all-seeing skull of the dead mistress in *The Revenger's Tragedy*. These vengeance-bound figures carry an audience with them, at least in some measure, enjoying what Walter Scott once called revenge: "the sweetest morsel to the mouth, that ever was cooked in hell." Every generation one erudite scholar or another publishes a volume demonstrating the carnage that Hamlet leaves in his wake, the horror of his refraining from killing Claudius in prayer lest the king go straight to heaven. Whatever Hamlet's violations of ethical orthodoxy, audiences refuse – the critics be damned – to be argued out of their thrilled identification with the Danish heir as he works through, or works up, his dream of passion. There is no purgation here – instead, a half-guilty (and all the more exciting) participation in the enactment of vengeance.

In an excellent recent book, Anne Pippin Burnett distinguishes between the functioning of revenge in ancient Greek tragedy and in English Renaissance tragedy. She rightly lays stress on the greater ambivalence in the English plays:

> So much doubleness leaves the spectator at a Renaissance revenge drama pleasurably confused. He is asked to applaud and also to condemn both the indignant criminal and the flawed order that the criminal attacks. And this bifurcated emotional response is extorted from him even as he is deprived of his ordinary identity by the sheer gory excess of the show. (Burnett, 1998, 29)

This is well said, but Burnett herself at points tries to put a little more order into the confusion. Thus she argues that the Renaissance "poets of revenge had put together a package of conventions by which they might pass, in their dramas, from a rebellious premise to a loyal conclusion." So that where "[A]t the opening, revenge was an honorable deed done in a context of degenerate public power . . . at the end, in the presence of a revived authority now laudable, godly and pure, it was shown as a dark and punishable crime." She concludes, "The English revenge play thus consists of a kind of extended Anti-masque, capped by the briefest of performances in praise of order and power" (1998, 22). This is true enough; but it does not quite capture the oneiric potency of the English revenge play, in which the ambivalence – the dogged insistence on having one's moral cake and eating the sweet morsel of revenge – proves omnipresent, and not merely sequential.

Take, as an example, the opening of Tourneur's (or Middleton's) *The Revenger's Tragedy* (probably written 1605–7). None of the major characters is named in the opening scene. Vindice (= Revenger) and his brother and accomplice Hippolyto address one another as "brother," and Vindice refers to the target of his vengeance, the lecherous and murderous Duke, only by title: Vindice speaks the first line of the play with "Duke; royal lecher; go, grey-hair'd adultery." We will learn that we are in Italy; at the moment we do not have a clue.

But when the play was first mounted, we had plenty of clues. For we were in the Globe theater watching the King's Men. The actor holding a skull, identifying for us the villainous royals as they process across the stage, is the same actor (bearing the same property skull) that we have seen on these boards as Hamlet. For good measure, we can guess that the actor playing Hippolyto also did Horatio; and that the royally lecherous Duke was enacted by the fellow who performed the role of King Claudius. In fact, the entire scene cries out to be read as an echo – paying tribute, but with an edge of mockery – to Shakespeare's earlier revenge play. Once we make the connection, we can hardly stop linking the plays. Thus after Vindice's 48 lines of soliloquy, Hippolyto enters with a question: "Still sighing o'er death's vizard?" – the same problem Hamlet presented to the Danish court.

So we are in Italy, but allusively we are in Hamlet's Denmark; and that is only the beginning of the story. Vindice will repeatedly explain his doings to the skull of his dead mistress. At the center of the play, Vindice will enlist that presiding stage property in his maximalist revenge: baited with poison, the skull is presented to the Duke as "the bony lady" procured as a new companion for his bed. One kiss from the "royal lecher" suffices to carry off the murderous trick. Triumphantly Vindice identifies the perpetrator to the Duke, who is dying in agony:

> Brother –
> Place the torch here, that his affrighted eyeballs
> May start into those hollows. Duke, dost know
> Yon dreadful vizard? View it well; 'tis the skull
> Of Gloriana, whom thou poisonedst last.
>
> (III.v.147–51)

At this climax of torture, the playwright reveals that the skull presiding over these nightmarish doings bears a name that was one of the key poetic designations of the recently deceased Queen Elizabeth. For a horrified moment, the transition of sovereigns that we recall from *Hamlet* merges oneirically with the transition in England. Our loss as Englishfolk and Vindice's as enraged Italian converge. The playwright toys with the guilty secret that we have busily been comparing our new monarch with our old, imagining what she would be doing different from her Scottish successor.

Even the horrid torture, then, has its stroke of political wit to enact. Our identification with the revenger enacts a thrilled guilt that he largely avoids – part of the joke here is how *unlike* Hamlet he is. We become the worrying Hamlets, vexed at the decline from this glorious monarch to this lesser creature.

This example of the opening and the middle of *The Revenger's Tragedy* will begin to suggest how wrong those commentators were in past generations who read such plays as simple blood-and-guts affairs. The major revenge dramas of the age look to one another with knowing insight; they invite us to enter the fabric of their politically fraught, morally thrilling nightmare vision. We can turn to any of the brilliantly unsettling works in the revenge tradition, from John Marston's *Antonio's Revenge* (c.1600), written for the child actors of Paul to ape the elder performers in the adult companies; through Henry Chettle's *Hoffman* (1602), a nightmarish fantasy on some themes of *Hamlet*; and Cyril Tourneur's sharply moralizing *Atheist's Tragedy* (c.1609), at once so like and so unlike *The Revenger's Tragedy*; to James Shirley's *The Cardinal* (1641), which carried Kydian motifs into the last decade of the pre-revolutionary Stuart monarchy.

Where to begin admits of no doubt: with the inaugural work of surviving English revenge plays: Thomas Kyd's *Spanish Tragedy*, which was among the most popular plays of the 1590s and the first decades of the seventeenth century. (For the rest of this discussion let the traditional attribution to Kyd stand.)

Kyd would have been surprised to learn that he had founded a sub-genre of tragedy, revenge tragedy, whose conventions and motifs would be assiduously gathered by nineteenth- and twentieth-century scholars. Ancient criticism knew of no such things as revenge tragedy; nor did sixteenth-century commentators in Italy or England. To be sure, tragedy often involved revenge – a prior deed of horror provoking the bloody business before the audience. Many a drama by Seneca or his sixteenth-century Italian followers began with the appearance of a miasmic revenant from the underworld who demanded vengeance with horrid speech. But that was tragedy *simpliciter*, not a sub-genre thereof.

Like any good poet, Kyd began with what his audience knew – and twisted it, surprising them. Spain was the great enemy of England in the last two decades of the sixteenth century. But Kyd places us for most of the drama in the Spanish court, where England goes barely mentioned. Moreover, Kyd opens the play with two visitors from the underworld who prove very different from the Senecan norm. These figures, who will remain visible to the audience throughout the drama, serving as a between-act chorus, are Revenge and the recently killed soldier Don Andrea. The former could not be more different from the typical Senecan Prologue figure from the underworld who demands a grisly vengeance. Slow, quiet, certain of what is to come, but evidently rather bored with it all, this Revenge will even fall asleep later in the drama. (We can hardly imagine a Senecan Prologue figure sleeping; he is a cauldron of wrath.) And Don Andrea, a handsome if bloodied soldier, tugs at his companion's sleeve anxiously: where am I, what am I doing? The brilliant induction grabs the audience's attention on its own terms; but viewers who know their Seneca will be especially thrilled. This is not at all how that brilliant Spaniard (from Córdoba) started his plays.

Soon we are in the Spanish court, and watching the middle-aged hero Hieronimo, knight marshal of Spain, gradually drawn into a web of vengeance. Balthazar, son of the Portuguese viceroy, has been captured by the Spanish forces – in particular, by Lorenzo, the king's nephew, and by Horatio, Hieronimo's son. The king has enough trouble dividing the ransom of the Portuguese prince between these two captors. But when Lorenzo's highly nubile sister Bel-Imperia (Don Andrea's former lady friend) passes her affection to Horatio, thwarting Lorenzo's machinations for an imperial wedding between his sister and the hapless Portingale, the enraged Lorenzo with his sidekicks interrupt a tryst between aspiring Horatio and the willing Bel-Imperia. A quotation of some length will establish the edgy power of Kyd's conception.

In act II, scene iv, the two lovers are moving from kisses to the coitus signaled by the usual Elizabethan term for orgasm ("to die"). "O stay a while and I will die with thee, / So shalt thou yield and yet have conquered me" (lines 48–9). At this point Lorenzo and his party "Enter . . . disguised"; the young woman is led away and "They hang him [Horatio] in the arbor" (SD).

> *Horatio*   What, will you murder me?
> *Lorenzo*   Ay, thus, and thus; these are the fruits of love.
>   *They stab him*

Bel-Imperia pleads for his life: "O save his life and let me die for him!" But the unintended erotic quibble further enrages her brother, who viciously summarizes the affair: "Although his life were still ambitious proud, / Yet is he at the highest now he is dead" (lines 60–1). Lorenzo here condenses several meanings of words. For him, Don Horatio had sought to climb above his station through his affair with Bel-Imperia; that is pride in one sense. Yet for the Elizabethans pride also meant sexual ardor, and the psychosexually depraved prince must punish the commoner's passion: the thrusts of his knife ("Ay, thus, and thus; these are the fruits of love") viciously mimic the sexual thrusts that they have forestalled. With the two senses of pride Kyd links two senses of "highest": that is as high as he will get in his social climbing, hanged on a tree; and (obscenely) with a view to a supposed consequence of hanging, jabbing at Horatio's maximal erection.

This is brilliant, thrilling, stuff – and dangerous for the actors in all sorts of ways. (A director of a production that I saw called this the toughest scene in the play: transferring Horatio to a hook on a tree or wall so that he looks like a hanging man turned out to be awkward, even physically risky for the performer.)

At this moment Hieronimo enters, observes the body of his son (hanging like the body of The Son; the body will be removed, mourned with elaborate visual echo of the crucifixion), and speaks the first of his various soliloquies that mark out his path to vengeance. The soliloquies must be read as if one had never heard Hamlet recite his. These are different, intensely stylized and rhetorical in ways that can put off a twenty-first-century reader or audience. The point is to see what the rhetoric is doing – something that Elizabethan viewers with even a secondary education could well have managed. If we did not know it from the comic pedagogues of the Renaissance stage, we could judge from surviving textbooks that youngsters were constantly asked, in reading Latin verse and prose, to identify the figure of speech at work here. These figures are superficial and pedantic if handled superficially and pedantically. Kyd knows how to capitalize upon them.

As an example take the opening of act III, scene ii. Hieronimo calls for some sign from the heavens to account for his son's death. After the first 23 lines of the speech a new day dawns blood-red: a letter written in Bel-Imperia's blood *"falleth"* to explain that Lorenzo and his pack are responsible. But here is the passage:

> O eyes, no eyes, but fountains fraught with tears;
> O life, no life, but lively form of death;
> O world, no world, but mass of public wrongs,
> Confused and filled with murder and misdeeds!
> O sacred heavens! if this unhallowed deed,
> If this inhuman and barbarous attempt,
> If this incomparable murder thus
> Of mine, but now no more my son,
> Shall unrevealed and unrevengéd pass,
> How should we term your dealings to be just,
> If you unjustly deal with those that in your justice trust?
> The night, sad secretary to my moans,
> With direful visions wake my vexed soul,
> And with the wounds of my distressful son
> Solicit me for notice of his death.
> The ugly fiends do sally forth of hell,
> And frame my steps to unfrequented paths,
> And fear my heart with fierce inflamed thoughts.
> The cloudy day my discontents records,
> Early begins to register my dreams
> And drive me forth to seek the murderer.
> Eyes, life, world, heavens, hell, night, and day,
> See, search, show, send some man, some mean, that may –
>> *A letter falleth*

The passage opens with a figure called in Greek *epanorthosis*, in Latin, more revealingly, *correctio* or correction. Hieronimo corrects, revises: "O eyes, no eyes" and the like. But soon Hieronimo passes on this power of revision to his surroundings: "night" as "secretary" wakes him with "direful visions"; the "day [his] discontents records." Hieronimo begins the soliloquy revising, correcting; but by the time the "bloody writ" falls into his hands it is he who has been revised, or corrected. Hell has corrected him, redirected his steps to the "unfrequented paths" of revenge. This passage is indeed a showpiece of rhetoric; but it also brilliantly shows the psychological development of Kyd's protagonist.

Only after readers have duly attended to the function of Kyd's rhetorical figures should they risk the all but unavoidable comparisons with *Hamlet*. And the comparisons should at first proceed from the earlier work, *The Spanish Tragedy*. For whoever composed the first *Hamlet* play very probably did so in response to that work: creating a prince visited by a royal father's ghost who incites revenge where the earlier drama had a court functionary father (observed but not addressed by his murdered son's ghost), begging the heavens for some guidance as to the identity of the murderer. The two plays speak to one another systematically; and if *Hamlet* gets the last word, the word it offers is a systematic transformation of the schemata developed in *The Spanish Tragedy*.

Kyd's play ends, as it began, with the Ghost of Andrea and Revenge alone on stage. Andrea confidently assigns the various characters whose deaths we have observed to places in the classical underworld: Don Lorenzo will replace Ixion upon the wheel of torture. The bewildered Andrea of the play's opening has become a confident dispenser of what he takes to be justice. And if various Spaniards are in for an eternity of torture, that is something the contented Elizabethan spectators can no doubt live with. They too have been thrilled by the action of the play, rendered confident of their future, and not merely the literary future of the new sub-genre of tragedy that *The Spanish Tragedy* inaugurates. Andrea's realized dream of vengeance is, unbeknown to him, the audience's as well.

[handwritten marginal note:] cathartic function of the play

REFERENCES AND FURTHER READING

Allman, Eileen Jorge (1999). *Jacobean Revenge Tragedy and the Politics of Virtue*. Cranbury, NJ: Associated University Presses.

Ardolino, Frank R. (1995). *Apocalypse and Armada in Kyd's "Spanish Tragedy"*. Kirksville, MO: Sixteenth Century Journal Publishers.

Baldwin, William (1547). *A Treatise of Moral Philosophy*. London.

Bowers, Fredson Thayer (1940). *Elizabethan Revenge Tragedy 1587–1642*. Princeton: Princeton University Press.

Burnett, Anne Pippin (1998). *Revenge in Attic and Later Tragedy*. Berkeley: University of California Press.

Foakes, R. A., ed. (1966). *The Revenger's Tragedy Attributed to Cyril Tourneur*. London: Methuen.

Hallett, Charles A. and Elaine S. Hallett (1980). *The Revenger's Madness: A Study of Revenge Tragedy Motifs*. Lincoln: University of Nebraska Press.

Hickman, Ruby Mildred (1938). *Ghostly Etiquette on the Classical Stage*. Cedar Rapids, IA.: Torch Press.

Kyd, Thomas (1989). *The Spanish Tragedy*, ed. J. R. Mulryne. New Mermaid, 2nd edn. London: A. & C. Black; New York: Norton.

Norland, Howard B. (1998). "Kyd's formulation of the conventions of revenge tragedy." In *Tudor Theatre: "Let there be covenants . . .": Convention et Théâtre*. Bern: Peter Lang.

Seneca (1928). "On anger." In *Moral Essays*, trans. John W. Basore, vol. I. Cambridge, MA: Harvard University Press.

24
Staging the Malcontent in Early Modern England

Mark Thornton Burnett

In the literature and culture of early modern England, the figure of the malcontent loomed large. Lawrence Babb's seminal study of melancholy, *The Elizabethan Malady*, associates this male type with a range of identifiable features. Discontent was the trait most readily attributed to the malcontent, with a predilection for satirical railing, for cultivating a neglected appearance and a scornful attitude, and for broadcasting a sense of unrewarded abilities (Babb, 1951, 80, 83). Later critics have extended this list to encompass the malcontent's immersion in Italian vices, split between public and private roles, alienation from women, and rebellious tendencies (Finkelpearl, 1969, 184; Gomez, 1992, 67; Lyons, 1971, 17). Given this range of characteristics, it is perhaps not surprising that the malcontent should have proliferated into a spectrum of typological possibilities. As well as the melancholy traveler, the malcontent could adopt the mantle of the villain, the cynic, and the scholar (Babb, 1951, 76). The fixed hold of the malcontent on the social imaginary was reflected in the variety of ideological homes to which he gravitated.

Certainly, in the prose work of the period, the malcontent is given pride of place, being commemorated in lengthy and rhetorically demonstrative descriptions. At once, matching this descriptive mode, he is credited with a worrisome linguistic facility. Joseph Hall, writing in 1608, states that the "male-content" allows "his lawless tongue to walk through the dangerous paths of conceited alterations" (Hall, 1924, 78); as the terms suggest, what is unsettling about the malcontent is the likelihood of verbal laxity jeopardizing carefully demarcated arrangements and precipitating upset. It was a small step, therefore, to the view that the malcontent constituted a transgressively thrilling and potentially disruptive political force. Thomas Nashe writes in *Pierce Pennilesse* (1592) that the "malecontent . . . eates not a good meales meat in a weeke . . . take[s] vppe . . . melancholy in his gate . . . and talke[s] as though our common welth were but a mockery of gouernment" (Nashe, 1966, I, 170). Implicit here is the idea of a willed identity, an assumed posture of dejection, and this is reinforced through the passage's linking of voluntary material hunger and anti-establishment discourse. For Thomas Lodge, too, writing in 1596, there was a powerful equation between the malcontent's moody self-fashioning and bristly relationship with officialdom. The "malecontent . . . put[s] on [a] habite," Lodge maintains, to malign "his countrie wherein he was bred, his gratious Prince . . . he . . . [raises] so many monsters, that no cittie in Italie hath beene vnstained with them, and no kingdome in Europe vnmolested" (Lodge, 1596, 17–18). Now the implication is that the malcontent holds out the threat of national hybridization; such is his behavior that notions of Englishness will be compromised through a quasi-magical conjuration of the spirits of dissidence. Juxtaposed with the inception of the nation-state is the malcontent's treacherous liminality.

malcontent assummes a guise of discontent

If the malcontent was at odds with authority in its political manifestation, he also fretted against government in a more local guise. Throughout contemporary representations, he is set apart from a familial location as well as a larger cultural environment. In a 1628 account, John Earle argues that the "disease" of the "Discontented Man" (a synonym for the malcontent) can be traced to his having fallen out with a "hard father" (Earle, 1924, 196–7). Earle's perspective introduces a complicating dimension to popular constructions, arguing, as it does, for an explanatory rationale for the malcontent, one that inserts the type into a network of patriarchal responsibilities and understands him as an alleged victim of domestic breakdown. In speech and manner, comportment and conduct, the malcontent, in friction with the father and the fatherland, stood on the peripheries of the early modern world's most treasured institutions.

But it was in the drama that the malcontent made his most memorable impact. The theater of the English Renaissance is rife with competitors for the malcontent's credentials, from Hamlet in his tortured anxiety to Bosola in his sulky conviction of rejection, Jaques in his condemnation of vanity and Vindice in his frenzy for revenge (see chapter 23 above). This chapter argues for the centrality of the malcontent as an early modern phenomenon and posits a connection between the dramatic attention given to the type and a cultural climate of inequity and instability. In particular, it seeks to establish an historical embeddedness for the figure in the political and professional transformations of the sixteenth and seventeenth centuries, a series of developments that touched upon patronage opportunities, social ambitions, and generational difficulties. By concentrating on the examples of John Marston and George Chapman, the chapter suggests that, rather than a willed pose, the malcontent identity provided a means whereby the experience of rejection, and the entertainment of unorthodoxy, could be addressed and negotiated. Both Marston and Chapman, then, will be seen to an extent as themselves displaced products of a culture of melancholia. In their dramas – namely, *Antonio and Mellida* (1599–1600), *Antonio's Revenge* (c.1600), *The Malcontent* (1603), and *Bussy D'Ambois* (1603–4) – can be glimpsed the processes with which a divided subjectivity is brought into play. In particular, the energies invigorating the malcontent sensibility are translated into a vexed attitude toward language, a heightened theatricality, an alternately vituperative and venerating treatment of women, and a flirtation with phallic aggressiveness. In this

purpose of this essay

sense, the malcontent stands finally as a creation of gendered projections and an example of cultural marginalization at one and the same time.

To identify the determinants shaping the malcontent's rise to prominence, we need to turn to the period's institutional structures, which reveal an order of checks and balances that invariably undermined aspiration, kept back advancement, exacerbated sedition, and promoted grievance. In short, in the ideological apparatuses that accompanied England's civic organizations, there was ample scope for the malcontent to prosper. First, for the ambitious writer, professional success was by no means guaranteed, chiefly for the so-called "university wits," such as Lodge and Nashe, caught between an enervated patronage system and the as yet inchoate community of commercial publishing. Such uncertainty of opportunity at the level of writing was matched by similar blocks to progress at the Elizabethan court. The crown in the sixteenth and seventeenth centuries made sure of the faithful service of its supporters by distributing money, grants, political privileges, titles, and gifts of office. Peers of the realm received traditional gifts of perquisites, while the gentry were able to bid for knighthoods, posts in the shrievalty, and commissions of the peace. Aspirants lower down the scale either sought annuities, monopolies, and leases or exploited extra-official profits, what MacCaffrey terms an "indeterminate but ceaseless flow of gratuities, *douceurs*, and reciprocal favours" (1961, 111). Yet, by the end of the sixteenth century, it seemed to many as if Elizabeth's customary parsimony had hardened into ingratitude. Feelings of courtier resentment gathered force: annual fees had not been modified in response to inflation, few posts were permanent, and there was fierce competition for prizes that were shrinking in number. In 1584, the dean of Durham inveighed against Elizabeth, complaining that "rewards were not bestowed by those in authority upon such as deserved them" and highlighting "niggardness at court" (Esler, 1966, 138). The growing conviction was that hopes had been stultified by a queen who was no longer uberous.

In many respects, the situation of the frustrated courtier was symptomatic of the conditions afflicting other disgruntled groupings swelling the social polity. Younger sons, for instance, were attracted to the court as a mecca for potential aggrandizement. All too often, however, as Thirsk (1969, 359) points out, the younger son faltered on the path to greatness, "sacrificed" on the altar of "primogeniture." A similar fate awaited aspirants aiming to carve out materially profitable military careers. According to Keller (1993, 78), "noblemen commanders were troubled by their own inability to promote themselves . . . This social immobility resulted from their . . . prolonged absences" from the political center. In view of the depth of professional disappointment at many levels, then, the explosive uprising of a figure such as Robert Devereux, the earl of Essex, is easily comprehensible. Archetypally resentful, Essex was evoked in contemporary representations in terms that equated him with his theatrically malcontented counterparts. As William Camden wrote in 1600, Essex "is shifted . . . to rage and rebellion . . . uttering strange words . . . and . . . entertaineth . . . men of broken fortunes, discontented persons, and such as saucily use their tongues in railing against all" (Harrison, 1938, III, 127, 132). The linguistic excesses of Essex, familiar as a trait of the malcontent, were translated into the famed revolt of 1602 with its catastrophic consequences. Significantly, Essex was finally provoked to rebel against his queen when refused the renewal of his sweet-wines monopoly and excluded from the Accession Day tilt; once again, a parallel can be drawn between the denial of favor and the onset of malcontented preoccupations.

Although the specificities of Essex's case need to be acknowledged, it is striking that many of the barriers to elevation that marked his concluding days continued to surface in different forms well into the next century. Clearly, Elizabeth and James as founts of patronage operated according to opposing principles; where one fostered scarcity, the other invested in abundance. However, because of the multiplication of favorites controlling rewards under James, there "were inevitably more disappointed suitors than satisfied ones" (Lockyer, 1998, 96), with the result that a dysfunctional patronage system both weakened governmental capacities and alienated those local elites it was designed to conciliate. Judged alongside the perpetuation of practices that tended to militate against preferment, the emergence in early Stuart England of what Curtis terms the "alienated intellectual" takes on a singular urgency. According to Curtis, universities at this time produced more "trained men" and "educated talent" (1965, 299) than could be accommodated by the existing regime. These "individuals" suffered "frustration in the pursuit of their professions or careers, for opportunities to use their [skills] . . . were not available . . . they frequently had to accept posts . . . which, no matter how remunerative, could not entirely satisfy them. These positions . . . left them restless and critical" (1965, 299). In particular, the period witnessed the coming into being of an over-supply of lecturers and ministers, a grouping that, despite its ecclesiastical flavor, took comfort in a sense of its own importance and maintained a competitive distance from the rest of the clergy (1965, 306, 311). Of course, the tide of religious opposition that was to precipitate the civil war and the overturning of the monarchy had not yet settled upon a group identity, yet in the patron–client deadlocks and intellectual impasses of the early seventeenth century one is perhaps privy to its first stirrings. —>This discontent sowed the seeds of civil war

Whigham has written that the "social self" is shaped "in the abrasive zone between emergent and residual social formations" (1996, 223), and his hypothesis offers an intriguing point of entry into the conflicted universes of early modern malcontented playwrights. For both Marston and Chapman, I suggest, participate in, and strive against, a transforming environment in which institutional arrangements, trapped in a disempowering nexus of specialization and adulteration, expansion and constriction, reform and decay, were in flux, to the extent that the acquisition of privilege or recognition appeared an increasingly unlikely prospect. Notably, Marston articulates a response to the unstable equilibrium of his moment by promulgating in his poems a persona shot through with testy animosity. In the shifting versions of the "malecontent" (Marston, 1961, 75) that people his satires, it might be argued, can be discerned quasi-biographical echoes of thwarted aspiration. If one speaker in *Certaine Satyres* (1598), for instance, cogitates gloomily on the theme of being in "seruitude" with "no promotions liuelihood" (1961, 74), another, sheltering under the cloak of the

sardonic traveller, frets at the *"corrupted age, / Which slight regard'st men of sound carriage"* (1961, 76). More generally in the satires, constructions of grievance and injury
come to the fore via addresses to imaginary audiences and petitions to forces of salvation. In class-related condemnations, Marston endeavors to separate himself from
an encroaching popular market, rejecting in *The Scourge of Villainy* (1598) the "base
muddy scum" (1961, 97) that threatens to consume his art. As the grotesque imagery
suggests, the speaker conceives of his work as floating free from degeneration and
rising above its earthly bases. To position himself further from the taint of the lower
populace, Marston indulges in a fantasy of a fertile matriarch who offers ultimate sustenance. *The Scourge of Villainy* contains a prefatory dedication to *"Thou nursing Mother
of faire wisedoms lore"* (Marston, 1961, 102). The problem, however, is that such a figure
simultaneously represents *"Ingenuous Melancholy"* (1961, 102) and thus constitutes a
contradictory amalgam, a mixture of longed-for intellectual possibility and a reminder
of brute embodied realities. Appealing to his female savior serves only to recall to the
speaker the discontent from which he agitates to escape.

Pincered between social constituencies and a compromised maternity, the speaker
of the poems finds relief in scenes of phallic aggressiveness. Marston relished using
his self-appointed pseudonym, "W. Kinsayder" (Marston, 1961, 101), a jokey reference to "kinsing" (the castrating or docking of a dog) which alerted readers to a sub-
sidiary pun on testicles and his own name – Marston/Mar-stone. The implied jest is
that Marston will disempower his detractors at the level of the pen–phallus by marring
or silencing their instruments of literary reproduction. Not surprisingly, Marston as
a phallic satirist proved yet another double-edged creation, solidifying with an erec-
tile resonance his critical qualifications but also providing material for his contemporaries stylistically to take him to task. Joseph Hall had pasted into a number of
copies of *Pigmalion's Image* (1598) a derisive verse that reversed the poet's castratory
capacity and saw *him* as the ungelded "madde dogge" (Marston, 1961, 164): the identification did not escape Marston's notice and elicited an amused but acerbic reply.
Similarly, in *The Second Part of the Return from Parnassus* (1601–2), Marston is branded
as "Monsier Kinsayder, lifting vp [his] legge and pissing against the world" (*The Second
Part*, 1949, 241). "Put vp man . . . for shame," one character exclaims, while another
adds: "he . . . Cutts, thrusts, and foines at whomesoeuer he meets" (1949, 242). More
than one idea is concatenated here, but prominent is the suggestion of Marston's
phallic exhibitionism, a tumescent revelation that challenges the world in its simultaneously penetrative and discharging antagonism. Inaugurating the theme of
Marston's relieving himself, but from a contrasting perspective, was Ben Jonson: his
Poetaster (1601) contains a scene in which Crispinus, a parodic portrait of Marston,
is, in T. F. Wharton's words, "made to take a purge and painfully disgorge various
gobbets of unmistakably Marstonian neologisms" (1994, 11). Because of the ways in
which phallic traits define the Marstonian persona, it is tempting to see in this representation an ejaculatory jibe. Finally, Marston's agonistic relationship with "villainy"
is allowed to come to a climax, but in such a manner as to belittle the author and
subject his verbal fireworks to humiliating exposure.

I have been suggesting that Marston's absorption in the malcontent represented an ideological reply to a culture fascinated by, and immersed in, discourses of repressed opportunity. Yet such a claim should not bypass the material specificities of Marston's own experience, the biographical realities that lent his work its tone of dissatisfied acidity. In many respects, Marston's career path anticipated the disgruntled experiences of the seventeenth-century "alienated intellectual," hallmarked, as it was, by exclusion, dispossession, and crushed expectation. Even in his origins (Marston was born to an English father and an Italian mother), one might argue, the inception of a displaced and divided identity can be discerned. Hints of a disappointed separateness persist later into Marston's professional life; he was, for instance, lent 40s. by Philip Henslowe on September 28, 1599, a possible indication of lean finances. But the most severe example of deprivation emerges in Marston's own relationship with the *paterfamilias*. In the 1599 will of John Marston, the poet–playwright's father, an extended history of unrealized hopes and dispirited resignation is visible. One passage in the will runs: "my law books . . . to my . . . son, whom I hoped would have profited by them in the study of the law, wherein I bestowed my uttermost endeavour. But man proposeth and God disposeth." The gloomy timbre of the words notwithstanding, John Marston's confession shows considerably more restraint than an earlier, deleted draft: the books were left to "him that deserveth them not, that is my wilful disobedient son, who I think will sell them rather than use them, although I took pains . . . therein; God . . . give him true knowledge of himself . . . to forgo his delight in plays and vain studies and fooleries" (Pascoe, 1997, 97). Several familiar motifs are here brought into play: there is the narrative of the "Discontented Man" who falls out with his father, the hint of economic hardship, the implication of professional rejection, the conviction of misplaced self-awareness, and the promise of either retribution or rescue. In brief, the will mimes the trajectory of the contemporary malcontent, and, in this connection, it is ironically appropriate that all Marston finally received at his father's death in November was a "black trotting gelding" (Pascoe, 1997, 97).

Perhaps as a by-product of familial estrangement, Marston assumed over the course of his career a highly ambiguous stance toward constituted authority. On the one hand, he took up a dissident position. In 1599, two books of his satires were publicly burned on the orders of Archbishop Whitgift of Canterbury and Bishop Bancroft of London; in 1605, he was imprisoned with Jonson and Chapman for risky references in *Eastward Ho* to the king's recently appointed knights; and, on June 8, 1608, he was committed to Newgate, possibly in connection with an offensive play satirizing James' mining policies. On the other hand, rather than flouting the establishment, Marston constructed himself as equally concerned to enter its fold. Over the course of the latter part of his career, he executed his most dramatic gesture, a complete withdrawal from the world of metropolitan theater. Following on from his marriage in 1605 (his father-in-law was a cleric), he was, in 1609, ordained as a deacon and then a priest. From 1616 to his retirement in 1631, he was the incumbent of Christchurch in Hampshire. The only indication of a continuing relationship with the stage came in 1633 when he intervened in the publication of an octavo edition of six of his plays, insisting that all traces of his name be removed. Death claimed Marston in 1634, but not before he had been able to have confirmed for his tombstone the inscription "*Oblivioni Sacrum*" – "Sacred to oblivion."

Clearly evident from this biographical excursus is the extent to which Marston was pulled and distorted in antithetical directions by his times. The author exemplifies a desire for public recognition and a will to eschew it completely. A need to be acknowledged by the professional community coexists with, and rubs against, a drive to secure anonymity. Challenges to official languages are issued in the same moment as there are efforts to write within and to preserve their essential outlines, suggesting a psychological stalemate between censured and approved discursive arrangements. To adapt Dollimore's formulation, Marston was a "prototype of the modern decentred subject" (1989, 50).

As far as Chapman is concerned, a comparably malcontented career pattern is evident. Cursed with the degradation of the younger son, Chapman's professional aspirations were hampered from the start. Typically for an upwardly driven artist of his condition, he received a paltry patrimony – only £100 and two silver spoons – and was obliged, as a young man, to pursue a fruitless military career in the Low Countries. Continually restrained from promotion by his stretched economic circumstances, Chapman was blighted by a run of financial and legal disappointments. In 1585, he entered into bonds with two brokers; in 1599, he was forced to sell his interest in the moiety of Shephall Manor in Hitchin; in 1600, he was imprisoned for failure to honor a debt; and in 1613, again in jail because of debt, he wrote to the master of the revels complaining that he had not been adequately recompensed for a masque. Indeed, Chapman's impoverishment seems to have been particularly critical at this time: although he had been appointed sewer-in-ordinary to Henry, prince of Wales, the position evaporated at his royal master's death, as did a promised life-pension. Not unrelated to Chapman's predicaments were his constant endeavors to secure a patron, to establish a network of male bonds that would permit him to rise above the vagaries of fortune. At different points during his dramatic trajectory, he appealed to Sir Francis Bacon; the earl of Essex; Thomas Hariot; Philip Henslowe (from whom he received advances on 15 occasions); Francis, lord Russell; and Sir Walter Ralegh; lending support to Tricomi's suggestion that Chapman "constituted" a member of "a new, truly underprivileged class" (1989, 113). With such contexts in mind, Chapman's choice of dramatic material follows a predictable logic: invariably in his plays, he either satirizes a spendthrift court or represents the plight of disaffected political subjects. Like Marston, however, to whom he is eerily linked, Chapman did not persist in a posture of political recalcitrance. Arguably disillusioned with fathers both real and metaphorical, he turned from 1612 onward toward a more contemplative existence, retiring from the theatrical arena, choosing to live in Hitchin, the rustic place of his birth, and, until his death in 1634, exercising his mind in moral symbolism and philosophical idealism, chiefly through Homeric translations. Via such modalities of stoic withdrawal, one might argue, Chapman was able to cultivate mythological fantasies and visions of an untempered classical history that helped intellectually to offset the vicissitudes of his urban experience.

In a recent study, Breitenberg has argued that, because of "profound changes in virtually all aspects of its economic, political and social fabric" (1996, 17), early modern England was witness to a crisis of seemingly ubiquitous "masculine anxiety" (1996, 1). According to Breitenberg, such anxiety is portrayed as a "site of . . . competing elements," and the "individual" who suffers from its symptoms is invariably "at war with himself" (1996, 18). Earlier parts of this chapter have suggested that the divided sensibilities of Marston and Chapman trace their origins to biographical misfortunes that were themselves refractions of a larger social malaise. But such an interpretation should not blind us to the gendered manifestations that the culture of the malcontent could assume. Indeed, one might go so far as to suggest that both the figure of the malcontent and the conflicted careers of Marston and Chapman discover masculinities in states of dangerous extremity. This becomes apparent when the term – "malcontent" – is approached by way of early modern orthography. As this chapter's opening extracts make clear, "malcontent" in the period was frequently printed "male-content," which could convey that "males" and "discontent" were familiar bedfellows. Two further instances will reinforce the point. *Leycesters Commonwealth*, an anonymously published 1584 satire, argues that "there are so many suspitious, every where . . . as we cannot tell whom to trust. So many melancholique in the Court, that seeme male-contented . . . and such like unpleasant and unsavery stuffe" (Burgoyne, 1904, 219). The culinary metaphor enlisted in the passage consorts with hints about sexual fastidiousness and male alienation to underscore the impression of a political world made nervous by its thrifty female sovereign. An associated utilization of the idea is reserved for an epigram on Marston himself. John Davies in his *The Scourge of Folly* (first published in 1611) writes:

> Thy *Male-content*, or Male-contentednesse,
> Hath made thee change thy Muse as some do gesse;
> If Time mispent made her a *Male-content*,
> Thou needst not then her timely change repent . . .
> > Thou shalt be prais'd, and kept from want and wo;
> > So blest are crosses that do blesse vs so.
> > > (1878, II, 33)

Because it refers to events in London from 1608 to 1610, it is almost certain that the verse highlights Marston's retirement from the theater and change in muses. It trades upon the image of a malcontented man vexed by Fortune, who is identified as female. A fresh security is hinted at in the switch from playwriting to piety: the new muse is Christ, a comforting male benefactor, whose presence is implicit in the concluding emblem of the "crosses" (although there is also the suggestion that Marston himself has taken on the burden of crucifixion in response to his sexually reformed figurehead). As he ventures out to embrace his role as priest, it is implied that Marston is able to leave behind the gendered anxieties of a malcontented past.

Attending to the intersecting narratives of the malcontent in early modern England – the connections between satire and dissatisfaction, the dissident potentialities of language, the effect of institutional imbalances, the complicating contribution of gender, and the popularization of notions of exemption – provides a contextual framework for an assessment of Marston and Chapman's dramatic interests. As Marston's plays move inexorably from levity to disillusionment, for instance, a set of malcontented underpinnings emerges clearly into view. *Antonio and Mellida* (1599–1600) makes such a perspective immediately available to its audience. A sense of an embittered author is ventilated in the dedication, where Marston images himself as "most servingman-like, obsequiously making legs and standing, after our free-born English garb, bare-headed" (lines 14–16). Not only do these remarks evoke the fraught personae of Marston's poetry; they also introduce the specter of downward mobility, a prospect that the invocation of emancipation makes doubly unattractive. Tied to Marston's personal signature on his work is the play's investment in canine discourse. On a later occasion, Felice lashes out: "Vengeance to such dogs / That sprout by gnawing senseless carrion!" (II.i.121–2). His comment illuminates a paradoxical imperative – a Marstonian will to social elevation coupled with a corresponding realization that such a rise hinges upon parasitic corruption. Moreover, given the fact that, as Lyons points out, the "dog" was "the most common animal symbol of melancholy" (1971, 107), an additional dimension of meaning comes into play – the possibility that melancholia represents an incurable condition rather than a state of affairs that can be transcended through poetic action.

Equally reminiscent of the Marston of the satires are metaphorical articulations in *Antonio and Mellida* of phallic disempowerment. Invariably in the play masculinity is glimpsed as a beseiged and eviscerated entity. The courtier Mazzagente is described as a "notchèd stick" (I.i.136) that will easily "snap" (I.i.137) and as "the flagging'st bulrush that e'er drooped" (II.i.184): associations of fragile rectitude and repeated detumescence mark the portrait. Manliness, then, is disabled, and mainly because women are envisaged as possessing a greater influence in rhetorical terms. Casting into shadow conventional diatribes against women are those scenes in which female characters manipulate a verbal dexterity that reduces men either to impotence or to profitless expostulation. Castilio states that Rosaline's "wit stings, blisters, galls off the skin with the tart acrimony of her sharp quickness" (II.i.60–1). The ways in which Rosaline is credited with reversing the traditional skills of the male satirist, to the extent that she strips her masculine opponents of all linguistic dignity, are arresting. At a deeper level, Rosaline is destabilizing, the play suggests, because she transforms men into a living anatomy, appropriating the functions of other traditional male professionals – the torturer, the anatomist, and the executioner.

By contrast, male protagonists in *Antonio's Revenge* (*c*.1600) appear unprepared for the rigors of rhetorical combat. In keeping, perhaps, with the early date of the drama, Marston presents his malcontented spokesmen as fledgling types, apprentices in the arts of protest. Dressed as Florizel, the Amazon, Antonio stands betwixt and between well-defined identities, a comic malcontent whose divided role is communicated through his gendered disguise. Like the pubescent boy actor, Antonio sits on the cusp of masculinity and femininity, on states of possibility, an index of an as yet unrealized performative power. Not surprisingly, his habitual practice is to fall to the ground, his action indicating both a loss of control and psychological and philosophical paralysis. As Antonio states, he cannot "find himself, not seize himself" (IV.i.3). For the character Felice, criticism comes more easily, particularly when he bluntly labels Piero a "thing" (V.ii.136), reducing the monarch to an object and robbing him of special status. However, Felice is simultaneously in training for his part and wavers in the targets he selects for abuse: he indulges in sleep, for instance, sleeplessness being one of the malcontent's distinguishing features.

If grievances are not consistently registered in representatives of masculinity, they are in repeated linguistic formulations. *Antonio's Revenge* is distinctive for initiating a spectrum of verbal motifs that were to serve Marston well throughout his theatrical life. In particular, imagery of strangulation, swelling (Induction.11–12), and exploding (III.ii.180) is exploited for its phallic properties to communicate an illusion of escalating tension and unsettling release. But the implication is not always pejorative. At the close, Piero's reformation is signaled in the play's customary stylistic modes, here inverted to undergird reconciliation. Thus Andrugio's "joy's passion" (V.ii.238) "chokes the current of his speech" (V.ii.239), while Balurdo "grow[s] stiff" (V.ii.268) with the "passion" (V.ii.266) of the moment. The instruments of the malcontented psyche are incorporated within a mannered finale, a curative maneuver that heals friction, reinstates a "healthy" sexuality, and promotes absolution.

Where particular languages in *Antonio and Mellida* are manipulated to make a concluding point, in *Antonio's Revenge* they constitute a focus of major anxiety. Indeed, in this play, the limits and possibilities of both words and theater are arguably the overriding preoccupations. Language, as Marston conceives it, simultaneously defines character and, as also for Jonson, precipitates a breakdown in personal relationships. Controlling means of verbal expression, in addition, ensures the acquisition of political privilege. When Piero warns his accomplice not to "stroke . . . the head / Of infant speech till it be fully born" (I.i.39–40), it is suggested that he acts as an arbiter of language and the midwife of its delivery, taking upon himself the powers attached to its subsequent development. In contrast, Antonio, still something of a junior malcontent, is tongue-tied, struggling for adequate articulation. Even Seneca's *De providentia*, which he peruses, fails to represent his frustrations accurately: "Pish! Thy mother was not lately widowed, / Thy dear affièd love lately defamed / With blemish of foul lust when thou wrot'st thus" (II.ii.50–2). Between the printed book and the gathering storm of Antonio's passions, there is an unbridgeable divide. By deciding upon revenge, therefore, Antonio is as much reacting against technologies of communication as he is striving to settle personal scores.

Characters do not only draw attention to themselves at the level of language; to represent their conditions they borrow from vocabularies of theatrical performance. As it progresses, the play constructs enmity in terms of acting styles; on the one hand, there is the "apish action" (I.ii.315) of stamping, weeping, and cursing arraigned by

Pandulpho; on the other, there are the transparent histrionics approved by a director-like Piero and imitated by his acolytes. Performing being the dominant modality of his universe, Antonio's decision to disguise himself as the court fool makes logical sense. He exclaims:

> there is no essence mortal
> That I can envy but a plump-cheeked fool.
> O, he hath a patent of immunities
> Confirmed by custom, sealed by policy
> As large as spacious thought.
>
> (IV.i.11–15)

Interestingly, the speech highlights a number of typically malcontented fantasies. It underscores the idea of donning a part; reminds us of the malcontent's harried lean-ness; focuses on the prospect of intellectual emancipation; stresses the legally approved character of Antonio's actions; and gives free rein to the discourse that challenges a prince. However, as the term "policy" suggests, Antonio, through his foolery, will simultaneously need to employ tactics of Machiavellian expediency: equally familiar here are hints of adulteration, of the disintegration of the malcontent's moral integrity.

To convey an impression of mounting frustrations, Marston sounds variations on tried and trusted stratagems. Desire for vengeance is etched first in imagery of break-ing or bursting out, as when Balurdo remembers his dream about the simile "belched up" (I.ii.127) by the ground: connotations of vomiting, linguistic parturition, and monstrous birth lend his recollection an agitated thematic intensity. Verbal patterns are replicated in stage incidents and stylized dramatic tableaux. For Pandulpho, the strictly demarcated limits of language collapse, and he laughs maniacally (I.ii.260). The moment is returned to when the ghost of Andrugio ruptures the con-fines of its resting-place to enjoin Antonio to execute revenge (V.i.17–25). Such episodes are highly charged in and of themselves, but they work primarily as the formal equivalents, both aural and visual, of the play's prevailing motifs. Second, Marston, true to the spirit of the popular construction of the malcontent, deploys familial metaphors to query patriarchal operations. At the start of the drama, Maria salutes Antonio in a speech that is a composite of commonplaces on the theme of the family ideal:

> Fair honour of a chaste and loyal bed,
> Thy father's beauty, thy sad mother's love
> . . . all the blessings that a poor . . . wretch
> Can pour upon thy head, take, gentle son;
> Live, gracious youth.
>
> (I.ii.160–1, 164–6)

Although virtue and conjugal harmony are pinpointed in the address, they are sen-sationally overturned by the appearance of the body of Felice, suspended and riddled with wounds. The revelation of the murder defamiliarizes Maria's words, replacing union with divorce, liquid benediction with mortal blood, and heteronormative desire with a perverse homoeroticism. Procreative suggestions are contravened by the presentation on the stage of a ghastly extinction, while religious associations are upset through the spectacle of an anatomy "*hung up*" (I.iii.192, s.d.), possibly in the form of a parodic crucifixion. Having lulled his audience into rhetorical security, the playwright promptly explodes the illusion to shocking effect.

Nowhere is *Antonio's Revenge* more unnerving than in its closing stages, which tie the play's considerations together in a particularly grotesque twist. A cluster of allusions to eating and gluttony (Balurdo's hunger and Piero's feasting) paves the way for the horror in the masque of the tyrant being pressed cannibalistically to ingest the remains of his own son, an apt punishment for his inordinate appetites. It is also hideously fitting that, having attempted to command speech, Piero should have his tongue forcibly taken out. Not only a realization of the revengers' claim to speak freely, the removal of Piero's linguistic instrument resembles another monstrous birth, a cesarean-type delivery that might bring about a new order. Finally, because Piero is dispatched within a species of play-within-a-play, theatricality is granted its most extravagantly summative statement. The degree of regeneration attendant on Piero's death, however, remains ambiguous. On being asked "Whose hand presents this gory spectacle?" (V.iii.115), all the revengers claim responsibility, creating a bickering triumvirate that recalls the jockeying machinations of their bloody victim. Venice has been decontaminated, but in the process something more dreadfully circular has emerged. The revengers' decision to "live enclosed / In holy verge of some religious order" (V.iii.149–50) exacerbates the irresolution by stressing the need for a compensating self-sacrifice. There is no celebration here, merely a Lenten abstinence; nor can language be resurrected, since cloistered silence will be the dominant characteristic. Familial reconstruction, too, proves untenable. Antonio states that, since Mellida "lives in me, with her my love is dead" (V.iii.157), and vows to occupy a "virgin bed" (V.iii.156): birth and sterility enmesh in the image of the pregnant lover who will never deliver his burden. It is possible to see in these gloomy declarations the coming of age of the malcontented sensibility: Marston's discontented protagonists are left to reckon up the costly consequences of fulfilled ambitions. More likely Marston is now driven to speculate about the void left behind when the model of the malcontent is no longer available as a representational resource. Crucially, therefore, the revengers are ultimately discovered as deformed abstractions, purged of embodiment (V.iii.163–8) and in seach of penitence. The play itself has given birth not to a political solution but to a prodigious absence.

If *Antonio's Revenge* concentrates on malcontents who exercise their powers only in the final moments, *The Malcontent* (1603), as its title implies, consistently privileges the vituperative wit of Malevole, its central satirical voice. This is also the play in which the barbed utterances of Marston's poems are given their most wide-ranging dramatic license. A number of derelictions vex Malevole, but prominent among his concerns is the social degeneration that has resulted in a universe of worryingly irreconcilable binary opposites. To Bilioso he remarks: "And how does my old muckhill overspread with fresh snow? Thou half a man, half a goat, all a beast, how does thy

young wife, old huddle?" (I.i.70–2). More than one polarity is mobilized in the statement: heat mixes strangely with cold, age with youth, purity with decay. There is
also the suggestion of dissolving boundaries (human and animal classifications are
drifting signifiers), which the allusion to hidden but ubiquitous excrement serves only
to emphasize. Malevole's Genoa is, then, a world of no fixed bearings, a territory whose
explanatory mechanisms share only the common denominator of a perceived venality.
In such a system, identities float and are confused, and even traditional gendered
arrangements are seen to be in flux. Distinctively, the play introduces antithetically
organized attitudes toward its female personalities. In the same moment, the category
of "woman" is judged from a variety of interpretive standpoints. According to Malevole, Maquerelle, the bawd, is noted for her "restoratives for your decayed Jasons? Look
ye, crab's guts baked, distilled ox-pith, the pulverised hairs of a lion's upper-lip, jelly
of cock-sparrows, he-monkey's marrow, or powder of fox-stones?" (II.ii.18–21). At
once it would seem as if this Jonsonian litany of material things is designed merely
to further the impression of a dramatic environment breaking up into its constituent
parts, melting into a set of dissociated fragments. Deeper in its interstices, however,
the description functions at a gendered level as a summary of the signs of a crushed
masculinity: all the creatures named were reputed libidinous. And although Maquerelle must claim responsibility for the process (the animals' essences are the chief
ingredient of her potions), she is also a vehicle of profane resurrection. Her melting-
pot of medicines, it is claimed, has the capacity to bring men back to a state of wholeness: as a result, the bawd figures simultaneously as an agent of sexual decline and as
a medium for miraculous recovery.

A closer look at *The Malcontent*, indeed, reveals that the play as a whole harps obses-
sively on themes of bodily and physical infraction. Whatever social abuses plague
Genoa, the drama implies, have their point of origin in a corrupted sexuality. When
Maquerelle asks Ferneze to "give me those jewels of your ears" and states that she "can
bear patiently with any man" (I.ii.6, 8), for instance, it is suggested that she is able
to trade state secrets for the pleasures of the bed: a mutually reinforcing relationship
is established between the subterfuge of prostitution and the circulation of political
knowledge. Elaborating upon this vision, Marston exploits two of his favorite stylistic idioms, the dog and the phallus. Phallic expletives such as "*Cazzo!*" ("prick":
I.i.137) and penile puns such as "pricked" (II.iv.113) come easily to Malevole, who
deploys his satire like a rudimentary male organ: it is the "privy key" (I.i.290) with
which he will both unlock and correct a court in disrepair. If he represents a refor-
matory penis, Malevole also performs as a metaphorical "hound" (I.i.53), pursuing
chosen quarries and spearheading the chase to rout out decadent prey. But, as the play
makes clear, the dog can operate no less powerfully as an emblem of servility (II.i.22)
and social inferiority (II.ii.56), and this sensitizes us both to Marston's touchy sense
of his own identity and to his frustrated relation to a perceived dependency. Thus
Maquerelle's sexually resonant disquisition on her "two court dogs, the most fawning
curs, the one called Watch, th'other Catch" (V.i.16–17) is intriguingly multivalent:
"I, like Lady Fortune, sometimes love this dog, sometimes raise that dog, sometimes

favour Watch, most commonly fancy Catch" (V.i.17–19). Mythological ironization, psychological encouragement, and phallic development all jostle with each other in the passage. Dominating, however, is a construction of professional stasis, a state of affairs vividly familiar to Marston and arguably realized in the arbitrary practices of his bawdy female creations.

Perhaps because of personal investment in this his most satirically dense work, Marston imbues *The Malcontent* with a particularly acerbic tone. Not surprisingly, Malevole's voluminous condemnations are likened to "bespurtling" (I.i.19), which evokes not only a dog's urinating and ejaculating but also marking ideological territory. As a malcontent, Malevole is not unsuccessful in his reconstructive design. True, he distinguishes himself from Maquerelle by using disguise eventually to engineer exposure rather than promote deceit. To Pietro he teaches the arts of governmental expediency, and in the false duke's religious conversion toward the end there is perhaps an echo of Marston's own departure for the world of the spirit. Yet Malevole is also flawed as the architect of a new regime. Like a later Shakespearean protagonist, Prospero, Malevole owes his downfall to a lack of political perspicacity; as he confesses, "I wanted those old instruments of state" (I.i.212). Thus, when he finally reveals himself to resume authority, questions about his own learning experience still circulate. Despite the reunions and banishments of the last scene, the reinstated oligarchy of Genoa can appear worryingly unchanged in its essential contours.

In contrast to Marston, who exploits the popular image of the malcontent in all of its manifestations, Chapman elects to take up the well-established traits of the figure only to subject them to inversionary treatment. To a large extent, the central protagonist of *Bussy D'Ambois* (1603–4) would seem at first sight to answer to all the relevant malcontented criteria. In his opening speech, Bussy lies down in a dejected pose to complain that:

> Fortune, not Reason, rules the state of things,
> Reward goes backwards, Honour on his head;
> Who is not poor, is monstrous; only Need
> Gives form and worth to every human seed.
>
> (I.i.1–4)

The defeatist productivity animating this rhetorical tour de force assists the articulation of a utilitarian perspective on an arbitrary universe. For Bussy, the only movement has been retrogressive, his comment on reversed direction encapsulating a fraught sense of inertia. Now need is the new deity, a realization that affords a potential conceptual reorganizing of the heavenly system. As the speech implies, Bussy is also constructed as an intellectual *manqué*, a creative force that has been taken up by the ruling order quickly to be discarded. "I am a scholar, as I am a soldier" (I.i.183), he states, "And I can poetise" (I.i.184). The claim resonates with the popular image of the malcontented soldier while simultaneously enhancing the representation of Bussy as an artist, one for whom, as the darkness in which he habitually conceals himself suggests, there has been scant regard. But rather than playing this malcontented music more loudly, Chapman steers his hero in some unexpected directions. Scenes of satiric objection are mostly understated, and, when an extended series of critical speeches is finally staged, it is set in the context of a flyting match between Bussy and Monsieur, a dramatic move which substitutes rhetorical showiness for purposeful arraignment. In general in the play, Bussy is presented as a railer only after he has been elevated and has shrugged off the root causes of his alienation; in this way, the playwright both limits and minimizes the effect of his outrage. The guiding imperative would seem to be to elaborate a Marstonian hint, to imagine the post-malcontented malcontent and the state of the world once his frustrations have been exorcized.

Over the course of the drama, the heroic protagonist emerges as a mélange of conflicting factors and energies. Apparently disconnected features cluster about Bussy, making a uniform judgment hazardous. On the one hand, he epitomizes qualities of *virtù* and prowess, as when he displays "sudden bravery, and great spirit" (II.i.2) in a duel with his opponents, the term "spirit" being frequently deployed to indicate Bussy's brand of chivalric masculinity. He is similarly credited with a regenerative ability, the power to bring greatness to others through deeds of personal magnificence. "In his rise . . . shall my bounties shine" (I.i.51), states Monsieur, imaging Bussy as a mirror of his own ambitions. On the other hand, the play seeks to stress the fragility of these virtues in the face of court intrigue. A reference to "apes, disfigur'd with the attires of men" (I.ii.50), for instance, looks forward to the entrance of Bussy dressed as a gallant, implying that he is falling prey to distortion, being possessed by processes he would ostensibly resist. On a later occasion, Bussy is envisaged as the king's "Eagle" (III.ii.4), but this is uncomfortably close to an earlier realization of "Envy" (II.i.4) as a "kite" (II.i.5), and suggests an unsettlingly rivalrous dimension to the monarch–favorite equation. Given such discontinuities, it is not to be wondered at that the play should be equally concerned to read characterological inconsistency in terms of political subversion. Indeed, Bussy is noted for his singularly unconventional institutional philosophizing, arguing for a type of native nobility that transcends his civil location. A latter-day Tamburlaine, Bussy can be seen as dangerous in that he constructs himself as his own ruler: he will bypass the law in favor of an order based on merit and his own sense of rightness.

Bussy D'Ambois, then, is no straightforward elaboration of the malcontent. Not so much the reformer of his environment, Bussy, like Bosola, is viewed more as its product, the variations in his character serving as an index to a disjointed universe. Such innovation in dramatic procedure extends, too, to the play's gendered discovery of its subjects. Typically, a malcontent play invests, even if ambivalently, in a discourse that convicts women of presumed infidelities. Chapman's work proves no exception, as is demonstrated in Friar Comolet's reflections on female dissembling (II.ii.225–36) or Monsieur's spun-out discussion of "the unsounded Sea of women's bloods, / That when 'tis calmest, is most dangerous" (III.ii.286–7), which naturalizes an idea of female treachery via references to the ordinary world. What is distinctive about *Bussy D'Ambois*, however, is the fact that few of these detractions issue from the mouth of its soldier hero. By excluding him from a culture of "masculine anxiety" about women, the play seeks, in fact, to create a dynamic alignment between Bussy and his lover, Tamyra, who is fashioned as his ideological equal. Once their mutual interest has been kindled, Bussy and Tamyra begin to acknowledge an uncanny kinship. For instance, Tamyra's recognition that her "fancy . . . rageth" (II.ii.38, 42) and cannot be contained recalls her lover's explosions of "spirit"; her desire for "Fortune" (II.ii.165) to cease revolving reminds an audience of his more despairing attitude toward the goddess; and her "constant . . . virtue" (III.i.53) complements Bussy's single-minded cultivation of similar attributes. One might argue that Chapman resolves the gendered dilemmas of many a malcontent by framing the figure's anxieties within a broader canvas. *Bussy D'Ambois* contains not one malcontent but two, and the piecing out of particularized preoccupations between male and female personalities allows the play to entertain a more interpretively capacious perspective. The dramatist exorcizes the ghosts of a homoerotically identified Marstonian malcontent (the male-content can also connote the male contented with or pleased by other men), replacing them with an offsetting, heteronormative male-content and "female-content." For Chapman, confrontation with the world is less a solitary enterprise than a shared endeavor between like-minded representatives of psychological pre-eminence.

Departures from a malcontented norm persist into the drama's closing stages. Notably, Tamyra is not straightforwardly punished for her transgressions. Admittedly, she is obliged to separate from the abused Montsurry, but the refusal to consign her to a generic bloodbath permits a fuller registration of her symbolic importance. On the surface, Bussy, too, would appear to be valorized. As death approaches, he confronts his murderers, rescues his lover from obloquy and "Envy" (V.iii.109), and is transmogrified into a new "star" (V.iii.269) in the "firmament" (V.iii.271), an abiding reminder of his extraordinary abilities. More cynically, the play finally represents Bussy as a victim of explanatory exhaustion, incapable, despite his intellectualism, of making sense of his experience. The soldier–poet can only remark that he has breathed a "Courtier's breath" (V.iii.132), that his moment of efflorescence came and went with the rapidity of a "thunderbolt" (V.iii.192), and that he resembles a "Roman statue" (V.iii.144), externally uplifting but petrified and robbed of a feeling interior. This, then, in spite of Chapman's experiments with and revisions to the type, is the fate of the malcontent, a vision of the nihilism attendant upon the achievement of long-frustrated aspiration. For both Marston and Chapman, the malcontented male and female were forever expressions of discontent, trapped in a world where new knowledges only exacerbated an awareness of irremediable crisis.

NOTE

My thanks to Ewan Fernie for his generous and stimulating comments on a draft of this chapter.

References and Further Reading

Babb, Lawrence (1951). *The Elizabethan Malady: A Study of Melancholia in English Literature from 1580 to 1642.* East Lansing: Michigan State College Press.

Breitenberg, Mark (1996). *Anxious Masculinity in Early Modern England.* Cambridge: Cambridge University Press.

Burgoyne, Frank J., ed. (1904). *History of Queen Elizabeth, Amy Robsart and the Earl of Leicester, Being a Reprint of "Leycesters Commonwealth".* London: Longmans, Green.

Chapman, George (1979). *Bussy D'Ambois*, ed. N. S. Brooke. Manchester: Manchester University Press.

Curtis, Mark H. (1965). "The alienated intellectuals of early Stuart England." In *Crisis in Europe, 1560–1660*, ed. Trevor Aston. London: Routledge and Kegan Paul.

Davies, John (1878). *The Scourge of Folly.* In *The Complete Works*, ed. Alexander B. Grosart. 2 vols. Edinburgh: Edinburgh University Press.

Dollimore, Jonathan (1989). *Radical Tragedy: Religion, Ideology and Power in the Drama of Shakespeare and his Contemporaries.* 2nd edn. Hemel Hempstead: Harvester Wheatsheaf.

Earle, John (1924). *Microcosmography.* In *A Book of "Characters"*, ed. Richard Aldington. London: Routledge.

Esler, Anthony (1966). *The Aspiring Mind of the Elizabethan Younger Generation.* Durham, NC: Duke University Press.

Finkelpearl, Philip J. (1969). *John Marston of the Middle Temple: An Elizabethan Dramatist in his Social Setting.* Cambridge, MA: Harvard University Press.

Gomez, Christine (1992). "The malcontent strain in Hamlet." *Hamlet Studies* 14, 67–73.

Hall, Joseph (1924). *Characters of Virtues and Vices.* In *A Book of "Characters"*, ed. Richard Aldington. London: Routledge.

Harrison, G. B., ed. (1938). *The Elizabethan Journals, 1591–1603.* 3 vols. London: Routledge.

Keller, James R. (1993). *Princes, Soldiers and Rogues: The Politic Malcontent of Renaissance Drama.* New York: Peter Lang.

Lockyer, Roger (1998). *James VI and I.* London and New York: Longman.

Lodge, Thomas (1596). *Wits Miserie.* London: A. Islip.

Lyons, Bridget Gellert (1971). *Voices of Melancholy: Studies in Literary Treatments of Melancholy in Renaissance England.* London: Routledge and Kegan Paul.

MacCaffrey, W. T. (1961). "Place and patronage in Elizabethan politics." In *Elizabethan Government and Society: Essays Presented to Sir John Neale*, eds S. T. Bindoff, J. Hurstfield, and C. H. Williams. London: Athlone.

Marston, John (1961). *The Poems*, ed. Arnold Davenport. Liverpool: Liverpool University Press.

Marston, John (1997). *"The Malcontent" and Other Plays*, ed. Keith Sturgess. Oxford and New York: Oxford University Press.

Nashe, Thomas (1966). *Pierce Penilesse.* In *The Works*, ed. Ronald B. McKerrow. 5 vols. Oxford: Blackwell.

Pascoe, David (1997). "Marston's childishness." *Medieval and Renaissance Drama in England* 9, 92–111.

The Second Part of the Return from Parnassus (1949). In *The Three Parnassus Plays (1598–1601)*, ed. J. B. Leishman. London: Nicholson and Watson.

Thirsk, Joan (1969). "Younger sons in the seventeenth century." *History* 54, 358–77.

Tricomi, Albert H. (1989). *Anticourt Drama in England 1603–1642.* Charlottesville: University Press of Virginia.

Wharton, T. F. (1994). *The Critical Fall and Rise of John Marston.* Columbia, SC: Camden House.

Whigham, Frank (1996). *Seizures of the Will in Early Modern English Drama.* Cambridge: Cambridge University Press.

25
City Comedy
John A. Twyning

In 1501, England's capital city could be described thus:

> London, thou art of towns *a per se.*
> 　　Sovereign of cities, seemliest in sight,
> Of high renown, riches and royalty;
> 　　Of lords, barons, and many a goodly knight;
> 　　Of most delectable lusty ladies bright;
> Of famous prelates in habits clerical;
> 　　Of merchants full of substance and might:
> London, thou art the flower of cities all.
> 　　(Dunbar, "In honour of the city of London,"
> 　　　　cited in Manley, 1986, 52)

Whatever the truth of this eulogy, with its organic sense of social harmony, this was the London ideal from which later city literature departed. By the 1590s this image was thoroughly satirized by writers like Thomas Nashe: "For Londoners are none more hard-hearted and cruel . . . The snake eateth the toad, the toad the snake. The merchant eats up the gentleman, the gentleman eats up the yeoman, and all three do nothing but exclaim upon one another" (McKerrow, 1958, II, 159). Nashe's organicism is base and bestial, as he measures class antagonism in menacingly apocalyptic terms. The flower of cities had developed an underworld which imaginatively and materially challenged the seemliness of its appearance. These two views, encomiastic and satirical, both from different literary traditions in English culture, crystallize the production of discourses of London in this period.

In the early sixteenth century, the flower of cities appeared predominantly in semi-official texts like panegyrics or chronicles. As the century bloomed, London generated a huge increase in the style, quantity, and development of texts which featured itself. A variety of popular prose literature unfolded, beginning in the 1560s, such as the rogue literature written by Thomas Harman, Robert Greene, and Thomas Dekker.

This work, like Harman's cony-catching pamphlet, *A Caveat for Common Cursitors*, purported to offer insights and warnings into the nefarious activities of London's developing underworld (Salgādo, 1972). The pamphlets established a number of things: a set of sub-urban characters, a rogues' gallery; a catalogue of the ways in which the honest denizen could be duped or deceived; and a lexicon by which these city types could be understood. A number of important developments accrued from the success of these prosaic pamphlets. Most notably, a new kind of urban reading constituency was forged, one which imaginatively charted and conceptualized London's unofficial places, its liberties, suburbs, and outer boundaries. Intimately connected to this constituency was a new breed of writers: men like Greene, Nashe, and Dekker, who, albeit reluctantly, wrote without patrons as they sold their work to bolster a burgeoning publishing industry. Such authors and audience provided the wellspring which nourished the rapidly growing theaters, the medium which generated city comedy toward the end of the sixteenth century.

Although the character of London sprawled on to the late sixteenth-century stage in mostly comedic form, a precise definition of city comedy eludes us. Some scholars make the point that terms like city comedy, Jacobean city comedy, and citizen comedy are no more than "convenient label[s] for the editor and critic" (Salgādo, 1975, 9). While there is some truth to this, the various terms speak to different ways of understanding what was happening on and off the stage in early modern London. In Brian Gibbons' formative and influential account, a group of 20–30 plays written between 1598 and 1616 constitute a specific genre: Jacobean city comedy.[1] As city comedy changed the scope of the politics involved in courtship and marriage toward satire and cynicism, it irrevocably tarnished the notion of romance which had been the hallmark of earlier comedies. For Gibbons, the writers responsible for this were Ben Jonson, John Marston, and Thomas Middleton: "these playwrights had self-consciously, sometimes aggressively, forged the new form, City Comedy, and the mood of the plays was notably hostile to the earlier tradition of non-satiric, popular, often sentimental London comedies such as Dekker's *The Shoemaker's Holiday*" (1968, 15).

The Shoemaker's Holiday has proven to be something of a touchstone in the assay of city comedy. Based on Thomas Deloney's romance, *The Gentle Craft*, Dekker's version is seen by many to echo sentiments which depict London blooming into a city of social harmony (Kastan, 1987). As he explores the impulse to suppress and reconcile social conflict in turn-of-the-century romances, Lawrence Manley cites Dekker's play: "By uniting an even broader range of social types, from the maimed apprentice to the King of England, Dekker's *The Shoemaker's Holiday* (1599) lays to rest in similarly romantic fashion a potential for class strife which the play identifies with the farcical cycle of predation" (Manley, 1995, 441). Whereas Gibbons makes the case that the satirical bounds of Jacobean city comedy are defined by their exclusion of such sentiments and structures found in Elizabethan romance, Manley sees the different forms as having a symbiotic or dialectical relationship. "There is probably no city comedy," he says, whereby "romantic and farcical, utopian and satiric possibilities are not in some sort of tension." Accordingly, "the dark, demystifying turn of Jacobean city comedy depended in many respects on the exploitation of the farcical potential that had been suppressed by the romantic bias of much earlier popular theater comedy" (Manley, 1995, 442). With its cross-class lovers and festive reconciliations, *The Shoemaker's Holiday*, along with plays like *Four Prentices of London* by Thomas Heywood and *The Merry Wives of Windsor* by Shakespeare, figures as such a moment of suppression. It is a definitive one, too: "much of the history of city comedy is a history of dissent against romance dynamics of the kind represented in Dekker's plays" (Manley, 1995, 444). Influenced by L. C. Knights, Gibbons does not admit Dekker, Heywood, or (for different reasons) Shakespeare as contributors to the genre. Even Dekker's *If This Be not a Good Play, the Devil Is In It* is excluded, though it precedes Jonson's *The Devil Is an Ass*, which is cited as the apotheosis of city comedy. Although Gibbons credits Middleton with the "establishment" of the "form" of city comedy after Jonson, comedies like *The Honest Whore* plays or *The Roaring Girl* (co-authored by Dekker and Middleton) are, perhaps, considered to be too contaminated by Dekker's sentimental pen to be included. If this be not a Dekker play, then it must be a city comedy. The point here is not to argue for the inclusion of Dekker, or to lament his exclusion, but to argue that critical categories have a profound impact on how we perceive comedy and the city in the early modern period. The question of genre, then, defines our sense of how we map London in terms of its social and dramatic dimensions.

One way to deal with *The Shoemaker's Holiday* and similar plays was to create a subgenre which addresses more precisely the content of these works. And, following Knights' taxonomic terminology (1937) – "Dekker, Heywood and Citizen Morality" – this is what Alexander Leggatt achieves in *Citizen Comedy in the Age of Shakespeare* (1973). Despite the title – Shakespeare never wrote a true citizen comedy – Leggatt explains the term "citizen comedy" as "comedy set in a predominantly middle-class social milieu" (1973, 3). Here, middle-class means "shopkeepers, merchants, and craftsmen who are rich enough to employ the labor of men . . . and usually are clearly identified as such in the drama" (1973, 3). Although the "plays are written *about* the middle-class, they are not necessarily written *for* them," Leggatt notes, except "the citizen heroes of Dekker and Heywood" (1973, 4). Thus the shoemaker Simon Eyre stands in this account as the paradigmatic figure of middle-class virtues; with *The Shoemaker's Holiday* exemplifying what Manley calls "a neofeudal burgher ethos" (1995, 442). By dint of his ability to enact the values of hard work and social harmony, Simon Eyre comes to represent an old-fashioned merchant "full of substance and might." He embodies the traditions set out in John Stow's *A Survey of London* (1603), which reconceptualized London's history to include a long line of bourgeois benefactors and citizen worthies (1971).

Yet, however much plays like Dekker's tapped the popularity of Stow's *Survey*, they cannot be accounted for by their being written "for" the middle class. Assessing the demographic makeup or class affiliation of the play's audience is difficult to do – but it is hard to imagine people flocking into the theaters to be inducted into a "morality that the average decent citizen would find acceptable" (Knights, 1937, 231). This is not to say that the audience was amoral; rather, the motive for playgoing should not be determined by the subject of the drama. In a broader, more formal and stylistic sense, "'citizen comedy' cuts across a variety of comic modes: we find ourselves dealing with the satiric, the didactic, and the simply amusing, with everything from lightweight farce to pieces that verge on domestic drama" (Leggatt, 1973, 4). Such a view allows Leggatt to consider a gamut of urban characters, which he couches in binary distinctions, to exemplify citizen comedy: citizen heroes and villains, prodigals, intriguers, chaste maids and whores. John Marston's *fabulæ argumentum* – "the difference betwixt the love of a courtesan and a wife is the full scope of the play, which, intermixed with the deceits of a witty jester, fills up the comedy" – in *The Dutch Courtesan* could be taken at face value. It seems that the "common factor" in citizen comedy is "how to get money, and how to spend it; how to get a wife and how to keep her" (Leggatt, 1973, 4).

To return to Jacobean city comedy, we should be mindful of Gibbons' conclusion that no author was more responsible for designing the tenets and form of the genre than Ben Jonson. It is Jonson's "potentially anarchic comic imagination . . . in tension with his classicist's discipline" which shapes and reshapes the plays (Gibbons, 1968, 18). "The approach to Jonson's plays is the key to the approach to city comedy as a whole, for Jonson fathered the genre, powerfully shaped its growth, and crowned its maturity with two great plays, *Bartholomew Fair* in 1614 and *The Devil Is an Ass* in 1616" (Gibbons, 1968, 18). Such dramatic peaks, however, were intimately connected to their surroundings, as Gibbons continues: "I have traced the chronological development of the *genre* to show how the playwrights – Jonson, Marston, Middleton and others – learned from each other's plays as they appeared, modifying, reshaping or copying them . . . and how the great plays of the *genre*, in their turn, drew on the riches stored in the convention" (1968, 18). The enduring strength of Gibbons' argument is that he demonstrates how city comedy articulates a profound critique of its age through its very form and style. Satire and the city are thoroughly integrated.

In many ways the central definitions of city comedy (anti-romantic satires of their contemporary milieu which deploy intrigues about sex, marriage, and money) and citizen comedy (the means by which contemporary London staged and tested middle-class mores) could be seen as tendencies which increasingly pervaded drama from the 1590s onward. Although it is possible to place certain plays in one category or the other, it is striking how these tendencies intermingle. For example, plays like *Eastward Ho*, *The Roaring Girl*, *A Chaste Maid in Cheapside*, *If This Be not a Good Play, the Devil Is In It*, and *The Knight of the Burning Pestle* all work to some degree across those definitions, the last play, by Francis Beaumont, quite self-consciously.

Since the Middle Ages London had always been growing, but the city of 1501 was a vastly different place from the metropolis it would become a century later (Beier and Finlay, 1986). Many factors contributed to this: the crown and court's permanent residence at Whitehall; the increased role of the legal and administrative institutions of the city of London; the city's expansion as a port and manufacturing center; and its place as a national and European market. But the overwhelming feature of London's growth and change was the nature and speed of its demographic growth. From the

Reformation onward, the pace of immigration to London accelerated. Thousands upon thousands came each year, by choice or by necessity, thereby irrevocably altering the city's topography, economy, and culture. Driven off the land by various changes in the rural economy, the majority of the country people who traveled to London were less equipped than the legendary Dick Whittington – certainly their hopes for advancement far outweighed their prospects of gainful employment. Conflict in Europe – religious, political, and economic – brought many refugees and ex-soldiers, including Huguenots from France and various craftsmen or tradesmen from the Netherlands, fleeing Counter-Reformation forces. The disenfranchised from Wales and Ireland, too, made their way east. By the end of the sixteenth century, a vast army of the dispossessed crowded the streets, swelling London's liberties and suburbs, stretching resources and services beyond their viable capacity. Not all the newcomers to the city were Mad Toms and masterless men; many estate owners decamped to the capital, preferring the kind of lavish lifestyle and opportunities to be found there. Smaller landholders also responded to economic pressure, sold up, and moved to London, seeking jobs or favor either at court or in the Inns of Court. Such men (like Froth in *Measure for Measure*), arriving with money in their purse and looking for the most profitable ways to spend it, quickly entered the new urban lexicon as gulls, gamesters, or conies – commonplace targets of prostitutes and thieves. They account for London's rapid expansion, growing from 50,000 in 1500 to 120,000 by 1550; and between 1550 and 1650 by more than another quarter million, with a sharp acceleration around 1600. At such a time city comedy was also expanding.

Thus figures like the Country Wench in *Michaelmas Term* "encapsulates the forces of immigration, and the moment of threshold, as she comes to London to sell herself" (Twyning, 1998, 56). She is a nameless and ubiquitous symbol of alienation and exploitation: her father nearly becomes her client in a vicious moment of misrecognition. Middleton's character economically traces the relationship between dislocation and opportunity which characterized habits of acquisition. As an index of London, prostitution appears as supra-metaphoric (Twyning, 1998, esp. ch. 2, 54–91). "O London, thou art great in glory . . . but there is much harlot in thine eyes," Dekker writes, contrasting the encomiastic with the contemporary (cited in Twyning, 1998, 65). For good reason, then, Jonson's famous lines appear as a blueprint for city comedy:

> Our scene is London, 'cause we would make known,
>   No country's mirth is better than our own.
> No clime breeds better matter, for your whore,
>   Bawd, squire, imposter, many persons more,
> Whose manners, now called humours, feed the stage.

City madams, Dutch courtesans, and honest whores fed the stage in extraordinary numbers in this period. The strumpet and the stage, topographically and imaginatively, occupied each other's space as brothels jostled cheek by jowl with London's

theaters. For Jean-Christophe Agnew this liminal place took on a transfigurative function as a threshold of exchange: "it transpired that in the early seventeenth century,
a new extraterritorial zone of production and exchange sprang up outside London's
ancient marketplaces and thus out of reach of their juridical, ceremonial, and talis-
manic protections – and restrictions" (Agnew, 1986, 50). Jonson's Ursula – suburban
bawd and whore, generating illicit production and exchange right under the well-
plucked nose of the authorities – embodies this view in *Bartholomew Fair*, just outside
the ancient walls of the city of London. The city's relationship to comedy, and the
exchanges between them, became more intense and complex, not least because they
functioned as interchangeable images of themselves.

Much lies behind Jonson's phrase "no clime breeds better matter." "Breeds" encodes
the perversely bestial notion of usury or interest. In *The Merchant of Venice*, Shylock's
comment on capital exemplifies this: "I make it breed as fast" (I.iii.91). *Twelfth Night*'s
Feste, upon being given a coin, follows suit: "would not a pair of these have bred?"
(III.i.50). Once money becomes a commodity, and a variable means of exchange
between other commodities, everything it touches is rendered liquid – or a "matter"
of liquidity. Money becomes the measure of value of everything that can be measured.
Money both dissolves and readjusts the value of almost anything in any transaction
– land, groceries, even aristocratic titles. Small wonder that Shakespeare's Feste notes
that "words are very rascals, since bonds disgraced them," meaning not just bonds or
"feudal ties" but the relationship between words and things (Marx and Engels, 1962,
36).

Henry Moody enjoys playing with a variety of financial metaphors in his tribute
to Philip Massinger in the poem "On his comedy called *A New Way to Pay Old Debts*."
After praising the author's ability to plot and instruct, he continues:

> The nobles are your bondmen, gentry, and
> All besides those that did not understand.
> They were no men of credit, bankrupts born,
> Fit to be trusted with no stock but scorn.
> You have more wisely credited to such,
> That though they cannot pay, can value much.

Bonds have clearly been disgraced, and only the author now, it seems, can affirm value
as one who perceives the problem. His reward for saving aristocratic assets, that for
which he is credited, is "fame." Such praise, anticipating the play, follows one of the
central principles of city comedy: some force personified – usually by old men who
are cantankerous, sterile, greedy, obstinate, inflexible, retrograde, and generally intolerant toward the desires of the young – is deemed to have threatened the social order,
its succession, or its ability to reproduce itself. Having established in whom this force
is embodied, the victims are duped, tricked, humiliated, and generally thwarted by
the rightful custodians of society and its values (usually young men about town, sometimes class-crossed lovers). Such instances of defeat and (re)establishment are cus-

tomarily accomplished by a generous intervention from the author, who often assists with a plot where commonplace expectations (what some might call realism, or realistic expectations) are overcome. Among the many plays which follow this pattern are *Epicoene, A Trick to Catch the Old One, A Chaste Maid in Cheapside*, and *The Shoemaker's Holiday*; others like *The Dutch Courtesan, Bartholomew Fair*, and *The Devil Is an Ass* come close. Studying the moral pattern of city comedies confirms much of the scholarship on them, especially disclosing a drama where the forces of satire are more likely to succeed than virtue. Such a reading makes strange authorial bedfellows. How else would we find Middleton (of whom it can be said that he held Puritan sympathies)[2] and Jonson (of whom it can be stated that he did not) sharing similar dramatic ethics?

What Jacobean city comedy presents "is a keen analysis in moral terms first and last," says Gibbons, and "such a concern is clearly less ephemeral and more profound than any economic analysis, and accounts for the permanent value of the *genre* as dramatic art" (1968, 29; see also Knights, 1937, 206). Ironically, it was the transitory aspects of the early modern economy which increased the focus, both on and off the stage, upon the moral economy. Agnew says: "the new liquidity of mercantile relations, like the growing fluidity of social relations, made itself most vividly felt in those literary genres most devoted to social description and moral instruction" (1986, 59). To understand city comedy and its criticism means coming to terms with the idea that moral scrutiny was and is a matter of economics. For Knights, *Volpone* and *The Alchemist* express "Jonson's general 'anti-acquisitive attitude'"; one which was, strictly, a moral posture. Consequently, "the essential function of art is moral," which means keeping it clean from the contamination of the "money-gett" world (Knights, 1937, 200, 206). This perspective is part of a long critical tradition of seeing city comedy as a satirical indictment of the emergence of a capitalist economy: for example, the harsh dramatic treatment of characters like the Yellowhammers in *A Chaste Maid in Cheapside*, or Meercraft in *The Devil Is an Ass*; not to mention an array of Puritan tradesmen, hucksters, and monopolists.

Knights' view is most effectively challenged along its own lines by Peter Womack's detailed reading of Jonson's work. Womack explains how Volpone disdains any "secondary accumulations" of "resources resulting from greed"; instead he devises "his own organization for tapping the source: his unique swindle is a machine for extracting money from greed itself . . . his business doesn't pass through material media such as agriculture, trade, or even usury: his commodity is, directly, human behaviour" (Womack, 1986, 65). From this distinction we realize that divorcing satire from the moral judgment that initiates it is an incredibly difficult task.

Perhaps more so than *Volpone, The Alchemist* is built on the complex relationship between accumulation and economies of representation. A couple of years before Jonson's play, Dekker wrote this about money: "(Golde) the strange Magick of it drave me straight into a strange admiration. I preceiv'de it to be a witch-craft beyond mans power to contend with . . . a poyson that had a thousand contrarie workings on a thousand bodies" (cited in Twyning, 1998, 69). Realizing that he is already too close

to the uncanny force which has seduced him, the writer details the infinitely meta-
morphic power of gold: the purest form of liquidity. Once the distillatory goal of
alchemy, gold itself is now perceived to be *the* transmutative medium. There is a thrill
in Dekker's lines generated by the tension between fear and admiration, one which is
intimately connected to the imagination. What better way to describe the theater
than a "strange Magick" working "on a thousand bodies"? Money, alchemy, and
theater are inextricably intertwined, as Womack's assessment of Jonson's moralism
makes clear:

> Thus to the transgressive images of theatre – alchemy, sexuality, plague, carnival – which
> play across Jonson's dramatic writing and fissure its ideological coherence, we can add
> that of capitalism. It's *written* as a demonic image, a negation of nature, good sense and
> legitimacy . . . [it is] an insidious attack on the solidity and integrity of people and
> things, it is *wholly* evil; and the theatre, as another, is *wholly* complicit with it. Conse-
> quently, a vital aspect of the text – the dimensions of linguistic play (in every sense)
> without which structured communication is inconceivable – is closed to the moral inten-
> tions of the author. It's this impediment to his moralism that prevents Jonson from actu-
> ally achieving the "natural" closures of language and character which his explicit
> aesthetic programme designates as proper to drama. (Womack, 1986, 145)

Although written about Jonson, much of Womack's analysis here is applicable to
tendencies in city comedies throughout the period. We can also see why the city took
to the stage in predominantly comic form, eschewing tragedy and Elizabethan
romance, because both forms seek (if not always find) resolutions to the problems
which they have dramatized in the harmony of marriage or the catharsis of death. The
problem with such climacterical moments in the drama is the same as that which
undermines the notion of a single moral perspective in city comedy. To do so would
result in the kind of straightforward didacticism and moral exactitude which contemporary critics like Stephen Gosson and Philip Stubbes leveled at the theater.
Or the drama might collapse in on itself, going into a self-reflexive spiral inevitably
producing absurdly ironic moments which obscure any complicity with the object of
its satire – Beaumont's *The Knight of the Burning Pestle* comes to mind in this respect.
For Jonson, Middleton, and Marston especially, the viciousness with which they
attacked certain characters in their plays suggests a pitiless overkill that could easily
disguise their own ambivalent position in relation to their dramatic medium. Having
admitted that the London scene has provoked both the "rage" and "spleen of comic
writers," Jonson's prologue to *The Alchemist* continues to tell us much about city and
comedy:

> Though this pen
> Did never aim to grieve, but better men;
> Howe'er the age, he lives in, doth endure
> The vices that she breeds, above their cure.
> But, when wholesome remedies are sweet,

And, in their working, gain, and profit meet,
He hopes to find no spirit so much diseased,
But will, with such fair correctives be pleased.
(Jonson, 1966)

It is not just that "gain" and "profit" are tantalizingly homologous, but that around this time profit increasingly referred to the surplus product of industry, rather than the "wholesome" advantage attached to a person or community. Equally ambiguous is the writer's place, somewhere between vice and cure. The prologue is a plan for the play. Face, Subtle, and Dol Common – Theatre, Alchemy, Money (gold as "common whore of mankind") – generate a surplus, through their conspiracy and industry, which is then acquired by Lovewit, the urban gentleman, by dint of his ownership of the house in which the play is staged. Jonson's conceit is that Lovewit gets the profit without messing in trade through the offices and concomitant rewards of and for the author; gain and profit meet, commensurably. It is hard not to see Lovewit as a figure which stands for the combination of the theater company's aristocratic patron with the calculating theater owner (a new urban businessman like Philip Henslowe).

In *Bartholomew Fair*, Jonson further plays out the relationship between city and comedy. As such, "eleven respectable citizens, various in rank and character, who visit the Fair lose themselves there," says Womack, because it is "a space where stable identities dissolve in ambivalently proliferating forms of desire and which, in its asymmetrical combination of utopianism and deception, is the theatre's own self-reflected image" (1986, 145). The Fair-folk and their world are a microcosm of or synecdoche for the forces which had changed London during the sixteenth century. Jonson brilliantly enacts the threshold of exchange which constitutes the city and deconstructs all motley feudal ties and citizen morality in an atmosphere of carnival, of which theater is a solid emblem. Having carefully atomized the families and alienated the visitors, Jonson reconstitutes them "as an *audience*." Only the playwright, it seems, could do this, because all the other ideologies and prejudices which had been brought to the Fair-city had been trashed, mocked, or rendered irrelevant.

If Jonson's play in *Bartholomew Fair* remakes the community – albeit as a product of his artistry – in the Fair-as-city, then Middleton's *A Chaste Maid in Cheapside* offers an interesting insight into the differences between the two playwrights and their contrasting projects in city comedy. *A Chaste Maid in Cheapside* also begins with a country visitor, Sir Walter Whorehound, whose arrival starts up the play and whose expulsion ends it. Although Cheapside bears all the hallmarks of the concentration on money in early seventeenth-century London ("cheap" meaning market, price, barter, and bargain), its total effect in the play is very different from the Fair. Working through the tropes of Lent, Middleton's urban nexus is depicted as a realm almost wholly corrupted by the reduction of all social interaction to exchange value – everything is a commodity. What we see is gold or money as a "poyson" working its deleterious "magick" on all the relations between people across the social spectrum. Crucially, in Middleton's Cheapside, this "poyson" does not tear asunder or dissolve the ties between people; rather, it utterly contaminates them. And, in a dramatic situation as complex as that which constitutes Bartholomew Fair, this produces a vicious set of plot convolutions based on exploitation and abuse. In sum, these amount to an overriding ironic effect: avarice, selfishness, and pride (as amoral products of the cash nexus) simultaneously bind and divide people from each other and from the community. A perversion of Lenten values, whereby the individual reflects upon his or her spiritual relationship to the community, this ironic gap is endlessly propagated in Cheapside – past, present, and future. And the play is continuously built on ironic distances: chaste maids are chased whores and vice versa; the family is a hollow sham; Puritans are hypocrites; the stupid appear clever, as the clever are crooks. Touchwood Junior's marriage to Moll may release some of the tensions which hold meaning and value apart, but this whiff of romance cannot wholly change its context. Once again, the author will need to intervene if there is to be any effective resolution.

With its savage satirization of city life, it seems as if *A Chaste Maid in Cheapside*, if not a splenetic outburst, is the product of moral outrage – enough, at any rate, to bolster much critical opinion about Middleton's dramatic didactic style, especially in this, his last city comedy. Middleton had close ties to London's guild and civic leaders, many of whom were Puritan sympathizers; and scholars like Margot Heinemann have invoked the seemingly antithetical concepts of "Puritanism and theater" in his name (1980, esp. ch. 5, 73–87). And, certainly, on occasion, Middleton's bleak views of a depraved world untouched by grace seem to lean substantially on Calvinist theology. Such things have helped to define Middleton as one of the most moralistic authors of city comedy in particular, and the Jacobean period in general. But when we consider the notion of providence (essential to Calvin's doctrine on the moral nature of man), Middleton's drama tends to complicate as much as it clarifies. It is not just the way in which Middleton makes vice an instrument to punish vice, but that providential aspects of the plot, its incredible turns and the resolutions which they provide, depend upon our faith in the will of the author. How else would Touchwood Junior and Moll get married, or Sir Walter be exposed? Whatever the influences of Calvinism or Puritanism on Middleton, his city comedies seem to uphold the view that the aristocracy should know its place, and that London's citizenry, high and low, should eschew avarice, live virtuously, and accept their rightful and dutiful position in a civilized urban society.

Although Middleton and Jonson are often considered together for the sake of generic definition, their aims differ, even if their topics do not. Jonson begins the prologue to *The Alchemist* with a dissertation on "Fortune" which, to some, could be a term for providence. But the dramas we are discussing here operate in profoundly dissimilar ways. The concept of Fortune appealed to the feudal aristocracy whose rule was preordained by what their critics would call "mere accident of birth." So important is this notion that it was extended into other areas where individual choice or free will might contaminate "chance." From the fifteenth century onwards, Valentine's Day rituals enacted the fantasies of Fortune. Lovers were determined by lot: names were inscribed on paper, folded, and then drawn by one's sweetheart. (Later, of course, this activity was commuted to one of personal choice, albeit a secret.) With Grace Wellborn (a name which snubs Calvinist theology and privileges aristocratic value) as the grand prize, *Bartholomew Fair* plays a traditional version of the Valentine's Day game. First, the Fair has to dissolve her ties to Bartholomew Cokes and Adam Overdo, then her Fortune becomes complexly integrated with the forces and context of the Fair. The relationship between words, grace, bonds, and rascals is difficult if not impossible to untangle. How much you believe Jonson determines Grace's future depends upon how much you think he determines the fate of the Fair. "Fortune," says Jonson in *The Alchemist*, "favours fools"; in Bartholomew Fair it also favors clever texts and their interpreters.

Altogether, city comedy made a strong impression on the early modern stage. To Gibbons' 20–30 plays it would be easy to add another dozen which have city-comedic tendencies, from George Chapman's 1597 play *An Humorous Day's Mirth* (arguably the first dramatized satire in an urban setting) (Salgãdo, 1975, 10), through *The Shoemaker's Holiday, Northward Ho, Timon of Athens, Measure for Measure, The Roaring Girl, The Knight of the Burning Pestle*, right up to the Caroline play *A New Way to Pay Old Debts*. What made it so popular – and in such a relatively short space of time? Did people really go to the theater for instruction, to be informed of "fair correctives," or for the pleasures of moral didacticism, to witness the follies of the age being scourged? Although these are compelling reasons – not least because many of the plays purport to offer such things – they seem inadequate when one thinks of a rapidly expanding entertainment industry and an increasingly sophisticated audience. Who, by 1613, did not know it was wrong to trade in human life, sell sex, or hide an illegitimate baby under some mutton during Lent? Was the audience meant to fulminate, be morally outraged, then shake its collective head, concluding that the world really had gone mad? If it is funny, and it is, why did they laugh? To answer this means thinking about the needs of the audience in relation to what they found entertaining.

Two of Jonson's earliest city comedies – *Every Man In his Humour* and *Every Man Out of his Humour* – play upon the conceit that certain behavior is the result of an imbalance of the humors. In *Every Man In his Humour*, for example, Old Kno'well's humor is manifest as an excessive but misguided concern for his son's morals. As he sets out to spy on him, what will become the usual suspects of city comedy are put into play: tricksters, gamesters, country gulls, deceptive servants, intriguers, disguisers. They were the same characters, the same city crew, who had evolved from the rogue literature a few years earlier. Perhaps Jonson alludes to one of those early writers, Thomas Harman JP, as he becomes Justice Clement, "an old merry magistrate" who purges them of their humors by making them aware of their follies. Whatever the technical definition of humors which Jonson was employing – and there has been much debate on this subject – he clearly makes the idea into a metaphor for articulating city behavior. By the time he writes *The Alchemist*, the list of characters – "whore," "Bawd," "squire," "many persons more" – who now inhabit the London stage are close to caricatures. Significantly, manners and humors are practically interchangeable terms. The earlier concept of everyman, a type that stands for all, has become "every man", and every woman, in city comedy. Every character, although he or she may have "one peculiar quality," is effectively just one of the catalogue of types who inhabit the city and "feed the stage." The need to fix characters according to their behavior, to ascribe names that fit with the audience's perception of the world around them, is connected to the anxieties many felt at the time. Every man and every woman who came to London had then to be someone else. Small wonder the world-as-stage was such a powerful metaphor. In *Every Man Out of his Humour*, the sarcastic Buffone explains how to be à la mode, or in the humor of a city gentleman:

> First (to be an accomplisht gentleman, that is, a gentleman of the time) you must give o'er house-keeping in the countrey, and live altogether in the citie among gallants: where, at your first appearance, 'twere good you turnd foure or five hundred acres of your best land into two or three trunkes of apparell.

Buffone's definition demonstrates how the gentleman loses his tenure to a fixed identity in exchange for the inventory of a small theater company. In one move, the feudal gentleman translates himself into a player, perhaps with a number of roles. But while this would have been profoundly disturbing for his sense of himself, even exciting, once in the city he would have become a type: a city gallant. For those lower down the social scale, those dismissed from their 500 acres, the options in the city were more limited, but the ease with which they could be categorized was not. They usually occupied the same positions as the lower section of the dramatis personae of almost any city comedy such as *Bartholomew Fair*.

London was made up of people who chose to refashion themselves in such a manner to qualify, in Agnew's terms, as "artificial persons" (1986, esp. ch. 3, 101–48). Uprooted landowners became "accomplisht" gentlemen or gulls; dispossessed rural workers became laborers or entered the rogues' gallery; and craftsmen and tradesmen found themselves increasingly tarnished by the function of exchange. Selling and whoredom became inextricably linked: Middleton's prostitute in *Michaelmas Term* asks, "doe not al Trades live by their ware, and yet called honest Livers?" (IV.ii.10–12). An air of dishonesty gathered around the marketplace. And just as the "whore" became synonymous with dissimulation, selling became increasingly perceived as theatrical. In Dekker's *If This Be not a Good Play, the Devil Is in It*, Barterville (likely canting slang for London) explains the need for donning a "Turke-Merchant-like" habit (both manner and clothing):

> That, for which manie their Religion,
> Most men their Faith, all chaunge their honestie,
> *Profite*, (that guilded god) *Commoditie*.
> Hee that would grow damnd-Rich, yet live secure,
> Must keep a case of many Faces, sometimes demure,
> Sometimes a grum-surly sir, now play the Jewe,
> Then the Precision; Not a man weele viewe,

But varies so. My selfe, (of bashfull nature)
Am thus supplyed by Arte.
                    (Dekker, 1953–61, III, 176 [IV.i. 7–15])

Despite the racism, we can see that for Barterville ethnic identities are just as mutable as structures of belief in a world evaluated through profit and the commodity and performed as enactment. Yet such a world enforces theatricality, and we can see how a repertory of "Faces" and characteristics are deemed necessary. Moreover, Barterville reveals how any person viewing another in the city knows him or her to be playing a role, and those being viewed know that they are being assessed in such a way. With so many faces, a seemingly infinite variety, both viewer and viewed tended to organize the world into patterns of behavior and types of people which they could imaginatively if not palpably control – to fix, or make (de)finite. Such categories and prejudices were often explored, tested, made, and remade in the very place where theatricality was licensed; the theater. Comprehending that the surfaces of the world, especially when "supplyed by Arte," are untrustworthy, if not lacking in "honestie," also came with the sense that one might have an honest or truthful characteristic – a humor, a manner, a peculiar quality, something which could denote a person truly – which unquestionably constituted the "self." Significantly, a quality such as a bashful nature superseded apparently metaphysical concepts like religion and faith when it came to defining the self. The conflicting anxieties and opportunities created by the way in which outward appearances were intimately connected to the characteristics which they obscured or disguised were the very stuff of city comedy. All the world was as much audience as it was stage. And those who made up the audiences of city comedy came to be enthralled and appalled as the security of their position as viewers was simultaneously reinforced and undermined. But whatever their experience, there was always another play.

NOTES

1   For the most extensive elaboration of the term "Jacobean city comedy', see Gibbons (1968).
2   For a convincing elaboration of this idea see Heinemann (1980).

REFERENCES AND FURTHER READING

Agnew, Jean-Christophe (1986). *Worlds Apart: The Market and the Theater in Anglo-American Thought, 1550–1750.* Cambridge: Cambridge University Press.

Altieri, Joanne (1988). "Against moralizing Jacobean comedy: Middleton's Chaste Maid." *Criticism* 30.2, 171–87.

Barton, Anne (1978). "London comedy and the ethos of the city." *London Journal* 4.2.

Beier, A. L. (1985). *Masterless Men: The Vagrancy Problem in England 1560–1640.* London: Methuen.

Beier, A. L. and Roger Finlay, eds (1986). *London 1500–1700: The Making of the Metropolis.* London: Longman.

Brown, John Russell and Bernard Harris, eds (1960). *Jacobean Theatre*. New York: St. Martin's Press.

Covatta, Anthony (1973). *Thomas Middleton's Comedies*. Cranbury, NJ: Associated University Presses.

Dekker, Thomas (1953–61). *The Dramatic Works of Thomas Dekker*, ed. Fredson Bowers. 4 vols. Cambridge: Cambridge University Press.

Finlay, Roger (1981). *Population and Metropolis: The Demography of London, 1580–1650*. Cambridge: Cambridge University Press.

Gibbons, Brian (1968). *Jacobean City Comedy: A Study of Satiric Plays by Jonson, Marston and Middleton*. Cambridge, MA: Harvard University Press.

Heinemann, Margot (1980). *Puritanism and Theatre: Thomas Middleton and Opposition Drama under the Early Stuarts*. Cambridge: Cambridge University Press.

Hutson, Lorna (1989). "The displacement of the market in Jacobean city comedy." *London Journal* 14.1, 3–16.

Jonson, Ben (1966). *The Alchemist*, ed. Douglas Brown. New York: W. W. Norton.

Kastan, David Scott (1987). "Workshop and/as playhouse: comedy and commerce in *The Shoemakers' Holiday*." Studies in Philology 84.3, 324–37.

Knights, L. C. (1937). *Drama and Society in the Age of Jonson*. New York: Norton.

Leggatt, Alexander (1973). *Citizen Comedy in the Age of Shakespeare*. Toronto: University of Toronto Press.

Leinwand, Theodore B. (1986). *The City Staged: Jacobean Comedy, 1603–13*. Madison: University of Wisconsin Press.

McKerrow, Ronald B., ed. (1958). *The Works of Thomas Nashe*, 5 vols. Oxford: Blackwell.

Manley, Lawrence (1986). *London in the Age of Shakespeare: An Anthology*. London: Croom Helm.

Manley, Lawrence (1995). *Literature and Culture in Early Modern London*. Cambridge: Cambridge University Press.

Marx, Karl and Frederick Engels (1962). *Manifesto of the Communist Party*. In *Karl Marx and Frederick Engels: Selected Works: Volume One*. London: Lawrence and Wishart.

Salgãdo, Gãmini (1972). *Cony-Catchers and Bawdy Baskets*. Harmondsworth: Penguin.

Salgãdo, Gãmini (1975). *Four Jacobean City Comedies*. Harmondsworth: Penguin.

Smith, David L., Richard Strier, and David Bevington, eds (1995). *The Theatrical City: Culture, Theatre and Politics in London, 1576–1649*. Cambridge: Cambridge University Press.

Stow, John (1971). *A Survey of London*, ed. C. L. Kingsford. 2 vols. Oxford Clarendon Press.

Twyning, John (1998). *London Dispossessed: Literature and Social Space in the Early Modern City*. Basingstoke: Macmillan.

Venuti, Lawrence (1989). "Transformations of city comedy: a symptomatic reading." *Assays: Critical Approaches to Medieval and Renaissance Texts* 3, 99–134.

Wells, Susan (1981). "Jacobean city comedy and the ideology of the city." *ELH* 48.1, 37–60.

Womack, Peter (1986). *Ben Jonson*. Oxford: Blackwell.

26
Domestic Tragedy: Private Life on the Public Stage
Lena Cowen Orlin

I

At about the time that the play *Arden of Faversham* was being staged in London, in early 1591, Alice Suttill was called before the Consistory Court of Canterbury.[1] Her husband William suspected her of committing adultery and seeking his death. The couple's servant, Margaret Christmas, testified to an unquiet household. Alice frequently railed at William, gave him no warning when she stayed out as late as 10.00 at night, once shut him out of their house, and boasted that she was "ordained to be a scourge and whip to plague and vex" him. Margaret reported one day's errands in particular detail: she was dispatched by Alice to Edward Winterborne's to fetch 20 shillings, was referred by Winterborne to a man named Ward, and when she eventually returned from Ward's found Winterborne at home with Alice. Clearly, Margaret believed that she had conveyed a prearranged signal to Winterborne and that her mistress had committed adultery with this man. As for the charge of homicidal intent, Margaret recalled the day she was dismissed from the Suttill parlor so that Alice could talk privately with a man named Thomas Fanshame. Complicated narratives about monies and services exchanged between Alice, Fanshame, and Fanshame's wife seem to establish that Alice had commissioned a "token" from the couple. This was a piece of paper that Alice had been seen to wear about her neck and had once hidden in a cellar woodpile. She claimed that the paper was a charm to make her husband love her again. William believed that it was inscribed with satanic writings threatening his life, and others testified that the death of a neighbor caused Alice to complain that according to Fanshame William was to have been the next in the parish to die. In the case of *Suttill contra Suttill*, William was granted the right to live separately from his wife.

Meanwhile, sometime between 1589 and 1592, *Arden of Faversham* is thought to have initiated the genre of "domestic tragedy" by dramatizing a notorious true crime: an adulterous woman and her lover succeed in murdering her husband after numerous failed attempts and with the aid of many willing collaborators. The crime dated back to 1550, but it had percolated slowly through the textual filters of local record and county chronicle before finally, in 1577, reaching a national audience in accounts compiled in the name of Raphael Holinshed. For the next century, other domestic crimes that caught the public imagination were likened to the Arden case for their degree of what Holinshed called "horribleness." The "horribleness" of the Arden story inhered both in Alice's murderous persistence despite her husband's many escapes and in the sheer number of her accomplices – the play describes seven who were executed and two who eluded justice.[2]

This overplus of plots and plotters would seem to have set the Arden story apart from its culture as an anomaly. As the case of Alice and William Suttill instead goes to show, the precipitating issues and anxieties dramatized by *Arden of Faversham* were not unique to it. A key difference between the Suttills and the Ardens was that if Alice Suttill had indeed commissioned black magic against her husband, it did not succeed. In this respect, the Arden story was the more sensational and the more stage-worthy. But sensation was by no means the only element of *Arden*'s public value. Like *Suttill contra Suttill*, the story played out some of the most bitter contestations of Elizabethan private life, with husband and wife competing for control of their home, with servants drawn into household conflicts, and with the larger community of neighbors and townspeople similarly dividing their allegiances. Unsettled power relations in betrothal and marriage, the nature of authority in the household and its uncertain gendering, and transgressions against social order and community responsibility were all real issues, and these may have been at least as compelling to the playgoing audience as was true crime.

There is one further, telling analogy between the Suttill and Arden stories: on the margins of both can be glimpsed public figures whose networks of political interest were entangled in these dysfunctional marriages. Edward Winterborne, Alice Suttill's alleged lover, was steward to one of the most powerful men in Kent, Richard Rogers, then bishop of Dover. When Alice suffered a breakdown, it is reported that she was cared for – and perhaps interrogated – in the bishop's house. When Alice charged Thomas Fanshame with practicing witchcraft, he was prosecuted before the same bishop of Dover. There are larger political implications of the Arden case, as well: Alice Arden was the stepdaughter of Sir Edward North, chancellor of the Court of Augmentations and member of both Parliament and the Privy Council. North's first clerk at the Augmentations was Thomas Arden, and North's steward was the man named Mosby who became notorious as Alice's lover and collaborator in murder. Arden himself represented a generation of social and economic change as one of the "new men" who established their wealth and influence in consequence of the dissolution of the monasteries and expansion of government bureaucracies.

These larger associations in the Suttill and Arden cases are chiefly discernible through what appear to be cracks in the public record. Holinshed's *Chronicles of England, Scotland, and Ireland* (1587) mention Mosby's connection with North, for example, but suppress those of Thomas and Alice. Erasures such as these make it all the more remarkable, first, that Holinshed chose to recount Arden's story and, second,

Holinshed cites this as for the reason for recording the story & preserving it

that he then apologized for doing so. "Horribleness" was his justification: "otherwise it may seem to be but a private matter, and therefore as it were impertinent to this history." But so uncertain a posture is entirely self-created. Given Arden's stature with the central government, his participation in landmark historical events, and the involvement of the Privy Council in the investigation of his murder, his tale could have been told in such a way as to make no apology necessary. While his connections may have been complicit in bringing his murder to public attention, the more potent cultural force of Arden's story evidently lay elsewhere, in the private realm to which the *Chronicles* refer. The contestations and contentions of private life may have required some public forum, and this, in its various recountings, the Arden story helped construct.

At nearly five text-heavy folio pages, the *Chronicles'* account of the "whole murder" is surprisingly detailed, describing how each accomplice was enlisted, how an innocent man was unjustly implicated, how the crime was finally perpetrated, how the subsequent investigation was conducted, and how those involved were exposed and punished. But while the *Chronicles* were clearly the play's primary source, *Arden of Faversham* focuses less strictly on these matters of "horribleness." Instead, private issues move even further to the foreground, so that the play derives at least as much of its energy from the motivations, internal conflicts, and interpersonal relations of its characters. Like a church-court case, with its variety of perspectives aired in sequential depositions, *Arden* shows each character viewing the world through his or her own fears and desires. There is Thomas Arden, resisting and ignoring his suspicions about Alice's unfaithfulness; Alice, prolonging his uncertainties by alternately lavishing affection on him, flaunting her disdain for him, and aggressively lodging her own accusations against him; Mosby, wavering from but then allowing himself to be reseduced to the love affair and the murder plot; and each new accomplice, succumbing to an approach shrewdly tailored to his own greeds and aspirations. The *Chronicles'* apology for representing a "private matter" has worked to obscure from us the ways in which that account in fact emphasized the sensational aspects of the story that most removed it from the relational concerns occupying the daily lives of *Arden's* audiences. For many years these had their best airing in neighborhood gossip and disputes of the sort that made their way to the church courts, as did the case of *Suttill contra Suttill* – until, that is, the initiation of the genre of domestic tragedy.

II

The term "domestic tragedy" was not applied to plays like *Arden of Faversham* in their own time. In 1831, John Payne Collier remarked certain distinguishing similarities among the anonymous *Arden of Faversham* (1592), the anonymous *Warning for Fair Women* (1599), Robert Yarington's *Two Lamentable Tragedies* (1601), the anonymous *Fair Maid of Bristow* (1605), and the anonymous *Yorkshire Tragedy* (1608).[3] These plays shared localized English settings, journalistic content, and unadorned style. Collier labeled them for their affinities to some eighteenth-century French plays Diderot had characterized as tragedies "domestique[s] et bourgeoise[s]" (1968, 49).[4] In 1884, John Addington Symonds added to the list Thomas Heywood's *Woman Killed with Kindness* (1607) and Thomas Dekker, John Ford, and William Rowley's *Witch of Edmonton* (*c*.1621), both of which contain fictional plots with the same domestic settings and concerns as the true-crime plays. The first fully fledged study of the genre was completed by Edward Ayers Taylor in an unpublished dissertation of 1925. Taylor included George Wilkins's *Miseries of Enforced Marriage* (1607) and William Sampson's *Vow Breaker* (1636).

Taylor also reported on lost plays which, had they survived, might have far expanded our notion of the popularity and cultural significance of the genre. From Henslowe's *Diary* alone come the following titles:

The History of Friar Francis (performed as an "old play" in 1594)
The Merchant of Emden (performed by the Admiral's Men in 1594)
The Witch of Islington (performed by the Admiral's Men in 1597)
Black Bateman of the North (a two-part play for which Henry Chettle, Robert Wilson, Michael Drayton, and Thomas Dekker were paid in 1598)
Page of Plymouth (for which Ben Jonson and Thomas Dekker were paid in 1599)
The Stepmother's Tragedy (for which Henry Chettle and Thomas Dekker were paid in 1599)
Cox of Collumpton (for which John Day and William Haughton were paid in 1599)
Bristow Tragedy (for which John Day was paid in 1602)
William Cartwright (for which William Haughton was paid in 1602)
Black Dog of Newgate (a two-part play for which John Day, Wentworth Smith, Richard Hathaway, and "the other poet" were paid in 1603)
Shore's Wife (for which Henry Chettle and John Day were paid in 1603)

Also mentioned often are *An History of the Cruelty of a Stepmother* (performed at court in 1578), *The History of Murderous Michael* (performed at court in 1579), and Thomas Dekker, John Ford, William Rowley, and John Webster's *Late Murder of the Son upon the Mother* (performed at court in 1624; this play was also known as *The Late Murder in White-Chapel* and *Keep the Widow Waking*). For many of these lost plays, popular pamphlets establish that their topic was probably a notorious actual murder, and this accounts for their suggested attribution to the domestic genre.[5]

With so many potential examples of the genre lost, with those surviving of unknown or collaborative authorship, without a "great-man" protagonist to compel interest of the traditional sort, and given the general sense that these were curiosities of a sensational and ephemeral nature, the domestic tragedies were critically scanted for some decades. In 1943, however, Henry Hitch Adams attracted significant scholarly attention with his *English Domestic or, Homiletic Tragedy 1575 to 1642*. For Adams, the one "invariable" characteristic of the genre was the "humble station" of its protagonists, always "below the ranks of the nobility" (1943, viii). With this single criterion, his canon expanded to include "plays from legend and history" like R. B.'s

Appius and Virginia (*c*.1564), dramatized from Livy and set in ancient Rome; Thomas Dekker's *Old Fortunatus* (*c*.1600), derived from an old German legend and presented as a comedy; and the anonymous *Life and Death of Jack Straw* (*c*.1591), based on a famous rebellion and more a chronicle history than a domestic tragedy. Subsequent critics have found Adams' inclusiveness unwieldy and misleading. Most would emulate him in adding to the canon Thomas Heywood's *1 and 2 Edward IV* (1599) and his *English Traveller* (1633), if only because the Jane Shore plot of the former and the Geraldine plot of the latter are so analogous to his *Woman Killed with Kindness*. But relatively few have followed Adams in including John Ford's *'Tis Pity She's a Whore* (1633), with its Italian setting, or *The Miseries of Enforced Marriage*, with its comic ending. The canon of surviving domestic tragedies is most often taken to comprise *Arden of Faversham*, *A Warning for Fair Women*, *Two Lamentable Tragedies*, *1 and 2 Edward IV*, *A Yorkshire Tragedy*, *A Woman Killed with Kindness*, *The Witch of Edmonton*, and *The English Traveller*. *Othello*, too, is often mentioned in discussions of the genre, as Shakespeare's nearest approach to the form.

If the canon is arguable, this may be because the defining characteristics of the genre are contested. As literary scholars have taken on board the work of social historians, many have come to understand the anachronism of Adams' assumption that the two terms "humble station" and "below the ranks of the nobility" are synonymous. *Arden of Faversham*, *A Yorkshire Tragedy*, and *A Woman Killed with Kindness* are largely populated with gentlemen and gentlewomen who, while certifiably "non-aristocratic," would never have been taken by their contemporaries to be "humble." The plays emphasize the wealth and status of their protagonists as landowners. Even *Arden* refers to its title character as a "gentleman of blood," thus elevating him above the taint of the "new" that obtained for his historical namesake. Of more "middling" stature are the merchant family of *A Warning for Fair Women*, the shopkeepers and apprentices in one of the *Two Lamentable Tragedies*, and the yeomen and servants of *The Witch of Edmonton*.[6] While rank thus varies widely across the genre, domestic tragedies cohere in locating their protagonists in centers of their own authority and responsibility, their households. In fact, the import of social history may be that Adams got things exactly backwards. For him, the "lowly social station of the tragic protagonist" was the "*sine qua non*" which had a "natural result": "playwrights set the action of their plays in the family merely because their plots inevitably concerned the everyday problems of the 'common' hero" (1943, 1). It may be that the business of everyday life was more the *sine qua non*, and that stature was variable within certain non-aristocratic, above-the-poverty-line parameters.

The least persuasive of Adams' theses has proven to be that proclaimed in his title: "homiletic tragedy." Arguing that domestic plays were strictly didactic, Adams was dismissive of the genre on aesthetic grounds. He asserted that each plot follows a monotonous moralizing formula: sin is committed, it is discovered, and the sinners repent, are punished, and seek divine mercy. "As long as domestic tragedy concerned itself with the things of the next world rather than with the things of this," wrote Adams, "it remained a subordinate genre, one really apart from the actual lives of the people, one whose products were largely ephemeral literature." The genre "failed" to develop "a real tragedy expressive of the actual problems of the citizen of England" (1943, 189–90). The burden of the analogy between the Suttills and Ardens goes to suggest that Adams had too limited a view of the "actual problems" of early modern English men and women.

Peter Ure soon objected that dramatic texts are not, Adams to the contrary, didactic tracts. He called *A Woman Killed with Kindness*, *Women Beware Women*, and *The Broken Heart* "marriage plays." Michel Grivelet (1957) and Andrew Clark (1975) followed this line in emphasizing the importance of marital and familial themes across the full canon of domestic tragedies. Adams' broadly regularizing, thesis-driven readings of the plays were also modified by those who did the important work of making individual domestic tragedies widely available in critical editions, among them A. C. Cawley, Barry Gaines, Arthur F. Kinney, Brian Scobie, Keith Sturgess, R. W. Van Fossen, and M. L. Wine.[7] Finally, a vital new form of critical intervention was inaugurated by Catherine Belsey's "Alice Arden's crime," which first appeared in 1982 and which demonstrated how richly rewarding this then-obscure text could be when read against the grain. Belsey showed how the dialogue that established the conflicted motivations and aspirations of the characters "invites a response which contradicts the play's explicit project." In subsequent scholarship, the feminist, materialist, and historicist criticisms to which *Arden* seems fruitfully to lend itself have demonstrated how deeply the genre of domestic tragedy was imbricated in contentious issues of its culture. A greater awareness of its social importance has resulted in a substantial body of new criticism on the genre, by David Attwell (1991), Ann Christensen (1997), Viviana Comensoli (1996), Frances E. Dolan (1992, 1994), Nancy Guitterez (1989), Richard Helgerson (1997, 2000), Diana E. Henderson (1997), Garrett Sullivan (1998), Frank Whigham (1996), and myself (Orlin, 1994, 2000).

III

Arden of Faversham seems not to have had much sense of occasion about its own generic impertinence in violating the traditions of *de casibus* tragedy, which chronicled the fall of a great man, most often a king, and dealt with matters of state. Judging from the titles of such lost plays as the 1578 *History of the Cruelty of a Stepmother* and the 1579 *History of Murderous Michael*, *Arden* may have been preceded in generic innovation. If so, it is the first domestic tragedy merely by default, as the earliest to have survived. *Arden* is apologetic only in its Epilogue and then only in asking pardon for matters of style, not substance. The play is termed a "naked tragedy," without "filèd points" or "points of glozing stuff" – even though there is more-than-passable poetry in Arden's report of a premonitory dream and in Mosby's recoil, Macbeth-like, from his own ambition. But "simple truth" has no need of rhetorical ornament, the Epilogue asserts. To the extent that the Epilogue justifies the play, it does so on the basis of a truth claim: "Thus have you seen the truth of Arden's death."[8]

Equally, however, *Arden* may not apologize in the terms we would expect because it found no apology necessary. There was warrant enough in prevailing cultural constructs. The comprehensive logic known as analogical thought thoroughly enmeshed the fate of the state with that of each individual household. In their popular domestic treatise of 1598, *A Godly Form of Household Government*, John Dod and Robert Cleaver began: "A household is as it were a little commonwealth." They echoed the conventional view which held any one sphere to be analogous to all others, with each hierarchized in parallel ways. Thus, the head in the body was like the father in his household was like the king in his kingdom was like Christ in his church. Analogical constructs incorporated the corporeal, the domestic, the political, and the divine in a single, satisfyingly complete world view, and an event in one sphere could be understood to resonate in all others. Thomas Arden's household, for example, was a microcosm of the kingdom.

During the sixteenth century, these principles of analogical thought were introduced into formulations of authority and obligation. Prevailing notions of obedience were premised on the fifth commandment: "Honor thy father and thy mother." By analogy, the biblical injunction regarding a child's obedience to his or her parent could be understood to pertain to a citizen's fealty to his or her monarch. While there were other justifications for state power in circulation, patriarchalism was uniquely suasive, drawing as it did on the model of a social unit, the family, that was thoroughly naturalized and easily grasped. By picturing itself as a family writ large, the state appropriated the divine sanction of the Bible for its own authority and thus required obedience less in its own name than, it could suggest, God's.[9] Thus it was in the state's own interest to reinforce the analogies between itself and the private sphere, to make each realm conceptually dependent on the other.

This mutual imprinting of domestic and political spheres had the further effect of giving the state cause to concern itself with order in all households and to enjoin good domestic governance as a public duty. The strategies of state control played themselves out in many ways, one of which the historical case of Thomas Arden perfectly illustrates. If Arden's household was a little commonwealth, and if he was the head of this petty commonwealth, then defiance of his authority was comparable to rebellion against that of the king, and Alice and the other members of the Arden household who sought Arden's death were as much insurrectionaries as murderers. Indeed, while the greater number of the conspirators against Arden were convicted of homicide, his wife and two servants were found guilty of petty treason and punished accordingly. Alice and a maidservant were burned at the stake, while Arden's manservant was hanged, drawn, and quartered.

The analogical world view also informs *Arden of Faversham*, where the adulterous partnership of Alice and Mosby is shown to be emotionally troubled but politically purposeful. Alice resents Arden's "control"; what right has he "to govern me that am to rule myself?" (i.274, x.85). Mosby is depicted as a usurper, seeking to secure "Arden's overthrow" and to best other aspirants to "Arden's seat," so that he may become "sole ruler of mine own" (viii.30–6). Meanwhile, Greene's loss of tenure in

[margin notes:] intersection of public & private — religious problems of the time — national problem at the time

lands seized by the crown following the dissolution of the monasteries is transmuted from grievance against the king to grievance against Arden, the crown's grantee: "Nor cares he though young gentlemen do beg" (viii.476). Reede comes before Arden as a humble petitioner for another "plot of ground" (xiii.12). Both thus invest Arden with larger political attributes. Arden is so much the petty monarch in the little world of Faversham that he is also given a councillor, Franklin, the only fictional character added to this tale of true crime. In these ways, this "domestic" tragedy operates on principles analogous to those of state tragedy, and it is similarly occupied with issues of order and obedience.

The domestic tragedy looks less like state tragedy to us, living in an age in which the boundaries between private and public are differently drawn, than it would have done in its own time. One landmark dividing the early modern from the modern was the year 1828, when the old statute of treasons was finally abolished. The system of analogies had fallen away sufficiently that mariticides were thereafter understood to have committed murder, not petty treason. In 1831, J. P. Collier surveyed the Elizabethan drama with eyes no longer acculturated by a system of thought that had been deemed outmoded just three years earlier, and *Arden of Faversham* suddenly looked sufficiently unlike the great orthodox tragedies that he developed the classification system that lastingly labeled the "domestic." If we recognize how much narrower the conceptual gap between the two forms of drama originally was, however, we come closer to understanding their cultural meanings in their own time.

Analogical thought is most familiar to us today as the doctrine outlined in E. M. W. Tillyard's highly influential *Elizabethan World Picture* (1959). In consequence of the pioneering materialist work of Jonathan Dollimore (1984), we have learned to be skeptical of Tillyard's tidy formulations. It is important to recognize, as Dollimore certainly did, that this "metaphysic of order" was in wide circulation in the early modern period, as the statute of treasons confirms. What Dollimore importantly demonstrated, however, is that the Elizabethan "world view" did not represent popular consensus about the nature of authority in the period. These doctrines would not have been endlessly repeated in sermons and homilies had they been as thoroughly naturalized as they liked to pretend; strategic and persistent reinforcement was necessary. The Janus faces of the "Elizabethan world picture" were critical to the domestic tragedy. On the one hand, analogical thought was so widely promulgated that it provided a conceptual structure for such plays. On the other hand, the application of analogical thought to doctrines of public order was never entirely successful, as both domestic tragedies and tragedies of state demonstrated. All tragedy required jeopardy and contestation to propel its action, and, however decorous its resolution, the greater part of a play's "two-hours' traffic" enacted challenges to the prevailing metaphysic of order. It could scarcely help but be what Dollimore termed "radical tragedy," confronting its audiences with the disorder that ideology could never sufficiently contain.

The principal agent of disorder in *Arden of Faversham* is Alice Arden. The 1592 title-page of the play purports to show "the great malice and dissimulation of a wicked woman," a "disloyal and wanton wife." In the play, however, Alice maintains an oppositional self-representation. Enlisting an accomplice, for example, she complains of her husband that "he keep[s] in every corner trulls." She also charges that she has received from Arden "froward looks, / Hard words, and blows" (ll. 494–7). The play gives us no reason to find her allegations credible; Alice's rhetoric is the stuff of church-court slander cases. There, most insults found expression in a sexual vocabulary which was, like a dead metaphor, detached from actual performance.[10] In a similar manner, when her husband bridled at "boarding" first her mother and then her sister, Alice Suttill retorted that he spent more on keeping his whores than her kin. She also claimed self-defense by describing actions taken out of fear of his "misuse . . . both by words and stripes" – although no witness came forward to confirm that she was abused. Even if the self-justifications of these women had little credibility in their own contexts, they help us read the women outside those contexts. We cannot but wonder if Alice Suttill took in her mother and sister as a way of creating a female support system in her troubled household. And of course we bring different political sensibilities to Alice Suttill's insistence that "I will go where I list," even as to Alice Arden's declaration that she will not have her husband "govern me that am to rule myself."

However, this is to limit the radical ideological import of the play to the characterologic. *Arden of Faversham* enacts larger, systemic challenges to prevailing cultural constructs, and these are visible even when reading *with* the grain of the play. Analogical thought was tidy and comprehensive in its abstract outlines but rife with irregularities and mismatches in practical application. In *Arden of Faversham* some of the incapacities of doctrine are represented in the fact that Thomas Arden receives such bad advice from his good councillor, Franklin. When Arden confesses his fear that his wife may be straying, Franklin recommends that he travel to London for a period. Thus, Arden misguidedly cedes territory to his challenger, as he eventually realizes: "that base Mosby doth usurp my room / And makes his triumph of my being thence" (iv.29–30). The play is at least as much a contest for control of his little kingdom as for Alice's affections. This is a point made in *Suttill contra Suttill*, too, as several witnesses paint verbal pictures of the emblematic moment when William Suttill was locked out of his own house, Alice having seized the advantage of her occupation of it.

In the proto-capitalist society of early modern England, the house was a more contested territory than prevailing ideology was prepared to admit. First, many households did not fit the notional norm, being headed by unmarried men or widowed women. Second, even in households with the normative demographics, the economic reality was that many husbands were required to work away from home. Most wives performed their own labors of cottage industry, market gardening, provisioning, child-rearing, cleaning, doctoring, and the various other forms of production and consumption that required them to supervise servants, exercise authority, and interact with the larger community from their home base. Political ideology could not acknowledge the female forms of social and economic power. Its principal aim was to

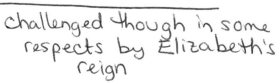

[handwritten marginal note] Challenged though in some respects by Elizabeth's reign

justify its own monarchic form of government, and such a project left no conceptual space for notions of shared governance and split authority. By persisting in formulating the household as a man's kingdom-in-little, ideology rendered itself incapable of addressing many of the real features and challenges of daily life in early modern England. *Arden of Faversham* showed some of the fissures in the dominant belief system – ways in which the patriarchal center did not always hold – and so did the murder plays that followed it.

IV

A Warning for Fair Women is often coupled with *Arden of Faversham* because it, too, concerns a fatal triangle: the "most tragical and lamentable murther" of a London merchant, George Sanders, "acted" by George Browne and "consented unto" by his wife. In fact, *Warning* has less sensation value but may finally be a more subversive play. While members of the *Arden* audience would easily have identified with the emotions and contentions of its principal characters, few could have related to the more exotic elements of its plot: countless collaborators and go-betweens, murderers-for-hire, poisoned crucifixes and portraits. Alice Arden, memorably characterized in the nineteenth century as a "bourgeois Clytemnestra," is one of the great overreachers of Elizabethan drama, undoubtedly recognizable to her contemporaries in her desires but estranged from them by her actions. By contrast, Anne Sanders is thoroughly grounded in the everyday pursuits of purchasing linens and gloves, minding her credit, asserting authority over her servant, monitoring the contents of her fruit closet, and bantering with her son "sir sauce." She is also an unimpeachably loyal wife, rebuffing George Browne when he accosts her. An outside agent, her neighbor Anne Drury, is required to effect her seduction, which is intellectual. Drury, feigning skill in palmistry, pretends to divine Anne Sanders' fate: George Sanders will die and the young widow will marry the gentleman recently met. Once persuaded that Browne will be her next husband, Anne is readily convinced that she owes him anticipatory obedience. Drury effectively enacts in Anne Sanders' private life the domestic analogue of the political formula "The king is dead; long live the king": George Sanders is (soon to be) dead; long live George Browne. Anne Sanders' unwilling complicity in murder is thus effected, ironically, by her deference to authority. From her slippery slope, however, Anne Sanders is then seen to slide so far as to deny her guilt. The play didactically details her doomed resistance, her eventual confession, and, finally, her pious admonitions as she faces the gallows. But the heavy-handed moralizing of this prolonged denouement cannot entirely erase the ideological contestation entertained in the main action. Anne Drury appropriates the very principles of patriarchalism to leave Anne Sanders no ethical safe harbor.

Heywood's two plays on *Edward IV* pose similar challenges to conventional thought. These are nominally history plays, but half their action concerns Edward's mistress Jane Shore, whose story unfolds like a domestic tragedy. Jane is a faithful wife to her goldsmith husband, Matthew, scrupulously attentive to her spousal responsibilities and reputation. When the king "besieges" her, however, she faces a crisis of authority. She is a subject in both domestic and political spheres, and the heads of the two spheres are in conflict. She can remain loyal to her husband and defy her king, or she can obey her king and betray her husband. Again, there is a neighbor of easier ethics, Mistress Blague, whose appetite for status and wealth serves to clarify for us Jane's earnest ambition to choose the right moral course. In time, the king "enforces" Jane's removal to court, and even Matthew then defers to royal authority. But the moral jeopardy is Jane's alone. She is in a position to understand the conflicted emotions of the two apparitors who direct her penance after Edward's death: "I know the King's edict / Set you a work – and not your own desires" (Heywood, 1874b, 165). As she dies in a gutter ("Shoreditch" is here given a false derivation), her final reconciliation with her husband is so heavily sentimentalized as to seem intended to be sympathetic. And in fact, some 15 years later a poem named "The Ghost of Richard III" recalled both the stage-play that had increased Jane Shore's "fame" and the way women in the early modern audience "commiserated" with her. The prevailing metaphysic of order had not equipped her for the moral predicament she confronted.

The true-crime plot of *Two Lamentable Tragedies*, the murder of chandler Thomas Beech by taverner Thomas Merry, is rooted in London's commercial culture of shop-keepers and tradesmen. Its fictional companion plot, the murder of the orphan Pertillo by his uncle Fallerio, centers on wealthy Paduan landowners. The play advances by means of alternating scenes awkwardly mediated by the bombastic choral figures Truth, Homicide, and – establishing a shared motive for these murders – Avarice. The London murder is a lurid one, with Merry striking Beech on the head with a hammer 15 times, carving up his "body" on-stage, toting the torso off to a ditch, and leaving the head and legs in a dark city corner for two watermen to trip over. Suspicious that Beech's shop assistant will identify him as the killer, Merry also attacks the boy, thus producing one of the Elizabethan theater's more memorable stage directions: "Brings him forth in a chair, with a hammer sticking in his head" (sig. D3ᵛ). For what may seem to be obvious reasons, *Two Lamentable Tragedies* has not been a critical success. But neither has it been given its due. Stripped of the usual plot device of sexual intrigue, it lays bare the political substructure of all these plays. Its unifying focus is on political subordinates and their ethical dilemmas. Merry's sister Rachel, an unmarried woman living in her brother's house and, thus, under his authority, is an unwilling accomplice. Her moral horror is movingly detailed, as is her unhappy decision that she cannot betray Merry. In the alternate plot, Allenso is appalled when his father, Fallerio, kills young Pertillo so that Allenso will inherit his cousin's estates, but he, too, reluctantly conceals the crime. He says tellingly that this is "obedience to unlawfulness" (sig. C2). Thus the political submission mandated by conventional thought leads to immoral action, and in this way some of the incapacities of that thought are exposed.

With humble persons as well as gentle, factual plot and also fictional, *Two Lamentable Tragedies* represents more than one strain of the domestic tragedy. It also exemplifies the way in which the murder plays came to shift their focus from female criminals to male. The Wife of *A Yorkshire Tragedy*, a type of the Patient Grissell, faces none of the moral choices and quandaries of Anne Sanders, Jane Shore, and Rachel Merry. Instead the ethical focus of this play is on the Husband, a gentleman who has dispersed an ancient fortune on gambling and riotous living. With his sons impoverished and his brother imprisoned for his debts, he finally recognizes that "That name, which hundreds of years has made this shire famous, in me and my posterity runs out" (iv.75–7). He perversely determines to spare his family further shame by murdering the members of his petty commonwealth: "Bleed, bleed rather than beg, beg. / Be not thy name's disgrace" (iv.105–6). He succeeds in killing two of his three sons and injuring his wife and a servant. In its closing passages, *A Yorkshire Tragedy* imputes these crimes to demonic possession, but once again the moral tone of the conclusion cannot completely erase the many other meanings in play through earlier scenes. There, the Husband seemed to rebel against his own ideologically mandated authority, charging all his difficulties to "the very hour I chose a wife, a trouble, a trouble" (ii.101–2) and to the responsibilities entailed by marriage and housekeeping. Although the Wife implausibly forgives all his crimes, there is little hope of divine mercy for the Husband. And there is no redemption for his radical resistance of his prescribed, patriarchal role.

The Witch of Edmonton is overridingly an issues play, addressing society's harsh treatment of the elderly poor and bastard children, the unhappy consequences of betrothal negotiations and enforced marriages, and the competing belief systems of religion and magic. The title plot is based on the true trial of Elizabeth Sawyer for witchcraft; there is a second plot involving the fictional domestic tragedy of Frank Thorney. Thorney, an impoverished gentleman in service to Sir Arthur Clarington, believes that he has fathered a fellow servant's unborn child. Sir Arthur requires Thorney to marry the pregnant Winifred. Meanwhile, Thorney's father compels him to marry Susan, a wealthy yeoman's daughter, in order to preserve the family estate. When Sawyer's familiar, a devil dog, rubs against him, Thorney is inspired to find a terrible way out of the bigamy to which these conflicting imperatives have impelled him. He murders Susan. Like Sawyer, who uses a matrimonial language to describe herself as "enforced" to witchcraft by poverty and intolerance (II.i.14), Thorney is a victim of the community's harsh moral economies. As do Allenso and Rachel in *Two Lamentable Tragedies* and the Wife of *A Yorkshire Tragedy*, Thorney also suffers from the fact that the ranking figure of his world-in-little is corrupt. Good intentions find no purchase in Sir Arthur's sphere of influence. Thorney's sense of responsibility for Winifred is misplaced, because Sir Arthur is the true father of her child. Winifred cannot succeed in her earnest resolution to reform "From a loose whore to a repentant wife" (I.i.193). And plain-speaking, direct-dealing Susan is murdered for no crime of her own. Even the intervention of the local magistrate, who eventually requires Sir Arthur to recompense Winifred with 1,000 marks, is not restorative. As the Justice intones in the last line of the play, "Harms past may be lamented, not redressed" (V.iii.170).

The main plot of *The English Traveller* is named for its protagonist, Geraldine, recently returned from a tour of Europe. Geraldine is at the center of at least three different affective triangles. First, the elderly Wincott competes so aggressively for

Geraldine's allegiance that his own father, Old Geraldine, forbids his son to see Wincott. Geraldine betrays his father in a midnight meeting which Wincott casts as perfidious on his part, as well ("Nor can be ought suspected by my Wife, / I have kept all so private," Heywood, 1874a, 68). Second, Geraldine's return to England revives his former relationship with Wincott's Wife. The two pledge to reunite, but, in deference to Wincott, to wait until after his death to consummate physically what may nonetheless be seen as emotional disloyalty. Third, it develops that Geraldine's friend Delavill is also interested in Wincott's Wife, although these two do not delay their liaison. Somewhat confoundingly, their adultery is depicted more as a breach of Geraldine's trust than of Wincott's. When Mistress Wincott conveniently expires from shame, leaving a deathbed request that because Geraldine has been "each way noble" Wincott should "love him still," Wincott enthusiastically pledges Geraldine in a "marriage of our love." Thus, formally, *The English Traveller* is not a tragedy. There is nothing to regret in the death of the sketchily characterized Mistress Wincott, and the resolution is clearly meant to be a triumph for Geraldine. Because Wincott's lands will eventually enrich the Geraldine estate, even Old Geraldine is reconciled to what the play insists on portraying as a happy ending. With Geraldine spending much of the play seeking to honor both Wincott's affection and Wincott's marriage, *The English Traveller* follows the strategy of other domestic tragedies in encouraging empathy for characters facing the relational dilemmas of private life – strained though Geraldine's morals are.

V

The most important of Heywood's domestic tragedies is generally agreed to be *A Woman Killed with Kindness*. In each of its two fictional plots, the honor of a house is jeopardized. First, John Frankford welcomes a guest, Wendoll, who eventually seduces Frankford's pliant wife, Anne, and threatens the good order of his household. Second, Sir Charles Mountford incurs so large a debt to his enemy, Sir Francis Acton, that to repay it would cost him his estate and his gentility; instead, he offers to prostitute his loyal sister Susan to Acton. The play acknowledges Frankford's accountability in encouraging Wendoll "to be a present Frankford in his absence" (vi.79). And Mountford's troubles are set in train when he kills two of Acton's servants during a hunting dispute. But *A Woman Killed* also strives mightily to persuade us that the subsequent corrective actions of these order figures are laudable. It terms Frankford "kind" because he does not kill or mutilate Anne. Instead, he exiles her. The members of the household who assemble to witness her expulsion include her children, servants Nicholas, Jenkin, Sisly Milk-Pail, and Spiggot, and also house-guest Cranwell; Frankford is particularly scrupulous to rescue the children from her "infectious thoughts" (xiii.127). Anne serves the play's moral message by thereafter refusing all sustenance and, on her deathbed, validating Frankford's actions. Similarly, Susan endorses the desperate measures her brother takes to salvage his estate. She plans to submit to rape but then kill herself. When Acton is moved instead to marry her, Mountford's tortured honor is presumably understood to be justified. In both plots, then, women's lives are sacrificed to the ethical trials of men whose honor is configured in the moral institution of the early modern household.

Like the other domestic tragedies, *A Woman Killed with Kindness* is occupied with the betrayal of traditional social contracts relating to marriage, service, and community. At issue also is the betrayal of a fading ideology. Heywood's moral universe was old-fashioned even as he replicated it on stage. As social and economic realities conspired to feminize the seventeenth-century household, he struggled to maintain his notion of it as a man's castle and fortress. The women of *A Woman Killed with Kindness* and *The English Traveller* lack the agency and subjectivity that might have made it more difficult for their protagonists to validate a male-centered world view upon them. But it is precisely because state ideology endorsed this masculinist belief system that early modern households had meanings that were peculiar to their time. The ideological mechanism of the domestic tragedies depended on a comprehensive scheme of analogies. In a different generic field, however, Holinshed's apology for including the Arden story was symptomatic of the cultural processes that would eventually trivialize the private sphere. Henry Hitch Adams (1943) and, more recently, Viviana Comensoli (1996) have interested themselves in the long phenomenon of domestic themes in drama, from medieval moralities through eighteenth-century sentimental drama to Ibsen. This has a distorting effect, because the "domestic" had different significances in different times. By the time Collier (1831) came to *Arden* and its fellows, "domestic" meant something far less "important" than had been true during the sixteenth and seventeenth centuries. *A Woman Killed with Kindness* in one of its aspects is a serious tract on the erosion of old ideals of friendship and hospitality and the challenges of the new order of "companionate" marriage and household governance.

This is not to say that the domestic tragedies had no entertainment value. They offered their audiences farcical humor as well as ethical dilemmas. Thomas Arden's countless escapes from his assassins are more comical than miraculous, as the blundering hired guns Black Will and Shakebag are clobbered by a shop shutter, foiled by a locked door, and stymied by heavy fog and their hapless fall into a ditch. *Two Lamentable Tragedies* gives us the shop boy with a hammer sticking out of his head as well as a neighbor who, when roused by the cry of "Murther!," replies "What, would you have some Mustard?" (sig. C4). Even Heywood adds to the second plot of *The English Traveller* the witty servant Reignald. And as a cast of characters gather at Anne Frankford's deathbed to sigh "I'll wish to die with thee," the pugnacious Nicholas – Frankford's household informant about her adultery – unsentimentally interjects "So will not I; / I'll sigh and sob, but, by my faith, not die" (xvii.99–100).

While Reignald is borrowed unapologetically from Roman comedy, Nicholas' best cognate may be found in another case from the Consistory Court of Canterbury.[11] In 1595, Robert Turner, a servant in the household of Thomas Cullen, described the day another servant named Stephen Smyth feigned illness, took himself off to his chamber in the stables, and was joined there by his mistress. Finding occasion to pass by the chamber, Turner observed the two in bed, Mildred Cullen with her clothes thrown up and Smyth with his breeches pulled down. Like Wendoll and Anne Frankford, they had taken advantage of the absence of their household's head. The Cullen case also had its Cranwell, a house-guest named Michael Barber who joined a family card game and unhappily deduced the relationship between Mildred and Smyth. Catherine Wallup, the Sisly Milk-Pail of the Cullen household, was taken on as a servant on December 22, 1594, and she was quick to note that when Mildred Cullen prepared to go to the Canterbury Christmas market, Smyth's hand slid high under her skirts as he helped her mount her horse. By then, it turns out, Cullen already knew of the affair, although in this case his informant is not named. Evidently anxious to avoid the confrontation Frankford engaged in, Cullen dismissed Smyth while Mildred was at the market. The spitefulness of Turner's testimony and the judgmentalism of various neighbors' remarks fade away, though, in the face of former servant Elizabeth Goldup's quiet report. Her deposition suggests that there was deep feeling as well as physical attraction between Mildred and Smyth. After Cullen had settled down for the night, Goldup would regularly fetch Smyth into the main house, where he and Mildred would sit by the fire talking quietly. And, we learn, Mildred endured Smyth's absence for but three days. On December 25, she walked out of the house, leaving the doors open behind her. Consistory Court depositions allow Mildred a subjectivity denied Anne Frankford, but the two women shared one tragic consequence of their actions. The justices of the peace intervened to require Mildred to leave her child with her husband. These were the human tragedies that brought private life to the early modern stage.

Notes

1 Canterbury Cathedral Archives and Library MS X.11.2, fols 215–78 *passim*; and CCAL MS Y.3.13, fol. 39. For an excerpt from the case, see my transcription in Ostovich and Sauer (forthcoming). The case is also briefly discussed in O'Hara (2000).

2 For a review of Arden's textual representations both before and after Holinshed, see especially works by Belsey, Helgerson, and Orlin listed among the "References and further reading." As the *Chronicles* had many authors, "Holinshed" is referred to for convenience rather than strict accuracy. Holinshed's report of the Arden case is excerpted in Wine's edition of the play, from which I cite.

3 Here and below, the dates given generally reference the first printing of a play. Each was probably written and performed some few years earlier. Where a date is proceeded by "*c.*," however, the first printing is demonstrably late, and so a reasonable assumption is made about first performance.

4 Here and below, the reader is referred to the "References and further reading" for full bibliographic information on the critical works cited. Space constraints prevent full acknowledgment of my many debts to these authors.

5 Although Taylor opened this line of conjecture about lost plays, I am indebted here to Henry Hitch Adams' Appendix A, "Lost domestic tragedies" (1943).

6 In a recent study of the genre, Viviana Comensoli persists in identifying those from "non-aristocratic ranks of society" with "merchants, housewives, labourers, farmers, shopkeepers" (1996,

3). But the plays are careful to make distinctions. Thus, for example, *A Warning for Fair Women* includes a scene at court that contrasts with those in Sanders' merchant home, *Two Lamentable Tragedies* features a second plot with wealthy landowners, and *The Witch of Edmonton* includes a knight and declining gentry as well as its yeomen. None of these characters is properly "middle-class" or "bourgeois," terms which imply a class-consciousness that had not yet developed.

7 These editions should be consulted for their introductions and notes as well as their texts. Editions used here are: Cannon (1975); Cawley and Gaines (1986); Dekker et al. (1998); Heywood (1874a, 1874b, 1961); Sturgess (1969); Wine (1973); Yarington (1913).

8 Here and below, the play-texts consulted are listed in the "References and further reading" (citations are of single-play editions rather than collections).

9 The classic work on this subject is Schochet (1975); see also Sommerville (1986).

10 See especially Gowing (1996).

11 CCAL X.11.5, fols 22–55 *passim*.

REFERENCES AND FURTHER READING

Adams, Henry Hitch (1943). *English Domestic or, Homiletic Tragedy 1575 to 1642*. New York: Columbia University Press.

Attwell, David (1991). "Property, status, and the subject in a middle-class tragedy: *Arden of Faversham*." *English Literary Renaissance* 21, 324–48.

Bach, Rebecca Ann (1998). "The homosocial imaginary of *A Woman Killed with Kindness*." *Textual Practice* 12, 503–24.

Belsey, Catherine (1982). "Alice Arden's crime." *Renaissance Drama* n.s. 13, 83–102.

Belsey, Catherine (1985). *The Subject of Tragedy: Identity and Difference in Renaissance Drama*. London and New York: Methuen.

Cannon, Charles Dale, ed. (1975). *A Warning for Fair Women*. The Hague: Mouton.

Cawley, A. C. and Barry Gaines, eds (1986). *A Yorkshire Tragedy*. Revels Plays. Manchester: Manchester University Press.

Christensen, Ann (1997). "Business, pleasure, and the domestic economy in Heywood's *A Woman Killed with Kindness*." *Exemplaria* 9, 315–40.

Clark, Andrew (1975). *Domestic Drama: A Survey of the Origins, Antecedents, and Nature of the Domestic Play in England, 1500–1640*. Salzburg: Institut für Englische Sprache und Literatur, Universität Salzburg.

Collier, John Payne (1831). *The History of English Dramatic Poetry to the Time of Shakespeare*. London: J. Murray.

Comensoli, Viviana (1996). *"Household" Business: Domestic Plays of Early Modern England*. Toronto: University of Toronto Press.

Dekker, Thomas, John Ford, and William Rowley (1998). *The Witch of Edmonton*, ed. Arthur F. Kinney. New Mermaids. London: A. & C. Black; New York: W. W. Norton.

Diderot, Denis (1968). "Second entretien sur le *Fils naturel*." In *Oeuvres esthetiques*, ed. Paul Vernière. Paris: Garnier Frères.

Dod, John and Robert Cleaver (1598). *A Godly Form of Household Government*. London.

Dolan, Frances E. (1992). "The subordinate(')s plot: petty treason and the forms of domestic rebellion." *Shakespeare Quarterly* 43, 317–40.

Dolan, Frances E. (1994). *Dangerous Familiars: Representations of Domestic Crime in England, 1550–1700*. Ithaca and London: Cornell University Press.

Dollimore, Jonathan (1984). *Radical Tragedy: Religion, Ideology, and Power in the Drama of Shakespeare and his Contemporaries*. Brighton: Harvester Press.

Gowing, Laura (1996). *Women, Words, and Sex in Early Modern London*. Oxford: Clarendon Press.

Grivelet, Michel (1957). *Thomas Heywood et le drame domestique Elizabethain*. Paris: Didier.

Guitterez, Nancy (1989). "The irresolution of melodrama: the meaning of adultery in *A Woman Killed with Kindness.*" *Exemplaria* 1, 265–91.

Helgerson, Richard (1997). "Murder in Faversham: Holinshed's impertinent history." In *The Historical Imagination in Early Modern Britain*, eds Donald R. Kelley and David Harris Sacks. Cambridge: Woodrow Wilson Center Press and Cambridge University Press.

Helgerson, Richard (2000). *Adulterous Alliances: Home, State, and History in Early Modern European Drama and Painting.* Chicago and London: University of Chicago Press.

Henderson, Diana E. (1997). "The theater and domestic culture." In *A New History of Early English Drama*, eds John D. Cox and David Scott Kastan. New York: Columbia University Press.

Heywood, Thomas (1874a). *The English Traveller.* In *The Dramatic Works of Thomas Heywood*, ed. R. H. Shepherd. London: John Pearson.

Heywood, Thomas (1874b). *The First and Second Parts of King Edward IV.* In *The Dramatic Works of Thomas Heywood*, ed. R. H. Shepherd. London: John Pearson.

Heywood, Thomas (1961). *A Woman Killed with Kindness*, ed. R. W. Van Fossen. Revels Plays. London: Methuen.

Holbrook, Peter (1994). *Literature and Degree in Renaissance England.* Newark: University of Delaware Press.

Holinshed, Raphael (1587). *The Chronicles of England, Scotland, and Ireland.* London.

Hyde, Patricia (1996). *Thomas Arden in Faversham: The Man Behind the Myth.* Canterbury: Faversham Society.

Newman, Karen (1991). *Fashioning Femininity and English Renaissance Drama.* Chicago: University of Chicago Press.

O'Hara, Diana (2000). *Courtship and Constraint: Rethinking the Making of Marriage in Tudor England.* Manchester: Manchester University Press.

Orlin, Lena Cowen (1994). *Private Matters and Public Culture in Post-Reformation England.* Ithaca and London: Cornell University Press.

Orlin, Lena Cowen (2000). "Chronicles of private life." In *The Cambridge Companion to English Literature*, ed. Arthur F. Kinney. Cambridge: Cambridge University Press.

Ostovich, Helen and Elizabeth Sauer (forthcoming). *Reading Early Women.*

Panek, Jennifer (1994). "Punishing adultery in *A Woman Killed with Kindness.*" *Studies in English Literature* 34, 357–78.

Schochet, Gordon J. (1975). *Patriarchalism in Political Thought.* New York: Basic Books.

Sommerville, J. P. (1986). *Politics and Ideology in England, 1603–1640.* London: Longman.

Sturgess, Keith, ed. (1969). *Three Elizabethan Domestic Tragedies.* Baltimore: Penguin.

Sullivan, Garrett (1998). *The Drama of Landscape: Land, Property, and Society Relations on the Early Modern Stage.* Stanford: Stanford University Press.

Symonds, John Addington (1884). *Shakspere's Predecessors in the English Drama.* London: Smith, Elder.

Taylor, Edward Ayers (1925). "Elizabethan domestic tragedies." Unpublished PhD dissertation, University of Chicago.

Tillyard, E. M. W. (1959). *The Elizabethan World Picture.* New York: Vintage Books.

Ure, Peter (1974). "Marriage and the domestic drama in Heywood and Ford." In *Elizabethan and Jacobean Drama: Critical Essays by Peter Ure*, ed. J. C. Maxwell. Liverpool: Liverpool University Press.

Whigham, Frank (1996). *Seizures of the Will in Early Modern English Drama.* Cambridge: Cambridge University Press.

Wine, M. L., ed. (1973). *Arden of Faversham.* Revels Plays. Manchester: Manchester University Press.

Yarington, Robert (1913). *Two Lamentable Tragedies.* Students' Facsimile Edition. Amersham: John S. Farmer.

27
Romance and Tragicomedy
Maurice Hunt

Romance

A strange silence surrounds English Renaissance dramatic romance. In *Hamlet*, Polonius announces that the players visiting Elsinore are the "best actors in the world either for tragedy, comedy, history, pastoral-comical, historical-pastoral, tragical-historical, tragical-comical-historical-pastoral" (II.ii.387–91) – apparently for every type of play except romance. Heminges and Condell created no category called romance in the 1623 Folio titled *Mr. William Shakespeare's Comedies, Histories, and Tragedies*. According to G. K. Hunter, Edward Dowden in 1876 "seems to be the first person to use the word 'romance' for the purpose of grouping together Shakespeare's last plays" (1997, 501) – *Pericles*, *Cymbeline*, *The Winter's Tale*, and *The Tempest*. The compilers of the First Folio left the first of these plays out of the book altogether, placed the second among the tragedies, and grouped the last two with the comedies. The title-page of one of the first extant English dramatic romances refers to "The Historie of The Two Valiant Knights, Sir Clyomon Knight of the Golden Sheeld . . . And Clamydes the White Knight" (*c*.1570–83; pub. 1599). When not called "histories," the English Renaissance plays we call "romances" were usually known as "comedies" or "tales."

This odd silence partly derives from Elizabethans' and Jacobeans' tendency to think of romance not so much as a kind of play like tragedy as the fable or "matter" of a dramatic tragedy, comedy, or history. Sir Philip Sidney in *An Apology for Poetry* (*c*.1581–3) suggests as much. He complains that elements we recognize as derived from Hellenistic and medieval romance inform English comedies and tragedies, fantastically multi-purpose elements such as an on-stage rock where three ladies walk in a garden, which then produces the report of a shipwreck, and out of the back of which comes "a hideous monster with fire and smoke" (Sidney, 1965, 134). And yet the titles of lost plays written throughout the 1570s suggest that generic romances were being performed. Audiences of this period could have seen "*Cloridon and Radiamanta* (1572), *Mamillia* (1573), *Preda and Lucia* (1573), *Herpetulus the Blue Knight and Perobia* (1574), *Panecia* (1574) . . . *The History of Cynocephali* (1577) . . . *The History of the Solitary Knight* (1577) . . . [and the] *Knight of the Burning Rock* (1579)" (Wilson, 1969, 120). To this non-exclusive list might be added *Lady Barbara* (1571), *Chariclea* (or *Theagenes and Chariclea*) (c.1573), and *Paris and Vienne* (c.1572) (Harbage, 1940, 42–3). Viewers of these plays may not have called them "romances," but many of them knew that their characters and plots derived from those of Hellenistic romance as well as from medieval chivalric romance.

The four best accounts of the ingredients of English Renaissance dramatic romance are given by Pettet (1949, 11–35), Salingar (1979, 28–75, esp. 31–9), Dean (1979, 1–166), and Henderson and Siemon (1999, 216–20). Dean neatly encapsulates the traits of Hellenistic romance. Homer's *Odyssey* constituted the prototype of Hellenistic romances such as Heliodorus' *Aethiopica* (trans. Thomas Underdowne c.1569), Achilleus Tatius' *Clitophon and Leucippe* (trans. William Burton 1579), and Longus' *Daphnis and Chloe* (trans. Angell Day 1587). Hellenistic romance consists of an episodic journey, of a hero's or a pair of separated lovers' wandering toward home or reunion. Along the way, they endure a series of hardships, including shipwrecks and seizure by pirates, as well as marvels and the intervention in their lives of deities. Essentially the characters are idealized – pious and chaste – although accounts of the young couple's interaction sometimes has an erotic quality that appealed to Elizabethans fond of Ovid. Usually the hero or heroine must disguise himself or herself, almost always as a person of a lower social class, at one or more moments during the quest. A token or mark generally precipitates the final reunion of romance between strangers, made so by lapsed time, great distances, and disfiguring suffering, who discover they are husband and wife or lovers. Hellenistic romance thus reaffirms the reality of a providential outcome for suffering, presumably as a reward for virtue maintained though beset by temptation and adversity, and often involving the fulfillment of the riddling terms of an early oracle or prophecy. Hellenistic romance shows seemingly lower-class characters revealed to be aristocrats or royalty, status that could be construed as compensation for enduring the slings and arrows of what appeared to be outrageous fortune. It thus – like medieval romance – appeals to some of the mind's deepest wishes for happiness and a beneficently designed world. While this cluster of traits can most clearly be seen in Shakespeare's *Pericles* and to a lesser extent in his *The Winter's Tale*, it also presumably informed the aforementioned anonymous lost play *Chariclea* (named after the heroine of the *Aethiopica*) as well as *The Queen of Ethiopia* (1578) and *The White Moor* (c.1594–1629).

Pettet describes three distinct strains of non-Hellenistic romance flowing into English Renaissance drama: native medieval romance such as *The Tale of Gamelyn*, *Sir Bevis*, and *The Morte D'Arthur* and foreign medieval romance such as *Amadis de Gaule* and the Spanish *Palmerin*; Italian romantic epics such as those of Boiardo, Ariosto, and Tasso; and certain Spanish and Italian novellas and tales of writers such as Montemayor, Boccaccio, Cinthio, and Bandello (1949, 12). The latter two

strains had their greatest influence on Sir Philip Sidney during the 1580s in his composition of the *Arcadia* and then (probably independently) on the dramatist Robert
Greene. The unknown writers of those 1570s dramatic romances listed earlier, to
judge by the chivalric names in many of their titles, turned for inspiration to the
original or translated pages of specimens of Pettet's first strain of romance: the older,
medieval variety. Here we find many of the basic traits of Hellenistic romance – the
knight's quest, his wandering through a maze of adventures and hardships toward
home, in this case often a redeeming tourney or the supposed location of the Grail.
Along the way, he is plagued by malign magicians, supernatural beasts and dragons,
infidels often in disguise. Binding episodes together is a chivalric code of service to a
lady, of a male fellowship of unbroken (and broken) oaths, and of incessant heroic
battles and single tourneys. Ceremonial pageantry is more apparent here than in
Hellenistic romance, while romantic love often has a darker, sometimes oedipal,
cast. (Shakespeare's Hellenistic romance *Pericles* represents the exception.) The story
of Launcelot's love for Guenever reads like that of a son for a mother, a son who
does not wish to overthrow the father-figure Arthur but brings disaster for him
nevertheless.

Literary historians generally agree that only three dramatic romances of the period
1570–86 are extant: the previously mentioned *Clyomon and Clamydes*, *Common Conditions* (1576 Stationers' Register), and *The Rare Triumphs of Love and Fortune* (c.1582).
All three are anonymous, though Thomas Preston may have written the first two.
Although it is sometimes cited in relationship with Shakespeare's *Cymbeline*, *The Rare
Triumphs* is the least important of the three for the history of Elizabethan dramatic
romance. Its text is a medley of fourteeners, poulter's measure, ten-syllabled couplets,
and blank verse. Classified as a "Mythological Moral" by Harbage (1940, 50–1), *The
Rare Triumphs* depicts the intervention of Jupiter in an agon between Venus and
Fortune to determine who is more powerful in human affairs. These two deities
disastrously shape a romance fable of sundered lovers, an old man maddened by
magical books, and children separated from parents that requires the Jovian imposition of concord, which illustrates the moral that wisdom controls both love and
fortune.

Clyomon and Clamydes, however, best represents the characteristics of pre-Greenian
dramatic romance. The knight Sir Clamydes, son of the king of Suavia, cannot marry
his beloved Juliana until he kills a flying serpent, which seizes virgins and wives to
"feed his hungrie paunch," and brings her its head. Meanwhile, Sir Clyomon, Juliana's
brother and the son of the Danish king, who vanished from court years ago, cleverly
substitutes himself for Clamydes when the latter's father attempts to knight him.
Knighted, Clyomon sets off on a series of adventures accompanied by a holdover of
the morality play tradition – the witty Vice, Subtle Shift (later known as Knowledge).
An off-stage encounter with the flying serpent interrupts Clamydes' vengeful pursuit
of the thief Clyomon. Having beheaded it, Clamydes, however, is charmed by the
mage Bryan Sans Foi, who steals Clamydes' shield and apparel along with the severed
head, intending to win Juliana by their means. A neat allegory thus implies that

Clamydes' faith is not yet strong enough to merit his lady. Meantime, Clyomon, ship-wrecked, is revived by Neronis, daughter of King Patranius of the Strange Marshes. But Thrasellus, king of Norway, thwarts their mutual love by abducting her. Escaping Norway's court, Neronis disguises herself for safety's sake in a male page's clothing. Wandering, she becomes a shepherd's boy. Clyomon finds and kills Norway; Providence descends and prevents Neronis from killing herself after believing mistakenly that Norway has killed her beloved. Neronis then becomes the squire/page of Clyomon unbeknown to him. Strangely disguised himself (his shield covered), he has vowed to fight on her mother's behalf against a knight of Mustantius, who threatens the matriarch. (Actually, the knight is Clamydes in disguise.) Like Jupiter in *The Rare Fortunes*, Alexander the Great appears and dissolves this conflict through the force of reasonable wisdom. In the other main action of the play, Juliana believes Bryan Sans Foi is Clamydes when the former character presents the serpent's head, and she promises to wed him. But the cowardly Bryan flies when challenged to combat by the disguised stranger, Clamydes, and the promise of two royal marriages concludes the romance.

Nowhere do Clyomon or Clamydes indicate that they have matured through the process of having to assume lesser personas and earn a heroic identity. As for romance recognition, Juliana at the play's end oddly keeps insisting that Clamydes is not Clamydes even though she looks into his face, and each of the two knights claims that he is the man. English Renaissance dramatic romance contains a remarkable opportunity for character development. Simply put, dramatic anagnorisis involves the protagonist's recognition of his or her true identity or better self. The physical disguises that a romance character adopts as he or she wanders toward an emotionally charged reunion offer a vehicle for the dramatization of romance anagnorisis, for the moments of their assumption and shedding encourage on-stage an examination of the self. But playgoers would have to wait until 1587–91 and certain romantic plays of Robert Greene for the realization of this rich possibility. Nevertheless, two aspects of *Clyomon and Clamydes* augur well for the development of character and for anagnorisis in later romances. Disguised Neronis once tells Clyomon that her name is *"Cur Daceer"* ("Heart of Steel"). The playwright thus suggests that a new identity and the entailed hardships are fostering a mannish endurance within the princess, a possibility fully realized decades later in *Cymbeline* when Imogen, disguised as the male servant Fidele, exclaims that suffering adversity in that guise in Wales has taught her the flinty virtues of men (III.iv.167–79). Contrasting with silly Subtle Shift as "Knowledge," Alexander the Great articulates a self-knowledge of modesty, a humility that empowers his reconciliation of the bloodthirsty knights. Even though this self-knowledge of Alexander is never absorbed by Clyomon and Clamydes, it represents a conclusive value of the play.

With the short-lived Robert Greene (1558–92), we come to a watershed in English Renaissance dramatic romance, to a writer who shaped diffuse materials into a relatively sophisticated romantic play. The Greene canon consists of four plays written apparently within a brief span: *Alphonsus, King of Aragon* (*c.*1590, pub. 1594); *Friar*

Bacon and Friar Bungay (*c.*1589–90, pub. 1594); *The Scottish History of James the Fourth* (*c.*1590, pub. 1598); and *The History of Orlando Furioso* (*c.*1591, pub. 1594). What most likely was Greene's first play – *Alphonsus* – was written in the wake of Marlowe's stunning *I and II Tamburlaine the Great* (*c.*1587–8). Modern commentators have identified a ten-act schema in Marlowe's related plays of *de casibus* tragedy, of the Scythian shepherd's rise and fall on a wheel of Fortune, perhaps turned by Providence's hand. But Brian Gibbons regards *Tamburlaine* as a heroic romance. "The romance elements of *Tamburlaine*," according to Gibbons, "its vast territorial scope, its wandering hero, the great exploits of love and war, the generation of emotions of sublime awe, wonder, horror, its gratification of wish-fulfilling fantasy, its providential design (however qualified), are in tension with its chronicle-history basis" (1990, 218). Greene's *Alphonsus, King of Aragon* is more obviously a heroic romance; analysis of it can help us understand the degree to which *I Tamburlaine* can be thought of as not only a heroic romance but a comedy as well. In the process, we discover a likely reason for the notorious absence of the term "romance" in surviving Elizabethan and Jacobean records and written accounts of plays.

The complete title of Greene's play in Thomas Creede's 1599 quarto is *The Comicall Historie of Alphonsus King of Arragon*. Analysis of the text reveals neither a clown nor humorous speeches. And yet in the Prologue Greene (through Venus) says that he will "describe *Alphonsus* warlike fame: / And in the maner of a Comedie, / Set down his noble valour presently" (Greene, 1905a, 101–3). Alphonsus' uncle deprived Carinus, Alphonsus' father, of the crown of Aragon, and Aragonians believe that Carinus and Alphonsus are dead. But both are alive, poor unknowns. Alphonsus becomes a base mercenary of Belinus, king of Naples, in his defensive war against evil Flaminius, the present king of Aragon. Alphonsus in battle kills Flaminius and thus begins his gradual climb to Tamburlainian supremacy. He dethrones Belinus and then aims to seize the Turkish crown. The middle of the play includes the romance trappings of the enchantress Medea, a deceptive dream vision of the Turkish monarch Amuracke, and an oracle of Mahomet spoken through a brazen head. Alphonsus defeats Amuracke and imprisons him, but the hero has fallen in love with Amuracke's daughter Iphiginia and she wins her father's release and pardon. Thus a romance laced with heroic combat ends in a projected marriage. Greene's rationale for having the goddess Venus speak prologues to the play as a whole and to each act lies in the concluding moral that love conquers all. In the Prologue to act II, Venus asserts that "Thus from the pit of pilgrim's pouertie / *Alphonsus* ginnes by step and step to climbe / Vnto the toppe of friendly Fortune's wheele" (Greene, 1905a, 352–4). Greene's play is a comedy in the traditional sense that can be traced to Chaucer and Dante: a main character rises from adversity to prosperity, a pinnacle whose drop on the other side of the wheel structure registers the tragic fall to adversity.

Alphonsus, King of Aragon is a heroic romance generating the comic experience. Only part one of *Tamburlaine* could be called a comedy, or – strictly speaking – a heroic romance. Shakespeare's *Henry V*, a play sometimes called a heroic romance, has the above-described comic form. Concluding, like *Alphonsus*, in a strife-ending marriage,

Henry V shows its hero, like Alphonsus and Tamburlaine, at the height of Fortune's (or God's) wheel. Terming *Alphonsus* a chivalric rather than a heroic romance, Charles Crupi judges that "Venus' promise of 'doughtie deeds and valiant victories' . . . recalls plays like *Clyomon and Clamydes*, not *Tamburlaine*, as do the sing-song cadence, stock phrases, and archaic diction of her description of Alphonsus going off to battle" (1986, 102). What romantic dramas such as *1 Tamburlaine*, *Alphonsus, King of Aragon*, and *Clyomon and Clamydes* all have in common is formal comedy – a protagonist's climb as an unknown, through battles and encounters with brazen heads, enchanters, and flying serpents, to romantic love, marriage, and the resolution of armed strife (momentary in the case of the macro-play *Tamburlaine*). Elizabethans may not have thought to apply the word "romance" to the episodic plays they saw that were derived from a tale of a hero of chivalry because they perceived them by and large to be formal comedies.

Greene's major accomplishment involved developing the component of romantic love in romance into relatively complex stories. Whether he was indebted to Sidney's accomplishment in this respect is unclear, for the revised *Arcadia*, first published in 1590 as *The Countess of Pembroke's Arcadia*, could have either closely preceded or followed the writing of every Greene play except *James IV*. Greene most likely read Ariosto's *Orlando Furioso* in the original, patterning after it his Orlando's madness and his character's climb from a "stragling mate" through intermediate identities to become the renowned French hero of Charlemagne's time. And yet Greene's enlightened portrayal of Angelica's and Orlando's love overshadows this sweep characteristic of romance. Greene breaks with patriarchal code when he shows Marsilius, emperor of Africa, urging his daughter Angelica to pick a husband she loves. She chooses the banished Orlando, a man of questionable heroism. Betrothed but not married, Angelica chastely rejects the amorous advances of the villainous politician Sacrepant, who in revenge then slanders her by getting Orlando to believe that she is having an affair with Medor. The situation thus anticipates Iachimo's poisoning of Posthumus' faith in his new wife Imogen in Shakespeare's *Cymbeline*. Sexual jealousy enrages Orlando much more than it does Posthumus, but Angelica throughout her ordeal remains as faithful as Imogen does to her misogynistic mate. Believing Sacrepant's slander, Marsilius puts Angelica in rags and banishes her. Not recognizing "the poore woman" Angelica, Orlando saves her from threatening Brandemart, thus atoning in a sense for his misplaced hatred of her. In *Cymbeline*, Posthumus forgives Imogen even though he believes she is an adulteress. Mad Orlando, however, soon sees the ragged woman as a squire he will knight. He learns of Angelica's innocence from the enchantress Melissa, who charms him into sanity. Melissa also divulges Sacrepant's policy, prompting Orlando as "a common mercenarie souldier" to gain his heroic status by raining blows in a formal fight on the shields of the peers of France, rescuing Angelica condemned by them and her father to death for supposed adultery. Orlando's revelation of Melissa's claims about the heroine's innocence exonerates Angelica in everyone's mind. Like Imogen at the play's end, she never blames her husband for his weak faith in her.

In Greene's *Orlando Furioso*, the lover's and beloved's character development, made possible by the adversity of romance and a series of disguised identities, thus stands midway between the potential for it in *Clyomon and Clamydes* and the self-generated learning seen in Shakespeare's Imogen and Posthumus and in Leontes in *The Winter's Tale*. Queen Dorothea's role in *James IV* perhaps moves Greene even closer in this respect. James authorizes the murder of his wife Dorothea so that he may freely lust after Lady Ida. Dorothea, informed of her husband's homicidal commission, flees the Scottish court disguised as a male squire. Wounded in a sword-fight with the tool–villain Jaques, she is rescued and healed by Sir Cuthbert Anderson, who never learns she is a woman. Meanwhile, rumor informs the king of England of James' part in the presumed death of the king's daughter, and he invades Scotland. Shaken, James prays for the miraculous restoration of his wife to end the slaughter of his blameless subjects. Dorothea anticipates Fidele's transformation into Imogen in *Cymbeline* – the epiphany of chaste, constant womanhood in a male identity – when she reveals herself to her husband, her father, and startled onlookers. Throughout her ordeal, Dorothea has prayed for James' recovery, never losing her self-sacrificial love for him. Romance anagnorisis occurs not within her but within those that her romance metamorphosis of character wonderfully affects. James especially is moved to revalue virtue and the importance of humility, vowing to banish flatterers and politicians from his court. He thus better understands who, as king, he ought to be.

We are close here to the atmosphere and dynamics of the final acts of Shakespeare's late romances. Although the history of *James IV* is basically fictional, Greene's play is a precedent for historical romance, for *Cymbeline* and for Shakespeare's and Fletcher's *Henry VIII* (1613). Between Greene's dramas and Shakespeare's late romances appear plays such as Thomas Dekker's *The Shoemaker's Holiday* (1599), which Hunter describes as a romance adventure play (1997, 370–1) and Gibbons portrays as "the celebration of the city as a land of romance and the citizen as hero" (1990, 231). Despite Greene's accomplishment, romances like *Clyomon and Clamydes* remained popular with plebeian audiences well into the seventeenth century. The most popular play of the English Renaissance was a romance, *Mucedorus*, written anonymously sometime between 1588 and 1598 and reprinted a staggering 13 times before 1639. Complete with a wild man, a bear, a seeming shepherd but an actual prince, and a romantic tale of exile from a court to a forest, *Mucedorus* reportedly was the play King James I most requested. Despite the incongruity, or crudity, of the mix of its elements, dramatic romance bolstered a beleaguered aristocracy's courtly values by presenting idealized aristocratic heroes and heroines. Shakespeare's *Pericles* was reprinted five times between 1609 and 1635. Furthermore, the majority of English dramatic romances show "beneficent [relatively] absolute monarchies all triumphant in the end" (Dean, 1979, 25).

Yet even as dramatic romances drew audiences until 1642, the criticism of Sidney and others that these plays violated classical dicta of drama, such as a tight conca-tentation of events and the so-called unities of time and place, continued to stereo-type them as inferior productions. Ben Jonson, in the Induction to *Bartholomew Fair*

(1614), asserts that he is "loath to make Nature afraid in his plays, like those that beget Tales, Tempests and such-like drolleries." Reinforcing this neoclassical criticism is a series of plays, beginning with George Peele's *The Old Wife's Tale* (c.1589, pub. 1595), that in one way or another poke fun at representative plots and characterizations of dramatic romance (or the taste that romance appeals to). Strongly satirical are John Day's *The Isle of Gulls* (1606) and Francis Beaumont's *The Knight of the Burning Pestle* (c.1607). Day's play reprises some of the characters and motifs of *Mucedorus* as well as several romance features of this highly popular play's source: Sidney's *Arcadia* (most likely as found in the 1593 *Countess of Pembroke's Arcadia*). Through two inset playlets, Beaumont satirizes a naive middling-class taste for a romance of an apprentice's upwardly mobile love affair and of chivalric fantasies like those in *Palmerin of England*. The two quarto printings of Day's play in 1606, and one of Beaumont's in 1613 and two in 1635, attest to a sustained market for the travesty of dramatic romance. Moreover, a survey of the later part of the most recent revised edition of the *Annals of English Drama* lists far fewer new romances introduced onto Stuart stages than was the case during Elizabeth's reign. A new kind of play – tragicomedy – may partly account for this shift.

Tragicomedy

Shortly after he complains that episodic romance contaminates the stage tragedies of his day, Sir Philip Sidney asserts that Elizabethan playwrights create works that are:

> neither right tragedies, nor right comedies . . . but [they] thrust in clowns by head and shoulders, to play a part in majestical matters, with neither decency nor discretion, so as neither the admiration and commiseration, nor the right sportfulness, is by their mongrel tragi-comedy obtained. (1965, 135)

Sidney could have used Thomas Preston's *Cambyses* (c.1558–69) to illustrate his notion of "mongrel tragi-comedy"; the play's full title is *A Lamentable Tragedy, Mixed full of Pleasant Mirth, Containing the Life of Cambyses, King of Persia*. Concerning such mixed-mode plays, Sidney continues:

> I know the ancients have one or two examples of tragi-comedies, as Plautus hath *Amphitrio*. But, if we mark them well, we shall find, that they never, or very daintily, match hornpipes and funerals. So falleth it out that, having indeed no right comedy, in that comical part of our tragedy, we have nothing but scurrility, unworthy of any chaste ears, or some extreme show of doltishness, indeed fit to lift up a loud laughter, and nothing else: where the whole tract of a comedy should be full of delight, as the tragedy should be still maintained in a well-raised admiration. (1965, 135–6)

Implicit in these judgments is the lament that England lacks an academy or a group of theoreticians who might have prescribed the rules for and thus shaped decorous stage comedy and tragedy (and perhaps even tragicomedy). Elizabethan mongrel tragi-comedy had evolved haphazardly, without rule or direction. As late as 1598, John Florio could define "tragicomedy" in his *Worlde of Wordes* simply as "halfe a tragedie, and halfe a comedie" (McMullan and Hope, 1992, 1).

Mid-Tudor playwrights found precedent for their mixed mode in the dramaturgy of the medieval miracle play, which – as in the York *Crucifixion of Christ* – included comic dialogue in tragic biblical episodes, apparently as reminders that the final divine comedy of Christian doctrine makes local human tragedy the catalyst for salvation (Hirst, 1984, 12). Nevertheless, they found a more authoritative model in the plays of the Christian–Terence tradition, which has been called tragedy with a happy ending. Terming his *Christus Redivivus* (*c.*1540–1) "comoedia tragica, sacra et nova" (Herrick, 1955, 217), Nicholas Grimald nicely illustrates the sub-genre, in which the formal structure of classical comedy is imposed upon the details of a somber but redemptive Christian story. In the course of the dramatic narrative, low, comic char-acters mingle with serious figures, and both groups speak diction approximating the urbane style of Terence.

The lone surviving play from the early part of Elizabeth's reign explicitly termed a "tragical comedy" in the text – rather than so implied on the title-page – is Richard Edwards' *Damon and Pithias* (Edwards, 1906, 4), "acted before the Queen at White-hall by Edwards's Children, probably during the Christmas season of 1564–5" (Wilson, 1969, 112). The Prologue craves that playgoers "with heedful ear and eye . . . hear the cause and see th' effect of this new tragical comedy" (5). The play's pagan setting and story of ideal friendship cannot conceal Edwards' reliance upon a Christian–Terentian conclusion for his ending. The tyrant Dionysius' conversion and subsequent pardon and enfranchisement of the eponymous friends, condemned to death as spies, formally delivers the promise on the title-page of the 1571 edition that audiences will see "the excellent *Comedie of two the moste faithfullest* Freends, Damon and Pithias." Moreover, the work is shot through with low comedy involving the servant Stephano, the lackeys Jack and Will, and Grim the Collier. Nevertheless, this is no formulaic tragedy with a happy ending. Armstrong (1958) has shown that the play is tragical in the sense that Damon and Pithias' ordeal, which no fewer than four characters on-stage call a "tragedy," produces the effect of tragedy according to Tudor dramatic theory – that is, the played spectacle of Damon and Pithias' friendship serves to reform a tyrant. Converted Dionysius does tell Damon and Pithias, "the immortal gods above / Hath made you play this tragedy, I think, for my behoof" (Edwards, 1906, 79). No one else would compose a "tragical comedy" in the spirit of Edwards' understanding of the phrase.

In 1604, John Marston's *The Malcontent* entered the Stationers' Register as a "*Tragiecomedia*," a designation apparently reflective of the influence of Giovanni Bat-tista Guarini's Italian tragicomedy *Il Pastor Fido* (1590; English trans. 1602) and his analysis of tragicomic form, *Compendio della poesia tragicomica* (1603) (McMullan and Hope, 1992, 5). Guarini's principles, however, are best understood in the explication below of John Fletcher's *The Faithful Shepherdess*, for the Italian's ideas are only partially evident in Marston's play (Herrick, 1955, 243–5). In "To the Reader," Marston calls his play a "comedy" and implies that it is a "satire" (ll. 26, 32) (Marston, 1964, 4). All five acts of *The Malcontent* (but mainly the first two) exhibit the comical satire (or satirical comedy) for which Marston is generally known. Nevertheless, the play appears headed for tragedy as the motive of revenge animates the protagonist, Giovanni Altofronto, plotting – disguised as the malcontent Malevole – to destroy his adversary, the wicked Mendoza, and punish Pietro Jacomo, the current duke of Genoa, for together deposing him. During a series of thwarted plots and counterplots among these three, Mendoza apparently kills Ferneze, the duchess's lover, and he seemingly murders Malevole with the fumes of a lethal poison, in both cases in full view of the audience. But playgoers later learn that Ferneze lives (to be pardoned for his adultery), and Malevole starts up from the stage, having had the foresight to substitute a harmless substance for the poison. Malevole's gradual awareness of the enormity of Mendoza's wickedness has the effect of converting him from a desire to revenge himself on Pietro to the resolve to league with him secretly to punish Mendoza. Mendoza's apprehension occurs during the concluding Masque of Mercury, a romance device that predicts reconciliation among Malevole, Pietro, and their wives and a non-fatal punishment for Mendoza. Guarini's influence appears in Marston's fashioning the danger, not the death, and in his "decorously" creating characters according to either tragic or comic conventions.

John Fletcher was "the first English dramatist to rescue the term 'tragicomedy' from its 'mongrel' status and to restore its standing in the world of letters" (Herrick, 1955, 261). He did so by constructing *The Faithful Shepherdess* (c.1608–9) according to Guarini's principles. While later praised by Ben Jonson, this pastoral tragicomedy was not popular with original audiences, who, according to Fletcher, expected to see the spectacle of "country hired Shepheards, in gray cloakes, with curtaild dogs in strings, sometimes laughing together, sometimes killing one another" ("To the Reader," ll. 5–7; Fletcher, 1976, 497). But a:

> tragie-comedie is not so called in respect of mirth and killing, but in respect it wants deaths, which is enough to make it no tragedie, yet brings some neere it, which is inough to make it no comedie: which must be a representation of familiar people, with such kinde of trouble as no life be questiond, so that a God is as lawfull in this as in a tragedie, and meane people as in a comedie. (ll. 20–6)

Certain late plays of Shakespeare – notably *The Winter's Tale* and *The Two Noble Kinsmen* (a collaboration with Fletcher) – have been called tragicomedies almost as often as they have been termed romances, mainly because they reflect traits of Fletcherian tragicomedy. Gods do control events in these plays so that elect mortals such as Posthumus and Perdita are spared tragic deaths. But Shakespeare's so-called tragicomedies, rather than wanting deaths, include them. Cloten and Cymbeline's Queen, Mamillius and Antigonus, Arcite – these characters die, apparently the middle two as scapegoats required by the wrathful god Apollo's providence.

On the contrary, Fletcherian tragicomedy would create a distinctive artistry out of the nearness by which characters would be brought to death's threshold and the serio-ludic tone of this staging. In *The Faithful Shepherdess*, Amarillis loves Perigot and seeks to divert his mutual love affair with Amoret by having the Sullen Shepherd dip her into a magical well that transforms her into Amoret. Her wanton wooing of Perigot convinces him that the true Amoret is morally loose, and he pursues Amoret and mortally wounds her. Thrown into the well by the Sullen Shepherd, she is raised and healed by the God of the River. Later, Amoret tells Perigot that she wants to die because she cannot convince him that she is chaste-minded. He obliges by severely wounding her! The Satyre, who earlier took wounded Alexis to the cunning herbalist Clorin, finds bloody Amoret and takes her to this healer. The exhausted Satyre's complaint – "Yet more blood, / Sure these wanton Swaynnes are wood [mad]" (IV.iv.184–5) – must have provoked laughter, giving a serio-ludic tone to the staging. Shakespeare approximates this feature of Fletcherian tragicomedy when in the middle of *The Winter's Tale* the grisly report of the bear devouring Antigonus almost coincides with the comic sight of it pursuing him off-stage and with the punchy dialogue of the Shepherd and his Son, especially the Son's pun that his father's charity would have lacked "footing" onboard the capsizing ship seen offshore.

Like Guarini, Fletcher in his pastoral tragicomedy attempts to characterize individuals decorously according to classical conventions of comedy and tragedy, and he devoted his fourth act to complicating his tragic situation apparently beyond remedy. Like Guarini, he sought to temper comic and tragic elements so that his denouement ultimately recommends the virtue of temperance. (Mowat, 1987, 85, 88; Yoch, 1987). Unlike Guarini, he introduces typically English bawdy humor and a god's direct intervention and magical agents for his resolution. Whether Fletcher achieves Guarini's single end of tragicomedy – the purging of melancholy in the playgoer's mind (Mowat, 1987, 92; Yoch, 1987, 117) – remains debatable. *The Faithful Shepherdess* includes many other features that would compose the signature of Fletcherian tragicomedy: an intricate story, articulated in architectonic symmetries and focused on varieties of love and lust, whose resolution settles questions of state; main characters subject to the expression of strong passions in extravagant poetry (later, a Burtonian "humour" would seriously flaw many of these figures); the sacrifice of the moral development of characters (and often the play as a whole) to opportunities for memorable arias and startling turns in events; the absurd reversal of stock theatrical conventions (as when Perigot stabs suicidal Amoret rather than trying to comfort her); and a vague, often unidentifiable providence underneath events. Beaumont and Fletcher's *Philaster* (c.1608–10) illustrates these qualities in addition to two related ones that would make up Fletcherian tragicomedy: a heavy dependence on physical or figurative disguise, frequently as the means for accomplishing an astounding act-V discovery that rights the play's tortured world. In *Philaster*, the hero's male page Bellario reveals herself to be disguised Euphrasia, Dion's bastard daughter, and thus dispels the slander that Bellario and Arethusa are lovers.

The complete cluster of the traits of Fletcherian tragicomedy appears in *A King and No King* (1611) (Hunt, 1990), which John Dryden called Beaumont and Fletcher's best play (Herrick, 1955, 269). Of the 50 plays in the Beaumont and Fletcher second folio (1679), approximately 15 are tragicomedies, 10 of them explicitly classified as such (Herrick, 1955, 268). After 1611, the best of these are *The Island Princess* (*c.*1619–21) and *A Wife for a Month* (1624). The serio-ludic tragic moment of inflicted wounds and/or apparent death found in *The Faithful Shepherdess* and *Philaster* tends to disappear in later specimens of Fletcherian tragicomedy, giving place to a greater, non-Guarinian emphasis on the building of suspense and the startling discovery of concealed identities. These concealed identities – never known by the audience until act V – also tend to become multiple within a play, suggesting that the primary attraction of this kind of tragicomedy had become playgoers' curiosity over how the dramatist would solve tragic complications, their listening for clues by which they might hypothesize the solution, and their delight and admiration once the discoveries occur. A detective plot overwhelmed the other Aristotelian elements of drama in the less memorable forms of Stuart tragicomedy.

Lee Bliss in chapter 35 below treats Beaumont and Fletcher's drama more fully. For my purposes, it is enough to say that Fletcher and his collaborators and their successors made tragicomedy the most important dramatic phenomenon in England between 1610 and 1650. A systematic writing of tragicomedy according to Guarinian principles never caught on among Stuart dramatists. While one might trace some of the methods of their tragicomedies to the precedents set by the Italian dramatist and theorist, Stuart playwrights were more eclectic, more selective, looser in their dramaturgy. Moreover, even as dramatic romance of the *Clyomon and Clamydes* variety remained popular with certain audiences well into the seventeenth century, so native-strain, hodge-podge English tragicomedy found playgoers until the closing of the theaters. Dekker, Rowley, and Ford's *The Witch of Edmonton* (*c.*1621) and James Shirley's *St. Patrick for Ireland* (*c.*1637–40) testify to this continuing interest. Reasons for the popularity of the different kinds of tragicomedy have been hard to come by. According to William Proctor Williams, for Jacobeans, "the death of Elizabeth I and the accession of James I were a triumph of royal authority – a true and real-life tragicomedy – for the transition of power had been relatively clean, efficient, and without political upheaval" (1987, 143). In this reading, dramatic tragicomedy became a repeated community celebration in a multitude of narratives of this near-miraculous event. On the other hand, others have speculated that, as England drifted toward civil war, tragicomedy became a vehicle of cultural wish fulfillment that showed impending tragedy averted in various scenarios of social life, both past and present.

After Fletcher, the principal Stuart tragicomic dramatists were Thomas Middleton, Philip Massinger, and James Shirley. John Webster wrote a tragicomedy, *The Devil's Law-Case* (*c.*1610–19), but it resembles more the earlier type of English tragicomedy than the Guarinian model, and resorts to the singular expedient of using the law and the courtroom – rather than a character or god – to avert tragedy and effect the tragicomic ending. Among the five Massinger plays labeled tragicomedies, *The Maid of Honour* (c.1621–32) may be his best. The title reflects a special interest of Middleton's, a preoccupation that would point tragicomedy toward Restoration themes. Middleton and Rowley's *A Fair Quarrel* (c.1615–17) creates a tragic complication by showing characters of honor trying to live in a complex world hostile to that virtue (Hunter, 1997, 521–2). Later, Sir William Davenant (1607–68), in tragicomedies such as *Love and Honour* (1634) and *The Fair Favourite* (1638), would anticipate the Restoration's hallmark literary opposition of love and honor. In Davenant's tragicomedies, "reason, love, and honor, as in seventeenth-century French tragicomedy, are all-important possessions and must co-exist in harmony before the noble characters can be happy" (Herrick, 1955, 306). John Ford's two tragicomedies, *The Lover's Melancholy* (1628) and *The Queen* (c.1621–42), respectively illustrate Shakespearean and Fletcherian tragicomedy. The first:

> has to do with the mystery of suffering, with [men and women] in [their] relation to the universe . . . [and with the union of] a tragic sense of loss with the comedy of restoration and renewal by fusing tragic feeling and comic potential, neither of which cancels out the other; [the second] comments on the vicissitudes of everyday social, especially sexual, relationships . . . [during which] the comic depends on the reversal and, in large part, negation of the potentially tragic. (Foster, 1987, 97–8, 99)

Finally, the argument can be made that nearly half of Shirley's 34 plays are tragicomedies in one sense or another. The best of these is *The Royal Master* (1638), in which Shirley most closely follows the pattern of Fletcherian tragicomedy. In fact, several Shirley tragicomedies could be said to outdo Fletcher's in "artfully concealed denouement, startling discoveries, and succession of final surprises" (Ristine, 1910, 139).

In 1668, John Dryden in "An essay of dramatick poesie" has Neander claim that "we have invented, increas'd and perfected a more pleasant way of writing for the Stage than was ever known to the Ancients or Moderns of any Nation, which is Tragicomedie" (1971, 46). Dryden wrote tragicomedies, his favorite *The Spanish Error, or the Double Discovery* (pub. 1681), but by 1695 he would condemn the genre as "'an unnatural mingle; for mirth and gravity destroy each other, and are no more to be allowed for decent than a gay widow laughing in a mourning habit'" (Herrick, 1955, 310). Essentially, however, tragicomedy died with the playwright who had claimed to be Shakespeare's son, William Davenant.

References and Further Reading

Anon (1913). *Clyomon and Clamydes*, ed. W. W. Greg. Malone Society Reprints. Oxford: Oxford University Press.

Armstrong, William A. (1958). "*Damon and Pithias* and Renaissance theories of tragedy." *English Studies* 39, 200–7.

Childress, Diana T. (1974). "Are Shakespeare's last plays really romances?" In *Shakespeare's Late Plays: Essays in Honor of Charles Crow*, eds Richard C. Tobias and Paul G. Zolbrod. Athens: Ohio University Press.

Crupi, Charles W. (1986). *Robert Greene*. Twayne English Authors Series, 416. Boston: Twayne Publishers.

Dean, John (1979). *Restless Wanderers: Shakespeare and the Pattern of Romance*. Salzburg Studies in English Literature, Elizabethan and Renaissance Studies, 86. Salzburg: Institut für Anglistik und Amerikanistik, Universität Salzburg.

Dryden, John (1971). "An essay of dramatick poesie." In *The Works of John Dryden: Prose 1668–1691*, eds Samuel Holt Monk, A. E. Wallace Maurer, and Vinton Dearing. Berkeley: University of California Press.

Edwards, Richard (1906). *Damon and Pithias*, ed. James S. Farmer. In *The Dramatic Writings of Richard Edwards, Thomas Norton, and Thomas Sackville*. Rpt 1966. New York: Barnes & Noble.

Fletcher, John (1976). *The Faithful Shepherdess*, ed. Cyrus Hoy. In *The Dramatic Works in the Beaumont and Fletcher Canon*, gen. ed. Fredson Bowers. Cambridge: Cambridge University Press.

Foster, Verna (1987). "Ford's experiments in tragicomedy." In *Renaissance Tragicomedy: Explorations in Genre and Politics*, ed. Nancy Klein Maguire. AMS Studies in the Renaissance, 20. New York: AMS Press.

Gesner, Carol (1970). *Shakespeare and Greek Romance*. Lexington: University of Kentucky Press.

Gibbons, Brian (1990). "Romance and the heroic play." In *The Cambridge Companion to English Renaissance Drama*, eds A. R. Braunmuller and Michael Hattaway. Cambridge: Cambridge University Press.

Greene, Robert (1905a). *The Comicall Historie of Alphonsus King of Arragon*. In *The Plays and Poems of Robert Greene*, ed. J. Churton Collins. Rpt 1970. Freeport, NY: Books for Libraries Press.

Greene, Robert (1905b). *The Historie of Orlando Furioso, One of the Twelve Peeres of France*. In *The Plays and Poems of Robert Greene*, ed. J. Churton Collins. Rpt 1970. Freeport, NY: Books for Libraries Press.

Greene, Robert (1970). *The Scottish History of James the Fourth*, ed. Norman Sanders. Revels Plays. London: Methuen.

Harbage, Alfred (1940). *Annals of English Drama, 975–1700*, rev. Samuel Schoenbaum and Sylvia Stoler Wagonheim. Rpts 1964, 1989. London: Routledge.

Henderson, Diana E., and James Siemon (1999). "Reading vernacular literature." In *A Companion to Shakespeare*, ed. David Kastan. Oxford: Blackwell.

Herrick, Marvin T. (1955). *Tragicomedy: Its Origin and Development in Italy, France, and England*. Illinois Studies in Language and Literature, 39. Rpt 1962. Urbana: University of Illinois Press.

Hirst, David L. (1984). *Tragicomedy*. Critical Idiom, 43. London: Methuen.

Hunt, Maurice (1990). "Conquering words in *A King and No King*." *South Central Review* 7.4, 23–39.

Hunter, G. K. (1997). *English Drama, 1586–1642*. Oxford History of English Literature, vol. 6. Oxford: Clarendon Press.

Ker, W. P. (1908). *Epic and Romance*. Rpt 1957. New York: Dover Publishers.

McMullan, Gordon, and Jonathan Hope (1992). "Introduction: the politics of tragicomedy, 1610–50." In *The Politics of Tragicomedy: Shakespeare and After*, eds Gordon McMullan and Jonathan Hope. London: Routledge.

Maguire, Nancy Klein, ed. (1987). *Renaissance Tragicomedy: Explorations in Genre and Politics*. AMS Studies in the Renaissance, 20. New York: AMS Press.

Marston, John (1964). *The Malcontent*, ed. M. L. Wine. Regents Renaissance Drama Series. Lincoln: University of Nebraska Press.

Mowat, Barbara A. (1987). "Shakespearean tragicomedy." In *Renaissance Tragicomedy: Explorations in Genre and Politics*, ed. Nancy Klein Maguire. AMS Studies in the Renaissance, 20. New York: AMS Press.

Pettet, E. C. (1949). *Shakespeare and the Romance Tradition*. London: Staples Press.

Ristine, Frank H. (1910). *English Tragicomedy: Its Origin and History*. Rpt 1963. New York: Russell & Russell.

Salingar, Leo (1974). *Shakespeare and the Traditions of Comedy*. Cambridge: Cambridge University Press.

Shawcross, John T. (1987). "Tragicomedy as genre, past and present." In *Renaissance Tragicomedy: Explorations in Genre and Politics*, ed. Nancy Klein Maguire. AMS Studies in the Renaissance, 20. New York: AMS Press.

Sidney, Sir Philip (1965). *An Apology for Poetry*, ed. Geoffrey Shepherd. Nelson's Medieval and Renaissance Library. London: Thomas Nelson & Sons.

Waith, Eugene M. (1952). *The Pattern of Tragicomedy in Beaumont and Fletcher.* Yale Studies in English, 120. New Haven: Yale University Press.

Williams, William Proctor (1987). "Not hornpipes and funerals: Fletcherian tragicomedy." In *Renaissance Tragicomedy: Explorations in Genre and Politics*, ed. Nancy Klein Maguire. AMS Studies in the Renaissance, 20. New York: AMS Press.

Wilson, F. P. ed. (1969). *The English Drama, 1485–1585,* with a bibliography by G. K. Hunter. Oxford History of English Literature, Vol. V. New York: Oxford University Press.

Wolff, Samuel Lee (1912). *The Greek Romance in Elizabethan Prose Fiction.* New York: Columbia University Press.

Yoch, James J. (1987). "The Renaissance dramatization of temperance: the Italian revival of tragicomedy and *The Faithful Shepherdess.*" In *Renaissance Tragicomedy: Explorations in Genre and Politics*, ed. Nancy Klein Maguire. AMS Studies in the Renaissance, 20. New York: AMS Press.

28

Gendering the Stage

Alison Findlay

The relationship between gender and performance has preoccupied early modern dramatists and critics alike, producing a fascinating, wide-ranging debate. This chapter cannot offer a comprehensive account, but by studying examples from 1559–1638, it will consider how, throughout the period, early modern drama articulates the complexities of gendered identity: interrogating stereotyped behavior for men and women, biological essentialism and performativity. The importance of space and the status of boy players and then female actors will be addressed as vital elements in the multi-faceted representations of sexual difference.

From the very beginning of Elizabeth I's reign gendering the stage was a complex process. When she passed through the streets of London on January 14, 1559, the day before her coronation, Elizabeth introduced herself to her population in theatrical terms. Richard Mulcaster, who recorded the event, noted the city was "a stage wherein was shown the wonderful spectacle of a noble-hearted princess toward her most loving people" (Mulcaster, 1999, 22). Elizabeth was greeted by pageants and speeches constructing her as an ideal Protestant monarch. Her interaction with these *tableaux vivants* allowed her to perform the virtues for which she was praised, harnessing the power of dramatic self-representation to establish herself politically. For example, Elizabeth expressed pleasure at the receipt of a Protestant Bible, dramatically kissing it as a "Book of Truth" (ll. 1083–91) (Hackett, 1995, 46–7). She spoke to assure the population, "I will be as good as ever queen was to her people," vowing to spend her blood for their safety (ll. 556–61).

Elizabeth's agency as the key actor and spectator in these proceedings signals a tradition of powerful female self-representation in non-traditional stage venues: spaces like the street, the royal court, the household arena. The development of a female theatrical aesthetic is a huge subject in itself, but will be touched on in the latter part of this chapter with reference to work by Anne of Denmark and Henrietta Maria. In the case of Elizabeth's entry into London, even though she dominated the spectacle, her powers of self-representation were also circumscribed, limited in ways which looked forward to commercial stage practice. When she approached Cornhill, Elizabeth was confronted with "One representing the Queen's Highness sat in this seat crowned with an Imperial crown" (ll. 349–50), a spectacle celebrating her as "prince of peerless fame" (l. 371). Elizabeth could not represent herself, but had to view herself impersonated by a boy. The masculinization of her power was a constant feature of Elizabeth's reign, but the incident broadcasts the marginalization of female identity that was to characterize the commercial theaters where boy actors represented women.

In Thomas Heywood's play *The Fair Maid of the West Part I* (c.1600), the curious pattern of glorification and substitution features again through the idealized heroine, Bess, who blushes to be "pattern[ed]" with "the only phoenix of her age" (V.i.98–9). While overtly denying direct comparisons between the aged queen and a 16-year-old character (played by a boy), the play nevertheless stages the challenges posed by the woman-on-top and tries to manage those within its romantic plot. Bess is a rare combination of traditionally masculine and feminine qualities who crosses boundaries, frequently disturbing the commonplace model of woman as chaste, silent, and obedient. She walks a tightrope, combining unconventional actions and stereotyped feminine virtue. While welcoming customers and their money to her inn, Bess rigidly maintains the modesty required of a woman usually confined to the domestic sphere: "beyond that compass / She can no way be drawn" (I.ii.60–2). When assaulted by Roughman, she dresses as a man to put down the braggart in a fight, but excuses her behavior as a defense of her household:

> Let none condemn me of immodesty
> Because I try the courage of a man
> Who on my soul's a coward; beats my servants
> Cuffs them, and, as they pass by him, kicks my maids
> Nay, domineers over me, making himself
> Lord o'er my house and household.
>
> (II.iii.27–32)

Bess's protection of herself and "my house and household" looks forward to Moll Cutpurse's wonderful defense of women in *The Roaring Girl*, when she overcomes Laxton (III.i.89–110) and champions her sex in a powerful rebuttal of male assumptions that all women are sexually insatiable, defining them instead as the victims of financial necessity and male lust.

The revelation of Roughman's cowardice is essentially comic, yet Bess's strength as a woman-on-top ("Lie down / Till I stride over thee" (II.iii.72–3)) hints at an underlying insecurity which troubles the men around her. Roughman remarks "I was ne'er so put to't since the midwife / First wrapp'd my head in linen" (III.i.13–14), suggesting that Bess's assertive behavior reduces him to infantile dependency. Her male attire gives her "manly spirit" (II.iii.5) but unmans him. Laura Levine has identified in discussions of cross-dressing and its supposed effeminizing effects an "unmanageable anxiety that there is no such thing as the masculine self" (1994, 24). Boy actors wearing female costume (like the boy playing Bess) and women-monsters like the cross-dressing character both disfigured the signs constituting gendered identity. In such a process, the traditionally dominant position occupied by the male is in danger of being stripped of its difference from the inferior female position. Janet Adelman (1992) has examined such a collapse in psychological terms as a return to the symbiotic relationship with the mother, whose presence threatens to suffocate the male figure's sense of individual identity. In Bess's reduction of a rough man to a baby swaddled by the midwife, the play comically hints at the consequences of Queen Elizabeth's powerful rule as mother of her country.

Since biblical authority forbade men to wear women's clothes and women to wear male attire, specifically armor (Deuteronomy 22:5), the military woman is usually shown as a witch or an unnatural beast, "a tiger's heart wrapped in a woman's hide" (*Henry VI Part 3* I.iv.138). However, Bess's transvestism is never condemned; it seems to be part of a festive tradition in which, according to David Cressy, cross-dressing was not seriously transgressive (1996, 461). Her romantic quest helps to diffuse the threat. Bess is dedicated to her lover Spencer, even when she believes he is dead, her constancy something "all lovers will commend" (III.iv.114). Cross-dressing to follow lovers into battle or to avenge their deaths was celebrated in a popular tradition on which Bess draws, comparing herself to "Mary Ambree or Westminster's Long Meg" (II.iii.13). The reappearance of Spencer and the happy resolution in the lines "we'll see thee crown'd a bride" (V.ii.147) promise the marriage destiny which Queen Elizabeth had refused. The romantic plot thus plays out what was lacking in the Maiden Queen, offering an illusion of marital containment which could not be achieved in Elizabethan England. (The fate of Bess the chaste wife was dramatized in *Part II*, staged before Charles I and Henrietta Maria in 1630/1631.) Hints of an excessive female energy even unsettle the ending of the play, though with comic surprise. In the Moorish court, Bess is about to be united with Spencer, and asks the king of Fez to favor her "brave" (handsome) gentleman, to which the king responds, "see him gelded to attend on us. / He shall be our chief eunuch" (V.ii.92–3). Bess's actions threaten to castrate the hero and reduce him to dependence on her "constancy" (V.ii.121) or her acceptance of a fiction in which she will fall back into the submissive position accorded to woman.

If, as *The Fair Maid of the West Part I* suggests, gender cannot be securely fixed by clothing or by traditionally gendered activities, perhaps the surest way of demarcating the sexes on stage was through representations of an essential biological process: reproduction. Even though the female body was absent from the public stage, the boy actor's performance of pregnancy could signify womanhood, and, implicitly, the subjection to male authority which was part of Eve's punishment. Representation was apparently not a problem: dramatists entrusted boys to play various stages of pregnancy in plays as diverse as *A Woman is a Weathercock*, *All's Well That Ends Well*, *The Winter's Tale*, *'Tis Pity She's a Whore*, and *Women Beware Women*, for example. Using the biological "certainties" of reproduction to secure the gender hierarchy on which early modern patriarchy relied was much more problematic, however, as can be seen from Middleton's *A Chaste Maid in Cheapside* (*c.*1611). The plots, involving a remarkable number of tropes of Jacobean womanhood, focus on a comic mismatch between the feminized world of the flesh and the masculine word or letter of the law. The ebullient fullness of the female body is a source of pleasure and regeneration, but difficulty in regulating its activities undermines homosocial control of the city. Touchwood Senior confesses to the audience: "I am the most unfortunate in that game / That ever pleased both genders: I ne'er played yet / Under a bastard" (II.i.54–6). Gaming is a metaphor for sex: the real gamble of the comedy. Even the promoters see sex as an essential part of the circulation of money (II.ii.69–74). Here, Touchwood Senior's pun on the word "bastard" (an illegitimate child and the losing card at the end of the game) touches on the basic insecurity at the heart of patriarchy. The female reproductive body could not be absolutely controlled. Paternity payments were sought in the case of unmarried mothers, and since biological paternity could not be proved or denied, potentially any man could be left with the charge of a bastard. The comic scenes in which the Country Wench accuses Touchwood Senior of fathering her child, receives payment from him, and then tricks the promoters into caring for it demonstrate "she that hath wit may shift anywhere" (II.ii.148). Female flesh literally outwits the masculine word of law: the Country Wench profits while the promoters lament "half our getting must run in sugar-sops and nurses' wages now" (II.ii.194–5).

Marriage, the institution designed to contain the regenerative female body, also held dangers for men. Legally, the child of a married woman was assumed to be her husband's unless non-access or impotence could be proved. The uncertainty of paternity within marriage is a classic example of masculine anxiety as "a necessary and inevitable condition" of early modern patriarchy (Breitenberg, 1996, 2). *A Chaste Maid in Cheapside* dramatizes Mark Breitenberg's thesis that such anxiety works simultaneously on two levels: first it reveals "the fissures and contradictions of patriarchal systems" and paradoxically it also "enables and drives patriarchy's reproduction and continuation of itself" (1996, 2). In Middleton's play, anxiety is expressed not by the cuckolds but by the wider male community. Cuckoldry is simultaneously the basis of strong cooperative bonds between the men, as, for example, the arrangement between Allwit and Sir Walter Whorehound. The cuckold Allwit proclaims this is the "happiest state that ever man was born to!" (I.ii.19–22), yet others are anxious on his behalf. One of his servants observes "he falls to making dildoes" (I.ii.60), hinting at his sexual inadequacy as well as his singing. Sir Walter despises him, claiming he has lost the "soul's pure flame" of manhood (II.ii.41–2).

A more literal instance of male insecurity serving to drive patriarchy's reproduction of itself is the impregnation of Lady Kix by Touchwood Senior, where the gap in male control allows for a happy ending to the sterile marriage. Sir Oliver is oblivious to the double entendres surrounding the "cure" which Touchwood Senior brings, but Lady Kix and her lover-to-be are all too conscious of her husband's failure to "stand" (III.iii.126–30). As well as providing the longed-for heir for Sir Oliver, adultery ironically serves to make Lady Kix into a proper woman:

Sir Oliver	Thou art nothing of a woman.
Lady Kix	Would I were less than nothing! [*Weeps.*]
Sir Oliver	Nay, prithee, what dost mean?
Lady Kix	I cannot please you.
Sir Oliver	I' faith, thou art a good soul; he lies that says it. Buss, buss, pretty rogue. [*He kisses her.*]

(III.iii.84–9)

This brilliantly observed scene, where the Kixes alternate "kissing or scolding" (III.iii.45), conveys their frustration in a comic mode that simultaneously disguises and expresses the desperation of a couple longing to have children. Only maternity confers identity, so the gossiping where "Everyone gets before me" (II.i.169) is a painful occasion for Lady Kix.

The gossiping scene (III.ii) emphasizes maternal presence in contrast to the uncertain absence of paternity. Its feminine bias is anticipated when the Wet Nurse equivocally tells Allwit that his daughter is "the best piece of work that e'er you did," reversing the usual preference for male children (II.ii.24–7). The scene begins with the direction for Mrs Allwit's bed to be "thrust out," a significant way of gendering the stage. In early modern England, the birthing room remained a closed, all-female space, its secrets guarded by a community of sisterly visitors. In 1633, a young man named Thomas Salmon was presented before the archdeacon's court for cross-dressing to join the celebrations at a birth room. As David Cressy has remarked, it was not Salmon's cross-dressing per se which the court found disturbing, but his invasion of a female space (1996, 464). In dramatic representations, spectators are confined to the masculine role of outside observers, as in the off-stage birth scenes of *The Duchess of Malfi* and *All is True*, although the onset of labor is shown by Thaisa in *Pericles* and the eponymous heroine of *The Dutches of Suffolke*. In act 3, scene ii, of *A Chaste Maid in Cheapside* the exclusivity of the birthing room overflows into the Christening feast. The male characters quickly retire, as if sensing their intrusion. Displaying a gossips' meeting on stage must have been a curiosity. Men in the audience would cast themselves, like Thomas Salmon, as transvestite spectators, while many female spectators would have been able to laugh knowingly from the privileged position of those with experience of the real event.

Masculine anxiety about what might happen at a gossips' meeting is suggested in the words of preacher Robert Hill, who recommended that in the case of the newly delivered woman, "all that are about her to avoid at this time effeminate speeches, wanton behaviour, and unseasonable mirth, which doth often accompany such meetings as this" (Cressy, 1997, 85). It is as though the event of birth, a messy, undignified, but hopefully joyful occasion, creates space for celebration of the material body, specifically the female body, traditionally the locus of all that was grotesquely unfinished, open, and opposed to the closed, proper, masculine body of the law and reason. The gossips' behavior in *A Chaste Maid* plays out Hill's worst nightmares: they consume sweetmeats voraciously and imbibe huge quantities of wine. The openness

of the female body, constantly dissolving boundaries, threatens to reduce male characters to infants, as in the case of Tim, whose indignation at being "served like a child,
when I have answered under bachelor" (III.ii.146) symbolizes the fragility of the
authoritative masculine word, the learning of Cambridge. The same insecurity haunts
sexual activity in the comedy. By arguing that the women are contained by marriage
at the end of the play, Gail Kern Paster fails to acknowledge the threat which the
leaky body continues to pose, secretly, silently, in the production of children whose
paternity always remains a mystery (Paster, 1993, 23–63).

Female confinement appears in a much more negative light in the romantic plot
of *A Chaste Maid*, where gender difference is explored at the crucial moment of
betrothal. Although mutual passion between Touchwood Junior and Moll Yel-
lowhammer humanizes the younger brother's interest in a rich prize, Moll is still an
object of exchange between her father and lover, even in a stolen match (I.ii.196–200).
For Moll, the household becomes a frighteningly claustrophobic space, like the coffin
into which she is placed. Her vow of love draws attention to the tyranny of confinement endured by many tragic heroines whose desire transgressed parental wishes:
"Though violence keep me, thou canst lose me never; / I am ever thine although we
part for ever" (III.i.57–8). Tim's determination to guard his sister with "Harry the
Fifth's sword" (IV.iv.57) mocks the predatory protection of woman as goods. As a late
entry into the dramatic debate over arranged marriage, *A Chaste Maid* critiques the
possessive "love" of the Yellowhammers in the public mourning over Moll's supposed
death.

Kathleen McLuskie suggests that *A Chaste Maid* may be a "travesty of theatrical
narratives" like *Romeo and Juliet* (McLuskie and Bevington, 1999), but the more playful
aspects of parody which could be achieved in performances by the boys' companies,
are, arguably, not as obvious in companies composed of adult and boy actors. If, as is
probable, *A Chaste Maid* was written for a combination of Lady Elizabeth's Men and
the Queen's Revels, then Moll and Touchstone Junior's fates could have given the play
a darker, tragicomic tone. Lisa Jardine notes that in tragedies, the boy actor's presence is effaced by tragic identification (1983, 23). The powerful cry of Webster's protagonist, "I am Duchess of Malfi still" (IV.ii.152), depends for its tragic effect on a
sense of female integrity, not awareness that a boy actor "lies" behind the role. Commendatory verses by Middleton and Rowley remark that the Duchess was so "lively
body'd in thy play" as to raise tears in the audience (1999, 567), suggesting immersion in the heroine's story. Fully representing the female self is also the keypoint of
Elizabeth Cary's *The Tragedy of Mariam* (1613). Although there are no records of a
seventeenth-century production of Cary's play, the text makes clear that its heroine
declares her emotions publicly in performance, debating her responses to each turn of
the plot and refusing to adopt an antic disposition to perform for her husband
(III.iii.47–8). Such unguarded representation costs Mariam her life, and even in a
"safe" household playing arena, she experiences self-division, imagining a fight
between the persona she identifies with, and the womanly model which Herod and
patriarchal society expect of her:

Had not my self against my self conspired,
No plot, no adversary from without,
Could Herod's love from Mariam have retired,
Or from his heart have thrust my semblance out.
                                                    (IV.viii.9–12)

Identity crises like this are not peculiar to female figures. Tragedy is just as much a staging of heroes' gender insecurities. In addition to cuckoldry, the performance of ambition and authority in a world governed by giddy fortune constantly challenges the masculine sense of self. Manhood, as constituted in early modern England, is a fleeting illusion, "a tale / Told by an idiot, full of sound and fury / Signifying nothing" (V.v.25–7), as Macbeth comes to realize.

Staging often added to the exposure of gender as a fragile, insubstantial pageant in tragedy. Spectators were sometimes confronted by scenes in which the boy actor's body was required to play the specifically female body as a site of difference; as, for example, by the revelation of a breast. In *Antony and Cleopatra*, Cleopatra dies with an asp at her breast, like a baby "that sucks the nurse asleep" (V.ii.305), and audience attention is focused directly on the physical body. Stallybrass remarks that at such crucial moments, we are presented with contradictory attitudes about sexuality and gender: first gender as a set of prosthetic devices, and, conversely, gender as the "given" marks of the body, signs of absolute difference. However, the stage undoes the essentialism of such difference, since those signs are located "upon another body," that of the boy actor (Stallybrass, 1992, 73–4). The paradox of presence and absence in the case of the female body is seen in *The Duchess of Malfi*, where the truth of the Duchess's pregnancy is hidden behind her "loose-bodied gown" (II.i.171), much to Bosola's annoyance. He teases the midwife for knowing "the trick how to make a many lines meet in one center" (II.iii.26–7), but of course at the center of the staged Duchess is the absence of the full womb. In such cases, "the fetishistic signs of presence are forced to confront the absences which mark the actor's body" (Stallybrass, 1992, 71). The body is also a false witness in *The Changeling*. Alsemero's fantasy of the ideal, chaste wife is a fiction, even though he tests Beatrice-Joanna's virginity with the glass M. By performing the correct symptoms, sneezing, gaping, and then falling into a "dull, heavy and lumpish" (IV.i.52) melancholy, the character mimics what the boy actor would have to do to perform female virginity (IV.ii.136–47).

The play of possibilities which the transvestite boy actor offered to dramatist, actor, and spectators was exploited to the full in plots which involved cross-dressing. It is impossible to pin down the effects such stage transvestism created, since the sexual dynamics shift from moment to moment in production, inevitably differing in each performance and for every spectator. A transvestite disguise can blur gender distinctions, teasing out the implications of the Galenic model for human anatomy, in which female genitalia are an inverse model of the male. Anti-theatricalists certainly argued that cross-dressing collapsed essential biological differences between the sexes in the eyes and minds of the beholders. Dramatists often seem to flirt with

Laconian post structuralism

the idea that signs, clothes, have the power to undo gender, to turn Galen's genital models inside out. In *Twelfth Night*, for instance, the mirroring of Sebastian and Viola suggests masculine sameness as much as difference on an early modern stage, thus undoing the heterosexual resolution in marriage which is deferred beyond the end of the play.

However, Janet Adelman has shown that the so-called "one-sex" model, derived from Galen, did not hold much sway in vernacular medical texts of the period, however attractive a tool it may be for analyzing transvestite theatre (1999). Such texts show more interest in sexual dimorphism, differences between male and female bodies. For spectators conscious of this distinction, the anti-theatricalists' complaints against the ungodly blurring of genders must have seemed exaggerated. Jonson's *Bartholemew Fair* caricatures and ridicules such ideas in the Puritan Busy, whose objections are outfaced by the puppet who *"takes up his garment"* to show *"we have neither male nor female among us"* (V.vi.114–25). Leatherhead uses the puppet to critique Busy's lack of theatrical awareness, implicitly arguing that any normal spectator can distinguish between art and life and read theatrical costume as simply that. In such cases, as Judith Butler argues, theater offers a "safe" containment of categories, since one can say "this is just an act," and even transvestite theater, which constitutes "a modality of gender that cannot be readily assimilated into the pre-existing categories of gender reality," refers back to a "discrete and familiar reality in which genders are distinct" (1990b, 278). The puppet's threat of "nothing" does not relate to a dissolution of gender boundaries, but an absence of gender distinction without performance. In early modern England, gender was not insecure because of a belief that the sexes were biologically very similar, differences between them likely to collapse. Rather, in a culture founded on sexual difference, the reiteration of that difference had to be constantly re-played or re-cited.

The disturbing relationship between biological difference and performance is central to the plots of Jonson's *The New Inn* (1629) and Brome's *The Damoiselle* (1638), which follow in the tradition of Jonson's *Epicoene* (1609), and use cross-dressing to trick the audience. *Epicoene* offers a wonderful *coup de théâtre* in the revelation that the heroine is a performance by a boy character, mirroring the reality (or fiction) of "her" representation on stage by the boy actor. *The New Inn* and *The Damoiselle* both feature cross-dressed characters called "Frank" whose gendered performances unaccountably shift register, and so can no longer be contained "safely" within the realm of playing. In *The New Inn* Frank is introduced as a beggar boy, the adopted son of the Host. He is dressed up as "Laetitia" by Lady Frances Frampul, to impersonate her long-lost sister and fool her suitors. Lord Beaufort falls for the beautiful bait and marries "Laetitia" at the inn. At the end of the play a series of unmaskings outwits the audience and all but two of the characters.

A comic denouement is staged by the Host and the ladies, who reveal Frank underneath the lady's costume, "a counterfeit mirth and a clipped lady" (V.iv.48). However, this is quickly upstaged by an Irish beggar-woman's surprise revelation that Frank is her daughter, so the marriage can stand (II.vi.25–7). In this second unmasking, the figure of Frank/Laetitia offers a fantasy of social integration and moral reform in the possibility of a cross-class match. A third unmasking finally reveals Laetitia as the cross-dressed character s/he was playing: the daughter of the estranged Lord and Lady Frampul (who had been disguised as the Host and Irish beggar-woman). The "true Laetitia" collapses the transvestite possibilities, and with them the social and political transgressions. Only Prudence, the lady's maid, is able to rise above her birth and marry into the nobility, and even her transformation to a lady is illusory. When Lady Frampul criticizes Pru's failure to read her mistress with the sisterly insight of a lady, the character begins to take off her gown, revealing the boy player's body, and protesting "I will not buy this play-boy's bravery / At such a price, to be upbraided for it / At every minute" (IV.iv.322–4). With this reflexive gesture, the performer acknowledges the fantasy of transcending sex and dependence on commercial theater, to become a lady in her own right.

Brome's *Damoiselle* seems to be deliberately constructed as a mirror image of Jonson's text, in that his "Frank" is a cross-dressed boy, the son of a ruined knight Brookeall. The "Rifling" (or raffling) of the Damoiselle's virginity is a money-making project set up by the knight Dryground, who disguises himself as a Host and offers to help Frank, to repair his crime of impregnating and abandoning Brookeall's sister. Unbeknown to the audience the Damoiselle is a fiction, the fantasy of Dryground's lost bastard daughter. Like Jonson, Brome uses the transvestite to critique the commodification of women and the corrupt capitalist world of self-interest, of which Caroline London offered notable examples. Frank represents woman as an idealized savior who can convert the whole city and the law from its corruption (Brome, 1873, p. 462).[1] The most extreme conversion is that of Wat, the villainous usurer's son, who condemns the prostitution of the Damoiselle and declares he will "take a Beggar, / And joyn in trade with her, though I get nothing" (p. 458). Brome substitutes a real child for the fantasy transvestite child to rewrite Jonson's pessimistic conclusion. Because Wat declares himself willing to marry the beggar Phillis, he is rewarded by the revelation that she is Dryground's real bastard daughter at the end of the play. Uncasing Brookeall's son Frank, Dryground declares "His Sonne's my Daughter" (p. 464), little knowing that his real bastard daughter has shadowed Frank's symbolic status throughout the play, begging to gain a dowry and getting her donors to compete in alms, almost as they would in dice. When Phillis steps into Frank's place, the fantasy of redemption can be sustained. From the perspective of the audience, however, "she" looks no different from the "Frank" who has just been uncased. "She" is still an illusion created by the boy actor. The play wryly acknowledges that its optimism for reform may be just as fantastic in the real world outside the theater.

In both plays "Frank" is a fantasy child, a figure for a lost, ideal wholeness, whose indeterminate identity as both a boy and a girl is, as Marjorie Garber remarks, "the ultimate 'transvestite effect'," the "signifier that plays its role only when veiled" (1992, 92). Reading both Franks in terms of the Lacanian model of comic phallic fetishism situates them as the equivalent of Lacan's third term, which exceeds and evades the conventional masculine and feminine positions of "having" or "being" the phallus, by

"seeming" or "appearing." To quote Lacan, the transvestite performer is "the intervention of a 'to seem' that replaces the 'to have' in order to protect it on the one side
and to mask its lack in the other" (1977, 289). The gender-swapping Franks enact
the undecidability of castration, an illusion of original wholeness. Such wholeness is
a fantasy, and by superimposing different performances of gender or "seeming" to trick
the audience, these plays push the boundaries of playing and being beyond the stage
to suggest that there is no final referent for "sex"; that sexuality is performative. In
both plays, the gender of "Frank" is what Baudrillard would call a simulacrum, "never
again exchanging for what is real, but exchanging in itself, in an uninterrupted circuit
without reference or circumference" (1988, 170). The boy actor is there behind both
male and female roles, but remains ambiguous, unreadable.

In *The New Inn* Lovel is told that Frank "prates Latin / And 'twere a parrot or a
play boy" (I.iii.4–5), but the "hidden" Frank who speaks Latin is simultaneously,
within the world of the play, a girl. In *The Damoiselle*, Frank's identity is also ambiguous. Dryground dismisses his supposed daughter by calling her both "Maid" and
"Frank," and reminding her of her housekeeping duties: "In Maides about your work.
And heare you Franck / Discharge the Butchers, and the Chandlers Bills" (p. 417).
To the audience, both these "Franks" are unreadable. Neither is perfectly Frank: they
point to a perfection of gender (either male or female) which is absent, beyond the
stage. Indeed, in *The New Inn* Frank is called "My Lady Nobody" (II.ii.54), signifying both the lack of a female performer (no/body) and her/his fantastic nature.

The transvestite does, however, create the possibility of reading the female body in
positive rather than negative terms, opening a space in which we can move beyond
Freud and Lacan, to where female subjectivity and desire can be articulated in positive terms. The unstable signifier of "Frank" undoes binary oppositions of male subject
and female object. For the heroines of *The New Inn*, entry into the symbolic order is
an unusual process. In act 2, scene ii, Jonson creates a mirror effect by placing the
cross-dressed Frank opposite her/his real sister, Frances:

Lady F	Is your name Francis?
Frank	Yes.
Lady F	I love mine own the better.
Frank	If I knew yours
	I should make haste to do so too, good madam.
Lady F	It is the same as yours.
Frank	Mine then acknowledgeth
	The lustre it receives by being named after.
Lady F	You will win upon me in complement.
Frank	By silence.
Lady F	A modest and well-spoken child.

(II.ii.19–26)

At one level Frank/Laetitia is playing the deferential social inferior or younger sister,
as befits convention (although in the latter case we have a fascinating example of an

all-female construction of female subjectivity). At another level, however, we see a redefinition of woman as lack. Lady Frances is constructed as the primary subject and the apparently male "Frank" is a second copy, who "acknowledgeth / The lustre it receives by being named after," and who plays feminine modesty and silence. This inversion of normal gender roles continues when Lady Frances creates a model or projection of her desires for agency by cross-dressing Frank as Laetitia, the woman with a phallus, in order to gull her suitors in the Court of Love. Frank/Laetitia, who appears to "have" the phallus, is the catalyst which allows Lady Frances to acknowledge and express her passion for Lovel. As we have seen, this arena of cross-dressing also inspires Prudence to perform as Queen of the Court, and ultimately provides the gateway to a cross-class wedding with Lord Latimer.

In *The Damoiselle* subject and object positions, masculine originals and female copies, are reworked by the elusive eponymous character. The name "Frank" and his/her French education link female agency and its relation to performance to the figure of Henrietta Maria. Frank's strangeness (as an alien in terms of nationality and gender – neither fully male nor female) exposes the English commodification of women. In the comic sub-plot, the Damoiselle coaches Magdalen Bumpsey and her daughter Jane in courtly French deportment, promising "Ile artifice you" (p. 455):

> for the Art of dressing, setting forth
> Head, Face, Neck, Breast; with which I will inspire you.
> To cover, or discover any part –
> Unto de best advantage.
>
> (pp. 455–6)

Here drag subversively repeats gender so as "to promote a subversive laughter in the pastiche-effect of parodic practices in which the authentic and the real are constituted as effects" (Butler, 1990a, 146). Frank shows how all women reproduce themselves as artifacts, effectively constructing themselves from the transvestite viewpoint of the male gaze.

The danger in this is that femininity is always "drag," even when performed by a woman, because masculinity is the norm and the original. However, in Brome's play the transvestite's Tiresias-like knowledge leads him into a discussion of male artifice which inverts subject/object positions and presents men dressing to please the gaze of the Other. The Damoiselle's lesson on how to "cover, or discover any part – Unto de best advantage" (p. 456) shows men imitating the feminine arts of performance, and reveals their anxiety to authenticate themselves through artifacts. On the fashion of bare neck and shoulders, Frank declares:

> 'Thas been suggested by invective men,
> Women, to justifie themselves that way,
> Began that Fashion. As one tother side,
> The fashion of mens Brow-locks was perhaps

Devis'd out of necessity, to hide
An il-grac'd forehead; Or besprinckled with
The outward Symptomes of some inward griefe.
As, formerly the Saffron-steeped Linnen,
By some great man found usefull against Vermine,
Was ta'ne up for a fashionable wearing.
Some Lord that was no Niggard of his Beauty,
Might bring up narrow brims to publish it.
Another, to obscure his, or perhaps
To hide defects thereof, might bring up broad ones.
As questionless, the streight, neat timber'd Leg,
First wore the Troncks, and long Silk-hose: As likely
The Baker-knees, or some strange shamble shanks
Begat the Ancle-breeches.

Magdalen   Sure the men
Took that conceit from us. What woman shewes
A Leg, that's not a good one? [*She shewes a swadled leg*]

Frank   These among men, are followed for the fashions,
That were invented for the better grace.
(As our attires) to set off Limb, or face.

Magdalen   Good lack! What knowledge comes from forraigne parts?
(pp. 456–7)

"Saffron-steeped Linnen," or yellow ruffs, were, of course, a form of masculine attire adopted by some aristocratic women, against which complaints were made in the 1620s. What is more important in this extract, however, is the way in which competition over costume, the ultimate artifice, functions as a metaphor for a comic battle of the sexes over primary subjectivity and self-determination. Who is copying whom, who is the original inventor of artifice? The knowledge that comes from foreign (male) parts – the Damoiselle's revelations about male fashions – is that these are performative constructs too. Magdalene exclaims, "What lack!" defining her sex as the positive originators of performative gender, and men the secondary imitators of such acting. The irony of the conversation is obviously increased on stage where the "original" women are all artificially represented. Brome's male transvestite Frank thus mirrors Jonson's original female Frank to prove that both are signifiers demonstrating the undecidability of signification. Both show it is impossible to be perfectly Frank.

Brome's preoccupation with female performance perhaps responded to an explicit regendering of the stage by the inclusion of female actors in court dramas (Findlay et al., 2000, 42–67). Henrietta Maria had built significantly on the tradition of female masque performance developed by Anne of Denmark in work like Jonson's *The Masque of Queens* (1609). Anne's innovation of an ante-masque advertised the difference between male imitations of women (the professional actors who played the hags or witches) and the aristocratic or royal women who represented the queenly embodiments of female virtues in the House of Fame. As Suzanne Gossett has pointed out, the sex discrepancy of the performers reinforced a central message "that 'real' women are, or should be, like the masquers" (1988, 99). In the main masque, the "choice of woman-kind" (ll. 377–8) is celebrated in Jonson's elision of performer and role. He concludes the text with the names of the lady masquers, reporting that there is no fitter epilogue *"than the celebration of those who were the celebrators"* (ll. 699–700). Jonson's attempt to recreate in printed form the presence of royal and aristocratic women testifies to the significance of a female presence on the court stage.

Henrietta Maria's court entertainments emphasized the inimitable quality of female performance. In *Tempe Restored* (1632), Circe (played by Madam Coniack) reproved the male masquer presenting Pallas with the words "Man-maid, begone!" (l. 268). Women moved center stage in the all-female production of *The Shepherds Paradise* in January 1633. This pastoral play, written by Walter Montagu, reversed English public theater tradition, since Henrietta Maria and her ladies played both male and female roles within a complex plot scripted in 3,858 lines, all of which were spoken by women. The pastoral tradition was appropriated by noble and royal women in dramatic forms beyond the public stage. In Sidney's *The Lady of May* Elizabeth perversely resisted the passive role usually assigned to women in pastoral; Mary Wroth's *Love's Victory* (c. 1614–16), Rachel Fane's household entertainments (c. 1630s), and Jane Cavendish and Elizabeth Brackley's *Pastorall* masque (c. 1645) again regendered the genre.[2] Henrietta Maria's production of *The Shepherds Paradise* can be seen as part of this alternative dramatic tradition. The pastoral retreat is governed by Bellessa, played by the queen, and although the paradise exists as a protectorate within the king of Castile's domain, its constitution creates a distinctive space of female autonomy. The queen is elected "by the plurality of the sisters voyces, from wch election the brothers are excluded" (Montagu, 1997, 732–3), and all subjects must dedicate themselves to chastity. The paradise idealizes Henrietta's court at Somerset House as a dependent yet semi-autonomous entity. Bellessa's vow *"To keepe the honor & the Regall due: / without exacting any thing that's new"* (ll. 719–20) declares the queen's position as consort. She "Reserve[s] *noe power to suspend the Lawes*" (l. 724). In theatrical terms, such modesty is somewhat disingenuous. By staging *The Shepherds Paradise*, Henrietta Maria was breaking every rule in the book, as William Prynne's notorious condemnation of female performance showed (Heywood, 1633). Far from allowing male actors and directors to keep the honor of dramatic performance, she was exacting something very new in the production.

James Shirley's *The Bird in a Cage* (1633) responds to the threat of the female actress by restaging an exclusive all-female production mounted by the imprisoned heroine Princess Eugenia and her ladies, as Kim Walker has remarked (1991). The written dedication mockingly apologizes to Prynne that the printed text lacked "much of that Ornament, which the Stage and Action lent it, for it comprehending also another Play or interlude, personated by Ladies, I must referre to your imagination, the Musicke, the Songs, the Dancing and other varieties, which I know would have pleas'd you infinitely in the Presentment" (Shirley, 1980, 3).[3] Shirley makes a complex metatheatrical joke, in which his play jests at the absence of the lady actors who are present as characters, playing the parts of men and women in their interlude, just as boy actors and men actors play the parts of both men and women in *A Bird in a Cage*. Simultaneous absence and presence is a theme that runs through the play, reiterating the unsettling connection between gender and citation found in Jonson's and Brome's texts.

The hero, Philenzo, is "a Paradoxe" (p. 11), a "peece made up of all performance" (p. 29), and even his romantic quest to win Eugenia's hand is built on a series of roles: his disguise as Rolliardo to get into the court, his disguise in the bird cage to get into Eugenia's palace, and then his pretence that he is the prince of Florence when he first reveals himself to Eugenia. The fool Morello physically disguises himself as a lady, in order to deceive his way into Eugenia's palace, telling the guards "I am neyther a man nor a woman, I am an Hermaphrodite" (p. 35). He is punished by having to "weare the petticote for a Month" as a court jester (p. 47). This comic representation of male transvestism comments on the court culture of 1633, since Henrietta Maria's lost Shrove-tide masque of that year featured cross-dressed aristocratic men (Ravelhofer, 1999).

In the interlude, Donella encourages her sister actors: "Doe not distrust your owne performance, I ha knowne men ha bin insufficient, but women can play their parts" (p. 42). Perhaps with a glance across to Continental traditions of female performance, Donella asserts that women are better actors because they can play the female self more naturally (as well as with more grace), without costume or prostheses, props which are required to supplement male insufficiency. In addition, the critique of men's performances carries a third possible meaning: that women can play "their parts" (the men's) better too. They are simply better performers, trained from birth to insert themselves into a series of roles within the patriarchal script rather than attempting to fashion a self of their own devising. The female actors still imagine themselves as objects of a male gaze, creating an imaginary audience of "Silke and Cruell Gentlemen in the hanging" (p. 53), but the play does not simply "recuperate women's acting for patriarchy" (Walker, 1991, 399). Working within a given script, the women demonstrate that all gender is performative and show themselves as the original performers. As in *The Damoiselle*, they are the originals and men are poor imitators, shown by Morello's buffoonery but also by the other men's difficulties in maintaining their masculine roles.

Although it seems that early modern English spectators read gender in terms of difference, appreciating the distinctive qualities of each sex, stage representations frequently interrogated the meanings attributed to such difference. The combination of adult male actors and boys on the public stage was a convention accepted by audiences, but it could be manipulated by dramatists or performers to produce comic or disturbing theatrical effects. Moments in which the art of acting was put under the spotlight, especially through the mouths or bodies of transvestite performers, unsettled the idea of fixed, perfect, gender difference. The presence of female performers in other theatrical arenas, such as court or household entertainments, inevitably complicated the issue. Against these, male representations of women often seem the products of both fear and desire, haunted by deep insecurity about masculine self-hood. Hamlet's confident declaration "what a piece of work is a man" (II.ii.305) implies the effort required to secure gendered identity: the work to construct oneself as different on a stage in which sexual distinctions can only be imagined. For women, fighting against myriad masks and representations, the problem was perhaps still greater, since they were largely denied access to formal theatrical modes of self-representation. However, even in all-male productions, theater retained its power of exposure. On stage, the perfect constitution of gender, as either man or woman, was relegated to the realm of fantasy, and the performative nature of sexual difference was fore-grounded. Recreating oneself as a credible man or woman was the professional actors' work; non-professional actors like Henrietta Maria were able to play at expanding the parameters of acceptable activity for a woman. For the spectators of early modern England, performing difference was the stuff of everyday living. Visiting the theater frequently reminded one of that invisible work.

NOTES

1 References are to page numbers as act, scene, and line numbers are not given in the 1873 edition.
2 See Findlay et al., 2000, 52–5, 59–66, 70–4, and chapter 33 below.
3 All references to this text are to page numbers as Senescu's edition does not give act, scene, and line numbers.

REFERENCES AND FURTHER READING

Adelman, Janet (1992). *Suffocating Mothers: Fantasies of Maternal Origin in Shakespeare's Plays*. New York and London: Routledge.

Adelman, Janet (1999). "Making defect perfection: Shakespeare and the one-sex model." In *Enacting Gender on the English Renaissance Stage*, eds Viviana Comensoli and Anne Russell. Urbana and Chicago: University of Illinois Press.

Baudrillard, Jean (1988). *Selected Writings*, ed. Mark Poster. Oxford: Polity in association with Blackwell.

Breitenberg, Mark (1966). *Anxious Masculinity in Early Modern England*. Cambridge: Cambridge University Press.

Brome, Richard (1873). *The Damoiselle* (1638). In *The Dramatic Works of Richard Brome Containing Fifteen Comedies*. London: John Pearson.

Burton, Robert (1964). *The Anatomy of Melancholy*, ed. Holbrook Jackson. London: Dent.

Butler, Judith (1990a). *Gender Trouble: Feminism and the Subversion of Identity*. London and New York: Routledge.

Butler, Judith (1990b). "Performative acts and gender constitution: an essay in phenomenology and feminist theory." In *Performing Feminisms: Feminist Critical Theory and Theatre*, ed. Sue-Ellen Case. Baltimore and London: Johns Hopkins University Press.

Cary, Elizabeth (2000). *The Tragedy of Mariam*, ed. Stephanie J. Wright. Peterborough, ON: Broadview Press.

Cressy, David (1996). "Gender trouble and cross dressing in early modern England." *Journal of British Studies* 35, 438–65.

Cressy, David (1997). *Birth, Marriage and Death: Ritual, Religion and the Life-Cycle in Tudor and Stuart England*. Oxford: Oxford University Press.

Drue, Thomas (1631). *The Dutches of Suffolke*. London.

Findlay, Alison (1994). *Illegitimate Power: Bastards in Renaissance Drama*. Manchester: Manchester University Press.

Findlay, Alison and Stephanie Hodgson-Wright, with Gweno Williams (2000). *Women and Dramatic Production 1550–1700*. Harlow: Longman.

Garber, Marjorie (1992). *Vested Interests: Cross Dressing and Cultural Anxiety*. New York: Routledge.

Gossett, Suzanne (1988). "'Man-maid, begone!': women in masques." *English Literary Renaissance* 18, 96–113.

Hackett, Helen (1995). *Virgin Mother, Maiden Queen: Elizabeth I and the Cult of the Virgin Mary*. Basingstoke: Macmillan.

Heywood, Thomas (1633). *Histriomastix*. London.

Heywood, Thomas (1968). *The Fair Maid of the West Parts I and II*, ed. Robert K. Turner Jr. London: Arnold.

Hibbert, Christopher (1990). *The Virgin Queen: The Personal History of Elizabeth I*. London: Viking Penguin.

Jardine, Lisa (1977). *Still Harping on Daughters: Women and Desire in the Age of Shakespeare*. Brighton: Harvester Press.

Jonson, Ben (1984). *The New Inn*, ed. Michael Hattaway. Manchester: Manchester University Press.

Jonson, Ben (1995). *The Masque of Queens*. In *Court Masques*, ed. David Lindley. Oxford: Oxford University Press.

Jonson, Ben (1999). *Bartholemew Fair*. In *Renaissance Drama: An Anthology of Plays and Entertainments*, ed. Arthur F. Kinney. Malden and Oxford: Blackwell.

Lacan, Jacques (1977). *Ecrits: A Selection*, trans. Alan Sheridan. New York: W. W. Norton.

Laqueur, Thomas (1990). *Making Sex: Body and Gender from the Greeks to Freud*. Cambridge, MA: Harvard University Press.

Levine, Laura (1994). *Men in Women's Clothing: Anti-Theatricality and Effeminization, 1579–1642*. Cambridge: Cambridge University Press.

McLuskie, Kathleen (1994). *Dekker and Heywood, Professional Dramatists*. London: Macmillan.

McLuskie, Katheleen E. and David Bevington, eds (1999). *Plays on Women*. Manchester: Manchester University Press.

Middleton, Thomas (1999). *A Chaste Maid in Cheapside*. In *Plays on Women*, eds Kathleen E. McLuskie and David Bevington. Manchester: Manchester University Press.

Middleton, Thomas and Thomas Dekker (1999). *The Roaring Girl*. In *Plays on Women*, eds Kathleen E. McLuskie and David Bevington. Manchester: Manchester University Press.

Middleton, Thomas and William Rowley (1999). *The Changeling*. In *Renaissance Drama: An Anthology of Plays and Entertainments*, ed. Arthur F. Kinney. Malden and Oxford: Blackwell.

Montagu, Walter (1997). *The Shepherds Paradise*, ed. Sarah Poynting. Oxford: Malone Society.

Mulcaster, Richard (1999). *The Queen's Majesty's Passage Through the City of London to Westminster the Day Before Her Coronation* (1559). In *Renaissance Drama: An Anthology of Plays and Entertainments*, ed. Arthur F. Kinney. Malden and Oxford: Blackwell.

Orgel, Stephen (1996). *Impersonations: The Performance of Gender in Shakespeare's England*. Cambridge: Cambridge University Press.

Paster, Gail Kern (1993). *The Body Embarrassed: Drama and the Disciplines of Shame in Early Modern England*. Ithaca: Cornell University Press.

Ravelhofer, Barbara (1999). "Bureaucrats and courtly cross-dressers in the Shrovetide Masque and *The Shepherds Paradise*." *English Literary Renaissance* 29, 75–96.

Rosenblatt, Jason P. and Winifred Schleiner (1999). "John Selden's letter to Ben Jonson on cross dressing and bisexual gods." *English Literary Renaissance* 29, 44–74.

Sedinger, Tracey (1997). "'If sight and shape be true': the epistemology of cross-dressing on the London stage." *Shakespeare Quarterly* 48, 63–79.

Shakespeare, William (1988). *The Oxford Shakespeare*, eds Gary Taylor and Stanley Wells. Oxford: Oxford University Press.

Shirley, James (1980). *The Bird In a Cage: A Critical Edition*, ed. Francis Frazier Senescu. New York and London: Garland.

Stallybrass, Peter (1992). "Transvestism and the 'body beneath': speculating on the boy actor. In *Erotic Politics: Desire on the Renaissance Stage*, ed. Susan Zimmerman. London and New York: Routledge.

Townshend, Aurelian (1995). *Tempe Restored*. In *Court Masques*, ed. David Lindley. Oxford: Oxford University Press.

Walker, Kim (1991). "New prison: representing the female actor in Shirley's *The Bird in a Cage*." *English Literary Renaissance* 21, 385–400.

Webster, John (1999). *The Duchess of Malfi*. In *Renaissance Drama: An Anthology of Plays and Entertainments*, ed. Arthur F. Kinney. Malden and Oxford: Blackwell.

29

Closet Drama

Marta Straznicky

Defined by most critics as a play that was either never intended for performance or never performed, closet drama has predictably been marginalized by generations of critics who, however varied their theoretical positions or scholarly interests, have taken Renaissance drama to mean drama written for performance. To be sure, there have been pockets of scholarship on certain clusters of closet plays, such as the neo-Senecan drama of the Sidney circle, the dramatic pamphlets of the civil wars, or, most recently, the variety of plays written by early modern women for whom there was no legitimate access to commercial theater.[1] But much of this work is also informed by what we might call a theatrical bias: an imputed preference for theater and performance that construes closet drama in terms of resistance or deficiency. While this scholarship has revealed much about the available forms of theatricality in the period, it has also obscured the place of closet drama within literary culture more generally and thus made it difficult to assess the form as a discrete tradition of dramatic writing.

The inclination in closet drama criticism toward theater and stageability is largely attributable to the genre's negative and stage-oriented definition: in one influential formulation, plays "that were never acted, and were never meant to be" (Greg, 1939–59, 4, xii). The opposition between closet and stage implied by this definition, however, was not a feature of Renaissance dramatic discourse, at least not with the kind of regularity that might allow us to take the term itself as current in the period. In fact, it was not until the late eighteenth century that the closet/stage dichotomy became embedded in critical language as a way of distinguishing certain types of plays as appropriate for performance and others for reading. Eighteenth-century playwrights and critics also infused the closet/stage dichotomy with the related distinction of private/public, a closet play being designed for solitary reading while a stage-play was meant to be performed at a commercial playhouse. While there was considerable debate in the period about which of the two dramatic types was preferable, the opposition between private closet and public stage was a core concept of late eighteenth- and then nineteenth-century theoretical discourse.[2] Until very recently, twentieth-century scholars adopted these terms without historicizing them, although the preference has shifted decidedly toward the performance tradition.

Without arriving at strict chronological distinctions between dramatic theories and conceptions of private or public space, attending to historical context does reveal that in some important respects closet drama of the sixteenth and seventeenth centuries was not understood as antithetical to the stage, regardless of performance history or authorial intention, nor was it in any fixed sense a private mode. Rather, closet drama or "dramatic poetry," the nearest equivalent Renaissance term, was a label that could be applied to *any* play – whether performed or not – that was or sought to be inscribed in literary culture, a culture that, informed as it was by ideas of reading as social practice and print as engagement with the public sphere, was not in stable opposition to "public" forms of theatricality.

Public versus Private, Closet versus Stage

One way of approaching early modern notions of private and public spheres as they apply to dramatic literature is through the architectural spaces underlying the closet/stage dichotomy. In an obvious sense, of course, late sixteenth- and seventeenth-century commercial theaters were public venues, accessible to any playgoer who could afford and wished to disburse the entrance fee. On the other hand, commercial drama was performed in theaters that were designated either "public" or "private," terms that most theater historians take as straightforward architectural distinctions between the purpose-built amphitheaters and the refurbished great halls of vacant monasteries. But while it is true that public and private generally refer to obvious structural differences, the terms are also suggestive of a complex cultural irony in that they imply mutually exclusive theatrical practices for what was, in fact, a largely unified field of commercial entertainment.[3]

We can tell from the title-pages of printed plays, plays being marketed to a readership, that the uses of "private" and "public" as they apply to commercial drama follow a discernible pattern, particularly in the first half of the seventeenth century. With the reopening of the Blackfriars theater in 1599 (see chapter 11 above), and the accompanying opportunity for developing a distinction between indoor and outdoor theatrical experience, "public" and "private" not only begin to figure prominently on title-pages, but reveal a gradual change in the value of these terms for publishers and readers. For the first two decades of the seventeenth century, plays advertised as having been "plaid publiquely" compete more or less even-handedly with "privately acted" productions, all of which had been given either at the newly reopened indoor playhouses or before an elite audience at court. Beginning around 1630, however, title-pages announcing public performances of any kind are extremely rare and, in nearly inverse proportion, the "private house" pedigree is *de rigeur*. The general pattern seems to be a decline in the promotional value of "public" performances, except where they are preceded by – and framed as repetitions of – the more prestigious, private, court productions, and a surge in references to "private" theaters as a marketing strategy for selling play-books.[4]

However slim the evidence of title-pages alone may be, it seems worth considering that the growing marketability of "private" drama parallels the increasing interest in modes of privacy (social, architectural, intellectual) evident in the early modern period generally (Ranum, 1989). But what exactly was meant by privacy in this context? What was it about the "private" theater that was so appealing to seventeenth-century playgoers? In what sense was the playgoers' experience "private" at theaters that accommodated as many as 700 paying spectators? A much-cited passage in John Marston's *Jack Drum's Entertainment* (1600) hints at an answer. One of the characters says of the audiences who attend the Children of Paul's plays:

> I'faith, I like the audience that frequenteth there
> With much applause: A Man shall not be choked
> With the stench of garlic; nor be pasted
> To the barmy jacket of a beer-brewer.
> 　　　　　　　　　　　(Gurr, 1987, 215)

Marston's distinction between private and public audiences is made not only in terms of status, but more immediately in terms of bodily experience. The spectators at the children's plays are not subjected to one another's offensive odors, nor do they endure contact with unwashed members of the audience; rather than being "choked" by and "pasted" to their neighbors they maintain a respectful distance from one another, their bodies segregated and untouched. To extend Marston's terms somewhat, "open" theaters mean "open" bodies, where physical boundaries between spectators are dangerously and offensively permeable; "closed" theaters, on the other hand, secure those boundaries and thus protect the integrity of the theater-going subject.

It is not surprising, therefore, that the cure for the playgoing disease is a kind of quarantine, a therapeutic regime that was also institutionalized in late sixteenth- and early seventeenth-century plague-orders (Slack, 1985, 284–310). "Let us but shut up our ears," advises one opponent of the public theater, "pull our feet back from resort to theaters, and turn away our eyes from beholding of vanity" (Gosson, 1974, 101), and in a later tract he urges his readers to "Enter every one into your selves" (1974, 191). Here the corrupt, open body of the playgoer is refigured as a closed site. Moreover, the closed body of the reformed spectator is positioned within spaces that are clearly delineated as private and domestic: one's house or rooms for those who refrain altogether from the theatrical, or, where some interest in theater is likely to continue, the study or closet, domestic spaces in which plays can be read but which preclude the physical conditions of the "public" theaters. William Prynne, for example, gives the following as a reason for permitting the reading of playbooks: "Stage-plays may be privately read over without any danger of infection by ill company, without any public infamy or scandal, without giving any ill example" (1633, 930). "When a man reads a Play," he continues, "he ever wants that *viva voce*, that flexanimous rhetorical State-elocution, that lively action and representation of the Players them-selves which put life and vigor into these their Interludes, and make them pierce more deeply into the Spectators' eyes, their ears and lewd affections" (1633, 930–1). Not only does private playreading secure corporeal boundaries, it also enables the subject to "pass by all obscene or amorous passages, all prophane or scurrill Jests, all hea-thenish oaths and execrations," thus restoring moral control over the theatrical illu-sion. "[No] such liberty," claims Prynne, is available to spectators, who are by contrast vulnerable to various forms of contagion.[5]

Closed bodies, private spaces, and the exercise of an independent critical intelli-gence are all associated by Prynne with playreading and are framed in opposition to the collective event of public playgoing. Interestingly, these same qualities emerge in descriptions of the "private" commercial theater, although Prynne for one was well aware that this was nothing more than a cultural fiction. The physical discomforts of attending the hall theaters focus on the "gentleman-like smell" of tobacco, what we might call an up-market odor compared with the garlic and onion of the "stinkards" at the amphitheaters (Gurr, 1987, 39, 221). Hall theater audiences tend to be described in terms of their clothing rather than their bodies, the visual field cluttered with brightly colored taffeta, starched ruffs, generously cut cloaks, and wide-brimmed, feathered hats, bulky if gorgeous outfits that interfere with sight lines and buffer one body from the next. More importantly, the critical faculties of playgoers begin to concern playwrights far more than rude conduct. Francis Beaumont, for instance, views the Blackfriars theater as a court where "a thousand men in judgment sit," a crowd, to be sure, but one that is daunting for the number of critical minds at work rather than for the throng of a massive, collective body (Gurr, 1987, 223). By contrast, it is precisely this kind of crowd that John Tatham in 1640 identifies with the Fortune theater: "Rabbles, Apply-wives and Chimney-boys, / Whose shrill con-fused Echoes loud doe cry, / Enlarge your Commons, We hate Privacy" (Gurr, 1987, 249).[6]

In practice, of course, and to the minds of those with anti-theatrical prejudices, the bodies of playgoers at the private theaters were no more secure than at the public venues (as the numerous references to pickpocketing, prostitution, and sexual touch-ing attest) and the crowds of spectators posed the same moral and health hazards. The residents of Blackfriars, for example, were not fooled by Burbage's proposal to build a "private" theater in their precinct. In their petition protesting what they insist on calling the "common playhouse," they warn of the very same conditions that civic authorities feared of the amphitheaters. No wonder the King's Men, once they were granted permission to perform at Blackfriars, were keen to portray their style of theater as "private" in spite of its frankly commercial aspect (Chambers, 1923, IV, 320; Gurr, 1996, 366–7). The closed space of the hall theater, it might be said, was an overdetermined site for a cultural practice that sought to dissociate itself from the "public."

At the same time, it is difficult to confer stability on the "private" space of the closet, the site toward which much stage drama, in the form of published play-books, was migrating and where it might more legitimately seek the prestige of privacy. Recent studies in the social and architectural history of the early modern closet have linked changes in the placement and use of this room with the increasingly specialized organization of domestic space and the concomitant desire for personal privacy. Since it was a small room, usually accessible only through an adjacent bedchamber and thus furthest removed from spaces such as the hall or gallery in which the household's more communal life was conducted, the closet was easily adapted to a variety of functions requiring some degree of controlled access: the storage of pharmaceuticals, costly household provisions, business and personal accounts, or coin and jewels; the entertainment of close friends; devotional exercises; or reading and writing more generally.[7] While none of these functions is unambiguously private, the fact that they involve the concept of concealment or retreat has led literary scholars to link certain closet practices (mainly the devotional, administrative, and literary) with the intersecting discourses of secrecy, surveillance, and subjectivity. But rather than finding clear distinctions between private and public spheres, current scholarship has shown that the spatial and metaphoric construction of the closet is fundamentally paradoxical: the private space of the closet, either literally or as a trope for an essential, inaccessible subjectivity, is constructed within public systems of representation: the gestures of privacy (concealment, withdrawal, control of access) only become meaningful if they are discernible and intelligible to others (Fumerton, 1991, 67–110; Stewart, 1995).

Closet Drama, Playreading, and Privacy

Set within this context, where privacy in both theatrical and architectural discourse is more a pragmatic than an ontological category, early modern plays designed for reading rather than performance, or those self-consciously making the transition from performance into print, are better understood as attempts to construct various kinds of liaisons between public and private than as embodiments of a stable "private" culture. First, there are very few plays of any kind which situate reading in a space that is explicitly closed and/or domestic, be it within a closet, a study, a bedchamber, or a library, and even those that do are not concerned thereby to distinguish between playreading and playgoing per se. Perhaps the best-known such example is from *The Roaring Girl* (1611), in which Thomas Middleton assures "the Comic, Play-readers" that the published play is "good to keep you in an afternoon from dice, at home in your chambers," but also that, like the real Moll Cutpurse, it may pass freely between the theater and the bedchamber: the "book . . . may bee allowed both Gallery room at the play-house, and chamber-room at your lodging." Conflating the play-book with its sexualized transvestite heroine in effect collapses the distinction that antitheatrical writers like Prynne would want to maintain between the corporeal public theater and the chaste private chamber. This may not surprise us in a play, successfully staged as it was at the popular Fortune theater, that has no apparent investment in aligning its cultural value with a specifically private domain.

But even plays that do represent the private space of playreading in opposition to public theater do not necessarily oppose reading to performance. Robert Wilmot's *Tancred and Gismund* (1591), "Newly revived and polished" for a readership, has an author's preface advising that the play "contain her self within the walls of your house" in order to elude the "Tragedian Tyrants of our time"; similarly, a dedicatory poem to Thomas Randolph's *The Jealous Lovers* (1632) would have the play "impaled lie / Within the walls of some great library" rather than making it "public to the common view." Both of these plays, however, were originally performed in what we can call genuinely private theaters, *Tancred and Gismund* by students at the Inner Temple for Queen Elizabeth, and *The Jealous Lovers* at Trinity College, Cambridge, before the court of Charles I, so that the desire to contain them "within the walls" of domestic space is not so much a conferral of privacy on the act of playreading as an attempt to preserve the plays' prior status as private theatricals and thereby distinguish them from "the vulgar people's sport." We find here an alliance, then, between domestic playreading and the courtly or academic stage, all three equally rooted in what is deemed to be a private culture.

We might also bear in mind that the early modern term for closet drama, dramatic poetry, does not point explicitly to a physical space of any kind, suggesting that the material condition of reading is not the definitive factor when a play either claims or refutes membership in literary culture, just as the material condition of playgoing is incidental, if not flatly contradictory, to the connotation of "private" in theatrical discourse. Ironically, the stakes in distinguishing a dramatic poem from the stage are most conspicuous in plays that deliberately make a transition from commercial performance into print, particularly in the case of amphitheater plays that were patently unsuccessful on stage, where the impulse to draw a line between a vulgar audience and a discriminating readership is at once a face-saving and a marketing device. One of the most explicit examples is John Webster's *The White Devil*, published in 1612 following a dismal failure at the down-market Red Bull theater (Gurr, 1996, 323). The Red Bull audience is an easy target, characterized by Webster as an "uncapable multitude," a mob likened to the "ignorant asses" who haunt stationers' shops looking for nothing but the newest books; his intended readers, by contrast, are presumed to be familiar with the "critical laws" of "sententious Tragedy." A similar distinction is made by Walter Burre, publisher of Beaumont's *The Knight of the Burning Pestle* (1613), which had flopped before the more rarefied audience at the "private" Blackfriars theater in 1607. Burre blames the play's failure on the crude interpretive skills of the Blackfriars audience, particularly on their inability to discern "the privy mark of Irony about it." This figurative quality of the play shows it to be "no off-spring of any vulgar brain," the spectators by contrast having a poor sense of literary judgment, capable only of "fond and merely literal interpretation, or illiterate misprision." Two related points seem worth drawing out from these examples: that the intended readers are opposed to spectators primarily in terms of literary expertise, but that the spectators are not by that token deemed illiterate. However much Webster and Burre decry the vulgarity of the theater audience, it is also clear that that audience is to some extent a readership. The more precise distinction, then, is between literary standards and kinds of intellectual labor rather than between private reading and public theater-going.

Representations of "learned" or "understanding" readers in early modern plays assume a specific kind of expertise: readers are presumed to have a well-developed sense of critical judgment, a familiarity with the conventions of classical drama, and an expectation that plays issued in print will repay the labor of reading. Thus, Webster, admitting that *The White Devil* "is no true Dramatic Poem," bolsters his credibility as an educated, serious writer by describing the literary conventions of which the Red Bull audience is utterly ignorant: dramatic poems are to be "senten-tious," "observing all the critical laws, as height of style; and gravity of person," and "enrich[ed]" with a "sententious Chorus" and "the passionate and weighty Nuntius." Similarly, Ben Jonson claims to have discharged the "offices of a Tragic writer" in *Sejanus* (1605) by observing "truth of Argument, dignity of Persons, gravity and height of Elocution, fulness and frequency of Sentence," even though a full embodi-ment of the "old state, and splendor of Dramatic Poems" would be pointless "in these our Times, and to such Auditors." Although neither Webster nor Jonson uses the terms "private" and "public" to label the distinction they are drawing between theater audiences and an elite readership, it is clear that for the commercial playwright aspir-ing to literary status, the tradition of scholarly playreading can be invoked to con-stitute a "private" realm, in the sense of belonging to an exclusive, educated minority.

The literary qualities and readership skills Webster, Burre, and Jonson associate with an intellectual elite drama constitute, in effect, the predominant closet drama tradition of the early modern period, stemming from the Greek and Roman classics and including academic translations, plays of moral or religious instruction, and the kind of topical political drama written by the Sidney circle in the late sixteenth and early seventeenth centuries. Such plays share a number of formal features that may be understood as "readerly" devices, orienting the reader as they do in the process of moving through the text or being particularly well suited to the intellectual focus that reading affords: an introductory argument outlining the context and action of the play, a list of speakers, division into acts, lengthy sententious speeches typo-graphically represented in continuous text columns, and a chorus serving to prompt and guide interpretation. The inscription of such plays within a literary rather than a theatrical culture is also signaled by the absence of the label "play" in their titles (instead they identify the genre or use non-theatrical terms like dramatic poem, dia-logue, history, work, or treatise), and by other textual cues such as dedicatory or com-mendatory epistle, marginal annotations, or scholarly aids of various kinds.

Perhaps most significantly, these closet plays – some by virtue of adopting the formal characteristics of the type, others by explicit statement– are situated within a playreading *tradition* rooted in the humanist pedagogical program and thus predicated upon a model of readership as labor rather than leisure, as public rather than private commodity. Although humanist theorists do not articulate a specific regime for the study of drama, the central role of the classical playwrights in the general reading program suggests that plays would have been read in the manner prescribed for all classical texts: diligently, repeatedly, with pen and paper at hand, and directed or at least assisted by a tutor.[8] The scene of reading thus conducted presupposes a very different function for the dramatic text than would, say, the chamber reading imagined by Middleton in the preface to *The Roaring Girl*. Taking place at a writing table, with tutor, fellow pupils, and reference works nearby, the scholarly playreading does not seek pleasure or even diversion as its goal, nor does it approach the play as a theatrical script: rather, it makes of the text first an object of linguistic and rhetorical instruction, scrupulously to be analyzed using every available technological aid, and second an instrument to be incorporated by the pupil and literally put into action in speech, writing, and conduct.

Leading as it does to the application of verbal and behavioral models, and this within an educational program with clearly conceived employment goals, scholarly playreading overtly intersects with social and political economies.[9] Although some sixteenth-century translations of Greek and Latin plays were strictly academic, printed as parallel texts or otherwise using typographical arrangements to guide readers through comparative linguistic analysis, the majority framed their function at least as much in terms of moral and political as of philological learning. Translation itself, of course, was considered work in service of the state, providing broad access to the foundations of humanist learning, fostering public morality and civic virtue, and augmenting the capacity of the English tongue. "A translator travaileth," wrote Nicholas Udall, "not to his own private commodity, but to the benefit and public use of his country" (Amos, 1920, 88). For the translators of classical drama, the public benefit or "profit" of playreading was in the moral and political lessons to be learned from the ancients. Alexander Nevyle, for example, advises the reader of his translation of Seneca's *Oedipus* (1563) to ignore technical proficiency and "Mark thou rather what is meant by the whole course of the History: and frame thy life free from such mischiefs." More overt is John Studley's preface to the reader in *Agamemnon* (1566), where he says he was persuaded to publish what was merely a private exercise, "rudely performed," in order "to serve my country withall," to "apply" his talent so that the "excellency of the matter" might benefit other young students.

In one sense, of course, proclaiming the moral function of these works is consistent with the dominant theory of literary value in the medieval and early modern periods. But in the mid-sixteenth century, the Act for the Advancement of True Religion (1543), which restricted the publishing of "songs, plays and interludes" to works that were "for the rebuking and reproaching of vices and setting forth of virtue," had given the ideal of literature as moral improvement a distinctly political edge (Walker, 1998, 20). We also need to consider that the rhetoric of public service in these translations is informed by some degree of professional ambition. In John Studley's translations, for example, second-party prefaces to the reader acknowledge that "graver age" or "hoary heads" might be more capable "to travel in this trade," and yet declare with confidence that the "riper wit" of "lusty youth" produces more lively expressions.[10] Furthermore, Studley's plays are dedicated to members of the Privy Council (*Agamemnon* to William Cecil, *Medea* to the earl of Bedford) rather than to respected or influential members of the academic community, suggesting that there is some attempt here to demonstrate one's ability to transfer "private exercises," or scholarly knowledge and skills, to a more explicitly political sphere.

The general culture and ideals of scholarly playreading can also be linked to non-classical closet dramas of religious instruction whose concern to be of public value was not so obviously infused with private motive, plays such as Nicholas Grimald's *Archipropheta* (1548), H. N.'s *An Enterlude of Myndes* (?1574), Arthur Golding's translation of Theodore Beza's *Abraham's Sacrifice* (1577), and George Buchanan's biblical tragedies. Unlike the majority of plays written before 1580, which were, as Greg Walker has shown, elite great-hall plays, products of the "moral economy of household life" (1998, 52) and thus anchored in the interests, views, and positions of a specific patron, this group of closet plays was devised for the moral instruction of a public, if still necessarily elite, readership. The use of readerly devices such as illustrative woodcuts, chapter headings, numbering of speeches, and elaborate allegorical descriptions of characters indicates that there was little uncertainty about the nature and function of these closet plays, the emphasis falling squarely on didactic content, as opposed, again, to printed texts of the great-hall plays, in which the presentational strategy is noticeably conflicted for much of this period (Walker, 1998, 16–19). Most importantly, the religious closet dramas of the sixteenth century formed a distinct and widely admired tradition of politicized playreading, approved even by the most vehement anti-theatrical writers, which immersed readers and writers in the public sphere. For instance, Robert Wilmot, whose hostility to the commercial stage we have already encountered, convinced himself that publishing *Tancred and Gismund* was "convenient for the common wealth" when he called to mind the examples of Buchanan's *Jepthes* and Beza's *Abraham's Sacrifice*. Buchanan's *Baptistes*, originally designed to represent "the death and accusation of Thomas More and set before the eyes an image of the tyranny of that time" (Phillips, 1948–9, 40), was praised by Stephen Gosson as a play containing "good matter" that "may be read with profit" in the specific sense of political influence: "So Bucchanus wrote his play of John Baptist for the king of Scots to read, that . . . He might learn to govern his own house, and beware what entreaty he gives to the Prophets of God" (1974, 178). Similarly, Prynne approves in political terms the value of reading "serious, sacred, divine" plays on the example of dramatists who, "in King Henry the 8. And Queen Mary's bloody reign, being restrained by Superior Popish powers to oppose received errors or propagate the truth and Doctrine of the Gospel in public Sermons, . . . did covertly vent and publish sundry truths . . . in Rimes, in Comedies, Tragedies, & Poems like to Plays" (1633, 833). Even more than the scholarly play translations, the instructional and polemical aims of these closet dramas and the overt politicization of playreading associated with them indicate a dramatic tradition that endows the acts of reading and writing with a meaningful and profitable public dimension.

The best-known closet dramas of the early modern period, the plays written by the literary and political coterie known as the Sidney circle in the late sixteenth and early seventeenth centuries, redeploy the generally public resonance of the genre for a more narrowly elite political debate. The very existence of any such "circle" has been questioned in recent years, but most scholars would agree that members of the Sidney and Leicester families shared a core set of political and literary values with which certain writers, courtiers, and clergymen became variously allied over the last two or three decades of the sixteenth century.[11] Varied as it was, the group was fundamentally reformist in its political sympathies and humanist in its intellectual endeavors, promoting popular sovereignty and limited monarchy, and developing a literary culture in which poetics, piety, and politics were uniquely combined. As the products of this intellectual milieu, the Sidnean closet plays span literary and political fields, private coteries and public readerships.

Drawing on the politicization of the genre in English and Continental precursors, the Sidnean closet plays are tragedies of state in Senecan form, exploring the issue of tyrannous authority from the viewpoint of characters who are variously disempowered. Mary Sidney is nowhere explicit about the political function of her *Antonius* (1592), although her decision to translate and publish a play which was itself an intervention in the political crisis in France in the 1570s suggests at least an awareness that she was working with potentially topical material, and had some interest in having it disseminated.[12] Samuel Daniel is equally subtle about the political intent of his companion play, *Cleopatra* (1594), but he was called by the Privy Council to answer for his critique of the Essex affair in *Philotas* (1605), a play written in the same tradition as *Cleopatra* and sharing the Sidney circle's concern over Elizabeth's increasingly autocratic rule. Forced into a public denial of the play's topical relevance, and protesting in a letter to the earl of Devonshire that "there is nothing in it disagreeing nor any thing . . . but out of the universal notions of ambition and envy, the perpetual arguments of books or tragedies" (Daniel, 1963, I, xxiii), Daniel managed to dodge the authorities but has failed to convince scholars that his intentions were politically innocent (Dutton, 1991, 165–71; Tricomi, 1989, 63–71). More explicit still about the place of closet drama in political culture is Fulke Greville's account of the rationale behind his two tragedies *Mustapha* (1609) and *Alaham* (1633). Intended to inspire "those that are weather-beaten in the sea of this world," the plays were an attempt "to trace out the highways of ambitious governors, and to show in the practice of life that the more audacity, advantage and good success such sovereignties have, the more they hasten to their own desolation and ruin" (Greville, 1986, 133–4). That such a general political message could well have had direct topical relevance is suggested by Greville's account of the reason why he "sacrificed in the fire" a third tragedy, about Antony and Cleopatra. Having given the play to some friends to read, and they finding in it the "personating of vices in the present governors and government," Greville decided to destroy the manuscript rather than risk legal correction (Greville, 1986, 93). Finally, even the apparently domestic orientation of Sidnean closet dramas such as Thomas Kyd's *Cornelia* (1594), Samuel Brandon's *Octavia* (1598), and Elizabeth Cary's *Mariam* (1613; see chapter 33 below) have been linked with the more overtly topical plays through their use of distinctly political discourses (e.g., Straznicky, 1994; Shannon, 1994).

In various ways, then, the majority of sixteenth- and early seventeenth-century closet plays were not inscribed in a cultural domain that was identified as "private," even if they never reached the size and breadth of audience attending the commercial theaters. In marked contrast to stage-plays that sought to be considered part of an exclusive, non-commercial, literary culture, the evidence of reading habits and authorial purpose for the closet plays suggests that this strain of dramatic writing did not confine itself to the closed spaces in which elite literary activities occurred (primarily colleges and private households), but sought instead to occupy a cultural position that could meaningfully intervene in social, religious, and political discourse. Perhaps because of this desired extension from private space to public sphere, early modern closet plays are generally not opposed to theatricality, even if none of them would have aspired to performance in a commercial venue. Academic drama, of course, was not only read but performed at the universities (see chapter 18 above), and this in a pedagogical context that, with only a few exceptions, treated the two activities as complementary.[13] The most reader-oriented classical translations make no attempt to distinguish themselves from performance traditions, either ancient or contemporary, and several include performative effect as part of their rhetorical commentary (e.g., Bernard, 1598; Sherburne, 1648).

The closet plays of moral and religious instruction are also either indifferent to the issue of theatricality or represent their own prior performance history without any sense that reading and seeing drama are conflicting activities, nor do the anti-theatrical writers who approve only of reading express any concern that some such plays had indeed been performed (as were, for example, the plays of Buchanan some 30 years before their appearance in print). Even the Sidnean closet plays, long considered an attempt to reform popular theater along classical lines, express no interest in commercial drama, and the writers – except for Fulke Greville – reveal nothing like a programmatic anti-theatrical position. Garnier's plays had been performed in France to popular acclaim, a fact of which Mary Sidney must surely have been aware but which apparently did not deter her from choosing Garnier as a source text. She herself was the dedicatee of William Gager's *Ulysses Redux* (1592), a neo-Latin academic play performed at Christ Church, Oxford; she also wrote a dialogue intended for performance and patronized at least one member of the acting profession (Lamb, 1990, 29; Gurr, 1996, 267). Thomas Kyd, of course, was a prominent commercial dramatist as well as the author of a closet play, and Samuel Daniel, appointed licenser of the Queen's Revels company in 1604, was not above releasing *Philotas* for commercial performance, however much he would later try to represent this as the desperate measure of a bankrupt professional writer (1963, I, xiii). Elizabeth Cary was reportedly fond of attending the public theaters; William Sheares, publisher of Marston's collected plays, dedicated the volume to her in 1633. Samuel Brandon's *Octavia* (1598) even has a stage epilogue that is indisputably evidence of a projected, if not actual, performance.

This diversity of interests in drama and theater among the group of writers whose closet plays have been viewed as manifestos against the popular stage, in addition to what we have already seen of the crossover in elite literary discourse between stage and closet drama, should caution us against using analytic categories that make firm distinctions between private and public modes of drama and theatricality. Even Sir Philip Sidney's famous critique of mixed genres in stage plays, a critique which many scholars have taken as a spur to the closet drama "campaign" of the Sidney circle, is in alliance with the critical theory prefacing one of the period's most sensational stage successes, Marlowe's *Tamburlaine* (1590). The play's printer, Richard Jones, explains in an epistle to "the Gentlemen Readers: and others that take pleasure in reading Histories," many of whom have seen the play on stage, that he has excised some "fond and frivolous gestures" in order to achieve the generic purity appropriate to printed drama: were comedy, he writes, "to be mixtured *in print* with such matter of worth, it would prove a great disgrace to so honorable and stately a history" (emphasis added). Although there is considerable continuity between the theater audience and the play's intended readership, Jones is concerned to shape the stage play into conformity with literary conventions – here, the consistently high style of "history" – suitable to a play in print. Sidney, on the other hand, seems scarcely aware that playreading constitutes anything like a separate dramatic tradition, although of course his knowledge of the rules of "skilful poetry" derive from textual study rather than theatrical experience (1966, 65). His references to classical plays refer to performance often enough to suggest that this is the reception context he considers normative for drama, and however critical he may be of the contemporary commercial stage, the ideal he embraces is theatrical rather than strictly literary. Thus he advises, following Aristotle, that comedies produce "delightful teaching" by portraying characters with a touch of the real, "a busy loving courtier" or "a self-wise seeming schoolmaster": "These if we saw walk in stage names, which we play naturally, therein were delightful laughter, and teaching delightfulness" (1966, 69). Interestingly, it is Buchanan, whose plays Sidney could only have read, who rouses "divine admiration" for achieving the same end in tragedy (1966, 69).

The significant distinctions in the field of early modern dramatic writing insofar as closet drama is concerned are drawn along the lines of moral purpose, intellectual labor, and rhetorical skill rather than theatricality or privacy. Plays certainly were written expressly for readers rather than playgoers, but rarely do they articulate a relationship to the commercial theater, let alone defend their legitimacy in any way. On the contrary, it is the stage drama that appears to have struggled for legitimacy, particularly when it sought a shift in cultural status to the very standard represented by the literary tradition to which closet plays already belonged. It would not be until the mid-seventeenth century, when the influence of humanism had waned and the prohibition of public theater lent playreading a sense of deficiency, that closet plays would begin to adopt a defensive posture (e.g., Anon., 1648).[14] The kind of resolution against performance we find expressed by John Milton or Anne Finch in the later seventeenth century has so little precedent among pre-revolutionary closet dramatists as to seem the product of a different culture, one in which the commercial theater had become the dominant venue for drama in terms of both status and popularity.[15]

For the earlier period, closet and stage drama were distinct but continuous traditions, their relations a site of negotiation between private and public, literary and theatrical culture.

NOTES

1 For a detailed account of the scholarship, see Straznicky (1998).
2 On the closet drama of the eighteenth and early nineteenth centuries, see Burroughs (1997, 8–12).
3 Gurr notes that the widespread use of these inaccurate terms coincides with the revival of the boy companies and may therefore have been an attempt on their part to avoid the licensing measures that applied to public theaters (1996, 337–8).
4 This pattern is clearly discernible in the title-pages transcribed in Greg (1939–59). See also Farmer and Lesser (2000, 91).
5 Elsewhere in the treatise, however, Prynne condemns the "frequent constant reading" (1633, 914) of plays. Although he does not explain this contradiction, he appears to be drawing a distinction between literary and theatrical plays.
6 For the full text of these and other references to playgoing, see Gurr (1987, 205–51).
7 The full range of functions served by the closet is discussed by Orlin (1998).
8 On the place of drama in the humanist curriculum, see Norland.
9 Grafton and Jardine (1986) discuss the relationship between humanism and the non-academic employment of scholars. On the public dimension of scholarly playreading, see Grafton and Jardine (1990) and Sherman (1996).
10 In *Agamemnon*, "H.C. To the reader"; in *Medea*, "W. F. in the Translatours behalfe."
11 For a challenge to the view that Mary Sidney patronized a circle of dramatists, see Lamb (1981).
12 On Garnier's context, see Jondorf (1969); on Sidney and the politics of translation, see Clarke (1997).
13 For arguments against the academic theater, see Rainolds (1599).
14 See Wiseman (1998) for a general account of the politics of drama during the Civil War period.
15 On Milton, see Sauer (1998); on Finch, Straznicky (1997).

REFERENCES AND FURTHER READING

Amos, Flora Ross (1920). *Early Theories of Translation*. New York: Columbia University Press.
Anon. (1648). *The Second Part of Crafty Cromwell*.
Beaumont, Francis (1613). *The Knight of the Burning Pestle*.
Bennett, H. S. (1970). *English Books and Readers, 1603–1640: Being a Study in the History of the Book Trade in the Reigns of James 1 and Charles I*. Cambridge: Cambridge University Press.
Bernard, Richard (1598). *Terence in English*. London.
Brandon, Samuel (1598). *Octavia*. London.
Burroughs, Catherine (1997). *Closet Stages: Joanna Baillie and the Theater Theory of British Romantic Women Writers*. Philadelphia: University of Pennsylvania Press.
Chambers, E. K. (1923). *The Elizabethan Stage*. 4 vols. Oxford: Clarendon Press.
Clarke, Danielle (1997). "The politics of translation and gender in the Countess of Pembroke's *Antonie*." *Translation and Literature* 6, 149–66.
Daniel, Samuel (1963). *The Complete Works in Verse and Prose of Samuel Daniel*, ed. Alexander B. Grosart. 5 vols. Rpr. New York: Russell & Russell.
Dutton, Richard (1991). *Mastering the Revels: The Regulation and Censorship of English Renaissance Drama*. London: Macmillan.

Farmer, Alan B. and Zachary Lesser (2000). "Vile arts: the marketing of printed drama, 1512–1660." *Research Opportunities in Renaissance Drama* 39, 77–165.

Fumerton, Patricia (1991). *Cultural Aesthetics: Renaissance Literature and the Practice of Social Ornament.* Chicago: University of Chicago Press.

Gosson, Stephen (1974). *The Schoole of Abuse* (1579) and *Plays Confuted in Five Actions* (1582). In *Markets of Bawdrie: The Dramatic Criticism of Stephen Gosson,* ed. Arthur F. Kinney. Salzburg: Institut für Englische Sprache und Literatur.

Grafton, Anthony and Lisa Jardine (1986). *From Humanism to the Humanities: Education and the Liberal Arts in Fifteenth- and Sixteenth-Century Europe.* Cambridge, MA: Harvard University Press.

Grafton, Anthony and Lisa Jardine (1990). " 'Studied for action': how Gabriel Harvey read his Livy." *Past and Present* 129, 30–78.

Greg, W. W. (1939–59). *A Bibliography of the English Printed Drama to the Restoration.* 4 vols. London: Bibliographical Society.

Greville, Fulke (1986). *The Prose Works of Fulke Greville, Lord Brooke,* ed. John Gouws. Oxford: Clarendon Press.

Gurr, Andrew (1987). *Playgoing in Shakespeare's London.* Cambridge: Cambridge University Press.

Gurr, Andrew (1996). *The Shakespearian Playing Companies.* Oxford: Clarendon Press.

Jondorf, Gillian (1969). *Robert Garnier and the Themes of Political Tragedy in the Sixteenth Century.* Cambridge: Cambridge University Press.

Jonson, Ben (1605). *Sejanus.* London.

Lamb, Mary Ellen (1981). "The myth of the Countess of Pembroke: the dramatic circle." *Yearbook of English Studies* 11, 194–202.

Lamb, Mary Ellen (1990). *Gender and Authorship in the Sidney Circle.* Madison: University of Wisconsin Press.

Marlowe, Christopher (1590). *Tamburlaine.* London.

Norland, Howard B. (1995). *Drama in Early Tudor Britain 1485–1558.* Lincoln: University of Nebraska Press.

Orlin, Lena Cowen (1998). "Gertrude's closet." *Shakespeare Jahrbuch* 134, 44–67.

Nevyle, Alexander (1563). *Seneca's Oedipus.* London.

Phillips, James E. (1948–9). "George Buchanan and the Sidney circle." *Huntington Library Quarterly* 12, 23–55.

Prynne, William (1633). *Histrio-Mastix.* London.

Rainolds, John (1599). *Th'Overthrow of Stage-Playes.* Middelburgh.

Randolph, Thomas (1632). *The Jealous Lovers.* London.

Ranum, Orest (1989). "The refuges of intimacy." In *A History of Private Life. III: Passions of the Renaissance,* ed. Roger Chartier. Cambridge, MA: Belknap Press.

Sauer, Elizabeth (1998). "The politics of performance in the inner theater: *Samson Agonistes* as closet drama." In *Milton and Heresy,* eds Stephen Dobranski and John P. Rumrich. Cambridge: Cambridge University Press.

Shannon, Laurie J. (1994). "*The Tragedie of Mariam*: Cary's critique of the terms of founding social discourses." *English Literary Renaissance* 24, 135–53.

Sherburne, Edward (1648). *Medea: A Tragedie.*

Sherman, William H. (1996). "The place of reading in the English Renaissance." In *The Practice and Representation of Reading in England,* eds James Raven, Helen Small, and Naomi Tadmor. Cambridge: Cambridge University Press.

Sidney, Sir Philip (1966). *A Defence of Poetry (1595),* ed. Jan Van Dorsten. Oxford: Oxford University Press.

Slack, Paul (1985). *The Impact of Plague in Tudor and Stuart England.* London: Routledge & Kegan Paul.

Stewart, Alan (1995). "The early modern closet discovered." *Representations* 50, 76–100.

Straznicky, Marta (1994). " 'Profane Stoical paradoxes': *The Tragedie of Mariam* and Sidnean closet drama." *English Literary Renaissance* 24, 104–34.

Straznicky, Marta (1997). "Restoration women playwrights and the limits of professionalism." *ELH* 64, 703–26.

Straznicky, Marta (1998). "Recent studies in closet drama." *English Literary Renaissance* 28, 142–60.

Studley, John (1566). *Seneca's Agamemnon*. London.

Tricomi, Albert H. (1989). *Anticourt Drama in England, 1603–1642*. Charlottesville: University Press of Virginia.

Walker, Greg (1998). *The Politics of Performance in Early Renaissance Drama*. Cambridge: Cambridge University Press.

Wilmot, Robert (1591). *Tancred and Gismund*. London.

Wiseman, Susan (1998). *Drama and Politics in the English Civil War*. Cambridge: Cambridge University Press.

PART FOUR
Dramatists

30
Continental Influences
Lawrence F. Rhu

The Renaissance in England derives its major impulse from Continental humanism, whose origins can be traced back to Italy in the fifteenth and even the fourteenth centuries. Writers such as Giovanni Boccaccio and Lorenzo Valla attest to the sense of a new culture's dawning, and the revival of the arts and learning signals for them the coming of a new epoch. The revival of classical culture especially characterizes the educational movement fostered by Continental humanists. The discovery of lost texts from antiquity and the recirculation of neglected ones in more authoritative editions helped provide humanists with a new canon. But such educators also chose to heighten their emphasis upon certain aspects of the medieval curriculum. The study of rhetoric in particular acquired greater importance, and the inherently theatrical nature of the art of persuasion made mastery of oratorical skills apt training for playwrights who would ultimately bring them to bear in works for the English stage.

The belated arrival of Renaissance culture in England made it coincide with the Reformation. Thus, English Protestants always felt a deep ambivalence about the Continental culture upon which so many of their achievements were founded. For example, in *The Schoolmaster* (1570), Queen Elizabeth's former tutor, Roger Ascham, urges *The Book of the Courtier* (1528) by Baldassare Castiglione upon English youth, for they can read it at home in England, especially since Sir Thomas Hoby has so ably translated it into their native tongue (Ascham, 1967, 50). Such reading can thus spare them the manifold hazards of travel in Italy, whose Circean allure, Ascham fears, would threaten English virtue at every turn.

When Thomas Nashe reviews the fortunes of humanism at the end of the sixteenth century in *The Unfortunate Traveler* (1594), Jack Wilton's Continental tour includes significant visits to Münster and Wittenburg as well as a long journey through major cities of Italy such as Venice, Florence, and Rome. Nashe's travelogue records a jaundiced view of Continental culture near the *fin de siècle*, when Elizabethan tragedy has already developed its own resources for registering profound skepticism about humanistic values that initially reached England trailing clouds of glory associated with their inaugural appearance in Italy. Hamlet, the Wittenburg scholar come home for his father's funeral and (as it turns out) his mother's hasty remarriage as well, epitomizes this perspective. "And yet to me what/is this quintessence of dust?," he asks, in what could be a melancholy gloss on the exemplary optimism of Pico della Mirandola's *Oration on the Dignity of Man* (1486).

Such sentiments, despite the skeptical viewpoint characteristic of tragic drama, supply some evidence for Jacob Burckhardt's oft-debated claim that, during the Renaissance in Italy, "man became a spiritual *individual*, and recognized himself as such" (1958, I, 143). Perhaps this alleged "discovery" of the individual occurred during the Renaissance, or perhaps it took place in Paradise after the Fall. One way or the other, it entails the simultaneous discovery of the isolation of the individual, which tragic drama in the English Renaissance eloquently explores. The tragic figures in an agonizing drama like Shakespeare's *King Lear* (1605), for example – Cordelia, Edgar (and Edmund), Kent, Gloucester, and Lear himself – all stand vividly alone in the face of a devastating ordeal, whether or not they represent definitive manifestations of a previously inaccessible individuality.

In his effort to fathom the world of this play, Stanley Cavell invokes certain Continental thinkers of the early sixteenth century whose writings can help to characterize the intellectual milieu in which English Renaissance drama was composed. The bearings he takes reproduce those evident in Roger Ascham's ambivalence in *The Schoolmaster* and in Jack Wilton's itinerary in *The Unfortunate Traveler*. For example, Cavell asserts the presence of "Machiavelli's knowledge of the world" in *King Lear*, and he discerns this knowledge not just in "attitudes of realism and cynicism" but in the "experience of the condition to which these attitudes are appropriate – in which the inner and outer worlds have become totally disconnected, and man's life is all public, among strangers, seen only from outside. Luther saw the same thing at the same time, but from inside" (1987, 67–8). The final proposition comes as an abrupt surprise. It is a striking collocation from opposite ends of a spectrum that can include such extremes as the Machiavellian ruthlessness of Edmund and Cordelia's uncompromising integrity of conscience or, in the *Duchess of Malfi* (1612–14), Bosola's shady connivance and the Duchess's heroic steadfastness. This surprising association of two such diverse thinkers can represent in small the effect of the wide range of Continental influences that permeates English Renaissance drama.

For example, when we encounter Shylock in *The Merchant of Venice* (1596–7), we must reckon with a confluence of developments readily signaled by allusion to both Machiavelli and Luther. Such references can again remind us that the belated appearance of Renaissance culture in England coincided significantly with the Reformation. Humanist scholarship and, especially, the increasingly historical philology that such scholars initially applied to pagan classics were soon directed toward the critical study of sacred texts. Such habits of reading authorized fresh responses to passages from scripture whose traditional meanings posed no threat to institutional arrangements. This new scholarship facilitated the spread of religious reform.

Thus, when Shylock seeks to justify usury, he summons as a proof-text Genesis 30:25–43 and retells the gist of that episode, Jacob's clever exaction of his final wages from Laban. Antonio, his primary interlocutor in this exchange, offers a rival response to the incident recounted:

> *Shy.*   This was a way to thrive; and he was blest;
>   And thrift is blessing, if men steal it not.
> *Ant.*   This was a venture, sir, that Jacob served for –
>   A thing not in his power to bring to pass,
>   But swayed and fashioned by the hand of heaven.
>   (I.iii.85–9)

However stereotypically "Jewish" Shylock may seem in this scene and elsewhere in this play, however "demonized" this victim of prejudice may become as the action unfolds, the reading that he offers of Jacob's ploy against Laban is quite idiosyncratic and thus bespeaks a Protestant dilemma: the proliferation of unlicensed interpretations of the Bible.

For example, in a sermon delivered at Paul's Cross in London in 1589, Richard Bancroft complains of text-torturing Protestant expositors. Although he clearly opposes what a later age would come to call the magisterium of the Catholic church (that is, its teaching function, especially in regard to biblical interpretation), Bancroft is also alarmed by unqualified readers of Holy Writ who put strains upon passages from that sacred text and wrest meanings from them that lead to heresy and schism. Thus, Bancroft cites Augustine to the effect that "faithful ignorance is better than rash knowledge"; and goes on to invoke Gregory of Nazianzus' assertion, "It falleth not within the compas of everie mans understanding to determine and judge in matters of religion: *Sed exercitatorum*: but of those that are well experienced and exercised in them" (Bancroft, 1588/9, 33–41). Bancroft's distress at the liberties taken by inexperienced readers participates in the mounting anxiety over Protestant tendencies that seem to be spinning out of control in the 1590s (see Weimann, 1996, 79–84).

Traditional exegesis, both Jewish and Christian, had gone to some lengths to make cosmetic improvements upon Jacob's habitual tricksterism. Such behavior in an official role model could occasion scandal and required interpretive redress (see Kugel, 1998, 208–10). Tudor Bibles, both radical and conservative, incorporate this approach to the episode Shylock recounts. The Geneva Bible (1560) pleads Jacob's defense in thus glossing Genesis 30:37, which describes Jacob's device: "Jacob herein used no deceit, for it was God's command." The Bishops' Bible (1568), with reference to Genesis 31:9, thus explains away Jacob's ploy: "It is not lawfull by fraude to seke recompence of iniurie; therfor Moyses sheweth afterwarde that God thus instructed Jacob." Thus, when Shylock offers his own self-justifying gloss on Jacob's ruse, he enacts an odd analogue to what Luther proclaimed as the priesthood of all believers. His appropriation of the official expositor's role strikes a distinctly Protestant note. To paraphrase a famous question Portia poses in the play, "Which is the Gentile here, and which the Jew?"

But Shylock's character also betokens transformations that Niccolò Machiavelli's reputation underwent in its north European reception. Barabas, the protagonist of *The Jew of Malta* by Christopher Marlowe (1589/90), probably served as the immediate dramatic stimulus for Shakespeare's creation of Shylock; and Barabas' affiliation with the Italian archetype of "politic" villainy occurs prominently at the outset of Marlowe's play. In one of the landmarks of mythic wickedness associated with "old Nick," Machevill (whose very name resonates with other such derogatory turns upon its original as "Match a Villain") thus begins the prologue:

> Albeit the world think Machevill is dead,
> Yet was his soul but flown beyond the Alps,
> And now the Guise is dead, is come to France
> To view this land, and frolic with his friends.
> But such as love me, guard me from their tongues,
> And let them know that I am Machevill,
> And weigh not men, and therefore not men's words.
>
> (Pro. 1–8)

Mention of the duke of Guise evokes this statesman's responsibility for the St. Bartholomew's Day Massacre of French Huguenots in August of 1572. Moreover, this French connection suggests a further Continental source of anti-Machiavellian feeling, which derives from resentment of the Florentine queen mother, Catherine de Medici's, powerful influence upon French affairs from 1559 to 1589. Her anti-Protestant policies, together with her foreign origins, served to focus anti-Italian sentiment upon both her and her "Machiavellian" favorites at court. Such an influential work as Innocent Gentillet's *Contre-Machiavel* (1576) thus emerged from a setting where the Florentine politician was thoroughly demonized, and it met with an English reception that readily affirmed that dark image.

Therefore, Machiavelli's resolutely secular humanism was promptly relocated into the context of religious strife so pervasive in English Renaissance culture as to destabilize that very label, "Renaissance," which too often overemphasizes continuities with classical antiquity and occludes the concomitant impact of the Reformation crisis upon English drama. Richard of Gloucester, who himself invokes "the murderous Machiavel" as a measure of the wickedness he means to exceed (*Richard Duke of York*, III.ii.193), can remind us enough of Shylock in the following self-description to demonstrate the confluence of developments that makes the perspectives of Luther and Machiavelli undeniable cohabitants of the dramatic worlds represented on late sixteenth- and early seventeenth-century stages in England:

> But then I sigh, and with a piece of scripture
> Tell them that God bids us do good for evil;
> And thus I clothe my naked villainy
> With odd old ends, stolen forth of Holy Writ,
> And seem a saint when most I play the devil.
>
> (*Richard III*, I.iii.332–6)

The demystification of religion and its consequent manipulability for purposes of gaining and maintaining power typify the cynical calculations of the Machiavellian politician as this figure emerges on the English stage. Reasons of state, which can traditionally signify a leader's concern for the public good, become merely a cover for selfish ambition that stops at nothing to advance its personal agenda; and Protestant scrupulosity about matters of conscience, as well as virulent anti-Italian sentiment, only intensify the demonization of such villainy. Whatever concern for the commonweal may constitute princely *virtù* in Machiavelli's guide for governors thus disappears in bringing this dark legend to the English stage in such figures as Richard of Gloucester and Edmund, the illegitimate son of the earl of Gloucester in *King Lear*.

The wheel of Fortune, a medieval emblem of the way of the world (especially for those in high places), epitomizes the kind of medieval tragedy labeled *de casibus*, which undergoes significant modifications in its deployment on the English Renaissance stage. Machiavelli's telling opposition of *virtù* to *fortuna* reflects a new dynamic of rival forces in the arena of human struggle that plays itself out in tragic agons. The ready moralization of overweening ambition now submits to revised criteria. In an arena where Fortune's sway no longer receives automatic acceptance and knowing nods from arbiters of public virtue, the previously low estimate of worldly wisdom and high regard for divine providence no longer saps the drama from the contest between *virtù* and *fortuna*. Machiavelli notoriously outraged conventional sensibilities with his blunt rhetoric, and we experience to this day a comparably shocked response when reading, in chapter 25 of *The Prince*, his characterization of Fortune. She is a woman who responds favorably to rough, even violent, treatment. Traditional iconography represented Dame Fortune being bound to her wheel by an elderly hermit symbolizing Wisdom or Poverty (Thomson, 2000, 20, illustration 23). This fresh assault upon her, recommended by Machiavelli, comes from self-serving policy ready to change its approach with the needs of the moment, not from self-sacrificing faith and steady forbearance despite mundane vicissitudes.

The realpolitik of Machiavelli stands in striking contrast to the Platonic idealism of *The Book of the Courtier* (1528). This manual of conduct for aspirants at court went through almost 80 editions during its first 90 years in print and thus enjoyed an exceptionally widespread circulation throughout Europe. Thomas Hoby's 1561 translation further guaranteed its accessibility in England. Though previous texts such as Plato's *Symposium*, Boccaccio's *Decameron*, and Bembo's *Gli Asolani* notably influenced the composition of Castiglione's vernacular classic, the chief model was Cicero's *De oratore*. This pre-text not only signals the pervasive presence of the rhetorical tradition in this exemplary work of Renaissance literature; it also demonstrates the impact of humanist scholarship upon the new literary culture of this era. For this dialogue of Cicero's on the ideal orator was first rediscovered and published during the fifteenth century, thus providing, paradoxically, an ancient classic of recent vintage for imitative appropriation.

Courtiers and courts, quite frequently in Italy, are staple characters and settings in English Renaissance drama. Such Italian settings need not represent actual locales; for in Tudor and Stuart England, Italy was as much a place in the heart as a place on the map. It was a state of mind where ordeals of conscience and political crises could play themselves out in dramatic conflicts. Or, as G. K. Hunter rather too emphatically puts it, "Italy became important to English dramatists only when 'Italy' was revealed as an aspect of England" (1960, 95). Thus, when critics mislocate the action of *The Changeling*, as several have done, and call its setting Italy rather than Spain, theirs is an edifying error (Jones, 1970, 251–2). They are referring to the spiritual homeland of moral corruption and religious error, also known as Italy in the English Renaissance imagination. In *Pierce Penilesse* (1592) Nashe thus allegorizes Italy as "the Academie of man-slaughter, the sporting-place of murther, the Apothecary-shop of poyson for all Nations" (Nashe, 1958, I, 186).

In such settings, whether explicitly situated in Italy or elsewhere, playwrights repeatedly strike keynotes of Castiglione's guide to conduct, which in turn makes intelligible ideals of behavior at court whose manifestation on stage takes innumerable forms during this period. The affectation of Osric in *Hamlet*, the high-mindedness (and consequent vulnerability) of Cassio in *Othello*, the ambition and sinister compliance of Oswald in *King Lear* – all bespeak facets of an institution and its habitués under analysis in *The Book of the Courtier*. These sentiments, which we encounter at the opening of John Webster's *The Duchess of Malfi*, reprise central terms and values of the moral discourse on courtliness that Castiglione's manual of conduct best epitomizes:

> a Prince's court
> Is like a common fountain, whence should flow
> Pure silver drops in general. But if't chance
> Some curs'd example poison it near the head,
> Death and diseases through the whole land spread.
> (I.i.11–15)

Webster's couplet signals the proverbial nature of such an observation, whose presence in Castiglione brings closure to an unusually complex moment. There the potentially beneficial uses of duplicity and deception win those typically disparaged qualities an endorsement in terms redolent of the Epicurean tradition. Using "the veil of pleasure," courtiers should "beguile" the prince "with salutary deception like shrewd doctors who often spread the edge of the cup with some sweet cordial when they wish to give a bitter-tasting medicine to sick and over-delicate children" (Castiglione, 1959, 294).

Such indirect means to ostensibly good ends easily raise suspicions. A world where virtue must operate under cover threatens to make virtue indistinguishable from vice. Elsewhere in Castiglione's manual of conduct the recommended flexibility of the self can seem mere hypocrisy – or, should we say, theater – rather than the exercise of civic virtue. As Federico Fregoso puts it:

I would have our Courtier bend himself to [obedience and the furtherance of his prince's wishes], even if he is by nature alien to it, so that his prince cannot see him without feeling that he must have something pleasant to say to him; which will come about if he has the judgment to perceive what his prince likes, and the wit and prudence to bend himself to this . . . But if our Courtier who is accustomed to handling affairs of importance should happen to be in private with his lord, he must become another person, and lay aside grave matters for another time and place, and engage in conversation that will be amusing and pleasant to his lord, so as not to prevent him from gaining such relaxation. (Castiglione, 1959, 110–13).

Of course, such pliability in thus fashioning the self entails a capacity for performance. The ideal of playing such a role in everyday life signifies the deep relation between the world of the stage and that of mundane ambition in pursuing a career at court. But it also signals the constraints of power, if not despotism, that hobble free expression at court and keep down dissent. As Federico Fregoso puts it in his next response to his interlocutor, Cesare Gonzago: "You see to what a great danger those men expose themselves who rashly enter into conversation in a prince's presence without being invited" (Castiglione, 1959, 114).

Moreover, Castiglione's guide to behavior at court reflects social crises often central to dramatic conflict in English Renaissance theater, where ordeals of change in society at large find compelling expression; for a social climber would be more willing to make such accommodations than an established aristocrat, whose sense of entitlement might balk at politic ingratiation. The very language of identity deployed in discussing the ideal courtier betrays the major faultline between upwardly mobile aspirants to places at court and the traditional aristocracy. The perfect courtier is often called a "cavalier," a term whose root meaning signals the horsemanship associated with knighthood and the ranks of the established nobility. As the Tudor monarchy became more centralized, legal and diplomatic and more generally "secretarial" skills increased in value. The adroit application of a humanistic education could serve one better than mere entitlement, and there arose a corps of bureaucrats contemptuously labeled "carpet knights" by resentful aristocrats.[1]

In *Twelfth Night* (1601–2), such tensions find further expression in the cruel tricks Sir Toby Belch and his cohorts play upon the steward Malvolio, whose ambition and self-importance leave him wide open for sadistic scapegoating. After all, in comparison with a blood relation to the titled lady of the house, just who does this merely domestic functionary think he is? Similar anxieties about status and kindred terms of social value come into play at the court of the Duchess of Malfi, where the careers of Daniel de Bosola and Antonio Bologna stand in marked contrast. The former, a "graduate," gains the provisorship of the Duchess' horse in exchange for his services as a spy in the employ of her brother the Cardinal. Antonio, her steward, having distinguished himself in jousting, participates in this exchange with Duke Ferdinand, her other brother:

Fer.   You are a good horseman, Antonio . . . what do you think of good
         horsemanship?
Ant.   Nobly, my lord . . . out of brave horsemanship, arise the first sparks of
         growing resolution, that raise the mind to noble action.

(I.ii.61–7)

When Duke Ferdinand then replies to Antonio, "You have bespoke it worthily," it is
well to remember that shortly before, in another conversation, the Duke has remarked,
"Methinks you that are courtiers should be my touchwood, take fire when I give fire;
that is, laugh when I laugh, were the subject never so witty" (43–6).

The tension between chivalric and courtly virtue becomes a topic in *The Book of
the Courtier* in terms both of the comparative value of letters and arms and of the
relationship between virtue and birth. That there should be dialogue about such
matters itself suggests the existence of social tensions and the questions they prompt.
That those studies called the humanities are deemed the crown of a courtier's –
or cavalier's! – accomplishments belatedly registers the triumph of humanistic
education, at least from Castiglione's nostalgic perspective (1959, 68, 70). That birth
and virtue should not be inextricably bound shows there remains considerable play
in the contest between Fortune and virtue, in whatever sense one construes that second
term.

For example, Malevole, in *The Malcontent* (1604), chafes Bilioso as "my dear
Castilio" in a scene (I.ii.89) reminiscent of Hamlet's raillery and exposure of Osric's
chameleon-like accommodations of the Prince's every whim. This ridicule of hypocrisy
by Hamlet, who is himself a playwright and actor within the play bearing his name,
ironically reveals the necessary complicity of both the virtuous and the vicious in the
theatricality of life at court – whether in an Urbinate palace such as Castiglione
idealizes or in a degenerate Elsinore whose treachery Hamlet must fathom and resist.
Malevole shares this skill for theatrical mastery, not only of trivial time-servers like
Bilioso, but also of his mightier and more sinister opposites at court in Genoa: first
Pietro Jacomo and Aurelia, the usurping Duke and Duchess, and then Mendoza, who
subsequently undermines their hold on power.

However, John Marston's representation of courtly intrigue and usurpation bears
the marks of a kind of play "writ in choice Italian" (*Hamlet* III.ii.240) but significantly different from *The Murder of Gonzago* or *The Mousetrap*, as Hamlet variously
identifies his selection for the evening entertainment at Elsinore. The play-within-a-
play in *Hamlet* reflects the tragic action whose pattern defines the work in which it is
embedded. *The Malcontent* decisively diverges from that pattern. Marston dedicated
this play to Ben Jonson, his former enemy in the notorious War of the Theaters, which
occurred only a few years before the first production of *The Malcontent* and which
Hamlet itself mentions in the remarks of Rosencranz and Guildenstern about why the
players have abandoned the city and gone on tour. In his dedication Marston labeled
it *asperam hanc suam thaliam* ("this his bitter comedy"). This Latin tag signals what
the entry of this play in the Stationers' Register confirms by identifying *The Malcon-*

tent as a tragicomedy: it is a conscious experiment in a genre recently the subject of literary debate in Italy (see chapter 27 above). At the center of that noteworthy controversy stood Battista Guarini's *Il Pastor Fido* (1590), a work whose popularity Jonson himself indicates through a speech of Lady Politic Would-Be's in *Volpone* (1605). This fatuous English tourist has previously claimed familiarity with the entire Italian canon of vernacular masters by asserting, quite simply, "I have read them all" (III.iv.81). But when she mentions Guarini's *Pastor Fido*, despite Volpone's exasperation with her incessant chatter, she becomes even more expansive:

> All of our English writers,
> I mean such as are happy in th'Italian,
> Will deign to steal out of this author, mainly;
> Almost as much, as from Montaignié:
> He has so modern, and catching a vein,
> Fitting the time, and catching the court ear.
> (III.iv.87–92)

The Malcontent abounds in borrowings from *Il Pastor Fido* that echo both the Italian original and the 1602 "Dymocke" translation into English. Moreover, the play employs the *de casibus* pattern to signal how its plot comes to rest at a station in the turning of Fortune's wheel well after the low point in that cycle characteristic of tragic endings (see Geckle, 1980, 108–24). It is a tragedy with a happy ending such as the Italian playwright and theorist Giraldi Cinthio had composed and described in the mid-sixteenth century; and it follows the pattern of pastoral tragicomedy such as Guarini had defended in his debates with Giason Denores in the 1580s and 1590s, and ultimately codified in his *Compendio della poesia tragicomica* attached to the 1602 Italian edition of *Il Pastor Fido*.

However, despite its extensive borrowings from Guarini, *The Malcontent* is by no means a pastoral play in its setting. It takes place exclusively at court and thus reflects, through the jaundiced eye of its railing protagonist, Malevole, the satirical or hard-pastoral mode of the mixed genre of tragicomedy rather than the soft-pastoral mode. These options within this hybrid kind were memorably pictured on the title-page of Ben Jonson's *Works* (1616), where a satyr and a shepherd flank the figure of Tragicomedy to indicate this genre's characteristic range of modes. Bosola, who is introduced as "[t]he only court-gall" in *The Duchess of Malfi* (I.i.23), embodies such a satirical perspective within this Italianate tragedy of Webster's; but Malevole's mordant commentary in *The Malcontent* occurs within a sequence of events leading to his restoration to the duchy of Genoa, which thus constitutes the *lieto fine* (happy ending) of a clearly tragicomic alloy.

The drive toward such merging of genres is audible in Guarini's immediate model and inspiration for *Il Pastor Fido*, Torquato Tasso's *Aminta* (pub. 1580). There the poet's alter ego, Tirsi, reveals how his efforts in heroic poetry have influenced him to include elements of that genre in his pastoral piping:

> né già suona
> la mia sampogna umil come soleva;
> ma di voce più altera e più sonora,
> emula de le trombe, empie le selve.
>   (I.ii.641–3)

(my humble pipe does not sing as before; but with a loftier and more sonorous voice, emulous of the trumpets, it fills the woods.)

The instruments (pipe and trumpet) bespeak generic codes (pastoral and epic, respectively) that had increasingly become intelligible signals of poetic kinds – as had the locale (the woods), which distinguishes pastoral in its "satiric" mode. For example, in Tasso's most famous passage of literary theorizing, when he aims to express the variety-in-unity or *discordia concors* that heroic poetry should aim to achieve, he employs a sort of geography of literary kinds that cover the globe, which thus amounts to a single site containing a multiplicity of significant landscapes (Rhu, 1993, 130–1).

Italian tragicomedy influenced English dramatists to undertake a variety of experiments in this generic hybrid, and this mixed kind has sometimes served critics to help decipher the diverse signals sent by those works of Shakespeare's belatedly termed "problem plays" and "romances." In a late play like *The Winter's Tale*, the language of place has become especially expressive, and Shakespeare puts it to noteworthy uses in the shifting scenes of that so-called romance as they range from Sicily to Bohemia and back, and from court to coast and pasture, before returning to court (see Henke, 1993; chapter 27 above). In the midst of tragic developments at Leontes' court, Shakespeare also introduces a brief evocation of the serene and beneficent "isle" of Delphos, in telling contrast to the scene being played out in Sicily and as a harbinger of alternative outcomes.

Moreover, *The Winter's Tale* stands as the final Shakespearean investigation of erotic jealousy in a sequence that runs the gamut of genres, beginning with the comedy *Much Ado about Nothing* (1598), and recurring in tragic form in *Othello* (1602). Both of these plays also derive in significant part from Italian *novelle*, a type of generally realistic narrative often fraught with lurid crime and sexual intrigue that nourished an English audience's appetite for sensational stories associated with Italian settings. John Webster's *The Duchess of Malfi*, which recounts details from an actual episode that took place during the sixteenth century, ultimately derives from a story in Matteo Bandello's *Novelle* (1554). This same collection of tales, along with an alternate version in Ludovico Ariosto's *Orlando Furioso* (1532), supplied Shakespeare with the Hero and Claudio plot in *Much Ado*.

Erotic jealousy in such plays as *Othello* and *The Winter's Tale* also provided Shakespeare with a means of representing the existential depths of the most far-reaching philosophical development in early modern thought, the emergence of skepticism, even before its full articulation in the work of René Descartes (Cavell, 1987, 7–12, 15–17). Standard accounts of this development in intellectual history attribute its origins, in significant part, to the circulation, in the 1560s, of the writings of Sextus

Empiricus (*c.* 200 CE). The fresh accessibility of these major texts of Pyrrhonian skepticism coincided with the widespread struggle for unquestionable criteria in the interpretation of the Bible that preoccupied Reformers, and their opponents who defended the traditional authority of the church of Rome. At the beginning of the modern age, radical doubt about the most basic assumptions of European culture increasingly occasioned a shaking of the foundations upon which that culture had been built (see Popkin, 1979; Larmore, 1992). In the skeptical line, Montaigne (a touchstone for Lady Politic Would-Be, as we have seen) is the chief Continental thinker whose writings undeniably influenced English Renaissance dramatists like Shakespeare and Marston and their contemporaries. Indeed, John Florio, who translated Montaigne's *Essays* into English (1603), enjoyed the patronage of the earl of Southampton, whose beneficence had also seen Shakespeare through hard times when the theaters were closed due to the plague in 1592–93.

The evolution of skepticism from Montaigne to Descartes entails what intellectual historians often term an epistemological crisis and a paradigm shift (see MacIntyre, 1977). In other words, ways of knowing and models of understanding altered drastically during this period when the modern age came into being. Stanley Cavell links this development of English Renaissance drama in the following manner:

> Nietzsche thought the metaphysical consolation of tragedy was lost when Socrates set *knowing* as the crown of human activity. And it is a little alarming, from within the conviction that the medium of drama which Shakespeare perfected also ended with him, to think that Bacon and Galileo and Descartes were contemporary with those events. We will hardly say that it was *because* of the development of the new science and the establishing of epistemology as the monitor of philosophical inquiry that Shakespeare's mode of tragedy disappeared. But it may well be that the loss of presentness – which is what the disappearance of that mode of tragedy means – is what works us into the idea that we can save our lives by knowing them. This seems to be the message both of the new epistemology and of Shakespeare's tragedy themselves. (1987, 93–4)

Of course, the message of the new epistemology was an optimistic one, promising a mastery of self and world that boded well for the future it envisioned. Although such a sanguine outlook would soon encounter disenchantments of its own with which to contend, Descartes evidently did experience some relief by coming up with a cogent proof of his own existence. But the agons undergone by figures like Lear and Othello, whose relentless demands for demonstrations of love and fidelity lead to catastrophe, express the darker side of the quest for knowledge in early modernity. As we can see in *Hamlet* and Nashe's *Unfortunate Traveler*, English Renaissance tragedy achieved its greatest expressive powers in a period of radical disenchantment with the high hopes of early humanists. Using the very instruments that humanism itself had made available – classical models in literature and rhetorical training in composition – tragic drama on the English Renaissance stage marked unforgettably the occasion both of its own passing and of the passing of the culture that had provided the conditions necessary for this unique dramatic achievement.

In *The Tempest*, the latest play for which we can confidently claim Shakespearean authorship throughout, we encounter a distinct reminiscence of Faustus, the over-reaching magus of Wittenburg, in the figure of Prospero. But the passions of the mind cause this Italian scholar to lose his dukedom, not his soul; and he ultimately averts tragedy by tempering revenge with forgiveness. The mitigated skepticism of Montaigne also pervades this tragedy. It is present, for example, in the utopian fantasy of Gonzalo that draws explicitly upon Montaigne's (1603) essay "Of Cannibals." The adaptation of a native American perspective upon European culture in this essay demonstrates the relativism already pushed to an extreme by the supreme humanist, Desiderius Erasmus, in *The Praise of Folly*. In his debate with Luther over freedom of the will, skepticism, which (Erasmus claimed) could become an occasion of faith by its exposure of the limits of human understanding, was deemed by the German reformer an inadequate premise in an argument for accepting the authority of the church of Rome. Having witnessed the bloodshed of religious warfare in which late sixteenth-century France was awash, Montaigne arrived at a conclusion comparable to that of Erasmus. Shakespeare, moreover, appealed to Montaigne at the moment of crisis in *The Tempest*, when revenge yields to forgiveness and a potential tragedy is transformed by a happy ending.

However, once it had been unleashed by a spirit of radical doubt, chaos, such as Othello fears, could indeed come again and not be contained by yieldings, such as Prospero's, of passion to restraint. Descartes entertains hyperbolic doubt precisely because it is the undeniable threat of extreme skepticism with which he feels forced to contend. In doing so he echoes the circumstances that Prospero readily calls to mind and easily dispels in soothing the disturbances of Ferdinand's senses, startled by the sudden disappearance of the masque celebrating his betrothal to Miranda.

"There may indeed be those who would prefer to deny the existence of a God so powerful, rather than believe that all other things are uncertain," Descartes opines in "Meditation 1." But, he continues, "at the end I feel constrained to confess that there is nothing in all that I formerly believed to be true, of which I cannot in some measure doubt" (Descartes, 1996, 61). Suppose it is all just dream, to put it bluntly and prosaically. That is the premise that Prospero encourages Ferdinand to accept, not about art but about life; and that is the question that Descartes forces himself to face in the *Meditations*. The interaction between Continental and English culture in many ways helps to produce such gestures of mind and imagination on the English Renaissance stage.

NOTES

All quotations from the plays of Shakespeare are taken from *The Norton Shakespeare*, gen. ed. Stephen Greenblatt (1997).

1 In *1 Henry IV* (1596–7), Hotspur's lengthy excursus in justification of his failure to supply the king with prisoners taken at Holmedon Hill vividly portrays an encounter between effeminate courtliness and macho chivalry from the perspective of aristocratic contempt (I.iii.28–47).

REFERENCES AND FURTHER READING

Ascham, Roger (1967). *The Schoolmaster (1570)*, ed. Lawrence V. Ryan. Ithaca: Cornell University Press.

Bancroft, Richard (1588/9). *Sermon Preached at Paules Cross*. London.

Burckhardt, Jacob (1958). *The Civilization of the Renaissance in Italy*. 2 vols. New York: Harper and Row.

Castiglione, Baldassare (1959). *The Book of the Courtier*, tr. Charles S. Singleton. New York: Doubleday.

Cavell, Stanley (1987). *Disowning Knowledge in Six Plays of Shakespeare*. Cambridge: Cambridge University Press.

Clubb, Louise George (1989). *Italian Drama in Shakespeare's Time*. New Haven: Yale University Press.

Descartes, René (1996). *Discourse on Method and Meditations on First Philosophy*, ed. David Weissman. New Haven: Yale University Press.

Doran, Madeleine (1954). *Endeavors of Art: A Study in Form in Elizabethan Drama*. Madison: University of Wisconsin Press.

Geckle, George L. (1980). *John Marston's Drama: Themes, Images, Sources*. Rutherford, NJ: Fairleigh Dickinson University Press.

Greenblatt, Stephen, gen. ed. (1997). *The Norton Shakespeare*. New York: Norton.

Henke, Robert (1993). "*The Winter's Tale* and Guarinian dramaturgy." *Comparative Drama* 27, 197–217.

Hunter, G. K. (1960). "English folly and Italian vice." In *Stratford-upon-Avon Studies* 1, *Jacobean Theatre*, eds J. R. Brown and B. Harris. New York: St. Martin's Press.

Jones, Robert C. (1970). "Italian settings and the 'world' of Elizabethan tragedy." *Studies in English Literature* 10, 251–68.

Jonson, Ben (1988). *Volpone*, ed. Philip Brockbank. New York: Norton.

Kugel, James L. (1998). *Traditions of the Bible: A Guide to the Bible As It Was at the Start of the Common Era*. Cambridge, MA: Harvard University Press.

Larmore, Charles (1992). "Scepticism." In *The Cambridge History of Seventeenth-Century Philosophy*, eds. Daniel Garber and Michael Ayres. 2 vols. Cambridge: Cambridge University Press.

MacIntyre, Alasdair (1977). "Epistemological crises, dramatic narrative, and the philosophy of science." *Monist* 60, 433–72.

Marlowe, Christopher (1979). *The Jew of Malta*, ed. T. W. Craik. London: A. & C. Black; New York: Norton.

Marston, John (1975). *The Malcontent*, ed. G. K. Hunter. Manchester: Manchester University Press.

Montaigne, Michel de (1603). *The Essays*, trans. John Florio. London.

Nashe, Thomas (1958). *Works*, ed. R. B. McKerrow. 5 vols. Oxford: Oxford University Press.

Popkin, Richard H. (1979). *The History of Scepticism: From Erasmus to Spinoza*. Berkeley: University of California Press.

Rhu, Lawrence F. (1993). *The Genesis of Tasso's Narrative Theory: English Translations of the Early Poetics and a Comparative Study of their Significance*. Detroit: Wayne State University Press.

Tasso, Torquato (1994). *Aminta*. Milan: BUR.

Thomson, Leslie (2000). *Fortune: "All is But Fortune"*. Washington, DC: Folger Shakespeare Library.

Webster, John (1983). *The Duchess of Malfi*, ed. Elizabeth M. Brennan. London: A. & C. Black; New York: Norton.

Weimann, Robert (1996). *Authority and Representation in Early Modern Discourse*. Baltimore: Johns Hopkins University Press.

31

Christopher Marlowe
Emily C. Bartels

If ever there were reason for the guardians of church and state to be wary of the politics being practiced, promoted, or critiqued within the Elizabethan theater, reason for Puritan activists such as Philip Stubbes to declaim against "all kind of sin and mischief" appearing on the Renaissance stage, or reason for Queen Elizabeth herself to authorize secretly the assassination of a popular playwright (as David Riggs has suggested she may have done to Marlowe), the plays of Christopher Marlowe provide that prompt.[1] *Dido, Queen of Carthage, Tamburlaine Parts I and II, The Jew of Malta, Doctor Faustus, Edward II,* and *The Massacre at Paris* draw the spectators into a world where transgression is not merely the source of crisis but also the motivating force behind identity, ideology, and the institution of meaning. It is no wonder that when the early Shakespeare creates his own extraordinary outcasts, such as Richard III and Aaron the Moor, whose notoriously evil intentions pave the way to power, his characterizations build on Marlowe. No wonder either that when Bertolt Brecht and Derek Jarman turn to Renaissance drama for an undertext that is certain to unsettle the status quo, they turn to Marlowe, to *Edward II*, to a dramatic milieu that announces itself as socially and politically outrageous. On Marlowe's stage, sodomy, necromancy, robbery, selective genocide, deception, erotic betrayal, treason, and murder provide the order as well as the disorder of the day.

Like Marlowe himself, a reputed atheist, sodomite, smoker, and spy, Marlowe's "heroes" bear the reputation of rebels, who indulge willfully in "unlawful things" (*Faustus* Epilogue 6), be they religious, social, sexual, or otherwise political.[2] Typecast in seeming stereotype, these figures represent controversial social positions and identities that Elizabethan authorities were vigorously scripting as taboo. Faustus is a notorious necromancer, who dismisses all clearly acceptable academic disciplines in favor of something, black magic, that puts him dangerously, if not damnably, on the "'ravishing' razor edge" of intellectual and spiritual thinking (Marcus, 1997, 18). Tamburlaine casts off the signs of class, the shepherd's "weeds" (*Tamb. I* I.ii.41), that mark him as a "paltry Scythian" and "thief" (I.i.53, 36) to become a ruthless imperialist, as bent on conquest as the Turk England at once admired and feared. Barabas is "the Jew," a subject officially banished from the realm centuries before. Dido is an African queen who plays erotically with the epic fate of Troy, and so of the "New Troy" (i.e. London); the Duke of Guise a French, Machiavellian Catholic, who "seeks to murder all the protestants" (*Massacre* I.i.31). Even Marlowe's English king, Edward II, is a confirmed and flagrant sodomite, one whose predilections get the Renaissance as close as it will come to imagining sodomitical acts as part of an ingrained sexual identity.

For the most part, these figures inhabit worlds outside the close confines of England. Dido occupies and *is* Carthage. Tamburlaine maps his story out across the East, bringing his spectators into contact with a whole range of exotic places and place names, from Scythia to Arabia, to Egypt, Morocco, Algiers, and Fez and to the seductively fetishized Persepolis, where he imagines he will "ride in triumph" (*Tamb. I* II.v.50) if for no other reason than the sound. The Jew of Malta runs his enterprises from Malta, a Mediterranean entrepôt where Spaniards, Turks, and Italians come to make their fortunes too. Although Faustus sits in his study in Germany, his fantasies take him across the globe, to "all corners of the new-found world," to an India full of "gold" and an ocean full of "orient pearl" (*Faustus* I.i.83–5), to an America whose "golden fleece" "yearly stuffs old Philip's treasury" (I.i.132–3), to "the hills that bind the Afric shore" (I.iii.107), as well as to "Olympus' top," where he:

> views the clouds, the planets and the stars,
> The tropic, zones, and quarters of the sky,
> From the bright circle of the horned moon
> Even to the height of *primum mobile*.
> (*Faustus* 3 Prologue 4, 7–10)

Even the England of *Edward II* is somewhat unfamiliar ground, caught as it is at a moment in medieval history when the powers of the king were up for grabs from a nobility that could claim competing rights. Although set in France, *The Massacre at Paris* is something of an exception, since it recreates a contemporary event, the massacre of Protestants that occurred in Paris in 1572, that resonated within Protestant England with a striking immediacy. Still, the erratic movement and sound-bite speed of action, whether Marlowe's invention or a consequence of textual "corruption," produce a world strangely out of time and out of joint.[3]

Yet if Marlowe's plays are therefore "fascinated by the idea of the stranger in a strange land," as Stephen Greenblatt has suggested, if they capitalize on turning unfamiliar, unseemly, and "unlawful" things into public spectacle for mass consumption, it is finally at the level of the self that they bring their stories pertinently home (1980, 194). For what comes with transgression in Marlowe is the illusion of self-hood – the illusion that individuation happens, as Greenblatt has put it, through "subversive identification with the alien" (1980, 203). It is telling that we know, or have imagined that we know, so little about William Shakespeare, despite the cult that has made him familiarly "ours," and so much about Christopher Marlowe, in contrast, since the historical documents that call him rebelliously into being are themselves products of questionable men and motives.[4] In history, in criticism, and in Marlowe's dramatic worlds, transgression sells as self. Ben Jonson may have been the boldest Renaissance writer to declare himself author of his "works." But Marlowe's subversive signature seems to have been written all over his plays, creating the illusion that there is indeed an author within and behind these texts. In *Renaissance Self-Fashioning*, Greenblatt sets Marlowe provocatively beside More, Tyndale, Wyatt, Spenser, and Shakespeare as one of the signal authors self-consciously invested in the processes of "self-fashioning" that were defining, transforming, if not also modernizing, the early modern subject. Though in Greenblatt Marlowe's rebels struggle in vain against a theatrical backdrop of self-consuming vacancy, their starting point, and ours – the point that Marlowe relentlessly questions – is the possibility and the promise that the alien subject can claim, maintain, and sustain a self-propelled, self-possessed, and self-authorizing presence (see also Maus, 1995, esp. 85–103).

Formally, the single most striking and original feature of Marlovian drama – after its innovative use of blank verse – is its almost obsessive preoccupation with the central figure, who, as he or she transgresses, controls and steals the show. Dido may have her Aeneas, Tamburlaine his Zenocrate (alive or, in Part Two, quite dead), Faustus his Mephastophilis, Barabas his Ithamore, and Edward his Gaveston, but in the end it is the protagonist whose subversive presence defines the dramatic landscape, whose radical will gets played out, and whose extraordinary fortunes determine the form. From start to finish, these figures dare, relentlessly, to desire, and it is their desire that provides the passion and cue for otherwise unthinkable action. We know from Tamburlaine's first appearance that he wants not only to "ride in triumph through Persepolis" and conquer Persia as a means to conquering Asia, but also "to be a terror to the world, / Measuring the limits of his empery / By east and west, as Phoebus doth his course" (*Tamb. I* I.ii.37–40). We know that Faustus wants "all things that move between the quiet poles" to be at his command (*Faustus* I.i.57), no matter how banal or comic, demonic or deadly. We know that Edward "will have Gaveston" (*Edward II* I.i.96), and after Gaveston, Spencer, that Dido will have Aeneas "sit in Dido's place" (*Dido* II.iii.93), and that *The Massacre at Paris*'s Duke of Guise will have anything and everything "that flies beyond [his] reach" (*Massacre* I.ii.42).

And in Marlowe, wants and wills become "means," with things ordinarily beyond reach becoming extraordinarily reachable. As the protagonists act on their desires, they act as authors who seem to write both themselves and the worlds they live in. With a simple change of costume and an awesome display of "working words" (*Tamb. I* II.iii.25), the Scythian shepherd Tamburlaine reinvents himself as an indomitable conqueror, with a sign system of his own. His terms become *the* terms of power (see also Thurn, 1989). At the beginning of Part I, we may believe that the "sweet fruition" of a single "earthly crown" (*Tamb. I* II.vii.29) can satisfy, may think that being king of Persia, soldan of Egypt, king of Fez or Morocco, or even emperor of Turkey is what "earthly crown" signifies for him. But as Tamburlaine maps his way, through conquest, across the watching world, marketing himself not only as king, but also as emperor, "monarch of the earth" (*Tamb. II* V.iii.217), and finally scourge of God, he changes that world's unit of organization from the local to the global to the godly. Under Tamburlaine's regime, nations give way to empires, empires to "the earth," the earth to the heavens as sites of power, with titles such as "monarch," "king," "lord," and even "scourge" losing their geographical specificity and registering instead an abstract, unbounded dominion. Generically, the play seems to follow suit. It forgets its *de casibus* obligations (see chapter 30 above) and exceeds its own bounds, producing a horizontal rather than vertical trajectory, with the episodic "progress" of Tamburlaine's "pomp" (*Tamb. II* Pro. 4) consuming Part One and being, then, almost randomly curtailed in Part Two by Tamburlaine's sudden, inexplicable, and arguably anticlimactic fall into a strange "distemper" (*Tamb. II* V.i.17) – as if the playwright is merely tracing, and not constructing, the dramatic pattern that Tamburlaine, the character, has set, as if there is finally no predictable pattern, no readable moral, that can contain the conqueror's force.[5]

Whereas in other plays of the period, figures seem to follow form, in Marlowe, consistently, form seems to follow figure. Consider the difference between, say, Hamlet, who is haunted, his story framed and formed, by a revenge plot he can neither fully answer nor fully evade, and the Jew of Malta, Marlowe's revenger par excellence, who (like most of Marlowe's protagonists) has no history, no past, and no ghosts to tie him down. Though in Hamlet's hands, revenge becomes an oppressive dictate from the past, which repeatedly blocks his attempts to articulate a new kind of self, for Barabas revenge is an improvisational product of the present, a vehicle of his shifting and shifty self-promotions which, at times, fool even us.

Or consider the difference between Marlowe's *Edward II* and its Shakespearean heir, *Richard II* (1595), both of which, as history plays, are generically bound by fact and function to tell the story of state. Both Shakespeare and Marlowe conflate the genre partially with tragedy to struggle against its terms, to find a place for an authorizing self amid the pressures and precepts of history. Yet in Shakespeare, tragedy ultimately gives way to history, the story of Richard II becoming consumed by an historical tetralogy that traces the rise of Henry V. And in *Richard II*, we can see the eclipse coming. From the start of his play, Richard is caught by feudal ceremonies that have obviously outlived their time, and he is unable to adapt his monarchical vision to accommodate noble subjects who put land before allegiance, property before propriety, and self before state. However much he figures and functions as a "poet king," his words do not translate into power. As he sits in prison after his deposition, his language fails utterly to express, secure, or recuperate a discrete or stable identity. In the end, Shakespeare presses Richard's history back into form, his death resonating not as a personal crisis for Richard but as a legitimation crisis for the Henrys and Henry plays that follow – a crisis that can itself be managed and ameliorated through ceremony, through the promise of pilgrimage which allows the new, ostensibly illegitimate kings to create in form the atonement they never quite deliver in person.

If Shakespeare's king is thus constrained by form, his tragedy almost inevitably restored to history, Marlowe's king and Marlowe's play insist on breaking through the pomp and circumstance that would otherwise limit Edward's story, and remake history in terms that make us rethink self as the crucial vehicle of state. The play opens on Edward's inscription of his royal will – "My father is deceas'd. Come, Gaveston, / And share the kingdom with thy dearest friend" (*Edward II* I.i.1–2) – which openly defies his father's dictate that Gaveston be forever banished from the realm, and establishes a world in which the political must be measured by the sexual, the sexual by the political. Edward will have Gaveston, and it is *by* and not *despite* having Gaveston that Edward stands his ground against the combative nobility, who would use the historical precedent set by Edward I to challenge Edward II.[6] The king's expression of desire becomes his site of power, his (and Marlowe's) means of disturbing the linear trajectory that otherwise augurs Edward's defeat. For once Gaveston has been killed and his saga ended, Edward turns his attentions to the Younger Spencer and starts episodically over, this time with an ambition that seems more political than it is sexual. To decipher the complex interplay of sex and politics, politics and sex here, we must read forwards and backwards, from Edward's embrace of Gaveston to the embrace of Spencer who at once replaces and reiterates Gaveston. Hence, as Edward's priorities shift, stall, and start again, in some senses so do ours, from reading history teleologically to reading it as circular and circumstantial, dependent upon the contingencies of character rather than the precedents of state. Like Richard, Edward, of course, will die. But his death – a violent murder which takes place graphically on stage and which may have approximated a sodomitical rape – reiterates, even as it attempts to eradicate, the terms of Edward's story. This final spectacle undermines the legacy, the promise of Edward III, the play offers in closing and turns attention back to the political cultivation of sexuality that defined the reign of Edward II as it would not the reign of Edward III. *Edward II* not only *is not* followed by an *Edward III*; given the play's resistance to historical linearity, it simply *cannot* be.

Indeed, Marlowe's plays are so compelled and controlled by their protagonists that when these figures die, there seems to be nothing left, even in the case of *Edward II*, where the future of the English monarchy is at stake. Although Tamburlaine passes on his global legacy to his eldest son Amyrath, the play offers no anticipation of a future. Amyrath himself cuts Tamburlaine's history off, dictating "here let all things end" (*Tamb. II* V.iii.250), scripting in a vacancy on the other side of the play with a finality notably more barren than that projected at the end of *King Lear*, whose survivors can only hope for a shortened future in which no one will "see so much" or "live so long" (*Lear* V.iii.327) as Lear.[7] When the deserted Dido brings her own and Aeneas' story to climax and closure by casting herself and the "relics" of their love into flames, making Aeneas "famous through the world / For perjury and slaughter of a queen" (*Dido* V.i.292–4), Anna and Iarbas, the subjects on the sidelines of that story, run suicidally into the flames after her, gestures which Marlowe invents, departing from his classical sources and exaggerating the final void. And when Faustus is gone, the author seems to have no choice but to end the play as routinely as the hour ends the day – "*Terminat hora diem, terminat Author opus*" – as if there is nothing, not even hell, on the other side. In Greenblatt, these vacancies suggest "the nothingness into which all characters fall at the end of a play" – a nothingness which pressures Marlowe's protagonists, if they are to survive, into a compulsive repetition of "self-constituting acts" and which betrays identity as "a theatrical invention that must be reiterated if it is to endure" (1980, 200, 201). Yet each of Marlowe's plays ends with the character as much as the character ends with the play, suggesting a double-edged theatricality which emphasizes, as much as it may challenge, the power of the player to set the terms of play.

And yet, while Marlowe puts such authorizing selves at the center of his plays and insists on their ability to figure over form, it is not finally their interiors, their isolated subjectivities or psyches, that we are asked to explore, experience, or evaluate. Most of Marlowe's plays qualify as tragedies, but not one offers a typical interrogation of the tragic self, who searches, and so prompts the spectators to search, the depths of his thought and feeling to find some meaning there. Barabas is no Hamlet, Edward II no Richard II, Tamburlaine no Othello, Antony, or Lear. No one in Marlowe asks what it means to be or not to be, or goes onto a vacant heath, risking madness and death, to confront "unaccommodated man" in his barest and basest element (*Lear* III.iv.106–7). No one looks into the interiors of body and soul to anatomize what "man" is made on, or confronts the skull beneath the skin, the body as a "box of wormseed" (*Duchess of Malfi* IV.ii.123), the mind as a seat of madness, uncertainty or despair.[8] Even Faustus, whose story in outline is a saga of soul, never really looks within, even when Mephastophilis prompts him to take his soul-selling seriously. With a certitude that wavers but never fails, Faustus treats hell as if it were a "fable" (*Faustus* II.i.128), sin as if it were a pageant to "feed [his] soul" (II.iii.163), and damnation and the soul as "vain trifles" (I.iii.62). In the background, the morality voices of the Good and Bad Angel try to make the spiritual consequences of Faustus' choices real. And periodically Faustus toys with the vocabulary, if not the concept, of repentance – though never with the level of self-scrutiny we will get even from *Hamlet's* decidedly unrepentant Claudius. However much Marlowe's play itself engages with the idea of soul, in *Faustus* soul-making or soul-breaking happens as a consequence of materiality rather than morality, as a social rather than spiritual choice, Faustus himself being driven by a desire to be resolved in action more than to be redeemed in thought.

In producing protagonists who are characteristically so resolved, so single-minded and consistent in their pursuits, so untroubled by internal complication, the plays, in fact, actively block our interrogation into their interiors. Because these figures do not stop to scrutinize who they are and what they want, we cannot. They dictate form, and the form dictates action, offering little time or space or prompt for us to look within, to the implicit demons and desires behind the explicit, externalized desires these figures posit as their passion and their cue. After all, it is only because Hamlet agonizes over why he, who has urgent cause to effect revenge, is mired in indecision and delay that we agonize, even in the face of knowing that what he proposes to do, for regicide as well as patricide is patently criminal. It is only because the Duchess of Malfi insists that she has "not gone about" in her secret, cross-class marriage "to create

/ Any new world, or custom" (*Duchess of Malfi* III.ii.111–12) that we question her motivation. And it is at least in part because Iago is so haphazard in rationalizing his motives and Othello so insistent in rationalizing his that we search the Moor's interiors, instead of the quasi-Marlovian Iago's, for "the cause" of the domestic tragedy (*Othello* V.ii.1). In contrast to the tragic "heroes" who will define, and internalize, the focus of Renaissance tragedy, Marlowe's protagonists do not wonder; they desire and do (cf. Yachnin, 1997, 93–107).

It is in the doing, in fact, that the source of self lies. For Marlowe's protagonists do not simply *have* desires that we are prompted to decipher; they *perform* desire in public. It is no accident that the plays seem schizophrenically split between tragedy and comedy. For as much as they focus on the designs and desires of their central subjects, they also embed those figures in a social context and insist on the import of audience.[9] As much as Marlovian drama is self-centered, that is, it is simultaneously audience-centered, its protagonists emerging as inextricably social subjects. Their characterizations may begin with soliloquy – with Faustus "settl[ing]" his studies (*Faustus* I.i.1), or with the Jew of Malta counting up the "infinite riches" that fill his "little room" (*Jew of Malta* I.i.37) or with Gaveston reading Edward's invitation to "come" "and share the kingdom." Yet soliloquy in Marlowe is relatively rare, especially compared to what we find in Shakespeare, in self-centered tragedies such as *Hamlet*, *Othello*, and *Lear*. Moreover, on the other side of solo moments in Marlowe, an audience waits and watches. Faustus' soliloquy is preceded, its self-enclosure compromised, by an opening chorus, which directs our gaze to "the man that in his study sits" (*Faustus* 1 Pro. 28), making us self-consciously aware that Faustus is being watched from the start, as he will be, by the Chorus, throughout the play. Similarly, Barabas' opening soliloquy is preceded and prescribed by Machevill, who, if he does not literally become the Jew in a likely doubling of roles, as audience previews the action of "the tragedy of a Jew, / Who smiles to see how full his bags are cramm'd" (*Jew of Malta* Pro. 30–1). In starting Edward II's story with Gaveston, Marlowe actually starts with audience, with a subject who gives voice and presence to the king by reading what will become the text and test of regal power – "My father is deceas'd. Come, Gaveston."

Although in these instances, the protagonists do not know that they are performing in public, it is never long before they themselves find an immediate audience for their self-productions. Tamburlaine, the master of "working words," is never without spectators, who precede and produce his appearance and who multiply excessively, almost parodically, as Tamburlaine moves and conquers from place to place to place. Edward II announces before a court full of clerics and nobles that he is ready to give up his kingdom and retreat to "some nook or corner" "to frolic with my dearest Gaveston" (*Edward II* I.iv.72–3). But that he never does so – that he, in fact, offers this solution only after recognizing that he "must speak fair" (I.iv.63) and placate the noble faction – only emphasizes how blatant his favoritism of Gaveston (and likewise Spencer) is. Barabas is a master at keeping himself and his criminal strategies hidden, to the point that he fakes a death even we cannot see through. Yet, he keeps tellingly at his side as witnesses a series of accomplices (whom he will ultimately betray), among them his daughter Abigail, his Turkish slave Ithamore, and, ironically, the Christian governor Ferneze – as if deception depends on display. Notably, too, as the play progresses, Barabas' plots, props, and spectacles get increasingly elaborate and visible. At first he simply hides and, in the sole presence of his daughter, recovers a store of gold beneath the floorboards of his house, and anonymously poisons a convent (his ex-house) full of nuns with a pot of rice, carried and envied by the ever-hungry Ithamore. At the end of the play, however, the false floor and pot are reiterated in visible excess, as Barabas constructs a public scaffold, whose floor gives way to a "deep pit past recovery" (*Jew of Malta* V.v.38) where a huge cauldron waits to catch the Turkish Calymath before the Christian governor and government. Even Faustus, who probably should be home scrutinizing his soul, takes his show on the road, proving himself a master conjurer in front of the German emperor, the duke and duchess of Vanholt, and, almost gratuitously, an unfortunate horse-courser – all this despite the fact that conjuring, like murder, sodomy, and conquest, puts these shows on the outer edge, if not way over the edge, of legitimacy.

What is particularly striking about Marlowe's protagonists, given the transgressive nature of what they do, is that they are so obviously, unabashedly "out." Even in seventeenth-century revenge tragedy, which picks up and habitually outdoes Marlowe's production of taboo, the illicit must be hidden. For when it comes to light, usually in a climactic moment of exposure, its tenure is through. In John Ford's *'Tis Pity She's a Whore* (c.1629–33), for example, Giovanni and his sister Annabella can carry out an incestuous relation only until her body, in pregnancy, gives their shocking desires away. Webster's Duchess of Malfi can freely, though discreetly, sustain a marriage and produce two children until her brother finds out who the unacceptable, because low-stationed, husband is. The action of these plays is propelled toward that brutal moment of discovery, when the intent and extent of a protagonist's incriminating deeds become publicly clear and accounted for, resulting usually in the annihilation of both deed and doer. As a consequence, we understand (and often sympathize with) the transgressively desiring subject as a figure restrained rather than sustained by a social order, which becomes, therefore, his or her (and to some degree, our) biggest foe.

In contrast, because Marlowe's protagonists make themselves the source and site of spectacle, because they insist on performing their transgressions not behind the scenes but flagrantly within them, there is no discovery, no climactic moment of exposure, no ritual undoing of the illicit deed and doer tied to a concomitant redoing of the social order. Audience emerges here not as an anathema to an otherwise self-actualizing subject, but rather as a necessary complement, a vital measure and marker of self. By and large, when their trees fall in the forest, Marlowe's protagonists want someone, if not everyone, to hear. In that, they are like Marlowe himself, who makes a provocative public spectacle of precisely those thoughts and actions that law, morality, the politics and policies of church and state would regulate, eliminate, or suppress.

This display of taboo is not, however, a sort of gratuitous hedonism we are to enjoy and indulge, uncontrollably. We do not get transgression here simply, luridly, outrageously, for transgression's sake. For importantly, while Marlowe's protagonists write themselves and write their worlds, their audiences write back, drawing crucial lines between good and bad, the decent and the damnable, prompting us to think about what makes the vital difference. Barabas may play into Christian society, marketing his vengeful theatrics, his spectacular Turk-trap, as a crucial vehicle that can free Christian Malta from the imposing control of the Turks, while he plans to bring "confusion" on the Christians anon (*Jew of Malta* V.v.90). But he is ultimately outdone by the Christian governor, who turns the treasonous trap on the Jew, pulling the floor out from Barabas to prove his own Christian control over Malta, displaying "the unhallow'd deeds of Jews" (V.v.97), and ultimately the Turk. Edward II is almost literally hoist with his own petard, as Lightborn calls for a spit, which the chronicles tell us may have been rammed up the unfortunate king's "fundament."[10] Although this spectacle does reiterate Edward's terms of power, as I suggested above, it also reminds us that the sword (or spit) is double-edged: if Edward's terms brand the play ideologically, the on-stage audience, in the figure of Lightborn, brands Edward materially. And while Faustus ravishes the world with his magic, in the end Lucifer and Mephastophilis seem to get the last word, at least Faustus' last words – "Ugly hell gape not, come not, Lucifer, / I'll burn my books, ah, Mephastophilis!" (*Faustus* V.ii.114–15) – as if Faustus sees himself now as subject to their terms, rather than they to his.

Whether *we* do or not, however, is another question. Our attempts to evaluate the protagonists, to decide whether the "form" of their "fortunes" is indeed "good or bad" (*Faustus* Prol. 8), must be filtered through the model spectators. Because Marlowe's protagonists play to them and they play back, they inhabit and mediate the contact zone between the aliens and us. We cannot take the Jew out of Malta or Malta out of the Jew, or understand Faustus apart from the onlookers who applaud, mimic, or condemn him in awe, emulation, or horror. We cannot read Marlowe's aliens apart from the world which reads them. For at the heart of Marlovian drama is an important tension between the alien subjects who would have the world at their command and the watching world which would produce (and even theatricalize) alienation on its own. At the heart of Marlovian drama, that is, there is a competition for the display, possession, and dispossession of otherness – one that makes it impossible for us to read the protagonists out of context, and evaluate the Jew as Jew, the black magician as black magician, the sodomite as sodomite, the African queen as African queen, as if the inscription of stereotype were simple, meaningful, and absolute.

To the contrary, in play after play, Marlowe puts the spectators on stage under critique for attempting to circumscribe the protagonist, and turns their efforts to condemn and denounce, to codify, prejudge, and predict, back against the speakers, exposing their discriminatory discourse as strategically constructed, unstable, and self-serving.[11] The more the on-stage audiences resist the alien, the more we resist them. Take, for example, *The Jew of Malta*, whose focal character, Barabas, comes to the stage costumed in a large nose and red beard, dripping with the stereotype engendered in the medieval mystery plays, in the inflammatory figure of Herod. At its start, the play does everything to typecast the Jew, beginning with Machevill's opening prologue, which insists that Barabas "favours" the Machiavel (*Jew of Malta* Pro. 35). Barabas himself prompts the question when he, asserting that his credit is as good as it is widespread, asks of Malta's merchants: "Tush, who amongst 'em knows not Barabas?" (I.i.68). Indeed, who among them, who among the audience, knows not the Jew? Yet before we have a chance to read Barabas through stereotype, we watch as others do – and do in a way that exposes *their* questionable cunning rather than *his*. We watch, for starters, as the Christian governor, scrambling for a way to get tribute money for the Turks, demonizes the Jew as an "infidel" "accursed in the sight of heaven," taxable because of the Christians' "sufferance of [the Jews'] hateful lives" (I.ii.65–7). If we are tempted to embrace those terms, we are cautioned by their instability – by the fact that Ferneze has already appealed to Barabas via "reason," as a "private man" who should sacrifice himself for the "common good" (I.ii.49, 102–3), before finally condemning him as one whose "excess of wealth" has led him towards the "monstrous sin" of "covetousness" (I.ii.127–8). We are cautioned as well when Ferneze, after getting the gold, authorizes Barabas to "live still" in Malta, "where thou gott'st thy wealth, / . . . and, if thou canst, get more" (I.ii.106–7) – an authorization which calls into question not only Barabas' status as an accursed "infidel" but Ferneze's status, if excess of wealth equals sin, as a model Christian.

Or consider the case of *Tamburlaine*, the first play which Marlowe brings, and the first play which brings Marlowe, to the public stage. Of all Marlowe's protagonists, Tamburlaine is the most dominating, his "working words" the most expansive, his spectacles – displays of wealth, crowns, defeated kings, colored tents, and slaughtered virgins – the most spectacular. Moreover, his history itself is explicitly about domination.[12] Yet importantly, even he must compete for stage space against a foreground of conquerors, who use images and ideas of him to define and defend their own potency. Notably in Part One, it is not Tamburlaine but those whom he will overthrow who anticipate and usher in each of his key episodes of conquest – first of Persia, then of the Turkish empire, and finally of Egypt. And in the opening scenes of Part Two, the Muslim Orcanes, the Christian Sigismund, and Bajazeth's captive son, Callapine, stake their claims against the conqueror, whom we first see (when we finally see him in scene iv) not on the battlefield but at home, surveying the strength of his sons, albeit in preparation for war. While this dramatic chronology does not necessarily annul the reality of Tamburlaine's advances (as advances), it does suggest his competitors' moves against him as offensive actions rather than simply defensive reactions, motivated by some things other than the conqueror himself.

Persia's hapless king Mycetes, for example, is the first to introduce Tamburlaine, not coincidentally at a moment when Mycetes' brother Cosroe has just openly denounced the king for turning what was once "the seat of mighty conquerors" into an "unhappy Persia," its provinces now threatened by invading "Turks and Tartars"

(*Tamb. I* I.i.6–7, 16). Under the pressure of this critique, Mycetes invokes "that Tamburlaine" as "the cause of [his] conceived grief," as a "fox in midst of harvest time" who "doth prey upon my flocks of passengers" and "pull my plumes" (I.i.29–33). As Mycetes announces a course of action – "to send my thousand horse incontinent / To apprehend that paltry Scythian" – he does so with an eye to proving his prowess as king and even asks the "honourable lords" at court, "Is it not a kingly resolution?" (I.i.52–5). The abstract pastoralism of Mycetes' representation clearly undermines the kingliness of his resolution, turning king into shepherd (the class position Tamburlaine will soon disdain) and reducing the threat of the enemy (in something of a mixed metaphor) to that of a plume-pulling fox. Yet the ill-fit of the imagery draws attention to the fact that this is a discourse in the making, one which reflects back (and here badly) on its speaker more than on its subject. In efforts to support the king, the more politically astute Meander progressively remakes the image into one of greater national import, accusing Tamburlaine, the "sturdy Scythian thief," first of robbing Persia's merchants, then of committing "incivil outrages" "daily" "with his lawless train," and finally of hoping "to reign in Asia" and "to make himself monarch of the East" "with barbarous arms" (I.i.36, 39–43). By the time Meander is through, what starts as a local nuisance becomes a global nightmare – a cause it would indeed be "kingly" to disarm. Cosroe, in turn, uses Tamburlaine to further his own resistance to the king, and his representations change significantly as *his* (not Tamburlaine's) situation changes, In under to undercut Mycetes' potency, Cosroe undercuts Tamburlaine, declaring it a "folly" for the king to expend his energies "warring with a thief" (I.i.96, 88). When Cosroe then joins in alliance with that thief, Tamburlaine becomes a "worthy" "wondrous man" (II.i.60, 32), and when Tamburlaine betrays and overthrows him, he becomes a "devilish shepherd" and a "monstrous slave" (II.vi.1, 7), and so on.

This is no local, peculiarly Persian, occupation. Part of what makes Tamburlaine such an indomitable global subject is that leaders the world over almost invite his approach by using him to propel their own conquests. Even the Turkish emperor Bajazeth, whose track record as an imperialist at first surpasses Tamburlaine's, himself invokes and categorizes the conqueror as part of a self-authorizing ploy, an attempt to justify and promote his siege of Constantinople before the African kings (of Fez, Morocco, and Argiers) whose forces he relies on. Although from what we see, at this point Tamburlaine is still preoccupied with his betrayal of Cosroe and conquest of Persia, Bajazeth persuades the "great kings of Barbary" that "one Tamburlaine," supported by "Tartars and eastern thieves," has begun to "bicker with your emperor, / And think[s] to rouse us from our dreadful siege / Of the famous Grecian Constantinople" (*Tamb. I* III.i.1–6). In response, the African leaders rally around the cause, as if there were some urgency. That urgency is immediately belied, however, as Bajazeth changes his terms and proposes to "take a truce" with the thieving, bickering foe because he "hears" that Tamburlaine "bears a valiant mind" (III.i.31–2). Of course, when Tamburlaine inevitably challenges "that Bajazeth," the Turk responds by debasing him as a presumptuous "Scythian slave" (III.iii.65, 68).

In Part One, the Soldan of Egypt may not need an approaching Tamburlaine as an excuse to censure his men as "fainted-hearted base Egyptians," who "lie slumbering on the flowery banks of Nile, / As crocodiles that unaffrighted rest / While thundering cannons rattle on their skins" (*Tamb. I* IV.i.8–11) or to take revenge as an affronted father whose daughter (Zenocrate) had been kidnapped and turned "concubine" by "the rogue of Volga" (IV.i.4–5). In Part Two, Orcanes may not need to position himself "'gainst proud Tamburlaine" (whom he readily imitates), as he decides to "parley" and make peace with Sigismund rather than to "meet him in the field" (*Tamb. II* I.i.11–12), in order to prove that "all Asia Minor, Africa and Greece / Follow my standard and my thundering drums" (I.ii.86, 81–2), without the aid of his new Christian allies, who therefore had better watch their step (and their backs). But it is notable that these competitors, like Mycetes and Bajazeth, initiate actions against Tamburlaine at the same time as they decide to assert authority over their own domains (a time which, in the Soldan's case, occurs substantially after the kidnapping he uses as a pressing imperative). And it is also notable, though by now not surprising, that their visions of Tamburlaine alter with the encounter.[13] For example, once it is clear that Tamburlaine means to "add more strength" to the Soldan's "dominions / Than ever yet confirm'd th' Egyptian crown" (*Tamb. I* V.ii.387–8), as well as to "invest" Zenocrate as "Queen of Persia" (*Tamb. I* V.ii.433), making the Soldan the fortuitous father-in-law to the "general of the world" (*Tamb. I* V.ii.390), the Soldan yields willingly to the man he has repeatedly condemned as a "sturdy felon" and "bloody," "base-bred thief" (*Tamb. I* IV.iii.11–12), the "base usurping vagabond" who, in "brav[ing] a king, or wear[ing] a princely crown" stands as "a blemish to the majesty / And high estate of mighty emperors" (*Tamb. I* IV.iii.19–22) – and yields "with thanks and protestations / Of endless honour" (*Tamb. I* V.ii.435–6).

This circumscription of Tamburlaine sets the stage for what carries across all of Marlowe's plays – a continual but discontinuous representation of the "alien" as a device to build power and save face. What does not carry, however, is any particular image, which is as transient and as circumstantial as the moment of articulation itself, and which stands next to a number of images that compete with and contradict it. In a sense, the strategies of the on-stage spectators backfire theatrically, alienating rather than orienting us. For even when the protagonists act in ways that seem to mark them as violent, dangerous, or deadly – when Tamburlaine, for example, has the virgins of Damascus or the Governor of Babylon executed and then hanged on the city's walls, or fatally stabs his own son, Calyphas, for cowardice, when Barabas poisons his daughter and orchestrates a fatal feud between her suitor and the governor's son, when Dido lures Aeneas into her embraces and takes the wind out of his divinely driven political sails, or when Edward endows his lover with political titles that both Gaveston and Kent, the king's sympathetic brother, acknowledge as exceeding Gaveston's "worth" and "birth" (*Edward II* I.i.157, 159) – we cannot condemn these figures without substantial pause.[14] For if, in Marlowe's theatrical universe, acts of discrimination always point incriminatingly back to their speaker, we can only question ourselves and wonder what is finally in it, in the articulation of otherness, for us.

If Marlowe's plays thus caution us against imposing any pat and easy judgment by exposing the fallacies of those that do, how are we to come to terms with the protagonists? If these figures are indelibly etched into a social context, as subjects of a discourse we cannot buy, why do we assign them a unique self-consciousness and self-possession? How can they have the power to write the worlds they live in, if that world is always writing back? How can their outrageous fortunes and transgressive desires define and determine form? In short, how and why do these extraordinary "heroes" prevail, and prevail as self-asserting subjects?

Significantly, Marlowe's protagonists stand out not only as the endlessly refashioned objects of their society's gaze but also as endlessly refashioning subjects, who meet that gaze, self-consciously, on their own – and not simply its own – terms. Marlowe's central figures play to audience actively rather than simply reactively, turning its passions and its cues back on itself in ways that advance and advantage their own agendas and desires. When Barabas wants to gain the loyalties of the enthusiastically criminal, unabashedly anti-Christian, and ever-greedy Turkish slave, Ithamore, he performs himself as a Christian-bating Jew who smiles to see "Christians moan" and deceives "Christian thieves," who "kill[s] sick people groaning under walls" and "poison[s] wells" (*Jew of Malta* II.iii.177, 180–2), who indulges in usury, "extorting, cozening, forfeiting" and other "tricks belonging unto brokery" (II.iii.196–7). When he wants to gain the trust (and the money) of the Christian governor whom he has overthrown and means to undo again, he offers "to procure / A dissolution of the slavish bands / Wherein the Turk hath yok'd" (V.ii.77–9) Malta and the Maltese government and, as the moment of truth arrives, even pretends not to want the "hundred thousand pounds" (V.v.21) he has demanded the Governor should pay. In the end, Ferneze out-trumps him, but not before we see Barabas thriving freely, because theatrically, within a society that repeatedly attempts to do him in (see Bartels, 1993, 96–108). Barabas' heir, Shylock, has his own claims to theatrical skill. But where Shylock turns *in* to escape castigation as a Jew, putting all his Christian spectators on the spot by asking "hath not a Jew eyes," "hands, organs, dimensions, senses, affections, passions; fed with the same food, hurt with the same weapons, subject to the same diseases . . . as a Christian is?" (*Merchant of Venice* III.i.59–61), Barabas turns *out*. He performs himself in different guises, as the Jew best suited to his changing audiences. And although we cannot then read *him* simply, solidly, reliably as "the Jew," what finally defines him for us is that, until the very end, he can read – and so evade and outsmart – *them*.

And so it is repeatedly across the Marlovian canon. Marlowe's protagonists may not always read flawlessly; Faustus proves a fatal instance there, and, in the end, Barabas obviously misses a cue. But as these figures make themselves public, putting their outrageous or unlawful actions on display, they do so by self-consciously scoping out and playing to the spectators on the other side.[15] When Cosroe allies himself with Tamburlaine, he automatically assumes (against all grounds of common sense) that the "thrice-renowmed man-at-arms" will serve, complacently, under him, as his "general lieutenant" and his "regent" (*Tamb. I* II.v.6, 8–9). In contrast, when

Tamburlaine garners his leaders to unseat the unwitting Cosroe almost immediately after, he tests their desires for kingship and power, asking and enticing Usumcasane and Theridamas: "Is it not passing brave to be a king?" (II.v.53). And when they suggest yes, he undermines those ambitions and the value of a crown by proving how easy it is – through but a "pretty jest" (II.v.90) – to gain one. Edward II throws his "will" in the nobility's face when he has a chance to contest them, but when he faces "the legate of the Pope" whom, he acknowledges, "will be obey'd" (*Edward II* I.iv.64), he backs off and "speaks fair," as one who wants not to rule but to "frolic."

What makes the representations of these protagonists different from, and to us more self-possessing than, the ones that hem them in is that they break the bounds of category and codification, defying expectation, prescription, comprehension, and apprehension. Where their audiences script the alien alternately into a place of either/or, "god, or fiend," "divine, or else infernal" (*Tamb. I* II.vi.15, 9), redeemable or damned, "good or bad," the protagonists write themselves into the more complex world of both/and. What makes Edward II and the Carthaginian Dido so intriguing is that we cannot determine whether they are using sex for power or power for sex, since they talk sex via power and power via sex. We cannot determine whether Faustus wants to evade or embrace all boundaries as he dismisses orthodox disciplines and signs away his soul, since he reaches after limitlessness by consigning himself to limit. Nor can we determine whether he really believes in the very hell, the magic, that sets him intellectually (and maybe literally) on fire, since he claims possession of his soul only at the moment that he dispossesses it and positions himself as both master and servant to Mephastophilis, whom he at once desires and denies. We cannot tell whether Tamburlaine is a man of honor or horror, beauty or barbarity, since he uses both words and swords, displays and destruction, to overthrow, descants on the "heavenly quintessence" of "beauty's worthiness" (*Tamb. I* V.ii.102, 107) while standing before a spectacle of "slaughtered carcasses" "hoisted up" on a city wall (*Tamb. I* V.ii.68), and finally marries and, after her death, glorifies the woman he has technically kidnapped, raped, and socially disgraced. And ironically, it is precisely because we cannot tell that we imagine self.

If we look to *Hamlet* as a touchstone in the early modern representation of selfhood, what is crucial and groundbreaking there is that its construction of self depends upon the unreadability of the subject. From the start, Hamlet announces that he has "that within which passes show," that cannot be accommodated by "the trappings and the suits" of court or custom (*Hamlet* I.ii.85–6). Nor does it seem to be accommodated by an available, concrete language, for each time Hamlet returns to the subject of being, his attempts to locate a self within produce an abstract, digressive discourse, one which gains a foothold only as Hamlet takes on the prescribed, but ill-fitting, role of revenger. Yet the drama is propelled by the fact that Hamlet, as much as he speaks and speaks of self, never fully expresses himself. We know the back story, the "overhasty marriage" (II.ii.57) and murder, that contribute to his "nighted color" (I.ii.68) and dis-ease. The characters on stage try, of course, to diagnose him into a readable place of madness, and although we may be tempted, therefore, to question

Hamlet's sanity too, their attempts to nail him down actually emphasize the inadequacy – and in Polonius' case the foolishness – of their prescripts, which are as blatantly self-serving as those we find in Marlowe. (Claudius needs Hamlet to be mad to cover his own murderous tracks just as Polonius needs Hamlet to be madly in love with Ophelia to advance or enhance his own centrality to the court.) But the suggestive holes within Hamlet's self-construction sustain the illusion, which Claudius' anxious surveillance enforces, that there is significantly more to Hamlet than meets the eye.

Marlowe will not go as far as Shakespeare in realizing a consciousness by marking its presence through its absence. Yet already Marlowe sets up a performative tension between the secondary characters, who attempt, from moment to moment, to confine the protoganists they watch to a single, stable, and predictable space of being, and the protoganists themselves, who move unpredictably between the spaces. If the evidence that Hamlet is uniquely self-possessed comes from that fact that he does *not* fit, and says he does not fit, any of the pre-fashioned roles his audiences would impose upon him, the evidence that Marlowe's central figures are as uniquely self-possessed comes from the fact that they *do* fit, and produce themselves as fitting, a number of pre-fashioned roles. And because they fit many, they never quite fit one, and emerge consequently as outrageously, transgressively, defiantly ever more than the sum of their society's parts. The possibility of individuation, self-assertion, and self-possession in Marlowe is, then, ironically, indelibly and profoundly social. Marlowe's protagonists take their being not, like Hamlet, from a private interior space *beneath* or *within* a staid and stated exterior, but in the public interstices *between* or *beyond* society's exteriors – a between or beyond that is itself always defined and bounded by social constructs. These self-realizing figures do not simply leave their mark by identifying subversively with the alien. They leave their mark by problematizing just what the alien can mean.

But importantly, not just the alien. For if Edward II is both a monarchical power-broker and a sodomite, and Dido, likewise, both queen and lover, if Tamburlaine is both a conquering monster and an honorable man, Faustus both a redeemable trickster and a damnable conjuror, the whole normalizing structure that would insist on the radical difference of the other falls as the other comes to resemble the normative self, state, or standard.[16] Repeatedly, Edward II, Dido, Tamburlaine, Faustus, and the Jew appear not so terribly different in their transgressions from the ostensibly nontoxic characters. Malta is teeming with greedy Machiavels, vying for economic advantage, from the Christian Ferneze to the Turkish Calymath to the Spanish king, who waits ominously in the wings to take his due. Dido is surrounded by rash and unwieldy lovers – by Iarbas, the African king who wants her or her power, and by her sister Anna, who, in turn, wants him. Almost everyone in *Tamburlaine* wants to be conqueror, from Mycetes to Cosroe to Bajazeth in Part One, to Orcanes, Sigismund, and Callapine in Part Two. *Faustus'* stage is filled with would-be conjurors, who include not only the clowns, Robin and Rafe, but also the scholars, Valdes and Cornelius, who share Faustus' renown. And while not everyone in *Edward II* qualifies as a sodomite, several (Gaveston, Mortimer Junior, maybe Isabella) use sex for power. If these surrounding characters represent the norm, that the protagonists can mimic them – or that they, despite themselves, mimic the protagonists – sets the whole system, and its inscriptions of difference, on its head. In the end, if anyone escapes, it is the alien, who understands social prescript as prescripts and discrimination as a flexible body of signs to be deployed rather than believed. And in the end, what comes from knowing the difference is self.

After Marlowe, the play of type and taboo will give way to a sort of realism where constructions are harder, and interiors easier, to find. Yet it is arguably because of Marlowe that type and taboo go underground, and self, of the kind Hamlet will claim, begins to come out. If, before Marlowe, an external articulation of otherness remains a viable strategy for self-assertion, its exposure in Marlowe demands thereafter a turning in, to "that" which lies not only *between* but *within* the gaps of social discourse. Barabas predicts and produces Shylock, Tamburlaine Othello, and even Faustus Hamlet, Marlowe's socially embedded aliens giving way almost inevitably to Shakespeare's socially alienated selves, the image of the alien to the effect of alienation.[17] And it may be in no small part because of Marlowe, because of his insistence that the delineation of the alien is crucial to the fashioning of the self, that those who follow and fill the Renaissance stage will present the self, in turn, as alien.

NOTES

1 From *The Anatomy of Abuses* (1583), quoted in McDonald (1996, 341).

2 Unless otherwise noted, all quotations from *Faustus* are from Keefer (1991). All other quotations from Marlowe are from Steane (1986).

3 On the textual problems and critical responses to those problems, see Potter (1996, 70–95). Because the text is of such questionable status, and its strategies and effects not, to my mind, characteristic or representative of Marlowe, I give the play only limited treatment here.

4 On the construction of Marlowe's biography and its reciprocal construction of culture, see Goldberg (1991, 75–82) and Riggs (1997).

5 On Marlowe's manipulation of *de casibus* tropes, see also Grande (1999, 44–72).

6 I develop this point at greater length in Bartels (1993, esp. 167–72). See also Bredbeck (1991, esp. 60–77), and Smith (1991, esp. 210–23).

7 All quotations from Shakespeare are from Evans et al. (1974).

8 All quotations from the play are from Webster (1993, 1998).

9 On the import of audience, see also Cartelli (1991).

10 See the account (and the uncertainty) in Holinshed (1807, II, 587).

11 This is one of the key arguments of Bartels (1993).

12 For a provocative discussion of one historical context here, see Wilson (1995).

13 This pattern is more evident in Part One than in Part Two, where representation seems to have reached a point, through excess, of exhaustion. See my discussion in Bartels (1993, 71–6).

14 The one exception would be the Duke of Guise, who seems to live up to the attacks against him.

15 Again, this is less true in *The Massacre at Paris*, where the emphasis falls more on the transgressive action than on the way that action enters discourse.

16 On the ways *Faustus* makes us question Christian orthodoxy, see, for example, Dollimore (1984, 109–19) and Sinfield (1997, 192–9).

17 For a treatment of the more direct and tangible influence of Marlowe on Shakespeare, see James Shapiro, *Rival Playwrights: Marlowe, Jonson, Shakespeare* (New York: Columbia University Press, 1991).

REFERENCES AND FURTHER READING

Bartels, Emily C. (1993). *Spectacles of Strangeness: Imperialism, Alienation, and Marlowe.* Philadelphia: University of Pennsylvania Press.

Bartels, Emily C. ed. (1997). *Critical Essays on Christopher Marlowe.* New York: G. K. Hall.

Bevington, David M. (1962). *From "Mankind" to Marlowe: Growth of Structure in the Popular Drama of Tudor England.* Cambridge, MA: Harvard University Press.

Blakemore Evans, G., et al. (1974). *The Riverside Shakespeare.* Boston: Houghton Mifflin.

Bredbeck, Gregory W. (1991). *Sodomy and Interpretation: Marlowe to Milton.* Ithaca: Cornell University Press.

Cartelli, Thomas (1991). *Marlowe, Shakespeare, and the Economy of Theatrical Experience.* Philadelphia: University of Pennsylvania Press.

Cheney, Patrick (1997). *Marlowe's Counterfeit Profession: Ovid, Spenser, Counter-Nationhood.* Toronto: University of Toronto Press.

Dabbs, Thomas (1991). *Reforming Marlowe: The Canonization of a Renaissance Dramatist.* Lewisburg: Bucknell University Press.

Dollimore, Jonathan (1984). *Radical Tragedy: Religion, Ideology and Power in the Drama of Shakespeare and his Contemporaries.* Chicago: University of Chicago Press.

Goldberg, Jonathan (1991). "Sodomy and society: the case of Christopher Marlowe." In *Staging the Renaissance: Reinterpretations of Elizabethan and Jacobean Drama*, eds David Scott Kastan and Peter Stallybrass. New York: Routledge.

Grande, Troni Y. (1999). *Marlovian Tragedy: The Play of Dilation.* Lewisburg: Bucknell University Press.

Grantley, Darryll and Peter Roberts, eds (1996). *Christopher Marlowe and English Renaissance Culture.* Aldershot: Scolar Press.

Greenblatt, Stephen (1980). *Renaissance Self-Fashioning: From More to Shakespeare.* Chicago: University of Chicago.

Holinshed, Raphael (1807). *Chronicles of England, Scotland and Ireland.* London: J. Johnson.

Keefer, Michael, ed. (1991). *Doctor Faustus: A 1604-version Edition.* Peterborough, ON: Broadview Press.

Kernan, Alvin, ed. (1977). *Two Renaissance Mythmakers: Christopher Marlowe and Ben Jonson.* Baltimore: Johns Hopkins University Press.

Levin, Harry (1952). *The Overreacher: A Study of Christopher Marlowe.* Cambridge, MA: Harvard University Press.

McDonald, Russ (1996). *The Bedford Companion to Shakespeare: An Introduction with Documents.* Boston: Bedford Books.

Marcus, Leah S. (1997). "Textual indeterminacy and ideological difference: the case of *Doctor Faustus*." In *Critical Essays on Christopher Marlowe*, ed. Emily C. Bartels. New York: G. K. Hall.

Maus, Katharine Eisaman (1995). *Inwardness and Theater in the English Renaissance.* Chicago: University of Chicago Press.

Nicholl, Charles (1992). *The Reckoning: The Murder of Christopher Marlowe.* Chicago: University of Chicago Press.

Potter, David (1996). "Marlowe's *Massacre at Paris* and the reputation of Henri III of France." In *Christopher Marlowe and English Renaissance Culture*, eds Darryll Grantley and Peter Roberts. Aldershot: Scolar Press.

Riggs, David (1997). "Marlowe's quarrel with God." In *Critical Essays on Christopher Marlowe*, ed. Emily C. Bartels. New York: G. K. Hall.

Shapiro, James (1991). *Rival Playwrights: Marlowe, Jonson, Shakespeare.* New York: Columbia University Press.

Shepherd, Simon (1986). *Marlowe and the Politics of Elizabethan Theatre.* New York: St. Martin's Press.

Sinfield, Alan (1997). "Reading Faustus's God." In *Critical Essays on Christopher Marlowe*, ed. Emily C. Bartels. New York: G. K. Hall.

Smith, Bruce (1991). *Homosexual Desire in Shakespeare's England: A Cultural Poetics.* Chicago: University of Chicago Press.

Steane, J. B., ed. (1986). *Christopher Marlowe: The Complete Plays.* London: Penguin.

Thurn, David H. (1989). "Sights of power in *Tamburlaine*." *English Literary Renaissance* 19, 3–21.

Webster, John (1993, 1998). *The Duchess of Malfi,* ed Elizabeth M. Brennan. London: A. & C. Black; New York: W. W. Norton.

White, Paul Whitfield, ed. (1998). *Marlowe, History, and Sexuality: New Critical Essays on Christopher Marlowe.* New York: AMS Press.

Wilson, Richard (1995). "Visible bullets: Tamburlaine the Great and Ivan the Terrible." *ELH* 62, 47–68.

Yachnin, Paul (1997). *Stage-Wrights: Shakespeare, Jonson, Middleton, and the Making of Theatrical Value.* Philadelphia: University of Pennsylvania Press.

32

Ben Jonson

W. David Kay

It is further covenanted, concluded and agreed, that how great soever the expectation be, no person here is to expect more than he knows, or better ware than a Fair will afford. . . . If there be never a servant-monster i'the Fair; who can help it? he says; nor a nest of antics? He is loth to make Nature afraid in his plays, like those that beget Tales, Tempests, and such like drolleries, to mix his head with other men's heels, let the concupiscence of jigs and dances reign as strong as it will amongst you. (*Bartholomew Fair*, Induction, 100–2, 112–18)

Jonson and the Elizabethan Popular Theater:
The Example of *Bartholomew Fair*

As his sly ridicule of the crowd-pleasing features in *The Tempest* and *The Winter's Tale* indicates, Ben Jonson's relationship to popular Elizabethan drama was conflicted and paradoxical. Although he began his dramatic career in the late 1590s as an actor in Pembroke's Men and as a collaborative playwright for Philip Henslowe's companies, he later reacted disdainfully to the commercial theaters where playwriting was a "trade." Determined to counter contemporary prejudice against the low status of dramatic authorship, he presented his plays as poetic "works" intended for judicious readers and conducted an ongoing campaign in his prefatory matter against the "ill customs" of the Elizabethan stage. Sometimes teasingly, sometimes indignantly, he condemned its improbable treatment of time and space, its love of spectacle, its romantic escapism, its bombastic rhetoric, its clownish fooleries, and its bawdy humor. His refusal to pander to the popular taste for shows, extraneous amusements, and immodest joking was partly inspired by Horace's condemnation of Roman theatrical entertainments and partly imitated from the playful self-promotion of Aristophanes and Plautus, who contrast their own comedies with the low humor and overworked type-characterization of their rivals. On a deeper level, as Jonas Barish

[handwritten marginal note: You can see this in the introduction of Every Man Out]

has noted, it was rooted in a philosophic "anti-theatricalism" that viewed acting, miming, and metamorphosis as inauthentic modes of being to be satirized rather than celebrated (1973, 27–53).

At the same time, Jonson used theatrical means to criticize false theatricality, and his creativity was continually nourished by his engagement with, and rivalry toward, the work of his fellow playwrights. Although he posed as a bold innovator or positioned his dramatic practice in opposition to Shakespeare's, he also pirated forms developed by his less-talented competitors as the basis for his own plays. Many of his comedies build on popular dramatic models, either cleverly parodying well-worn theatrical motifs or reworking them more artfully. Often he employs several of these strategies at once, developing a rich web of intertextual allusions that can be fully appreciated only if we recognize their sources in the popular dramatic repertory. And even while posing as the amusingly eccentric "Ben" who attacked public taste to win a hearing for his distinctive mode of dramatic satire, he kept in mind the particular demands of the theatrical troupes or occasions for which his comedies were first intended.

Bartholomew Fair is itself an excellent example of his inventive theatrical intertextuality and his ability to craft a play for the conditions of its performance. Written at the height of his powers in 1614 for presentation at the Hope Theater, which doubled as a bearbaiting arena, it exploited the theater's stockyard atmosphere in order to stage the annual horsefair held in Smithfield outside the Church of St. Bartholomew each August. Jonson's evocation of the fair's tawdry attractions forms the backdrop to his satire on self-righteousness and folly, though the play's gritty realism prevents us from celebrating what Mikhail Bakhtin calls "the lower bodily stratum" in a spirit of festive release. Despite his disclaimer, Jonson does include a servant-monster in his Fair, a tapster aptly named Mooncalf (see *The Tempest* II.ii.106, 135), who, like Caliban, is called an "errant incubee" or devilish offspring (II.ii.75). However, rogue comedy, not romance, is his inspiration, for Mooncalf's employer, Ursula the Pig-Woman, condemns him for being devilishly slow to learn the tricks of her trade, such as short-filling ale-mugs and adulterating tobacco.

Yet Jonson neither celebrates the trickery of the Fair's cheats nor takes a simple moralistic perspective. His theme is self-knowledge in the face of human imperfection. Reversing the pattern of disguised-ruler plays such as Shakespeare's *Measure for Measure* and Middleton's *The Phoenix*, where the play's authority-figure throws off his disguise at the last moment to punish hidden abuses, his Justice Adam Overdo attempts to uncover the "enormities" of the Fair's fraud and debauchery, only to learn that he has mistaken Edgeworth the cutpurse for an "easy and honest young man" and that his own wife has naively been recruited as a prostitute. Overdo's fellow opponent of the Fair, the Puritan Zeal-of-the-Land Busy, is similarly silenced when his accusation that the puppets are an abomination because of their cross-dressing — a common Puritan charge against the players — is answered by the revelation that they are sexless. Jonson's caricature of Puritan gluttony, hypocrisy, and over-zealousness was calculated to amuse King James, who viewed the play at court the day after its opening. However, Busy's identification of the Fair and its denizens with "the three enemies of man, the world, . . . the devil, . . . and the flesh" (III.vi.32–3) also evokes the emblematic staging of the old morality drama, as does the moment when all three "righteous" opponents of the Fair (Busy, Overdo, and the irascible Humphrey Wasp) are placed in the stocks, an ironic parallel to the persecution of the virtues by the vices in the early Tudor moralities. Jonson thus creates a complex perspective on his fictive world, satirizing it as a version of Vanity Fair on the one hand, while ridiculing those who consider themselves exempt from the frailties of "flesh and blood" on the other.

Jonson further points up his difference from popular playwrights by drawing extensively on Henry Chettle and John Day's very successful comedy *The Blind Beggar of Bednal Green*, a quasi-historical romance that also features "the merry humor of Tom Strowd," an incongruous hybrid who is part gull and part yeoman hero. Tricked out of his satin suit even before the play begins, Strowd is further robbed of his cloak, his sword, and his father's 100 pounds by a trio of cheaters, who pose first as gypsies and then as operators of a puppet show. In the play's climactic scene, however, he proves "a Norfolk Yeoman right" by joining with Lord Momford to defeat the rogues in a trial by combat, armed only with his ashen staff. This confused comedy is exactly the type of romantic hack-work Jonson scorned, but it nevertheless inspired such features of *Bartholomew Fair* as the repeated fleecing of Justice Overdo's idiotic nephew Bartholomew Cokes, the inclusion of Edgeworth, and the puppet show written by John Littlewit. In every case, Jonson gives the borrowed motifs fuller development, a more consistent satiric point, and fuller integration with his play's themes. His fairpeople stage a virtuoso demonstration of criminal tricks exceeding that in *The Blind Beggar*, including two suspenseful purse-stealing scenes (II.vi and III.v) in which Quarlous and Winwife's choric commentary directs our attention to the clever means by which Edgeworth gets Cokes' money and then passes it off deftly to the balladsinger Nightingale. Unlike the contradictory Strowd, Cokes is a thorough-going simpleton whose childish antics and spontaneous enthusiasm for every new attraction in the fair are at once appropriate to his imbecilic nature and yet symbolic of human concupiscence in general. His victimization by the cheaters and his loss of his fiancée to the gamester Quarlous help to characterize Bartholomew Fair, and by extension the world at large, as a deceptive place where the naive or foolish are exploited by the shrewd.

Jonson also uses the puppet-play motif in a richly complex way, transforming the brief, aborted performance in *The Blind Beggar* into a critique of public theater. The violent slapstick, bawdry, and scatology of Littlewit's script, acted out in Punch-and-Judy style, not only mirror the passions of the fair-goers in little, but also exemplify the corrupted theatrical taste Jonson had condemned some years before in the dedication to *Volpone*. Though his defense of the puppets against Busy's Puritanical objections now seems to endorse such crude entertainment, Cokes' enthusiastic spectatorship makes it clear that the vulgar show he delights in is a theater for idiots. Jonson's development of the latent possibilities in Chettle and Day's work tacitly affirms his superiority to popular writers he considered to be "rogues" and illustrates the creative alchemy by which he transmuted the base stuff of his competitors into artistic gold.

"Monstrous" Humors, Comical Satire, and the War of the Theaters

Jonson's realistic and critically detached view of the human scene led him to affirm repeatedly that the subject of his plays was the actual behavior of men and women. In the prologue for the revised *Every Man In his Humour*, written shortly after *Bartholomew Fair* for the 1616 Folio edition of his *Works*, he promises:

> deeds and language, such as men do use:
> And persons, such as Comedy would choose,
> When she would show an image of the times,
> And sport with human follies, not with crimes.
>
> (ll. 21–4)

Glancing once more at fantastic figures like Caliban, he teasingly concludes by hoping that the audience's laughter at "popular errors" will prove that "You, that have so graced monsters, may like men" (l. 30). Yet as Peter Womack perceptively observes, he paradoxically presents the follies of his realistic characters as equally monstrous because they subvert ideals of human rationality and dignity or violate ethical norms (1986, 47–75). Jonson's conviction that his plays should fulfill the Ciceronian definition of comedy as *"the imitation of life, the glass of custom, the image of truth*; a thing throughout pleasant, and ridiculous, and accommodated to the correction of manners" was stated as early as 1600 in *Every Man Out of his Humour* (III.vi.179–81). By "ridiculous" he means "full of ridicule" – the derisive laughter Sir Philip Sidney describes when he says that comedy represents "the common errors of our life . . . in the most ridiculous and scornefull sort that may be; so as it is impossible that any beholder can be content to be such a one" (Smith, 1904, II, 176–7).

In Jonson's early comedies, as in plays like Porter's *The Two Angry Women of Abington* and Shakespeare's *The Merry Wives of Windsor*, that derision is directed first of all at disruptive emotions like jealousy and anger. *The Case Is Altered* (performed by Pembroke's men, 1597) combines the plots of Plautus' *The Captives* and *The Pot of Gold*, achieving its happy ending through the discovery of identities, but a major source of its comic effects is excessive passion, which frequently illustrates the temperamental differences Elizabethans ascribed to the dominance of one of the four bodily fluids or "humors." So Count Ferneze is portrayed as a quick-tempered man whose natural choler is compounded by grief, his daughter Phoenixella is given to melancholy, and the sanguine or mirthful temperament of her sister Aurelia encourages lively wit-combats like those in *Love's Labour's Lost*. The merry cobbler Juniper, who misuses language exuberantly, and the miserly Jaques, whose fears of losing his daughter and his gold recall Shakespeare's Shylock, provide additional comedy. Jonson never melds this derivative mix of characters into a plot with the high level of intensity required for effective farce, but in *Every Man In his Humour* (Chamberlain's Men, 1598) he was more successful. Adapting the formula of George Chapman's *A Humorous Day's Mirth*, where Lemot, the witty minion of the French king, both stimulates the jealousies and exhibits the formulaic speech of his fellow aristocrats, *Every Man In* directs our laughter at a variety of passionate humors and at three affected pretenders. In the tradition of Terence's *The Brothers*, the anxious cares of the elder Knowell (so named in the revised Folio version) about his son's possible prodigality are manipulated by his clever servant Brainworm, while the self-induced jealousy of the merchant Kitely and the choler of Squire Downright are further provoked by Wellbred, friend to young Edward Knowell. Kitely's growing frenzy as his suspicious fantasies spiral out of control drives the action to an effective climax. As in *A Humorous Day's Mirth*, the confusion is resolved happily by a good-natured authority, the eccentric Justice Clement, and by the obligatory New Comic marriage of Edward to Wellbred's sister Bridget.

Jonson skillfully orchestrates his characters' emotions for comic effect, but his major contribution to the development of humor comedy was to transform Chapman's limited satire on linguistic affectation into a thorough-going critique of social performance. By redefining humor metaphorically as "a gentlemanlike monster, bred in the special gallantry of our time by affectation, and fed by folly" (III.ii.164–6), he made satire on current modes of self-presentation the central business of comedy. His trio of pretenders – the country gull Stephen, the poetaster Matthew, and the braggart soldier Bobadill – ape the forms of gallantry, but lack the social grace, wit, or courage to support their pretensions. Endowed with an energetic forwardness, they eagerly try to impress each other with their airs, needing only the slightest encouragement from Edward Knowell and Wellbred, who act as satiric "presenters." Jonson gives each an extensive repertory of poses, gradually highlighting their singularities of dress or mannerism while undercutting their posturing with dramatic irony. So Bobadill's tobacco-taking and his modish costume of Spanish leather boots, padded hose or "slops," silk stockings, and jeweled earring (which he is forced to pawn at one point) mask the poverty that necessitates his lodging at Cob's, just as his demonstration of Italian fencing strokes, his unusual oaths, and his nonsensical tales of military prowess are exposed as empty sham by Downright's challenge and beating. Bobadill's quick recovery from embarrassment has led some commentators to suggest that Jonson secretly favors his performance, but he is rebuked in the end by Justice Clement and excluded from the wedding feast along with Matthew, whose poetry is shown to be plagiarized. Scornful dismissal, rather than comic reintegration into society, is the general fate of Jonson's fools.

Although he chose *Every Man In* to lead off the 1616 Folio, Jonson's reputation as the age's leading "humorist" was not fully established until the production of *Every Man Out of His Humour* (Chamberlain's Men, 1599), popular enough to be published in three editions in 1600. Identified on its title-page as a "comical satire" and introduced by his Juvenalian persona Asper, who threatens to anatomize "the time's deformity . . . / With constant courage and contempt of fear" (Induction, 120–2), it stages the whole gallery of social types ridiculed by contemporary prose and verse satirists. Jonson's shift to satiric comedy has been attributed to the official ban on the works of Nashe, Marston, and others issued in June 1599, but it is a logical outcome of his own dramatic development. Though his description of *Every Man Out* as "strange, and of a particular kind by itself, somewhat like *Vetus Comoedia*" (Induction, 228–9) seems to characterize it as a dramatic experiment inspired by Aristophanes, it is merely a conventional humor comedy stripped of its New Comic frame, leaving the process of displaying, heightening, and frustrating the foolish humors as the main business of the plot. Running commentary by the "Grex" or on-stage chorus of Mitis and Cordatus, the author's surrogate, and by his two satiric presenters – Carlo Buffone, a sarcastic jester, and Macilente, an envious scholar – encourages the ironic detachment that is an essential feature of Jonsonian comedy, directing attention to the characters' false "outsides" and inviting our judgment on their absurdity. As in *Every Man In*, where the witless Stephen mimics the affected behavior of Matthew and Bobadill, Jonson establishes a social and intellectual hierarchy among his pretenders, playing off shallow aristocrats like the proud Lady Saviolina and the clothes-conscious Sir Fastidious Briske against their upwardly mobile imitators, the aspiring countryman Sogliardo and his nephew Fungoso, an Inns-of-Court reveller whose doomed efforts to match Briske's ever-changing wardrobe leave him perpetually behind the fashion. Gabrielle Bernhard Jackson has pointed out that Jonson's humor characters are so absorbed in their role-playing that they are incapable of true interaction, but their attempts at self-display bring them together in such gathering-places as the center aisle of St. Paul's Cathedral, the court at Whitehall, and the Mitre Tavern (1969, 23–34). The play's artful recreation of the rhythms of urban life and its satiric depiction of the London scene helped initiate the vogue for city comedy.

In *Cynthia's Revels, or The Fountain of Self-Love* (1600) Jonson narrowed the scope of his comical satire to courtly self-fashioning. Written for the Chapel children at Blackfriars, whose youthful precociousness invited parody of rival repertories and of their own elite audience, it caricatures the ideal of *sprezzatura* or artful nonchalance advocated by Baldassare Castiglione (see chapter 30 above), and lays bare the competitive impulses behind the vapid parlor games and courtly rituals by which Renaissance nobles affirmed their social distinction. To modern tastes *Cynthia's Revels* is too tedious an anatomy of out-dated manners, but it is not entirely without theatrical wit. Jonson's cleverest stroke is to include a Cupid like those who initiate love complications in the plays of John Lyly, only to have him find that drinking from the Fountain of Self-Love has made the courtiers impervious to his arrows. In the final masque the false courtiers, disguised as their opposing virtues, are exposed by Cynthia and sentenced to do penance under the guidance of Arete ("Virtue") and the masque poet Crites, a poor scholar suspiciously like Jonson. His self-idealization and the confident tone of the epilogue – "By [God], 'tis good, and if you lik't, you may" – provoked a response from his old associates, John Marston and Thomas Dekker. Uneasy relations between Jonson and Marston had already led the latter to insert some satire on Jonson's scornful attitudes in his *Histriomastix* (1598–9) and *Jack Drum's Entertainment* (1600), which Jonson answered in the 1600 Quarto of *Every Man Out of his Humour* by briefly parodying Marston's abstruse poetic vocabulary. Their mutual irritation now broke out in an exchange of dramatic satire often called "The War of the Theaters" because it drew in both private theater companies and the Chamberlain's Men, with whom Jonson had disagreements over the staging of *Every Man Out*.

Originating as a response to Jonson's particular modes of literary rivalry, this "Poetomachia" or "Battle of the Poets," as it was first known, was conducted partly by literary parody and partly by adding personal allusions to standard type-characters. In *What You Will* (1601) Marston cleverly reverses the pattern of *Cynthia's Revels* by showing his scholar–poet Lampatho Doria to be unfit for the court, where he woos awkwardly and his moralistic comedy *Temperance* is rejected by the pleasure-loving duke. Jonson responded with *Poetaster, or The Arraignment*, written for the Chapel children in fifteen weeks to forestall a second attack by Dekker. Set in Augustan Rome, it is a dramatic apology for poetry contrasting the self-indulgent eroticism of Ovid with the high public art of Vergil. Defending his own satiric practice through the language of his chief model Horace, Jonson depicts Marston as the Roman poetaster Crispinus (here identified with the bore of Horace's *Satires* I.9) and Dekker as the desperate Demetrius, "a dresser of plays about the town." Urged to accuse Horace of treason by the swaggering Captain Tucca, modeled on the character of Tubrio from Marston's own verse satires, Crispinus is himself condemned to take an emetic which makes him vomit up obscure Latinate terms ("oblatrant," "furibund," "fatuate,") used by Marston and earlier "inkhorn" writers. Tucca's untrustworthy behavior in voting against Crispinus is punished by his being forced to don a pair of masks like the "vizarded-bifronted-Janian-rout" of two-faced hypocrites targeted in Marston's Satire I, thereby cleverly turning Marston's satire back upon himself. In Dekker's *Satiromastix, or The Untrussing of the Humorous Poet*, presented by both the Paul's Boys and the Chamberlain's Men, Tucca and Crispinus are given their revenge in an amusing parody of Jonson's own style, exposing Horace's boasting, his backbiting of his patrons, and his obsequiousness when challenged. However, whereas Jonson's caricatures wittily conflate traits of Marston and Dekker with characters from Horace's own satires, Dekker's "self-creating Horace" is a thinly disguised personal portrait, undercutting Jonson's proud pose as a priest of Apollo with nasty taunts at his pock-marked face, his experience as an itinerant actor, his bricklaying, his arrest for killing the actor Gabriel Spencer in 1598, and his slowness of composition. Dekker's vigorous attack reminded Jonson of his beginnings in the commercial theater and questioned his ability to compete there on even terms.

Roman Tragedy: *Sejanus* and *Catiline*

In the "Apologetical Dialogue" written to defend *Poetaster* Jonson announced that he would turn his energies to tragedy "since the Comic Muse / Hath proved so ominous to me" (ll. 220–1). This was not a new enterprise. Francis Meres had listed him among "our best for Tragedy" in 1598, and Henslowe's account books record advances in 1598–9 and 1602 for collaborations with Dekker, Chettle, and others on English historical and domestic tragedies. His two surviving tragedies are Roman plays – *Sejanus His Fall* (1603–4) and *Catiline His Conspiracy* (1611), both produced by the King's Men. Neither play was successful with the theatrical public, for Jonson's austere neoclassic formula for tragedy emphasized "truth of argument, dignity of persons, gravity and height of elocution, fullness and frequency of sentence [that is, sententious maxims]" while keeping the violence of revenge tragedy off-stage. However, *Sejanus* and *Catiline* were held in high regard by many readers in the seventeenth century for bringing Roman history to life in ways that paralleled the times.

Sejanus His Fall is a Senecan tragedy that demonstrates the instability of Fortune when its villain–hero is torn to pieces by the Roman mob. Although the play incorporates an impressive range of Roman sources, it is based primarily on the *Annals* of Tacitus, a clear-sighted analysis of monarchic power that was read variously by Jonson's contemporaries as a handbook of political intrigue or as a guide to prudent conduct under a tyrant. Jonson's Tiberius is a cunning Machiavel who retreats from Rome to enjoy his private lusts while employing the ambitious Sejanus to eliminate his enemies, the followers and children of the dead prince Germanicus. Sejanus too is deviously "politic," poisoning Tiberius' son Drusus and aspiring to marry his widow Livia, a fatal misstep that alerts Tiberius to his imperial ambitions. Blinded by his overconfidence and by Tiberius' seeming inattentiveness, Sejanus is trapped by Tiberius' tool Macro into attending a Senate meeting where his fall from favor is gradually made clear in a circuitous letter from the emperor. Jonson's ending lacks theatrical power, but the play presents a chilling image of a tyrannical state in which the systematic repression of liberty is made possible by a servile Senate. The prosecution and defiant suicide of Silius, unjustly accused of treason by Sejanus' henchmen, and the arrest of Sabinus by spies hidden in his bedroom ceiling dramatize the precarious position of the opposition. Restrained by the orthodox monarchist belief that "No ill should force the subject undertake / Against the sovereign" (IV.163–4), the Germanicans, like the Jacobeans, can do little but lament the loss of republican virtues. Although the indignant asides of Arruntius point up their inaction, Lepidus' successful recipe for survival – to "live at home, / With my own thoughts, and innocence about me" (IV.296–7) – seems to endorse an ideal of passive virtue.

Jonson's depiction of a nightmarish world of surveillance, censorship, and politically motivated trials was not fanciful. Silius' spirited defense against unproven charges echoes the treason trial of Sir Walter Ralegh, found guilty on circumstantial evidence in 1603 of plotting with his old enemy Spain, and the suppression of John Hayward's life of King Henry IV in 1599 offers a direct parallel to the burning of the historian Cremutius Cordus' books in Act III. The play's application to the times was brought home directly when the earl of Northampton, who had joined with Sir Robert Cecil to bring down Ralegh and Lord Cobham, accused Jonson to the Privy Council of treason because of it.

Jonson's use of Roman history in *Catiline His Conspiracy* also points up similarities between the classical past and Jacobean England. The Chorus to Act I, lamenting Rome's decay, sounds the themes of his own satire on Jacobean excess and corruption, while the play's subject – Catiline's plan to burn the city and seize power in a violent coup – is an inescapable analogy to the Gunpowder Plot of 1605. Although his treatment resists being read as a direct allegory, Jonson heightened the topical parallels by describing the date of Catiline's coup, actually October 28, as "the fifth (the kalends of November)," by emphasizing the conspirator's use of sulfur, and by having Cicero reassure the wavering Curius that "no religion binds men to be traitors" (III.369). Catiline's status as an anti-social monster is signaled immediately by the ghost of Sylla, whose introduction of him as his heir in cruelty recalls the beginning of Seneca's *Thyestes*, but his downfall is counterpointed by the heroic action of Cicero, a "new man" who illustrates Jonson's humanist creed that virtue is the source of true nobility. Jonson's concern for "truth of argument" is once again shown by his synthesis of historical sources – Sallust's *The War with Catiline*, Plutarch's *Lives*, and Cicero's orations, one of which is translated entire in act IV, to the detriment of the theatrical action. However, under the influence of *The Conspiracy of Catiline* by Constantius Felicius Durantinus, he modifies Plutarch's view that Cicero was cowardly, stressing the false slander Cicero must endure and his skill in winning over Curius, and he implicates Caesar and Crassus in the conspiracy. Their critical asides have led some commentators to argue that Jonson views Cicero negatively, but their speeches are regularly countered by Cato or the Chorus, and Cicero is celebrated throughout as a "careful" and virtuous magistrate forced by circumstances to use espionage to counter the hidden evil of Catiline's threat. Although Jonson's indictment of Roman decadence invites application to Jacobean England, his view of the arts of rule is much more positive here than in *Sejanus*.

Trickster Comedy: *Volpone* and *The Alchemist*

Jonson had taken up comic writing again in the summer of 1605 by working with Chapman and Marston, with whom he was now reconciled, on *Eastward Ho*, a subtle parody of prodigal-son plays. The three authors skewer citizen and courtier alike, contrasting the officious moralism of Touchstone the goldsmith and his son-in-law Golding with the riotous behavior of the bankrupt knight Sir Petronel Flash and the delinquent apprentice Francis Quicksilver, whose surprising fifth-act repentence produces a mock happy ending in which all are reconciled. Satire on King James' Scots courtiers, however, led to Chapman's and Jonson's imprisonment and to the threat that they would have their noses and ears cut. Jonson's next comedy, his famous *Volpone, or The Fox* (King's Men, 1606), is set safely in distant Venice, noted for its opulence, its sensuality, and its rigorous justice. As in *Catiline*, both *Volpone* and its later counterpart *The Alchemist* (King's Men, 1609) satirize a modern "Age of Gold" by showing how greed corrupts a variety of "estates" or representative social types, and as in *Sejanus*, both feature a group of intriguers who manipulate victims for their profit but contend among themselves as well. Jonson's construction of his plots according to the neoclassical scheme of *protasis* (exposition), *epitasis* (complication), *catastasis* (counterturn), and *catastrophe* (conclusion) builds the action effectively toward a dramatic fourth-act crisis, only to raise dramatic tension again with a new complication that brings down the cheaters in the end.

The Alchemist and *Volpone* also illustrate Jonson's drive to produce the quintessential treatment of each motif he reworks, combining classical and modern materials into a rich new compound that surpasses his individual models. In *Volpone* he combines satire on legacy-hunting from Petronius' *Satyricon*, Lucian's *Dialogues of the Dead*, and Horace to produce a multi-layered structure of ironies. Volpone's impersonation of a dying man to extract gifts from his suitors is based on Petronius, whose description of legacy-hunters and their victims as "carcasses to be torn to pieces, and crows to tear them" (Loeb ed., 289) may have suggested the names Voltore, Corbaccio, and Corvino (vulture, raven, crow) for Volpone's suitors. Volpone's own identity is inspired by bestiary accounts of foxes playing dead to attract scavengers and by Caxton's *The History of Reynard the Fox*, where Reynard rapes the Wolf's wife as Volpone tries to rape Celia. As in *Sejanus* and *Catiline*, where the vicious nature of the villain–heroes justifies their title of "monster," Jonson's beast fable signals the depravity of the hypocritical suitors, eager to hasten Volpone's death, just as the freakishness of Volpone's servants – fool, dwarf, and hermaphrodite – symbolizes his perverted sensuality and wit. His blasphemous claim that gold is "the best of things . . . far transcending / All style of joy, in children, parents, friends" (I.i.16–17) is proven true in the play's world by the willingness of Voltore to commit perjury, the jealous Corvino to prostitute his wife, and Corbaccio to disinherit his son in order to obtain Volpone's treasure. These corrupt Venetians are contrasted with two comic English visitors, the parrot-like chatterers Lady Politic Would-Be, whose relentless discourse torments the supposedly bedridden magnifico, and her husband Sir Pol, eager to appear a knowledgeable insider about European politics. In act V Sir Pol's efforts to hide by crawling about under a tortoise-shell when tricked by the sharp-witted Peregrine form a humorous parallel to Voltore's feigned possession by spirits before the Venetian court.

Voltore's sham is given thematic weight by the First Avocatori's stern comments on the gold-fever that possesses the characters (V.xii.101–2), yet despite the moral seriousness of the main action, Volpone's suitors appear ridiculous because they are gulled out of their own wealth while trying to obtain his. The senile Corbaccio's foolish certainty that he will outlive Volpone, Voltore's excitement at being told he is sole heir, and Corvino's mistaken belief that Volpone cannot hear the insults he shouts in his ear are delicious ironies shared among Volpone, his parasite Mosca, and the audience, positioned to observe the suitors' false hopes as well as the skillful acting of the tricksters. It is important, however, to remember Robert C. Jones's caution that "we can share a knave's enjoyment of his own sport at a foolish victim's expense without likening ourselves to him" (1986, 6). Although Volpone wins admiration for "the cunning purchase" of his wealth, Jonson encourages our detachment from him in a variety of ways. His extravagant, narcissistic rhetoric in the seduction scene, which focuses on the fantasied roles Celia will play for him, is based ironically on classical accounts of Roman excess, and his attempted rape and subsequent prosecution of Celia and Bonario to cover his misdeeds prevent our continuing identification with him.

Moreover, Jonson adds a new level of irony to legacy-hunting satire by making Volpone a victim of his own overconfidence and of Mosca's deception, foreshadowed immediately when Mosca flatters money out of him in the opening scene. Volpone's decision to announce his own death and to declare Mosca his heir, which allows Mosca to spring his "Fox-trap," compensates for Mosca's needling about his anxiety during the courtroom proceedings in act IV, and he compounds his error when, disguised as a court officer, his jeers at the suitors' frustration lead them to reconvene the tribunal in act V. Jonson builds suspense here by depending on the audience's awareness of two possible disguise-play models – Chapman's *The Blind Beggar of Alexandria*, where Cleanthes seduces several women in his multiple disguises and escapes scot-free by killing off his alter egos, and Middleton's *Michaelmas Term* (1605), where the crafty usurer Quomodo traps himself by disguising himself and announcing his own death to see how his family will respond. When Mosca tries to gain the advantage by insisting that his master is dead, Volpone – like Quomodo – can salvage his dignity and gain credit for his performance only by revealing his identity and admitting his crimes. Although his undoing satisfies the Elizabethan taste for seeing the cheater cheated, the harsh sentences meted out by the court darken the comic tone. Volpone's appeal in the epilogue for the audience to distinguish between the legal punishment he deserves as a character and the delight he has given them as an actor does not fully right the balance, but the play's rich ironies have kept it on stage continually for four centuries.

In *The Alchemist*, Jonson returned to a London setting and refined the formula used in *Volpone*, blending together a broad range of alchemical satire and rogue literature to create a more complex fraud, a less stable group of rogues, and a more genial resolution. Once again he improved on a lesser-known dramatic model, taking his cue for his pairing of the roguish "Captain" Face and the fraudulent "Doctor" Subtle from the anonymous comedy *The Puritan, or The Widow of Watling Street* (pub. 1607), which featured two cheaters of the same type, satire on Puritan hypocrisy, and a marriage scheme involving a widow. As in Heywood's *The Wise Woman of Hogsden* (1604), whose title-character conducts many different kinds of scams, Jonson's Subtle pretends to be an alchemist only to Sir Epicure Mammon and the Puritans Tribulation Wholesome and Ananias. To the law clerk Dapper, he is a conjurer dealing in necromantic spirits; to the apothecary Abel Drugger, a palm reader, astrologer, and cunning-man; and to the wealthy Kastril and his widowed sister Dame Pliant, an instructor in quarreling and a marriage broker. The cheating of Dapper, stripped of his valuables in anticipation of seeing the Queen of Fairy and then left to languish in the privy with a gingerbread gag in his mouth, is based loosely on an actual fraud involving one Thomas Rogers and on the tricks of the cunning-woman Judith Philips. The scene in which

Mammon's hopes of riches are literally exploded by "a great crack and noise within" after he is caught by Subtle with Dol Common is based on a hint in Erasmus' colloquy "Alchemy," brilliantly elaborated so that Mammon thinks his own sin has lost him the philosopher's stone.

Jonson found the terminology of alchemy absurd, and he was particularly amused by the pretensions of Paracelsus' claims for the "Spagyric" art. By opposing Surly, who considers alchemy a fraud, with Mammon, the true believer, and by having Subtle catechize Face about "the vexations, and martyrizations / Of metals" (II.v.20–1) to intimidate Ananias, he ridicules Paracelsus' presentation of alchemy as a quasi-religious system of belief. His primary targets, however, are the greed, lust, and credulity of the gulls, which the tricksters transmute into profit by heightening their desires. Face's role is to con the gulls into seeking (and paying) more, as, for example, when he translates Drugger's initial request for help with intestinal worms into one for a mystic shop plan and sign, and then into hopes of marriage to the rich Dame Pliant. Mammon, on the other hand, needs little encouragement. His soaring fantasies of the sensual delights he will enjoy with the philosopher's stone are expressed, like Volpone's, in rhetoric so excessive it becomes grotesque, but rhetoric made even more comic because, unlike Volpone's, his wealth is merely illusory. Jonson's satire on Ananias and Tribulation Wholesome repeats but far exceeds the ridicule of hypocritical casuistry in *The Puritan*, distinguishing between Tribulation's conscious manipulation of his flock for profit and Ananias' knee-jerk outbursts against anything that smacks of Catholicism. His zeal adds a manic energy to the comedy that is best seen when he is recruited to drive Surly out of the alchemist's shop because of Surly's Spanish costume.

Jonson invests his three tricksters with impressive abilities, but he also depicts their collaboration as transitory and limited. Subtle the "sovereign," Face the "general," and Dol the body-politic form an anti-social state that preys on and is "entrenched" against the conventional world (see III.iii.33–8), yet this "venter tripartite" is unstable and dependent on conditions beyond their control. The scatological insults and animal epithets of Face and Subtle's opening quarrel establish their base nature, and their struggle for supremacy evolves by stages from a contest to see "who shall shark best," to rivalry for possession of Dame Pliant, to a scramble for the profits. As sharkers, they are virtuoso performers capable of playing multiple parts, each with its own vocabulary, mannerisms, or costume. Thus Subtle shifts from a fearful, reluctant conjurer with Dapper to a pious "father" with Mammon; Face alternates between acting as the laboratory drudge Eulenspiegel and as a captain or pimp; and Dol switches from Queen of Fairies to an aristocratic madwoman, spouting apocalyptic commentary on the book of Daniel. At the same time, we are repeatedly reminded that they are operating on borrowed time in the house of Lovewit, Face's master, and their difficulty in keeping the eager gulls in line while they shift roles puts them on an accelerating treadmill that speeds out of control. Their temporary success in defeating Surly's threat of exposure in act IV is reversed by the return of their angry victims in act V and by the appearance of Lovewit, who forms a new alliance with Face, now reduced to his old role as Jeremy the butler but in much greater favor for winning his master a chest of treasure and a wealthy young wife. Like Quarlous in *Bartholomew Fair*, Lovewit is presented not as an ideal figure but as a self-interested man of the world. His willingness to strain his "candor" to acquire the tricksters' ill-gotten gains assures a modicum of poetic justice without the rigorous moralizing of *Volpone*.

Marriage and Misogyny: *Epicoene* and *The Devil Is an Ass*

Jonson's ability to orchestrate an elaborate trickster plot into a sequence of big scenes marked by a growing crescendo of noise and action is demonstrated in a new key in *Epicoene, or The Silent Woman* (Queen's Revels, late 1609). Written to the capacities of a children's troupe, which allowed a greater number of women's parts, it reworks motifs from other recent private theater plays about gender roles and the contest for power in marriage. Jonson's division of his cast into a female-dominated couple (the Otters), a male-dominated couple (Morose and Epicoene), aggressive society women (the Ladies Collegiates), emasculated gallants (Sir Amorous La Foole, Sir Jack Daw), and witty intriguers (Truewit, Clerimont, and Dauphine) parallels that of *Every Woman In Her Humour* (pub. 1609), a spin-off of Jonson's own humor comedy that also satirizes gender inversion, effeminate manners, women's extravagance, and face-painting. Although based mainly on Libanius' declamation about a man who could endure no noise yet married a talkative wife, Jonson's Morose may also have been inspired by the title-character of Beaumont and Fletcher's *The Woman Hater* (1606) and by that of Chapman's *Monsieur D'Olive* (1604), who complains, "What a hell 'tis . . . to have a man's house pestered with a whole country of guests, grooms, panders, waiting-maids, etc! I careful to please my wife, she careless to displease me . . . all she does must be law, all she says gospel!" (I.i.347–54). Dauphine's plot to trick Morose, who has threatened to disinherit him, into marriage with the silent Epicoene, and then, when she discovers her voice and turns shrewish, offer Morose a divorce on Dauphine's terms, translates these hints into splendid comedy as wave after wave of talkative guests and musicians pours into Morose's house in act III and Epicoene takes command. Tom Otter's drinking match and his fight with Mistress Otter in act IV, punctuated by drum rolls and fanfares, and the contentious argumentation of the divorce proceedings in act V sustain the noisy energy of this "comedy of affliction." Surprisingly, although the play's language of monstrosity characterizes the Otters and Madam Centaur as freakish hybrids who deviate from norms of male dominance and female submissiveness, Morose's tyrannical household management makes him seem no less a "portent" or "prodigy" capable of turning hearers to stone than "that Gorgon, that Medusa," Mrs. Otter, and he is criticized by Truewit because he would be friends with his wife "upon unconscionable terms, her silence" (IV.iv.38–9).

The geographical and social world of *Epicoene*, in which gallants enjoy "high fare, soft lodging, fine clothes" and ladies shop at the China houses or the New Exchange in the Strand, mirrors that of the Whitefriars Theater audience, and Jonson chooses satiric presenters who move easily in this court-oriented society. Although he criticizes them individually for their indolence, egotism, and heartlessness, respectively, Clerimont, Truewit, and Dauphine serve as a collective model of urbane wit and manly aggressiveness that contrasts with the idle chatter and cowardice of La Foole and Daw, who allow themselves to be blindfolded and physically abused to avoid dueling with each other. La Foole's boasting about the feasts he gives and the gold jerkin he wore when knighted (I.iv.39–52) continues the satire on conspicuous consumption begun in *Every Man Out*, but Jonson now shifts the emphasis to women's behavior, updating anti-feminist satire from Juvenal, Ovid, Martial, and Plautus to comment on the use of cosmetics and the growing market for luxury goods in Jacobean London. Truewit's reworking of Juvenal's Satire VI on women's vices in II.ii is purposefully exaggerated to discourage Morose from marriage, but his warnings against women's lust and extravagance are confirmed by the Ladies Collegiates' pursuit of Dauphine and their advice that Epicoene demand coaches, gowns, and servants.

Jonson sets a new standard for ironic wit in Truewit's adaptations from Ovid's *Art of Love*, substituting a subtler mode of mock encomium for the broad paradoxes found in other private-theater plays like Chapman's *All Fools*, where unchaste wives and cuckoldry are praised ingeniously. Truewit's remarks about cosmetic artifice in I.i ridicule face-painting while seeming to defend it, and his ironic advance to Dauphine and Clerimont on male courtship in IV.i, where he advocates practices Jonson usually satirizes, are frequently mistaken as straightforward advocacy. Similarly, Dauphine's pretended love for the Collegiates (see IV.i.118) has the effect of exposing their superficial judgment, while his creation of Epicoene, which reveals how gender is socially constructed and performed, belies his feigned ignorance about women's practices. Epicoene's unmasking at the end proves Dauphine to be the master wit, embarrasses the Ladies Collegiates for revealing their secrets to a male, and deflates the sexual boasting of Daw and La Foole, who claim to have slept with her. As in *Volpone*, the exclusion of any romantic interest and the substitution of divorce for the customary comic marriage confirm the play's status as dramatic satire.

Epicoene was much admired by Dryden and other Restoration comic writers, but its paradoxical wit seems to have puzzled its original audience. *The Devil Is an Ass* (King's Men, 1616) revisits many of the same topics from a different angle. Jonson's central conceit, communicated through his parody of the Tudor morality play Vice in the first scene, is that in Jacobean England vice and virtue can no longer be distinguished because modern vice is too subtle. Borrowing the main plot-motif of William Haughton's *Grim the Collier of Croyden, or The Devil and His Dame* (1600), where the fiend Belphagor is cuckolded by his earthly wife, Jonson depicts an old-fashioned devil, Pug, who finds himself outwitted at every turn by modern Londoners. Assigned by Satan to the household of the jealous Fabian Fitzdotterel, Pug first tries unsuccessfully to seduce his mistress, then spitefully prevents her affair with the clever young Wittipol. Tricked out of a diamond ring by the cozening Merecraft and his man Trains, Pug is imprisoned for theft and finally carried back to Hell by the vice

Iniquity in an explosive exit, proving that "now, the evil out-carries the Devil" (V.vi.77). Jonson's witty inversion of morality conventions thus makes a moral point while rejecting the cruder representations of devilry in popular works like *The Merry Devil of Edmonton*.

Despite its clever thesis, however, the play offers a narrower spectrum of fools than Jonson's other middle comedies. Called a truer "prodigy" than all the monsters of Africa and America (I.v.7–9), Fitzdotterel is the most complex, displaying his foolishness by his willingness to let Wittipol court his handsomely dressed wife before his face in exchange for a rich cloak, his delusion that Merecraft's project for draining the fens will make him "Duke of the Drowned-lands," and his passionate attraction to the Spanish lady, played in broadly comic fashion by the very tall Wittipol in disguise. His female counterparts, Lady Eitherside and her friend Lady Tailbush, whose hopes of a cosmetics monopoly provoke dreams of coaches and attendants, form a fellowship like that of the Ladies Collegiates. Their discussion with the Spanish lady about the sexual freedoms of courtly women and their interrogation of Pug about a gentleman usher's duties make him exclaim, "There is no hell / To a lady of fashion" (V.ii.14–15). Both Fitzdotterel and Lady Tailbush are milked for cash by Merecraft, whose expansive plans for monopolistic projects ranging from the sensible (licensing the production of forks) to the absurd (making wine from raisins) ridicule the financial schemes floated to enrich courtiers and the royal treasury at the expense of the Jacobean public. Sir Paul Eitherside's belief in Fitzdotterel's feigned spirit possession in act V, abetted by Merecraft, satirizes credulous or incompetent justices and frauds like those exposed by King James early in 1616.

Of particular interest is Jonson's treatment of Wittipol and Frances Fitzdotterel, which breaks new ground by staging an adulterous attraction that is mutual, yet resisted. Like Celia in *Volpone*, Mrs. Fitzdotterel is the victim of a husband at once jealous and yet willing to encourage behavior she considers immodest, but her character is developed more fully than most of Jonson's women. Embarrassed by her husband's folly and fetishism, she is attracted by Wittipol's courtship in I.vi, where his speech on her behalf when she is forbidden to speak indicates sympathy for her shame, and in II.vi she permits his sexual attentions, scripted by the erotic language of Jonson's "A Celebration of Charis," until her husband interrupts. However, her moving plea in IV.vi for assistance in assuring her financial security, seconded by the intervention of Manly, diverts Wittipol from seduction to friendship, thereby establishing a pattern for later sentimental comedy. Although Jonson's ending denies us a sense of romantic closure, recent professional productions have proven that the play is good theater.

The Late Plays

A ten-year gap separates *The Devil Is an Ass* from Jonson's next play, *The Staple of News* (King's Men, early 1626), the last of his works to attempt a massive synthesis of classical and English materials. With its system of emissaries or reporters, Master Cymbal's staple, or commercial office, represents both the syndicate of London print-ers authorized to publish news-sheets about the Thirty Years War and the network of professional letter-writers corresponding about domestic affairs. Jonson ridicules the news-sheets' confusion of rumor and fact and the popular appetite for sensational lies, but despite the topicality of his references, his insight into the commodification of the news media has led to renewed interest in the play. The Gossips who comment between the acts and the covey of Jeerers who trade insults and provoke discussion of various professional jargons, even though they do not comically illustrate them, provide additional satire on abuses of language. The framing action, inspired by Lucian's *Timon*, Aristophanes' *Plutus*, and moralities like *The Contention between Liber-ality and Prodigality*, is an allegory in which the three Peniboys, representing the Aris-totelian mean of liberality and its two extremes, contend for control of Clara Aurelia Pecunia (money), but the treatment of prodigality and miserliness is much darker here than in Jonson's early works. In contrast to the extravagant Asotus in *Cynthia's Revels*, the prodigal Peniboy Junior does not simply spend his mistress Pecunia into a swoon, but blazons her attractions to the Jeerers, whom he invites to court and kiss her. The nastiness of Peniboy Senior's thrift, more repulsive than Jaques' comic anxiety in *The Case Is Altered*, is heightened by the scatology and beast imagery of his con-frontations with the Jeerers and by the mad trial of his dogs, modelled on that in Aristophanes' *The Wasps*. Unfortunately, however, Jonson is unable to draw his various materials into a coherent whole, and the play never achieves the dramatic or satiric power of his great middle comedies.

Jonson's three Caroline plays – *The New Inn, or The Light Heart* (King's Men, 1629), *The Magnetic Lady, or Humors Reconciled* (King's Men, 1632), and *A Tale of a Tub* (Queen's Men, 1633) – and the unfinished pastoral *The Sad Shepherd* show the aging dramatist striking out in new directions and reworking earlier motifs in new ways. The tender, playful relationship between Robin Hood and the spirited Maid Marian and the sentimental laments of Aeglamour in *The Sad Shepherd* portray romantic love in a manner never attempted in Jonson's satiric comedies, while his evocation of the woodland landscape and his knowledgeable use of witch and fairy lore show his ability to handle Shakespearean materials he otherwise avoided except in his masques. *The New Inn* also offers belated homage to Shakespeare in its romance plot, which reunites Lord Frampul, living disguised as the Host of the Light Heart, his wife, and daugh-ters after years of separation, though Lady Frampul's change from a comical Irish nurse merely by removing her eye-patch and altering her accent has left critics debating whether Jonson is parodying the form or playing it straight. However, acting is here uniquely viewed in Jonson's comedy as a mode of discovery, not as falsification, for Lovel's speeches on Platonic love and true valor in the mock Court of Love lead Lady Frances Frampul to realize her affection for him, and the chambermaid Pru's perfor-mance as the court's sovereign moves Lord Latimer to make her a lady indeed. The disclosure in act V that Lord Beaufort, thought in act IV to have married the Host's son Frank in disguise, has actually married the real Laetitia Frampul, gives the ending of *Epicoene* one further turn of the screw. Once again Jonson tries to improve on rival treatments, adopting the inn motif from Fletcher's *Love's Pilgrimage* and the Court of Love from Massinger's *The Parliament of Love* (1624), but *The New Inn* was hissed off the stage at its first performance, and it has only recently been given a professional revival by the RSC.

The Magnetic Lady and *The Tale of a Tub* return to the plotting of intrigue at which Jonson was so skilled. *A Tale of a Tub*, an amusingly condescending view of village life in rural Finsbury-hundred during the late 1550s, shows signs of being an early work that was thoroughly revised in the 1630s to incorporate satire on Inigo Jones, Jonson's uneasy collaborator on the Stuart masques. Full of the punning name-jokes characteristic of his earliest and latest plays, it finds comedy in the differences in status among members of the rural hierarchy as they compete for possession of Audrey Turfe, daughter of the local constable, in a plot whose multiple disguisings and sudden reversals recall those of Anthony Munday. *The Magnetic Lady*, by contrast, is an urban comedy in which the valiant Captain Ironside and the shrewd Master Compass navigate through various straits and passages to the wealth of Lady Loadstone and her niece the true Pleasance, switched at birth with her nurse's daughter, Placentia. As in *The Alchemist*, the women in these plays are agreeably "pliant" – content to accept the winner in the competition of wit for wealth that gives edge to the satire. Jonson self-consciously presents *The Magnetic Lady* as "the shutting up" of his artistic circle, begun in his two *Every Man* plays, but he is much less interested here in the folly of humorous affectation or irrational passion than in the fact that each man has his price. The "humors" of the money-man Sir Moth Interest and the court politician Bias are reconciled by Interest's purchase of Bias's influence with his lord, just as Compass is able to persuade the lawyer Practice to relinquish his claims to Pleasance in exchange for a reversion to court office. The contrast between the whimsical judgments of Justice Clement and these tough negotiations, set against a background of court corruption, are an index of how much Jonson accommodated his satiric comedy to the changing spirit of the times.

REFERENCES AND FURTHER READING

Barish, Jonas A. (1960). *Ben Jonson and the Language of Prose Comedy*. Cambridge, MA: Harvard University Press.

Barish, Jonas A. (1973). "Jonson and the loathed stage." In *A Celebration of Ben Jonson*, eds William Blissett, Julian Patrick, and R. W. Van Fossen. Toronto: University of Toronto Press.

Barton, Anne (1984). *Ben Jonson, Dramatist*. Cambridge: Cambridge University Press.

Boehrer, Bruce Thomas (1997). *The Fury of Men's Gullets: Ben Jonson and the Digestive Canal*. Philadelphia: University of Pennsylvania Press.

Brady, Jennifer, and W. H. Herendeen, eds (1991). *Ben Jonson's 1616 Folio*. Newark: University of Delaware Press.

Burt, Richard (1993). *Licensed by Authority: Ben Jonson and the Discourses of Censorship*. Ithaca: Cornell University Press.

Butler, Martin (1992). "Late Jonson." In *The Politics of Tragicomedy: Shakespeare and After*, eds Gordon McMullan and Jonathan Hope. London: Routledge.

Butler, Martin, ed. (1999). *Representing Ben Jonson: Text, History, Performance*. Basingstoke: Macmillan.

Chapman, George (1961). *The Plays of George Chapman: The Comedies*, ed. Thomas Marc Parrott. 2 vols. Rpr. New York: Russell & Russell.

Dessen, Alan C. (1971). *Jonson's Moral Comedy*. Evanston: Northwestern University Press.

Donaldson, Ian (1970). *The World Upside Down: English Comedy from Jonson to Fielding*. Oxford: Oxford University Press.

Donaldson, Ian (1997). *Jonson's Magic Houses: Essays in Interpretation*. Oxford: Clarendon Press.

Duncan, Douglas (1979). *Ben Jonson and the Lucianic Tradition*. Cambridge: Cambridge University Press.

Dutton, Richard (1983). *Ben Jonson: To the First Folio*. Cambridge: Cambridge University Press.

Dutton, Richard (1996). *Ben Jonson: Authority: Criticism*. Basingstoke: Macmillan.

Evans, Robert C. (1994). *Jonson and the Contexts of his Time*. Lewisburg: Bucknell University Press.

Haynes, Jonathan (1992). *The Social Relations of Jonson's Theater*. Cambridge: Cambridge University Press.

Jackson, Gabriele Bernhard (1968). *Vision and Judgment in Ben Jonson's Drama*. New Haven: Yale University Press.

Jackson, Gabriele Bernhard, ed. (1969). *Ben Jonson: Every Man in His Humor*. New Haven: Yale University Press.

Jones, Robert C. (1986). *Engagement with Knavery*. Durham: Duke University Press.

Jonson, Benjamin (1981). *The Complete Plays of Ben Jonson*, ed. G. A. Wilkes. 4 vols. Oxford: Clarendon Press.

Kay, W. David (1995). *Ben Jonson: A Literary Life*. Basingstoke: Macmillan.

Kay, W. David (1999). "*Epicoene*, Lady Compton, and the gendering of Jonsonian satire on extravagance." *Ben Jonson Journal* 6, 1–33.

Kernan, Alvin (1959). *The Cankered Muse: Satire of the English Renaissance*. New Haven: Yale University Press.

Leggatt, Alexander (1981). *Ben Jonson: His Vision and his Art*. London: Methuen.

McDonald, Russ (1988). *Shakespeare and Jonson: Jonson and Shakespeare*. Lincoln: University of Nebraska Press.

Marcus, Leah S. (1986). *The Politics of Mirth*. Chicago: University of Chicago Press.

Maus, Katherine Eisaman (1984). *Ben Jonson and the Roman Frame of Mind*. Princeton: Princeton University Press.

Riggs, David (1989). *Ben Jonson: A Life*. Cambridge, MA: Harvard University Press.

Rowe, George E. (1988). *Distinguishing Jonson: Imitation, Rivalry, and the Direction of a Dramatic Career*. Lincoln: University of Nebraska Press.

Sanders, Julie, Kate Chedgzoy, and Susan Wiseman, eds (1988). *Refashioning Ben Jonson: Gender, Politics, and the Jonsonian Canon*. Basingstoke: Macmillan.

Shapiro, James (1991). *Rival Playwrights: Marlowe, Jonson, Shakespeare*. New York: Columbia University Press.

Slights, William W. E. (1994). *Ben Jonson and the Art of Secrecy*. Toronto: University of Toronto Press.

Smith, G. Gregory, ed. (1904). *Elizabethan Critical Essays*. 2 vols. Oxford: Oxford University Press.

Tiffany, Grace (1995). *Erotic Beasts and Social Monsters: Shakespeare, Jonson, and Comic Androgyny*. Newark: University of Delaware Press.

Watson, Robert N. (1987). *Ben Jonson's Parodic Strategy: Literary Imperialism in the Comedies*. Cambridge, MA: Harvard University Press.

Womack, Peter (1986). *Ben Jonson*. Oxford: Blackwell.

Yachnin, Paul (1997). *Stage-Wrights: Shakespeare, Jonson, Middleton, and the Making of Theatrical Value*. Philadelphia: University of Pennsylvania Press.

33

Sidney, Cary, Wroth

Margaret Ferguson

Introduction

Twenty years ago, the three women named in my title would not have been grouped together as playwrights in a companion to English Renaissance drama. Each might, however, have been mentioned separately as a minor contributor to the emergent nation's dramatic culture. Mary Sidney (1561–1621) was a patron of drama, as was her husband the earl of Pembroke; and her 1592 translation of Robert Garnier's *Marc Antoine* is the first English dramatic version of Plutarch's famous story of love and empire. Her translation influenced Shakespeare's *Antony and Cleopatra* of 1607 as well as a number of other plays that use ancient history to comment on contemporary English politics.[1] Elizabeth Cary's *Tragedy of Mariam* is one of the plays indebted to Sidney's example. This drama about a tyrant who was appointed to rule the Roman colony of Judea by Mark Antony, and who executed his beloved Jewish wife Mariam in a fit of jealousy created in large part by his sister Salome's machinations, was popular among Continental dramatists of the sixteenth century (Valency, 1940; Cary, 1613/1994, 23–6); Cary is the first to render the story as an English drama. Her tragedy circulated in manuscript for some years before it was printed in 1613, without the author's full name on the title-page. Although *Mariam* may have influenced, or been influenced by, Shakespeare's *Othello*, Cary's play was not printed again until 1914 and was read only by a few scholars until the 1990s, when it suddenly became a quasi-canonical text in some university courses reflecting the renewed interest in early modern women's writing. The fact that Cary (*c*.1585–1639) allowed her play to be published at all, and in a way that made her identity as a noble lady legible to an elite readership, suggests that she shared Mary Sidney's interest in developing a polit-ical (and theological) voice under the veil of feminine modesty.

Mary Wroth (*c*.1586/7–1651/3) seems, at first glance, to be an even less significant contributor to English drama than Sidney or Cary. Wroth is noted in literary histories as participating in several of Queen Anne's court performances, including Ben Jonson's *Masque of Blackness* of 1605 in which 12 ladies, according to a disapproving contemporary observer, appeared dressed "too light and curtisan-like," with "their Faces and Arms up to the Elbows . . . painted black" (letter of Dudley Carleton, cited in Wynne-Davies, 1992, 88). And she wrote a pastoral tragicomedy, *Love's Victory*, that circulated in manuscript to a coterie audience and that may have been privately performed in the 1620s. Since *Love's Victory* was published only in the twentieth century, however, Wroth has not been studied as a playwright until very recently. Her play, moreover, belongs to a different era, as well as a different genre, from those of Cary and Sidney, so it may seem somewhat arbitrary to group Wroth with the earlier playwrights even in the context of this volume. Mary Sidney, however, was Wroth's aunt and either still living or very recently dead when Wroth wrote her play. In it, she makes Mary Sidney both an actress in and a spectator of a plot that wittily alludes to, and transforms, Antony and Cleopatra's tragedy.

Although modern readers require more information to decode Wroth's allusions than did her initial coterie audience, we are now in a better position to appreciate Wroth's dramatic art than any previous audience has been except the first one. Thanks to the recent publishing and critical labors of feminist scholars, we can now read Wroth's play, as well as those by Sidney and Cary, in ways that allow us to decipher some if not all of the layered historical messages such dramas contain. In Wroth's case, one of those messages undermines Mary Sidney's dominant historical reputation as a pious servant of God – and of her brother Philip's literary heritage. Wroth presents a contrasting image of Sidney as a servant of Venus; and in so doing, the niece named for her aunt calls attention to the elder Sidney's accomplishment as the writer not only of psalms but also of a secular play about love. Wroth rereads her aunt's play in a way that wittily develops the Shakespearean conceit that tragically dying lovers like Antony and Cleopatra are in truth actors who will awake both to love again and to act in another play, perhaps a comedy.

Sidney, Cary, and Wroth make significant contributions to our understanding of English dramatic traditions despite the fact that none of these women wrote for the public theater or published (via the medium of the press) an original play under her own name. Their complex literary personae are tied to their membership of privileged families for whom the institution of dynastic marriage was a crucial means of maintaining and/or extending social power. These women lived in stately houses where there were many servants, many books, and also sufficient money for paper and quills. Each woman received an extraordinarily good education that allowed her not only to read literature in more than one language but also to write in a courtly, metropolitan dialect that speakers of the modern "standard" language can still understand.

Mary Sidney and Mary Wroth belonged to a prominent family alliance that controlled "approximately two-thirds of the land under Elizabeth's rule."[2] Mary Sidney added luster to her family by marrying the immensely wealthy and much older Henry Herbert, earl of Pembroke and owner of Wilton House, among other properties

(Beilin, 1987, 124; Hannay, 1990). Elizabeth Cary was not so well-born as the Sidney women but she was marked, as they were, both by her family of birth and by the family she entered through marriage. Cary's father, who acquired a knighthood, and hence gentry status, only in 1604, used money gained from his tenants and his lawyer's fees to give his only child an attractive dowry that allowed her to be married, in 1602, to a man whose noble connections on the maternal side made him a good prospect for a peerage. He became viscount of Falkland in 1620, having spent his wife's dowry and having attempted to spend her jointure – the money settled on her by her father – as well. On the title-page of *Mariam* the author is referred to as that "learned, vertuous, and truly noble Ladie, E. C."; but later in her life Cary signed herself "Elizabeth Falkland," or "E. F." According to the biography of Cary by one of her Catholic daughters, Sir Henry Cary married his 15-year-old bride "only for being an heir, for he had no acquaintance with her."[3]

While their membership in privileged families enabled Sidney, Cary, and Wroth to write, it also worked to constrain their choice of genres and their modes of reaching a public audience. Well-read in contemporary Christian religious discourses as well as in ancient and modern literary works, these women had ample opportunity to see that the humanist goal of literary fame, rooted in a classical ethos of competition, stood in considerable tension with Christian tenets about humility, self-hood, and the afterlife. The tension was even more acute for aspiring women writers than it was for men, because the notion of literary fame (or "glory") was antithetical to the maintenance of the "good name "connected to the cultural ideal of the wife as the husband's property, "chaste, silent, and obedient" (Hull, 1982; Jones, 1986, 75–95). As the Chorus – a voice of "doxa" or common opinion – explains in Cary's *Mariam*, a wife who seeks "to be by public language grac'd" will wound her "fame" in the paradoxical sense that word carried when it applied to females: for them, fame denoted the specifically "private" virtue of chastity – or at least a perfectly maintained appearance thereof. As the writers discussed here sought to negotiate the complex and often competing value systems given to them by their education, their social status, their gender, and their (differing) religious views, they repeatedly dramatize women's fears of and desires for some kind of fame. In so doing, particularly in their experiments with the dramatic and quasi-dramatic literary genres examined here, these women interrogate their culture's theories and practices of censorship, sometimes in surprising ways.

Modern readers may expect female authors to protest censoring forces in their society, and at times these writers, and their heroines, seem to do just that; but these writers' attitudes toward censorship are, on close inspection, very complex, not only because the writers are concerned with their reputations and adept at courtly modes of indirection (in his *Arte of English Poetrie* of 1589, Puttenham called "allegoria" the "courtly figure"); but also because the culture offered some positive – and politic – models for self-censorship. Sidney and Cary draw on Stoic philosophical traditions that advocate self-censorship as a noble response to situations of political oppression. And Cary, who was interested in Catholicism even as a young woman, long before her "public" conversion in the 1620s, was already interested in Jesuitical theories of equivocation when she wrote *Mariam*. Such theories, adapted to the problems faced by English Catholics suspected of treason (as were all subjects who refused to accept the monarch as "head" of an "English" church), sought to legitimate modes of spoken or written discourse that disguise one's "inner thoughts" from hostile authorities.

Censorship works both as a major theme in a number of these women's works – some of which were not printed in their lifetimes – and as a pressure on their efforts to fashion authorial personae compatible with their social status and gender. The pressure colors, albeit in different shades, their reflections on two related questions: what constitutes proper female behavior, on the one hand, and, on the other, what constitutes proper behavior for a Christian political subject – female or male – who may harbor serious doubts, as Elizabeth Cary and Mary Sidney clearly did, about their monarch's governance of the English body politic. Wroth was less concerned than Sidney and Cary were to reform the realm through allegorical drama; but Wroth followed her aunt's example in using drama to comment critically on her society. Her autobiographically inflected tragicomedy offers, as Barbara Lewalski has argued, a "challenge to both generic and cultural norms" (1991, 105).

Sidney

Sidney (plate 10) made her most influential contribution to English drama with her translation of Robert Garnier's play *Marc Antoine*; she also wrote a short dramatic poem, "A Dialogue betweene two shepheards, Thenot and Piers, in praise of Astrea." The latter was written, probably in 1599, to entertain the queen during a planned visit to the Pembroke estate at Wilton, and the dialogue has usually been read as a conventional pastoral poem of praise. In the dialogue as in her translation of Garnier, however, Sidney uses the cover of drama's multiple voices to explore political and theological problems. A master of "admonitory flattery" (Hannay, 1990, 126; 1985), Sidney sought to speak truth to power without getting punished for her act. In *Antonius* and the "Dialogue," she focuses critical attention on the ruler's temptation to become an "idol" in his or her own eyes as well as in those of some of his gullible subjects.

For her translation of Garnier, Mary Sidney used the 1585 text of *Marc Antoine*, a text "known to have been substantially revised by the author, who was still living when she began her translation" (Herbert, 1998, 147). Garnier died in 1590, poor and in political disgrace because of his decision to support the League, a group of Catholics extremely opposed to the monarchy. Completed in the year of Garnier's death, Sidney's play was first published in 1592 in a small quarto volume that also contained Sidney's translation (in prose) of another French work, the Protestant Philippe de Mornay's *Discours de la vie et de la mort*. The aristocratic female translator's name is prominently (and unusually) displayed on the title-page of the first edition,

Plate 10 Mary Sidney, Countess of Pembroke: engraving by Simon Van der Passe. By courtesy of the National Portrait Gallery, London.

which reads: *"Discourse of Life* and Death Written in French by Ph. Mornay. *Antonius* A Tragedie written also in French by Ro. Garnier. Both done in English by the Countesse of Pembroke." In 1595, Sidney's translation of Garnier was reprinted by the same publisher, William Ponsonby, under the title *Antonie* and without de Mornay's text.

Sidney's version of Garnier's play begins with Antony berating Cleopatra for fleeing with her boats from the battle of Actium. Assuming that she deserted him because she sought to please Caesar and thus save her own crown, Antony rehearses misogynist stereotypes to avoid blaming himself in any way for his plight (he lost the battle spectacularly by following her rather than fighting). First attributing his downfall to "the cruell Heav'ns" (l. 2) and then to Cleopatra – she "only hast me vanquisht" (l. 34) – Antony describes the Egyptian queen as a sorceress whose "poisned cuppes" spoiled his reason.[4] He pities himself, moreover, in the repeated phrase "Poore *Antonie*," as the feminized slave of a cruel, perjuring, traitorous woman (ll. 18–20). Antony's view of things does not, however, go uncontested. A Chorus representing the perspective of the Egyptian people on the acts performed by the "great ones" remarks, at the end of act I, that "Nature made us not free / When first she made us live" (ll. 175–6). Thus countering Antony's view of himself as enslaved by Cleopatra, the Chorus introduces an idea central to Stoic ethics: the wise man should direct his desires "inward toward those things that are strictly within his own control" (Straznicky, 1994, 115).

Cleopatra offers another counterpoint to Antony's opening perspective when she enters the play (in act II) questioning how she could have "betraide my Lord, my King" (l. 396). In striking contrast to Antony, Cleopatra accepts full responsibility for her error ("I am sole cause: I did it, only I," l. 455) while also opening a breach between motive and act. She does not deny that she broke her "vowed faith," but she does not explain either to herself or to the audience/reader what led her to her crime; and her subsequent dialogue with her maid Charmian shows that she now utterly rejects the idea Antony had ascribed to her, that of saving herself and her crown by seeking Caesar's favor. While leaving unresolved the mystery of her flight at Actium, Garnier's and Sidney's plays invite admiration for the eloquent Cleopatra as she takes responsibility for her mistake, laments it, remains steadfast in her love for Antony, and finally resolves on suicide rather than become Caesar's captive. Sidney's Cleopatra, in an interesting addition to Garnier's text, explains her fear of becoming Caesar's prisoner in terms that imply a concern for her future fame: she does not wish to become part of the spectacular "triumph" Caesar will stage upon returning to Rome (ll. 1644–5).

Sidney's play, like its French original, belongs to the sub-genre usually described as "Senecan" or neo-Senecan closet drama (see chapter 29 above). Plays in this tradition typically observe the Aristotelian unities of time and of action; they also observe "unity of place," although this rule was actually first formulated not in antiquity but rather in Renaissance Italy, by Lodovico Castelvetro in 1571 (Sidney, 1970, 74–5n.). Plays in the Senecan tradition usually have five acts divided by meditations of the

Chorus, and the major characters deliver long soliloquies "alternating with dialogues between a protagonist and a minor character" (Herbert, 1998, 141) The major characters do not speak to each other – in Garnier's play, Antony meditates on his actions in acts I and III, Cleopatra meditates on hers in acts II and V, while Octavius Caesar speaks (with some interjections from the minor character Agrippa) in act IV. Garnier's play is typical in its use of a *nuntius* or messenger to report action that occurs offstage, and it also has a "rhetor," or semi-professional speaker, who characteristically comments on the meaning of events. In Garnier's play, this role is played by Philostrate, who makes one long speech at the beginning of act II elaborating the destruction caused to the Egyptians by the protagonists' love. Most importantly, perhaps, plays in the Senecan tradition draw on Stoic doctrines to explore psychological conflicts that have serious political causes – and effects.

Why, in 1590, did Sidney choose to render into English a neo-Senecan play by a French Catholic? Why, in particular, did Sidney choose, from several plays on Roman historical themes by Garnier, one about two royal personages who lost their political power, harmed their subjects, disinherited their children, and committed suicide for the sake of love? Critics have offered many different answers to this question, accompanying radically contrasting judgments of the play's qualities both as a translation and as an influence on the development of English drama. Is Sidney's translation "accurate . . . faithful to [its] original in style and mood," as one set of recent editors maintain (Herbert, 1998, 147)? Or is it, in the words of another such set, "remarkably free," involving a "rejection" of Garnier's verse form and many of his meanings in favor of a "more natural" English style and a proto-feminist vision of Cleopatra (Cerasano and Wynne-Davies, 1996, 15)?

From the mid-nineteenth century until quite recently, Sidney's translation was generally seen – as was Mary Sidney herself – as a faithful handmaiden to her brother's literary legacy. In the *Apology for Poetry* (written *c.*1581–3, published posthumously in 1595 by the same publisher who printed the 1592 and 1595 editions of Mary Sidney's translation), Philip Sidney had attacked English tragedies and comedies – along with the "mongrel tragicomedy" – for their failure to observe the rules of "honest civility" and of "skillful poetry"(Sidney, 1970, 74; see chapter 27 above). With the significant exception of *Gorboduc*, a tragedy of 1562 concerned with the problems of royal succession, English drama, in Sidney's view, lacks the "stately speeches and well sounding phrases, climbing to the height of Seneca his style." Such "high" speeches are necessary if poetry is to fulfill its end of "delightfully teach[ing]" (1970, 75). When Mary Sidney's translation is seen as an attempt to "improve" English drama along the classicizing lines her brother had prescribed in the early 1580s, it is easy to cast both the female writer and her work as an enemy of the true English people. This, as Margaret Hannay points out, is what Alexander Witherspoon does in a book first published in 1924 and reprinted in 1968. He sees Mary Sidney as the leader of a conspiracy against "the popular drama" because she undertook "that Reformation of English tragedy which her brother had so desired" (cited in Hannay, 1990, 121). He further describes her as a "bluestocking" who could not handle "the tragedies

. . . of the popular stage," which "were of masculine inception and for masculine consumption." Somehow, Mary Sidney, her interest in a French play about a feminized Roman hero, her influence on others who wrote "closet dramas" on Roman themes, and her era itself – an era of "female ascendancy" when an aging queen was refusing to secure the succession – all become linked in Witherspoon's mind. His final chapter, entitled "The failure of Lady Pembroke's movement," articulates an assessment of English "closet drama" – often called "Sidnean" closet drama (Straznicky, 1994, and chapter 29 above) – that still persists in many quarters, today.

Providing a quite different answer to the question of why Sidney translated Garnier's play, Mary Ellen Lamb suggests that Sidney wanted her 1592 volume to contribute to the tradition of discourse about how to die well (*ars moriendi*). By translating a play in which the main characters' chief ethical decision is whether to surrender to Octavius or to take their own lives, Sidney chose a text that raises some of the same moral questions posed in the prose *Discourse on Life and Death* that she printed with *Antonius*. Lamb further argues that Sidney attempts to "apply Mornay's philosophy to the situation of Renaissance women" through the portrayal of Cleopatra's Stoic death. Garnier's portrait of Cleopatra as a loyal wife offers an "unusual suppression of Cleopatra's sexual nature" and therefore "suggests insights into the way in which the resolve to die cleanses a heroine of sexual taint" (Lamb, 1981a, 129, 131–2). Some critics, however, have suggested that Sidney would have expected her readers to see Cleopatra (and Antony too) as illustrating how not to die well from either a Stoic or a Christian perspective (Skretkowicz, 1999, 9–10). De Mornay does explicitly condemn suicide, and Garnier's play may seek to soften the problem of suicide for his Christian readers by leaving it unclear at the end whether Cleopatra has actually applied the asps or not (Herbert, 1998, 143) Since there is a thin line, in some historical and literary instances, between Stoic suicide and Christian martyrdom, however, Sidney could well have chosen to juxtapose Garnier's and de Mornay's texts to promote thought about a much-debated problem rather than to provide clear ethical answers.

Many neo-Senecan dramas deploy the humanist rhetorical technique of arguing "on both sides of the question," leaving the reader or spectator to ponder the answer. In any case, it seems likely that Sidney was indeed drawn to Garnier's play because of her interest in the art of dying – an art exemplified in various ways by Sidney's brother, by both of her parents, and by Garnier himself in the years leading up to her act of translation. Moreover, her interest in death seems to include an element of baroque eroticism that Lamb does not fully explore, since it goes against her view that Sidney ennobles Cleopatra by "suppressing" the attributes of sexual voraciousness she has in Plutarch's *Life of Antony* and in many of the later European treatments of her story.[5] Echoing Catullus' famous poem to Lesbia, Sidney's Cleopatra ends the play with the following lines:

A thousand kisses, thousand thousand more
Let you my mouth for honors farewell give;

> That in this office weake my limbes may growe
> Fainting on you, and fourth my soule may flowe.
>
> (ll. 2013–22)

Garnier ends with a distinctly less positive image of dying: his Cleopatra "vomits" her soul onto Antony's body as she performs the last funerary rites.[6] "Vomir" has a more metaphorical meaning in French than it does in English, as Eve Sanders remarks; Sidney clearly saw that a literal translation would not do for her final lines, although earlier in the play – when Antony describes the death in battle he would like to have experienced – she renders his image of vomiting blood and life literally (ll. 1090–1; noted by Sanders, 1998, 110). For Cleopatra, however, Sidney offers a more allitera-tive and liquid image of death than Garnier does; and the "images of arousal and climax in the final two lines" of Sidney's text combine with a "confusion of subject and object," as Sanders observes, in a way that "evokes images of reciprocal erotic expression" (1998, 117). The images of merged beings, one dead but immortal, one still alive, look ahead to lines in Sidney's dedicatory poem to the "Angell spirit" of her brother Philip. Describing their "coupled work" of translating the psalms in a poem of 1599, Sidney writes, "So dar'd my Muse with thine it selfe combine, / as mortall stuffe with that which is divine" (Herbert, 1998, 110, ll. 5–6).

Several recent critics have indeed suggested an authorial sympathy or even a partial identification with Cleopatra as one of Sidney's reasons for translating Garnier's version of the queen's story. Garnier's Cleopatra is a complex character who struggles with her conflicting identities and duties. She is an anxious mother who suffers, unlike most of her other literary incarnations, when she parts from her children; she is also a ruler who laments causing her people's oppression at Caesar's hands, and a lover who wants to think of herself as a loyal "wife," although she "scarcely" is one, as her servant. Charmian reminds her (l. 598); Sidney, like Shakespeare, tells us with irony that Antony married Octavia to bring "amity" between him and his wife's brother, Octavius. Garnier's and Sidney's texts suggest that part of Antony's attraction to Cleopatra rather than to the more conventionally "chaste, silent, and obedient" Octavia comes from her powers of language. Garnier presents Cleopatra's verbal skills as superior even to her beauty (ll. 719–24), and he thus creates a hierarchy of Cleopa-tra's graces, whereas Plutarch, and his sixteenth-century translators Jacques Amyot and Thomas North, simply juxtapose Cleopatra's physical graces with her linguistic skills. Garnier's Cleopatra uses her voice, accompanied by hand gestures such as those that might be used by an actor, to conduct affairs of state. As Sidney's text puts it:

> hir training speache,
> Her grace, hir Majestie, and forcing voice,
> Whither she it with fingers speech consorte,
> Or hearing sceptred kings embassadors
> Answer to eache in his owne language make.
>
> (ll. 728–32)

The lines could be a reference to Sidney herself, as a skilled translator; they could simultaneously offer an elegant if ultimately sobering compliment to Queen Elizabeth, whose skill in languages and in diplomacy was famous. An implied analogy between Cleopatra and either the queen or Sidney herself was, however, quite risky, as Eve Sanders has noted (1998, 114). Sanders shows Sidney generally following Garnier very closely while nonetheless making changes that make Cleopatra even more heroic than she is in the source text. Although modern critics disagree about whether Sidney's translation is "faithful" or "free," her originality arguably consists not in a romantic deviation from Garnier but rather in a complex political collaboration with him across lines of language, gender, and religion.

In Garnier's play, which was performed in France as well as read, Sidney found a vehicle for speaking publicly while not seeming to do so in a way that provoked censure. Ladies, in the eyes of many Renaissance educators, should eschew public speech altogether and should also eschew all contact with cultural objects and experiences – secular books, for instance, and attendance at public playhouses – that allegedly fostered women's innate desires for illicit kinds of knowledge and love. To an aristocratic Englishwoman aspiring to a public voice prohibited by the dominant norms of femininity, the genre of Senecan drama being written and staged in France – in various "private" theatrical venues as well as the one Parisian theater available for public performances after the Counter-Reformation censoring of popular theater in 1548 – Garnier's plays would have looked more appealing as an object of imitation than they do to most modern readers.

These dramas belong to a humanist tradition that gives the human voice greater symbolic value than classical Senecan dramas did. The voice, both as theme and as vehicle for self-expression, is in fact central to the set of plays on biblical and classical Roman themes to which Garnier's *Marc Antoine* belongs. Written in 1578 during the French civil wars, Garnier's play, like its main French precursor, Etienne Jodelle's *Cléopâtre Captive,* illustrates Gordon Braden's argument that French neo-Senecan tragedy "can make up for its indifference to action or even conflict with an appreciation for the special courage and authority of the human voice" (1985, 128). Valuing the voice both as an instrument of moral reflection and as a dramaturgical equivalent for action (on the seventeenth-century French stage, as d'Aubignac asserts in his manual of "practical" theater, "speech is action"),[7] Garnier's play about a woman using her voice to conduct affairs of state had much to offer an Englishwoman interested in current debates about the relative merits of monarchical versus republican forms of government. Garnier gave Sidney a model for using Roman history to explore current political problems. The most compelling recent interpretations of Sidney's *Antonius* see it, in Danielle Clarke's formulation, as a "carefully timed use of the Garnier text to illuminate issues of rule, government, and morality" (Clarke, 1997, 151).[8] The first edition of Garnier's play included a dedication lamenting the parallels between "the civil wars of Rome" and "our domestic dissensions" (cited in Herbert, 1998, 39: my translation). Sidney shared Garnier's interest in allegorically probing "domestic dissensions" caused, in part, by a monarch's self-indulgences. Moreover, Sidney's trans-

lation of Garnier's "treatment of the death of a queen and concern with the consequences of a disputed succession would have struck clear chords in a decade constantly
anxious about the threat of civil war following Elizabeth's anticipated demise" (Clarke,
1997, 154).

Although some critics have attempted to unlock Sidney's and Garnier's political
allegories by finding one-to-one correspondences between the ancient characters in
the play and contemporary figures, neither Sidney nor Garnier, it seems to me, offers
an easily legible topical allegory. Both were highly aware of the need to veil their
meanings and both may have harbored complex, even changing, views about their
country's governors. Garnier had been a loyal servant of the French monarchy and its
system of justice (he served, by direct appointment of the king, as chief justice for
the Le Mans region), before coming, late in life and disillusioned by the civil wars,
to join the Catholic opposition to the monarchy (Garnier, 1975, intro.; Jondorf, 1969).
His play is a searching inquiry into the relations between rulers and those they rule.
The latter are given a voice, albeit a highly stylized one, in Garnier's Choruses, which
Sidney interestingly renders in short, rhymed lines that contrast with the blank verse
typically spoken by her royal protagonists. Using a stylistic contrast to suggest a difference in characters' social status, she anticipates a technique used by Shakespeare;
as she does by showing us gloriously eloquent royal protagonists who eventually suffer
the indignities of being ruled – by their passions, by the great leveler Death, and also
by Octavius Caesar. Garnier's critical attitude toward Octavius is important to Sidney,
and also to our assessment of the kind of cultural work her translation performed. By
Englishing the work of a French Catholic, Sidney underscores Clarke's contention that
there was a good deal of "shared theoretical ground" between Catholic and Protestant
theories of resistance to tyranny (1997, 153).

In striking contrast to Etienne Jodelle's Cleopatra, who coyly asks the emperor's
pardon and hands over her treasure to him in exchange for a promise of her children's
life, Garnier's and Sidney's heroines scorn Caesar and choose to follow Antony in death
without bargaining at all with the emperor. The lovers are noble but flawed; Caesar,
in contrast, seems ignoble and dangerously greedy in both Garnier and Sidney's plays.
Sidney conveys Caesar's quality of pride and, like Garnier, marks it as strikingly sinful
from a Christian point of view: "No Towne there is, but up my image settes," declares
Octavius (act IV, l. 1382, translating Garnier's "Il n'est ville ou de moy l'on ne dresse
une idole"). Proud and idolatrous, Garnier's Caesar, like Sidney's, highlights a moral
problem at the heart of the imperial desire for conquest over others. This is a problem
Jodelle too addresses in his portrait of Caesar, but his critique of the emperor's pride
is blunted by his desire to flatter Henry II as a new and "greater" emperor than Octa-
vian was. His play leaves open the question of whether such greatness is compatible
with Christian humility and pity.

The story of Antony and Cleopatra had been repeatedly dramatized in Italy and
France during the sixteenth century, but Sidney's version first brought the story across
the Channel.[9] Her play has been seen as influencing a set of 11 plays classified by literary historians as "neo-Senecan" or (more recently) as "Sidnean" closet drama (see

Straznicky, 1998, and chapter 29 above). This set of plays includes Samuel Daniel's *Cleopatra* (1594), which he describes in his dedication to Sidney as "the worke the which she did impose" in order to lead him from love poetry to the "higher" and, as we have seen, politically charged genre of tragic drama (cited in Herbert, 1998, 41).[10] The set also includes Thomas Kyd's *Cornelia* (1594), which translates Garnier's *Cornélie*; Samuel Brandon's *Tragicomeoedi of the Vertuous Octavia* (1598); and Cary's *Mariam*, which Marta Straznicky sees as the only play in the closet drama group to reappropriate "for the disempowered female the political power of stoic heroism" (1994, 124).

The influence of Sidney's *Antonius*, however, extends beyond the closet-drama group to plays written for the public stage and, in at least one case, to a play about Antony and Cleopatra "sacrificed to the flames" by an author who feared being censored for his version of a play about Antony and Cleopatra. As Straznicky remarks, standard definitions of closet drama as "plays that were never performed" or "never meant to be performed" tend to conflate authorial intent with lack of extant evidence about historical performances in various venues (Straznicky, 1994).[11] This problem is taken up by recent critics – and directors – who have argued that we should not confuse the "unperformed" with the "unperformable" (Findlay et al., 1999). As applied to a play like Cary's *Tragedy of Mariam*, which was successfully acted by the Tinderbox Theatre Company in 1994, in a production directed and described by Stephanie J. Hodgson-Wright, the phrase "closet drama" may lead us into presuming a simpler relation between public and private cultural domains – and between modes of communication and transmission of materials across political and linguistic boundaries – than in fact obtained in early modern Europe.

Cary

According to the account of Cary's life given by one of her Catholic daughters writing in the 1650s from a convent in France, Cary gave up playgoing after her husband's death in 1633; the biographer implies that Cary's "love" for theatrical productions, evidently indulged before her husband's death, was a kind of sin that needed chastisement: "she went no more," the *Life* melodramatically states, "to masques nor plays, not so much as at the court, though she loved them very much, especially the last extremely; nor to any other such public thing" (Cary, 1613/1994, 224). Although the biography mentions nothing about Cary's interest in writing plays, its description of her "extreme" love of the spectator role nonetheless provides an interesting gloss on the dialectic between pleasure and renunciation (often figured as self-censorship) that Cary explores in *Mariam* and that Garnier and Sidney had explored in their dramas as well. The passage also provides an interesting gloss on Paul van Somer's court portrait of Cary (1621; plate 11), which presents her "as though she is standing on a stage"; the red curtains on either side of the figure recall the theater's "discovery space" (Findlay et al., 1999, 132). The absence of historical records about any performance

Plate 11   Elizabeth, Lady Falkland: by Athow from a painting by Paul van Somer. By permission of the Ashmolean Museum, Oxford.

of Cary's drama(s) should not be taken as indicating Cary's own lack of interest in theatrical spaces and modalities of (self-)publication.

Probably written between 1603 and 1609, Cary's *Mariam* is described by her teacher Sir John Davies as the as yet-unprinted product of a Muse who moves "in Buskin fine, / With feete of State" (Davies, 1612/1878). The description neatly conflates the image of the classical tragic actor's booted feet with an allusion to Cary's metrical feet; her play is in iambic pentameter lines rhyming abab throughout, except for occasional rhyming couplets, some arranged to embed Elizabethan sonnets in the play's text. Both in its concern with English poetic form and in various aspects of its content, the play shows its debt to a Sidnean muse. Adapting a story from Josephus'

Antiquities of the Jews (*c.*90 CE) to her own political and theological purposes, Cary is also indebted to Thomas Lodge's 1602 translation of Josephus' works. The actual references to Cleopatra in Cary's play present her as a sensual "anti-type" to Mariam, and hence as a figure resembling Shakespeare's dangerous Egyptian more than the noble figure who emerges (eventually) in the pages of Garnier's and Sidney's plays. But Cary's Mariam also reincarnates aspects of Cleopatra's shifting historical persona; and in doing so, Mariam begins to look strangely like her enemy, Herod's Machiavellian sister Salome, as well as like the historical queen of England whose reputation was even more hotly debated after her death in 1603 than it had been during her life.

The events dramatized in *Mariam* occurred around 29 BCE, when the man later known as Herod the Great, having been appointed tetrarch or governor of Judea by Mark Antony, married the Maccabean princess Mariam and thereby secured his "title" to the throne of Judea.[12] The moral legitimacy of that title is rendered doubtful, however, by Cary's Argument, which serves as a preface to the play and signals that it participates in that task of commenting on affairs of state that was so often performed – at risk of censure – by neo-Senecan dramas.[13] Cary's play is less statically declamatory than Sidney's and Garnier's – indeed Cary's protagonists meet and look at and talk with each other, often sharply; moreover, two minor male characters actually engage in a somewhat comical sword-fight over Salome. Nonetheless, Cary's play follows the Sidnean model in having long soliloquies of considerable moral complexity, and in being fundamentally concerned with a form of tyranny that includes a strong tendency toward idolatry. The various subalterns resisting Herod include not only his second wife, Mariam, but also his first wife, Doris, his brother, Pheroras, who wants to marry a slave girl, Graphina, against Herod's will, and two young men who have been hidden by Salome's husband, Constabarus, since Herod decreed their death after they resisted his initial usurpation of the throne. These young men, the sons of Babus, die in the play, as Mariam does, because of Salome's Iago-like plotting, but also because they make the mistake of publishing their thoughts in a premature and politically naive way. Intriguingly, the only character who resists Herod successfully is his sister Salome; indeed she uses her powers of politic eloquence to manipulate the plot, arrange Mariam's death, and, in a striking departure from the norms of tragedy, escape discovery and punishment at the play's end. Babus' sons, like Graphina and Mariam, play a symbolically significant role in the play's meditation on when – and to whom – it is safe to speak or write one's inner thoughts. In the landscape of Cary's play, as in that of early Jacobean England, equivocation, as a way of hiding potentially treasonous ideas, was a much-debated practice for both Catholics and Protestants.

The play's Argument alerts us immediately to Cary's concern with the problem of tyranny: Herod is described as "having crept by the favour of the Romans" into the Jewish monarchy; he then attempts to consolidate his dubious claim to the throne by replacing his wife Doris with Mariam. She is the only member of the royal family whom Herod allows to live (Cary, 1613/1994, 67). The Argument suggests many reasons why the Judeans should resist Herod's authority. He has displaced and murdered, on a spurious charge of treason, Mariam's grandfather, the "rightful" male king who is also his people's priest; he has "repudiated" a wife who had given him heirs; and he has killed his new wife's brother (under cover of "sport") in order to appropriate a title which, Cary's phrasing suggests, belongs by right to his wife.

Both the setting and the plot of *Mariam* suggest an analogical relation between Judea in the years just before Christ's birth and England in the years after its traumatic break from the church of Rome. In England's domestic spaces as in the imperial nation at large, the distinction between friend and enemy, loyalist and traitor, could be extremely labile. Cary represents this lability in her drama, where a husband who is also a king ultimately censors his wife in the most extreme fashion – by "dividing" her body from her head – after the wife refuses to censor herself. "I cannot frame disguise, nor never taught / My face a look dissenting from my thought," she declares, refusing to smile obediently when Herod bids her to (IV.iii. 145–6). Her response of non-responsiveness "vexes" him, and the exchange seems to confirm the servant Sohemus' view that Mariam brings on her own death by refusing to "bridle her tongue." The play, however, suggests multiple causes for the heroine's death and its tragic consequences: madness for Herod and hence disorder for the state. Readers are invited to ponder these multiple causes along with the play's layered allegorical allusions to contemporary history. The play begins with the heroine asking questions about her behavior and about the mysterious relation between her present and past selves: "How oft have I with public voice run on / To censure Rome's last hero for deceit" (I.i. 1–2). Mariam's self-questioning opening, which takes us abruptly into the interior theater of the heroine's mind, recalls the interrogative opening of Cleopatra's first soliloquy in Sidney's play: "That I have thee betraid, deare Antonie, / My life, my soule, my Sunne? I had such thought?" (Herbert, 1998, ll. 394–5). Cary's play, like Sidney's, seems to live on unanswered questions that tease the reader into joining the play of the mind as it considers difficult questions about the past and the present.

Wroth

Mary Wroth's one exercise in drama also teases the reader into entering a labyrinth of literary and historical allusions. Wroth's play lightens the labor of interpretation, however, with many instances of comic relief. Comedy is absent from Sidney's *Antonius* and only fleetingly present – mostly through the agency of Salome – in Cary's *Mariam*. Wroth, however, suggests that comedy too can be a sharp instrument for social commentary. Recalling the games played in Castiglione's *Courtier*, Wroth's text, like the image of her holding a lute in the portrait owned by Lord De L'Isle (plate 12), is enigmatically stylized. Poetry, like lute playing, may be an ornamental accomplishment for court ladies, but poetry, at least in Wroth's hands, can bite.

Wroth's play is like Cary's in being laden with puns, some of them bawdy, and in its allegorical reflection on its own mode of existence on the border between public

Plate 12 Lady Mary Wroth. Reproduced by kind permission of Viscount de L'Isle, from his private collection at Penshurst Palace.

and private domains. It represents courtly shepherds engaging in "sports" and games that may reveal serious secrets. One of these games, a fortune-reading riddle game in act II, depicts the pastoral characters performing just the kind of ingenious matching of texts to individual identities that the play invites its own readers to attempt. Most of Wroth's writings have a "roman à clef" topicality, and most, including *Love's Victory*, complicate the game of historical decoding by giving us characters whose names allude to more than one member of the extended Sidney–Herbert circle. Thus Musella, the heroine of *Love's Victory*, is at once a figure for Mary Wroth herself and for Penelope Rich, the "Stella" beloved by Wroth's uncle Philip and represented as his Muse in the Petrarchan sonnets of *Astrophil and Stella*.[14] The historical Philip himself is figured in Philisses, Musella's lover, and echoed in some of his speeches (Wynne-Davies, 1999, 53). But Philisses also represents William Herbert, Mary Sidney's eldest son and the man beloved by Wroth before, during, and after her marriage to Robert Wroth. He appears in the play as the comic and literal-minded character "Rustick" and is the occasion for many of Wroth's puns on her married name. Because Rustick also represents Robert Rich, who married Philip Sidney's beloved and whose name also generates jokes, a multi-layered discourse arises that pits spiritual richness against worldly wealth and the institution of arranged marriage designed to transfer wealth from one generation to another. Rich and Wroth are "worthless" as lovers although aristocratic parents valued them as husbands, the character "Silvesta" suggests after Musella has apparently died rather than agree to be married to Rustick:

> She's happy, yet in death, that she is free
> From such a worthless creature. Can this be?
> Such virtue should in her fair breast abound,
> Yet to be tied where no worth could be found.
>   (V.v. 112–15)[15]

Most critics have dated the play from the early 1620s on the grounds of an overlap between its plot and the "Vale of Tempe" episode in the second part of the *Urania*. Marion Wynne-Davies, however, has recently argued for an earlier date of composition, between 1615 and 1618 (1999, 57). This places the drama after Robert Wroth's death (1614) – which seems highly plausible, given the ways in which the drama satirizes Rustick. The play has many features reminiscent of the courtly entertainments in which Wroth herself had participated in the early years of the century; among these was Jonson's *Masque of Blackness* and perhaps also his lost play *The May Lord*.[16] The play contributes, as Lewalski (1993) has shown, to the new "mixed" Renaissance genre of pastoral tragicomedy. Tasso's *Aminta* (1580) and Guarini's *Pastor Fido* (1590) were the main Italian exemplars of the new "kind," which had prompted much critical debate and which had come to England in such works as Fletcher's *Faithful Shepherdess* (1610) and Daniel's *Hymen's Triumph* (1615; see chapter 27 above). The *Aminta* had been performed at the court of Ferrara in 1573–4, and had quickly circulated among elite readers in Europe and England; it was translated into English by Abraham

Fraunce as *The Countess of Pembroke's Ivychurch* (1592; Lewalski, 1993, 298). Most of the plays in this emergent international genre seem to have been designed both for reading and for performance in some kind of theatrical space. These ranged from courts and great houses to "private" theaters like Blackfriars and even to public theaters like the Globe: Shakespeare's *The Winter's Tale*, arguably an experiment in pastoral tragicomedy, was presented both at court and at the Globe in 1611.

Plays in this loosely defined and culturally contested genre typically have five acts, gods or their oracles shaping the action, "lyrical songs and choruses, stock characters and a miraculous ending" (Waller, 1993, 238). In *Love's Victory*, as in *The Winter's Tale*, the "miracle" consists in a theatrical illusion created by a female character to rescue another female. The shepherdess Silvesta saves Wroth's heroine Musella from a forced marriage by giving her and her beloved Philisses a "sweet potion." This allows them, they believe, to die rather than be parted by Musella's marriage to Rustick. The love-death proves, however, to be only a sleep. After being displayed in a striking tableau described thus in Wroth's stage direction for act V, scene vii – "The temple, the dead bodies on the altar" – the lovers awake into the prospect of a blissful and fruitful marriage blessed by the "mother" who had previously opposed it. Rustick, educated by the pseudo-tragedy, is matched instead to Dalina, and one other couple, Simeana and Lissius, are also united in the happy ending. The fourth couple, Silvesta and the Forester who loves her, remain outside the "triumph" of Venus because Silvesta, like the goddess Diana and Queen Elizabeth, has dedicated herself to a life of chastity. Her role in stage-managing the play's generic turns (from comedy to apparent tragedy and back to comedy) suggests that she is one of the play's figures for the playwright.

Wroth's choice of genre in *Love's Victory* is intimately bound up with the statement about love made in its network of historical and literary allusions. Sir Philip Sidney had attacked the "mongrel Tragicomedie" in his *Apologie*, in a passage cited above. He had also, however, explicitly approved of "some Poesies" that "have coupled together two or three kindes, as the Tragicall and Comicall, whereupon is risen the Tragi-comicall . . . if severed they be good, the coniunction cannot be hurtfull" (cited in Lewalski, 1991, 91). Many critics have debated the apparent contradiction between Sidney's two passages; Lewalski plausibly argues that his attack on the "mongrel" tragicomedy is directed toward the "use of comic scenes" in English tragedies written before 1580 rather than toward the "new" tragicomedies being performed and written in Italy. A tension remains, however, because one of the chief items in Sidney's complaint – the mixing of clowns and kings – was also a staple in Italian attacks on the "new" plays, which were held to violate canons of social as well as artistic decorum (indeed it is often hard to distinguish a social from an artistic flaw in this critical discourse). Given that the famous "golden age" chorus in Tasso's *Aminta* had mounted an attack on all laws that suppress pleasure ("s'e piace, è lice," "if it pleases, it's allowed"); and given also that Wroth herself violated laws of decorum both by writing "vain" and "idle" books, as one contemporary called them, and by engaging in a semi-public extra-marital affair that produced two illegitimate children; it seems fair to surmise that her play both reflects on and plays with licit and illicit modes of coupling.

Love's Victory performs joining acts across linguistic and temporal borders: it alludes not only to classical and Italian texts (including, most prominently, Petrarch's *Trionfo d'Amore*) but also to many works of English literature, among them Spenser's *Faerie Queene*, Shakespeare's *Much Ado* and *Romeo and Juliet*, and various works by various members of the Sidney–Herbert family, in particular Philip, Mary, and Wroth's father Robert. Each of her characters' names joins at least two generations of the Sidney–Herbert circle into a single alphabetic rebus. "Simeana," for instance, Philisses' sister in the play, probably alludes both to Mary Sidney and to Wroth's friend Susan Herbert, who was married to William Herbert's brother and to whom the *Urania* is dedicated (Wynne-Davies, 1999, 52). By coupling the historical Mary Sidney with a character romantically linked to one "Lissius" in the play's plot, Wroth demonstrates her powers to reveal secrets about couplings her society considered illicit. If Mary Sidney, who died in 1621, was still alive when Wroth's play first circulated in manuscript (or, as some critics have inferred from the play's stage directions, was performed in a great house by amateur actors and actresses),[17] she might not have appreciated finding a play on the letters of her name in "Simeana." Mary Sidney's reputation as a chaste matron and author only of "pious" writings is gently but distinctly put at risk through her niece's representation of her as the lover of "Lissius," for the letters of his name insistently recall the historical doctor, Matthew Lister, with whom the widowed Mary Sidney traveled to Europe in 1613, generating much court gossip (Wynne-Davies, 1999, 52).

Wroth's relations with her aunt were complicated.[18] In *Love's Victory*, Mary Sidney may be figured not only in Simeana but also, as Marion Wynne-Davies has argued, in the character of Musella's mother. As the enforcer of a law of "licit" coupling, promoting her daughter's marriage with Rustick in accordance with the will of a dead father, Musella's mother is a female version of the "blocking" figure of traditional comedy, the *senex*. The mother is, however, educated into accepting the more pleasurable coupling of Musella and Philisses (historically an illicit union, although it is idealized as a marriage in the play). In begging Musella's pardon, the mother makes an interesting rhetorical gesture of self-censorship:

> Joy, now as great as was my former woe,
> Shuts up my speech from speaking what I owe
> To all but mine, for mine I joy you are,
> And love, and bliss, maintain you from all care.
> (V.vii. 77–80)

Playing on the married name of her author in a way that emphasizes Wroth's role as a writer or "maker," Musella replies: "Pardon me first, who have your sorrow wrought."

We do not know whether Wroth's play was composed before or after Lord Denny warned her to "repent" her writing of "lascivious tales and amorous toyes" and instead follow "the rare, and pious example of your vertuous and learned Aunt, who translated so many godly books and especially the holly psalmes of David" (cited from Wroth, 1983, 238–9). But we can see that the warning is full of historical ironies. Denny has apparently forgotten that among the books Mary Sidney translated was Garnier's drama about a passionate illicit romance. Wroth's *Love's Victory* harks back to her aunt's *Antonius* in a curious way: Wroth takes her aunt's tragedy, which had ended in Cleopatra's highly eroticized death scene, and rewrites it as a tragicomedy where the lovers' death turns out to be a theatrical illusion that only appears to "sacrifice" their bodies on an altar symbolizing (among other things) the laws of dynastic marriage.

In the baroquely pagan (or, from a Protestant perspective, papist) death scene, Venus' priests act as a Chorus calling for justice on Silvesta, the perpetrator of the supposed murder but in truth the agent of the plot's happy ending. The priests' final line, "Death she procured, and for death, life shall give," ironically echoes Mary Sidney's rendering of de Mornay's final advice in the treatise printed with her *Antonius*: "Die to live, Live to die" (*A Discourse of Life and Death*, cited in Beilin, 1987, 128). Under the authority of those priests, Venus, Cupid, and the shadowy figures of Wroth herself, as Musella and Silvesta, Mary Sidney in her allegorical guises is made to witness a love-death transformed into life. She thus is symbolically persuaded to imitate her own Cleopatra by putting the laws of love above all others. Here, those beneficent laws conspicuously include children as well as erotic partners. Henceforth, according to the play, the mother will paradoxically censor the speech society approves, while allowing free utterance to the speech that gives joy to "mine owne."

Even Wroth's verse forms underscore the theme of coupling: her characters speak in rhyming couplets of iambic trimeter, tetrameter, and pentameter; and sometimes lines are divided between two lovers. Urging Musella to live despite his own (imagined) death, Philisses says, "You may be happy." Musella finishes the next five syllables of the pentameter line by turning his supposition into an incredulous question: "Happy without thee?" The poetry is full of echo-effects, in its own movements and in its complex allusions to literary and historical subtexts. Through its allusive tactics, it provides a kind of analogue for a principle of speech enunciated by Wroth's Musella: "[S]ometimes I faine would speake then straite forbeare / knowingt itt most unfitt," she remarks to Philisses (III.i. 77–8). Despite the many differences in their social visions, all three female writers studied here use versions of the rhetorical strategy Musella models in these lines: she wittily articulates a desire to speak something "unfit" and performatively fulfills that desire even as she gestures obediently toward the social rule whereby ladies should "forbear" from illicit speech.

Conclusion

Sidney, Cary, and Wroth are still not well known as writers. Those who do know Wroth's work tend to be more familiar with her love sonnets and the first part of the

Urania than they are with *Love's Victory* – or with the two masques in part II of the *Urania*. This is a text that was extant in only one manuscript until its publication in 1999. Clearly, Wroth's contribution to English drama must be considered slight if we measure it by sustained cultural presence in the form of books in print, or by the kind of "influences" recorded in standard literary histories. If, however, we allow for other historical lines of influence to emerge; and if we entertain an idea central both to feminist criticism and to the new historical or cultural materialist approaches to Renaissance literature that have flourished in the US and in the UK in the last few decades – the idea that our ability to "see" aspects of that foreign culture which is the past is always partly determined by our investments in the present – then we can read figures like Sidney, Cary, and Wroth with considerable interest and even with surprise at features of their writing unremarked by previous generations of readers.

A concluding example is Wroth's decision to include masques in the second (unpublished and unfinished) part of her *Urania*. One of these masques is presented by a black man, the King of Tartaria, who is described as supremely beautiful. He also acts as "one of the twelve masquers" in an allegorical representation of Honor triumphing over Cupid (Wroth, 1999, I, 46). Presented by the character whom the heroine Pamphilia eventually marries, in a coupling her society would have considered quite as shocking as Desdemona's with Othello, the black king's masque seems to allude to Wroth's own early role in the *Masque of Blackness*. Queen Anne, as recent feminist studies of the masque have suggested, should be considered one of the historical masque's co-creators, along with the scene designer Inigo Jones. Although modern readers know the masque as Ben Jonson's literary property, he himself credited his queen with the drama's "controlling idea": "Because it was her majesty's will to have them blackamores at first," Jonson wrote, "the invention was derived by me" (cited in Lewalski, 1993, 31; see also Wynne-Davies, 1992). Wroth, we might speculate, activated the bilingual pun in Jonson's term "black-amore" when she embedded the King of Tartaria's masque in *Urania*. Using the cultural capital given to her by her education in foreign tongues, as Sidney and Cary had also done in their dramatic exercises in cultural translation, Wroth constructed a play in which the black lover at once directs and takes part in the plot. Like his female author, he uses the conventional idea that Honor should triumph over Love to pursue unconventional ends, both political and erotic.

NOTES

1   For Mary Sidney's influence on Shakespeare's *Antony and Cleopatra*, see the editors' introduction to *Antonius* in Herbert (1998, 39–40).

2   On the land owned by the Sidney and Dudley families, see Hannay (1985, 153). For Wroth's biography, see Lewalski (1993, 243–307) and Waller (1993).

3   For Cary's biography, see the Introduction to Cary (1613/1994); this volume includes the daughter's biography, *The Lady Falkland: Her Life*. The quotation is from p. 188 and all references to *Mariam* are to this edition.

4 All citations are from *Antonius*, the 1592 text, in Sidney (1998); references henceforth given by line number.

5 For other treatments of the *Antony and Cleopatra* story, see Morrison (1974), Barroll (1984), Williamson (1979), and Hughes-Hallett (1990).

6 "Et qu'en un tel devoir mon corps affoiblissant / Defaille dessur vous, mon ame vomissant"; Garnier (1975, 166, l. 1999). All citations of the French text are from this edition.

7 "là, *Parler*, c'est *agir*": d'Aubignac, *Practique du theatre* 4. 11, cited in Braden (1985, 129).

8 See also Skretkowicz (1999), Straznicky (1994), and Hannay (1990) for (differing) interpretations of the play's political meanings.

9 On the Italian versions, see Herbert (1998, 139).

10 Straznicky provides a complete list of the "Sidnean" closet dramas (1998, 143).

11 On the pejorative connotations of the phrase, see Freer (1987).

12 The chapters of Lodge's translation relevant to Cary's play are reprinted in Cary (1613/1994, 277–82).

13 On the political implications of Cary's choice of genre, see Fischer (1985), Raber (1995), Shannon (1994), Straznicky (1994), and Gutierrez (1991).

14 For Musella as a figure for Wroth, see Wynne-Davies (1999, 49); for Musella as Penelope Rich, see McClaren (1990, 289–90).

15 All references to Wroth, *Love's Victory*, are to the edition by Cerasano and Wynne-Davies (Wroth, 1996).

16 Jonson mentions "Lady Wroth" as one of the persons to whom "names are given" in his unprinted "pastoral intitled the May Lord"; it is not known whether the pastoral was ever produced. See Lewalski (1993, 361 n. 31).

17 For evidence of a possible performance, see Brennan's edition of *Love's Victory* (Wroth, 1988, 13–14).

18 For a generally positive account of these relations, see Hannay (1991).

REFERENCES AND FURTHER READING

Barroll, J. Leeds (1984). *Shakespearean Tragedy: Genre, Tradition, and Change in Antony and Cleopatra*. Washington, DC. Folger Shakespeare Library.

Beauchamp V. W. (1957). "Sidney's sister as translator of Garnier." *Renaissance Notes* 10, 8–13.

Beilin, Elaine (1987). *Redeeming Eve: Women Writers of the English Renaissance*. Princeton: Princeton University Press.

Bradby, David (1995). "France." In *The Cambridge Guide to the Theater*, ed. Martin Bedham. Cambridge: Cambridge University Press.

Braden, Gordon (1985). *Renaissance Tragedy and the Senecan Tradition: Anger's Privilege*. New Haven: Yale University Press.

Brashear, Lucy (1976). "A case for the influence of Lady Cary's *Tragedy of Mariam* on Shakespeare's *Othello*." *Shakespeare Newsletter* 16, 31.

Brennan, Michael (1988). *Literary Patronage in the English Renaissance: The Pembroke Family*. London: Routledge.

Bullough, Geoffrey (1964). *Narrative and Dramatic Sources of Shakespeare*. London: Routledge.

Callaghan, Dympna (1994). "A re-reading of Elizabeth Cary's *The Tragedie of Mariam, Faire Queene of Jewry*." In *Women, Race, and Writing in the Early Modern Period*, eds Margo Hendricks and Patricia Parker. London: Routledge.

Cary, Elizabeth, Lady (1613/1914). *The Tragedie of Mariam,* eds A. C. Dunstan and W. W. Greg. London: Oxford University Press, *Malone Society Reprints*; repr. 1992, with "A supplement to the introduction" by Marta Straznicky and Richard Roland.

Cary, Elizabeth, Lady (1613/1994). *The Tragedy of Mariam, the Fair Queen of Jewry. With The Lady Falkland: Her Life. By One of Her Daughters*, eds Barry Weller and Margaret W. Ferguson. Berkeley: University of California Press.

Cerasano, S. P. and Marion Wynne-Davies, eds (1996). *Renaissance Drama by Women: Texts and Documents.* London: Routledge.

Clarke, Danielle (1997). "The politics of translation and gender in the Countess of Pembroke's *Antonie*." *Translation and Literature* 6, 149–66.

Cotton, Nancy (1980). *Women Playwrights of England, c.1363–1750.* Lewisburg, PA: Bucknell University Press.

Davies, John (1612/1878, repr. 1967). *The Muses Sacrifice.* In *The Complete Works* of John Davies of Hereford, ed. Alexander B. Grosart. New York: AMS Press.

Ferguson, Margaret (1991). "Running on with almost public voice: the case of E.C." In *Tradition and the Talents of Women*, ed. Florence Howe. Urbana and Chicago: University of Illinois Press.

Findlay, Alison, Gweno Williams, and Stephanie J. Hodgson-Wright (1999). "'The play is ready to be acted': women and dramatic production, 1570–1670." *Women's Writing* 6, 129–48.

Fischer, Sandra K. (1985). "Elizabeth Cary and tyranny, domestic and religious." In *Silent But for the Word: Tudor Women as Patrons, Translators, and Writers of Religious Works*, ed. Margaret Hannay. Kent, OH: Kent State University Press.

Freer, Coburn (1987) "Mary Sidney: Countess of Pembroke." In *Women Writers of the Renaissance and Reformation*, ed. Katharina M. Wilson. Athens: University of Georgia Press.

Garnier, Robert (1975). *Two Tragedies, Hippolyte and Marc Antoine*, eds Christine M. Hill and Mary G. Morrison. London: Athlone Press.

Guttierrez, Nancy (1991). "Valuing *Mariam*: genre study and feminist analysis." *Tulsa Studies in Women's Literature* 10, 233–51.

Hannay, Margaret P. (1985). "'Doo what men may sing': Mary Sidney and the tradition of admonitory dedication." In *Silent But for the Word: Tudor Women as Patrons, Writers, and Translators of Religious Works*, ed. Margaret Hannay. Kent, OH: Kent State University Press.

Hannay, Margaret P. (1990). *Philip's Phoenix: Mary Sidney, Countess of Pembroke.* Oxford: Oxford University Press.

Hannay, Margaret P. (1991). "'Your vertuous and learned Aunt': the Countess of Pembroke as mentor to Mary Wroth." In *Reading Mary Wroth: Representing Alternatives in Early Modern England*, eds Naomi J. Miller and Gary Waller. Knoxville: University of Tennessee Press.

Heinemann, Margot (1990). "Political drama." In *The Cambridge Companion to English Renaissance Drama*, eds A. R. Braunmuller and Michael Hattaway. Cambridge: Cambridge University Press.

Herbert, Mary Sidney, Countess of Pembroke (1998). *The Collected Works of Mary Sidney Herbert, Countess of Pembroke*, Vol. 1, *Poems, Translations, and Correspondence*, eds Margaret P. Hannay, Noel J. Kinnamon, and Michael G. Brennan. Oxford: Clarendon Press.

Hughes-Hallett, Lucy (1990). *Cleopatra: Histories, Dreams and Distortions.* New York: Harper & Row.

Hull, Suzanne (1982). *Chaste, Silent, and Obedient: English Books for Women, 1475–1640.* San Marino: Huntington Library.

Jondorf, Gillian (1969). *Robert Garnier and the Themes of Political Tragedy in the Sixteenth Century.* Cambridge: Cambridge University Press.

Jones, Anne Rosalind (1986). "Surprising fame: Renaissance gender ideologies and women's lyric." In *The Poetics of Gender*, ed. Nancy K. Miller. New York: Columbia University Press.

Jones, Anne Rosalind (1990). *The Currency of Eros: Women's Love Lyric in Europe, 1540–1620.* Bloomington, IN: Indiana University Press.

Kegl, Rosemary (1999). "Theaters, households, and a 'Kind of History' in Elizabeth Cary's *The Tragedy of Mariam*." In *Enacting Gender on the English Renaissance Stage*, eds Viviana Comensoli and Anne Russell. Urbana and Chicago: University of Illinois Press.

Krontiris, Tina (1992). *Oppositional Voices: Women as Writers and as Translators of Literature in the English Renaissance.* New York: Routledge.

Lamb, Mary Ellen (1981a). *Gender and Authorship in the Sidney Circle*. Madison: University of Wisconsin Press.

Lamb, Mary Ellen (1981b). "The myth of the Countess of Pembroke: the dramatic circle." *Yearbook of English Studies* 11, 104–202.

Lewalski, Barbara K. (1991). "Mary Wroth's *Love's Victory* and pastoral tragicomedy." In *Reading Mary Wroth: Representing Alternatives in Early Modern England*, eds Naomi J. Miller and Gary Waller. Knoxville: University of Tennessee Press.

Lewalski, B. K. (1993) *Writing Women in Jacobean England*. Cambridge, MA: Harvard University Press.

McClaren, Margaret Anne (1990). "An unknown continent: Lady Mary Wroth's forgotten pastoral drama, *Loves Victorie*." In *The Renaissance Englishwoman in Print: Counterbalancing the Canon*, eds Anne M. Haselkorn and Betty Travitsky. Amherst, MA: University of Massachusetts Press.

Morrison, Mary (1974). "Some aspects of the treatment of the theme of *Antony and Cleopatra* in tragedies of the sixteenth century." *Journal of European Studies* 4, 113–25.

Pearse, Nancy Cotton (1976–7). "Elizabeth Cary, Elizabethan playwright." *Texas Studies in Language and Literature* 18, 601–7.

Purkiss, Diane (1999). "Blood, sacrifice, marriage: why Iphigeneia and Mariam have to die." *Women's Writing* 6, 47–64.

Quilligan, Maureen (1989). "Lady Mary Wroth: female authority and the family romance." In *Unfolded Tales: Essays on Renaissance Romance*, eds George M. Logan and Gordon Teskey. Ithaca: Cornell University Press.

Raber, Karen L. (1995). "Gender and the political subject in *The Tragedy of Mariam*." *Studies in English Literature* 35, 321–43.

Sanders, Eve Rachele (1998). *Gender and Literacy on Stage in Early Modern England*. Cambridge: Cambridge University Press.

Shannon, Laurie J. (1994). "*The Tragedie of Mariam*: Cary's critique of the terms of founding social discourses." *English Literary Renaissance* 24, 135–53.

Sidney, Mary, trans. (1592). *Antonius. A Tragedie written also in French by Ro. Garnier*. London.

Sidney, Philip (1970). *An Apology for Poetry*, ed. Forrest Robinson. Indianapolis: Bobbs Merrill.

Skretkowicz, Victor (1999). "Mary Sidney Herbert's Antonius, English philhellenism and the Protestant cause." *Women's Writing* 6, 7–26.

Straznicky, Marta (1994). "Profane Stoical paradoxes: *The Tragedy of Mariam* and Sidnean closet drama." *English Literary Renaissance* 24, 104–34.

Straznicky, Marta (1998). "Recent studies in closet drama." *English Literary Renaissance* 29, 142–60.

Swift, Carolyn Ruth (1989). "A feminine self-definition in Lady Mary Wroth's *Loves Victorie* (c.1621)." *English Literary Renaissance* 19, 171–88.

Trill, Suzanne (1996). "Sixteenth-century women's writing: Mary Sidney's *Psalms* and the 'femininity' of translation." In *Writing and the English Renaissance*, eds William Zunder and Suzanne Trill. London and New York: Longman.

Valency, Maurice Jacques (1940). *The Tragedies of Herod and Mariamne*. New York: Columbia University Press.

Walker, Kim (1996). *Women Writers of the English Renaissance*. New York: Twayne.

Waller, Gary (1979). *Mary Sidney, Countesse of Pembroke, a Critical Study of her Writing and Literary Milieu*. Salzburg: Salzburg Studies in English Literature.

Waller, Gary F. (1993). *The Sidney Family Romance; Mary Wroth, William Herbert, and the Early Modern Construction of Gender*. Detroit: Wayne State University Press.

Westfall Suzanne (1990). *Patrons and Performance: Early Tudor Household Revels*. Oxford: Clarendon Press.

Williamson, Marilyn (1974). *Infinite Variety: Antony and Cleopatra in Renaissance Drama and Earlier Tradition*. Mystic, CT: Lawrence Verry.

Wroth, Lady Mary (1933). *Loves Victorie*, ed. C. H. J. Maxwell. M.A. thesis, Stanford University, 1933. [An edition of the incomplete Huntington ms. (HM 600).]

Wroth, Lady Mary (1983). *Poems*, ed. Josephine A. Roberts. Baton Rouge: Lousiana State University Press.

Wroth, Lady Mary (1988). *Lady Mary Wroth's Love's Victory*, ed. Michael G. Brennan. London: Roxburghe Club. [An edition of the Penshurst ms.]

Wroth, Lady Mary (1996). *Love's Victory*. In *Renaissance Drama by Women: Texts and Documents*, eds S. P. Cerasano and Marion Wynne-Davies. London: Routledge.

Wroth, Lady Mary (1999). *The Second Part of the Countess of Montgomery's Urania*, ed. Josephine Roberts, completing eds Suzanne Gossett and Janel Mueller. Medieval and Renaissance Texts and Studies, xxiv. Tempe, AZ: Renaissance English Text Society in conjunction with Arizona Center for Medieval and Renaissance Studies.

Wynne-Davies, Marion (1992). "The Queen's Masque: Renaissance women and the seventeenth-century court masque." In *Gloriana's Face: Women, Public and Private, in the English Renaissance*, eds S. P. Cerasano and M. Wynne Davies. Hemel Hempstead: Harvester Press.

Wynne-Davies, Marion (1999). "'Here is a sport will well befit this time and place': allusion and delusion in Mary Wroth's *Love's Victory*." *Women's Writing* 6, 147–63.

34

Thomas Middleton
John Jowett

Thomas Middleton wrote an acerbic and skeptical drama that spanned the genres of city comedy, tragicomedy, and tragedy. His intense social awareness, his concentration on urban life, his commitment to explore the harsher aspects of human behavior, his exposure of ideology and sentiment, and his acceptance of discontinuities in experience and self-hood – these are among the characteristics that give him a special significance. Against the model of Shakespeare as universal genius may be set the model of Middleton as a dramatist of unremitting focus on his own times and so, indirectly, of particular relevance to ours.

Criticism of Middleton has often found him a writer hard to comprehend except in fragments. To T. S. Eliot, he was virtually a personification of the inscrutable author, a writer "who has no message; he is merely a great recorder"; his name almost arbitrarily binds together a handful of great plays (1951, 169–70). This admiration for an essential passivity can be found too in more recent criticism that engages with historical and cultural approaches. For Richard Dutton, Middleton is "a voice of the tensions between an earlier festive culture and an evolving competitive work ethic, of new economic and social structures rubbing shoulders with those of the old landed gentry, of the old oral and scribal culture coexisting alongside the world of print, of deeply spiritual anxieties running through a time intensely attuned to material and sensual realities" (1999, xv–xvi). Middleton is typically a reticent, anonymous, and unfetishized author figure who differs radically in kind from a self-promoting one such as Ben Jonson. The present attempt to define what is particular to Middleton's contribution to early modern drama is set in tension with that passivity, a tension that is in itself Middletonian.

Life and Works

Middleton was shaped by a city and a family. He was born in London in 1580. His father, a thriving businessman and member of the Tilers' and Bricklayers' Company, died when his son was six, leaving his mother Anne a prosperous widow. She remarried disastrously to a younger man named Thomas Harvey. The following years brought Middleton into close quarters with the harsh economic realities that could confront women. Anne lost control of her own estate to her impoverished, litigious, and opportunistic new husband, and struggled over many years to protect her children's inheritance from him. Middleton was brought up in an environment of domestic turmoil and lawsuits, interrupted only when his stepfather was in prison or at sea. The effect on him must have been considerable, and it can perhaps be traced in his plays. Most specifically, the plot involving Fidelio, Castiza, and the Captain in the early play *The Phoenix* (1603–4) seems to have been influenced by Middleton's early experiences, and his wider skepticism toward sexual and financial relationships may have been shaped here too.

At the age of 17 he set out as a poet of precocious gravitas by writing a long verse paraphrase of *The Wisdom of Solomon* (1597). The following year he entered Queen's College, Oxford, to begin the only period of his life when, as far as is known, he was not resident in London or its environs. Middleton sold his patrimony in order to finance his studies, but left Oxford with his education incomplete; by 1601 he was reported to be in London, "daylie accompaninge the players."

He thus became a professional writer at the lower end of the London literary marketplace: satirist, pamphlet-writer, and dramatist. As with many playwrights of his generation, his earliest dramatic writing was for the Lord Admiral's Men. Here Middleton learned to write both in collaboration and single-handedly. One Middleton play mentioned in the financial manager Philip Henslowe's *Diary* survives: "the pasyent man & the onest hore" (*The Patient Man and the Honest Whore*, more familiar as *1 Honest Whore*), which was written in collaboration with Thomas Dekker in 1604 and printed in the same year.

Middleton showed himself to be an innovator in the series of city comedies he wrote single-handedly for the boys' companies such as the Children of Paul's in the early years of the seventeenth century. Where earlier city plays such as Dekker's *The Shoemakers' Holiday* had been typically sentimental celebrations of London citizenry, Middleton made the genre a vehicle for wit and satire. In plays such as *Michaelmas Term* (1604–6), *A Mad World, My Masters* (1605–6), *A Trick to Catch the Old One* (c.1605), and *The Puritan Widow* (1606) he dissected the economic and sexual life of contemporary London. By 1607 the boy companies were closed or in decline (see chapter 22 above); later, however, in 1613 Middleton revived the genre for an adult company, Lady Elizabeth's Men, in *A Chaste Maid in Cheapside*. This, one of Middleton's best-known and finest plays, combines a brilliant complexity of plot structure with a Rabelaisian poetics of the consuming and leaking body. A labyrinthine vision of eroticized humanity contends with a depiction of an aggressively expanding commercial marketplace that treats people as commodities (Wells, 1981, 58). Middleton would return again to depicting city life in a late comedy written with John Webster, *Anything for a Quiet Life* (1621), a play dealing with clothes as the most obvious marker of class, and with the trade in clothing.

However, Middleton diversified after the collapse of the boys' companies by writing different kinds of plays, sometimes with new collaborators and for different companies. His most immediate turn was to writing tragedy, where he diversified from the early Senecan experiment with Dekker in *The Bloody Banquet* (*c.*1601–3). For the King's Men he supplied a share in the otherwise Shakespearean study of misanthropy, *Timon of Athens* (*c.*1605), the intense little domestic drama of *A Yorkshire Tragedy* (1605–6), and the crazily violent and witty *sprezzatura* of *The Revenger's Tragedy* (*c.*1606; see chapter 23 above). A few years later, in 1611, the same company performed his *The Lady's Tragedy*, a play Algernon Swinburne would later describe as a "strange and strangely beautiful tragic poem."

Middleton's most stable longer-term professional affiliation proved to be not with any single theater company but with the city of London. Like Jonson and Webster, Middleton was a Londoner by birth and upbringing; his plays focused on London life to an extent that even Jonson could scarcely rival. Here the world inhabited by the audience and the world shown on the stage are brought into sometimes startling proximity. His 1611 collaboration with Dekker, *The Roaring Girl*, was a fictionalized celebration of the notorious London low-life personality Mary Frith, known as Moll Cutpurse. She apparently herself showed up at the Fortune theater, where, according to the *Consistory of London Correction Book*, she "sat there vppon the stage in the publique viewe of all the people there *presente* in mans apparrell & playd vppon her lute & sange a songe."

Elsewhere Middleton marked the more formal aspects of London's here-and-now. As of 1613, the year of *Chaste Maid*, he began regularly to write civic pageants, elaborate and emblematic processional shows that celebrated the city before street audiences of thousands (Bergeron, 1971; see chapter 21 above). In the hands of Dekker, Anthony Munday, and especially Middleton, they inculcated a sense of civic consciousness at a time when London was widely felt to be a predatory city that inflicted deprivation, dearth, and social chaos (Paster, 1985). The pageants seek to disperse some of the anxieties about alienation within the civic community and economic insecurity that had been reflected in the city comedies (see chapter 25 above). In 1620 Middleton was appointed City Chronologer, responsible for recording the contemporary history of London and consolidating its traditions.

Middleton's mature playwriting ran alongside his commitments to the city, although it does not always reflect city matters in any obvious way. Indeed, another concern suggests itself. Play titles such as *The Roaring Girl*, *No Wit/Help like a Woman's* (1611), *Chaste Maid*, *The Widow* (1615 or later), *The Witch* (*c.*1616), and *More Dissemblers Besides Women* (1619?) reflect an interest in questions of gender, often drawing on the Jacobean pro-female/misogynist debates on the role and nature of women (Woodbridge, 1984). The list can be expanded to include the scrutiny of male roles and masculinity in plays such as *The Patient Man and the Honest Whore* and Middleton and Thomas Rowley's tragicomedy of duelling, *A Fair Quarrel* (1616–17). The later tragedies, *Hengist King of Kent* (1619–20), *Women Beware Women* (1621?), and *The Changeling* (again with Rowley, 1622) all sustain this focus on gender. *Hengist* is a history play dealing with the Saxon invasion of England, though the theme of sexual violence takes the foreground for much of the play. *Women Beware Women* reverts to the fantasy Italy of lust and murder at court that Middleton had already presented spectacularly in *The Revenger's Tragedy* and *The Witch*. Yet in this play, and even more so in *The Changeling*, the extravagance is strongly tempered by a sense of material and psychological reality. Apparently ordinary people, men and women leading mundane lives, get drawn into inner and outer maelstroms that they would not have thought possible.

Politics, in a broad sense of the word, runs persistently through all Middleton's representations of civic and courtly life (Heinemann, 1980; Chakravorty, 1996). Yet in the early seventeenth century the distinctly modern politics of political parties and public campaigns over contentious issues had scarcely begun. Middleton contributed in some measure to their inception. In his masque *The World Tossed at Tennis* (1620), commissioned by Prince Charles to entertain his father King James, Middleton espoused the Protestant cause in Europe, urging the king to abandon his cautious pacifism. Middleton's last known state play, *A Game at Chess* (1624), has the actors play out a game in which the black chess-pieces represent the Catholics and the white pieces the Protestant English; Philip of Spain and James of England are the respective kings. The play is a scathingly funny account of political intrigue, painting harsh, caricatured portraits of leading Catholic statesmen (Cogswell, 1984; Howard-Hill, 1995). Most notable is the Spanish Ambassador Gondomar, and the King's Men achieved a scatalogical *coup de théâtre* when they managed to obtain the "chair of ease" designed to give the ambassador relief from his anal fistula. The merciless and sometimes cruel humor affirms Middleton's capacity to suggest that the most bizarre moments of theatrical invention have a correlative in authentic social life. The play was a London sensation until it was closed down. Middleton died about three years later, in 1627.

An Elusive Canon

Unlike those of Shakespeare, Jonson, and Beaumont and Fletcher, Middleton's works were never gathered together in prestigious folio format. With the exception of the civic pageants, they were published haphazardly, if at all. It is symptomatic that he is probably the only unacknowledged dramatist whose writing was smuggled into both the Shakespeare Folio of 1623 and the Beaumont and Fletcher Folio of 1647 (see chapter 35 below). The latter is an authorially indiscriminate gathering, and *The Nice Valour* (1615–16) and *Wit at Several Weapons* (*c*.1613) are both now attributed to Middleton, the latter along with Rowley (Jackson, 1979). As for Shakespeare's more rigorously canonical Folio of 1623, Middleton's hand in *Timon of Athens* makes him the only playwright thought to have collaborated with Shakespeare between his early works and the late Shakespeare–Fletcher plays. Middleton is also, as far as we know, the only dramatist whom the King's Men entrusted to revise a Shakespeare play, and he did so twice. The introduction of the Hecate scenes into *Macbeth* has long been attributed to Middleton, revising the play in about 1616. He evidently also made alterations to *Measure for Measure* in 1621. Lucio and his companions' discussion of the impending peace with the king of Hungary in act I, scene ii, reflects an engagement with the politics of the Thirty Years War that has already been noted in *The World Tossed at Tennis* and *A Game at Chess*. The curious seepage of Middleton's writing into Shakespeare's would continue: *A Yorkshire Tragedy* and *The Puritan Widow* (1606) found their way into the supplementary "Apocrypha" collection in the 1664 edition of the Shakespeare Folio.

Although Middleton as a living writer had a determinate literary output, no one, with the doubtful exception of Middleton himself, would have been able to conceptualize that output as an authorial canon. Over a third of his extant plays were written in collaboration with Dekker, Rowley, and others. For an early modern professional dramatist this is not in itself exceptional, but it compounds with other factors. First editions of Middleton's plays were spread over six decades (1604–62). Most plays ran to only one or two editions, and so would have been unavailable when later works came out. The "Middleton" available in print in one decade would therefore differ radically from that in another. Moreover, at any one time only a minority of his writing in print would be identified as his. Important works such as *Chaste Maid*, *Hengist*, *The Changeling*, and *Women Beware Women* were not printed until after Middleton's death, and two extant plays, *The Witch* and *The Lady's Tragedy*, survive only in manuscript. Plays such as *The Bloody Banquet*, *The Revenger's Tragedy*, *A Yorkshire Tragedy*, and *The Lady's Tragedy* were unattributed or misattributed in the early texts, and indeed were not attributed to Middleton with any confidence until the 1950s. A number of works are certainly lost.

Modern scholarship is still grappling with the problems of establishing the corpus of writing that falls under the heading "Middleton." Few authors have been transformed as radically by redefinition of the range of their works (Lake, 1975). The Oxford *Collected Works* (Middleton, 2002) defines the canon for the purposes of this chapter and is the source for quotations. But in the edition the term "Middleton" remains provisional and open-ended. The edition's focus on the theatrical and textual culture in which his works appeared aims to break the very authorial boundary that it might seem to assume.

Realism and Religion

Critics attempting to define the specific qualities of Middleton's work have often drawn attention to a realism appropriate to an urban writer. It can be found in the casual but symptomatic details of material existence: references to cups and spoons, to satin and velvet, to laces and cushions, to pewter and silver, to rings and chains of pearls, to tennis courts and battledores, to comfits and fools, to dice and tobacco. These and countless other details are perceived not only as things in the world, but also as the elements of social life, the means whereby people define themselves in relation to others; they are objects of aspiration, objects that are significant to acquire whether by theft or by exchange. Goods are in circulation; people are jostling to display them or conspicuously to consume them. Money figures prominently, often in specifically numbered sums, and most frequently in the form of debts, bonds, and inheritances.

Material goods therefore provide the physical furnishings for Middleton's social realism, but also underpin it by virtue of their symbolic function, for the objects emblematize something about the figures who own or aspire to them or about the process of exchange in which they take part. The chain of pearls in *Your Five Gallants*, an expensive material object in its own right, doubles as a potential token of love that foretells erotic reward, and also as a symbol of the irregular circulation of commodities through trickery, exchange for sexual favors, and theft. It is always in transition of one kind or another to a new owner, and, as its own circular form suggests, it will eventually return to its starting point. This symbolic dimension of the material object is one means whereby Middleton opens onto other realms of realism: psychosexual realism, the fetishization of material objects, conflict and competition. The materialism that begins with objects ends in people as self-interested materialist beings.

But Middleton goes further than portraying a society of acquisitive Hobbesian automatons. From a Christian point of view, to desire, or to deprive, or to take pride in possession is an act of sin. Whether a religious perspective constitutes the ultimate truth may not be clear, for such habits of thought may, even to Middleton in early Jacobean England, have seemed in danger of becoming disturbingly beside the point. What matters is that Middleton's emblematic language enables him not only to represent an acquisitive and materialist society, but also to find a religious and ethical way of thinking about it.

A diction arising from a dark, obsessive Calvinism is threaded throughout Middleton's work (Stachniewski, 1990). It can be seen at its strongest in his early non-dramatic verse:

> O see destruction hovering o'er thy head,
> Mantling herself in wickedness' array,
> Hoping to make thy body as her bed,
> Thy vice her nutriment, thy soul her prey.
> Thou hast forsaken him that was thy guide,
> And see what follows to assuage thy pride.
>   (*The Wisdom of Solomon*
>   *Paraphrased*, ll. 109–14)

What anticipates the style of Middleton's more mature dramatic writing is the interweaving of abstraction and concrete physical detail relating to the human body. The dichotomy between body and soul is always apparent in Christianity, though at critical moments it can be dissolved so that the spiritual condition is made manifest on the body. The abstract idea "destruction" in the passage quoted is not only an abstract metaphor; the abstraction is overlaid with connotations of the supposedly real physical torments of hell.

But the image also has a classical resonance; the hovering female devourer is implicitly a Vergilian harpy, like the terrifying figure that snatches away the banquet in Shakespeare's *The Tempest*. Her intention to devour the body has further connotations of a sexually aggressive woman who will "make thy body as her bed" in quite another sense. There is, then, a complete interflux between the concrete act and its moral meaning, within an imaginative world that is at once Calvinist, misogynist, and perhaps, as a consequence, deeply neurotic. Middleton's ability to ironize and theatricalize such obsession would come later, but the habit of thought is recurrent. At the end of *Women Beware Women* the Duke laments that "Upon the first night of our nuptial honours, / Destruction play her triumph."

Irony and Verbal Puns

Early plays such as *A Trick to Catch the Old One* cleverly juxtapose different styles, such as Juvenalian satire (as modified by Thomas Nashe, and as attempted by Middleton in *The Black Book*, 1604), the intricate witty plotting of Roman comedy (which throws the emphasis of city comedy away from the artisans and onto the figure of the young gentleman trickster), and the tradition of the morality play (seen in character names such as Lucre, Hoard, and, more ominously, Dampit). The distinctive wit of Middleton's language arises typically through a kind of code-switching, between the moment and its meaning, the material and the emblematic, cynically indulgent acceptance and moralistic outrage, festivity and disgust. The quality of style for which Middleton is best known is irony. That is precisely what emerges where one style or one discourse rubs up against another.

Irony is dialogic, for it happens when the hearer is made to hold two (or more) perspectives at once. Irony is dangerous, because it empowers with voice the perspective that is positioned as unethical; it is the reprehensible figure who has utterance in the first instance. This opens up the troublesome possibility that the ironist is not the author making an implied comment on the speaker, but the actual speaker. At the point where the speaker has control over the ironic meanings, the text swerves vertiginously toward amorality. By such a reading the usurer exults in his viciousness, the duke exults in his power over the woman; they do it knowingly, they enjoy it, and they use it to enforce their power over the victim. If we read Middleton as a cynic, we will say that he shows these figures outrageously defying the moral codes to which they allude, and that the pleasure of the text lies in our enjoying their shocking cynicism. If we read Middleton as a didactic satirist, we will insist that irony exposes the rapacity of the speaker, and our enjoyment is to appreciate how limited an understanding the characters have of it. But how can we tell how far the speaker controls the language he uses, or how far the ironization flows through him so that he stands accidentally condemned in his own words? It would be absurd to try to determine in each and every case.

Even in the midst of high cynicism the suggestions of mortal consequence cannot be ignored. The sensuality of the moment can become loaded with implication of the utmost seriousness, as when Livia in *Women Beware Women* justifies her connivance in the seduction of Bianca by aligning sinful sexual pleasure with the bliss of heaven: "Sin tastes at the first draught like wormwood-water, / But, drunk again, 'tis nectar ever after" (*Women Beware Women*, II.ii.475–6). Throughout Middleton, images of touching, tasting, and swallowing all veer between the consumption of food, sexual pleasure, and the dangers of sin – haunted, perhaps, by the warning in the Anglican Holy Communion service that those who take the Communion without repenting their sins "eat and drink our own damnation." That sound likes a Middletonian thought, which is to say both that Middleton writes on the back of early modern religious language, and that we can read the Prayer Book differently as a consequence of reading Middleton. The Middletonian shadow of seriousness that is punningly cast over flippant or everyday language in his plays is of uncertain definition and coloration: it might be a mere glance, the slightest breeze disturbing the glassy surface of everyday reality. And it is an effect of wit. It is metaphysical in the sense of intimating a level of reality beyond the mundane and the everyday; and also metaphysical in the sense applied to John Donne's poetry, of involving mental dexterity and cleverness. That element of wit can only add to the overall indeterminacy of the point of view. Irony resists secure interpretation because there is a structural insecurity in the way Middleton uses it.

Middleton's puns are a special case of irony. A statement belonging to one discursive realm suddenly lurches into another, or rather collides with another. Christopher Ricks has written brilliantly on the various pressures applied to specific individual words. In *The Changeling*, terms such as "servant," "serve," and "service" revolve around the connotations of the chivalric lover, the household servant, and the town bull, as De Flores and Beatrice-Joanna negotiate their relationship (Ricks, 1960). Ricks indicates the care and precision of Middleton's deployment of such words.

Yet the sheer density of sexual and scatalogical innuendo is one of the most obvious features of Middleton's language. Perhaps not surprisingly, the speakers are usually (though not always) male. The effect is often distanced from any possibility of homosocial bonding with the male members of the audience; the humor is conditional, often at the speaker's expense. When Allwit in *Chaste Maid* wishes to give an example of how he enjoys material benefits such as a good supply of fuel for burning as a result of his wife's affair with Sir Walter Whorehound, he says:

> Look in my backyard, I shall find a steeple
> Made up with Kentish faggots, which o'erlooks
> The water-house and the windmills; I say nothing,
> But smile and pin the door.
>   (*A Chaste Maid in Cheapside*, I.ii.25–30)

The water-house and the windmills are mentioned as prominent physical structures on the cityscape of London, two sources of essential supplies. The steeple is the spire of the church that traditionally dominates the village or, as in this case, the city. According to Allwit it continues to do so despite competition from newer industrial buildings (the water-house for the "New River," a canal bringing an improved water supply to the city, was opened in the same year as Middleton wrote this play). But Allwit is not describing a steeple; his house is no church. On the contrary, it represents a combination of sinful sexual activity and material prosperity; it is in effect an exclusive brothel, and there is obvious irony in its having the equivalent of a church steeple. The moralized cityscape also incorporates elements of the lower human body. Within this frame of allusion, the water-house and the windmills allude to the parts of the body that produce urine and flatulence, just as one might speak of "water-works" and a "wind tunnel" today. The new steeple Sir Walter Whorehound has erected in Allwit's backyard is unignorably phallic, and the "backyard" itself has an unmistakable anal connotation. So the urogenital and anal regions of the body – Allwit's body, his wife's body, the collective symbolic body of their household – are dominated by the intrusive presence of the phallus. As Allwit complacently bolts the gate of his backyard, he contains the intruding steeple of faggots securely within the geography and economy of his household.

If the pun enables Middleton to apprehend simultaneously two (or more) different conceptualizations of the material world, references to the spiritual can operate in exactly the same way. That is, they equivocate between a realm of religious experience and a world whose very materiality is an affront to religion. The nuances can be quiet compared with a scatalogical pun. In the second scene of *More Dissemblers* a group of lords enter and draw back a curtain to reveal the Lord Cardinal seated at his books. He greets them saying:

> My lords, I have work for you. When you have hours
> Free from the cares of state, bestow your eyes
> Upon those abstracts of the Duchess' virtues,
> My study's ornaments. I make her constancy
> The holy mistress of my contemplation.
> Whole volumes have I writ in zealous praise
> Of her eternal vow. . . .
> [*Rising*] Here I stand up in admiration,
> And bow to the chaste health of our great Duchess,
> Kissing her constant name.
> (*More Dissemblers Besides Women*, I.ii.1–15)

Things, and indeed people, have been placed within a mentality of abstraction: "virtues," "constancy," "chaste health," and "constant name." The Cardinal's "holy mistress" might be thought of as the saintly opposite of the harpy Middleton described in *The Wisdom of Solomon Paraphrased*. She is an object of veneration, not just saintly in herself but constituted as saintly through acts of pious contemplation and "zealous praise." When the Cardinal kisses her "constant name," the phrase works as a kind of declined opportunity for punning along the lines of Hamlet's "country matters." Instead, he is kissing the pile of books he has written in praise of her: "those abstracts of the Duchess' virtues, / My study's ornaments." The Duchess is at once fetishized and disembodied: the Cardinal has *abstract*ed her key essence from her person and realized it in the form of writing, of material signifiers that in themselves become the objects of veneration. "Kiss the book" is a phrase that usually relates to the Bible. Here the Cardinal's writings replace the Bible, and the Duchess herself replaces God. The speech implies a strong and parodic critique of Catholicism, and the Cardinal's speech stands at the threshold of open hypocrisy. Beneath the spoken surface, linguistic and erotic anarchy stands ready to burst forth, as it does freely elsewhere in this play when the punning becomes explicit and runs to excess.

It is possible to think of Middleton's languages as working on a premise of repression: things that should not be articulated and are given no formal space in the economy of speech nevertheless keep bubbling up and making themselves visible. In some situations it is primarily the libido that is denied but that cannot ultimately be repressed; in others, it might be anxieties or convictions associated with a religious sensibility. The suggestion is that things underneath or beyond are unignorable, and are seriously different from their apparent surface.

Along with the characteristics noted here, one might recognize the sheer uncontainable ridiculousness of Middleton's humor; the casual but idiomatically energetic conversational surface that he produces with strainless ease; the exuberant use of languages: Latin, Dutch, Italian, Spanish, Welsh, Gypsy, and utter nonsense; and the concrete everyday detail mentioned above. All add to the Rabelaisian excess of Middleton's writing, which resists any Jonsonian sense of classical decorum. All contribute to an undercurrent of an anarchic, festive laughter that sometimes borders on horror and hysteria. In contrast there is the limpid and nervously isolated transparency of poetic language that so impressed Swinburne and Eliot. Throughout, Middleton's writing shows more interest in collisions than in messages. Its frisson lies in that vertiginous quality of leaving us not quite sure where we are.

Visual Puns and Dramatic Technique

In one sense, of course, we are in the theater. And comparable properties characterize Middleton's use of theatrical space. Space emblematizes human relationships. Middleton resists centered groupings so as to explore the stage as a site for separation, either as isolation or as a disharmonious composition of separate elements. Different voices reading the same encounter differently constitute a macrocosmic version of the pun. The result is a kind of alienation that, as much as Middleton's anti-sentimental and political reading of human situations, has analogies with the theater of Bertolt Brecht.

R. V. Holdsworth has drawn attention to the use of repeated kisses in *Women Beware Women* to build up a picture of "estrangement and betrayal" (1990, 250), and he notes ironic patterning through tableaus such as the Duke looking up to Bianca at her window during his procession through the city. Examples of two characters who articulate their separation rather than communicate together are numerous. To take one case, the second act of *A Game at Chess* opens with the naive and pious White Queen's Pawn reading a book that, though devotional, is designed to corrupt her. It is a Jesuit work urging obedience to the commands of a confessor, and the Black Bishop's Pawn has fed it to her. The latter at once enters to overhear her as she meditates on this advice. Staying, presumably, some distance from her so as to remain unnoticed, he congratulates himself that "She's hard upon't." But before he can accost her he stumbles upon a text of his own to read, a sealed note that is addressed to him. In it, the Black King notes his "late intelligence" of the Black Bishop's Pawn's schemes, and urges him to follow up his intended seduction of the White Queen's Pawn by using her as an instrument in the king's own designs on the White Queen herself, "whose fall or prostitution our lust most violently rages for." This larger political and sexual entrapment hinges on two parallel acts of reading that are taking place at the same time, both symptomatic of private self-dialogue. The moment has the erotic charge of voyeurism upon the white pawn's moment of private meditation and temptation. This combines with the overdetermination of desire as it stems from both the black pawn and his king. An encounter between the pawns will happen once their contrasted modes of thinking aloud give way to interaction. Meanwhile it is the alienated voices of the two readers that are presented.

The same technique, with variations, can be seen in encounters such as those between Isabella and Hippolito in *Women Beware Women*, or De Flores and Beatrice-Joanna in *The Changeling*. Often the dislocation between separate subjects is highly charged, but the apparently unresolvable conflicts of outlook and experience can also generate irony and even humor. The stage picture in *A Game at Chess* is itself ironic, and has qualities akin to a pun. It at once presents a man and a woman, a priest and a novice nun, a bad and a good, a subtle violator and an innocent victim. The action plays out psychosexually, politically, and theologically, all at the same time.

These are simple instances in terms of their staging, but the device of an ensemble scene used to stage social or existential fragmentation is just as characteristic. *No Wit/Help like a Woman's* is constructed around two such scenes. The first is a farcical banquet in which the staging takes its shape from Weatherwise's device of having the banqueting table arranged with emblematic place-settings based on the signs of the Zodiac. The guests cynically undermine the host, mocking his Zodiac conceit, and puncturing his efforts to court Lady Goldenfleece. His attempt politely to allegorize his guests is reduced to ridicule by their disruptive conversation. This episode is given further complexity when Mistress Low-water joins the feast disguised as an uninvited young gentleman. The second ensemble scene uses the comparably universalizing emblematic figure of the Four Elements in order, once again, to subvert it. This happens in the masque devised to mark the wedding of Lady Goldenfleece. The purpose of the masque as a celebration is never realized, because the masquers replace the script with their own speeches. They are Lady Goldenfleece's former suitors, who now use the masque as an opportunity to unleash their vicious denunciations. But the occasion is itself flawed from the outset, as the "man" whom Lady Goldenfleece has married is none other than the disguised Mistress Low-water. Neither the masque nor the wedding is what it purports to be.

Anti-Court Satire

The play-structure based on the midway banquet and the catastrophic final masque is repeated in another mode in *Women Beware Women*, where the setting is the ducal court in Florence. In such episodes there is a complex interplay between theatrical and social artifice, grounded in the original audience's awareness that banqueting and masquing at the court of King James were highpoints in the social life of the wealthiest and most powerful people in the land. Such occasions were visible, ostentatious, and theatrical to the few who could participate and observe (and these included the players of the King's Men, who helped to stage court entertainments), but known indirectly and by often scandalized report to the many. Middleton's masques and banquets are, then, theatrically and socially allusive episodes. The Platonic frame of reference that habitually enabled the court masque to use extravagant display as an expression of the court's excellence in virtue is persistently demolished, and the play-masques end up displaying on stage the putrefaction that was meant to stay hidden within.

This viewpoint is not confined to the horrified re-visions of court masques. *The Revenger's Tragedy* opens with Vindice saying "Duke: royal lecher." Later, the Duke's son Spurio describes how he was conceived as a bastard "After some gluttonous dinner. Some stirring dish / Was my first father, when deep healths went round, / And ladies' cheeks were painted red with wine" (I.ii.179–81). The opening scene of *The Witch* develops into a banquet with a bizarre toast that is drunk, at another Duke's insistence, in the skull of the Duchess' father. More macabre still, the Tyrant in *The Lady's Tragedy*, having killed the Lady he loves, removes her body from its tomb and installs it at court, where it becomes the object of a perverted necrophiliac courtship. In Middleton's plays the social theater of court decadence is repeatedly presented on altered terms on the public stage, which is thereby constituted as artistically, politically, and morally hostile to the court. Specific targets include the abusive and much-criticized Court of Wards, whereby the court farmed out the upbringing of rich orphans for profit (Tricomi, 1989). There are several specific allusions to the sexual decadence and murder at court that were revealed through the Overbury trials of 1615–16 in plays such as *Women Beware Women*. These references suggest disturbing similitudes between the Jacobean court and the exotic courts of Middleton's plays.

Some of the ground on which Margot Heinemann (1980) established Middleton as a political Puritan has subsequently been eroded (Bawcutt, 1999), and some of the "oppositional" positions Heinemann finds in Middleton reflect the policies of leading courtiers (Cogswell, 1984; Límon, 1986). But Middleton looks with an outsider's eye. It remains plausible to see him embracing a political Calvinism whereby the corrupt court shown on stage not only echoed the Catholic monarchies and dukedoms at their real or imagined worst, but also extrapolated from the example found more locally in King James's extravagance and absolutism.

Patriarchy

"Patriarchy" was not a word current in Middleton's time, but he clearly had a notion of it. A politicized and male-gendered reading of the fifth commandment, "Honor thy father and thy mother," is clearly laid out in the trial scene of *The Old Law* (with Rowley, 1615–19):

> Cleanthes, there is none can be
> A good son and a bad subject, for if princes
> Be called the peoples' fathers, then the subjects
> Are all his sons, and he that flouts the prince
> Doth disobey his father.
> (*The Old Law*, V.i.196–200)

The didactic plainness of utterance may here derive from Rowley. Nevertheless, no early modern dramatist offers a more rigorous and wide-ranging analysis of patriarchy as a term that encompasses human life from high politics to all domestic and personal relationships between men and women than does Middleton. Some critics have found his position to be ambivalent or even misogynist, though it should immediately be pointed out that Middleton's men are no better than his women, and are given less excuse.

One of Middleton's most compelling studies of abusive male behavior is to be found in *A Yorkshire Tragedy*. Here it is the claustrophobic space of a country gentleman's house that is the little kingdom for a man to rule, and the outside influences of city, county, and university act as a potentially healthful but ineffective antidote to the obsessive violence of the man as husband and father that takes place within the home. This play, written shortly after Middleton's early city comedies, shows the same satiric impulse, now toughened by a strong sense of outrage and a strong commitment to display the disturbing actuality of aggressive and irrational behavior.

But more often the actual distortions of authority that is supposed theoretically to be beneficent take place on the larger stage of state, and there is no appeal to higher secular authority. In *Women Beware Women*, Bianca's husband Leantio, a lowly merchant's agent, lives in fear of the Venetian aristocrats from whom he has "stolen" his wife, a fear that becomes refocused, all too late, on the Duke of Florence's invasive interest in her. To Leantio she is his prized commodity, a "most unvalued'st purchase" to be locked out of sight. The Duke, however, can and does exert his power variously: as alluring display, as seduction, as actual or potential rape, as bribery, and as advancement to a position at court where Bianca herself becomes the gratified object of display. Elsewhere Middleton uses the phrase "constrained consent" to describe Castiza's behavior in the dumb-show depicting her forced marriage to Vortiger: "*then bring in Castiza, who seems to be brought in unwillingly, {by} Devonshire and Stafford, who crown her and then give her to Vortiger, she going forth with him with a kind of a constrained consent*" (*Hengist*, II.ii.s.d.17–20; Raynulph, the commenting chorus, say less equivocally that they "force the maid, / That vowed a virgin life, to wed" (II.ii.11–12). In both cases the text emphasizes the woman's forced accommodation, suggesting that where there is a grotesque imbalance of power the weaker party's ability to grant or withhold consent is precisely what is denied.

Middleton's other major late tragedy, *The Changeling*, explores a contrasting scenario: what if the woman makes her escape from a lack-luster relationship by forming an initially unwanted bond not with a duke but with a servant? Beatrice-Joanna aims to replace Alsemero with Alonzo, but by enlisting De Flores as an assassin she finds herself bound to the manservant by a debt of obligation that he refuses to discharge with mere money. The question of rape arises here too, and the woman's accommodation to her role as mistress is again disturbing.

These tragedies both combine an uncompromising picture of power with an awareness of female psychology often considered unequalled in early modern drama; *The Changeling* gives intense focus too on the viewpoint of the more usually marginal figure of the domestic manservant. What remains an enigma is the ultimate origin of the bloody debacles that end these plays. Is it the flaws of patriarchy, or is it a potential for evil inherent in the daughters of Eve? The answer will be critical in positioning Middleton as either a proto-feminist or a misogynist. But the plays do not invite any straightforward answer based on this binary choice.

Critics such as Stachniewski (1990) have argued that the leading figures in the tragedies are, in a Calvinist sense, born to be damned; their lives will show the seed of innate wickedness growing to display itself by the necessity of predeterminism. Seen thus, the growth into consciousness of self is also one into consciousness of damnation. It is the women who come under special scrutiny, with the men occupying the position of the serpent as well as that of Adam. Bianca's marriage to Leantio is founded on a disobedience to the authority of her parents that is reproduced more spectacularly in her revolt against Leantio. The relationship between Isabella and Hippolito in the same play is still motivated by incestuous feelings even though Isabella has been told that Hippolito is not, after all, her uncle. Beatrice-Joanna's exceptionally virulent hatred toward De Flores early in the play is a form of denial of a destructive and perverse lust that already lies embedded within her, and that correlates with her all-too-easy decision to have her suitor killed. She eventually discovers her latent sexual fascination with De Flores' gross ugliness and brutal efficiency, as her repulsion turns to horrified recognition that sex with him is inescapable, and then to admiration for this "wondrous necessary man" (*The Changeling*, V.i.92) in his capacities of both henchman and lover: "The east is not more beauteous than his service . . . Here's a man worth loving" (V.i.71–6).

Such readings are persuasive in that they recognize both the Calvinist background to Middleton's thought and the psychological power and complexity of his drama. From a feminist perspective, however, they position him unfavorably. On the other hand, these plays make a strong point of showing the forms of oppression to which women are subjected, to the extent that their actions and choices can be seen as logical products of the communities to which they belong. It is a visible and structural fault in the societies of these plays that they offer no evident position between passivity and whoredom. The women often find that they have been appointed to a way of life whose only alternative is the morally negative position to which their culture assigns the unpassive female, and they seek out this role as though it were destiny. Acts that Calvinism calls sinful are, of course, far from exclusive to the women. What singles them out is that, as figures existing in an ideologically hostile world, they are positioned critically in the struggle between self-will and social determinism. Within this frame of being, self-will is a destructive force, and it achieves, with deep irony in the case of Beatrice-Joanna, a new form of subjugation to a man who is neither king, father, nor husband. For critics such as Cristina Malcolmson (1990), Beatrice-Joanna's acquiescence is a mark of Middleton's failure fully to realize the radical potential of his play. It could equally be accounted as his refusal to embrace purely utopian solutions to intractable problems of female existence as an observant male saw them.

Elsewhere, Middleton's plays repeatedly show women who have escaped from the two-celled cage of passivity and whoredom. In the first half of *Women Beware Women*, Livia is one such figure. Placing herself beyond direct involvement with men, she manipulates the sexual fortunes of all those around her, becoming both the philosopher and the engineer of an amoral sexual libertarianism. The play potentially avoids its tragic outcome for as long as Livia keeps control of both her own sexual energies and the plot. Her unlikely cousins include Mistress Low-water in *No Wit/Help Like a Woman's*, who uses disguise as a man to secure comic vengeance on Lady Goldenfleece. Mistress Low-water puts her characterless husband into the shadows, while steering Lady Goldenfleece into that duplicitous and potentially lesbian marriage with her in her male persona. Moll Cutpurse in *The Roaring Girl* is another such figure. Her transsexual dressing (which, unusually, does not hide her female gender) is a rebellious statement against male hypocrisy. It also allows her to indulge in sexual punning without attracting the opprobrium that would usually be the reward of a woman using such language. Moll acts as a self-appointed warrior for the right of women to say what they please, act in their own right, and not be treated as sexual and economic properties:

> Thou'rt one of those
> That thinks each woman thy fond flexible whore:
> If she but cast a liberal eye upon thee,
> Turn back her head, she's thine; or amongst company,

By chance drink first to thee, then she's quite gone,
There's no means to help her . . .
How many of our sex by such as thou
Have their good thoughts paid with a blasted name
That never deserved loosely or did trip
In path of whoredom beyond cup and lip?
                                        (*The Roaring Girl*, v.72–84)

Even the courtesan Jane in *Trick to Catch the Old One* belongs to the same camp, proving at least as wittily resourceful, and on her own terms finally as successful, as her partner Witgood.

Endings and Extremes

Jane usurps the position of the male wit in the closing moments of the play. She has achieved her aim of financial security, and this enables her triumphantly to announce her reformation from vice. But her priorities are certainly compromised: she is accepting marriage to a miserly old man. The roaring girl retains her independence, but pays the price by finally failing to gain acceptance (Rose, 1984). More damning, Livia succumbs to an overwhelming lust for Leantio that tilts the whole action of *Women Beware Women* toward its tragic final scene. These are admonitory outcomes that reflect another tension: between Eliot's great recorder and Middleton the dramatist who cannot fail to acknowledge the structural imperatives by which plays end. Or perhaps the tension lies between the moralist (both Calvinist and Horatian) and the anarchic libertarian for whom structures and morals will always be fractured. By either account, the outcome cannot be clear-cut.

Middleton's endings risk excess. Like other Jacobean playmakers, he will venture far into sensationalism rather than understate corruption and its consequences. The effect can be disorienting. Scenes of spectacular violence manage in one moment to convey extremes of louche decadence, harsh irony, playful wit, and didactic hostility. A reader or stage audience may justifiably feel unsure as to the appropriate response. Is this failure? Perhaps Middleton is ripe for fuller acknowledgement in a critical climate that distrusts the notion that authors should dictate meanings. He is not directive; but neither is he indifferent. Middleton is a paradoxically self-anonymizing author, writing a sharp, socially and politically analytic drama at the point where detachment fuses with distinctively inflected passionate vision.

References and Further Reading

Bawcutt, N. W. (1999). "Was Thomas Middleton a puritan dramatist?" *Modern Language Review* 94, 925–39.
Bergeron, D. M. (1971). *English Civic Pageantry, 1558–1642*. London: Edward Arnold.

Bromham, A. A., and Z. Bruzzi (1990). *"The Changeling" and the Years of Crisis, 1619–1624: A Hieroglyph of Britain*. London and New York: Pinter.

Bruster, D. (1992). *Drama and the Market in the Age of Shakespeare*. Cambridge: Cambridge University Press.

Chakravorty, S. (1996). *Society and Politics in the Plays of Thomas Middleton*. Oxford: Clarendon Press.

Cogswell, T. (1984). "Thomas Middleton and the court, 1624: *A Game at Chess* in context." *Huntington Library Quarterly* 47, 273–88.

Dutton, R. (1999). "Introduction." In *"Women Beware Women" and Other Plays* by Thomas Middleton, ed. R. Dutton. Oxford: Oxford University Press.

Eliot, T. S. (1951). "Thomas Middleton." In *Selected Essays* 3rd edn. London: Faber and Faber.

Heinemann, M. (1980). *Puritanism and Theatre: Thomas Middleton and Opposition Drama under the Early Stuarts*. Cambridge: Cambridge University Press.

Holdsworth, R. V. (1990). "*Women Beware Women* and *The Changeling* on the stage." In *Three Jacobean Revenge Tragedies: A Casebook*, ed. R. V. Holdsworth. Basingstoke: Macmillan.

Howard-Hill, T. H. (1995). *Middleton's "Vulgar Pasquin": Essays on "A Game at Chess."* Newark: University of Delaware Press; London: Associated University Presses.

Jackson, MacD. P. (1979). *Studies in Attribution: Middleton and Shakespeare*. Salzburg: Institut für Angelistik und Amerikanistik, Universität Salzburg.

Lake, David J. (1975). *The Canon of Thomas Middleton: Internal Evidence for the Major Problems of Authorship*. London: Cambridge University Press.

Leinwand, T. B. (1986). *The City Staged: Jacobean Comedy, 1603–1613*. Madison: University of Wisconsin Press.

Límon, J. (1986). *Dangerous Matter: English Drama and Politics in 1623/4*. Cambridge: Cambridge University Press.

Malcolmson, C. (1990). "'As tame as ladies': politics and gender in *The Changeling*." *English Literary Renaissance* 20, 320–39.

Middleton, T. (2002). *Collected Works*, gen. ed. Gary Taylor. 2 vols (vol. 1, *Works*; vol. 2, *Companion*). Oxford: Oxford University Press.

Paster, G. K. (1985). *The Idea of the City in the Age of Shakespeare*. Athens: University of Georgia Press.

Ricks, C. (1960). "The moral and poetic structure of *The Changeling*." *Essays in Criticism* 10, 290–306.

Rose, M. B. (1984). "Women in men's clothing: apparel and social stability in *The Roaring Girl*." *English Literary Renaissance* 14, 367–91.

Rowe, G. E. (1979). *Thomas Middleton and the New Comedy Tradition*. Lincoln: University of Nebraska Press.

Stachniewski, J. (1990). "Calvinist psychology in Middleton's tragedies." In *Three Jacobean Revenge Tragedies: A Casebook*, ed. R. V. Holdsworth. Basingstoke: Macmillan.

Steen, S. J. (1993). *Ambrosia in an Earthen Vessel: Three Centuries of Audience and Reader Response to the Works of Thomas Middleton*. New York: AMS Press.

Tricomi, A. H. (1989). *Anti-Court Drama in England, 1603–1642*. Charlottesville and London: University Press of Virginia.

Wells, S. (1981). "Jacobean city comedy and the ideology of the city." *ELH* 48, 37–60.

Woodbridge, L. (1984). *Women and the English Renaissance: Literature and the Nature of Womankind, 1540–1620*. Brighton: Harvester Press.

35

Beaumont and Fletcher

Lee Bliss

Two of the most important playwrights of the seventeenth century, Francis Beaumont and John Fletcher, are today seldom produced, their plays of interest largely to students of Renaissance drama. Yet in the first decade of the reign of James I they worked out distinctive versions of the dramatic "kinds" – particularly tragicomedy – that dominated the stage both before and after the Civil War. Each wrote early solo work, but it is as collaborators that they found success (see chapter 36 below). As early as 1612, in the epistle to *The White Devil* that lists the playwrights he admires, John Webster mentions "Master Beaumont, and Master Fletcher" after Chapman and Jonson but before the "copious industry" of Shakespeare, Dekker, and Heywood. With Jonson and Shakespeare, Beaumont and Fletcher received the distinction of prestigious folio collections of their plays, and when the first folio appeared in 1647, containing 34 plays and a masque, it was prefaced by 37 commendatory poems. Ironically, while the title-page ascription served to keep their names linked for posterity, the volume contained almost nothing of Beaumont's. When the 1679 second folio added previously printed plays, bringing the total to 50, Beaumont's contribution was still small; most of the plays were written after Beaumont left the partnership. Beaumont's name obviously still had commercial cachet, and the publishers used it shamelessly. Yet in another sense they were not so far off the mark. The distinctive style was developed in this collaboration, in which Beaumont was apparently the dominant presence, and the most famous works in the "Beaumont and Fletcher" canon are indeed truly Beaumont and Fletcher plays.[1] With some justice, then, beyond the constraints of space, this chapter will limit itself to Beaumont and Fletcher and to the works written, solely and together, before Beaumont's marriage and retirement to Kent in 1612 or 1613.

John Fletcher was born in 1579, the son of Richard Fletcher, whose meteoric career – chaplain to Queen Elizabeth, dean of Peterborough, bishop of Bristol, Worcester, then London – ended disastrously when his second marriage so displeased the queen that she suspended his episcopal functions. He died in debt in 1596 and seems to have consigned his eight children to the care of his brother Giles, who had nine of his own and meager financial resources. The "John Fletcher of London" admitted in 1591 to Bene't College, Cambridge (his father's college), probably refers to the future playwright. After his father's death he presumably lived in London at his uncle's house, although certainly Giles was in no position to provide patronage for his or his brother's children. Implicated in the Essex conspiracy, John Fletcher received no significant patronage thereafter under Elizabeth and, despite early promises from James, nothing materialized under the new king. Whether or not John Fletcher agreed, Giles and his children blamed their poverty directly on King James. Though John Fletcher's childhood had been spent in bishops' palaces, as far as is known as a young adult he lacked any secure social or financial position. He went on, of course, to fame and relative fortune and became Shakespeare's successor as principal playwright for the King's Men, the most prosperous and prestigious theatrical company of the time. He died in 1625, according to anecdotal evidence because he tarried in London waiting for a new suit and caught the plague.

Francis Beaumont's social pedigree was more illustrious than Fletcher's. In the preface to the 1647 folio, publisher Humphrey Moseley says he tried to obtain a portrait of Beaumont from "those Noble Families whence he was descended" as well as from his gentlemen acquaintances at the Inner Temple. After the Reformation, in 1539, Francis' grandfather had acquired the recently dissolved priory at Grace Dieu, Leicestershire, that became the family seat where young Francis was born in 1584 or 1585. The dramatist's father became a lawyer, an influential member of the Inner Temple, and finally a justice of the Common Pleas. Young Francis matriculated, with his two older brothers, at Broadgates Hall, Oxford, in 1597 and, in the family tradition, followed them to the Inner Temple in 1600. By the time young Beaumont met Fletcher, they may have been in analogous circumstances, for although Francis' eldest brother Henry did not survive long after inheriting the family estate, brother John outlived Francis by many years, and the dramatist remained a younger son. The family's finances were themselves threatened by persistent recusancy (apparently not shared by Francis). During the whole of Francis' playwriting career, two-thirds of the family land and goods were allotted to a Scots companion of King James, and brother John was confined to Grace Dieu. Neither Beaumont nor Fletcher had reason to favor James's ideology or his court.

While at the Inns of Court, both Francis and John Beaumont showed more interest in literary pursuits than legal studies. Francis composed a satiric "Grammar Lecture" for one of the Inns' Christmas revels and in 1602 published an Ovidian narrative poem, *Salmacis and Hermaphroditus*, a late contribution to the gentlemanly fad for writing erotic epyllia (little epics), while brother John began his poetic career with the mock-heroic *Metamorphosis of Tobacco*. Even after turning playwright Beaumont kept up his ties to the Inns, for he wrote *The Masque of the Inner Temple and Grays Inn* to help celebrate the marriage of Princess Elizabeth to the elector palatinate in February 1613. The first certain record of Beaumont's turning to the stage, and of his friendship with Fletcher, is *The Woman Hater*, a satiric comedy written for the

Children of Paul's in 1606, possibly with some revisions by Fletcher for the 1607 quarto.[2] The children's companies earned a reputation for social satire and, more excitingly, for the politically inflammatory allusions that finally brought about the suppression of the Blackfriars' troupe in 1608 (Paul's boys had ceased playing in 1606; see chapter 22 above). In *The Woman Hater* Beaumont tries to satisfy that taste, in part by borrowing from his more established colleagues. The title figure, Gondarino, and his counterpart in the primary sub-plot, Lazarello, show an obvious debt to the "humors" characterizations of Jonson and Chapman, and there are echoes of several Marston plays, especially *The Dutch Courtesan*. Beaumont's chaste but outspoken heroine Oriana, the first in a line of bold and witty women, is modeled on Marston's Chrispinella.[3] Beaumont juggles four plots with considerable ease, offering a bit of something for everyone: farce, bawdy wit, court satire, and a "high" romantic plot. He uses the Prologue to establish an ironic distance by wittily situating his play in its dramatic and political context. It alludes to the political environment in which satire might threaten an author with "the dear loss of his ears," as it had Jonson, Chapman, and Marston the preceding year (Beaumont and Fletcher, 1966–97, I, 157, ll. 11–12); he tells any informers with "table books" to leave, or stay to enjoy a simple entertainment offering the currently popular Italian setting and duke. With a final tongue-in-cheek general guarantee against city comedy's "ordinary and over-worn trade of jesting at lords and courtiers, and citizens," he assures the audience that the author "did never think but that a lord born might be a wise man, and a courtier an honest man" (ll. 19–26).

The play, of course, violates its Prologue's disclaimer. *The Woman Hater* proceeds to skewer the common targets of contemporary satire: new knights and upstart courtiers, royal favorites, government informers. The Duke's primary role is as lover of Oriana, not statesman, yet there is enough talk about how "princes" govern and the kind of court over which the Duke presides to indict him as complacent and self-indulgent. His lengthy prose disquisition on courtly patronage makes him (perhaps safely) representative as well as cynical: "We princes do use to prefer many for nothing, . . . whom we do use only for our pleasures" (I.i.63–4).[4] Count Valore, the play's chief plot manipulator, gives his sister a more grotesque version of the "fine sights" she expects to see at court: "you shall see many faces of man's making" and "you shall see many legs, too. Amongst the rest you shall behold one pair, the feet of which, in times past sockless, but are now through the change of time . . . very strangely become the legs of a knight and a courtier" (I.iii.12–17). Valore seems to be the play's satiric spokesman, though as privy councilor he is in part responsible for the corruption he excoriates; like the Duke, Valore seems detached, watching a spectacle put on for his entertainment. In this, Valore sets our holiday mood – "This day I am for fools, I am all theirs" (I.iii.229) – and when he manipulates Lazarello, the intelligencers, and the pompous would-be statesman Lucio for his own amusement, it is for ours as well. Yet it is also with Valore that the play stumbles in controlling the balance of tones among its plots. As satiric targets the intelligencers show themselves to be ambitious for power, money, influence; they enjoy being feared by their neighbors. Within the eavesdropping scene arranged by Valore, however, they are comic figures, wrenching disconnected phrases into a plot whereby Lazarello, who wants only his gourmet umbrano fishhead, intends to "burn the palace, kill the Duke, and poison his Privy Council" (III.ii.106–7). This sudden allusion to the real world and the increasing use of "intelligencers" after the Gunpowder Plot scare in 1605 returns in Valore's judgments on those his games have exposed. Lucio, who believed the intelligencers, is let off lightly, but the intelligencers themselves are dismissed as blood-sucking leeches who "grow fat and full fed by fall of those you rise by" (V.ii.101–2). This sharp, topically satiric note unsettles the resolution of this mini-plot and, to some extent, that of the play itself.

The Woman Hater employs other conventions besides the satiric commentator figure, and it more smoothly integrates these borrowings into the dominant comic mood. The lover's twist on the disguised-duke plot does end with his proposing to Oriana, but most of this plot concentrates not on his wooing but on the battle of the sexes between Gondarino and Oriana, determined to punish him for slandering her whole sex. Inverting the convention of male wooing, she becomes talkative, amorous, and aggressive; she chases Gondarino all over his house, forcing on him the language of courtly compliment. Violations of decorum in language and behavior are even more crucial to our delight in the farcical sub-plot. Most of the play's funniest parodies are Lazarello's borrowings from contemporary tragedies. This endlessly verbal gourmand also presses into service most of the (outmoded) literary languages of his day – Petrarchan love poetry, euphuism, the rhetoric of chivalric romance. Despite some disturbing undercurrents in its young aristocrats' irresponsibility and its vicious misogynist, *The Woman Hater*'s tone is largely controlled by Lazarello and by its mischievous heroine and comic exploration of the battle between the sexes. Amatory skirmishes between rakish gentlemen and well-born ladies became the hallmark of the romantic comedies Beaumont and Fletcher contributed to both private and public theaters in the next few years (*The Coxcomb*, *The Scornful Lady*) and of the comedies Fletcher later wrote himself.

The Woman Hater also reveals Beaumont's talent for lightening his satire with farce and, especially, linguistic parody as well as an apparent delight in running his own riffs on established theatrical conventions. Both features come to full flower in Beaumont's next comedy, *The Knight of the Burning Pestle* (1607). The Prologue to *The Woman Hater* had said, presumably as much tongue-in-cheek as the rest of that speech, "Inductions are out of date." In *The Knight* Beaumont takes this convention's opportunities – an initial frame of actors-playing-spectators who may remain on stage to comment on, even join, the play's action – and expands them to engulf the playhouse's intended offering. The Blackfriars children are about to present a city comedy called "The London Merchant" when two citizens, grocer George and his wife Nell, climb onto the stage to join the gentlemen spectators on stools. Rejecting a play he fears will satirize citizens, George demands a play of another genre, one that exalts London citizens as a class and typically stars apprentices accomplishing heroic deeds, often in exotic places. The Prologue-boy finally strikes a compromise by which the citizens, with the help of their apprentice Rafe, will make up a "play" (which they want to call "The Grocer's Honour") scene by scene out of the stock characters, situations, and rhetorical style of their favorite literature, chivalric romance. The players bawdily re-christen this impromptu effort "The Knight of the Burning Pestle" and agree to allow it to be staged between the scenes of their own production.

Initially, Beaumont seems to be doing just what his citizens feared: George and Nell prove to be imperious and egocentric, placated only by alternating scenes of spectacle and violence. Since they are willing to pay as well as threaten to stage their fantasies, they also exemplify the corruption of art by commerce. Yet George and Nell do not remain satiric stereotypes. They demonstrate good qualities as well as bad, and they are more vital and interesting than the citizens portrayed in "The London Merchant." In their interruptive commentary on both interior plays we see their importance to *The Knight* is less their taste in plays than their naivety as playgoers (and playmakers). Beaumont thus sets himself the task of juggling three narratives: the professional actors' production of the scripted "London Merchant"; the audience-created scenes of Rafe's chivalric quest; and the story of Nell's (and possibly George's) first visit to the theater. The citizens know neither the conventions of appropriate audience behavior nor those of genre needed to understand "The London Merchant," much less such theatrical basics as plot and probability. Yet their objections to "The London Merchant," based on how they as tradespeople would react to a runaway apprentice of their own, show up the artificiality of the conventional prodigal-son narrative: it may, as a boy player claims, have "plot" and obey the laws of cause and effect, but the little world of art may have nothing to do with life beyond the theater door. In fact, Beaumont's triumph is to seem to have brought "real life" in from the streets of London and onto the Blackfriars stage. Obstreperous, insisting on the immediate gratification of their desires, Beaumont's citizens allow him to explore something more fundamental to the theater's life and function than etiquette or the academic "rules" of art: theater as a place where the imagination satisfies its hunger to transform every-day reality and explore its own powers.

As a result, the stage which was to have presented a rather insipid, albeit professional, play turns into a place of carnivalesque energy, wish-fulfillment, and an "indecorous" variety of linguistic registers. And it is not only George and Nell who revel in a release from everyday economic concerns. An ardent amateur actor with at least *1 Henry IV*, *Mucedorus*, and *The Spanish Tragedy* in his repertory, as well as a reader of the popular translations of Iberian romance, Rafe is well prepared to turn the citizens' situational requests into full-blown scenes of knight-errantry, complete with the appropriate "parts" and rhetoric. He even adroitly manages the three final stipulated episodes that return him to London and his "real" apprentice status, adapting a different rhetorical style for his speech as May Lord, for the mustering of his soldiers at Mile End, and for his own death speech. The professional players, too, find a kind of improvisational release: they briefly stop "The London Merchant" to create new parts for themselves and two scenes for Rafe's knightly romance. Players have been pitted against customers, the boundary between plays (and their genres) breached. Beaumont's final twist on conventions comes at the end. "The London Merchant" has a generic comic conclusion to reach, and the players push through to it in acts IV and V. Suddenly grasping at least one dramatic principle, the need for closure, George for once feels helpless: "I do not like this. . . . Everybody's part has come to an end but Rafe's and he's left out" (Zitner, 1984, V.276–8). The players refuse to help, but Nell intervenes with the only real-life "end" she knows. A player objects that it will violate decorum for Rafe to "die . . . upon no occasion, and in a comedy too," but Beaumont allows her a mad logic: if the plotless story of Rafe's adventures is looked at as a loose chronicle history, it does find a fitting resolution in the death of the adventurer himself. So *The Knight* ends with a double denouement: one comic and one technically (and hilariously) tragic. Presiding over all is the aptly named father in "The London Merchant," Merrythought, whose singing humor fills the play with melody and whose song of the good life and its basis in "mirth" ends the play. Beaumont doubles the song's moral, and its inclusiveness, by giving the Epilogue to Nell, who not only hopes the gentlemen spectators think Rafe acquitted himself well but, reaching across status barriers, invites them home for wine and tobacco.

This appeal failed to move its auditors and, unfortunately for us, Beaumont wrote no more solo plays. It is often conjectured that *The Knight* flopped commercially because its mockery of citizens was not severe enough for a Blackfriars audience. Perhaps it was too even-handed, since present-day "knights" also receive harsh treatment. Instead of failure being explained in terms of class, it may have been a matter of content. Despite the fact that meta-dramatic investigations of the working of the imagination in the theater, or the interaction between audience and players, were not uncommon, such moments were usually confined to Inductions or comic sub-plots. Beaumont may have begun writing Pirandello's "theater trilogy" a few hundred years too soon. Ironically, *The Knight* is now the most admired, and most frequently acted, play in the whole Beaumont and Fletcher canon. For whatever reason, Beaumont's next play was a fairly evenly shared collaboration with Fletcher, the genre was tragedy, and the plot was based on Sir Philip Sidney's prose romance the *Arcadia*.[5] In *The Knight* Beaumont had borrowed the Don Quixote motif to mock hack-work translations of Iberian romances, but the *Arcadia*, like Edmund Spenser's *The Faerie Queene* (from which Fletcher also borrowed for *The Faithful Shepherdess*), was one of the monuments of high Elizabethan culture. Perhaps because Beaumont and Fletcher were new to fully shared collaboration, they chose to stick closely to their single source. Although John H. Astington (1979) argues that it was the success of *Cupid's Revenge* that convinced the King's Men to enlist Beaumont and Fletcher's talents when it took over the Blackfriars theater in late 1608 or 1609, posterity's judgment has not been as kind. In *Cupid's Revenge* Beaumont and Fletcher prove only slightly more adept at dramatizing prose romance than *The Knight*'s hapless George and Nell.

Part of the problem is that to enlarge Sidney's two-paragraph tale of Cupid's punishment for sacrilege committed by the daughter of the foolish Duke of Licia, Beaumont and Fletcher try grafting to it another, unrelated story from later in the *Arcadia*. The two families are combined, so there is now a guilty son (Leucippus) as well as father and daughter, and the action becomes a family tragedy held together by the continuity of some characters and by Cupid's direction of their fates by means of human agents (one of whom, the Machiavellian servant Timantus, is borrowed from yet another story in a different book of *The Arcadia*). The additive rather than integrated nature of the plotting makes the play a curiously broken-backed affair, and it is mirrored, even more damagingly, in the characterization of the putative tragic hero, Leucippus. He is whatever he is needed to be at any particular moment in the conjoined plots. In act I he encourages his sister's folly in urging chastity, for the play needs him to be another target of Cupid's revenge; in act II he seems a very up-to-date Jacobean rake joking callously with his mistress Bacha; when his doting father marries Bacha, Leucippus alters again and in the last acts he becomes a noble-minded victim of his villainous mother-in-law's plots. Beaumont and Fletcher have never been known for consistency in characterization, and conversions are common, but these leaps are huge. It undermines Leucippus' stature and authority when he is as easily duped by Bacha and Timantus as his foolish father. Problems in controlling tone appear everywhere and subvert any cumulative tragic effect. Sidney's main plot is tragicomic and his sophisticated narrative voice allows us to laugh at his heroes' follies while still seeing them as worthy young men. In *Cupid's Revenge* the comic and tragic dramatic cues clash and, despite seven deaths, the play is only technically a tragedy. Beaumont and Fletcher will not again be so constrained by a single source, though elements of the joint style are established here, from specific incidents (the citizen rescue of a prince, the stabbing of a woman disguised as a page) to the types and arrangement of the characters. When they turn to tragicomedy, what they take from *The Arcadia* are not borrowed plots but the predominantly thematic structure and a dramatic approximation of Sidney's sophisticated, self-mocking tone.

Much of this development is accomplished in Fletcher's *The Faithful Shepherdess*. Although he models his title on Giovanni Battista Guarini's Italian pastoral tragicomedy *Il Pastor Fido* (see chapter 27 above), and for his combative defense of the new genre in the prefatory epistle to the quarto (1609) borrows from Guarini's own justification, *The Faithful Shepherdess* is quite original. It reworks *Cupid's Revenge*'s spectrum of love ranging from chaste devotion to lawless lust, but also more fruitfully employs Sidney's thematic patterning, so that *The Faithful Shepherdess*'s interest lies in its shifting configurations of lovers rather than in "plot" in any conventional sense. A dramatic model for the confused lovers' night in the magical wood is borrowed from *A Midsummer Night's Dream*, and to this enchanted setting Fletcher adds incidents from *The Faerie Queene* as well as his own blend of gods and shepherds. The goal now is a mixed mode, and instead of comic and tragic effects undermining each other, Fletcher learns to subordinate tragic potential to comedy's final reconciliations. He discovers in practice what the 1609 definition outlines in theory: a conception of tragicomedy as a sophisticated blend of genres governed by tonal and thematic unity, marked by its own style and effect, not a crude yoking of kings and clowns. Guarini's defense looked for classical precedent and found it in, among others, Ovid, whose apparent authorial detachment and elegant style keep us above the often violent amatory action (Yoch, 1987, 123). Fletcher provides this kind of verbal artifice; we admire the overall patterning and do not become deeply engaged with the threatened rape or scenes in which one young shepherd twice stabs his beloved by mistake. We are offered a sophisticated double view of love: both its importance to the individual and the way powerful emotion makes any obstacle seem tragically significant, but also the pageant of folly impetuous young lovers can present to uninvolved spectators.

The stage failure of *The Faithful Shepherdess* may have been due to the audience's lack of sophistication, as Fletcher charges in his epistle. The play may also have been too long, too static, too uncompromisingly pastoral – in short, too like a masque for an audience that had come to see something more recognizably a "play." Dropping the purely pastoral and adding a bit more plot, Beaumont and Fletcher achieve their first real successes collaborating on romance tragicomedy and tragedy for the adults. Perhaps freed to rethink their style by the need to satisfy customers at the public Globe theater as well as Blackfriars, Beaumont and Fletcher become original as well as eclectic. For *Philaster* (1609) the character types borrowed from Sidney are retained, but the plot situation develops out of another sixteenth-century romance, Alonso Perez' continuation of Montemayor's *Diana*, by way of Shakespeare's *Hamlet*. Philaster's situation as deposed prince of Sicily living at the usurping king's court makes this an obvious dramatic model; more important, *Hamlet*'s mood of moral bewilderment proved congenial. Since *Philaster*'s genre was to be tragicomedy, alterations begin early. There is no murdered father to avenge, and the usurping king is rightful monarch of Calabria, to which he can return. Although titular hero, Philaster is structurally less prominent, and his is not the play's dominant consciousness. After act I, scene i, Philaster's primary concerns are amatory; matters of state are largely left to the court lords for commentary and to the citizens for active resolution.

Philaster establishes its juxtaposition of tones as well as its sexual politics from the outset. Three court lords comment cynically on the chastity of court ladies and the proposed marriage of the King's daughter Arethusa to the visiting Spanish prince Pharamond. While this might be a serious topical allusion, since King James intended foreign dynastic marriages for his children (an unpopular Spanish alliance for Prince Henry), the court lords and ladies keep our focus on Pharamond's physical attractiveness. This is a court of sexual, not political, intrigue. Pharamond's prominence in the early part of the play also helps shift the tone toward comedy, for he is laughably unsuitable – foreigner, sensualist, and stereotypical comic braggart. And the brave Philaster who defied the King in act I, scene i, becomes the comically tongue-tied lover in his private interview with Arethusa in the next scene, where she is forced to invert gender stereotypes and woo him. In terms of overall plotting, romantic comedy veers toward tragedy when Megra, caught trysting with Pharamond, accuses the princess of the same sexual misconduct with Bellario, Philaster's page. No one believes Arethusa's innocence, and Philaster initially fails this test of love's faith. The slandered-beloved plot can end tragically, as it does in *Othello* (which *Philaster* at this point echoes), or, if the slander can be disproved, happily, as it does in *Philaster* and Shakespeare's contemporary *Cymbeline*. Apparently betrayed spiritually as well as sexually by the two people he most loved and trusted, Philaster's world collapses; coming upon them in the woods, the suicidal Philaster asks Arethusa to kill him and, when she refuses, wounds her and later the sleeping Bellario. Philaster is kept from killing Arethusa by the intervention of a Country Fellow, and this sensational scene was apparently the play's highpoint, for the subtitle in the first quarto (1620) was "Love Lies a Bleeding" and the frontispiece was a woodcut of this scene. Slander has led to arias of despair from all three of the principal characters as well as to violence. When Philaster and Bellario are carried off to prison in Arethusa's custody, the play offers one of its several possible happy endings.

The first is from the world of romance. The disastrous pastoral interlude paradoxically produced its own resolution. By defending Philaster even after he has wounded them, Bellario and Arethusa prove their constancy. Reconciled, they try to engineer a comic conclusion. Bellario, dressed as Hymen, presents Arethusa and Philaster to the King in a solemn mini-masque. The King, however, refuses his cue to forgive Philaster and accept this love match. We re-enter the play's political world, where Philaster's execution is prevented by an armed rising of the citizens, who capture Pharamond as hostage. Fear of political revolt brings the King's repentance and the restoration of Philaster's power. Philaster quells the rebellion with this news, and the play "ends" again, but threatens to repeat itself when Megra renews her accusation against Arethusa and Bellario. Act V spirals to a new crisis, finally solved by another romance convention. Bellario reveals that "he" is really Euphrasia, who disguised herself as a page to be near Philaster, whom she loves in vain. The play can end happily, again, yet its final mood, appropriately, is more mixed than either of the early, more conventional attempts. It focuses on Bellario/Euphrasia, her long description of how she fell in love, her refusal ever to marry, her request to continue service to both Arethusa and Philaster. Here the self-consciously created pathos of a devotion that must remain forever platonic coincides with the titillating implications of this future ménage à trois.

One of the ways *Philaster* achieves its tragicomic mixed mood lies in this alternation of generic cues about where the play is headed. It juxtaposes different kinds of scenes, characters, and language (from highly wrought verse to earthy prose), and different perspectives on its own action. The cynical realism of the choric lords, Megra, Pharamond, and the King exists in one world, the idealized love of Philaster, Arethusa, and Bellario in another, yet they coexist in the same play, and the juxtaposition of scenes from each offers a kind of internal commentary. In the most cited example, two opposed perspectives oscillate in the same scene. When Philaster wounds the willingly sacrificial Arethusa, the Country Fellow appears to remind us what this event looks like to an outsider: "hold, dastard, strike a woman?" (Gurr, 1969, IV.v.86). Berated as "ill-bred" for intruding on "our private sports and recreations," he brings a dash of reality as well as an audience laugh: "I know not your rhetoric, but I can lay it on if you touch the woman" (IV.v.97–8). Two incompatible interpretations confront each other and force upon us that detachment characteristic of Beaumont and Fletcher's mature tragicomic style. We can still appreciate the heightened rhetoric and despairing self-abandon of the lovers' emotional crisis while acknowledging their artificiality and enjoying the self-conscious artistry that is providing us these pleasures.

In its political topicality *Philaster* allows the same sort of double vision, presumably the reason that it, as well as *The Maid's Tragedy*, successfully played at court as well as at the Globe and Blackfriars. The King's passion for hunting and for political absolutism, and Philaster's protest that "I am no minion," might point toward specific Jacobean targets, as general allusion to James' favorites or specific reference to the current star, Robert Carr. To the King's absolutist claims, Lord Dion offers a spirited denial – subjects must obey monarchs only when they "command things possible and honest" (IV.iv.35) – that may glance at the struggle between James and the common lawyers over whether the king is above the law. A successful armed citizen rebellion could have been a dangerous scene to stage. To those humanist theorists who condoned rebellion against a monarch, tyrannous rule was the justification; a prince's ethics were as important to his legitimacy as his birth. Yet any potentially ill-advised implication is muted by the fact that the play's King is usurper as well as tyrant. So too the citizen rebellion: it is not against monarchy but in aid of the rightful prince, and it is staged as comedy, with the voiced threats directed at Pharamond. Contemporary political relevance is there for those inclined to see it, but apparently sufficiently diffuse not to alarm the censor.[6] References to a benevolent providence working to restore justice by means of Arethusa's love for Philaster allow us to take the convoluted plot as validating belief in such a deity, but in its final focus on Bellario's ambivalent status, the play refuses to exemplify any divine tidiness. We are most conscious of the artistry of the dramatists who have rescued this world of moral ambiguity and human helplessness by manipulating their own fiction.

Politics is more central to *The Maid's Tragedy* (*c*.1610), for its amatory crises revolve around the King, and that (again generic) King is both a tyrant and legitimate. Extending the "tradition of a sexualized politics in which desire defines sovereignty and tyranny," Beaumont and Fletcher present a king whose private life may be read as "both a metaphor for and a microcosm of his government" (Bushnell, 1990, 163).[7] To provide a cover for his affair with Evadne, the King commands Amintor to break his betrothal to Aspatia and marry Evadne (although Amintor will not be allowed to sleep with his new bride). In protecting his private pleasure the King puts his absolute power in conflict with moral law: he interferes with his subjects' private lives and dishonors Amintor, Aspatia, his lord chamberlain (Aspatia's father), and Evadne's brother Melantius, the King's chief military commander. He forces his subjects to question their allegiance. The play's focus is not the King but the crisis he provokes for each of those his lust affects, since not only allegiance is at stake but the social structure, indeed the whole world view justifying divine-right monarchy. Traditional concepts of honor, heroism, and nobility, as well as the individual's relation to the state, are problematized.

These reactions are woven into a dramatic structure that also experiments with its audience's relation to both action and character. For all of act I we are in the position of the court, unaware of the real reason for the switch in brides. The deserted Aspatia appears briefly to darken the scene, but act I centers on the happy bridegroom's reunion with his best friend Melantius (now prospective brother-in-law) and on the gorgeous wedding masque that occupies most of act I, scene ii, celebrating the conventional assumptions about premarital chastity, the sanctity of marriage, and royal integrity. Not until Evadne's wedding-night revelations to Amintor do we learn that public self-portrait is a sham. Amintor had believed the facade and included himself in it as idealistic Petrarchan lover. When Evadne explodes the myths by which he has lived, Amintor psychologically collapses as he faces the new identity that has been forced on him: "husband" to Evadne, "father" to the King's bastards. He grasps at the divine right of kings to salvage his own honor: he will remain loyal to the office even though his own monarch has betrayed him. Evadne's response creates the scene's grotesque comedy: Amintor's conventional horror provokes impudent self-assurance. Both passionate and ambitious, Evadne has freely embraced the reality behind society's moral platitudes. A Hobbesian world of aggression, power, and lust offers her a scope impossible within the patriarchal political and social system. So wholly has she accepted the reduction of all values to negotiable social currency that she later shocks even the King. Should his "fortune" change, she "would bend to him / That won your throne" (Craik, 1988, III.i.173–4). Evadne will be turned back to traditional ideals of female honor not by Amintor but by her brother. She will be convinced that only killing the King can blot out her shame. This startling reversal arises from Melantius' very different response to the situation. He had earlier maintained his right to independent judgment: "where I find worth, / I love the keeper, till he let it go, / And then I follow it" (I.i.23–5). Melantius asserts a value higher and older than kingship: the code of personal and family honor. Dishonored as brother and as soldier by the King for whom he fought, Melantius refuses to find, as Amintor had, the name of "king" a "sacred" one. When the converted Evadne cannot kill the King because "the gods forbid it," he confidently answers, "No, all the gods require it: / They are dishonoured in him" (IV.i.145–6). Later, defending himself to the dead King's brother, he asserts a subject's right to choose his loyalties: "Whilst he was good, I called him king, and served him" (V.ii.40).

The Maid's Tragedy does not, of course, straightforwardly advocate regicide, nor does it propose Melantius as its "answer" to the issues it raises. It plays with revenge conventions to deflect that conclusion. Melantius – the wronged male subject – does not actually commit the murder, nor is it public. Vengeance is enacted by a sexually wronged woman and is taken in the King's bedchamber. It is bracketed with the bawdy comments of the attendant gentlemen, and the actual revenge is initially grotesquely comic: when the King awakens to find himself tied to his bed, he eagerly anticipates some sadomasochistic "love-tricks." He is not a regal figure but a lecher killed by his mistress, called not "king" but "my shame." An hysterical Evadne in the final scene commits suicide, and this scene's focus points us away from both the killing of the King and Melantius' defense to the play's passionate heart: the personal devastation caused by the failure of traditional beliefs. Aspatia and Amintor are both driven to doubt the existence of justice and order. Disguised as her avenging brother, Aspatia seeks death on Amintor's sword; dying in Amintor's arms, she reveals her identity and he, unable to bear this, or his own deeds, or Evadne's regicide, kills himself. The scene's deft choreography recalls the conjunction of the despairing Philaster, Arethusa, and Bellario in the woods in *Philaster*, but here the wounds are fatal and self-inflicted. Despite the "success" of his vengeance, Melantius is destroyed by its personal cost, and the play ends anti-climactically, with Melantius stunned and himself threatening suicide while the new King blandly asserts the traditional values whose disintegration we have witnessed.

The world of *The Maid's Tragedy* is a dark one, but not so very different from that of the tragicomedies, whose characters feel equally betrayed and helpless. This is particularly true of *Philaster*, which respects the tragic potential of its material.[8] In Beaumont and Fletcher's last tragicomedy, *A King and No King* (1611), that balance tips toward the comic emphasis that Fletcher seemed to find more congenial. In spirit it approaches the kind of tragicomedy Fletcher was to continue to write, and it looks more squarely toward later English practice in both tragicomedy and heroic drama. *A King and No King*'s dramatic world is less dense and fully realized than *Philaster*'s; its characters are flatter, its central situation more extreme, and its surprise ending tidier. In *A King and No King* the terror and despair caused by Arbaces' apparently incestuous love for his sister is redefined as the love-at-first-sight of a legitimate romantic couple when Lord Gobrius reveals that "King" Arbaces is really his son and therefore not Princess Panthea's brother. The substitute-baby trick does not entirely resolve the issue, to be sure. The violence of Arbaces' passion leads him to feel that if he cannot marry his sister he will be forced to rape her and then kill himself. Such love can be legitimated but not retroactively idealized. The play in other ways, too, distances us from both Arbaces and his plight, and it signals more insistently than *Philaster* that all will be well. The interspersed scenes of cowardly Bessus and the Sword-men are pure comedy. The use of a morality-play structure – Arbaces poised between good angel (soldier–confidant Mardonius) and bad (Bessus) – provides two characters who externally determine our attitude toward the king. Another perspective is afforded by the semi-parallel Tigranes, the defeated Armenian king whom Arbaces intended (before he sees his sister) as a royal match for Panthea, for in falling in love with Panthea Tigranes is breaking his bond to his betrothed, Spaconia. Mardonius, Bessus, and Tigranes each in some way diminishes Arbaces and keeps him, much more than Philaster, the comic butt of our laughter.

The importance of Tigranes to the play's portrait of the arbitrary force of passion overturning traditional aristocratic ideals of love and honor also deflects attention from Arbaces. Both kings have a conscience, but Tigranes needs no plot twist to save him from passions he cannot control. As Arbaces sinks toward bestiality, Tigranes exercises both the reason and will that Arbaces conspicuously lacks. He refinds his identity and self-respect by rejecting his "unmanly . . . sudden doting" and recommitting himself to Spaconia, for she "so much lov'd thee that in honesty / And honor thou art bound to meet her virtues" (Turner, 1963, IV.ii.18–19). Arbaces is saved by the playwrights' manipulation of plot elements, within the play by their surrogate Gobrius, whose ambition placed his son on the throne and whose "witching letters" predisposed Arbaces to fall in love with his "sister" (thus assuring that Arbaces would remain king, though by marriage, not by birth). Frankly human plotting has provided this happy ending, not fate, and Tigranes' refound constancy adds the possibility of the traditional comic resolution of marriage for all. *A King and No King* lacks the bittersweet mood of *Philaster*'s final focus on Bellario/Euphrasia.

Through the reigns of the early Stuarts and during the Restoration, the most popular Beaumont and Fletcher plays were these last three collaborative works and a comedy, *The Scornful Lady* (*c*.1610, largely Fletcher's). The first collaboration proved seminal, and perhaps these plays' quality, relative seriousness, and engagement with social and political issues should be attributed to Beaumont, or to his influence. Beaumont and Fletcher have now fallen almost completely out of favor, in part because, while we forgive Shakespeare his lapses, we are still heirs of the classicist hierarchy of genres – tragedy first, then comedy – and distrustful of experimental mixtures. Celebrated modern tragicomedies tip toward the tragic and the philosophic, like the plays of Samuel Beckett. Beaumont and Fletcher's use of frankly artificial plot twists to rescue their heroes and restore them from despair to happiness makes their tragicomedies seem morally flimsy to us, hence the usual charges of empty sensationalism or cynical escapism. They have been seen as both apolitical and as royalists writing for a courtly audience; more damning for a modern audience is their sexualization of politics, which seems an evasion not of censorship but of the serious issues of governance. Then, too, some of the features natural to Renaissance tragicomedy – flat characters, external characterization, theatricalized emotion, and heightened rhetoric – no longer appeal to a taste shaped by realistic, character-centered novels and plays. And despite the fact that collaboration was the norm of Renaissance theater practice, the subsequent romantic elevation of the singular artistic genius makes us distrustful of multiple authorship.

This chapter has argued against some of these responses. In recent years, historicist criticism has tried to restore Beaumont and Fletcher to their proper theatrical milieu (Masten, 1992, 1997) and political context – the country aristocracy, not the court (Finkelpearl, 1990; McMullan, 1994). The massive shift in taste since the seventeenth century, however, makes it unlikely that their tragicomedies will be resurrected as other than theatrical curiosities. What made these plays so appealing in their own time? Many of the commendatory verses in the first folio effusively praise their intricate plotting. Beyond being "well made," to seventeenth-century taste, the plays were sensational in subject matter, both politically and in centering on the darker aspects of romantic passion. In this they were not alone. Shakespeare's late plays also explore how quickly love can turn to suspicion, jealousy, and hatred. It is relevant that *Othello* was revived and in the 1611–12 season played at court with *The Winter's Tale* and *A King and No King*. In larger terms, Beaumont and Fletcher's plays appealed to an audience that sensed it was caught between worlds – an as yet unpredictable future (whose seeds were already present) and an Elizabethan past that, when James

I proved disappointing as monarch, was given the nostalgic glow of an era distinguished by an ideal queen and social, moral, and political certainties (Heinemann, 1990, 161–2). The tragicomedies' double perspective allowed its audience to share in the virtues and values of that golden world – nobility, valor, honor, friendship, Petrarchan love – while also participating in the playwrights' acknowledgment that that world no longer exists, its assumptions are no longer adequate.

The vacillating, self-absorbed young protagonists – Leucippus, Philaster, Amintor, Arbaces – are baffled by the apparent failure of these values. One reason for their confusion is that the whole patriarchal system is dramatized as breaking down. This is not merely a "crisis of the aristocracy," but a more general crisis of authority. There are no strong, admirable, or able kings in these plays. Philaster, Amintor, and (to his knowledge, before the last scene) Arbaces have no fathers. Strong, witty women may be rewarded at the end of the tragicomedies, but before that Arethusa and Spaconia suffer from patriarchy's instinctive disbelief in their chastity. The King in *The Maid's Tragedy* orders Amintor to desert patriarchy's ideal – the loving, chaste, patiently suffering Aspatia – while promoting the sexually transgressive Evadne. Crushingly, it is Amintor's reputation for being honorable that makes him the perfect candidate for the King's dishonorable plan. Loyalty to absolutist tyrants proves crippling, yet rebellion and regicide turn out to be personally devastating. Social status is equally unstable. Gobrius' plan successfully promotes his commoner son to the Iberian throne, and Spaconia advances to become Tigranes' queen. Despite the exotic settings and extreme situations, these plays offered their audience fictional versions of its own experience; they staged the clashing ideological constructions of a specific historical period. That Beaumont and Fletcher deconstructed their play-world without providing an alternative vision is a significant part of the milieu in which and for which they wrote. When the social and political world restabilized in the late seventeenth and eighteenth centuries, critical taste and audience milieu had changed, and this broader ideological appeal no longer resonated.

NOTES

1 The most extensive attempt to establish who wrote what is Cyrus Hoy's, in seven articles separately numbered under the general title "The Shares of Fletcher and his Collaborators in the Beaumont and Fletcher Canon" (1956–62). Hoy's methods and assumptions have been challenged by Masten (1992, 341–4) and McMullan (1994, 148–9). Even in Hoy's account, of Fletcher's several collaborators Beaumont is the most difficult to differentiate, and in this discussion I will not try to apportion scenes.

2 It is possible they knew each other as early as 1602, if the prefatory verses to *Salmacis and Hermaphroditus* signed "A. F." in 1602 but "J. F." in the 1640 quarto refer to John Fletcher. We also do not know when Beaumont wrote the lost play entered in the Stationers' Register (June 29, 1660) as "*The History of Madon, King of Brittain*, by F. Beamont."

3 These liberated heroines seem to have contributed to Fletcher's success, or so the prologue to the second issue of the second quarto (1649) of *The Woman Hater* claims: Fletcher "to the stars, your sex did raise; / For which, full twenty years, he wore the bays" (Beaumont and Fletcher, 1966–97, I, 236, ll. 23–4; quotations from this old-spelling edition are modernized).

4　Upton argues for specific satiric thrusts at James I and at favorites Philip Herbert and James Hay (1929, 1053–65). James D. Knowles finds "parallels between Lazarello's pursuit of the umbrano and the attempts to reform the royal household by reducing the number of diets" (1988, 935).

5　Fletcher may have been already working on his first solo effort, *The Faithful Shepherdess*. Whether *Cupid's Revenge* preceded *The Faithful Shepherdess* in 1608 cannot with certainty be decided, and I am somewhat arbitrarily discussing *Cupid's Revenge* first. For different ways the scanty information can be interpreted, see Astington (1979); Bliss (1987, 56); Finkelpearl (1990, 129); Savage (1948).

6　The differences between Q1 (1620) and Q2 (1622) have been attributed to censorship by Savage (1949); Gurr in his edition surveys the evidence against this view (1969, lxxv–lxxviii).

7　Wallis notes that after the Civil War Charles II is rumored to have banned playing *The Maid's Tragedy* (1947, 137); in the Restoration Edmund Waller rewrote the fifth act to convert the play to tragicomedy.

8　In 1763 George Coleman the Elder tidied up the "ribaldry" and "unmanly" elements but left the happy ending largely intact; in the printed edition he defended retitling it *Philaster, A Tragedy* (1778, 7).

References and Further Reading

Astington, John H. (1979). "The popularity of *Cupid's Revenge*." *Studies in English Literature* 19, 215–27.

Beaumont, Francis (1984). *The Knight of the Burning Pestle*, ed. Sheldon P. Zitner. Revels Plays. Manchester: Manchester University Press.

Beaumont, Francis and John Fletcher (1966–97). *The Dramatic Works in the Beaumont and Fletcher Canon*, gen. ed. Fredson Bowers. 10 vols. Cambridge: Cambridge University Press.

Blau, Herbert (1986). "The absolved riddle: sovereign pleasure and the baroque subject in the tragicomedies of John Fletcher." *New Literary History* 17, 539–54.

Bliss, Lee (1983). "Defending Fletcher's shepherds." *Studies in English Literature* 23, 295–310.

Bliss, Lee (1984). " 'Plot mee no plots': the life of drama and the drama of life in *The Knight of the Burning Pestle*." *Modern Language Quarterly* 45, 3–21.

Bliss, Lee (1987). *Francis Beaumont*. Boston: Twayne.

Bushnell, Rebecca W. (1990). *Tragedies of Tyrants: Political Thought and Theater in the English Renaissance*. Ithaca: Cornell University Press.

Coleman, George, ed. (1778). *Philaster, A Tragedy*. London: printed for John Bell.

Craik, T. W., ed. (1988). *The Maid's Tragedy*. Revels Plays. Manchester: Manchester University Press.

Crawford, Julie (1999). "Fletcher's *The Tragedie of Bonduca* and the anxieties of the masculine government of James I." *Studies in English Literature* 39, 357–81.

Danby, John F. (1952). *Poets on Fortune's Hill: Studies in Sidney, Shakespeare, Beaumont and Fletcher*. London: Faber and Faber.

Davison, Peter (1963). "The serious concerns of *Philaster*." *ELH* 30, 1–15.

Finkelpearl, Philip J. (1971). "Beaumont, Fletcher, and 'Beaumont and Fletcher': some distinctions." *English Literary Renaissance* 1, 144–64.

Finkelpearl, Philip J. (1990). *Court and Country Politics in the Plays of Beaumont and Fletcher*. Princeton: Princeton University Press.

Gayley, Charles Mills (1914). *Beaumont, the Dramatist*. 1969 repr., New York: Russell & Russell.

Gurr, Andrew, ed. (1969). *Philaster*. Revels Plays. London: Methuen.

Heinemann, Margot (1990). "Political drama." In *The Cambridge Companion to English Renaissance Drama*, eds A. R. Braunmuller and Michael Hattaway. Cambridge: Cambridge University Press.

Hoy, Cyrus (1956–62). "The shares of Fletcher and his collaborators in the Beaumont and Fletcher canon." *Studies in Bibliography* 89, 115.

Knowles, James D. (1988) *Times Literary Supplement*, August 26.

McLuskie, Kathleen (1992). "'A maidenhead, Amintor, at my yeares': chastity and tragicomedy in the Fletcher plays." In *The Politics of Tragicomedy*, eds Gordon McMullan and Jonathan Hope. London: Routledge.

McMullan, Gordon (1994). *The Politics of Unease in the Plays of John Fletcher*. Amherst, MA: University of Massachusetts Press.

Masten, Jeffrey A. (1992). "Beaumont and/or Fletcher: collaboration and the interpretation of Renaissance drama." *ELH* 59, 337–56.

Masten, Jeffrey A. (1997). *Textual Intercourse: Collaboration, Authorship, and Sexualities in Renaissance Drama*. Cambridge: Cambridge University Press.

Miller, Ronald F. (1978). "Dramatic form and dramatic imagination in Beaumont's *The Knight of the Burning Pestle*." *English Literary Renaissance* 8, 67–84.

Mizener, Arthur (1940). "The high design of *A King and No King*." *Modern Philology* 38, 133–54.

Neill, Michael (1970). "'The simetry, which gives a poem grace': masque, imagery, and the fancy of *The Maid's Tragedy*." *Renaissance Drama* n.s. 3, 111–35.

Neill, Michael (1981). "The defence of contraries: skeptical paradox in *A King and No King*." *Studies in English Literature* 21, 319–32.

Samuelson, David A. (1979). "The order in Beaumont's *Knight of the Burning Pestle*." *English Literary Renaissance* 9, 302–18.

Savage, James E. (1948). "The date of Beaumont and Fletcher's *Cupid's Revenge*." *ELH* 15, 286–94.

Savage, James E. (1949). "The 'gaping wounds' in the text of *Philaster*." *Philological Quarterly* 28, 443–57.

Shullenberger, William (1982). "'This for the most wrong'd of women': a reappraisal of *The Maid's Tragedy*." *Renaissance Drama* n.s. 13, 131–56.

Turner, Robert K. Jr. (1961). "The morality of *A King and No King*." *Renaissance Papers, 1961* 93–103.

Turner, Robert K. Jr., ed. (1963). *A King and No King*. Regents Renaissance Drama. Lincoln: University of Nebraska Press.

Turner, Robert Y. (1984). "Heroic passion in the early tragicomedies of Beaumont and Fletcher." *Medieval and Renaissance Drama in England* 1, 109–30.

Upton, Allbert W. (1929). "Allusions to James I and his court in Marston's *Fawn* and Beaumont's *Woman Hater*." *PMLA* 44, 1048–65.

Waith, Eugene M. (1952). *The Pattern of Tragicomedy in Beaumont and Fletcher*. New Haven: Yale University Press.

Wallis, Lawrence B. (1947). *Fletcher, Beaumont and Company: Entertainers to the Jacobean Gentry*. New York: King's Crown Press.

Woodson, William C. (1978). "The casuistry of innocence in *A King and No King* and its implications for tragicomedy." *English Literary Renaissance* 8, 312–28.

Yoch, James J. (1987). "The Renaissance dramatization of temperance: the Italian revival of tragicomedy and *The Faithful Shepherdess*." In *Renaissance Tragicomedy: Explorations in Genre and Politics*, ed. Nancy Klein Maguire. New York: AMS Press.

Zitner, Sheldon P., ed. (1984). *The Maid's Tragedy*. Revel Plays. Manchester: Manchester University Press.

36

Collaboration

Philip C. McGuire

Let us begin with a disparity, long-standing and still persisting, that hinders the study of Renaissance plays that are the products of collaboration.[1] The disparity involves the gap between the significance such plays had for the culture within which they came into being and the importance accorded them in recent and current work. As evidence of that importance, consider the two-volume *Drama of the English Renaissance*, the dominant collection of non-Shakespearean drama of the sixteenth and early seventeenth centuries since its publication (Fraser and Rabkin, 1976). Of the 41 plays in that collection, five are identified as products of collaborative writing practices. That ratio of roughly one in eight prolongs the (mis)impression that collaboratively written plays are a relatively small subset of Renaissance drama, which consists overwhelmingly of plays composed by a single dramatist writing individually.

The disparity I have in mind comes into focus when one places those figures in relation to evidence from the sixteenth and early seventeenth centuries, particularly Henslowe's diary, which Gerald Eades Bentley characterizes as "far and away the most detailed record of authorship that has come down to us" (1971, 199). "In the case of the 282 plays mentioned in Henslowe's diary," Bentley observes, "nearly two-thirds are the work of more than one man . . . as either collaborator, reviser, or provider of additional matter" (1971, 199). Of collaboration specifically, Bentley says, "The number of collaborations attested by Henslowe's records is very great. Indeed they show that the majority of the plays he bought for both the Lord Admiral's company and for the Earl of Worcester's men were not individual compositions but collaborations" (1971, 199). In *A Companion to Henslowe's Diary*, Neil Carson, focusing more narrowly on plays produced during 1598 at the Rose theater, observes that " 'collaborated plays accounted for 60 per cent of the plays completed in the Fall–Winter 1598, and an astonishing 82 percent in Spring–Summer 1598' " (quoted in Masten, 1997a, 357–8).

Undervaluing the significance of "collaborated plays" in the commercial theaters of early modern London is itself symptomatic of a more fundamental problem. As

Jeffrey Masten has explained, collaboratively written plays precede, elude, and resist "categories of singular authorship, intellectual property, and the individual that are central to later Anglo-American cultural, literary, and legal history" (1997a, 361–2). The extended dominance of those categories has, until very recently, made it extremely difficult to come to grips with jointly written plays on terms compatible with the cultural conditions within which they came into being, conditions in which, Masten contends, "collaboration was the standard mode of operation within the early modern English theater, not a problem to be confronted only after considering singularly authored plays" (1997a, 358).

Among the professional dramatists of the English Renaissance whose plays were performed in the commercial theaters of London, including those whom later centuries have come to cherish most highly on the basis of plays that they wrote single-handedly, it is difficult to find one who did not also engage in collaborative writing during his career. The most conspicuous case is Shakespeare, who since the eighteenth century has been regarded as the epitome of a (primarily post-Renaissance) conception of authorship based on the notion of a unique artistic consciousness exercising singular, dominant control over the production of a text and its meanings. He is considered, in Masten's phrasing, "*the* individual Author and the author of individuality – the very anti-type of collaboration" (1997b, 10). In the earliest published collection of Shakespeare's plays – the First Folio of 1623 entitled *Mr William Shakespeares Comedies, Histories & Tragedies* (1623) – John Heminges and Henry Condell claim, in their address "To the great Variety of Readers," to present the plays "as he conceived them." It is not difficult to hear in that "he" a rejection of even the possibility of the involvement of any other playwright(s), yet scholars have long accepted that Shakespeare wrote one of those plays that "he conceived," *Henry VIII*, in collaboration with John Fletcher, who later succeeded him as the principal playwright of the King's Men. There is also broad scholarly agreement that the same collaborative pairing wrote *The Two Noble Kinsmen*, which, although not among the plays published in the First Folio, has long been acknowledged as Shakespeare's (and Fletcher's). In a controversial move that established the groundwork for further inquiry into Shakespeare's participation in collaborative writing practices, the editors of the Oxford *Complete Shakespeare*, Stanley Wells and Gary Taylor (1986), identified *Timon of Athens* – a play included in the First Folio – as jointly authored by Shakespeare and Thomas Middleton.

As further evidence of the extensiveness of collaboration, consider the fact that not only Shakespeare but also every dramatist to whom this book devotes a separate chapter – Christopher Marlowe, Thomas Middleton, John Webster, John Ford, Ben Jonson – engaged in collaborative writing. Jonson's situation is particularly revealing. Evidence abounds that he participated in a variety of collaborative writing practices involving *Eastward Ho* and several plays now lost, including *The Isle of Dogs*, *The Page of Plymouth*, *Hot Anger Soon Cold*, and *Robert the Second, or The Scot's Tragedy*.

Jonson's engagement in collaborative dramatic writing is especially indicative of the prevalence of such activity. At a time when the scripts that dramatists wrote were legally owned by the acting companies that performed them, he came to insist upon his singularity and sovereignty as a dramatist to an extent that sets him apart from his contemporaries (see chapter 32 above). In doing so, he both contributed to and anticipated the then-developing conception of the author as "sole controller of the text" (McMullan, 1994, 155) that became dominant in subsequent centuries and remained unchallenged until the concluding decades of the twentieth. He became intensely concerned with claiming as his own, for himself, plays that he had written, singlehandedly or collaboratively, for sale to and performance by various acting companies. For example, when *Sejanus* was first published in 1605, he explained in an "Address to the Readers" that the play as published is different from the play as it "was acted on the public stage" by the King's Men in 1603. The difference on which Jonson concentrates is the presence in the performed version of the work of a collaborator, "a second pen [that] had good show,"and Jonson takes pains to explain that, in the published version, he has chosen to replace the contributions of the unnamed collaborator with words "weaker (and no doubt less pleasing) of mine own."

Jonson's effort with *Sejanus* to make a play-text in which a collaborator had a share into one that is entirely "mine own" inversely complements what happens with *Volpone*. In the Prologue to the play, first acted in 1606 and first published in 1607, Jonson finds it appropriate to declare that this play comes exclusively "From his own hand": " 'Tis known, five weeks fully penned it / From his own hand, without a co-adjutor, / Novice, journeyman, or tutor." This assertion of singlehanded authorship makes sense, Bentley cogently observes, only if Jonson were convinced that those who first heard those words spoken in the theater or read them on the printed page assumed that plays were written collaboratively (1971, 207–8).

Bentley goes on to declare:

> Collaboration between two or more dramatists, especially professional dramatists, was a common method of composition in the greatest days of the English drama. . . . Well known collaborations like those of Beaumont and Fletcher or Middleton and Rowley or Shakespeare and Fletcher should not be looked upon as oddities, but as common occurrences in the careers of professional dramatists of the time. (1971, 234)

Recent commentators have moved beyond Bentley's use of "common." Masten asserts, "In a scholarly field dominated by the singular figure of Shakespeare, it is easily forgotten, that collaboration was the Renaissance English theatre's dominant mode of textual production" (1997b, 14). Concentrating more specifically on the years of King James's reign (1603–25), Gordon McMullan declares, "It is thus essential to emphasize that active collaboration was the *norm* of Jacobean theater" (1994, 142).

The "Chronological table" of surviving plays provided in *The Cambridge Companion to Renaissance Drama* attests to the persistence of collaborative dramatic writing. Although that table "does not include plays the texts of which have not survived" and is "a full but not complete list of plays of the period 1497–1642" (Braunmuller and Hattaway, 1990, 419), it shows that at least one multiply authored play was written every decade from the appearance of *Gorboduc* in 1562 until the closing of the theaters in 1642 – a span covering eight decades and the reigns of Elizabeth I, James I, and Charles I. The list also offers instances of collaboratively written plays in each of the major dramatic genres – not only tragedies (such as *The Changeling* and *The Fatal Dowry*) but also comedies (such as *The Roaring Girl* and *A Cure for a Cuckold*), and histories (such as *Sir Thomas Wyatt* and *Henry VIII*). Jointly authored plays were particularly crucial to the emergence, during the first decade of the 1600s, of tragicomedy, the distinctive features of which were defined in large measure by the collaborative work of Francis Beaumont and John Fletcher in such plays as *Philaster* and *A King and No King* (see chapters 27 and 35 above).

Collaborative dramatic writing was most intense in James' reign, during which 56 of the 73 jointly written plays listed in the *Cambridge* table were composed or first performed. Between 1603, when James became England's king, and 1609, 18 jointly composed plays first appeared, 22 between 1610 and 1619, and 16 between 1620 and the year of James' death, 1625. The number written or first performed during each of those sub-periods exceeds the number that the *Cambridge* table lists for the entirety of either Elizabeth's reign (12) or Charles' (five).

The performance records of the King's Men, the pre-eminent theatrical company of the era, give further evidence of the degree to which collaborative dramatic writing practices were "common," "dominant," "*norm*[ative]." Between 1616 and 1642, Bentley notes (1971, 210), they performed 46 plays published in the Beaumont and Fletcher folio as the joint work of those playwrights,[2] compared to 16 attributed solely to Shakespeare. The same pattern is visible in the company's performances at court between 1616 and 1642: "42 performances (including repetitions) are," Bentley reports, "of plays from the Beaumont and Fletcher folios, compared to 18 performances of plays written by Shakespeare, and 7 performances of plays written by Jonson" (1971, 210).

The company's use of collaboratively written materials changed in revealing ways during the years between its founding in 1594 (as the Lord Chamberlain's Men) and its dissolution after 1642. According to the *Cambridge* table, the seven jointly written plays that first appeared after the company's founding and before Elizabeth's death in 1603 were owned not by them but by rival adult acting companies, with the Lord Admiral's Men, owners of five of the plays, in a controlling position. After 1603, however, the situation began to change decisively. Of the 18 jointly authored plays listed for the years 1603–9, two are not affiliated with a specific company, eight belonged to companies of boy players, and adult acting companies owned the remaining eight. Five of those eight were the property of the King's Men, while one was the property of the Prince's Men (formerly the Lord Admiral's Men), and a third adult company, the Queen's Men, owned two. Thus, the King's Men went from being a company that, according to the *Cambridge* table, did not perform new collaboratively written plays during its first eight years of existence to one that, during the first seven years of James' reign, acquired and first performed more such plays than did all other adult companies combined.

One possible explanation for that change is that, in turning to collaboratively written plays, the King's Men were adapting to changes in their situation flowing from James' accession and, in those new and unpredictable circumstances, to the competitive pressures exerted not only by rival adult companies but also, and perhaps especially, by the boy companies, who between 1603 and 1609 added to their repertories eight new plays that were collaboratively written: four for the Children of the Queen's Revels, three for the Children of St. Paul's, and one for the Children of the King's Revels (see chapter 22 above). Collaborative writing was particularly advantageous, Kathleen McLuskie points out, when speedy composition was needed. She offers as an example "*Sir John van Olden Barnaveldt* (1619), which was written [by John Fletcher and Philip Massinger], acted, censored, and acted again within six weeks of the Dutch patriot's trial and execution" (1981, 172). If dramatists could produce scripts for performance more quickly by working together than by working solo, then companies that did not have consistent access to such scripts would have found themselves disadvantaged. After 1603, the King's Men, reversing their previous practice, apparently made sure they were not so disadvantaged. They acquired and performed more collaboratively written plays than any of their competitors.

The numbers for the years 1610 through 1619 show the King's Men's use of collaboratively written plays increasing both absolutely and relative to their rivals. For that decade, during which the last of the boy companies ceased functioning, the *Cambridge* table lists 22 collaboratively composed plays, for four of which there is no company affiliation. Of the remaining 18 plays listed, 13 were first performed by or written for the King's Men – a more than two-fold increase from 1603–9. During the same years, three other adult companies first performed or had written three jointly authored plays, while one was performed by or written for a boy company. Thus, during that decade, the King's Men brought more collaboratively written plays to the stage than the rest of the acting companies combined.

The pattern of dominance established from 1610 through 1619 continued during the years 1620–5, for which the *Cambridge* table lists another 16 collaboratively written plays. Ten of them are plays for the King's Men, and the remaining six are for three other adult companies, each of which owned two. All in all, the table indicates that during the years from 1603 through 1625, the King's Men acquired or first performed (no fewer than) 28 of the 56 collaboratively written plays listed for that period. That is more than the total of such plays, 22, with which all the other acting companies – boy or adult – are affiliated in the *Cambridge* table, which includes six plays that are not linked to a specific company. The boy companies as a group are listed as affiliated with nine jointly written plays, approximately one-third of the King's Men's total; the other adult companies are affiliated with 13, fewer than half as many as the King's Men. The two specific companies with the highest totals after the King's Men are the Prince's Men and the Children of the Queen's Revels, each of which is linked with five multiply authored plays – a figure that is less than one-fifth of the 28 owned by the King's Men.

After Charles I succeeded to the throne in 1625, the number of collaboratively written plays declined sharply, the *Cambridge* table shows, but the dominance of the King's Men became total. Between 1626 and 1642, when the commercial London theaters were closed, five such plays made their first appearance – far fewer than any comparable period during the reign of James I. According to the table, all five of those plays belonged to the King's Men, and if the table is accurate, they were, during those years, the sole professional acting company that acquired and performed new collaboratively written plays. That situation is a full reversal of the company's initial relationship to collaborative dramatic writing. The King's Men went from being a company that, in contrast to their rivals, performed no new collaboratively written plays listed in the *Cambridge* table during their first years of operation, 1594–1602, to being, during what would turn out to be their (and their rivals') final years of existence, the only company performing such plays.

During 48 years of operation, the King's Men became and, equally impressively, remained the pre-eminent acting company in England, in the process coping effectively with various challenges, among them extensive changes in personnel over the years, including the loss of such crucial founding members as their leading playwright Shakespeare and their leading actor Richard Burbage. Many elements contributed to the King's Men's sustained pre-eminence, and one of them may well have been, after 1603, their increasing and eventually total dominance of collaboratively written plays. That dominance would have given them more new plays more quickly than their competitors, but it may also have conferred another advantage.

In an unpublished essay, William W. B. Slights (1999) has proposed thinking of collaborative dramatic writing as a process, analogous to systems of dowers and dowries, by which the properties – skills, techniques, stratagems, practices – of each participating dramatist would have been made available to, shared with, passed to, circulated among his fellow collaborators. The Beaumont and Fletcher Folio of 1647 – *Comedies and Tragedies Written by Francis Beaumont and John Fletcher, Gentlemen*[3] – offers evidence that such transmission occurred. Studies have established that most of the plays published in that volume as by "Beaumont and Fletcher" were not in fact written by that pair, but by other playwrights, including Fletcher, working alone or in collaboration. Bentley, for example, observes that "at least thirty of the plays were written after Beaumont's death" (1971, 208) and refers to "reasonable evidence" (1971, 209) of Philip Massinger's involvement in 19. By current standards, those plays are inauthentic, but their inclusion in the volume suggests that, in the view of those who organized it and those to whom it was marketed, playwrights other than the Beaumont–Fletcher team succeeded in writing plays so like those actually written by the era's most renowned collaborative pair as to be considered *by* Beaumont and Fletcher in the sense of having the properties of, being near or akin to, being classifiable with, the plays they penned together. In 1647 "*by*" Beaumont and Fletcher seems to have meant not only written collaboratively by them but also written by others who had acquired the capacities needed to (re)produce plays with properties that marked them as convincingly – which is to say, vendibly – in the Beaumont and Fletcher mode.

To the extent that transmission through collaboration did occur, the King's Men's domination of collaboratively written plays after 1603 would have given them an additional competitive edge by enhancing their access to a wider, fuller endowment or inventory of dramaturgical resources and practices. Almost certainly the key figure in such a process was John Fletcher, who, after Shakespeare's retirement, became the company's principal playwright and remained so until his death in 1625, the year in which James I also died. The sharp drop in the number of new collaborative plays performed in subsequent years almost certainly has as much, if not more, to do with Fletcher's passing than with James' death and the accession of Charles. Before and after succeeding Shakespeare, Fletcher wrote plays not only singlehandedly but also collaboratively, working with various dramatists in a network of interconnecting relationships: initially Beaumont, then Shakespeare, Nathan Field, William Rowley, Thomas Middleton, and, toward the end of his career, Philip Massinger, his successor as the principal playwright of the King's Men. Those relationships interconnected with others; Rowley, for example, wrote with (among others) Thomas Dekker, Thomas Heywood, John Ford, and John Webster as well as Middleton, whose collaborators included not only Rowley but also Dekker, Webster, and, arguably, Shakespeare.

The precise character of specific working relationships remains unclear. It is tempting, for example, to think of Fletcher as Shakespeare's "junior partner" (McMullan, 1994, 143) during their collaborations in 1612–13, when Shakespeare's career was drawing to a close, and then of Fletcher as the dominant partner in his collaboration with Massinger, who seems to have specialized in the openings and conclusions of the plays they wrote together. Whatever their particular configurations and dynamics, the collaborative relationships within which early modern English professional dramatists regularly worked were elements of interlacing networks, in which one wrote not just with a particular collaborator or collaborators but also, by proxy, with those with whom he and they had previously collaborated. Intertwined and overlapping, such networks were common in the sense of being frequent but also common in the sense of being open or conducive to extensive sharing and wide participation. They both presumed and fostered the dramatists' knowledge of one another's working practices, which were thus more easily and efficiently kept in circulation, pooled, and transmitted, remaining available for use by an acting company and those writing for it even after the retirement or death of a particular dramatist.

As one instance of such transmission, consider the following dialogue in *A Cure for a Cuckold*, written by Webster and Rowley:

> *Pettifog* I'll tell you how he was served: this informer comes into Turnball Street to a victualling house, and there falls in league with a wench –
>
> *Compass* A tweak, or bronstrops: I learnt that name in a play.
>
> *Pettifog* – had belike some private dealings with her, and there got a goose.
>
> (IV.i.120–6)

The exchange calls attention to Compass' use of "bronstrops," which means bawd, by having him comment, apparently in response to Pettifog's wordless reaction, that he "learned" the term "in a play." René Weis explains that "bronstrops" – a corruption, ultimately, of "bawdstrot" – "is a phrase frequently used by Middleton with whom both Webster and Rowley had collaborated" (Webster, 1996, 428).[4] Rowley is generally credited with writing scenes and passages involving Compass (a part he might also have played), but regardless of whether he or Webster is individually responsible for "bronstrops," the presence of the word, with its origin "in a[nother] play" marked conspicuously, attests to the process of circulation and transmission fostered by specific acts of collaboration and the networks of which such acts were elements.

Another example of collaborative transmission, this time involving non-verbal elements, occurs in the opening scene of *The Fatal Dowry*, collaboratively written by Massinger and Field for the King's Men and, in the *Cambridge* table of plays, tentatively dated 1617, the year after Shakespeare's death. Attired in "sable habit" (I.i.55) in sorrowful remembrance of his recently deceased father, Charalois says nothing for the first 50 lines, yet dominates the scene. The use of costume and the absence of speech to draw a character to the audience's attention make the scene, as both McLuskie (1981, 178) and Sleights (1999, 14) have observed, dramaturgically akin to the first court scene (I.ii) in *Hamlet*, where Hamlet is a silent, black-clad, yet conspicuous figure. There is no evidence that either Field or Massinger wrote collaboratively with Shakespeare, but each worked with Fletcher, who had worked with Shakespeare, and thus it is possible to see Field and Massinger as participants in and, in this instance, beneficiaries of a collaborative network that reached beyond each of them. Those networks sometimes extended across different acting companies; Rowley, for example, collaborated with Middleton in writing *The Changeling* for the Lady Elizabeth's Men, with Dekker and Ford in writing *The Witch of Edmonton* for the Prince's Men, with Heywood in writing *Fortune by Land and Sea* for the Queen's Men, and with Webster in writing *A Cure for a Cuckold* for the King's Men. As the company that came to dominate the performance of new collaboratively written plays, the King's Men were at the center of more of those networks, advantageously positioned to benefit the most from them. Given that position, it may have been no accident that, in choosing Fletcher to succeed Shakespeare as their principal playwright and then Massinger to succeed Fletcher in that capacity, the company, facing on both occasions a moment of transition that would crucially affect its future, each time selected a dramatist who had collaborated with his predecessor.

Twentieth-century scholarship on collaboratively written plays concentrated almost exclusively on matters of attribution, trying to determine which dramatist wrote what part(s) – act, scene, character, speech, line – of a given play by attending to "the traces of individuality (including handwriting, spelling, word choice, imagery, and syntactic formations) left in the collaborative text" (Masten, 1997a, 372). The work of Cyrus Hoy, especially his series of articles "The shares of Fletcher and his collaborators in the Beaumont and Fletcher canon" published in *Studies in Bibliography* (1956–62), is exemplary of such scholarship, which continues to be published. In recent years, however, efforts have begun to develop and apply alternative approaches that are, by current standards, more attuned theoretically and historically to the cultural situation(s) within which collaboratively written plays were composed and first performed in early modern England. Masten, for example, has both mounted a powerful critique of standard attribution studies and situated collaborative writing practices for the theater "at the complicated intersection of homoeroticism, male friendship/conversation, and domestic relations" (1997a, 369), including the living arrangements of Beaumont and Fletcher as described in John Aubrey's *Brief Lives*: "They lived together on the Bank side, not far from the Play-house, both bachelors; lay together . . . had one wench in the house between them, which they did so admire; the same cloathes and cloake, &c., between them" (quoted in Masten, 1997b, 61).

In his psychoanalytic study of texts collaboratively written mostly between 1885 and 1922, Wayne Koestenbaum employs a paradigm in which he posits "that men who collaborate engage in metaphorical sexual intercourse, and that the text they balance between them is alternately the child of their sexual union, and a shared woman" (1989, 3). The paradigm has limitations, including the assumption that men write in pairs, which is the most common but by no means the only configuration in which English Renaissance dramatists wrote together. On the other hand, the "shared woman" tallies with Aubrey's report of the "one wench" whom Beaumont and Fletcher "had . . . in the house between them," and Koestenbaum's paradigm offers a perspective on what promises to become, as the study of jointly written plays moves in new directions, a major area of inquiry: the relationship between the thematics and the poetics of such plays – between the issues and problems they engage and their collaborative mode of production.

A play likely to be at the center of that inquiry is *A Cure for a Cuckold*, written by Webster and Rowley for the King's Men. One plot line in the play involves a woman shared sexually by two men and the paternity of the child she bears – a situation that aligns with the metaphors of Koestenbaum's paradigm. Upon returning home to Blackwall, near London, after an absence of more than three years, the sailor Compass, who has been presumed lost at sea, learns from two boys that the wife whom he left childless is now the mother of "a brave boy" (II.i.29) who is less than a year old. His wife Urse tearfully acknowledges "my fault" and tells him, "'Tis true, I have a child" (ll. 116, 130). Compass responds by asking her to acknowledge, in defiance of biological certainties, that the child is his, and he does so using terms that are explicitly theatrical:

> Ha, you? And what shall I have then, I pray? Will you not labour for me as I shall do for you? Because I was out o'th' way when 'twas gotten, shall I lose my share? There's better law amongst the players yet, for a fellow shall have his share, though he do not play that day. If you look for any part of my four years' wages, I will have half the boy. (II.i.131–6)

The sexual, the marital, the theatrical, and the economic coalesce in Compass' lines. Just as sharers in an acting company who do not "play" on a given day receive their portion of the revenue, so, Compass reasons, he should have his "share," his "half," of the boy born of his wife, even though, absent and "out o'th' way," he played no part in the child's conception. When Urse replies, "If you can forgive me, I shall be joyed at it," Compass insists that she had done nothing requiring his forgiveness: "Forgive thee? For what? For doing me a pleasure?" (ll. 137–8). Then, in terms that register his determination that the child be accepted as his, he asks: "And what is he that would *seem* to father *my* child?" (ll. 138–9; my emphases).

That "he" turns out to be Master Franckford, a merchant, whose wife Luce has remained childless during their marriage. Confronting Urse and Compass at the place where the child is being nursed, Franckford insists that child is his, not theirs: "The child is mine. I am the father of it. . . . / I do acknowledge, and will enjoy it" (III.ii.70–2). When Compass challenges Franckford's assertion of paternity and thus of ownership, pointing out that "You may be as far off the father as I am" (ll. 74–5), Urse acknowledges the fact of Franckford's paternity but asserts that the child is hers: "He's the begetter, but the child is mine: / I bred and bore it, and I will not lose it" (ll. 79–80). Demonstrating a tolerance for marital infidelity as accommodating as Compass', Franckford's wife Luce replies by supporting his right to the child:

> The child's my husband's, dame, and he must have it.
> I do allow my sufferance to the deed,
> In lieu I never yet was fruitful to him,
> And in my barrenness excuse my wrong.
>
> (ll. 81–4)

Each party threatens to take the dispute to court, but instead, in an informal tavern gathering that verges on a mediation session, Justice Woodroff, Franckford's brother-in-law, declares, "The law is on the mother's part" (IV.i.182). Franckford accepts the judgment, telling Compass, "The child's your wife's; I'll strive no further in it" (l. 190), and he pledges neither to seek compensation for the expenses he has borne nor to "take back / The inheritance" (ll. 93–4) he has made to the child. The law that Woodroff applies is not the "law amongst the players" that Compass invoked when appealing to Urse to allow him his "share" in the child, yet Woodroff's ruling in favor of "the mother's part" is voiced in language that, with the word "part," has theatrical resonances, and the ruling confirms the "share" in the child that Compass earlier sought from Urse.

As the scene closes, Compass and Urse take action to cure the cuckoldry inflicted on him. They agree to make a "flat divorce," then "Within two hours" to "Woo and wed afresh" (ll. 211, 213, 214). The play concludes on the next day as they come from that wedding, accompanied by, among others, Franckford, Luce, Nurse, and the child. In response to a question from Woodroff, Franckford initiates an exchange that both complicates and clarifies the terms "son" and "father":

Woodroff   Brother, are you a helper in this design too?
Franckford   The father to give the bride, sir

Compass	And I am his son, sir, and all the sons he has; and this is his grandchild, and my elder brother; you'll think this strange now.
Woodroff	Then it seems he begat this before you?
Compass	Before me? Not so, sir. I was far enough off, when 'twas done; yet let me see him dares say this is not my child, and this my father.

(V.i.393–400)

Franckford's words are accurate in at least two respects: as the "begetter" of the child, he is "the father" who presents Urse to her new husband, and he is "the father" of the bride in the sense that his act of begetting the child set in motion the events that have led to the wedding just concluded. Franckford is also Compass' "father" not just because he is the "father" of the woman Compass marries "afresh" but also because he has "fathered" Compass in the sense of making him a father. Franckford is the man who "begat this" child whose legal (but not biological) father Compass has become by virtue of having been, and being, Urse's husband. In different but equally valid ways, both Franckford and Compass are – and each one is – the father(s) of the child, whose on-stage presence here, for the first and only time in the play, helps theater audiences appreciate the complexities of its paternal situation.

Compass' final words to Franckford, his co-father, merit careful consideration:

Come, father,
Child, and bride. And for your part, father,
Whatsoever he, or he, or t'other says,
You shall be as welcome as in my t'other wife's days.
(ll. 425–8)

Because "child," not "bride," follows "father," the language draws attention to Franckford's role ("part") in biologically fathering the child, and Compass' assurance of future welcome should Franckford come to visit (the child?) holds open the possibility that he might play that part again, fathering upon Urse additional children of whom, of course, Compass would also be the father.

In *A Cure for a Cuckold*, fathering involves both begetting and rearing, and paternity is both biologically determined and socially constructed. Koestenbaum's paradigm makes it easier to appreciate that the presentation of how the child, who is never named, is doubly fathered alludes to the processes of collaborative writing in which Webster and Rowley engaged and from which he and every other character in the play took their initial, doubly begat being. Such multiple begetting was a fundamental feature of commercial theater in early modern England.

NOTES

1   My focus is on the collaborative compositional practices of professional dramatists writing together and concurrently (synchronously) for the commercial theater industry of early modern London

between roughly 1590 and 1642. Thus, I do not discuss entertainments, masques, or plays written by amateur dramatists. I also do not discuss revision, a common practice in the theater of that period. In my view, revision is best seen as a form of sequential or diachronic collaboration because it involves a dramatist changing, usually by means of additions, deletions, and substitutions, a play-text previously completed by another dramatist (or dramatists) that the company owning it wants to perform again, in altered form, after some lapse of time. For discussion of revision, see the chapter on the subject in Bentley (1971) and Rasmussen (1997).

My thanks to the members of the "Rethinking collaboration" seminar at the 1999 meeting of the Shakespeare Association of America.

2 My phrasing seeks to indicate that, as discussed later in this chapter, most of the plays published in that volume as by "Beaumont and Fletcher" were not in fact written by that pair, but by other playwrights, including Fletcher, working alone or in collaboration (see chapter 35 above).

3 See the discussion of this volume in Masten (1997b), esp. ch. 4.

4 Weis also explains that "got a goose" refers to "swelling in the groin from venereal disease, known as Winchester goose" (Webster, 1996, 428).

REFERENCES AND FURTHER READING

Bentley, Gerald Eades (1971). *The Profession of Dramatist in Shakespeare's Time, 1590–1642*. Princeton: Princeton University Press.

Braunmuller, A. R., and Michael Hattaway, eds (1990). *The Cambridge Companion to English Renaissance Drama*. Cambridge: Cambridge University Press.

Carson, Neil (1988). *A Companion to Henslowe's Diary*. Cambridge: Cambridge University Press.

Fraser, Russell A., and Norman Rabkin, eds (1976). *Drama of the English Renaissance*. Vol. I: The Tudor Period. Vol. II: The Stuart Period. New York: Macmillan and Collier Macmillan.

Hoy, Cyrus (1956–62). "The shares of Fletcher and his collaborators in the Beaumont and Fletcher canon." *Studies in Bibliography* 8–15.

Hoy, Cyrus (1976). "Critical and aesthetic problems of collaboration." *Research Opportunities in Renaissance Drama* 19, 3–6.

Koestenbaum, Wayne (1989). *Double Talk: The Erotics of Male Literary Collaboration*. New York: Routledge.

McLuskie, Kathleen (1981). "Collaboration." In *The Revels History of Drama in English*, eds Philip Edwards, Gerald Eades Bentley, Kathleen McLuskie, and Lois Potter. Volume IV: 1613–1660. London: Methuen.

McMullan, Gordon (1994). *The Politics of Unease in the Plays of John Fletcher*. Amherst, MA: University of Massachusetts Press.

McMullan, Gordon (1996). "'Our whole life is like a play': collaboration and the problem of editing." *Textus* 9, 437–60.

Masten, Jeffrey (1992). "Beaumont and/or Fletcher: collaboration and the interpretation of Renaissance Drama." *ELH* 59, 337–56.

Masten, Jeffrey (1997a). "Playwrighting: authorship and collaboration." In *A New History of Early English Drama*, eds John D. Cox and David Scott Kastan. New York: Columbia University Press.

Masten, Jeffrey (1997b). *Textual Intercourse: Collaboration, Authorship, and Sexualities in Renaissance Drama*. Cambridge: Cambridge University Press.

Orgel, Stephen (1981). "What is a text?" *Research Opportunities in Renaissance Drama* 24, 3–6. Reprinted in *Staging the Renaissance: Reinterpretations of Elizabethan and Jacobean Drama* (1991), eds David Scott Kastan and Peter Stallybrass. New York: Routledge.

Rabkin, Norman (1976). "Problems in the study of collaboration." *Research Opportunities in Renaissance Drama* 19, 7–13.

Rasmussen, Eric (1997). "The revision of scripts." In *A New History of Early English Drama*, eds John D. Cox and David Scott Kastan. New York: Columbia University Press.

Shakespeare, William (1986). *The Complete Works*, eds Stanley Wells and Gary Taylor. Oxford: Clarendon Press.

Slights, William W. E. (1999). "Dower power: communities of collaboration in Jacobean drama," unpublished essay.

Webster, John (1996). *A Cure for a Cuckold*. In *"The Duchess of Malfi" and Other Plays*, ed. René Weis. New York: Oxford University Press.

37

John Webster

Elli Abraham Shellist

Many readers coming to Renaissance drama for the first time will know John Webster (*c*.1580–*c*.1634) only as a character from the popular 1998 movie *Shakespeare in Love*, in which he is portrayed as a sadistic 13-year-old who tortures mice, spies on the principal characters in the act of coitus, and attributes his love for theater to the moment in Shakespeare's ultra-violent *Titus Andronicus* (*c*.1593) "when they cut heads off . . . and the daughter [is] mutilated with knives." His artistic credo is, "Plenty of blood. That's the only writing." As we shall see, this particular representation is a personification (and most likely a parody) of a traditional – and somewhat antiquated – critical view of Webster as a misogynistic, hack playwright obsessed with sensationalistic violence and melodramatic horror. In many ways, this moralizing criticism merely deflected what it perceived to be the sins of Jacobean drama onto Webster and his three major plays: the tragedies *The White Devil* (*c*.1612) and *The Duchess of Malfi* (*c*.1614), and the tragicomedy *The Devil's Law-Case* (*c*.1618). The advent of the New Historicism in the late 1970s provided us with better ways of understanding Webster's plays and the ways they dramatize the cultural conflicts of Jacobean England, but the caricature from *Shakespeare in Love* is worth mention if for no other reason than to show how his gothic reputation dogs him even today.

Most of what we now know about Webster's life we have gleaned from Mary Edmond's research on his father.[1] John Webster senior ran a coach-making business in Cow Lane, just outside of the London city walls. Apparently business was good: he was a freeman of the Merchant Taylors' Company, an important member of his community (a councilman in his parish) with servants, apprentices, and connections with both the theater and publishing industries. He provided wagons for the actor Edward Alleyn, among others, and was neighbors with William White, the stationer who printed Shakespeare's *Love's Labour's Lost* (*c*.1595). Webster senior married Elizabeth Coates in 1577, which lends credence to a 1579 or 1580 birthdate for the playwright. More telling is a line from the dedication to the younger Webster's 1624 poem *Monuments of Honour*, a pageant written for the inauguration of another member of the

Merchant Taylors, as lord mayor of London, that refers to having been "borne free" of that company (Lucas, 1966, III, l. 14). Most likely this refers to Webster's inheritance of his father's place in the Merchant Taylors, upon the latter's death in 1615.

Whether Webster attended the prestigious Merchant Taylors' school is a bit hazier; some scholars have noted his ability with classical languages would seem to fall short of what one might expect of a graduate of that school.[2] If he did indeed attend, he probably would have entered the school around 1588 or 1589. We are certain that a John Webster was admitted to the Middle Temple from the New Inn in 1598. It seems likely that this was the playwright for two reasons: first, the time is right; and second, Webster's knowledge of the law as demonstrated in his plays is clearly extensive. Two of his major solely authored plays, *The White Devil* and *The Devil's Law-Case*, feature trial scenes which are among the finest in Jacobean drama, and the theme of inquisition is hardly absent from *The Duchess of Malfi*. Furthermore, the John Webster who entered the Middle Temple did not graduate from there, leading us to imagine a Webster who wandered from law school to the theater and did not return, having already mined the former for all of the dramatic material he could find.

Webster's dramatic career took a curious form: three (perhaps four) solely authored plays performed between 1612 and 1618, bookended on either side by collaborative work. The first mention of him is made by Philip Henslowe in 1602, who refers in his *Diary* to a play entitled "sesers ffalle" (*Caesar's Fall*), ostensibly co-written by "antoney munday & mydleton mihell drayton, webester & the rest." Henslowe also refers to a play called *Two Shapes*, possibly an alternative title for the same play. The same year saw Henslowe disburse money to Webster, Henry Chettle, Wentworth Smith, Thomas Dekker, and others for *Lady Jane*, a play which survives as *Sir Thomas Wyatt*; and to Webster, Chettle, and Dekker for *Christmas Comes but Once a Year* (Heywood may also have had a hand in this play, now lost). In 1604, he collaborated with Dekker on a city comedy, *Westward Ho*, for the Children of Paul's, and wrote the Induction to John Marston's famous play *The Malcontent*. The Induction is interesting insofar as it is a meta-dramatic piece, featuring Richard Burbage and others of the King's Men "playing" themselves.

The next year brought another collaboration with Dekker, *Northward Ho*, as well as another partnership – on March 18 Webster married Sara Peniall, the daughter of the warden of the Saddlers' Company. The couple had at least five children in their first 11 years of marriage, the eldest a son named John. Between 1610 and 1620, Webster wrote his four non-collaborative plays, and one of these, the now lost "Guise" (*c*.1614), may possibly have been a revision of Marlowe's *Massacre at Paris* (although this seems unlikely – Webster refers to "Guise" in the same breath as *The White Devil* and *The Duchess of Malfi* in the dedication to *The Devil's Law-Case*). In this time, the only other literary works to which he seems to have applied himself were some commendatory verses for Heywood's famous *Apology for Actors* (1612), a poem from *A Monumental Column* (a series of elegies for Prince Henry printed in 1613), and 32 "characters" to be added to the sixth edition of Thomas Overbury's *Characters*, which Webster edited in 1615. After 1620, he seems to have stopped writing solo pieces altogether, and resumed his collaborative career, co-authoring plays with Middleton, Ford, Rowley, Dekker, Fletcher, Massinger, and Heywood (see chapter 36 above). One of these, *A Late Murther of the Son upon the Mother, or Keep the Widow Waking* (1624, with Dekker, Ford, and Rowley), is lost; as for the others – *A Cure for a Cuckold* (1625, with Rowley), *The Fair Maid of the Inn* (1626, with Fletcher, Ford, and Massinger), and *Appius and Virginia* (1627, with Heywood) – it is very difficult to discern to what extent Webster participated in their composition. Sometime during this period (1621–7) he also collaborated with Middleton on *Anything for a Quiet Life*, but Middleton is credited with writing the bulk of this play. Webster's participation in *Appius and Virginia* is the last concrete evidence we have of him, so he may have died as early as 1628. At any rate, he was almost certainly dead by 1635, when Heywood published his *Hierarchie of the Blessed Angels*, a long poem in which Webster is mentioned in the past tense, along with Shakespeare, Marlowe, and others. Webster's plays continued to be performed and published as late as 1671, before falling into relative obscurity until the early nineteenth century.

Before Mary Edmond's research established where Webster came from, scholars seeking information relied heavily on a handful of references to him by his contemporaries, as well as the self-portrait he paints in the prefatory material to his plays. Some of Edmond's research confirmed things that were already suspected, such as the nature of the Webster family business. Webster's younger brother Edward (who appears to have taken over the business upon John Webster senior's death) is mentioned in William Hemminge's satirical poem *Elegy on Randolph's Finger* (*c*.1632): "websters brother would nott lend a Coach: / hee swore thay all weare hired to Conuey / the Malfy dutches sadly on her way" (ll. 38–40).[3] More biting was Henry Fitzjeffrey's reference in "Notes from Blackfriars," a poem printed in *Certain Elegies done by Sundry Excellent Wits* (1617), to "crabbed Websterio, / The playwright-cartwright (whether either!)" (Bentley, 1941–68, V, 1242). Fitzjeffrey's burlesque of Webster has also been often quoted for its pointed references to the latter's apparently slow rate of composition. Fitzjeffrey describes Webster as:

> the Crittick that (of all the rest)
> I'd not haue view mee, yet I fear him least,
> Heer's not a word cursiuely I haue Writ,
> But hee'l Industriously examine it.
> And in some 12. monthes hence (or here about)
> Set in a shameful sheete, my errors out.
> (Bentley, 1941–68, V, 1242)

Most critics believe that Webster is answering Fitzjeffrey in the preface to *The White Devil* when he writes of "those who report I was a long time in finishing this tragedy" (ll. 27–8),[4] a charge to which he responds:

> with that of Euripides to Alcestides, a tragic writer: Alcestides objecting that Euripides had only in three days composed three verses, whereas himself had written three

hundred: "Thou tell'st truth", quoth he, "but here's the difference: thine shall only be read three days, whereas mine shall continue three ages." (ll. 30–5)

Webster's response, however arrogant, has a ring of truth to it – Fitzjeffrey's only claim to fame today is his portrait of a writer whose work has indeed lasted for ages. But Fitzjeffrey's charges were indeed "truth": when writing alone, Webster seems to have worked at a snail's pace.

The preface to *The White Devil*, as well as the prefatory materials to Webster's two other major plays (and dedications written by his colleagues), provide us with a great deal of insight into the playwright's character, particularly in terms of his professional aspirations and his middle-class identity. We know from the retort to Fitzjeffrey that Webster had a high opinion of his own work, a sentiment bolstered by his blasting of the "ignorant asses" who gave *The White Devil* a lukewarm reception when it opened at the Red Bull, claiming that it was "the breath that comes from the uncapable multitude" that poisoned the play's success. We also know that he was relatively ambitious: he was fond of quoting from Martial at the start of his work: *non norunt, haec monumenta mori* – "These are the monuments that do not know how to die." In the preface to *The White Devil*, the quotation refers to:

> other men's worthy labours, especially of that full and heighten'd style of Master Chapman, the labour'd and understanding works of Master Jonson; the no less worthy composures of the both worthily excellent Master Beaumont and Master Fletcher; and lastly (without wrong last to be named) the right happy and copious industry of Master Shakespeare, Master Dekker, and Master Heywood. (ll. 40–7)

Like many of the playwrights of his day who were influenced by Ben Jonson (the use of the word "works" is telling in this capacity; see chapter 32 above), Webster was deeply concerned with the immortality of his own works, and of his own reputation as an artist: he follows this who's who of his contemporaries (about the only major figures missing are Middleton and Ford, both of whom would later write commendatory verses to be published with *The Duchess of Malfi*) with the wish that "what I write may be read by their light" (ll. 47–8).

Perhaps the most interesting feature of Webster's prefatory materials is how they emphasize personal achievement, privileging it over more established modes of cultural identification, even the traditional social hierarchies of Renaissance England. In the dedication of *The Duchess of Malfi* to George Harding, baron of Berkeley Castle, Webster writes, "I do not altogether look up at your title – the ancientist nobility being but a relic of time past, and the truest honour indeed being for a man to confer honour on himself" (ll. 14–18). Webster goes on to point out that Harding's "learning strives to propagate" this honor, citing Harding's "approv'd censure" – in this context, his established literacy – as the criterion for patronage, rather than his rank. In itself, this is nothing unusual: poets often complimented their patrons' literary acumen. But the line about "nobility being but a relic of time past" is more pointed than most statements of this nature, and moreover, Webster would go on to recycle it in *The Devil's Law-Case*, as we shall see. As for the idea of conferring honor upon oneself, the sentiment is closely echoed in Thomas Middleton's dedicatory poem to *The Duchess of Malfi*:

> To trust to others' honourings, is worth's crime,
> Thy monument is rais'd in thy life-time;
> And 'tis most just; for every worthy man
> Is his own marble, and his merit can
> Cut him to any figure, and express
> More art than Death's cathedral palaces,
> Where royal ashes keep their court.
>
> (ll. 7–13)

As with Webster's words to Harding, there is an emphasis in these lines on the pre-eminence of personal achievement in the acquisition of merit, preferring it even to the more class-based, lineal inheritance implied by the image of "royal ashes" keeping court in the tomb. This kind of rhetoric is essential to an understanding of Webster's work for two reasons. First, it is not confined only to the prefaces and dedications of his plays; rather, it is explicitly voiced by several of his characters. Second, and more importantly, the issue of social mobility, so manifest in questions of whether honor is inherited or earned, is the source of cultural conflict that is most frequently and intensely enacted in Webster's plays.

All three of the non-collaborative plays have issues connected with social mobility at their core. The changing status of both class and gender, increasing commercialism, the function of marriage in a metamorphosing society, and the gains and losses of identity that accompanied these changes are all dealt with in these plays, usually dramatized in a trial-like fashion showing evidence of legal understanding and perhaps legal study. Sometimes this evidence manifests itself through Webster's obvious familiarity with legal discourse (in itself a form of theater), on display in the trial scenes in *The White Devil* and *The Devil's Law-Case*. There is also a rhetorical structure to his plays that indicates an inclination to see things in terms of evidence, precedent, and rigid – although sometimes inadequate – systems for determining innocence or guilt.

Webster's legal sensibility reveals itself on several structural levels: in the way he forms his plots, in his process of character development, and in his use of *sententiae* (rhetorical commonplaces). As for the first, he seems to have been drawn to stories that foreground cultural conflicts. The principal characters in *The White Devil*, for instance, are a degenerate Duke, his married lover, and her brother, who acts as go-between for them in order to elevate his own social standing. Webster based the bulk of the plot on actual events he had drawn from several accounts of the murder of Vittoria Accoramboni in Italy in 1585. The Duke, Brachiano, and Vittoria's brother Flamineo arrange to have Brachiano's and Vittoria's existing spouses murdered; the rest of the play recounts the fall-out after the deed is done. It becomes a revenge tragedy in many ways, as the friends of Brachiano's wife seek to destroy first the affair, then the participants. But the "white devil" of the title is Vittoria, and the story is remarkable for the ways in which it focuses on her role in the affair and the murders, despite the fact that Brachiano and Flamineo are equally or more culpable than she. The play's centerpiece is the trial scene, in which the charge of murder against her is conflated with accusations of harlotry. Webster greatly expands the role of her brother from that in the original sources, making him in many ways the central character and his quest for advancement at any cost one of the play's central themes. The sensationalism of the original story takes a backseat to the examination of the social forces that it dramatizes – Vittoria's sexual and Flamineo's social mobility.

The Duchess of Malfi, also based on actual events, is even more overtly driven by cultural concerns. The entire play revolves around one remarkable event: a widowed Duchess secretly marries her steward, who is far beneath her in rank, against the wishes of her corrupt brothers, a Duke (Ferdinand) and a Cardinal. Eventually the couple is discovered by one of Ferdinand's spies, a discontented servant named Bosola. Bosola murders the Duchess on the brothers' orders, and when he is not given his due reward, he becomes her avenger. In the process, her husband and all but one of their children are murdered. The Duchess is clearly the hero of the play, despite her death in the fourth act, but, like Vittoria, she is the character put on trial. Hers is not a literal trial like Vittoria's, but rather a methodical inquisition into the strength of her convictions performed by Bosola, who occupies so central a role in the play that many critics have been tempted to call him the tragic hero. Modern criticism does not lend this view much credence, but it is safe to say that in many ways Bosola does bear the responsibility of witness to and commentator on the play's action and the cultural conflicts it embodies.

The last of the plays through which Webster's dramatic vision can be fairly assessed is *The Devil's Law-Case*, a tragicomedy with a labyrinthine plot primarily of the playwright's own invention. Briefly, the play is about an unscrupulous merchant, Romelio, whose attempts to enlarge his fortune include tricking his sister's suitors into an almost mutually destructive duel, almost murdering one of them himself, and almost passing his illegimate child (the mother is a nun) off as his sister's, in order to annex the fortune of one of her supposedly dead suitors. But for these "almosts," the play would share the same tone and themes as the tragedies that precede it; even without a tragic ending, it is a dark examination of the roles of money and social rank, whether earned or inherited, in the changing English cultural landscape. Indeed, the play often conflates the two, most notably in the law-case of the title, in which Romelio's mother tries to take both fortune and rank from him by accusing *herself* of infidelity to her husband, thus placing the stigma of illegitimacy on her son. She is foiled in this attempt, and even vilified for making it, but the fact remains that once again, the character at the center of Webster's dramatic "trial" is female, and once again, the play's ethos is conveyed primarily through a hero–villain who is practically an avatar of the clash of cultural forces beyond his control.

If Webster's plots and the cultural conflicts they dramatize are the largest building blocks of his "trials," his method of character development and even his process of assembling other writers' commonplaces into a whole of his own are equally important aspects of his unique dramatic mode. For instance, characters like Romelio, Bosola, Flamineo, Vittoria, and the Duchess, as psychologically complex as they are, can often be readily recognized as rhetorical commonplaces in and of themselves. This practice goes beyond generic convention or stereotyping; Webster's characters are part of a tradition of character study that was a genre in itself in Jacobean England. Charles Forker (1986) gives a fine account of the history of the so-called "prose character"; suffice it to say that volumes such as Joseph Hall's *Characters of Vertues and Vices* (1608) and Thomas Overbury's *Characters* (first printed as *A Wife* in 1614 and put through 11 more editions, the last in 1622) were very popular in Webster's England. Webster, we recall, was an associate of Overbury. The most famous character Webster contributed to the 1615 edition is *An Excellent Actor*, which may have been based on Richard Burbage. Forker describes the prose characters as literary exercises designed:

> to build up a generic portrait, whether idealized or satiric, by presenting a random but more or less typical collection of details — mental habits, beliefs, opinions, social mannerisms, moral attitudes, clothes, pastimes, occupational activities — that in combination would reveal the essence behind the façade. The purpose, of course, was didactic. (1986, 123)

Even a cursory reading of Webster's solely authored plays will reveal a similar process at work. The early acts of these plays are intensely devoted to revealing the essential nature of the primary characters; this process is so methodical that it seems inadequate to write it off as simply "character-driven." The first scene of *The Duchess of Malfi* reads almost like a dramatized series of Overbury's characters. Bosola enters and is "introduced" by Antonio to Delio (and the audience) as "The only court-gall," whose:

> railing
> Is not for simple love of piety;
> Indeed, he rails at those things that he wants,
> Would be as lecherous, covetous, or proud,
> Bloody, or envious, as any man,
> If he had the means to be so.
> (ll. 23–8)

Ferdinand and the Cardinal are critiqued in a similar manner: the Cardinal is identified as "a melancholy churchman," one who, "where he is jealous of any man, he lays worse plots for them than ever was impos'd on Hercules, for he strews in his way flatterers, panders, intelligencers, atheists and a thousand such political monsters" (ll. 86–90). No specific epithet is given to Ferdinand, but the description of this "perverse and turbulent nature" who "Dooms men to death by information" and "ne'er pays debts, unless they be shrewd turns" (ll. 96–109) serves the same purpose as the others given by Antonio, as well as those in the actual *Characters*. The same process is applied to "the right noble duchess," whose "nights, nay more, her very sleeps, / Are more in heaven than other ladies' shrifts" (ll. 130–1). It is almost as if Webster is introducing witnesses to a court and carefully establishing their credentials.

A final structural element of Webster's dramatic "trials" is his frequent use of *sententiae*. His reliance upon the words of other writers is extensive, even by Renaissance standards, and his plays are densely packed with "borrowings" from Erasmus, Sidney, Montaigne, the fellow playwrights he catalogues in the preface to *The White Devil*, and dozens of lesser writers. For instance, when Cornelia runs mad in the fifth act of *The White Devil*, she gives flowers to her murderous son, Flamineo, with the following speech:

> There's rosemary for you, and rue for you,
> Heart's-ease for you. I pray make much of it;
> I have left more for myself.
>
> (V.iv.78–80)

Taking his hand a moment later, she says "Here's a white hand: Can blood so soon be washed out?" (ll. 82–3). Anyone familiar with the mad scenes of Ophelia and Lady Macbeth will recognize Shakespeare in these lines. Imitation was an accepted and even an approved literary practice in Renaissance England. It was encouraged in schools, courts, and other repositories of humanist thought as both a mnemonic device and an effective argumentative strategy. R. W. Dent (1960) demonstrates that often, in any given scene from one of Webster's plays, one can discern entire long passages that can be traced to specific sources. In some instances the characters quite literally exchange various *sententiae* in dialogue. Sometimes Webster's derivative technique works extremely well, but some critics have found fault with it for a variety of reasons: for repetitiveness, for invoking imagery inappropriate to the scene at hand, for being too obviously sententious, to name a few (Dent, 1960). Webster's work as a whole reveals a tendency to recycle the same commonplaces frequently, even within the same play. Sometimes those commonplaces are his own: like many authors, he has a predilection for repeating certain images, often word for word. Because the frequency of Webster's imitation is so high in comparison with many of his contemporaries, some modern critics have seen his self-referencing as a sign of unoriginality.

Yet even Fitzjeffrey does not seem to have a problem with Webster on that front. Instead, he focuses on Webster's tedious process of composition, which was no doubt made the more tedious by the constant consultation of a commonplace book. "Was euer man so mangl'd with a *Poem*?" Fitzjeffrey writes:

> See how he drawes his mouth awry of late,
> How he scrubs: wrings his wrests: scratches his Pate
> A *Midwife*! Helpe By his *Braines coitus*,
> Some *Centaure* strange: Some huge *Bucephalus*,
> Or *Pallas* (sure) ingendred in his *Braine*,
> Strike Vulcan with thy hammer once againe.

If anything, this critique can be read as an attack not upon Webster's use of commonplaces, but upon his failure to integrate them gracefully into his work. The images of monstrosities formed in a definitively reproductive process (Webster's "*Braines coitus*") reveal an implicit aesthetic critique, as opposed to an ethical one.

There is an element of the baroque in Webster's borrowing, as Ralph Berry points out (1972). Webster's mode of mixing disparate literary elements into a pastiche of his own conception works on much the same principle as baroque architecture's tendency to blend different architectural styles into a unified whole. To return to the original point vis-à-vis Webster's borrowing, it also reveals a faith in his audience – or at least "the full and understanding auditory" to which he refers in the Preface to *The White Devil* – to accept the words of other writers as received wisdom, a kind of literary precedent.

Webster's plays seem designed to test the parameters of Jacobean England's rapidly shifting social strata through the actions of his characters, primarily those characters whose identities have been, in the words of Frank Whigham, "achieved, not ascribed, in a society where such identity has not yet been accepted as fully substantial" (1985, 175). All three of the major plays feature characters whose social mobility (or lack of it) is alternately dramatized as either dangerous or ideal. This tendency is most obvious in the upward mobility of the characters who most clearly represent the "middling sort," such as *The White Devil*'s Flamineo, *The Duchess of Malfi*'s Bosola, and Romelio from *The Devil's Law-Case*. The first two are failed scholars forced to seek preferment through service to dissolute aristocrats; the last is a self-made merchant resolved never to serve anyone. His description of "gentry" is a direct echo of Webster's dedication to Harding:

> 'Tis nought else
> But a superstitious relic of time past;
> And sift it to the true worth, it is nothing
> But ancient riches.
>
> (I.i.33–5)

But Romelio's words become more and more qualified as the play goes on; he may be a self-made man, but he is also a would-be murderer (of noblemen, no less) who goes so far as to identify himself with Marlowe's Barabas. He would thus seem to function as an embodiment of Webster's society's struggle with the legitimacy of self-advancement. His rejection of inherited worth is radical in that it is an attack on an institution that was hardly dead when the play was performed (the play itself is dedicated to a gentleman, Sir Thomas Finch), but his actions for the remainder of the play are practically a negative object lesson on the dangers of unrestrained social mobility.

In *The White Devil*, Romelio's forerunner Flamineo occupies a similar position, but gives more substantial reasons for his villainy. A second son, he has converted a worthless education and a demeaning occupation – that of pander between his employer and his sister – into an impetus for a destructive kind of liberation from conventional notions of service. He posits self-determination as the cornerstone of his identity, as one who can claim to have "made a kind of path / To . . . mine own preferment" (III.i.37–8). When this path reaches a violent termination, he doggedly insists upon his freedom from service: "This is my resolve: / I would not live at any man's entreaty / Nor die at any's bidding" (V.vi.46–8). Even in the moment of his death, in which he mourns the error of his ways, his language still seeks to eradicate the influence of others upon his destiny: "I do not look / Who went before, nor who shall follow me; / No, at myself I will begin and end" (V.vi.254–6). Ultimately, however, he cannot escape self-doubt, instantly qualifying these defiantly self-containing lines with a sentiment that clearly prefigures Bosola's final speech: "While we look up to heaven we confound / Knowledge with Knowledge. O I am in a mist" (V.vi.256–8).

It is this terrifying doubt of the possibility of a truly self-determined identity that carries over into *The Duchess of Malfi*, embodied and observed at once by Bosola. In the first act, Bosola seems a continuance of Flamineo, playing the "court-gall" and providing the audience with wry commentary on the corruption of the aristocracy, but at the same time serving that aristocracy in a demeaning capacity. Yet his first line, addressed to the Cardinal, "I do haunt you still" (I.i.29), qualifies this appearance, rendering him a ghost-like adherent to the traditional, antiquated mode of service. He appears eager to serve Ferdinand and the Cardinal, but constantly voices the antithetical position of discontent. "Miserable age, where only the reward of doing well, is the doing of it!" he cries at one point (I.i.31–2); at another, "who would rely upon these miserable dependences, in expectation to be advanc'd tomorrow?" (I.i.54–6). Bosola's speeches throughout the play are replete with such sentiments, and yet he spends most of his time executing the Aragonian brothers' worst commands.

Whigham explains this ambivalence as a socially informed reaction to "the complicated new problems that arise from [Bosola's] status of *employee*." Bosola, in Whigham's words, is "the first tragic figure whose isolation is formulated in terms of employment by another" (1985, 177). In Jacobean England, "service was undergoing the momentous shift from role to job, and the ways in which it could ground a sense of self were changing":

> Here human beings create themselves in the process of work. But in the Renaissance, when this insight began to be visible, it seemed a loss rather than a liberation. The obligation to found identity on one's actions seemed to sever the transindividual bonds that bound the polity together; it left one on one's own, save for the new power of cash, which would buy knighthoods, even titles. (1985, 177)

Whigham's seminal analysis of *The Duchess of Malfi* shows how New Historicism has shifted the emphasis in Webster studies from the moralizing criticism of the later nineteenth and early twentieth centuries to a focus on the plays' dramatization of the cultural conflicts that informed the ways in which Jacobeans understood themselves and the world around them. Whigham sees Webster as a playwright with a keen per-

ception of these conflicts, who wrote *The Duchess of Malfi* "to dissect the actual workings of the normative ideology" that the Duchess' actions subvert, in part to recover
the "stifled voices" of people victimized by that ideology. We have seen how Whigham
accounts for the characters laboring under what Shakespeare's Iago called "the curse
of service" (*Othello*, I.i.36). More importantly, he sheds some light upon what is at
stake in the play's central event – the Duchess' marriage to Antonio, and Antonio's
resultant upward leap in rank. This radical example of upward mobility inspires profound reactions from the play's principal characters, because the "problem of ontological mobility, or mobility of identity, is palpably at the center of the cultural
consciousness, certainly in London, nowhere more than in the theater, where . . . it
shaped depictions of sexual and marital patterns" (Whigham, 1985, 168). Webster's
plays enact the clash of two cultural views with radically different major premises
about the nature of social rank. The view that had held sway in England for hundreds
of years was imagined in terms of the "great chain of being," which placed the gentry
above the middling sort in a supposedly natural hierarchy. The other view is that
voiced by Webster and Middleton in the prefatory materials discussed above: namely,
that "every worthy man / Is his own marble, and his merit can / Cut him to any figure"
(ll. 11–12).

But questions of whether a culture should be an aristocracy or a meritocracy do
not take place in a vacuum – every other aspect of a society is affected by such considerations, including notions of sexuality or marriage. Webster's body of non-
collaborative work, as small as it is, is replete with instances – and examinations – of
this dynamic. Indeed, the lion's share of Webster criticism has been in one way or
another about his dramatizations of women and marriage, particularly that of the
Duchess. We have already noted that his "trials" of cultural conflict tend to revolve
around his female characters, in the form of Vittoria's arraignment, Leonora's law-case
against Romelio, and the Duchess' battle of words with Bosola before her murder.
Each of these scenes is arguably the central moment in its play, and also the moment
when the nature of the conflict at hand is broached most directly. In all three cases,
the play's primary female character can be seen as both being attacked and attacking,
in the sense that adherents of the more traditional ideologies of the English Renaissance – even those who question those ideologies themselves, like Bosola – are
inevitably the judge, jury, and executioner of women who represent the possibilities
of the emergent counter-culture. In all three cases, criticism has taken the form of, in
Whigham's words, "psychological inquiry and . . . moral evaluation." In the case of
the Duchess in particular, critics have focused on her sexuality and/or her ethics. But
if the play is seen as an effort "to articulate and construe the friction between the
dominant social order and the emergent pressures toward social change," then the
Duchess' decision to marry Antonio must not be seen in such reductive – and usually
conservative – terms, but rather as a conflict between the old, aristocratic world view
represented by Ferdinand and the burgeoning, upwardly mobile meritocracy represented by the Duchess. Seen from this point of view, the Duchess' elevation of
Antonio:

is . . . threatening to Ferdinand because it suggests that the supposedly ontological class categories are brittle and imperiled by the powers of flexible self-determination exhibited by the duchess and her base lover. Such rewriting of the rules threatens to reveal the human origin, and thus the mutability, of the ultimate elevation on which he rests himself. (Whigham, 1985, 170)

Whigham's arguments are taken up by Mary Beth Rose, who points out that the Duchess' status as a widow makes her an even greater threat to the world view represented by Ferdinand because of her freedom to run her own household and/or choose a husband. This posed a threat to many Jacobeans because, on the one hand, "an independent woman running her own household presented a contradiction to English patriarchal ideology; on the other, a widow who did remarry was criticized as lustful and disloyal, particularly in the threat her remarriage posed to a family's retention of property" (Rose, 1988, 165). The fact that the Duchess is a *royal* widow would have made her an even more troubling figure for Webster's audience because she simultaneously embodies the autonomy of the aristocracy and the subordinate social position of her gender. She is the perfect character for one of Webster's dramatized "trials," because "with her conjoined, paradoxical attachments to present, future, and past, to status granted at birth as well as status gained by achievement, to female independence and female subordination, the Duchess is in a position as fluid and anomalous as the social conditions of Jacobean England" (Rose, 1988, 159–60).

While Rose agrees with Whigham's assessment of the Duchess as "the first fully tragic woman in Renaissance drama," she believes that Webster's portrayal of the Duchess is in many ways qualified by the tragic genre. Rose acknowledges that Webster "clearly recognizes the radical potential of female heroism in the process of cultural change," but points out that Webster's decision to remove the Duchess from the active resolution of the conflicts of the play and grant her instead the indirect role of inspiration diminishes the scope of Webster's radicalism. Rose sees the Duchess as a representative of an emergent Jacobean dramatic discourse, the "heroics of marriage," which finds its origins in a distinctly Protestant idealization of marriage that was slowly replacing the traditional, dualistic view of women as either paragons of chaste virtue or creatures of sin. The Duchess' defining action is to conflate the categories of marriage and social rank by selecting a husband for love and his merit, as opposed to his birth. Rose posits that "it is the full recognition of the importance of private life, here claiming equal status with public concerns, that makes her tragic stature possible; in turn, the Duchess's heroics helps to define and clarify the heroics of marriage" (1988, 163).

Rose is quick to point out that the fact that the Duchess' marriage is the focal point of a tragedy qualifies the extent to which Webster is advocating the values that made such a marriage possible. "The contradictions about rank, status, gender, and power that characterize the heroics of marriage perpetuate rather than resolve the conflicts between past and future," she writes, because "the function of tragedy is not simply to represent irreconcilable ambiguity, suffering, and injustice, but also to contain these ruptures precisely by defining them, giving them meaning and form. Tragedy's unique role in this process is to underline the moment at which the previously meaningless becomes legible and articulate" (1988, 175). The Duchess' marriage and values underlying her decision to go through with it are rendered visible by the tragedy that ensues; Webster clearly reveals the possibilities of the emergent culture of merit-based mobility and the potential of marriage to enable it. But because the nature of tragedy is to elegize the past and the residual cultural structures that define that, the possibilities represented by the Duchess are negated to an extent, and "the sympathy and value assigned to her life are unambiguously allied instead with a compelling tribute to the lost past" (Rose, 1988, 172).

Many of the facets of Webster's work that drew critical fire before the advent of New Historicism have since been revealed to be his greatest strengths. His propensity for linguistic borrowing, his involvement in such decidedly popular ventures as the *Characters*, and his predilection for stories of sometimes violent inquisition were all once considered signs of unoriginality and what T. S. Eliot (1964) called a "very great literary and dramatic genius directed toward chaos." But by looking at the ways in which Webster's plays dramatize the cultural conflicts of Jacobean England, particularly those springing from changing conceptions of social mobility, it is evident that these supposedly negative qualities are indispensable aspects of a rhetorical strategy designed to test the boundaries of conflict in a methodical way.

NOTES

1 Edmond's work was first published in the *Times Literary Supplement* December 24, 1976, and updated in *TLS* (March 11, 1977; October 24, 1980).
2 It should be noted that Webster's supposed lack of ability in the classical languages is mere conjecture, based on the fact that he is heavily reliant on English translations of original texts. On the other hand, it would make no sense for the son of a merchant taylor not to attend the school.
3 Thomas Randolph, a poet, lost a finger in a tavern brawl. Hemminge's poem describes a mock funeral procession for the finger (Smith, 1923).
4 Unless otherwise stated, all quotations from Webster's plays have been taken from Dollimore and Sinfield (1983).

REFERENCES AND FURTHER READING

Bentley, G. E., ed. (1941–68). *The Jacobean and Caroline Stage*. Oxford: Clarendon Press.

Belsey, Catherine (1985). *The Subject of Tragedy: Identity and Difference in Renaissance Drama*. London: Methuen.

Berry, Ralph (1972). *The Art of John Webster*. Oxford: Clarendon Press.

Dent, R. W. (1960). *John Webster's Borrowings*. Berkeley: University of California Press.

Dollimore, Jonathan (1984). *Radical Tragedy: Religion, Ideology, and Power in the Drama of Shakespeare and his Contemporaries*. Chicago: University of Chicago Press.

Dollimore, Jonathan and Alan Sinfield (1983). *The Selected Plays of John Webster*. Cambridge: Cambridge University Press.

Eliot, T. S. (1964). *Elizabethan Essays*. New York: Haskell House.

Forker, Charles R. (1986). *Skull Beneath the Skin: The Achievement of John Webster*. Carbondale: Southern Illinois University Press.

Goldberg, Dena (1987). *Between Worlds: A Study of the Plays of John Webster*. Ontario: Wilfrid Laurier University Press.

Gunby, D. C. (1995). "Introduction." In *Webster: Three Plays*. London: Penguin.

Gunby, David, David Carnegie, and Anthony Hammond, eds (1995). *The Works of John Webster*. Vol. I. Cambridge: Cambridge University Press.

Henslowe, Philip (1968). *Diary*, eds. R. A. Foakes and R. J. Rickert. Cambridge: Cambridge University Press.

Lucas, F. L., ed. (1966). *The Complete Works of John Webster*. New York: Gordian Press.

Moore, Don D., ed. (1981). *Webster: The Critical Heritage*. London: Routledge and Kegan Paul.

Pearson, Jacqueline (1980). *Tragedy and Tragicomedy in the Plays of John Webster*. New Jersey: Barnes and Noble.

Ranald, Margaret Loftus (1989). *John Webster*. Boston: Twayne.

Rose, Mary Beth (1988). *The Expense of Spirit: Love and Sexuality in English Renaissance Drama*. Ithaca: Cornell University Press.

Smith, G. C. Moore, ed. (1923). *William Hemminge's Elegy on Randolph's Finger*. Oxford: Blackwell.

Stone, Lawrence (1965). *The Crisis of the Aristocracy, 1558–1641*. Oxford: Clarendon Press.

Stone, Lawrence (1977). *The Family, Sex and Marriage in England, 1500–1800*. New York: Harper & Row.

Whigham, Frank (1985). "Sexual and social mobility in *The Duchess of Malfi*." *PMLA* 100, 167–86.

38

John Ford

Mario DiGangi

John Ford has long been one of the most enigmatic of Renaissance dramatists. A Caroline playwright who thoroughly immersed himself in Elizabethan and Jacobean dramatic traditions yet also twisted and unraveled those traditions in striking ways, he has been subject to radically different assessments. The polarization of opinion that has come to define the critical tradition on him had its seeds in the early nineteenth century, when his plays were praised by Charles Lamb for depicting "grandeur of the soul" and disparaged by William Hazlitt as "extravagant" and "artificial." Later nineteenth- and early twentieth-century critics perennially disputed whether or not Ford had succumbed to a supposed Caroline moral "decadence." In his *Elizabethan Essays* of 1932, T. S. Eliot shifted the focus of debate from Ford's morals to his style, which he found superficial and derivative; while Eliot has had his supporters, dissenting voices have praised Ford's skill at depicting psychological conflicts and reviving dramatic conventions (Ide in Anderson, 1986, 62–3; Anderson, 1972, 134–7). Since the 1950s, as the emphasis of Renaissance dramatic scholarship has moved away from considerations of aesthetics and morality and toward the analysis of politics and society, scholarship on Ford has also taken new directions. Nonetheless, assessments of his work are still fiercely divided.

The diversity of critical opinion on Ford stems in part from the irregular shape of his career. Shakespeare's career is often imagined as a coherent progression from comedies and histories, through the transitional "problem comedies" and great tragedies, to the late tragedies and romances. In contrast, Ford did not even begin to write plays until he was nearly 40 years old. Born in 1586 into a Devonshire gentry family, he entered the Middle Temple of the Inns of Court, London's law schools, in 1602; it is generally assumed that he subsequently made his living in the legal profession. Between 1606 and 1620 he produced several non-dramatic works: elegies and encomiums (*Fame's Memorial, Honor Triumphant*), ethical treatises (*The Golden Mean, The Line of Life*), and a religious poem (*Christ's Bloody Sweat*). The first stage of Ford's theatrical career occurred between 1621 and 1625, when he collaborated with well-established playwrights like Thomas Dekker, Thomas Middleton, and John Webster (see chapter 36 above). Of these collaborative plays, three are lost and at least four survive (Anderson, 1972, 33–46), including the much-admired *Witch of Edmonton* (1621). Also lost are three plays Ford wrote independently during the 1620s. His reputation thus rests on a small number of extant plays, of uncertain date and order of composition, written independently between 1628 and 1638. His most accomplished works, with approximate dates, are *The Lover's Melancholy* (1628), a tragicomedy; *The Broken Heart* (1629), *'Tis Pity She's a Whore* (1630), and *Love's Sacrifice* (1631), all tragedies; and *Perkin Warbeck* (1632), a history play. Of lesser interest are *The Queen*, a tragicomedy published anonymously in 1653 but probably written early in Ford's career, and the tragicomedies *The Fancies Chaste and Noble* (1635–6) and *The Lady's Trial* (1638), his last play.

Despite the irregularity and belatedness of his dramatic career, we can confidently situate Ford within Caroline theatrical culture. In contrast to amateur courtier dramatists like William Davenant and Thomas Carew, Ford was one of four professional dramatists (along with Philip Massinger, James Shirley, and Richard Brome) who regularly wrote for the commercial theaters. Ford's first three independently written plays were performed by the King's Men at the fashionable Blackfriars theater; from 1630 on, his plays were staged at the Cockpit (or Phoenix). Both the Blackfriars and the Cockpit were small, enclosed halls that offered erudite, elegant fare to an audience largely comprised of gentry, ladies, prosperous merchant citizens, and young gentlemen from the Inns of Court (Gurr, 1996, 183; see chapter 11 above). According to Andrew Gurr, whereas the Blackfriars showcased the amateur dramatists' witty, "audacious" language, the Cockpit instead featured the more restrained, lyrical style of the professional dramatists. Hence Gurr proposes that Ford moved to the Cockpit in 1630 because he recognized that its relatively traditional repertory was more suited to his "economy and simplicity of dramatic language" (in Neill, 1988, 92).

The Cockpit was also located near the Inns of Court, Ford's long-term residence and a vibrant, influential literary milieu. Ford must have been aware of what Martin Butler calls the "narrow but demanding" dramatic tradition he inherited from fellow law students John Marston and Webster, whose plays are characterized by "sophisticated literary self-consciousness" and "violently opposed tones and styles," as well as an interest in "politics, sex, and scepticism" (in Neill, 1988, 201). Ford's own literary self-consciousness is evident from his reworking of plots, characters, and motifs from Shakespeare, Christopher Marlowe, George Chapman, and John Fletcher in addition to Marston and Webster. Butler maintains that the meta-theatrical dimension of Ford's work would have appealed to the sophisticated Inns of Court residents and their acquaintances who regularly attended performances at the Cockpit. Ford's self-reflexivity, which strikes some readers as artificial and derivative, may well attest to his appreciation of the specialized knowledge this audience brought to his plays.

In addition to examining Ford's social milieu, recent scholarship has considered the possible impact on his writing of his political convictions. It is generally held that he avoids direct engagement with contemporary political and religious controversies. Nevertheless, recent studies by Ira Clark and Lisa Hopkins have detected a pronounced political conservatism in his plays. Contending that the primary focus of Fordian drama is neither moral nor psychological but social, Clark argues that Ford's identification with the nobility explains his characters' strict adherence to the conservative doctrines of "obeying one's monarch, submitting to one's assigned station in the hierarchy, and playing out the child, gender, and occupational roles" dictated by society (1992, 78). Hopkins attributes Ford's conservatism to his possible links with a Catholic gentry coterie (1994, 1–2). She finds evidence of Ford's alignment with traditional Catholic rituals and customs in his treatment of food, language, and the body, subjects on which Protestant and Catholic attitudes sharply diverged. Although novel interpretations such as Hopkins' have been and doubtless will continue to be challenged (see Wymer, 1998), they have drawn much-needed attention to the political dimension of plays frequently approached as apolitical depictions of psychological and moral conflicts.

Whatever Ford's connections to gentlemen of the Inns of Court, aristocratic families, or Catholic factions, it must be stressed that theatrical performances in Renaissance London were socially heterogeneous events that accommodated diverse perspectives and identifications. Caroline drama no less than earlier Renaissance drama "dr[e]w strength from the conflicting prejudices and aspirations coexisting richly in its audience" (Butler, 1984, 5). The business practices of the theatrical companies also render problematic any neat generalizations about social divisions among playgoers and playhouses. Caroline theaters regularly staged Elizabethan and Jacobean plays as well as new, more topical, fare; moreover, the same play might be presented at a "public" theater like the Red Bull or Globe as well as a "private" theater like the Cockpit. Ford's career illustrates this fluidity between popular and elite theatrical venues. *The Lover's Melancholy*, for instance, was performed at both the Globe and the Blackfriars. During his later association with the Blackfriars and Cockpit, moreover, Ford can hardly have forgotten his experience during the 1620s collaborating on plays for the Fortune and Red Bull. Finally, even if his prose works and dedications express conservative values, the staging of his plays doubtless precipitated scrutiny of social and political orthodoxies. Imagine the possible reactions of those London citizens who in 1630 saw *'Tis Pity She's a Whore* performed at the Cockpit. Might not some of them have recognized the operations of political ideology in the Cardinal's mystification of aristocratic class interests as divine justice? Might not they have recognized the operations of gender and class ideology in the Cardinal's denunciation of Annabella – a merchant's daughter who rejects her role as an object of marital exchange between gentlemen – as a whore? These playgoers may well have left the theater with a more radical experience of John Ford than that of the more privileged who purchased his writings or knew of his connections with nobility.

Today, Ford's role in shaping the aesthetic, social, and political parameters of Caroline drama can no longer be ignored. Nonetheless, his work is still markedly underrepresented in Renaissance dramatic scholarship. A modern edition of his complete dramatic works does not exist. Important books by Margot Heinemann, Martin Butler, and Lawrence Venuti that have demonstrated the ideological complexity of Caroline drama unfortunately bypass Ford. Although Rowland Wymer's recent *Webster and Ford* (1995) provides valuable insight into the performance dimensions of Fordian drama, his distaste for political modes of criticism leaves unexamined those aspects of Ford's plays that might be illuminated through feminist or materialist approaches. Simply in terms of attention, Ford scholarship has not kept pace with the upsurge in Renaissance dramatic scholarship since the early 1980s: a search for "John Ford" in the *MLA International Bibliography* produces just 74 entries from 1980–9 (25 of which derive from two essay anthologies), and 53 entries from 1990–9 (15 of which are "notes" or very brief articles). Not including the two essay anthologies, Wymer's book, and the brief coverage of Ford in Julie Sanders' *Caroline Drama* (1999), only four book-length studies of Ford have appeared since 1980.

By paying attention to the multiple registers of meaning in Ford's plays, I hope to indicate productive directions for further study. My analysis will center on three plays that demonstrate the diversity and range of Ford's dramatic accomplishments: *The Lover's Melancholy*, *'Tis Pity She's a Whore*, and *Perkin Warbeck*.[1]

"Violence of Affection": The Lover's Melancholy

In *The Lover's Melancholy*, a broken society is reunified through the powers of art – embodied in a court physician – and of compassion – embodied in a chaste, dutiful daughter and a loyal, plain-spoken counselor. A tragicomedy in the tradition of Shakespeare's *Cymbeline* and Fletcher's *Philaster* (see chapter 35 above), *The Lover's Melancholy* features the basic plot devices of this genre: the reunion of family members, redemption of past wrongs, and sudden avoidance of impending disaster. A brief plot summary will reveal this tragicomic pattern. Two years before the action of the play begins, Palador, the current prince of Cyprus, and Eroclea ("true love"), eldest daughter of the counselor Meleander, were betrothed. The marriage was prevented when Palador's late father, King Agenor, attempted to rape Eroclea. Accompanied by the courtier Rhetias, Eroclea escaped to Athens, where she lived disguised as a young man called Parthenophill ("lover of virginity"). As the play opens, Menaphon brings Parthenophill back from Athens to a grief-torn Cyprus. A virtuous young gentleman, Menaphon suffers from unrequited love for Thamasta, a haughty aristocrat; Palador and Meleander have long been afflicted with melancholy at the loss of Eroclea; and Thamasta's brother Amethus is prevented from marrying Cleophila, Meleander's younger daughter, who devotes herself entirely to her father's care. These social and emotional problems are gradually resolved through the virtue of Eroclea, the wisdom of Rhetias, and the diligence of Corax, a court physician. By the end of the play, Palador and Meleander are healed, Thamasta has learned humility and accepts Menaphon's suit, and Eroclea is reunited with her father and lover. The orchestration of three marriages brings the play to a comic close.

To explain the centrality of melancholy to this play, some scholars have turned to Robert Burton's *Anatomy of Melancholy* (1621), which influentially analyzed the various causes, symptoms, and effects of mental perturbation. Defining melancholy as a "commotion of the mind, o'ercharged / With fear and sorrow," Corax faithfully follows Burton.[2] Yet while Corax's medical discourse may explain the "violence of affection" in grieving men like Palador and Meleander (V.ii.195), Burton's theories are not as central to the play as might initially appear. For instance, the Masque of Melancholy staged by Corax depicts neuroses like lycanthropia and hydrophobia as described by Burton; however, such extreme delusions illuminate neither the causes nor the symptoms of Palador's and Meleander's afflictions. Moreover, Corax does not follow Burton's recommendations for curing melancholy (Anderson, 1972, 50). *The Lover's Melancholy* clearly does not constitute a theatrical version of Burtonian psychological theories.

Rather, the project of curing melancholy in the play represents the arduous task of purging society from the consequences of a king's violent passions. It is productive to think of Ford's play in terms of Nicholas Radel's description of Stuart tragicomedy as "paradoxically revolutionary and conservative": "part of an ongoing struggle in the processes of constituting and deconstructing authority" (1997, 175). A pertinent illustration of this political complexity is supplied by Kevin Sharpe, who shows that Caroline courtier playwrights used representations of love to provide "didactic counsel and moral prescription" to the court (1987, 270). For instance, these playwrights advocated in public as well as private affairs "a middle course between unregulated passion and the suppression of man's natural appetite" (Sharpe, 1987, 286). That *The Lover's Melancholy* might be advancing a similar moral and political agenda (albeit to a broader audience) is corroborated by Ford's discussion of passion in *The Golden Mean*:

> The minde of a Wise and Noble man is such, that what or how many gusts and tides of adversitie assault him, they may at all times rather arme, then at any time oppresse him, since his resolution cannot overflow with the rudenesse of passion; for that his excellent and refined temperature will ever retaine the salt of judgement and moderation; the one proving a *Wise*, the other a *Noble* man. (Stock et al., 1991, 242)

Because princes were regarded as "the soul of the commonwealth," it was especially crucial that they governed their passions and appetites through reason and moderation (Sharpe, 1987, 272). As *The Lover's Melancholy* shows, a king's inability to govern his sexual passions could create social wounds that festered long after his death.

Also a victim of excessive passion, Palador lapses into a passive, "effeminate" languor that recalls the erotic indolence of Marlowe's Edward II. Just as Edward II's irresponsibility precipitates civil war, so Palador's sickness infects the entire state: the commons "murmur," the nobles "grieve," the court "grows wild," and neighboring states seek retaliation for Agenor's crimes (II.i.4–5). To avert such disaster, Rhetias delivers the "good counsel" regarded as central to "good kingship" (Sharpe, 1987, 272). Chastising Palador – "Princes who forget their sovereignty and yield to affected passion are weary of command" (II.i.132–3) – and reminding him of Agenor's misdeeds, Rhetias begins to shake the prince from his melancholic inertia.

According to traditional readings of the play, the powers of art, love, and providence ultimately cure Palador's melancholy. However, as Rhetias' political intervention suggests, *The Lover's Melancholy* is also open to readings that would demystify such seemingly timeless and transcendent categories. Corax's theatrical art is authorized by a system of royal patronage he finds coercive; hence he strives to heal Palador not simply out of compassion and fealty, but also out of a self-interested desire to be "discharged from [his] attendance / At court, and never more be sent for after" (III.i.126–7). Corax clearly regards his courtly duties as an imposition: "I need no prince's favour; princes need / My art" (III.i.90–1). Thus the providential designs of "eternal mercy" in restoring Palador to health are served by a scheme for personal gain (IV.iii.135). Moreover, in portraying the physician as a benevolent scholar who uses theater to reform society, Ford might be promoting his own interests by defending his profession against hostile critics (Bulman, 1990, 368).

The evils of cross-dressing, of course, were a frequent target of anti-theatrical hostility in Renaissance England. Although Eroclea's theatrical art also proves socially curative, the homoerotic complications that arise from her disguise belie any simple notion of the purity of her emotional impact on Thamasta and Palador. Thamasta's overwhelming attraction to Parthenophill delivers a salutary blow to her pride. Her humiliation evokes similar episodes in *Twelfth Night* and *As You Like It*, in which proud women (Olivia and Phebe) pursue cross-dressed women (Viola and Rosalind) who reject them. Yet whereas Olivia and Phebe experience shock and embarrassment at the public revelation of their "mistake," Thamasta firmly reasserts her desire after Eroclea has confessed the truth of her identity:

> It will be
> A hard task for my reason to relinquish
> The affection which was once devoted thine;
> I shall awhile repute thee still the youth
> I loved so dearly.
>   (III.ii.176–80)

Thamasta's insistence on her emotional constancy recalls her earlier reprimand of her brother for appropriating her romantic agency: "My freedom is my birth's; I am not bound / To fancy your approvements, but my own" (I.iii.24–5). Does Thamasta's refusal to relinquish her desire for Eroclea indicate that her pride has been insufficiently purged, or rather that she has discovered a further reason for resisting the obligations and restrictions of marriage?

Regardless of Thamasta's "freedom" to desire Eroclea, a same-sex partnership is no more a serious possibility here than it is in the comic sub-plot involving the foolish courtier Cuculus and his female page Grilla, who unbeknown to him is actually a cross-dressed boy. Although Ford's comic plots are sometimes dismissed as irrelevant, this parodic same-sex relationship between master and servant not only emphasizes the socially disorderly implications of Thamasta's pursuit of Eroclea, but acts as a foil to the idealized same-sex bond between Menaphon and Amethus. In the first scene of the play, Amethus vows to Menaphon that they will never part until "death leaves the one of us behind / To see the other's funerals performed" (I.i.47–8). Intimate male friendship provides a model for conjugal harmony because both relationships depend on an "equal love" between two souls (IV.iii.53; Opie in Neill, 1988, 246). Eroclea and Palador must achieve the harmonious union already enjoyed by Menaphon and Amethus before the play can end happily.

The memorable reunion scene between Eroclea and Palador reveals both the power and the danger of theatrical artifice. Having shed her disguise as Parthenophill, Eroclea addresses Palador in the somber, measured tones that are hallmarks of Ford's lyrical mode (Madelaine and Gibson in Neill, 1988, 43–4, 61–2). She intends to elicit in Palador a "moderate joy" at her return that will gently purge his melancholic passion (V.i.14):

> Minutes are numbered by the fall of sands,
> As by an hour-glass; the span of time
> Doth waste us to our graves, and we look on it.
> An age of pleasures, revelled out, comes home
> At last and ends in sorrow; but the life
> Weary of riot, numbers every sand,
> Wailing in sighs, until the last drop down,
> So to conclude calamity in rest.
>
> (IV.iii.56–63)

Heightening the emotional tension of this encounter, Palador perceives the speaker of these lines not as Eroclea, but as Parthenophill in female disguise, come to him as a "seducing counterfeit" (IV.iii.106). Even though Palador's longing to see Parthenophill had served as an important catalyst for his reunion with Eroclea – "Parthenophill is lost, and I would see him, / For he is like to something I remember / A great while since, a long, long time ago" (IV.iii.28–30) – his horror at Parthenophill's evident seduction attempt now equates same-sex desire with treacherous artifice and unruly passions (Radel, 1997, 167). The dangers of art are introduced at the beginning of the play in Menaphon's account of the musical duel between Parthenophill (art) and the nightingale (nature) that ends in the exhausted bird's death. In order fully to cure Palador, the play suggests, Eroclea must abandon theatrical art for the "natural" sentiments of affectionate "piety and duty" that define the wife's role in marriage (V.ii.119). Illustrating Sharpe's theory that Caroline dramatists "looked to marriage as the course by which body and soul, passion and love are reconciled in society" (1987, 286–7), the ceremonious reunion of Palador and Eroclea develops into an emblem of social and political harmony.

The Lover's Melancholy ends with an emotional, ritualistic scene that restores to Meleander his honors, his daughter, and his senses. The ceremonial elements

characteristic of Fordian dramaturgy – visual emblems, soft music, intricate patterning, formal speech – work here to further the sense that peace and sanity have been
restored. Yet the characteristic ambiguity of Ford's endings also intrudes on the joy
of this scene. Finally reunited with his daughter, Meleander nonetheless evokes the
distress of Shakespeare's broken King Lear – "Great, gracious sir, alas, why do you
mock me? / I am a weak old man, so poor and feeble" (V.ii.233–4) – while he somberly
anticipates his impending death. Larry Champion has observed that this resolution
"issues in gnawing ambiguities concerning both the individual's and society's ability
to achieve genuine renewal" (Anderson, 1986, 127). The tonally mixed conclusion of
The Lover's Melancholy may well elicit discomfort or doubt. Nonetheless, the subtle
probing of this lyrical tragicomedy can scarcely rival the assault on moral and social
certainties that drives Ford's most celebrated tragedy, *'Tis Pity She's a Whore*.

"A Nearer Nearness in Affection": *'Tis Pity She's a Whore*

No play of Ford's has generated more debate than *'Tis Pity*. In this tragedy of love
and revenge Ford explores the subject of incest more seriously than any of his contemporaries, emphasizing the complex social forces surrounding the illicit relationship between a young brother and sister from a respectable merchant family of Parma.
The conflicts that push the play toward its tragic conclusion emerge from Giovanni's
and Annabella's disastrous negotiations with the repressive demands of family, church,
and community. Examining the siblings' transgressive behavior in light of the social
pressures that produce, shape, and constrain their desires necessarily complicates the
moral frameworks through which the play has often been read.

Significantly, *'Tis Pity* does not begin with a prurient erotic encounter between
Giovanni and Annabella; rather, incest first arises as a topic of philosophical and
theological debate. Ford sharply delineates the contradictory epistemological assumptions that prevent mutual understanding between Giovanni and the Friar: whereas
Giovanni desperately grapples with his spiritual dilemma, the Friar retreats to blind
faith: "Dispute no more . . . for better 'tis, / To bless the sun, than reason why it
shines" (I.i.1, 9–10). Not only does the Friar's injunction fail to persuade Giovanni,
who like Marlowe's Dr. Faustus has been taught that logical disputation leads to
knowledge, but his example of the sun as a divine mystery best left unexamined might
have appeared willfully ignorant to a seventeenth-century audience, who had themselves been faced with new knowledge of the sun's place in the universe. For his part,
Giovanni provokes the Friar's anxious reprimands by speciously arguing that because
he and his sister shared "one father" and "one womb," they are therefore bound by
nature, reason, and religion "to be ever one: / One soul, one flesh, one love, one heart,
one all" (I.i.28, 33–4). Instead of refuting Giovanni's flawed logic, the Friar more
strenuously urges his repentance.

Although the Friar hesitates to engage Giovanni's arguments, his warnings reflect
orthodox church doctrine on incest: the "leprosy of lust" that brings death and damna-

tion (I.ii.74). Christian tradition since Thomas Aquinas had condemned incest as an extreme manifestation of the sin of lust, as an unnatural reproductive act responsible for prodigious births, and as a violation of the mandate for the extension of kinship bonds through marriage (Marienstras, 1985, 189–91). Given the monstrousness of incest, the Friar, like his counterpart in *Romeo and Juliet,* understandably pities and seeks to reform his erring pupil; nevertheless, his own limitations defeat his purpose. Because he is unable to respond with sufficient compassion to Giovanni's emotional crisis, his stern injunctions fail to relieve Giovanni's spiritual crisis. The Friar has more success with Annabella, whom he terrifies with a vivid description of hell. Because this lecture echoes passages from Ford's *Christ's Bloody Sweat,* it might represent the author's own theological tenets; nonetheless, many readers have found the Friar excessively harsh and manipulative in this scene, his lecture a "ruthless exploitation" of a distraught young woman's emotions (Farr, 1979, 45). Even more perplexing, the Friar offers Annabella the morally dubious, if admittedly pragmatic, advice that she hide her pregnancy by marrying Soranzo, a nobleman who has already committed adultery. Whatever his intentions, the Friar's spiritual principles are exposed as inadequate guides in the brutal world of social action.

Against the Friar's spiritual faith Giovanni poses his own fiercely held belief in the "Elysium" promised him by his sister's "immortal beauty" (I.ii.254, 207). The intensity and tenacity of Giovanni's passion exert a strong claim on our sympathy and admiration, despite his apparent flaws. For instance, Giovanni's narcissistic pride at having sexually conquered his sister is counterbalanced by his idealized yearning for the emotional and spiritual harmony of love. Giovanni and Annabella indeed appear to achieve that harmony when in their mutual vows they express a tenderness and devotion otherwise absent from the play. Ford's ambiguous representation of Giovanni as a sympathetic advocate of incest is further complicated by the use of meta-theatrical allusion. Giovanni might seem especially appealing, even heroic, as the Fordian type of the "dispossessed lover" who defies the established order (Robson, 1983, 4). Giovanni's exalted stature as a romantic hero diminishes, however, if perceived as the "naturalist-atheist villain" or the bloodthirsty revenger of Jacobean tragedy (Ide in Anderson, 1986, 74). For Marion Lomax, Giovanni occupies precisely such a liminal position, "trapped between dramatic traditions – love tragedy and revenge drama – and also between dramatic roles: noble hero or immoral villain" (1987, 174). Ironically, Giovanni does not realize that his actions, which he perceives to be self-willed, are being determined by Ford's manipulation of generic expectations and stock character types (1987, 174).

Lomax's meta-theatrical reading of Giovanni eschews the anachronistic assumption that characters in Renaissance drama must possess psychological consistency and coherence. The subjectivity of a dramatic character can instead be analyzed as a performative, (inter)textual, and ideological construct. Hence Martin Butler attributes the prevalence of decentered characters in Fordian drama to the plays' pronounced intertextuality: "Ford's metatheatrical forms necessarily involve a denial of the centered self" (in Neill, 1988, 226). Annabella's character illustrates the dispersed subjectivity produced by meta-theatrical forms. For his heroine, Ford draws upon various models of theatrical femininity: the sexually assertive heroine of romantic tragedy, as in *Romeo and Juliet*; the witty heroine of romantic comedy, as in *The Merchant of Venice* (McLuskie, 1989, 129); the wealthy merchant's daughter of Jacobean city comedy, as in Middleton's *A Chaste Maid in Cheapside* (Foster in Neill, 1988, 186–7); the physically abused wife of Jacobean tragedy, as in Chapman's *Bussy D'Ambois* (McLuskie, 1989, 153–6); and the beautiful (but ultimately destroyed) idol of Stuart love tragedy, as in *Othello* (Diehl, 1996, 122). The mingling of these incompatible conventions in a single character like Annabella accounts for the shifts of behavior and tone that confound a modern reader's expectations of psychological consistency. Yet through this skillful manipulation of dramatic tradition Ford achieves the particularly rich kind of layered meaning available only to what Richard Ide calls the "belated" dramatist (in Neill, 1988, 64). Even the stylistic incoherence sometimes charged against Ford might reflect, McLuskie proposes, not lack of skill but the ideological slipperiness of his preoccupation with "female chastity and the relations of sexual power," culturally fraught matters that "cannot be adequately represented on the stage" and "whose conclusions seem so problematic" (in Neill, 1988, 124).

Like his manipulation of dramatic conventions, Ford's often-remarked patterning of bodily language and imagery illuminates aspects of character and ideology. Many critics have discussed the images of wounded and dismembered bodies that contribute to Ford's "poetry of death" in *'Tis Pity* (Gibson in Neill, 1988, 64–5). In an explicitly political reading of *'Tis Pity*, Terri Clerico has productively argued that the play's "complex semiotics of blood" conveys the social anxiety surrounding marriage between mercantile and aristocratic families (1992, 413). The siblings' incestuous bond can therefore be understood as a "defensive act designed to fend off the implied conditions of exogamous [outside the group] alliances" (1992, 416). In contrast to his father's desire for familial advancement through aristocratic alliance, Giovanni enacts a conservative fantasy of restricting sexual alliance to the self-contained sphere of the family (1992, 424). Clerico's sociological account of the conservative implications of incest gains support from Richard Marienstras' anthropological account of the boundaries between family and community in *'Tis Pity*. Although sexual relations within the family may be unacceptable, he observes, so are the "normative" interactions of violence and revenge that constitute Parmesan society (1985, 198–9). Marienstras concludes that in the corrupt world portrayed by Ford the "unnatural nearness" of relatives who should be farther apart inverts the image of "terrifying distance" between neighbors who should be closer together (1985, 198).

If the boundary between family and community emerges in *'Tis Pity* as a site of social definition and struggle, so too does the gendered boundary between Annabella and Giovanni. Idealizing incest as a union of perfect similitude, a neo-Platonic sharing of "one beauty to a double soul" (I.ii.228), Giovanni consistently misrecognizes the gender differential that puts Annabella in a subordinate relation of power to himself and other men. For instance, he diminishes the cultural weight of Annabella's virginity by calling it a "pretty toy" that being lost " 'tis nothing, / And you are still the same" (II.i.10, 11–12). When Soranzo woos Annabella, Giovanni fears in her the inconstancy and sensuality generally attributed to the female sex: "Sister, be not all woman: think on me" (III.ii.11). Annabella's marriage to Soranzo only accentuates her vulnerability, for her enraged husband threatens to "rip up [her] heart" if she refuses to identify the man who impregnated her (IV.iii.53). In an analysis of this scene, Susan Wiseman explains that incest in early modern England was a "much more extreme and confused crime" than bastardy, because without a confession of the father's identity the crime itself would remain unknown (1990, 185). The importance of the pregnant woman's agency in revealing or concealing her sexual secrets helps to explain why Annabella's pregnant body should become an object of such anxious speculation and interrogation not only for Soranzo, but for Giovanni. Whereas Giovanni and Soranzo previously describe Annabella's body through the elevated discourses of neo-Platonism and courtly love (Wiseman, 1990, 191), once they lose control over that body they satirize it as sexually voracious. Soranzo blames the "close tricks" of Annabella's adultery on her "hot itch and pleurisy of lust" (IV.iii.11, 8); Giovanni likewise believes that Annabella has discarded him for a sophisticated "trick in night-games" discovered by Soranzo (V.v.2). It is her precarious status as both wife and sister, not simply personal remorse, that leads Annabella to abandon the incestuous relationship to which Giovanni remains so firmly committed.

Prevented by Annabella's repentance and Soranzo's possessiveness from continuing in his role as the illicit lover, Giovanni decisively takes up the role of the just revenger. The pathos of this development is that in embracing the dominant revenge ethic of Parma Giovanni exchanges the "glory / Of two united hearts" for the "glorious death" he associates with hypermasculine subjectivity: "Be all a man, my soul" (V.iii.11–12, 76, 74). By murdering Annabella, Giovanni believes that he has acted honorably in saving her from Soranzo's revenge and sacrificing her as a martyr to their sacred love. Nonetheless, he speaks the exultant idiom of the Marlovian conqueror or the Senecan revenger when, upon entering Soranzo's banquet with Annabella's heart on his dagger, he describes himself as "trimmed in reeking blood / That triumphs over death; proud in the spoil / Of love and vengeance!" (V.vi.10–12).

The gruesome and shocking spectacle of the excavated heart has generated much critical commentary. However one interprets this potent image, it is crucial first to recognize its multiplicity of meanings. For instance, Richard Madelaine considers the many possible meanings of Giovanni's dagger – a "token of a sincere lover's violent griefs," a "phallic symbol," an "instrument of murder and revenge," an "executioner's knife" – before concluding that it constitutes a "sensational' stage image" of "lust and its consequences" (in Neill, 1988, 33). Michael Neill reaches a very different conclusion by cataloging the "bewildering set of alternative meanings" Giovanni himself attributes to the heart: it is a "spectacular token" of his masculine power, a "symbol of profane sacrifice," a "bizarre erotic parody of the eucharist," a "conventional petrarchan emblem of his own passion," an allusion to "the spectacular imagery of public justice," an "emblem of Envy," and, most strangely, "the newly delivered offspring of their passion" (Neill, 1988, 162–3). For Neill, this dizzying accumulation of possible interpretations paradoxically empties the heart of significance, rendering it a piece of "raw meat" whose "atrocious physicality" thwarts any attempt to wrench stable meaning, and hence social stability, from such hideous butchery (1988, 163). By the end of the play, not only Annabella's heart, but the corpses of Giovanni, Soranzo, and Florio, testify to the irreducible horror of this tragic denouement.

The Cardinal's attempt to reassert social order seems only to compound rather than diminish doubts about the possibility of justice in Parma. Earlier in the play, the Cardinal pardons Grimaldi for the murder of Bergetto, an innocent citizen, simply because Grimaldi is "no common man, but nobly born" (III.ix.55). Yet in this scene the Cardinal orders that Annabella's servant Putana be burned at the stake for her knowledge of the incestuous relationship, a transgression for which she has already been brutally punished by Soranzo's servant Vasquez, who orders that her eyes be put out. That the weakest member of this community receives the harshest punishment confirms the suspicion that justice in Parma is largely the privilege of aristocratic men. After doling out his partial justice and confiscating the valuables of the deceased parties, the Cardinal delivers, as the last words of the play, a disturbingly glib and unfeeling assessment of these tragic events: "'Tis pity she's a whore" (V.vi.156). Susan Wiseman insightfully comments that in declaring Annabella a "whore," the Cardinal seeks to make cultural sense out of incest, an act that unsettles the ideological subordination of nature to culture that justifies his own moral and political authority (1990, 194). *'Tis Pity* is more than skeptical about the possibility of resolving moral dilemmas; rather, it interrogates the ideological, epistemological, and metaphysical "truths" upon which moral order itself is based.

"We Reign in Our Affections": Perkin Warbeck

The problem of truth is central to *The Chronicle History of Perkin Warbeck*, Ford's sole history play. Perkin Warbeck emerged in late fifteenth-century England as a pretender to the throne of the Lancastrian King Henry VII, who in 1485 had overthrown the Yorkist King Richard III. Claiming to be Richard of York, the prince whom Richard III supposedly had murdered in the Tower, Warbeck designated himself the rightful king of England. By presenting this familiar material in a "chronicle history," Ford announces his play's affiliation with a familiar Elizabethan theatrical form: *Perkin Warbeck*'s dramatization of Henry VII's reign serves as a sequel of sorts to Shakespeare's *Richard III.* In the Prologue, Ford further emphasizes the simplicity of his aim to provide a "true" account of English history based on credible English historical writings, not a fantastic tale "forged" in Italy, France, or Spain (ll. 16, 17).

Under closer scrutiny, however, the play's complete title – *The Chronicle History of Perkin Warbeck, A Strange Truth* – reveals the stress points of Ford's rhetorical claim to truth. First, the play's generic status is less stable than at first appears: this "chronicle history" was originally designated a "tragedy" in the Stationer's Register, and the subtitle's emphasis on "strange" evokes the fantastic adventures of tragicomedy (Wymer, 1995, 139–40). Interpretations of Perkin will be influenced by the generic expectations an audience brings to his tale of an exiled prince returned to claim his throne. This tale can be plausibly accommodated within the conventions of tragedy (the pitiful fall of a great man), romance (the providential redemption of loss), and chronicle history (the epic struggle to establish and maintain monarchical authority). More significantly, whereas the play's subtitle presents "truth" as a singular (if "strange") entity, the action of the play insistently suggests that truth is always partial, contested, and, like Perkin himself, fugitive.

The elusive quality of truth accounts for much of what makes *Perkin* such a fascinating, troubling play. Just as he invests the incestuous siblings of *'Tis Pity* with attractive qualities, so in *Perkin Warbeck* Ford attributes considerable dignity and integrity to a figure whom his historical sources unconditionally disparaged as a "'mischievous and dismall wretch'; a 'Mawmet'; an 'Idol of definance,' a 'lump of deformity,' a puppet, a player, a counterfeit stone, a sycophant, a juggler, and so forth" (Barish, 1970, 157). Ford's departures from his two principal sources, Thomas Gainsford's *True and Wonderful History of Perkin Warbeck* (1618) and Francis Bacon's *History of the Reign of Henry VII* (1622), leave tantalizingly ambiguous the fundamental issue on which the historians are absolutely clear: Perkin was an impostor, a Flemish merchant's son posing as an English prince. Whereas the historians report Perkin's ultimate confession of his humble parentage, Ford's Perkin at no point recants his story. Moreover, Ford invents an encounter between Perkin and Lambert Simnel, a former pretender to the throne who after admitting to his imposture accepted a position in Henry VII's household. The humiliated Simnel unsuccessfully urges Perkin likewise to confess and fall upon Henry's mercies; instead, Perkin scorns Simnel – "Thou poor vermin! / How dar'st thou creep so near me?" (V.iii.54–5) – and goes to his death declaring his endurance of a "martyrdom of majesty" (V.iii.74). In so altering his sources and investing Perkin with the resolution of his tragic heroes, Ford raises some difficult interpretive questions. How does the possibility of Perkin's actually being Richard of York impact on our assessment of his failure to achieve the crown? What is the difference between "being" a king and "playing" a king? Are there "kingly" qualities that bestow on Perkin a different kind of legitimacy or truth, if not that which secures possession of the throne? What, in short, is the relationship between "Truth" and "State" (Prologue l. 26)?

Such questions are woven into the play's intricate patterning of contrasts and correspondences among Henry VII of England, James IV of Scotland, and Perkin Warbeck. Structured through alternating scenes set in England and Scotland, the play's first act, in which Perkin does not appear, establishes the different monarchical styles of Henry and James. Henry's court evokes the dynastic conflicts and political machinations of Shakespeare's history plays, especially *1 Henry IV*. Like Shakespeare's Henry IV, Ford's Henry VII opens the play lamenting his troubles establishing his authority after having overthrown the previous king:

Still to be haunted, still to be pursued,
Still to be frighted with false apparitions
Of pageant majesty and new-coined greatness,
As if we were a mockery king in state.

                                                        (I.i.1–4)

To have lost his monopoly on the outward signs of kingship – "majesty," "greatness," and "state" (dignity) – is tantamount to being considered a "mockery king," instead of the true king Henry believes he is. Thus, despite his habitual use of theatrical metaphors to discredit Perkin's claims to royalty – "The player's on the stage still, 'tis his part; / 'A does but act" (V.ii.68–9) – Henry recognizes that kingship is to some degree a matter of performance. Yet whereas Henry can quell a popular uprising through military and financial strength or discover a traitor in their midst with the aid of a court informant, he cannot prevent Perkin from "new-coining" a royal persona on the "common stage of novelty" (I.i.106).

As Henry's outraged denunciations of his nemesis attest, Perkin's theatrical "witch-craft" is a threateningly potent source of the political support and personal sympathy he manages to obtain from the Scottish court (III.i.34). Because Perkin's performances are so charismatic, it might seem that Ford is celebrating the "actor as hero" and ele-vating style to "an absolute moral principle" (Neill, 1976, 118). At his first appear-ance on stage, Perkin indeed commands the attention of his on-stage audience, who marvel at his eloquence and bearing. Perkin's courtly, elevated mode of address – "You are a wise and just king, by the powers / Above, reserved beyond all other aids / To plant me in mine own inheritance" (II.i.85–7) – immediately convinces King James of his veracity: "He must be more than subject who can utter / The language of a king, and such is thine" (II.i.103–4). While some of the Scottish nobles greet Perkin (and his low-bred followers) with skepticism and scorn, King James' susceptibility to Perkin's refined demeanor and lofty goals derives from his own valuation of chivalry, pageantry, and "high attempts of honour" (II.i.113). Nor is it surprising that James, who staunchly professes the essential difference between subjects and kings, attrib-utes his perception of Perkin's true royalty to an "instinct of sovereignty," a seemingly unfaltering empathy between true kings (II.iii.42). James, in short, is no objective appraiser of Perkin's claims, and he certainly has more mundane reasons than "instinct of sovereignty" for championing this challenger to a rival monarch. Just such prag-matic and politic considerations will lead James to abandon Perkin when an alliance with Henry proves the wiser course.

Unlike James, Henry has already mastered the art of pragmatic statecraft. Skill-fully manipulating his reputation for being as "wise as he is gentle" (I.iii.19), Henry keeps a firm grasp on his subjects through cunning deployment of his financial, mil-itary, and ideological resources. Although he openly rejoices at being enthroned in his subjects' hearts, Henry also knows that "[m]oney gives soul to action" (III.i.29), and it is this combination of piousness and ruthlessness that strikes some readers as Machi-avellian. Henry has been condemned for "spiritual hollowness" (Edwards, 1979, 186), and for being "a king with the soul of an unscrupulous merchant banker" (Barton,

1977, 85). Other readers, however, admire Henry's political adroitness, which is only magnified by Perkin's political ineptitude. Jean Howard, for instance, calls Perkin a "gorgeous but ineffectual figure who cannot seize a throne, rouse a following, command an army" (in Neill, 1988, 264). Coburn Freer similarly observes that Perkin offers his supporters only a "constant appeal to a future of hope" (in Anderson, 1986, 133), an imaginary time when "we shall, in the fullness of our fate– / Whose minister, Necessity, will perfect– / Sit on our own throne" (III.ii.100–2). Perhaps Verna Foster, who finds Perkin *theatrically* less compelling than Henry, builds the most damaging case against the pretender. Whereas Perkin's "unrelenting eloquence" strikes Foster as monotonously artificial, Henry's aloofness and craftiness, she finds, confer upon him a multi-faceted and dynamic stage presence (1985, 148).

Wherever our sympathies might lie, we are finally confronted with Perkin's spectacular failure to achieve his kingdom. For some readers, his virtues make him the true victor nonetheless. For Neill, "[w]hat principally justifies Perkin's claim to truth is constancy" – his constancy to his own values as well as the "constant troth" or loyalty he wins from his followers (1976, 132). It might be argued along these lines that even though Perkin loses a geopolitical kingdom, he gains a domestic kingdom: "Even when I fell, I stood enthroned a monarch / Of one chaste wife's troth, pure and uncorrupted" (V.iii.125–6). Through Katherine's unshakeable loyalty, Perkin even triumphs over his ostensible conqueror: "Spite of tyranny, / We reign in our affections, blessed woman!" (V.iii.120–1). In Perkin's paradoxically triumphant failure we might detect the "strange truth" announced in the play's subtitle or the pun on "Truth and State" that concludes the Prologue. For despite his inability to displace Henry as the embodiment of one king of truth and state – "historical truth and good statesmanship" – Perkin achieves another kind of truth and state – Katherine's "truth" (or troth) to him, his truth to his own ideals, and the "state" (dignity) of his lofty aspirations (Wikander, 1986, 71). Hence Wymer feels that the "question of Perkin's 'truth' comes to seem less important than his wife's 'troth'" (1995, 152), and Jonas Barish finds Perkin's "ethical kingship" more important than an actual kingship (1970, 165). Although these interpretations are comforting, by valuing the private over the public sphere they seem to echo Perkin's own desire to redeem his failure in the eyes of posterity. Yet Perkin himself never concedes that his domestic or ethical superiority to Henry compensates for the loss of the kingdom. To the contrary, he goes to his execution still denouncing the "Duke of Richmond's" (Henry's) usurpation of his crown (V.iii.28). Perkin's personal achievements, then, must be carefully weighed against his indisputable and irretrievable political failure.

The possibility of interpreting Perkin in such antithetical ways underscores the difficulty of situating *Perkin Warbeck* in its contemporary political moment. Ford's only history play has often been taken as a critical commentary on the reigning monarch. For instance, Anne Barton argues that the stellar Perkin represents what King Charles should be, whereas the autocratic Henry represents what Charles is (1997, 81). Conversely, Henry has been regarded as the model of good kingship against which Charles' deficiencies are to be measured (Foster, 1985, 157). In a provocative reinterpretation of the play, Hopkins maintains that through the character of Henry VII Ford admonishes Charles to honor and to accept counsel from his trusted nobles (1994, 44). Most surprisingly, Hopkins proposes that Ford, like some of his contemporaries, might have believed that Perkin was the true Richard of York and that he also left heirs to his claim. Ford's refusal to resolve the mystery of Perkin's identity would thus serve to warn Charles that usurpation was possible and that only the support of his nobles could prevent it (1994, 62).

I want to end with a telling instance of scholarly disagreement over *Perkin Warbeck* that epitomizes the pervasive tension in Ford's plays between residual and emergent cultural forms. Using identical terminology to analyze the different models of kingship in the play, Barton and Howard reach antithetical conclusions. Barton argues that Perkin, like Shakespeare's Richard II, represents a "traditional" model of ceremonious kingship, whereas the bureaucratic Henry represents a "modern," debased, model of kingship (1977, 81, 85). Conversely, Howard draws on Renaissance gender discourses (and their operation in Shakespeare's *Henry V*) to describe the effeminate, histrionic Perkin as a "modern" figure who eschews the patriarchal absolutism of the "traditional" Henry (in Neill, 1988, 264, 277). According to these readings, then, Ford's original audiences could have responded to Perkin with a nostalgic longing for a traditional and anachronistic ideal of kingship (Barton), or, just as plausibly, with an unsettling apprehension of the passing of traditional ideals of gender difference and monarchical legitimacy (Howard). That this difference of perspective turns on the matter of backward-looking and forward-looking elements in *Perkin Warbeck* is particularly significant in light of the critical tradition of Ford. He himself has often been antithetically positioned as on the one hand an "anachronistic" figure – a Caroline playwright who worked with Elizabethan forms – and on the other hand a "modern" figure – a Caroline playwright who anticipated novelistic subjects and techniques. The point, of course, is not to determine whether Ford is best grouped with his literary predecessors or successors. Rather, the "strange truth" of his historical positioning can be taken to indicate that we still have much to learn about the fertile conjunction in Ford's drama of convention and innovation, and about its contribution to the emergent modernity of Caroline England.

NOTES

1 Unfortunately, considerations of space require that I omit discussion of *The Broken Heart*, regarded by some as Ford's finest play.
2 Ford (1995, III.i.106–7). I will cite from this edition throughout. In addition to the three plays discussed herein, this readily available edition also includes *The Broken Heart*.

REFERENCES AND FURTHER READING

Anderson, D. K., Jr. (1972). *John Ford*. New York: Twayne.
Anderson, D. K., Jr., ed. (1986). *"Concord in Discord": The Plays of John Ford, 1586–1986*. New York: AMS Press.

Barish, J. A. (1970). "*Perkin Warbeck* as anti-history." *Essays in Criticism* 20, 151–71.

Barton, A. (1977). "He that plays the king: Ford's *Perkin Warbeck* and the Stuart history play." In *English Drama: Forms and Development. Essays in Honour of Muriel Clara Bradbrook*, eds M. Axton and R. Williams. Cambridge: Cambridge University Press.

Bulman, J. (1990). "Caroline drama." In *The Cambridge Companion to English Renaissance Drama*, eds A. R. Braunmuller and M. Hattaway. Cambridge: Cambridge University Press.

Butler, M. (1984). *Theatre and Crisis, 1632–1642*. Cambridge: Cambridge University Press.

Clark, I. (1992). *Professional Playwrights: Massinger, Ford, Shirley, and Brome*. Lexington: University Press of Kentucky.

Clerico, T. (1992). "The politics of blood: John Ford's *'Tis Pity She's a Whore*." *English Literary Renaissance* 22, 405–34.

Diehl, H. (1996). "'Bewhored images and imagined whores': iconophobia and gynophobia in Stuart domestic tragedy." *English Literary Renaissance* 26, 111–37.

Edwards, P. (1979). *Threshold of a Nation: A Study in English and Irish Drama*. Cambridge: Cambridge University Press.

Farr, D. M. (1979). *John Ford and the Caroline Theater*. New York: Barnes and Noble.

Ford, John (1995). *'Tis Pity She's a Whore and Other Plays*, ed. Marion Lomax. Oxford: Oxford University Press.

Foster, V. A. (1985). "*Perkin* without the pretender: reexamining the dramatic center of Ford's play." *Renaissance Drama* n.s. 16, 141–58.

Gurr, A. (1996). *Playgoing in Shakespeare's London*. 2nd edn. Cambridge: Cambridge University Press.

Heinemann, Margot (1980). *Puritanism and Theatre: Thomas Middleton and Opposition Drama under the Early Stuarts*. Cambridge: Cambridge University Press.

Hopkins, L. (1994). *John Ford's Political Theatre*. Manchester: Manchester University Press.

Lomax, M. (1987). *Stage Images and Traditions: Shakespeare to Ford*. Cambridge: Cambridge University Press.

McLuskie, K. (1989). *Renaissance Dramatists*. Atlantic Highlands, NJ: Humanities Press.

Marienstras, R. (1985). *New Perspectives on the Shakespearean World*, trans. J. Lloyd. Cambridge: Cambridge University Press. (Original work pub. 1981).

Neill, M. (1976). "'Anticke pageantrie': the mannerist art of *Perkin Warbeck*." *Renaissance Drama* n.s. 7, 117–50.

Neill, M., ed. (1988). *John Ford: Critical Re-Visions*. Cambridge: Cambridge University Press.

Radel, N. F. (1997). "Homoeroticism, discursive change, and politics: reading 'revolution' in seventeenth-century English tragicomedy." *Medieval and Renaissance Drama in England* 9, 162–78.

Robson, I. (1983). *The Moral World of John Ford's Drama*. Salzburg: Salzburg University.

Sanders, J. (1999). *Caroline Drama: The Plays of Massinger, Ford, Shirley, and Brome*. Plymouth: Northcote House.

Sharpe, K. (1987). *Criticism and Compliment: The Politics of Literature in the England of Charles I*. Cambridge: Cambridge University Press.

Stock, L. E., Giles D. Monsarrat, Judith M. Kennedy, and Dennis Danielson, eds (1991). *The Nondramatic Works of John Ford*. Binghamton, NY: Medieval and Renaissance Texts and Studies.

Venuti, Lawrence (1989). *Our Halcyon Dayes: English Prerevolutionary Texts and Postmodern Culture*. Madison: University of Wisconsin Press.

Wikander, M. H. (1986). *The Play of Truth and State: Historical Drama from Shakespeare to Brecht*. Baltimore: Johns Hopkins University Press.

Wiseman, S. J. (1990). "*'Tis Pity She's a Whore*: representing the incestuous body." In *Renaissance Bodies: The Human Figure in English Culture c. 1540–1660*, eds L. Gent and N. Llewellyn. London: Reaktion.

Wymer, R. (1995). *Webster and Ford*. New York: St. Martin's Press.

Wymer, R. (1998). "Review of *John Ford's Political Theatre*, by L. Hopkins." *Medieval and Renaissance Drama in England* 10, 310–14.

Index

Printed in the United States
121756LV00001B/1-12/P